A Cypriot village of late antiquity:
Kalavasos-*Kopetra* in the Vasilikos valley

JOURNAL OF ROMAN ARCHAEOLOGY

SUPPLEMENTARY SERIES NUMBER 52

General Editor: J. H. Humphrey

AN INTERNATIONAL JOURNAL

ISBN 1-887829-52-0 ISSN 1063-4304 (for the supplementary series)

 Printed by Thomson-Shore, Dexter, Michigan

This and other supplements to the *Journal of Roman Archaeology*® may be ordered from:
JRA®, 95 Peleg Road, Portsmouth, RI 02871, U.S.A.
Telephone (+USA) 401 683 1955 telefax (+USA) 401 683 1975 e-mail: jra@JournalofRomanArch.com
Web site: JournalofRomanArch.com

A CYPRIOT VILLAGE OF LATE ANTIQUITY

KALAVASOS-*KOPETRA* IN THE VASILIKOS VALLEY

by

Marcus Rautman

based on fieldwork organized with Murray C. McClellan

with contributions by

L. Benson, S. C. Fox, M. D. Glascock, B. Gomez,
M. C. McClellan, H. Neff, W. O'Brien and D. S. Reese

PORTSMOUTH, RHODE ISLAND
2003

Table of contents

List of figures

List of Tables

1
Exploring Kopetra

Introduction

The web of cultures that today overlies the E Mediterranean constitutes only one recent moment of a complex and evolving process of land use and occupation. Through the millennia varied mainland polities, from mountainous Anatolia down the long Levantine shore to coastal Egypt, have looked to their common sea as source of colonial gain and means to advance national ambitions. The legacy of this enduring competition is inescapable in the richly textured palimpsest of artifacts and monuments found across the area. As in prehistoric, classical, and mediaeval times, diverse regional interests still converge at the E end of the Mediterranean, at the focus of which lies the island of Cyprus.

Few moments in this history have had greater consequence than late antiquity. Between the 4th and 7th c. the classical world passed through one of the most momentous turning-points known to the peoples of Europe and the Near East, with fundamental changes occurring on all levels of Roman society. Modern historians have followed classical writers in focusing primarily on the empire's large cities, where classical culture attained its fullest expression. Much less attention has been directed to the small towns and rural villages that occupied the lower rungs of the settlement ladder. Contemporary authors spare little praise for the remote and precarious hinterland, and recent scholarship generally has overlooked this poorly documented level of habitation. Archaeology has the unique potential to redress the imbalance of traditional historical sources, and in recent years regional survey projects have identified increasing numbers of settlements. While few of these newly discovered sites have been systematically explored, their widespread identification underscores an important gap.

Cyprus has yet to contribute to this emerging discussion. The island was a prosperous Roman province from the 1st c. B.C. and a strategic component of the Late Roman frontier until the post-Roman Dark Ages, when it became jointly subject to Constantinople and Damascus. Despite its reputation as a cross-cultural meeting place between east and west, Cyprus has been largely overlooked and its settlements unevenly explored. Excavated sites include large cities like Paphos, Soloi, Kourion, Amathus, and the provincial capital at Salamis-Constantia, where study has focused primarily on luxury villas, temples, churches, and other public buildings. Systematic research in the north was interrupted in 1974 by Turkish military intervention and many regions remain inaccessible to study. Problems of Roman urban organization, which are difficult to resolve even at excavated sites, have been infrequently addressed. Small places of Late Roman occupation have been noted by diachronic surveys carried out across the island, but few have been verified by excavation.

The site of Kalavasos-*Kopetra*, referred to simply as Kopetra in this report, provides an opportunity to raise these concerns. The locale comprises a bluff overlooking the Vasilikos river plain about 4 km from the island's S coast. While lacking epigraphic documentation and standing monuments, a Late Roman settlement was noted here in 1978 during extensive reconnaissance of the lower valley by the Vasilikos Valley Project (VVP). Eight years later the laying of irrigation pipes across the area dramatically underscored its potential for both archaeological research and agricultural development. As a result, Murray McClellan and I approached Kopetra in the late 1980s with two main objectives: to record aspects of an unknown archaeological site that was threatened by increasing development, and to explore questions of cultural change on rural habitation. Our goal was to provide a detailed view of one modest settlement of the late empire as a counterbalance to the literary and material evidence from the great cities of the island.

Our initial season (1987) focused on clarifying the topography and surface remains. Guy Sanders and Lee Ann Turner conducted a topographic survey of the ridge using local benchmarks derived from official survey-markers in the valley. Guided by our new plan, Susan Langdon helped us establish a transect across the site which we sampled using various collecting methods. These trial survey finds, together with material salvaged from the pipeline trenches, offered my first lessons in the pottery of Cyprus. For comparison at this early stage and throughout our project we were fortunate to be able to draw upon the collections of study materials previously assembled by Ian Todd for the VVP in Kalavasos and the Cyprus American Archaeological Research Institute (CAARI) in Nicosia.

Over the next 4 summers we conducted further survey of the ridge and excavation at several locations. We began at Kalavasos-*Sirmata* or Area I (1988), where we recorded the eroding remains of a small basilica, the east church, that had been damaged by earlier road-building activities. The presence of an adjacent courtyard and suite of surrounding rooms suggests that the ensemble housed a small monastery in the early 7th c. The dramatic end of the complex was preserved in the courtyard cistern, which contained human and animal skeletal remains dating to *c.*650, the time of widespread Arab raids in Cyprus. During the third and fourth campaigns (1989 and 1990) we turned to the main settlement area and at Area II explored at length a second basilica, the south church. This building was similarly constructed of local materials and the sanctuary originally contained floor and apse mosaics. Among the excavated débris we found a great deal of sculpture made of gypsum plaster, including Corinthian and floral capitals, images of birds and animals, and figural scenes. Despite its fragmentary condition, this ornament constitutes the most extensive program of architectural stucco so far recovered from an early Cypriot church. At the same time we undertook a trial sondage at Area III in order to test an otherwise featureless area marked by abundant surface pottery. During the fifth season (1991) we carried out limited excavations in three other parts of the survey area. Work near the apparent center of habitation revealed a domestic quarter with evidence of agricultural processing and light industry (Area IV). A second, larger residential structure with small rooms opening off a paved courtyard was identified nearby (Area VI). Fine ceramics, glass, and metal artifacts recovered here attest the relative affluence of its occupants, who may have been local landowners. Excavation near the N edge of the inhabited site located a third basilica, the north church, with traces of an apse mosaic and an *opus sectile* floor in the sanctuary (Area V). We discussed our progress in a series of preliminary reports (McClellan and Rautman 1989, 1991, and 1994; Rautman and McClellan 1987, 1988, 1989-90, 1990, 1991, and 1992).

Study of the survey and excavation evidence has produced the picture of an island village that flourished in the 6th and early 7th c. Most of the recovered pottery and coins date from this interval during which the three churches were built and repaired. The settlement's modest size, open siting, and rural orientation strongly suggest a culture based primarily on farming, mining, and trade. The successful exploitation of local resources is seen most clearly in the building of multiple churches and their decoration in stucco, mosaic, and imported marble. The valley's economic vitality also appears in goods, pottery, and rooftiles imported from other parts of Cyprus and across the Mediterranean. No less significant is the occurrence of a major crisis in *c.*650, when all known parts of the settlement were severely damaged. The immediate result was sharp physical contraction with makeshift repairs carried out within the ruins of two of the churches, but the paucity of later finds suggests that most residents soon relocated elsewhere. The abandonment of the ridge amid the political and economic dislocations of the 7th c. reflects changes that were felt across the E Mediterranean region. This report offers a fresh perspective of the Cypriot countryside during these closing years of antiquity.

Our original timetable envisioned 5 years of fieldwork followed by 5 years of study. In the event, this schedule was tempered by other commitments and the path of post-excavation research. From 1992 to 1995 I spent 4 to 6 weeks each summer studying the finds, building remains, and other sites in the valley and across the island. I prepared most of the survey and pottery chapters and an early form of the architectural report in 1992-93 with the support of a research leave from the University of Missouri-Columbia. During this period Basil Gomez and I also began an archaeometric investigation of Kopetra's ceramics in collaboration with Michael Glascock and Hector Neff of the University of Missouri Research Reactor (Rautman *et al.* 1993). Funding from the Getty Grant Program allowed Basil and me to undertake a broad analytical program that included prehistoric through modern pottery from different sites as well as clay samples from representative outcrops across the island (Gomez *et al.* 1995, 1996; Rautman 1995a; Rautman *et al.* 1999). In 1995 Murray McClellan and I completed the study of all survey and excavation materials remaining in Kalavasos and submitted them to the Department of Antiquities at the Larnaca District Archaeological Museum. Further research during the preparation of this report led me to consider some of the larger implications of our work (Rautman 1998, 2000, 2001a, 2001b). A research leave from the University of Missouri-Columbia in 1999-2000 enabled me to return briefly to Cyprus and provided time to put most of this text in final form. The prolonged gestation has led to a more detailed evaluation of this small site and its world.

This report is organized in 4 main parts. Chapter 2 introduces the Vasilikos valley and the site of Kopetra. The first section briefly characterizes the geographic setting and identifies its main environmental features. The second section describes the surface survey of Kopetra and its immediate environs. It reviews the problems and methods used, summarizes the evidence found, and assesses its contribution. It also presents the results of our trial sondage at Area III.

The excavated buildings are presented in chapt. 3. Introductory observations are followed by discussion of the architectural features of each Area or sector. The third part of each section includes a list of catalogued artifacts and additional objects arranged by stratigraphic Lot. Quantified pottery tables are included for each sector and for most closed deposits containing more than a handful of diagnostic sherds. The fundamental analysis of the site stratigraphy was done by McClellan, who also provided the descriptions of selected glass artifacts. Where possible, each Lot summary includes an estimated date (or range) based on recovered artifacts (listed or included in parentheses) or other stratigraphic grounds. A few topics of particular interest are discussed separately. Chronology and significance are summarized at the end of each section.

Chapters 4, 5, and 6 present three essential kinds of artifacts: coins, ceramics, and glass. The few identified coins come from excavated contexts and are included in a brief catalogue. The ceramics chapter presents an overview of the Roman and Late Roman pottery and rooftiles found in survey and excavation. The catalogue is arranged by functional category, ware, and shape. The results of compositional analysis of representative examples, discussed in detail in earlier articles, are summarized in Appendix 3. A concluding section evaluates the contribution of the pottery to an understanding of the site as a whole. The glass artifacts are presented by McClellan.

Chapter 7 offers an interpretative summary of this Late Roman village and its place in the Vasilikos valley, Cyprus, and the E Mediterranean. This overview begins with our fieldwork but draws upon a variety of other sources. I have tried to indicate the strengths and limitations of the evidence in reconstructing the relationship of this rural community with its contemporaries. The chapter concludes with a glance at the pivotal 7th c., when lifeways across the region were dramatically transformed. One small site can offer at best a modest contribution to understanding such far-reaching social changes but hopefully the landscape, artifacts, and questions raised at Kopetra will draw further attention to this period in Cyprus.

While the Kalavasos-*Kopetra* Project is the result of many hands, this summary is largely a personal view. I have tried to present both a candid narrative of our work and an accessible synthesis of our discoveries. For this reason I have tended to minimize descriptive detail for its own sake in favor of discussing features of broader historical interest. My goal has been to harmonize the views of my Kopetra colleagues while recognizing both differences of interpretation and the essentially constitutive basis of archaeological research.

Conventions used in this report

The village at Kopetra was inhabited primarily during the Late Roman period, which in Cyprus can be said to encompass the 4th through mid 7th c. Elsewhere efforts have been made to distinguish Early Roman (mid 1st c. B.C. to 1st/2nd c. A.D.) and Middle Roman (2nd to 3rd/4th c. A.D.) as distinct cultural periods (e.g., Riley 1979: 98; essentially the same as Early Roman 1, 2, and Late Roman 1 in Lund 1993: 137-39). Neither period is well represented at Kopetra, and the latter is difficult to detect in the Vasilikos valley and many other parts of the island. Rather than extend an Early Roman phase down to the late 3rd c. or posit a Middle Roman void, it seems preferable to call these centuries Roman, beginning with the appointment of a provincial governor in 58 B.C. and including the time Cyprus was administered from Italy. The use of Late Roman instead of Early Byzantine — terms sometimes used interchangeably (except when discussing numismatics) — emphasizes the island's cultural continuity until the Arab campaigns of the mid 7th c. The entire interval, from the mid 1st c. B.C. to the mid 7th c. A.D., is referred to as the Roman era in the text and pottery tables. The ensuing Dark Ages and the restoration of Constantinopolitan authority from Nikephoros Phocas until the time of Isaac Komnenos (*c.*965-1191) witnessed important changes in town and country, and are better described as Byzantine.

Field recording is based on the project's site grid, which is derived from the 500-m Universal Transverse Mercator Grid, Zone 36 (International Spheroid, European Datum), published at 1 : 5000 scale by the Cypriot Department of Lands and Surveys as D.L.S. 17 Sheet 55/XII (1978). A point slightly west of *Sirmata* lies at 5285(00)E/38460(00)N, and is expressed as 8500/6000 on the 1-m site grid (fig. 2.4).

All objects are identified as coming from one of 4 contexts: the 1986 pipeline trenches (expressed, e.g., K86-Tr. A), general surface finds (K-gen), systematic surface survey (e.g., SG10), or stratigraphic excavation. Excavation and recording procedures generally followed the system employed at the Neolithic site of Kalavasos-*Tenta* (see Todd 1987: 22-23; *RDAC* 1989: 160). Most trenches were square units laid out at 5-m intervals on the site grid and are identified by the NW corner co-ordinates (e.g., 8520/6015). As a rule 0.5-m balks were left on each side, so the actual excavated area of each 5-m square was 16 m^2 (4 x 4 m). The resulting balks between contiguous trenches facilitated access and were excavated separately; they are identified with respect to the original 5-m unit (e.g., the S balk 8520/6015S). Area IV constitutes the main exception where trenches were not laid out on the grid and are identified by letter (e.g., Tr. A).

Each trench was excavated as a series of baskets making up sequential units designated 1.1, 2.1, 2.2, etc., 3.1, 3.2, etc. After excavation was concluded and the artifacts recorded, the hundreds of excavation units were grouped for each Area or sector into a series of Lots or deposits (e.g., Lots I-1, I-2, etc.). The first Lot of each Area includes finds from the surface and topsoil. Other Lots are numbered arbitrarily. Structural features in each area have unique feature numbers (e.g., F010, F210).

Artifacts discussed in this report are identified in bold-face by either a catalogue number (**C1-C13** for coins, **1-225** for pottery and rooftiles, and **226-314** for glass), or an additional object number by Area and Lot (e.g., **II-3-1**). Artifacts submitted to the Department of Antiquities in years before 1995 are identified by a unique site inventory number (e.g., KK91-5; below, Appendix 7).

Preliminary Kopetra reports are referred to directly in the text (e.g., *RDAC* 1989). All other citations refer to sources listed in the bibliography. I have not been able to take fully into account publications appearing after 2000, including the important compilations of economic history edited by Kingsley and Decker (2001b) and Laiou (2002). Abbreviations are drawn primarily from the *American Journal of Archaeology* 104 (2000) 10-24.

Other abbreviations include the following:

ARS	African Red Slip	km	kilometer(s)
asl	above sea level	l.	length
ASOR	American Schools of Oriental Research	LRC	Late Roman C/Phocean Red Slip
avg.	average	m	meter(s)
B.P.	before present	max.	maximum
CAARI	Cyprus American Archaeological Research Institute	N	north
CRS	Cypriot Red Slip	p.	preserved
CS	Cypriot Sigillata	RBH(S)	rims, bases, handles (sherds)
diam.	diameter	S	south
E	east	s.u.	survey unit
est.	estimated	th.	thickness
g	gram(s)	Tr.	trench(es)
h.	height	VVP	Vasilikos Valley Project
ha	hectare(s) = 10,000 m^2	W	west
INAA	instrumental neutron activation analysis	w.	width
kg	kilogram(s)	wt.	weight

Dimensions are given in meters unless otherwise noted.

Acknowledgements

The Kalavasos-*Kopetra* Project has enjoyed the financial and institutional backing of a number of individuals and organizations. Funding for the initial season of fieldwork came from the Museum of Art and Archaeology of the University of Missouri-Columbia, which for many years promoted archaeological field-work in the Mediterranean region. Dumbarton Oaks granted additional support for the survey in 1988, and the Center for Field Research provided research stipends and 5 teams of enthusiastic Earthwatch volunteers in 1988 and 1989. We were joined at the site in 1989 by the Brock University Archaeological Practicum led by Margaret Morden and Bernice Cardy, and by a field school from Emory University. Two field schools led by Murray McClellan for Boston University came for the 1990 and 1991 seasons. The participation of expedition staff and graduate archaeology students was sponsored in part by the Museum of Art and

Archaeology and the University Museum at the University of Pennsylvania. The University of Missouri-Columbia supported my work through research leave and summer research fellowships. Expenses for travel, compositional analysis, and other ceramic research were met by a collaborative research award from the Getty Grant Program in 1992-94. Archaeometric work at the University of Missouri Research Reactor was supported by the National Science Foundation (SBR-9600334, SBR-950305). A Weldon Spring award and Research Board grant from the University of Missouri underwrote post-excavation expenses. Both field and publication phases of the project were affiliated with the American Schools of Oriental Research through its Committee on Archaeo-logical Policy.

This report owes much to many people. Our first and greatest debt is to the people of the Republic of Cyprus and especially the inhabitants of Kalavasos, our hosts and friends over 10 summers in the Vasilikos valley. We appreciate the support of the successive Directors of the Department of Antiquities — Vassos Karageorghis, Athanasios Papageorghiou, Michael Louloupis, Demos Christou, and Sophocles Hadjisavvas — all of whom encouraged and facilitated our project while working to safeguard the island's rich archaeological heritage. Other members of the Department of Antiquities, including Pavlos Flourentzos, Maria Hadjicosti, Andreas Hadjisavvas, Ioannis Hadjisavvas, and Eleni Prokopiou, advised and assisted us in varied ways. Staff members of the Cyprus Museum and Larnaca District Archaeological Museum provided a hospitable and supportive environment during our post-excavation research. Ian Todd, director of the VVP, welcomed us to the area and showed us its archaeological potential. Like many students of Cyprus, we have benefitted from Ian's comprehensive knowledge of the early history of the island and his intimate familiarity with the valley he calls home. Stuart Swiny, director of CAARI while the project was in the field, did much to support our efforts. Other members of the CAARI staff, in particular Vathoulla Moustoukki and subsequent directors Nancy Serwint and Robert Merrillees, helped in various ways. Kypros Kyprianou, then President of the Republic of Cyprus, granted us the use of a helicopter one bright summer afternoon.

I especially appreciate the efforts of the many students, volunteers, and specialists who joined us at Kopetra. Graduate archaeology students formed the core of our staff and their contributions are difficult to enumerate. They brought energy, enthusiasm, and a wealth of practical experience and fresh insights. We were fortunate to be joined by some of the best students then attending our home institutions. Lisa Benson, Victoria Nevius, Danielle Parks, Guy Sanders, and James Terry joined us from Missouri. Paul Scotton came to us from Pennsylvania and Mark Greco traveled from Boston. All these staff members have completed their graduate studies and are making their own contributions to the field. William Andreas, Larry Bruce, Sotiri Hadjicharalambos, and Rena Nestoros also helped supervise excavation and other fieldwork in multiple seasons. Undergraduate students from different colleges participated under the auspices of field schools from Emory, Boston, and Brock universities. Friends and volunteers organized by Earthwatch joined us for two of our 4 excavation campaigns.

A number of specialists who had previous experience working with Cypriot material helped us along the way. Claire Dean, Sharon Taylor, Howard Wellman, and Andreas Hadjisavvas of the Cyprus Museum offered conservatorial assistance while we were in the field and afterwards. Susan Langdon helped me organize the surface survey, supervised trenches at Areas I and V, and provided moral support in Cyprus and at home. Julie Hansen took time from her work with the VVP to advise us in recovering botanical materials; the summary of results in Table 3.1 is based on a senior honors' thesis written by Wendy O'Brien under Hansen's supervision at Boston University. Paul Goldberg undertook the petrographic study of structural and decorative plasters. Paul Croft assisted us in the field and reviewed the faunal remains from the site, especially from the cistern at *Sirmata*. Pamela Russell reviewed our Late Bronze Age pottery from the perspective of her work at Kalavasos-*Ayios Dhimitrios*. Basil Gomez shared with us his knowledge of the local terrain and geology of Cyprus as a whole; his analysis of the valley's alluvial sedimentation and landscape stability is included here as Appendix 2. David Reese's identification of shells from the site appears in Appendix 4. Sherry Fox joined us for parts of several seasons, during both excavation and publication phases, as she prepared her study of the human skeletal remains; her preliminary report is presented as Appendix 5. Other specialist reports are expected to appear elsewhere.

Excavation notebooks and field accounts provide the primary documentation on which this report is based. The site plan is derived from the original 1987 survey carried out by Guy Sanders and Lee Ann Turner. Architectural recording for the 1988 season was done by Virginia Delaney, who established a foundation on which I was able to build in subsequent seasons. Danielle Parks helped me survey the excavated features upon which my plans, sections, and reconstructions are based. Catherine Alexander completed the stratigraphic sections. Many of the architectural fragments were drawn in the field by Janie Ravenhurst, and several of these were inked by Leslie Hammond in Columbia. William Andreas and Susan Langdon helped me set up the recording system used for processing finds in the expedition *apotheke*. Bill

Andreas designed and maintained the expedition data-base; the numbers that form the foundation of this report result from his many hours of effort. I also appreciate Bill's preliminary observations on the excavated coins that are incorporated in chapt. 4; the photographs were provided by the Cyprus Museum. Lisa Benson and Jane Jalutkewitz offered special comments on the mosaics and architectural decoration. Murray McClellan defined the stratigraphic Lots for all 6 sectors and took many of the site photographs.

Over 15 years of work in Cyprus I have enjoyed fruitful discussions of Kopetra and related archaeological matters with many colleagues, both on the island and elsewhere. Among those who have followed and contributed to our progress are Charalambos Bakirtzis, Slobodan Ćurčić, Wiktor Daszewski, Stella Demesticha, Jane Fejfer, Pavlos Florenzos, Timothy Gregory, Maria Hadjicosti, John Hayes, John Lund, Sturt Manning, Peter Megaw, Henryk Meyza, Demetrios Michaelides, Eleni Prokopiou, James Russell, Kathleen Warner Slane, Jean-Pierre Sodini, Alison South, Ian Todd, Roberta Tomber, and Michael Toumazou. John Nesbitt suggested the reading for the incised table monogram from Area II. I have benefitted from the excellent libraries of the University of Missouri-Columbia, the University of North Carolina-Chapel Hill, and CAARI in Nicosia.

Finally, I owe special thanks to my co-director, Murray McClellan, who first recognized the potential of working at Kopetra. Over the course of our project Murray introduced me to Cyprus, organized the excavations, and resolved many of the day-by-day problems. Our running dialectic, apparent to all who visited the site, underlies my thinking about Kopetra and its historical significance. His sense of adventure, humor, resourcefulness, and integrity made possible both our fieldwork and this summary account.

2

A place in the country

An island landscape

The Vasilikos river originates in the ephemeral mountain streams of the Troodos Massif, the dominant landform of western Cyprus. For most of its length the river drains steep forested slopes and high pastures that range in elevation from 200 and 1200 m asl. Descending from this rugged terrain underlain by igneous rock, it weaves through eroded foothills and passes by the new rockfill dam about 4 km above the thriving village of Kalavasos. Between dam and village, from roughly 100 to 200 m asl, the river is embraced by steep walls enclosing a sheltered flood-plain and low flanking terraces (fig. 2.1). The valley narrows at about 100 m asl, near Kalavasos, but below this it opens into a broad, gently-sloping coastal plain of chalky marls covered by thin calcareous soils that continues into the neighboring Pentakomo and Maroni valleys (fig. 2.2). The flow of the lower river has long been intermittent and subject to rapid flooding in winter and spring. The Kalavasos dam, completed in 1985 to govern a total catchment of almost 100 km^2, has effectively reduced the natural rhythm of seasonal inundation in favor of controlled irrigation of the coastal plain. The surviving river-channel reaches the Mediterranean coast near the industrial complex at Vasiliko, about half-way between the large port cities of Limassol and Larnaca (fig. 2.3).

Broadly speaking, the Vasilikos valley shares the typically Mediterranean climate found across much of Cyprus and the surrounding coastlands. The lower elevations experience dry summers with average maximum temperatures approaching 30° C. Winters tend to be mild and rainy with an average low temperature of 7°. Moderate rainfall produces annual accumulations averaging 400-600 mm, almost all of which occur between October and May (Christodoulou 1959; Thirgood 1987: 19-23; B. Gomez and J. M. Wagstaff in Todd 1987: 3-5). Local climatic conditions are influenced by the valley's proximity to the sea, topographic orientation to the southeast, and gradient and shape of the surrounding hills. Pronounced sea breezes ascend the valley in the late morning and afternoon, particularly during the summer. Toward evening, the cooling mountain slopes can lead to occasional temperature inversions, with potentially damaging frost in winter and early morning fog throughout the year.

Fig. 2.1. Vasilikos valley, view to N from above Kalavasos (1987).

Fig. 2.2. Kopetra, view to S toward coast (2000).

Geology, slope, and climate yield a complex and varying distribution of soils and natural vegetation. The light, humus-carbonate soils of the steep upper slopes are home to forests of Aleppo, Brutia, and Troodos pine (*Pinus halepensis, brutia*, and *nigra*), holm and golden oak (*Quercus ilex* and *alnifolia* Puech.), and hawthorn (*Crataegus alnifolia*); lower elevations normally are covered with scrubby bush species and low aromatic shrubs (Christodoulou 1959; Thirgood 1987; J. Hansen in Todd 1987: 6-7). Strabo (14.6.5) and Theophrastus (*Hist. Pl.* 5.8.1) noted the thick forests that once covered much of Cyprus; even though degraded they continued to be harvested in later antiquity. Vast quantities of Cypriot timber must have been needed for copper smelting near the mines at Kalavasos-*Spilios* and *Petra* in the upper valley. The scale of such human intervention, together with the grazing of animals and cultivation of lower slopes and valley floor, has had a significant impact on long-term ecological patterns. The extent to which the landscape changed between Roman times and the mid 20th c., however, remains less certain (below, Appendix 2).

The Vasilikos valley is known to have been inhabited as early as the Aceramic and Ceramic Neolithic periods, and important settlements of this era have been noted at Kalavasos-*Tenta*, *Kokkinoyia*, and Mari-*Paliambela* (in general Todd 1985 and forthcoming). Chalcolithic settlements have been found at *Paliambela* and Kalavasos-*Ayious*, and minor habitation sites are known across the valley. Settlements, tombs, and other signs of activity in the Middle and Late Bronze Ages have been identified throughout the area, the most important being the large administrative complex at Kalavasos-*Ayios Dhimitrios*. Like many other parts of the S Cypriot coast, the Vasilikos valley was widely and sometimes intensively occupied from at least the mid 1st millennium B.C. through the mid 1st millennium A.D. The rich terra rossas and alluvial and colluvial soils that have developed on the valley's lower slopes and floor today mostly support the dry farming of cereal crops together with scattered olive (*Olea europea*) and carob (*Ceratonia siliqua*). Olive groves, often intercultivated with cereals (mostly wheat and barley), and a few grape vines (*Vitis vinifera*) are found on upper valley terraces.

The present villages of the Vasilikos catchment are not known before the late mediaeval or early modern periods (Goodwin 1984; J. M. Wagstaff in Todd 1987: 8-10). The small upland settlement of Asgata is found at 180-200 m asl in a western tributary valley of the Vasilikos, the Argaki tis Asgatas. Kalavasos, apparently the oldest and today the largest settlement in the vicinity, lies about 4 km to the southeast; it stretches along the W bank of the Vasilikos river

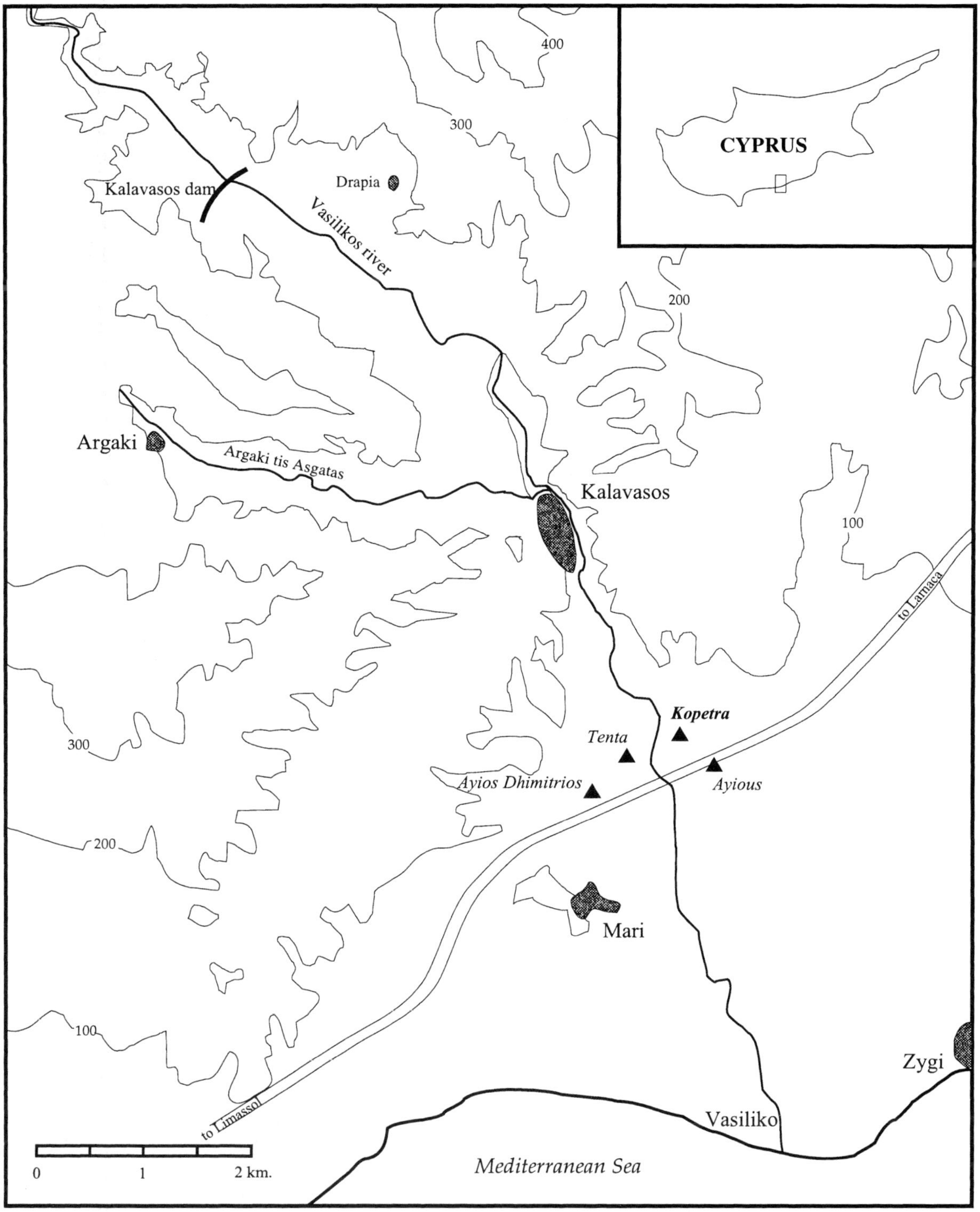

Fig. 2.3. Vasilikos valley, topography, modern settlements, and major excavated sites.

at 80-100 m asl, some 5-6 km from the sea. Mari is a more compact village, formerly of comparable size, that occupies an isolated hill at *c*.85 m asl. It dominates the W side of the lower valley from its location 3 km south of Kalavasos and 2 km from the shore. The small fishing village of Zyyi, once an important center of carob processing, lies on the coast 4 km southeast of Mari and 2 km east of the river outlet. A succession of khans, shops, and private dwellings has grown up over the years along the main highway traversing the valley and the road leading from Zyyi to Kalavasos. Recent land-consolidation efforts and expanded methods of irrigation and intensive cultivation have encouraged the construction of country houses and related agricultural structures across the lower valley and coastal plain. Today most of the region falls within the administrative district of Larnaca, whose urban center lies *c.*30 km to the northeast.

Memory and settlement

'Kopetra', or *'Kopetra me Ayious'*, is the name traditionally associated with the higher part of a bluff near the middle of the lower Vasilikos valley, about 75 m east of the river bed and 4 km from the coast. The name is of uncertain origin but presumably was current before the early 20th c., when British surveyors recorded it and other local toponyms on valley cadastral maps (although note the political context of such names observed by Şevketoğlu 2000: 121-23). *'Kopetra'* is said to mean 'hard rock' in Cypriot dialect.[1] The term may originate in the nearby gypsum quarries to the northeast, which provided the main building material used by local inhabitants and whose stony remains still cover these fields. Alternatively, *'Kopetra me Ayious'* may refer to hollows cut into the local rock by Chalcolithic residents that were explored recently on the more southerly part of the ridge known as *Ayious* (Todd 1985: 86-87; Todd and Croft forthcoming). A low nearby hill to the southeast is called *'Sirmata'*. The Cypriot form *'Syrmata'* is said to derive from the Greek for 'wires', and has also been used as a toponym near Kyrenia (Goodwin 1984: vol. II, 1563). The former alternate name was *'Saranda Ayious'*, a conventional reference to the Forty Saints (*Tessarakontes*) of Byzantine hagiography found elsewhere on the island (e.g., *Sarandi* near Lagoudhera in the N Troodos, *Sarandalaris*, and perhaps the *Kirklar Tékké* near Tymbou in E central Cyprus). The term's historical relevance to this place is unclear. Not inconceivably it reflects a distant commemoration of earlier people who — in prehistory as well as late antiquity — lived and were buried in the area.

That Kopetra was the site of significant Late Roman habitation has been known for over 20 years. The abundance of pottery and building débris across this largely undeveloped landscape recommended a systematic approach to recording its surface remains. Our procedures were intended both to complement local excavations and to evaluate the effectiveness of field survey as a guide to the early history of the island.

Natural and artificial features clearly define the study area (fig. 2.4; for an aerial view of the vicinity see Todd 1987, frontispiece). On the W side the coastal terrace drops away from an elevation of *c.*84 m asl into the Vasilikos river plain, providing an expansive view both toward the coast and up the valley (figs. 2.2 and 2.5). Evidence of Roman activity spreads across the

Fig. 2.5. Kopetra, view to N toward upper valley (1991).

1 Goodwin 1984: vol. I, 431; as *'chakimakopetra'*, a local term for chert; cf. *'Sandoukopetra'* near Paleokastro on Cape Kormakiti in Jeffery 1918: 281

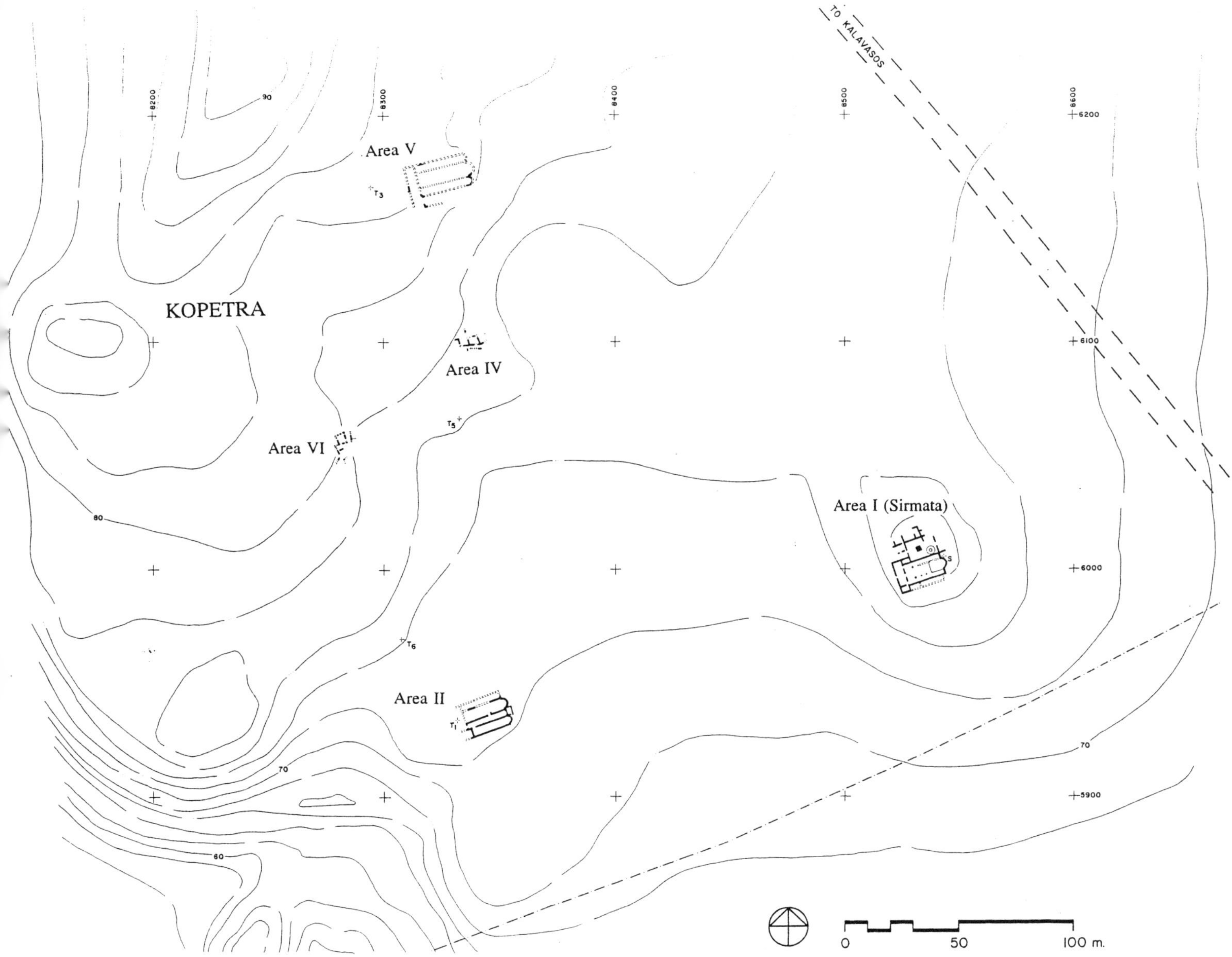

Fig. 2.4. Kopetra area, topography and excavated features.

undulating surface of the ridge, which slopes gently downward to south and east (figs. 2.6-2.7). Approximately 300-400 m to the east of the bluff runs the present road to Kalavasos, the E limit of our study area. The southern boundary is the exit ramp of the new highway from Limassol, which cuts through the ridge at *Ayious*. Excavated débris from this route, which was built in the early 1980s, was incorporated into a massive terrace at *Mangia,* on the N edge of the survey area. No natural source of water is known within these limits. The cadastral maps for the Vasilikos valley, which are derived from the General Survey of 1909-29, show the terrain to be partitioned into a number of small holdings. Several fields on the flatter E part of the plateau were under intense cultivation and unavailable for study: individual plots had been resurfaced with rich terra rossa soils (*kokkinoyia*) from another region and many were sheltered by light-weight plastic-covered *thermokipeia* (greenhouses). The effects of large-scale earthmoving and terracing appear clearly in the contour lines of the central part of the site plan (fig. 2.4). Prior to 1986 owners of these fields had built two houses and several support buildings along the dirt track between the mound at *Sirmata* and the Kopetra ridge. The rest of the vicinity preserves little trace of activity between the Late Roman and modern periods. Low terrace walls of recent date separate some of the fields, reflecting the fragmented landholdings typical of the island (Christodoulou 1959: 80-88; Karouzis 1977: 61-72; Thirgood 1987: 47-58). Two large steel pylons carry high-voltage cables across the N part of the site. Fields of grain, carob, olive, and fruit trees occupy much of the area.

Fig. 2.6. Kopetra, central ridge, view to W (1987).

Fig. 2.7. Kopetra, lower ridge (Area II), view to E toward *Sirmata* (1988).

The installation of an extensive network of irrigation pipelines in 1986 brought important changes in local farming practices; with each passing year additional fields have been graded, terraced, or otherwise renewed with fresh soils and fertilizers. Recognizing this impending development, between 1987 and 1989 we took advantage of favorable field conditions, tract visibility, and available personnel to sample the surface. Data gathered during these seasons were analyzed, selectively verified, and used to select excavation sectors in 1990 and 1991 (Areas III-VI). Since the conclusion of our fieldwork, additional fields have been resurfaced and enclosed by *thermokipeia* and more country houses have appeared along the Kalavasos road. While limited by time and funding and overtaken by local development, the survey nevertheless was able to sketch the approximate extent of this small settlement and summarize its surface remains.

Previous archaeological survey in Cyprus

The development of archaeological survey in Cyprus has paralleled the growth of field prospection elsewhere in the Mediterranean region (Barker 1991: 1-9; for a critical review of Cypriot survey see now Sevketoğlu 2000: 8-24). Early travelers and antiquarians from W Europe provide detailed, occasionally vivid glimpses of the rural landscape in the 18th and 19th c. (e.g., Martin 1998, 1999). During his years in Cyprus, Luigi Palma di Cesnola (1877 and 1894) explored cities such as Kourion and Salamis as well as opening tombs across the island, thereby stimulating public interest in its early history. In 1887 David George Hogarth traveled widely in Cyprus and briefly described almost 50 archaeological sites (1889). The British, French, and Swedish expeditions that followed in the early 20th c. initially focused on major urban settlements but occasionally looked to smaller, neighboring sites. E. Gjerstad *et al.* (1934: vol. 1, 277) early recognized the importance of surface material in developing a chronology of the island's prehistoric occupation. Together with large-scale excavations undertaken at Kition, Kourion, Soloi, and elsewhere, this early phase of field survey led to the creation in 1935 of the Cypriot Department of Antiquities under the direction of J. R. Hilton, who was succeeded the next year by A. H. S. Megaw (Karageorghis 1985b: 2). Establishing a systematic regional inventory of archaeological sites was an important part of P. Dikaios' (1936) exploration of Erimi and other early sites for the Department. Most surface survey over the next 20 years was directed to inspecting land for development (e.g., Megaw 1951, 1952, and 1953). In 1955 the Archaeological Survey department was organized within the Department of Antiquities under the direction of H. Catling and charged with recording archaeological sites and monuments across the island. During the initial season, an area of 100 sq. miles (*c.*259 km^2) in the vicinity of Cape Kormakiti was surveyed and the visible remains of over 400 Neolithic to mediaeval sites were recorded (Megaw 1955: 41). The next 4 years saw systematic reconnaissance of the N and central parts of the island, which noted many additional sites and set the island's settlement history on tangible foundations (Catling 1962 and 1982). This activity also led directly to excavations at several small but important Late Roman sites, including Kormakiti-*Panayia*, the Kornos cave, and the pottery-works at *Mersineri* near Dhiorios (Megaw 1958: 34; Catling and Dikigoropoulos 1970; Catling 1972). Since 1960 the Cyprus Survey has focused primarily on compiling basic regional inventories (e.g., Hadjisavvas 1977, 1983, 1991, and 1997) and on conducting salvage excavations at threatened sites.

As in Greece, the larger potential of surface study in Cyprus was first perceived by prehistorians, who initiated a second survey phase through a number of projects carried out on catchment and sub-regional levels. Systematic surveys of the Analiondas region in central Cyprus and the vicinity of Phlamoudhi near the N coast were conducted in 1971-72 (Stanley-Price 1972; Symeonoglou 1972). A diachronic survey of the Khrysokhou valley traced long-term settlement-patterns in W Cyprus (Adovasio *et al.* 1975). The Lemba Archaeological Project was initiated in 1976 to explore relationships among a number of prehistoric sites in the Ktima lowlands beyond Paphos (Peltenburg 1979; Peltenburg *et al.* 1983). The same year the Vasilikos Valley Project began its extensive survey of this S central valley, which led to subsequent excavations at several prehistoric sites (South 1984; Todd 1982, 1985, and 1987; Todd and Pilides 1993). The Canadian Palaipaphos Survey Project encompassed about 665 km^2 in the Ezousas, Xero Potamos, Dhiarizos, and Khapotami river valleys (Rupp *et al.* 1984, 1986, and 1992). Despite their diverse aims and methods, these regional studies played an increasingly important rôle in archaeological syntheses of the early history of the island (Stanley-Price 1979: 53-57; Keller and Rupp 1983: 321-40; Şevketoğlu 2000: 15-24).

Apart from noting potential sites for excavation, this second phase of Cypriot field survey contributed relatively little to the development of classical archaeology on the island (Tatton-Brown 1985). Only since the mid 1980s have systematic sampling methods been consistently applied to historical periods by surveys designed to explore the larger geographical settings of long-running excavations at Kourion (Leonard 1987) and Amathus (Petit *et al.* 1989, 1991, and 1996). The increasing contribution of surface reconnaissance is seen in recent coastal inventories (Giangrande *et al.* 1987; Hohlfelder 1992; Leonard 1995), projects combining regional survey and excavation (Fejfer and Mathiesen 1991 and 1992; Fejfer 1995; Manning and Conwell 1992; Manning *et al.* 1994 and 2002), and non-settlement studies (Knapp *et al.* 1992 and 1994; Given *et al.* 1999 and 2002; Maliszewski 1994, 1995, and 1999; Toumazou *et al.* 1998).

Site-specific survey has been particularly slow to develop in the E Mediterranean. For various reasons the intensive sampling strategies pioneered in North America in the 1960s were late to reach the Mediterranean region in general and classical archaeology in particular (see examples in Keller and Rupp 1983; Barker and Lloyd 1991; cf. Redman 1987). In 1986, the closest available models were found in Greece, where several large urban sites in Boeotia had recently been sampled as part of broader landscape inventories. In the late 1970s and early 1980s the Bradford-Cambridge Boeotia Project used existing field-boundaries to examine the sites of Askra, Haliartos, and Thespiai (Bintliff and Snodgrass 1988a and b). An expedition from McGill University employed a 5-m grid to record the 2.5-ha site of Khóstia (Fossey 1986). A team from Ohio State University carried out site-specific reconnaissance with 30-m collection circles at Thisbe as well as several sites near Corinth (Gregory 1985 and 1986). Subsequent surveys have used 1-m squares to sample the fortress at Isthmia (Gregory and Kardulias 1990), existing field-boundaries at Phlius (Alcock 1991), and 50-m transects at Koressos on Keos (T. Whitelaw and J. Davis in Cherry *et al.* 1991: 274-76). Except for the very intensive survey of the Isthmia fortress (total area 2.1 ha), most of these projects addressed large settlements ranging from 10 to 30 ha in size, with Phlius and Thespiai perhaps exceeding 100 ha. These complex sites have multiple chronological components, and in most cases a primary research goal was to trace long-term urban evolution from the early Iron Age down to mediaeval times.

Few synthetic surveys have been conducted at the site level in Cyprus. Early exploration of the sprawling settlements at Salamis and Soloi involved informal fieldwalking as a prelude to selective excavation (Picard 1993). Identified sites usually were sampled by unspecified means. Surface inventories undertaken prior to excavation employed various strategies but were rarely systematic and less frequently published. In 1972 two brief surveys sought to apply more systematic procedures to individual settlement sites. In the spring of that year a team from Edinburgh University investigated surface remains over a 15-ha area in central Cyprus, including the Neolithic site of Kataliondas-*Kourvellos*. Working with aerial photographs and topographic features, the survey team established a network of 20-m squares across two parts of the site. All (25) squares in the W part of the survey area were intensively sampled, while alternate squares (12 of 22) in the E part were collected (Watkins 1979: 12-14). The mapping of relative frequencies for chipped and ground stone suggested broad differences in early activities. The ASOR expedition to Idalion constitutes another early exception. During a two-week season that year, a 30-m grid was superimposed on the lower city, an area of about 20 ha. Thirty-four of these squares (one out of every 8) were systematically collected, representing 12.5% of the area (Walker and Bieber 1974). Reported surface densities ranged from 0.15 to 1.64 sherds per sq. m. Sherds were characterized as Geometric, Archaic, Classical, and Hellenistic/ Roman, and their totals were plotted on a series of phase plans. Little allowance was made for variable topography and field conditions, and time did not permit differentiating sherds by function or shape. Despite their limited sample size and unadorned presentation of results, both of these early reports offer a reasonable impression of how cultural material was locally distributed.

Survey objectives and methods at Kopetra

The Kopetra survey sought to apply intensive collection-techniques to a relatively small habitation site with a narrow chronological range. The primary objective was to define the

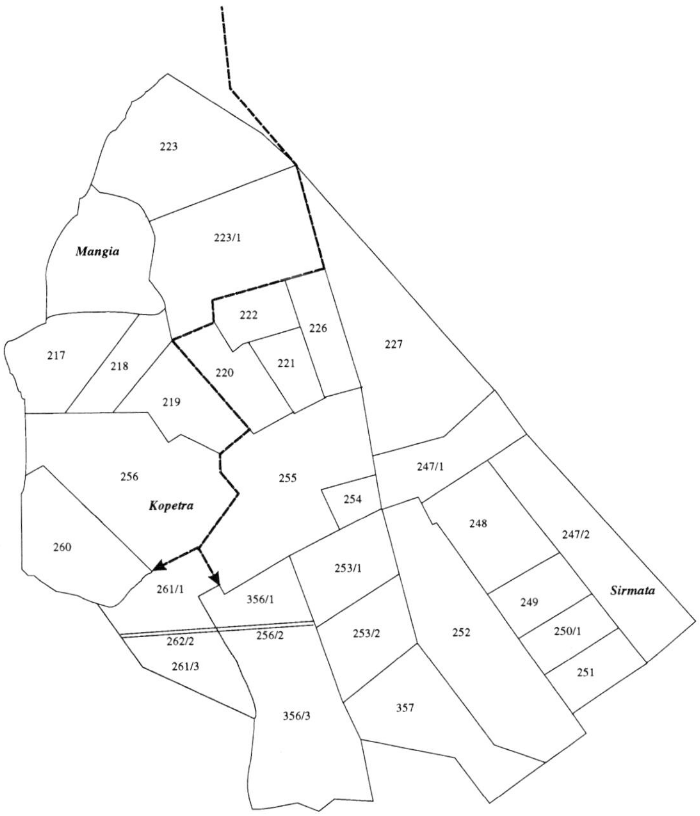

Fig. 2.8. Kopetra area, present field boundaries (based on cadastral map sheet LV.20, Mari Village, 1917, revised 1981), with 1986 irrigation pipeline.

maximum extent of the settlement. We further hoped that mapping the distribution of selected artifact types would reveal something of its historical development and internal organization. The project offered opportunities to test different survey methods through multiple sampling techniques and selective excavation, although its scope was too modest to support extended statistical analysis (cf. Shennan 1985). A broader goal was to help refine field methods for investigating an under-explored period (late antiquity) in a region (Cyprus) that faces increasing development.

The survey area presented both drawbacks and advantages. The recent construction of roads, houses, irrigation lines, and agricultural shelters significantly limited the available terrain and the extent to which we could explore the vicinity. Regular ploughing of the surface clearly enhances artifact visibility but constitutes an unknown variable in the organization of surface scatters (Lewarch and O'Brien 1981; Dunnell and Simek 1995; Boismier 1997; Taylor 2000). On the positive side, much of the Vasilikos catchment had been previously sampled by cross-valley transects, which first identified the site (Todd 1979a: 284; id. 1979b: 32). This broader background offered the potential of understanding an important habitation center within a well-documented geographic setting. Moreover, visible surface remains suggested that Kopetra's archaeological history was of relatively brief duration. The S part of the ridge included pottery and ground stone from the Chalcolithic settlement at *Ayious* (Todd 1985: 86-87, and forthcoming). To the northeast, several Late Bronze Age tombs had been recorded near *Mangia* (McClellan *et al.* 1988). Geometric to Archaic sherds and terracottas recovered from the N part of the ridge suggested the presence of early Iron Age activities. Apart from these peripheral scatters, the vast majority of surface artifacts seemed to date from the 5th to 7th c. A.D. A dense blanket of architectural débris, including cut gypsum slabs, blocks of mortared fieldstones, and rooftiles, pointed to the higher, W part of the ridge as the habitation center. Farther east, tumbled wall fragments of similar construction lay atop the *Sirmata* mound. Isolated masonry fragments appeared across the surface, as did stray examples of worked stone. The open fields of the upper ridge offered an attractive opportunity to refine this first impression.

The excavation of a series of irrigation trenches in 1986 produced the first detailed information about the site. In July the Cypriot Department of Public Works cut over 200 linear meters of 1-m-wide trenches through the central part and along the E edge of the ridge (fig. 2.8). The zig-zag course of this random transect encountered many features of an archaeologically rich landscape, including the *Mangia* cemetery. Trenches also sectioned mortared walls, benches, and floors in the E part of the ridge, which were recorded by McClellan before backfilling (fig. 2.9). A selection of pottery retrieved at the time confirmed the 6th- to 7th-c. date of the buildings and illustrated the variety of local ceramics.

The 6-ha survey area encompassed about 22 individual plots, whose boundaries appear on Cypriot cadastral maps (fig. 2.8, based on sheet LV.20, Mari Village, 1917, revised 1981). Indi-

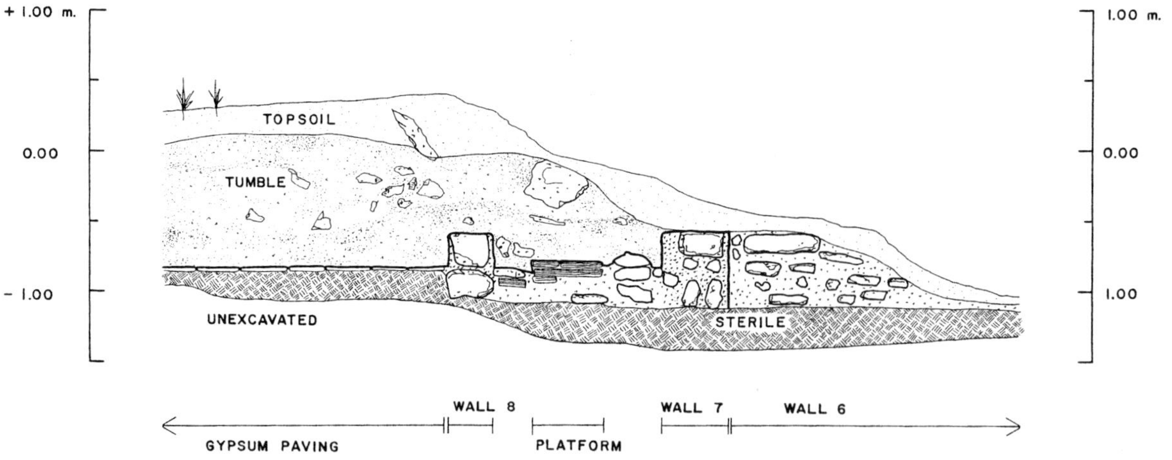

Fig. 2.9. Kopetra, section of irrigation trench (1986).

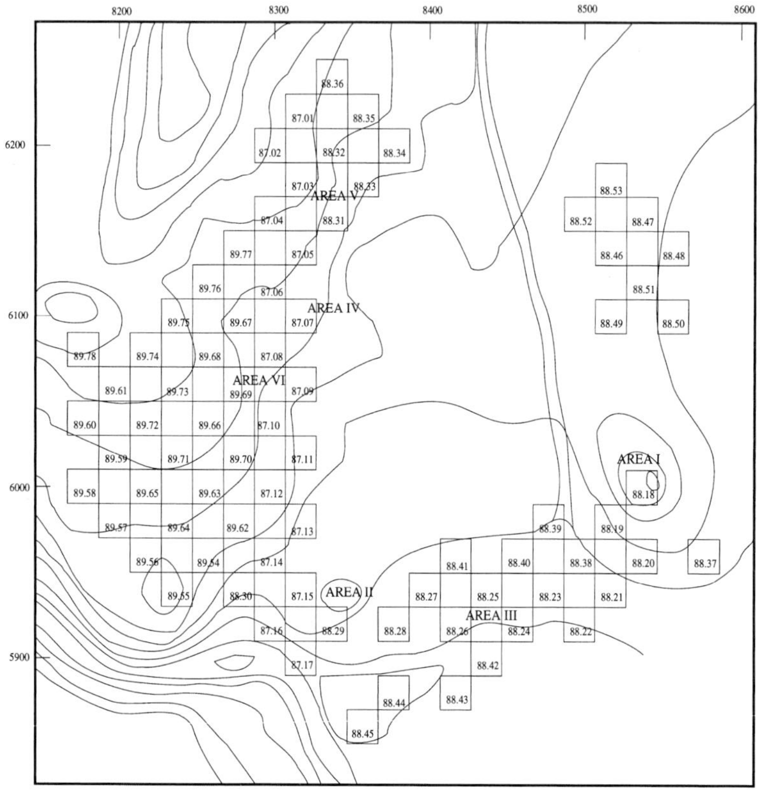

Fig. 2.10. Kopetra, survey units and excavation areas.

vidual fields are irregular in size and area, the result of Ottoman land-codes and the progressive subdivision of family estates. The traditional Cypriot disdain for clear physical demarcation by walls, terraces, or other permanent features recommended that we produce a new map and use a schematic grid (Christodoulou 1959: 84; Karouzis 1977: 61-72). The local topography was surveyed (by G. D. R. Sanders and L. A. Turner) during a 4-week campaign in 1987 and was recorded on the 1 : 500 site map (fig. 2.4). Data-points of the official Cyprus survey were used to generate a uniform grid that was superimposed across the area and anchored by 5 semi-permanent reference points (fig. 2.10). Co-ordinates were derived from nearby government markers and abbreviated for use here (above, p. 12).

The use of a schematic grid presented clear advantages over the existing cadastral system for both collecting and analyzing information. Once established, local benchmarks allowed the grid to be extended with reasonable accuracy across the site by a two-person team. Collection units could be defined at a scale and intensity that seemed appropriate for both site and staff resources. Finally, samples of consistent area could be more readily compared and mapped. Of course, abstract grids also present practical drawbacks. In addition to being cumbersome to establish, any grid offers the illusion of greater precision than can be consistently achieved. We used a Nikon NT-3A theodolite to establish long transects, 30-m and 50-m tape measures to anchor points, and tapes and knotted nylon cords to define individual squares. Occasional backsighting from fixed datum-points helped control cumulative error. The uneasy relationship of grid to field boundaries and archaeological features was more problematic. Only complete 20-m squares were sampled. Several potentially important units were partially obscured by roads, buildings, or terraces, and for this reason were omitted. Informal walking of these unsampled areas often produced interesting surface artifacts that lay outside the survey grid and so were recorded as stray finds.

Survey methods were worked out in 1987 by drawing a trial transect across the site. An extended dry period during the previous winter and spring had led to the year's barley crop being ploughed under, which produced optimal conditions for surface collection. A N–S axis was established near the middle of the ridge, along the 8305 line, and alternate 20-m squares were staked along this baseline (SG [survey grids] 1-17). The

20-m square initially seemed to be a unit that would ensure timely coverage by a small team while remaining sensitive to inter-site variations. Adjacent squares were easy to establish and the collection of alternate units achieved a 50% sample of the site. However, generous quantities of artifacts recovered in the first two squares immediately showed that total collection of such large units was impracticable. We revised procedures to sample separately the NW quadrant of each 20-m square for all artifacts (pottery, terracottas, glass, coins, metals, rooftiles, worked stone, and lithics). Data from this intensive sample were recorded by 100 m^2 units and represent a 12.5% sample of the ridge. Diagnostic pottery (rims, bases, handles, painted sherds, and fine wares) and all other artifacts except rooftiles were collected from the remaining 300 m^2 of each square; recorded separately, this extensive survey represents a selective ('judgement') sample of 37.5% of the vicinity. The result is actually two parallel surveys — one intensive, the other extensive — that offer complementary views of the ridge.

Field procedures remained constant throughout the project. A team of 1-6 members typically was deployed for shifts (3-4 hours) in the early morning or late afternoon, when visibility was best. Working from local markers and using theodolite, tape measures, and knotted cords, the survey team established a small group of contiguous squares, which were numbered in order of collection (SG1-78). For each grid unit, the 10-m square (e.g., SG10A) was collected first. A descriptive form included time of day and names of team members. Survey conditions were evaluated subjectively on a 5-point scale, ranging from excellent (5) to poor (1). The collection of each intensive square usually continued for about half an hour until no visible artifacts remained; this flexibility helped compensate for differing levels of visibility. Rooftiles were assembled, sorted by fabric and shape, and counted in the field; all other moveable artifacts were bagged for recording in the lab. Attention then turned to gathering diagnostic artifacts from the companion sample area (the remainder of the original 20-m square, e.g., SG10), for which a similar form was completed. In addition to terracottas, glass, coins, and metals, this 'judgement' sample focused on ceramic rims, bases, handles, and fine or painted body sherds, and continued until only plain body sherds and rooftiles remained. All collected artifacts were taken to the lab for recording.

Table 2.1 records our progress from 1987 to 1989. The first season included 17 survey units (6800 m^2) arranged along the 340-m trial transect (8305/5890-6230). This transect was designed to pass through the apparent habitation center and define its limits to north and south. During the following summer, 35 squares (14,000 m^2) were sampled from the E part of the survey area, primarily east of Area II and around *Sirmata*, in order to explore the settlement's apparent periphery. In 1989, 25 new survey units (10,000 m^2) were collected along the highest part of the ridge. Two squares of the original transect were re-sampled as a control on both collection procedures and the effects of seasonal farming. The total survey effort involved 168 person hours distributed over 30 working days, for an average intensity of 183 m^2 per person-hour. Field conditions remained relatively constant, ranging from an average of 4.1 (on the 5-point scale) in the first season to 3.1 in the third. With total coverage of only 0.03 km^2 (50% of 0.06 km^2), this highly localized survey was far more intensive than most regional surveys on Cyprus, which have averaged 24-30 person-hours per km^2 (Held 1988).

TABLE 2.1. SURVEY AT KOPETRA, 1987-89

Season	*Area (sq. m)*	*Person hours*	*Intensity (sq. m/hr.)*	*Pottery (intensive)*	*Pottery (extensive)*	*Rooftiles (intensive)*
1987	6,800	38	179	1409	674	2754
1988	14,000	66	212	2397	1450	3380
1989	10,000	64	156	1278	541	2491
TOTAL	30,800	168	183 (avg.)	5084	2665	8625

The dual survey strategy roughly doubled the amount of time needed to cover the site. A total of 89.9 person-hours was invested in intensive collection, while the extensive sample occupied 78.6 person-hours, not counting the time spent establishing the grid. The greater quantities of artifacts yielded by the intensive sample naturally included a higher proportion of non-diagnostic finds but also presumably many datable sherds that would have escaped collection by the extensive survey. On average, each intensive square was examined for a little over 1 person-hour (70 minutes, or 1.4 m^2 per minute), compared with 61 minutes (or 4.8 m^2 per minute) at the extensive level. The time commitment was greatest in the first season while we were working out survey procedures; subsequently it varied with field visibility. Considering the effort needed to establish the grid, this represents a very marginal saving of field time. Applying judgement methods to the same number of 10-m (or even 3-m) squares would have saved few hours while providing a dramatically smaller (12.5% or 2.25%) sample. Even allowing for additional time spent recording finds after collection, this level of coverage seems justified for exploring a limited settlement area.

TABLE 2.2. POTTERY FROM SURVEY, SUMMARY (INTENSIVE AND EXTENSIVE DATA COMBINED)

Survey	*rim*	*base*	*handle*	*sherd*	*sum*	*weight*	*avg. sherd wt.*
Chalcolithic	4	2	1	102	109	2440	22.39
Bronze Age	4		3	12	19	485	25.53
Early Iron Age	42	19	128	58	247	23785	96.30
Classical-Roman	3	6		5	14	275	19.64
Other Pre-Roman	9	3	18	85	115	3630	31.57
PRE-ROM. TOTAL	62	30	150	262	504	30615	60.74
Roman Fine	462	210	10	197	879	16565	18.85
Roman Plain	31	48	18	52	149	5360	35.97
Roman Amphora	342	46	1148	2289	3825	168235	43.98
Roman Cook	69	10	127	288	494	5845	11.83
Roman *Pithos*	431	73	34	274	812	163540	201.40
Roman Other	37	23	115	836	1011	18025	17.83
ROMAN TOTAL	1372	410	1452	3936	7170	377570	52.66
Post-Roman	17	2	9	47	75	1470	19.60
SURVEY TOTAL	1451	442	1611	4245	7749	409655	52.87

	rim	*base*	*handle*	*sherd*	*sum*
CRS 1	6	2			8
CRS 2	25	3		4	32
CRS 3	1			1	2
CRS 7	4	1		1	6
CRS 8	16	12		6	34
CRS 9	3	4			7
CRS 9A	65	22		12	99
CRS 9B	47	34		14	95
CRS 9C	18	9		7	34
CRS 10	9	1		1	11
CRS 11	17	5	9	10	41
CRS other	22	53		48	123
CRS total	233	146	9	104	492
LRC 3	37	13		7	57
LRC 3A	1				1
LRC 3B	1				1
LRC 3C	20	1		2	23
LRC 3D	2				2
LRC 3E	3				3
LRC 3F	7	1		2	10
LRC 3G	6				6
LRC 3H	1	1			2
LRC 5	2	1		2	5
LRC 9		2			2
LRC 10	16	1		1	18
LRC 10A	75	6		8	89
LRC 10B	9			3	12
LRC 10C	19			10	29
LRC other	1	20		14	35
LRC total	200	46		49	295
ARS 99C	1				1
ARS 104B	1				1
ARS 104C					
ARS 106		1			1
ARS 107	3				3
ARS 109	1				1
ARS other	1	7		25	33
ARS total	7	8		25	40
ERS	7	4		4	15
Other	15	6	1	15	37
FINE TOTAL	462	210	10	197	879

	rim	*base*	*handle*	*sherd*	*sum*	*weight*
LR1	283	29	811	1550	2673	126010
LR2	1		1	7	9	235
LR3			1		1	60
LR4	7		20		27	1550
LR5/6	1		3	6	10	500
LR7				1	1	100
KAmp1			3	27	30	715
KAmp2	3	5	58	82	148	6760
KAmp3	3	1	8	7	19	820
KAmp4			8	19	27	930
KAmp5	3	2	5	3	13	1075
KAmp6		1	16	16	33	2085
KAmp7	1		3	3	7	325
Other	40	8	211	568	827	27070
AMPH. TOTAL	342	46	1148	2289	3825	168235
Plain A	3	4	1	3	11	465
Plain B	8	31	11	31	81	1295
Plain D	20	13	6	18	57	3600
PLAIN TOTAL	31	48	18	52	149	5360
Cook A	14		13	19	46	585
Cook B	2				2	30
Cook C	4			1	5	275
Cook D	49	10	114	268	441	4955
COOK TOTAL	69	10	127	288	494	5845
Pithos A	47	13	2	22	84	15450
Pithos B	30	4		39	73	15055
Pithos C	45			5	50	10920
Pithos D	309	56	32	208	605	122115
PITHOS TOTAL	431	73	34	274	812	163540

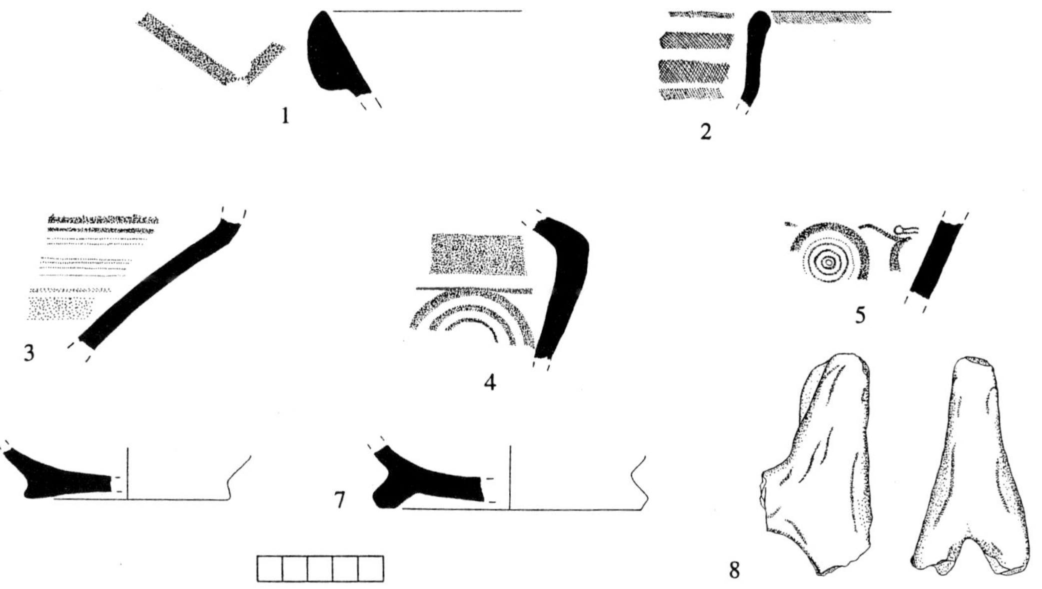

Fig. 2.11. Selected Early Iron Age artifacts from survey.

Artifacts

All survey artifacts were cleaned, sorted, and recorded in the *apotheke* in Kalavasos. Infrequent stone, metal, glass, and terracotta finds other than rooftiles were not systematically quantified. A total of 7749 sherds weighing almost 410 kg was entered into the survey database (Table 2.2). Most of the fine wares and amphoras fit comfortably into existing typologies and were readily quantified. Less familiar plain, cooking, and coarse wares were grouped in broad fabric categories, which are better understood from the excavation sectors. About 21% of the remaining Roman-era sherds were left unassigned, yielding a diagnostic level of 79% (comparable to diagnostic levels of 68% for Early Roman and 87% for Late Roman pottery obtained at Methana; H. Bowden and D. Gill in Mee and Forbes 1997: 84). About 8600 rooftiles were counted and left behind near the center of each survey unit. A significant amount of surface material was not closely datable but, like most of the diagnostic finds, probably dates to late antiquity.

Most signs of prehistoric activity take the form of ceramics and stone artifacts. Isolated Neolithic sherds were noted in the vicinity by the VVP survey and a few examples turned up during excavation of Late Roman levels. Both the valley and Kopetra surveys found Chalcolithic material widely distributed across the ridge. Chalcolithic pottery and worked stone artifacts reached peak densities south and southwest of *Sirmata* and around Area II, which marks the N limits of the Chalcolithic settlement at *Ayious*. The most common Chalcolithic wares were made in a coarse-grained local fabric with a distinctive red slip. Late Bronze Age material appears most clearly to the northeast of Kopetra, near the tombs at *Mangia*. The wider distribution of Chalcolithic pottery (1.4% of all survey sherds by count, 0.6% by weight) compared with Late Bronze Age wares (0.2% of all survey pottery by count, 0.1% by weight) may reflect differences between settlement and cemetery contexts (cf. below, Table 5.1). In fact, 95% of the excavated Late Bronze Age sherds came from deep fills at *Sirmata*, the closest excavation sector.

The early Iron Age is better attested and accounts for 3.2% by count (5.8% by weight) of the survey collection; it is the second best represented period at the site. An Archaic tomb was excavated at Kopetra by the Department of Antiquities in 1986 (Todd forthcoming). The valley survey noted the presence of some Geometric and Archaic material at the site, which we localized at the N edge of the ridge, toward *Mangia* (fig. 2.11 for a representative selection). While dumped highway débris nearby caused some confusion, excavation at Area V also found a variety of residual Geometric and Archaic sherds (especially thick, rolled amphora handles) in Late Roman contexts (6.3% by count, 14.1% by weight). By contrast, all other excavation sectors report less than 2%.

The Classical, Hellenistic, and early Roman periods are poorly represented among the surface finds, with few sherds or other artifacts assignable to these dates. The valley-wide VVP survey observed a similar marked decrease of activities during the early Iron Age. This coincides with the growth of Amathus as an independent island power, with domains that probably included most of the Vasilikos catchment (cf. Rupp 1997: fig. 3). A late Hellenistic/early Roman revival found elsewhere in the valley seems largely to have bypassed Kopetra. The scarcity of material from the later 1st through 4th c. agrees with larger economic trends noted elsewhere in the E Mediterranean (cf. Lund 1992 and 1996).

Roman-era finds account for 92% by count of all survey pottery (below, Table 5.1). Most fine and plain wares, amphoras, and cooking vessels clearly belong to the 4th to 7th c. Less familiar plain, cooking, and coarse wares, like rooftiles, were attributed to the period on the basis of this preponderance and their presence in datable excavation strata. To some extent the abundance of Late Roman material reflects the greater visibility of chronologically later artifacts, yet the lack of significant earlier assemblages — either surface or buried — supports the view of a single-component site that was occupied primarily during late antiquity. The horizontal distribution of finds offers a glimpse of local habitation as well as some of the field processes affecting its reconstruction.

Fine wares document the high end of local pottery use and provide the most detailed chronological information about the site (Table 2.2). The intensive survey recovered 388 sherds weighing 6.6 kg; the extensive sample collected 491 sherds weighing almost 10 kg. With an average sherd weight of 18.9 g (17.2 g intensive, 20.2 g extensive), fine wares comprise 12.3% of all Late Roman pottery by count but only 4.4% by weight (Table 5.2). Over half of the fine ware sherds are rim fragments. Most shapes were placed within the typologies proposed by Hayes (1972) and date to the 5th through 7th c. The results of excavation indicate that most of this material predates the settlement's sharp reduction from 650 (below, p. 209).

Cypriot Red Slip accounts for half to two-thirds of all fine ware from the survey; the intensive data indicate this proportion may actually have been slightly higher (below, Table 5.3). The average sherd weight of 22.6 g suggests that Cypriot Red Slip was the most durable of locally-used table wares, with its thick walls and rims consistently surviving in large fragments (compare a similar finding in Palestine at Tell Keisan, in Landgraf 1980: 66 and 92). Ten basic forms were distinguished, although a quarter of the survey examples remained unassigned. Early shapes like forms 1 and 2, traditionally dated to the 5th and early 6th c., comprise about 8% by count of all Cypriot Red Slip sherds, while *c.*7% by count can be assigned to the form 8 bowl with flat rim (late 6th to 7th c.). Roughly half of all Cypriot Red Slip sherds belong to forms 9 and 10 which are dishes characteristic of the late 6th and 7th c. The form 11 basin accounts for *c.*8% of the total survey sample, with rare and unassigned forms making up the balance. Most examples date to the late 6th and 7th c.

Phocean Red Slip (Late Roman C) constitutes between a quarter and a third of all fine ware from the survey and offers a similar chronological picture. The fine walls and brittle, hard-fired fabric yield an average sherd size of 13.8 g. About 88% of survey examples could be assigned to one of 13 basic shapes. The polymorphous form 3 dish/bowl, which was produced from the early 5th to mid 6th c., comprises a third of the ware. At least half of all assignable Phocean Red Slip sherds belong to the distinctive late 6th- and 7th-c. form 10 dish/bowl. Conventional dating of the type-series suggests that the ware established an early presence at Kopetra and continued to reach the site in quantity through the first half of the 7th c.

Other fabrics make up less than 10% of the survey pottery. African Red Slip accounts for *c.*5% of the fine wares. The average sherd weight of 18.1 g reflects the characteristically thick walls of the later forms. Over 80% of survey examples are unassignable body fragments; the half-dozen identified shapes (forms 99C, 104B and C, 106, 107, and 109) belong primarily to the late 6th and 7th c., showing that the ware continued to arrive into the A.D. 600s. The scarcity of Egyptian Red Slip (less than 2% by count) is somewhat surprising in view of the site's late date and location. Some sherds may have been misassigned, but other examples of these coarse-grained, inconsistently-fired fabrics may not have survived well in the ploughzone. A few examples of Egyptian Red Slip occur elsewhere in the Vasilikos valley, but the ware is rarely reported by field surveys outside Egypt (e.g., none is mentioned in Lund 1993).

Plain wares constitute barely 2% by count of all collected pottery compared with 3 to 9% by count of the excavated pottery (Table 2.2; cf. below, Table 5.2). This slight representation can be attributed to two factors: their overlooking by the 'judgement' sample and the poor visibility of small sherds in the field. Despite these circumstances, the fact remains that plain wares are consistently outnumbered by all other ceramic categories, including fine wares. Part of this disparity may result from counting some closed body sherds as amphoras, although the scarcity of rims, bases, and handles confirms their relative rarity. Another factor may be the availability of Cypriot Red Slip, which in addition to bowls and dishes was used for more utilitarian basins and jugs. The popularity of these shapes may have encouraged the production of high-footed jars and straight-walled basins in the unslipped wares. The most common plain ware (54.4% by count, 24.2% by weight) includes group B fabrics, which have a smooth, hard-fired texture that breaks easily into small fragments (average sherd weight 16 g; below, Table 5.4). The fabric of many examples resembles Cypriot Red Slip; indeed, the two wares are compositionally related. Other plain wares include a variety of flat base bowls, basins, and lids in thick, darker red fabrics.

Amphoras make up roughly half of all pottery from the survey (Table 2.2; cf. below, Table 5.2). Six of the most common types of E Mediterranean amphoras were distinguished, as well as 7 minor types or fabrics of uncertain origin. About 70% by count (75% by weight) of all survey amphoras belong to the panel-ridged LR1 variety, which occurs in three primary fabrics, identified as LR1(1), LR1(2), and LR1(3) (Table 5.5; for definition of the fabrics, see below, pp. 168-70). The standard fabric (LR1[2]) is the best represented (36.5% of the total by count, 33.2% by weight); its sandy texture and hard, thin wall, usually fired a strong pink to orange color, yield a relatively small average sherd weight (27.2 g). A closely related fabric (LR1[3]) appears dull yellow or light brown in color with a mottled surface (20.1% by count, 26.1% by weight). Handles account for a disproportionately large number of examples of this fabric and give an average sherd weight of 45.4 g. Compositional analysis indicates that both fabrics originated on the mainland, probably in Cilicia or N Syria. A third fabric (LR1[1]), known to be of Cypriot origin, is distinguished by its gritty yellow to light red fabric with many large, dark angular inclusions and has an average sherd weight of 36.8 g; such amphoras account for 12.3% by count, 14.1% by weight. Other types of amphora were noted infrequently by the survey. Amphora types LR2 and LR3 generally are rare on Cyprus. Both of the widely distributed Palestinian amphora types LR4 and LR5/6 account for less than 1% of all amphoras and have an average sherd weight of 20-30 g. Apart from a few N African vessels, the only other amphora type to occur in significant quantities (4% of the total) is KAmp2, a thick-walled carrot-shaped vessel with solid toe that apparently came from the N Syrian coast; the average sherd weight in the intensive sample is 45.7 g.

A very limited picture of the cooking wares emerges from the survey data (Table 2.2; cf. below, Table 5.4). The small size and poor visibility of individual sherds account for their disproportionately low presence: less than 7% by count (1.6% by weight) of all Late Roman pottery, with an average sherd weight of 18.1 g. Almost 60% of all cooking ware sherds were body fragments, with rim sherds constituting only 13.8% of the total. Three minor fabrics were distinguished. Group A vessels, which include finely ridged thin-walled casseroles and pots in a hard red fabric perhaps coming from Palestine, account for 9.3% by count (10% by weight) of the survey's cooking wares, with an average sherd weight of 15.4 g. Two examples of a highly micaceous cooking fabric presumably from Asia Minor belong to group B. Group C includes a distinctive series of handmade pots with heavy rolled handles in a coarse-grained, dark red to brown fabric; the average sherd weighs almost 80 g. Similar pots were excavated in exclusively 7th-c. contexts. The remaining cooking ware sherds, mostly coming from deep pots, were assigned to group D, whose fabrics and shapes seem to be of Cypriot origin.

The heavy walls and thickened rims of storage *pithoi* are regular features of the surface finds, with the large average sherd weight (201.4 g) ensuring their high visibility (Table 2.2; cf. below, Table 5.4). Excavated examples confirm the basic forms that were used in Late Roman times, presumably for domestic and commercial storage. Most *pithoi* have a flat discoid base and a thickened rim with heavy rolled handles. The large size and awkward shape are unsuited to transport and the coarse-grained fabric includes many sand-size and larger igneous inclusions of local origin. Three types of *pithoi* were differentiated on the basis of shape and surface decoration. Group A (at *c.*10%) presents a triangular rim below which are lightly incised wavy and zig-zag lines. Group B (*c.*9%) is distinguished by a less pronounced rim and a thick dark red to brownish slip. Group C (*c.*6%) bears a band of pinched corded decoration about the neck. The remaining 75% (Group D) present plain rounded or thickened rims without special decoration; small unslipped sherds can be difficult to tell from coarse-fabric rooftiles.

The survey distinguished only two categories of rooftiles. A set of distinctive tiles of curved section (for convenience termed Laconian-style) was made in a fine-grained red clay believed to originate in W Cyprus. Corinthian-style tiles appear in two standard sizes and fabrics: smaller tiles in a fine-grained yellow to light pink fabric originating in the lower Mesaoria valley of E Cyprus, and larger tiles in a coarse-grained, dark red to brown fabric that were made in the environs of the Vasilikos. Not initially appreciating the significance of these fabrics, we counted all Corinthian-style tiles as a single group. Other forms and fabrics were not apparent among the generally small fragments.

Very little mediaeval material was noted.

The survey found other objects and features that probably date to the Late Roman period as well. Most of the coarse pottery and rooftiles, though not intrinsically datable, was assigned to this primary occupation phase. Lithics and worked stone present other problems. Most of the small fragments of vesicular basalt probably come from Late Bronze Age grinders (i.e., querns and rubbers), although some may have been part of Roman-era millstones (Elliott *et al.* 1986: 80-85; Flourentzos 1996: 28-30). One worn fragment clearly belonging to the lower part of a hopper mill (max. w. 0.38 m, preserving one rectangular handle) was found near Area V on the N edge of the site (not illustrated; SG33, KK94-33). Many diorite grinders and pounders were noted, especially in the S part of the survey area, and undoubtedly derive from Chalcolithic activity at nearby *Ayious*. There is no reason to assume such handy utilitarian objects were not also used during late antiquity, as shown by excavated examples at Areas IV and VI. Many of these well-worn implements would suit myriad tasks in a farming village of any period and some are so used today. Small lithics equally served prehistoric and early modern valley residents. A heap of chipped flints found atop the low mound at Area II may have been gathered as *dhoukanes* for a threshing sled in recent times (cf. Stanley-Price 1972: 21; Fox and Perlman 1987; Toumazou *et al.* 1998: 170-72; Whittaker 1999: 8-9).

Several dry-laid terrace walls oriented roughly SW–NE across the site reflect current land-use patterns and seem to be of recent date (cf. Rackham and Moody 1992; Wagstaff 1992). Higher and less regular stony balks near the S edge of the settlement area and at Area VI reflect generations of pushing rubble to the field margins. Several large stone blocks used for agricultural processing were noted among these accumulations. One rectangular sandstone block includes a raised boss and several rectangular sockets (fig. 2.12 no. 1). A massive press-weight hewn of coarse-grained gypsum was recorded near the S edge of the settlement (fig. 2.12 no. 2; SG15). The large cylindrical block (h. 0.75 m, diam. 1.04-1.25 m) preserves a circular central hole and two lateral mortises. Similar weights have been found at other agricultural sites on the island and mainland (Hadjisavvas 1992: 61, type 2[a]; cf. Callot 1984 and Frankel 1997). Both objects were left in the field. A smaller suspension weight (possibly once serving as an anchor) was found in the extreme SW part of the site (fig. 2.12 no. 3; SG58, KK91-58). The weight has irregular dimensions (*c.*0.26 x 0.30 m) with a maximum thickness of 0.125 m. It was cut out of a large block of gypsum and pierced by a narrow hole. Similar weights have been noted elsewhere on the island, including the Hellenistic/Late Roman pressing complex discovered at Mari-*Kopetra* in the lower Vasilikos valley (Catling 1972: fig. 10; Hadjisavvas 1992: 34-40, 60-61, types 1[a] and 1[b]; Todd, forthcoming). Other pressing equipment was noted on the surface near Area IV (below, p. 134).

Further examples of worked stone include fragments of architectural decoration. A large limestone console block was discovered by villagers while ploughing the N central part of the ridge (fig. 2.12 no. 4). Its face measures 0.62 by 0.28 m. A band 0.22 m high of finely articulated acanthus leaves is carved in relief on three sides. The style of carving recalls general trends in 5th- and 6th-c. sculpture. The large size and good condit-

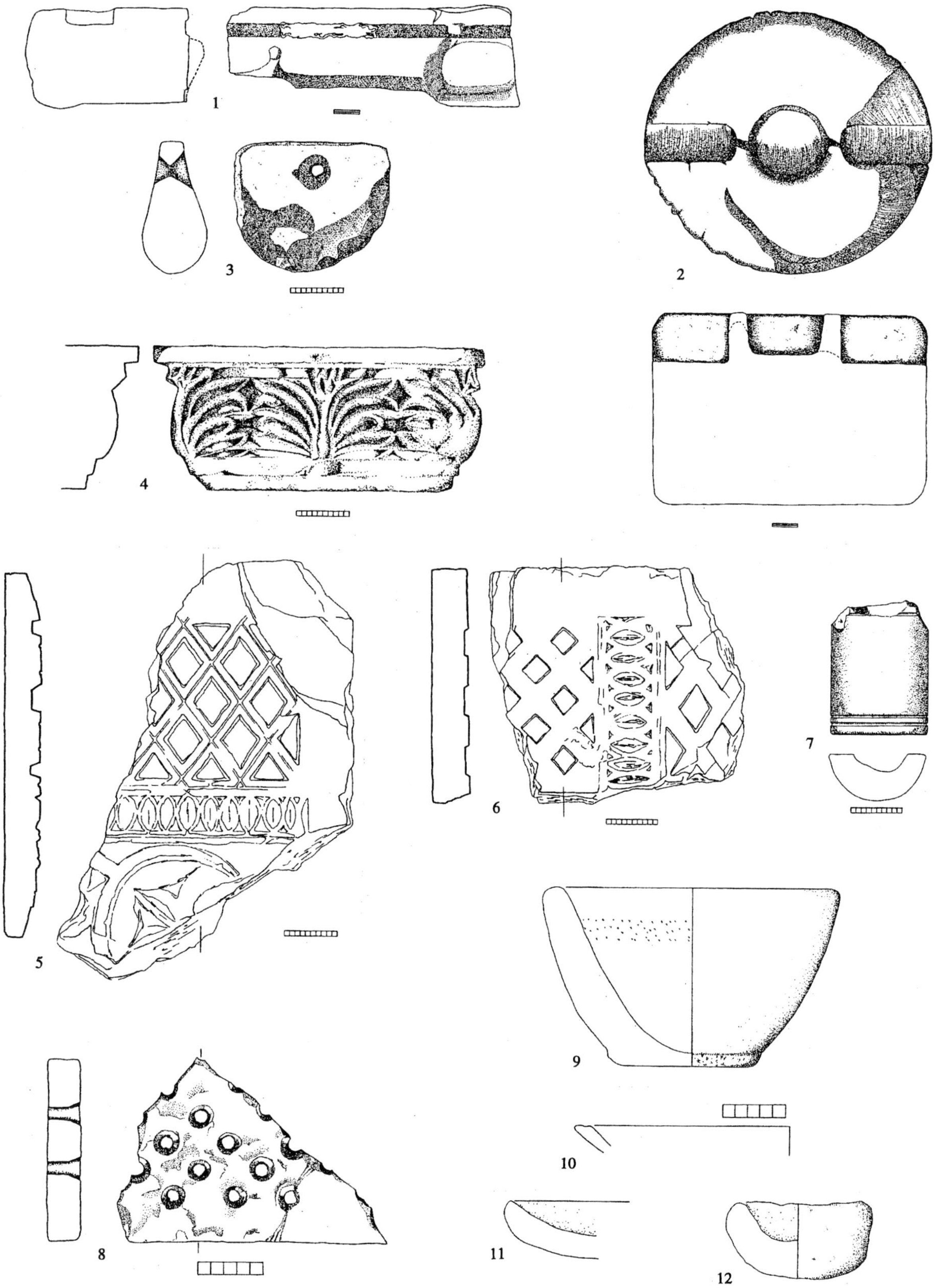

Fig. 2.12. Selected stone artifacts from survey.

ion of the block indicate that it had not traveled far from its original location, which may have been the north church at Area V. Two fragmentary relief plaques also were found in this area. Both slabs of gypsum were distinctively carved. One (fig. 2.12 no. 5; KK88-8, 0.85 x 0.55 m) presents a panel of diagonal reticulation, a horizontal leaf band, and a circular medallion (perhaps enclosing a cross with flaring arms). The same leaf band separates two reticulate panels on the second slab (fig. 2.12 no. 6; KK88-9, 0.46 x 0.49 m). Size and decoration of both plaques seem appropriate for panels of a chancel screen surrounding the *bema* or sanctuary of an early church. While no parallels were excavated at Kopetra, the form and technique are appropriate to the period and similar examples are known on the island. These elaborate plaques may also have come from the north church. Smaller architectural fragments include a semicircular colonnette shaft with moldings (fig. 2.12 no. 7), and a fragment of a pierced gypsum panel or screen (fig. 2.12 no. 8; SG12), similar to examples found at Area I and elsewhere at the site (below, pp. 86-87).

The survey identified pieces of several stone bowls. One large fragment of a deep, nearly hemispherical limestone bowl closely resembles other vessels of the period (fig. 2.12 no. 9; SG71A, KK88-12). The wall rises 0.14 m from a slightly offset base to a plain rounded rim (est. diam. 0.23 m). The roughly picked interior surface, together with signs of wear, suggests that it may have been used for processing household foods (cf. Hadjisavvas 1992: 41 fig. 69). A small fragment of a carefully-worked white marble bowl came from the same part of the upper ridge (fig. 2.12 no.10; SG73A, KK90-4). The shallow vessel has a thickened rim with top groove (est. diam. 0.34 m). The delicate form and fine-grained texture reflect its special status as an object that was brought from the mainland (cf. Patrich 1988a: 132 no. 70, pl. XI; Acconci 1998: 495 nos. 69-71). Both of these objects may have come from houses near the central part of the site. Fragments of smaller, less finely-finished limestone bowls found during survey are not closely datable (figs. 2.12 nos. 11-12; SG19A and 73A).

Distribution and analysis

Spatial analysis of survey artifacts offers insight into the size, history, and internal structure of local settlement. Successful interpretation depends on identifying factors that underlie the movement of artifacts and affect their recording. The approach is not without problems and the scepticism that dogs large-scale reconnaissance projects applies especially to small sites. The limited scale of our project may be partially offset by the geomorphological stability of the study area, the relatively good visibility and working conditions, and the wealth of quantified information they allowed. More importantly, survey was carried out in tandem with a limited excavation program, which informs the interpretation of its results.

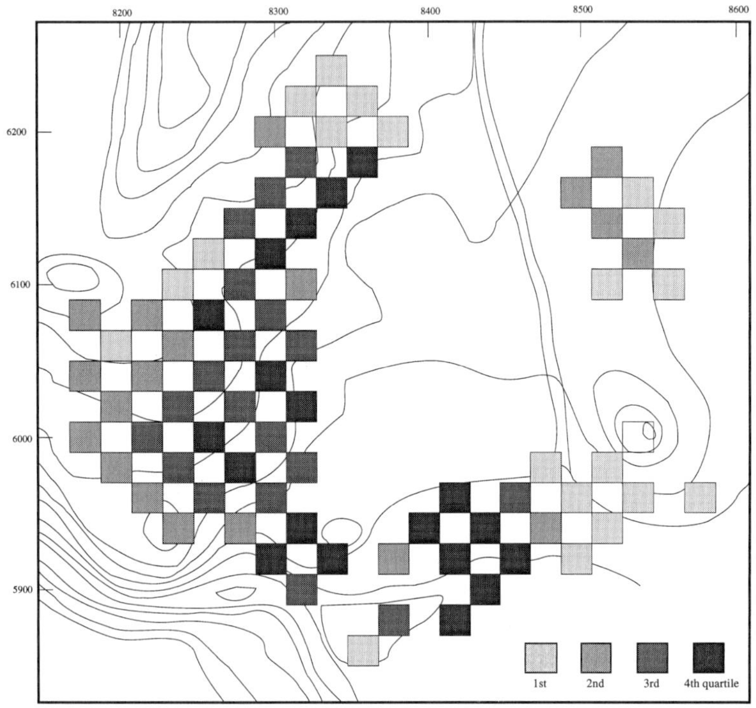

Fig. 2.13. Distribution of all pottery and rooftiles per survey unit, by quartile.

One main goal at Kopetra was to determine the settlement's maximum spatial extent as a step toward understanding the place it occupied in the Late Roman landscape. This question can be approached in terms of relative density and spatial distribution of period artifacts. The 77 quantified survey units (SG18 was collected as part of Area I) report a wide variety of objects, ranging from close to zero to a maximum of 700 sherds and rooftiles (SG26A). Elsewhere the distribution of multiple artifact categories has been identified as a better indicator of habitation area than single types alone, and when quantified along a continuous scale can suggest different activity levels (e.g., Sullivan 1992). The limited scale of our survey does not support such fine distinctions; instead, quartiles are used to distinguish broad contrasts within the data (fig. 2.13). Individual artifact categories exhibit considerable variation but broadly correlate across the site, which reinforces their usefulness as a guide to tracing early activities (see figs. 2.16-20).

The most important threshold lies between on-site and off-site areas. Much attention has been paid to defining rural 'sites' and the problems involved in their identification in different geographical and historical settings. Several recent surveys on the Greek islands have noted a minimum density in the range of 0.30-0.50 artifacts per sq. m for identifying small, nucleated settlements (Cherry *et al.* 1991: 46, Table 3.4; Alcock *et al.* 1994: 139). For this purpose 20 contiguous high-scoring units on the central ridge (average artifact density 2.40 per sq. m) were taken as representing the main inhabited area at Kopetra. Another 20 low-scoring units (average artifact density 0.37 per sq. m) from the survey's N, E, and S perimeters were assumed to lie peripheral to the settlement. Indeed, the low artifact levels found in some units within 100-200 m of the habitation center reflect a sharp decline over a short distance and a limited 'halo'. Rooftiles, which have been shown elsewhere to be a good indicator of settlement area (Gaffney and Gaffney 1986: 66-68), exhibit a similar distribution (cf. figs. 2.19-2.20). Tabulation of these two groups (Table 2.3) illustrates a clear contrast between the inhabited site and its near periphery. (The on-site to off-site ratio of 6.5 : 1 still reflects sustained activity in the vicinity, however, as compared with much larger differentials observed by broad area surveys in Greece, e.g., 127 : 1 at Methana, 133 : 1 in Boeotia, and 314 : 1 at Keos; see Mee and Forbes 1997: 36, 41 n.13; Cherry *et al.* 1991: 46-47, Table 3.4). Between these two extremes lies the settlement margin, which should reflect an intermediate level of activity in transitional artifact values. This perimeter, lacking outer walls or other defined physical limits, can be understood as less a static boundary than a fluctuating, multi-purpose zone lying between the inhabited built area and surrounding gardens and fields. The transition appears less clearly among the data thanks to the varied uses of the periphery for monastic habitation (Area I), agricultural processing (Area IV and the S settlement margin), and residential dumping (Area III). We found no trace of tombs or other burials, which may have been very modest. Considered together with excavated evidence, surface artifacts suggest the village occupied an area of about 4 ha, extending *c.*200 m N–S by at least 200 m E–W along the upper ridge.

TABLE 2.3

AVERAGE CERAMIC DENSITIES OF SELECTED SUB-SITE SURVEY AREAS (intensive data only)

	Objects/sq. m off-site (1)	*Objects/sq. m on-site (2)*	*Objects/sq. m Area III (3)*	*on-site : off-site*	*III : off-site*	*III : on-site*
All artifacts	0.37	2.40	4.27	6.5	11.5	1.8
All pottery	0.19	0.64	2.45	3.3	12.7	3.8
Fine ware	0.01	0.04	0.26	3.8	26.0	6.8
Plain ware	0.01	0.02	0.04	2.1	5.7	2.7
Amphoras	0.11	0.37	1.20	3.4	11.1	3.3
Pithoi	0.01	0.09	0.16	10.3	18.0	1.7
Rooftiles	0.18	1.76	1.83	9.8	10.2	1.0
Avg. sherd weight	29.88	51.91	31.85	1.7	1.1	0.6

(1) Off-site: SG1, 2, 19A-22A, 32A, 34A-38A, 46A-53A; n=20

(2) On-site: SG5A-14A, 62A-71A; n=20

(3) Area III: SG24A-27A, 41A-42A; n=6

Some sense of the settlement's population and economic vitality can be inferred from the frequency of artifacts within this area. Relative densities of finds are readily expressed as peak values per sq. m observed in individual survey units, e.g., all artifacts = 7.13 per sq. m (SG26A), rooftiles = 6.71 per sq. m (SG31A), sherds = 3.27 per sq. m (SG26A), fine ware = 0.45 per sq. m (SG26A); average values for on-site and off-site units are included in Table 2.3. Unfortunately, there is little available evidence to compare with Kopetra. Many surveys in the E Mediterranean use linear transects or irregular field boundaries and do not normally produce similarly quantified data. Different collecting strategies, influenced by variable local conditions, yield varying levels of intensity; the results, moreover, are variously expressed as peak (or average) numbers (or weights) of all (or period-specific) artifacts (or sherds) obtained over different areas. Under some circumstances it may be necessary to compensate mathemati-

TABLE 2.4. DENSITY AND SAMPLE SIZE AMONG SELECTED AEGEAN AND CYPRIOT SITE SURVEYS

Survey	*Peak density/sq. m*	*Sample size*	*Reference*
Vathy (Boeotia)	118 artifacts		Gregory 1986: 169
Methana MS67	56.5 artifacts		Mee and Forbes 1997: 41 n.9
Thisbe (Boeotia)	46.25 artifacts	30-m circles	Gregory 1986: 167
Isthmia fortress	37.51 artifacts	1 sq. m	Gregory and Kardulias 1990: 488
Maroni-*Petrera*	12.5 artifacts	20-m squares	Manning *et al.* 1994: 364
Akra Sophia Site 2 (Corinthia)	8.78 artifacts	1 sq. m	Gregory 1985: 420-21
Koressos (Keos)	>8 sherds	50-m transect	Cherry *et al.* 1991: 274
Kenchreai (Corinthia)	7.91 artifacts	2-m squares	Gregory 1986: 162
Kopetra	**7.13 artifacts**	**10-m squares**	
Evraionisos (Corinthia)	5.3 artifacts	2-m squares	Kardulias *et al.* 1995: 9
Khóstia (Boeotia)	>4.8 sherds	5-m squares	Fossey 1986: fig. 19
Akra Sophia Site 6 (Corinthia)	4.5 artifacts	1 sq. m	Gregory 1985: 423
Kopetra	**3.27 sherds**	**10-m squares**	
Kouveli island (Corinthia)	2.39 artifacts	207 sq. m	Gregory 1986: 169
Thisbe plain (Boeotia)	1.69 artifacts avg.		Gregory 1986: 168
Idalion (Cyprus)	1.64 sherds	30-m squares	Walker and Bieber 1974: 31
rural Keos	1.57 artifacts	"small"	Cherry *et al.* 1991: 46
rural Boeotia	1.20 sherds		Bintliff and Snodgrass 1988a: 176
E Corinthia	0.35 artifacts		Gregory 1985: 421

cally for uneven survey conditions (e.g., Bintliff 1999). Table 2.4 records peak artifact or sherd densities identified by several other projects. Despite the seeming abundance of material, Kopetra's artifact values can appear relatively modest when compared with some site surveys. Intensive collection of one 400-m^2 unit at nearby Maroni-*Petrera* obtained a total exceeding 12.5 artifacts per sq. m, a figure no doubt resulting from recent bulldozing of the area (Manning, *et al.* 1994: 346; cf. the high rooftile count from the recently damaged features at Area V recorded in SG31). The survey of the Isthmia fortress, for example, employed 1-m^2 collection units and produced mean artifact totals of 37.51 artifacts per sq. m (Gregory and Kardulias 1990: 488). The use of 2-m^2 collection units at Kenchreai yielded an average of 7.91 artifacts per sq. m. Artifact peaks of 46.25 per sq. m have been reported at Thisbe and 118 per sq. m at Vathy in Boeotia, presumably using similarly small collection units (Gregory 1986: 168-69). These values, much higher than we found at Kopetra, may reflect a genuine contrast between Greece and Cyprus, or different levels of settlement or economic activity, but it is equally likely that they derive in part from different survey techniques. It would be possible to identify isolated spots of similar density at Kopetra, yet our much larger (100 m^2) samples produced average values that are appreciably lower, if arguably more representative of the site as a whole. Possibilities of inter-site comparison, a perennial problem for archaeological survey, are complicated by such variation.

The growth of this small place emerges most clearly from the chronological distribution of the pottery, which also reflects its main commercial contacts (fig. 2.14; cf. below, fig. 5.20, for Kopetra as a whole). Among the fine wares, a modest supply of early Phocean Red Slip forms suggests the presence of a small 5th-c. community that expanded rapidly during the later 500s, when Cypriot Red Slip came to dominate the local market. The site's regional setting appears clearly in the predominance of amphoras from Cilicia, N Syria, Palestine, and Cyprus itself. The end of local settlement is less clear: fine wares apparently dwindled during the 7th c. and, apart from a few fragments of handmade cooking pots, there is little sign of later activity before the Middle Ages. Understanding the fuller significance of these handmade wares, and the demise of the village *c.*650, depends on excavation.

Within these parameters does the survey pottery offer any clues to the settlement's internal development? Assuming that site-formation processes remained constant, one would expect the

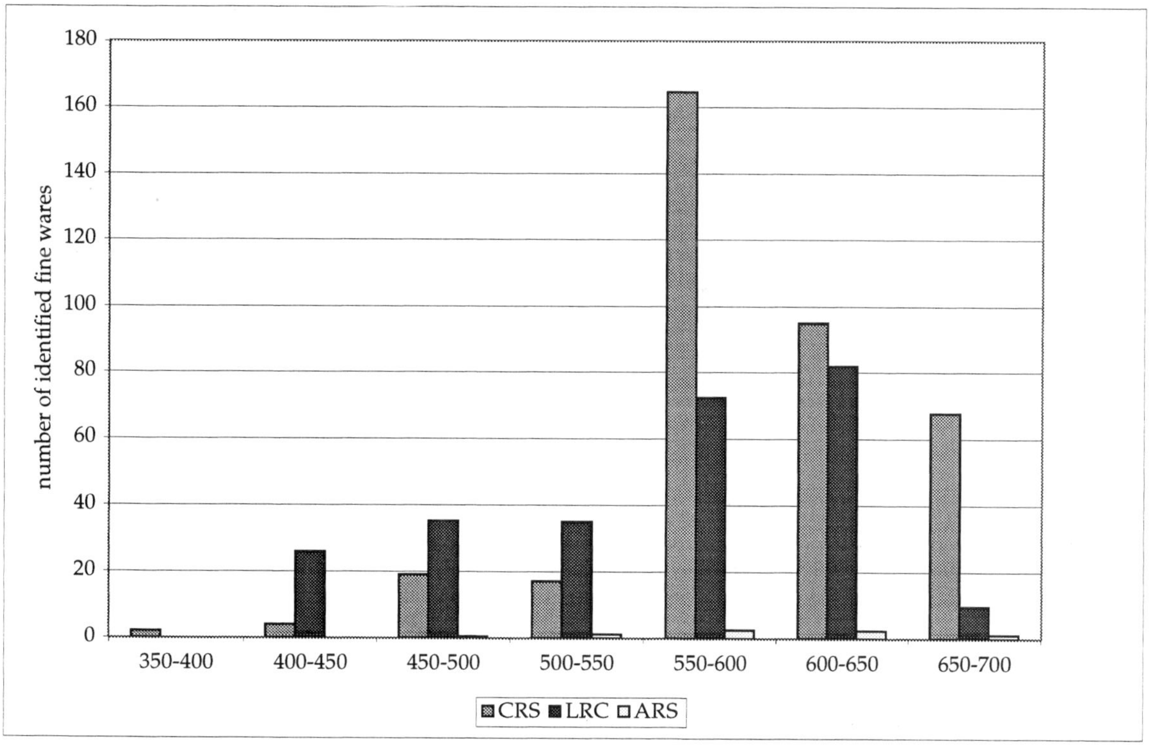

Fig. 2.14. Chronological distribution of dated fine wares from survey by half-century (n=636).

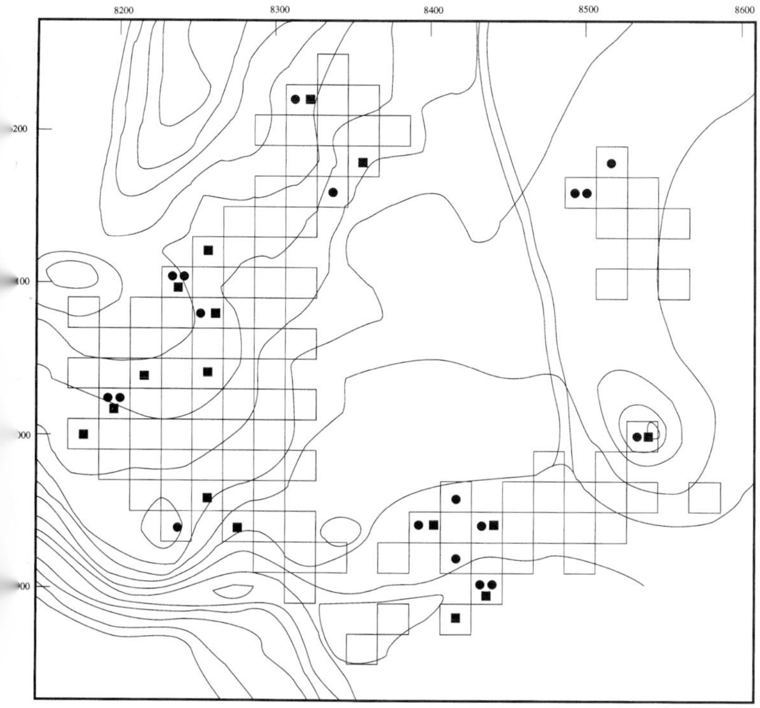

Fig. 2.15. Distribution of 5th-c. (circles) and 7th-c. (squares) diagnostic finds from survey.

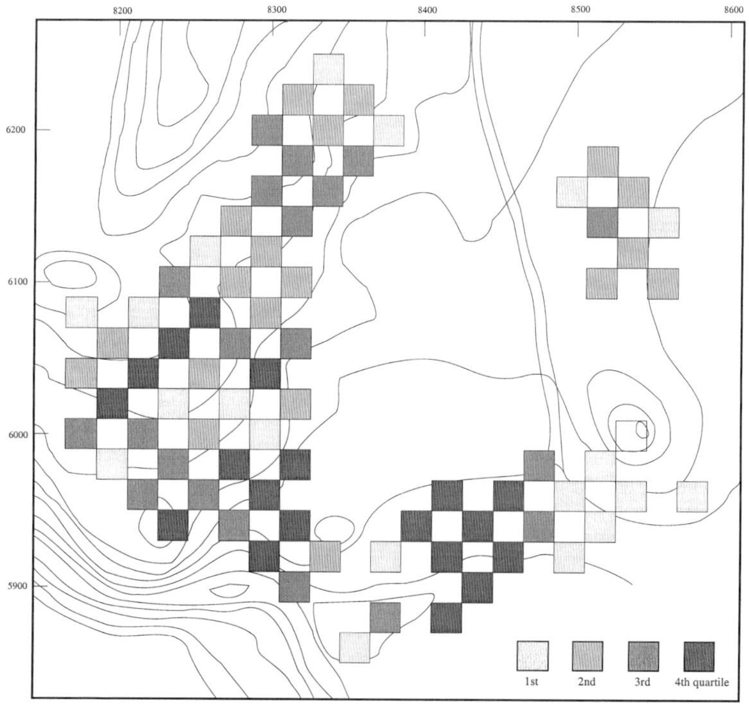

Fig. 2.16. Distribution of fine wares per survey unit, by quartile.

occurrence of early pottery forms to correspond with the earlier parts of the village, while later forms overlie its later phases. Fine pottery again offers the most closely datable evidence. Figure 2.15 records the appearance of selected chronologically diagnostic sherds. Forms of exclusively 5th-c. date appear on the upper ridge, at Area III, and north of Area I. The few exclusively 7th-c. forms, with handmade cooking ware sherds, appear similarly distributed on the upper ridge and at Area III. In both cases we are limited by the small number of closely datable objects. To some extent this incidence reveals as much about prevailing ceramic chrono-

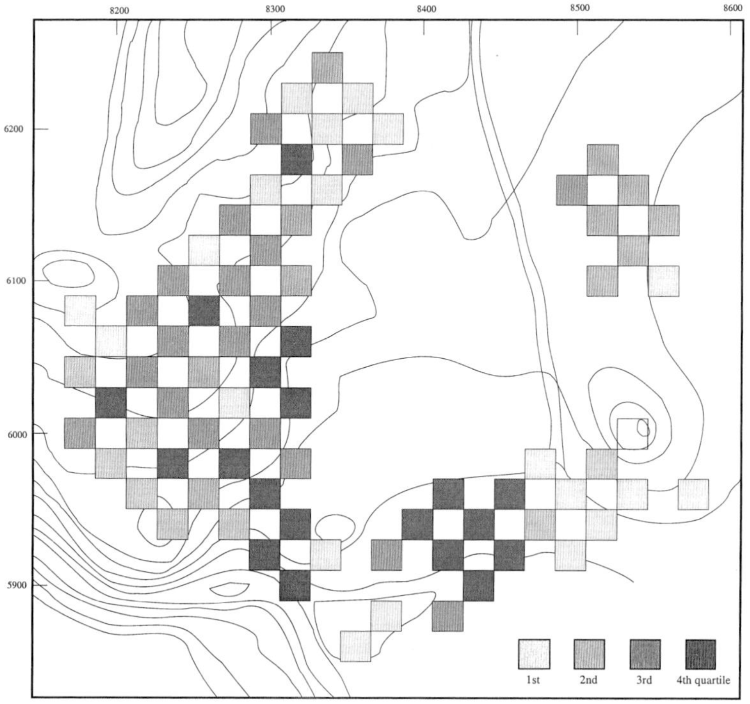

Fig. 2.17. Distribution of amphoras per survey unit, by quartile.

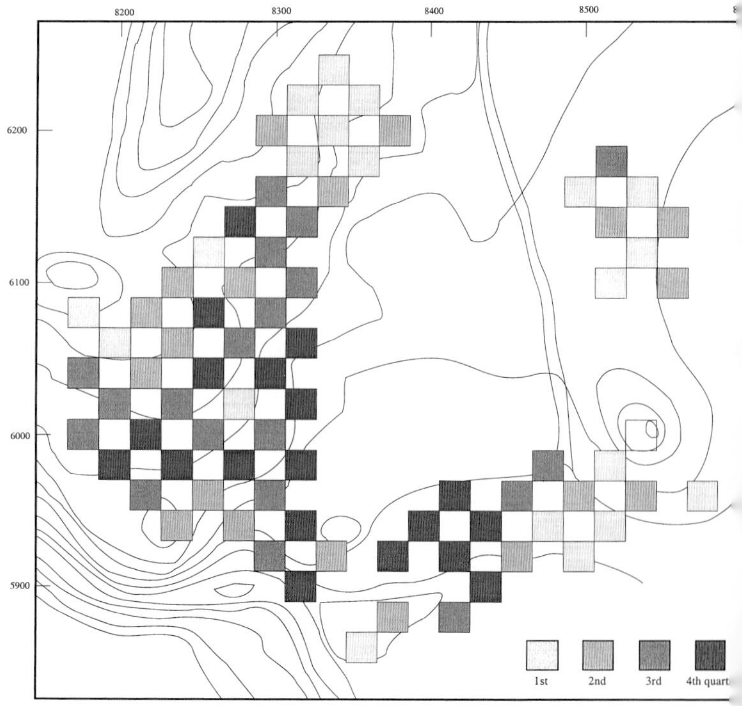

Fig. 2.18. Distribution of *pithoi* per survey unit, by quartile.

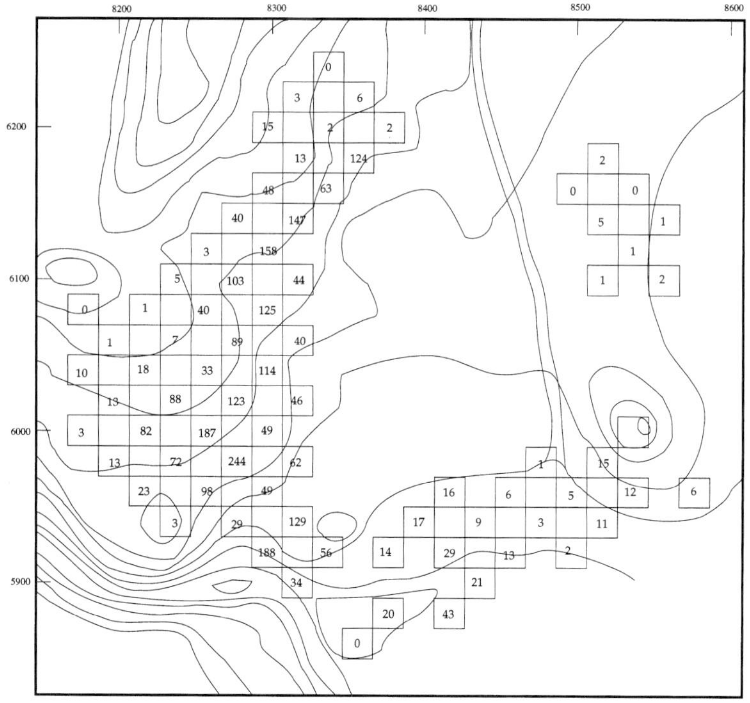

Fig. 2.19. Distribution of red-fabric rooftiles per survey unit.

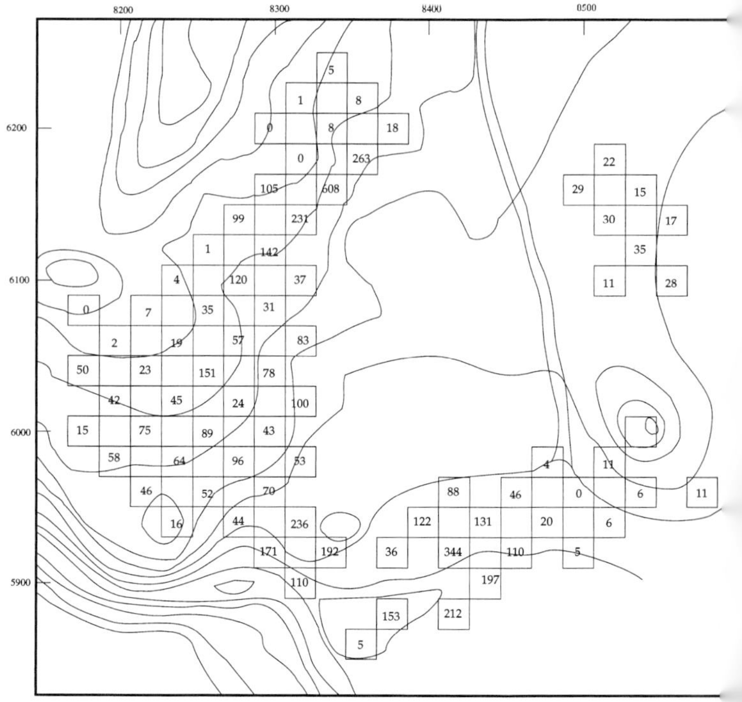

Fig. 2.20. Distribution of all other rooftiles per survey unit.

ogies as Kopetra's development over time, with forms assignable to the 500s or a broader chronological span far better represented. Yet the distribution of these few distinct examples points to the upper ridge as the center of use and discard. Excavation largely supports this view: the early 6th-c. north church on the upper ridge apparently belongs to the site's earlier phase, the south church having been built around the mid 6th c. as settlement grew in this direction; the late 6th-c. east church at *Sirmata* stands quite apart from the inhabited center.

The distribution of different kinds of artifacts presumably reflects something of the site's functional organization. Fine wares are concentrated in 4 areas: three clusters along the W, N, and S edges of the central habitation zone, and a smaller scatter near the center (fig. 2.16). The N and S clusters lie near the basilicas at Areas II and V. The well-built Area VI residence lies at one end of the W cluster. The largest scatter (at 0.26 sherds per sq. m) is at Area III and apparently represents dumped occupation débris. Amphoras, by contrast, appear less differentiated, with plentiful quantities occurring across the site (fig. 2.17). Large storage *pithoi*, intrinsically less mobile objects, appear across the central ridge and at Area III (fig. 2.18). The full significance of these artifact patterns remains unclear. The data-base technologies employed in an early form at Kopetra are increasingly able to track artifact categories by ware, shape, and fragment, yet the meaning of these spatial differences is not always apparent. Quantified interrogation of larger survey sets can test individual clusters against broader averages and highlight spots of particular interest (e.g., Dore 1992: 116 for variance mean ratios at Leptiminus). So verified, statistical constructs still require interpretation, and ultimately stratigraphic confirmation.

Rooftiles offer tangible evidence of building activity and perhaps the clearest measure of permanent occupation. Excavation demonstrated that the three main types of tiles were used to cover public (religious) buildings as well as some residential structures (Area VI); more modest dwellings (e.g., Area IV) may also have used slabs of *marmara* or fieldstone or packed earth, as elsewhere in the region (cf. Sinos 1984; Ionas 1988: 74, 161; Wright 1992; Hirschfeld 1995: 243-44). The relatively static nature of rooftiles in the archaeological record appears clearly around *Sirmata*, where low levels were observed on all sides of the Area I complex. Table 2.3 above reveals the 10-fold contrast in tile density between on-site and off-site areas.

Subtle differences underlie the distribution of the two rooftile types. Corinthian-style tiles are far more common, with a recorded total of over 5500 examples compared with almost 3100 Laconian-style tiles. This predominance is widespread, with Corinthian-style tiles outnumbering Laconian-style tiles in 52 of the 77 survey units (figs. 2.19-2.20). No doubt our failure to distinguish the two Corinthian sub-types has enlarged this disparity, yet it seems significant that these tiles dominate among the off-site units and especially at Area III. Assuming a constant rate of breakage, this suggests that Corinthian-style tiles may have been put into use earlier and enjoyed a longer period of discard around the settlement periphery.

TABLE 2.5. AREAS OF PEAK ROOFTILE DENSITY
(contiguous survey units where no. tiles >100)

Rooftile type	*no. s.u.*	*total tiles*	*avg.*
Corinthian-style			
Area II	4	769	192
Area III	7	1269	181
Area V	6	1469	245
Laconian-style			
Area II	2	317	159
Area IV	4	532	133
Area VI	4	668	167

This impression gains plausibility by identifying the 'hot spots' or areas of peak density for both tile types. One arbitrary criterion is the presence of contiguous squares with more than 100 tiles of either type (Table 2.5). Three such clusters of Corinthian-style tiles occur at Area II (4 survey units), Area III (7 units), and extending between Areas IV and V (6 units). Laconian-style tiles appear concentrated around Area II (2 survey units), near Area IV (4 units), and south of Area VI (4 units). The preference for Corinthian-style tiles in the N part of the settlement, near the early 6th-c. basilica at Area V, supports the view that this part of the village developed earlier. Relatively smaller quantities of Laconian-style tiles at Areas II and V may derive from later repairs to the two churches. Laconian-style tiles are significantly more numerous among the scant surface finds surrounding the late 6th-c. church at *Sirmata* (and were common at the early 7th-c. acropolis basilica at Amathus; see Hadjichristophi 1989: 878).

Use of Laconian-style tiles can be further localized by identifying those survey units in which their number is more than double that of Corinthian-style tiles. Setting aside 6 peripheral units reporting only a handful of fragments, 4 squares meet this criterion (SG8, 62, 63, 70). These units (together with 2 more — SG54 and 71 — that nearly qualify) extend south from Area VI across the lower part of the main settlement area. Interestingly, this area lies apart from the known churches and may reflect differences of function or patronage. In either event, the distribution of tiles constitutes an important view of the inhabited part of the site.

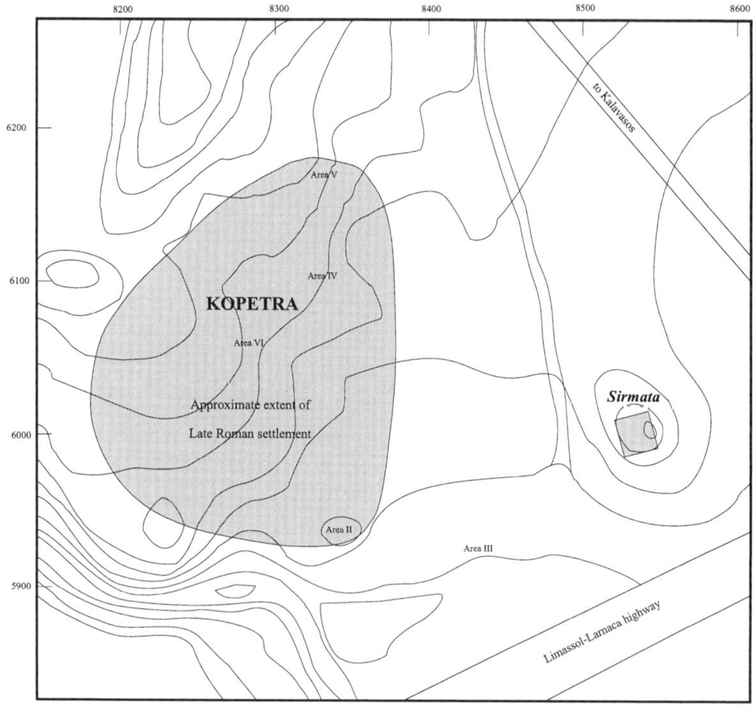

Fig. 2.21. Kopetra, approximate extent of settlement area.

The apparent 4-ha extent and apparent internal organization of surface material can be used with care to estimate the settlement's size (fig. 2.21). While lacking comparable evidence for Cyprus, village populations in many parts of the Near East have been found to range between 120 and 200 persons per ha, with the greater densities noted in more nucleated landscapes and at enclosed sites (Russell 1958: 77-83, 92-93; Hassan 1981: 66-75; Sumner 1989; Zorn 1994: 31-48). The presence of several other inhabited places within 1 or 2 km of Kopetra suggests that the Late Roman occupation of the Vasilikos valley was relatively dispersed (below, p. 237, fig. 7.1). The absence of a clear perimeter wall or other boundary points to an internal density toward the lower end of this range, perhaps about 125-150 person per ha. By this reasoning, the settlement at its greatest extent may have had a population of 500-600 individuals. This figure roughly coincides with the estimated capacity of the three identified local churches, which have a combined internal area of about 600 sq. m. Such approximations deserve considerable caution, but they at least suggest a plausible upper range for habitation of the village as well as a social scale for its economic activity.

Verification

The picture of any site or landscape derived from survey data, whether presented as a vertical profile of occupation or a broad mosaic of artifact densities, gains credibility when tested by other means. Our survey procedures at Kopetra sought to standardize coverage by collecting parallel samples across a uniform grid. The resulting assemblages nevertheless reflect depositional factors that vary from year to year. Geophysical survey by electrical resistivity or ground-penetrating radar, not attempted here, would offer a deeper view of the area. Ultimately, sampling in depth (i.e., by excavation) is needed to anchor artifacts stratigraphically and establish their relationship with sub-surface features (Barker 1991: 5; Keay *et al.* 1991; Millett 2000).

Two complementary but distinct views of the site emerge from the survey data. Both the 12.5% intensive collection and 37.5% extensive sample yielded similar pictures of how different pottery classes were distributed (Table 2.6). Within the larger categories (e.g., LR1 type amphoras) one can observe the general correlation of RBH counts too. Plain and cooking ware data correspond less closely, perhaps as a result of the small sample size.

TABLE 2.6. ROMAN SURVEY SHERD TYPES AND AVERAGE WEIGHTS

Ware/sample	*rim*	*base*	*handle*	*sherd*	*total no.*	*total wt.*	*avg. sherd wt.*
Fine							
Intensive	202	95	2	89	388	6660	17.16
Extensive	260	115	9	107	491	9905	20.17
Plain							
Intensive	11	27	8	39	85	2420	28.47
Extensive	20	21	10	13	64	2940	45.94
Amphora							
Intensive	151	12	440	2022	2625	81985	31.23
Extensive	191	34	708	267	1200	86250	71.88
Cook							
Intensive	31	3	60	240	334	2660	7.96
Extensive	38	7	67	48	160	3185	19.91
Pithos							
Intensive	157	39	17	234	447	73480	164.38
Extensive	274	34	17	40	365	90060	246.74
Other							
Intensive	15	16	62	754	847	12170	14.37
Extensive	22	7	53	82	164	5855	35.70
TOTALS							
Intensive	567	192	589	3378	4726	179375	37.95
Extensive	805	218	864	557	2444	198195	81.09

Some of this variation can be attributed to the fact that the intensive survey, as expected, recovered smaller sherds than the extensive sample. The weight (17.2 g) of the average fine ware sherd from the intensive survey compares with 20.2 g for the extensive sample. Sherds of the most common type of plain ware averaged 28.5 g in the intensive survey and 45.9 g in the extensive. Cooking wares presented the greatest proportional disparity, averaging 8.0 g in the intensive survey and 19.9 g in the extensive. Circumstances of collection, including time, visibility, and the experience of survey personnel, may have contributed to these differences.

Another question concerns the inter-seasonal visibility and variability of surface material. The Kopetra ridge is subject to bi-annual ploughing, a practice of long-standing in Cyprus (Christodoulou 1959: 43; Halstead 1987: 82; J. Wagstaff in Todd 1987: 7-8). Previous work has produced no consensus on the effects of continuous cultivation on the distribution of surface artifacts. It is to be expected that multiple surveys of the same terrain will produce different data as a result of changing land-use and survey conditions. Scale — both topographic and chronological — is an important factor, with small assemblages appearing more vulnerable to disturbance. Broad, diachronic trends emerge more consistently from re-surveys of large sites and wider areas; in some cases collection may actually be enhanced by regular ploughing (e.g., Lewarch and O'Brien 1981; Mattingly 1992; Boismier 1997).

The Kopetra survey sought to address this problem in three ways. First, ground visibility was subjectively evaluated at the time of collection. Second, sampling was carried out over three years, with adjacent squares yielding largely consistent data in different seasons. Third, two survey units (SG8 and 10) near the central part of the ridge were revisited in order to check the effects of repeated ploughing on a small area. Both squares were initially collected in 1987 and were resurveyed in 1989 (Table 2.7). In both cases total sherd counts fell (by over 40%) between the two years, while rooftile quantities rose by about 50%. This is unsurprising since we routinely removed sherds from the site but left tiles at the center of each collection square.

It is interesting that both re-sampled units gave broadly similar total sherd counts, which might be coincidental or the result of a constant rate of renewal by ploughing (cf. Ammerman and Feldman 1978; Shennan 1985: 44; Taylor 2000). Correlations between the two samples are rather broad but lie within the normal range of local surface material.

TABLE 2.7. COMPARATIVE SURVEY OF SG8 AND SG10
(intensive and extensive data combined)

SG8&10	*1987 count*	*1989 count*	*1987 weight*	*1989 weight*
CRS 9	14	2	350	85
CRS other		10		115
LRC 3	1	1	35	20
LRC 10	2		50	
ARS	3		75	
Plain D	1	2	230	95
LR1	115	52	6410	2570
LR2		1		40
LR3		1		30
LR5		1		70
KAmp2	3	1	65	75
KAmp6		9		520
Other amphora	44	30	1550	1270
Cook D	17	8	310	140
Pithos A		1		1070
Pithos C		1		270
Pithos D	41	31	10350	6735
Other	38	9	945	105
Pre-Roman	4	5	670	775
Post-Roman	1		5	
TOTAL	284	165	21045	13985

Stratigraphic excavation carried out in 6 parts of the site offers the best control of surface patterns. Like the survey, our excavation program was limited by practical concerns of access and logistics, which favored peripheral areas lying near field boundaries. In 4 cases architectural features were visible or otherwise apparent on the surface before digging. The two sectors without such surface features yielded either minor buildings (Area IV) or no structural remains at all (Area III). Information from these 6 sectors provides the opportunity to check apparent patterns of artifact differentiation and correlate survey and stratigraphic evidence.

Area III illustrates the uneasy relationship that can exist between surface and buried strata. The sector lies on the lower ridge about half-way between Areas I and II. This topographically undistinguished terrain occupies an open wheat field about 100 m WSW of *Sirmata* (fig. 2.7 above). The lack of any significant slope or evidence of modern disturbance recommended the area for intensive survey, which identified peak densities of 7.0 artifacts and 3.27 sherds per sq. m. These are, in fact, the highest levels noted anywhere at Kopetra. Finds appear to be concentrated near 8430/5950 (SG26), with large quantities of artifacts noted in 5 other survey units in the immediate vicinity. Artifact densities drop by half at radiate distances of 20-40 m, and beyond this they drop to background levels. The aggregate data from these 6 survey units constitute a major sub-site scatter that is chronologically and functionally homogeneous (Table 2.8).

Comparison of the surface finds from Area III with those from other parts of the site underscores their unusually rich composition (Table 2.3). All ceramic categories are much better attested than for both off-site and on-site survey units, the 4.3 artifacts per sq. m average noted for Area III being almost twice the level of the main settlement area and almost 12 times great-

TABLE 2.8. AREA III, ROMAN SURVEY POTTERY, SUMMARY
(intensive data only)

Area III-Survey	*rim*	*base*	*handle*	*sherd*	*sum*	*weight*	*avg. sherd wt.*
Fine	89	32	1	34	156	2520	16.15
Plain		10	2	12	24	435	18.13
Amphora	58	3	178	482	721	25930	35.96
Cook	6	1	17	46	70	540	7.71
Pithos	36	12	7	42	97	11270	116.19
Other	7	6	34	351	398	5125	12.88
ROMAN TOTAL	196	64	239	967	1466	45820	31.26

	rim	*base*	*handle*	*sherd*	*sum*	*weight*
CRS 1	2				2	35
CRS 2	8			1	9	130
CRS 8	2	1		2	5	110
CRS 9A	14	2		2	18	270
CRS 9B	7	10		3	20	415
CRS 9C	3	1			4	75
CRS 10	1				1	15
CRS 11		1	1	3	5	190
CRS other	3	8		9	20	370
CRS total	40	23	1	20	84	1610
LRC 3	6	3		1	10	135
LRC 3B	1				1	10
LRC 3C	1				1	10
LRC 3D	1				1	20
LRC 3E	1				1	15
LRC 3F	2				2	30
LRC 3G	5				5	100
LRC 3H	1	1			2	10
LRC 10A	23	2		2	27	340
LRC 10C	2				2	30
LRC other		1		2	3	25
LRC total	43	7		5	55	725
ARS 104B	1				1	20
ARS other				4	4	40
ARS total	1			4	5	60
ERS-A	2	2			4	75
Fine other	3			5	8	50
FINE TOTAL	89	32	1	34	156	2520
LR1	49	1	122	409	581	20345
KAmp1			2	6	8	215
KAmp2	1	1	15	21	38	1610
KAmp3	1		1		2	115
KAmp4			3	1	4	210
KAmp5			1		1	160
Other	7	1	34	45	87	3275
AMPHORA TOTAL	58	3	178	482	721	25930
Plain A		1		2	3	100
Plain B		9	2	10	21	335
PLAIN TOTAL		10	2	12	24	435
Cook D	6	1	17	46	70	540
Pithos A	5	9	1	13	28	2425
Pithos B				6	6	280
Pithos D	31	3	6	23	63	8565
PITHOS TOTAL	36	12	7	42	97	11270

er than outlying areas. The contrast is strongest among the fine pottery, whose average density of 0.26 sherds per sq. m at Area III is almost 7 times greater than is found in the primary habitation zone. The number of fragments of *pithoi* and rooftiles (large objects that tend to be spatially inert) more closely resembles data for the settlement area.

In 1990 we excavated a 1 x 4-m sondage at 8425/5950 in order to test the relationship between survey pottery and sub-surface features. Excavation reached sterile soil at a depth of 0.6 m without identifying any occupation levels. This limited undertaking recovered 759 sherds weighing 5.7 kg, of which 98% were assigned to the Roman era (Table 2.9; cf. below, Table 5.1). Datable pottery ranges from the late 5th-/early 6th-c. Cypriot Red Slip form 2 dish (5 exx.) to late 6th-/early 7th-c. forms in the three main fine wares (11 exx.).

TABLE 2.9. AREA III, ROMAN EXCAVATION POTTERY, SUMMARY

Area III-Excav.	*rim*	*base*	*handle*	*sherd*	*sum*	*weight*	*avg. sherd wt.*
Fine	22	3		40	65	350	5.38
Plain	9	1	3	15	28	260	9.29
Amphora	4		6	300	310	3155	10.18
Cook	3		23	53	79	275	3.48
Pithos	1			13	14	360	25.71
Other				250	250	1170	4.68
ROMAN TOTAL	39	4	32	671	746	5570	7.47

	rim	*base*	*handle*	*sherd*	*sum*
CRS 2	5				5
CRS 9A	1				1
CRS 11	1				1
CRS other	2	1		18	21
CRS TOTAL	9	1		18	28
LRC 3	4				4
LRC 10	5				5
LRC 10A	3				3
LRC other		2		20	22
LRC TOTAL	12	2		20	34
ARS 107	1				1
ARS other				2	2
ARS total	1			2	3
FINE TOTAL	22	3		40	65

	rim	*base*	*handle*	*sherd*	*sum*	*weight*
LR1	4		3	209	216	2360
LR4			2	13	15	190
LR5/6				13	13	105
LR7				1	1	10
KAmp2				21	21	205
KAmp4			1	8	9	90
KAmp5				3	3	30
Other				32	32	165
AMPHORA TOTAL	4		6	300	310	3155
Plain A	1	1		1	3	80
Plain B	6		3	14	23	155
Plain D	2				2	25
PLAIN TOTAL	9	1	3	15	28	260
Cook D	3		23	53	79	275
Pithos B				8	8	120
Pithos C	1				1	85
Pithos D				5	5	155
PITHOS TOTAL	1			13	14	360

The lack of walls and surfaces at Area III confirms the anomalous character of this surface assemblage and the absence of permanent habitation. There is no sign of unusual erosion or other surface processes, which minimizes the likelihood that buildings have been lost to systematic land-clearance. The absence of walls and floors does not necessarily prove the lack of occupation, which more extensive excavation might turn up. Exposure was limited and not pursued by a second sondage. After all, two of the trenches excavated at Dhiorios-*Mersineri* found no structural features, despite their proximity to Late Roman pottery kilns and related buildings (cf. Catling 1972: 17, Trenches C and Q). Yet the ceramic testimony of Area III, particularly the small size of excavated sherds, reinforces doubts about the nature of local activities.

No less than the survey finds, the excavated pottery from Area III stands apart from the other sectors (Tables 2.9-2.10; cf. below, Tables 5.2-5.5). Fine wares, for example, comprise 8.8% by count (6.3% by weight) of all Roman-era pottery here, a higher percentage than elsewhere. This strong showing can be explained in large part by the average sherd weight of barely 5 g, much less than the 17.6 g average for Kopetra as a whole. Some of this can be attributed to routine ploughing of Area III, since all sherds came from within 0.6 m of the surface, but it still falls far below the average sherd weight of nearly 19 g noted among the fine wares from the survey. Closer study confirms the small size of all categories of excavated sherds from Area III, ranging from 25.7 g for *pithoi* to 3.5 g for cooking wares. The disparity in sherd weight strongly suggests that Area III is essentially a surface scatter without deeper substance. Surface pottery from the main settlement area represents only a small portion of a larger sub-surface deposit and is regularly renewed by ploughing, a process well illustrated by the re-sampling of SG8 and 10 (Table 2.6). By contrast, peripheral or off-site sherd scatters are shallow, almost two-dimensional assemblages that lack underlying structure. The unusually small sherds recovered here by survey and excavation are best understood as secondary refuse derived from non-settlement deposition, probably the routine dumping of residential débris (cf. Bradley and Fulford 1980).

TABLE. 2.10. AREA III, ROMAN SURVEY AND EXCAVATION POTTERY COMPARED

Area III	*Excavation % count*	*Survey % count*	*Excavation % weight*	*Survey % weight*
Fine	8.8	10.6	6.3	5.5
Plain	3.8	1.6	4.7	1.0
Amphora	41.6	49.2	56.6	56.6
Cook	10.6	4.8	4.9	1.2
Pithos	1.9	6.6	6.5	24.6
Other	33.5	27.1	21.0	11.2
TOTAL	100.0	100.0	100.0	100.0

The possibility of dumping is supported by the abundance of much used domestic wares and their broad chronological range. Both 5th- and 7th-c. forms are well represented on the Area III surface and appear as distinct sub-site clusters in plan (fig. 2.15; Table 2.8). Their presence here suggests that dumping began in the 5th c. and continued over the life of the settlement. This interpretation gains support from the relative scarcity of two kinds of artifacts that are closely linked with habitation: *pithoi* and rooftiles. Excavated *pithos* sherds, which normally reflect domestic or commercial storage, are under-represented at Area III, comprising fewer than 2% by count (6% by weight) of the total, compared with 8% (33% by weight) for the site as a whole (Table 2.7; cf. below, Table 5.2). Moreover, excavated *pithos* sherds from Area III have an average weight of *c.*26 g — less than a quarter the size of *pithoi* from surveying Area III and only one-sixth the average for the survey as a whole. As for the other kinds of pottery, the small sherd size illustrates the effects of repeatedly ploughing a meager surface assemblage. Rooftiles offer a more complex view of this area. The greater numbers of Corinthian-style over Laconian-style tiles support the early appearance and long use of this type of tile. Yet unlike all other ceramic categories, tiles are scarcely better represented at Area III than at the settlement itself (Table 2.3; figs. 2.19-2.20). Recalling that the distribution of rooftiles, like other building materials, is usually a reliable indicator of the presence of structures, one can suggest that this departure reflects a functional separation between the activities (pottery) and place (rooftiles) of Late Roman habitation. In this light, Area III appears to have been the scene of residential discard that took place outside the village proper. The anomalous composition and small average sherd size reflect a dwindling supply of surface material. The agreement of survey and excavation data helps validate both methods while underscoring the need for their cautious interpretation.

Conclusions

Like most archaeological projects, the Kopetra survey represents a compromise among competing interests. The main objective was to salvage information from a rapidly changing landscape in a limited time and with few personnel. The use of multiple sampling strategies offered an opportunity to test some of the assumptions and methods of Mediterranean field survey in the context of Late Roman Cyprus.

The survey material provides an effective guide to the physical and chronological extent of local habitation. The area had been sparsely inhabited since Chalcolithic times but saw renewed activity in the early Iron Age. Neglected during the early years of Roman rule, in the A.D. 400s it became home to a minor settlement that expanded rapidly over the following century. Water probably was drawn from the river and nearby springs and surely was conserved by local inhabitants as they worked in the surrounding fields. Flourishing even into the early 7th c., this unwalled village at its apogee occupied an area of about 4 ha and may have been home to nearly 600 people. Selective excavation confirms this impression of rural prosperity by adding details of daily life and clarifying its sudden demise and brief re-occupation in the mid 600s. It is through the judicious synthesis of both kinds of evidence — surface and stratigraphic — that we can most fully envisage this small place in late antiquity.

3

The fabric of settlement

Still, the hammered gold in rooms all through
Byzantium conceals the pictureless underworlds
Of mortar slathered by the workmen's trowels ...
Gjertrud Schnackenberg, *A gilded lapse of time* (1992)

MATERIALS AND METHODS

The complexities of human settlement find their most enduring expression in architectural form. Domestic structures reflect the routines of daily life as pursued by individual families. Public buildings — whether intended for civic activities, religion, or popular entertainment — embody the concerns of the larger group, acknowledging the occasion and shaping the space for common assembly. The structural remains found at Kopetra show how one village addressed these recurring needs with houses and churches in the 6th c., and how later generations led their lives within them.

Building materials

The inhabitants of Kopetra employed a broad range of materials, both local and imported, in giving shape to their community. Identified buildings include three churches and two residential structures; other remains of uncertain purpose are evident across the site. All were assembled primarily of materials from the immediate vicinity. The bluff-top location in the central valley allowed ready access to local deposits of sedimentary rocks, igneous rocks, and alluvial fills from the Vasilikos river-bed, and timber from the Troodos foothills. Surface outcrops of gypsum provided structural stone and raw materials for making cement and plaster. Clays drawn from the river plain and upper valley were used to manufacture rooftiles as well as household pottery. Wood, little preserved today, was employed in various capacities during the building process, for structural timbers in floors and roofs, and as fuel for domestic and industrial purposes. Less common are imported materials, such as basalt grinder and millstone fragments, and fine marbles for interior furnishing and decoration. At least two types of rooftiles were brought in large quantities from elsewhere on the island.

Stone

One of Kopetra's most striking features is the blanket of gypsum and limestone rubble, regularly ploughed, that extends across the ridge surface. This architectural débris was found in equal abundance during excavation and reflects the most commonly used building materials in the valley during prehistory, later antiquity, and more recent times (cf. Christodoulou 1959: 65; Ionas 1988: 135-42). Most of this rubble consists of small fragments, relatively fine grained and rarely larger than 0.2 m in diameter. More substantial are irregular and roughly shaped limestone blocks with banded chert, some as large as 0.4-0.5 m on a side. Theophrastus (*Lap.* 64-66) knew that "a large quantity of gypsum is produced in Cyprus and can be seen everywhere, because it is found as soon as they dig and take away a little soil" (in Wallace and Orphanides 1990: 58). At Kopetra three varieties of gypsum were used in unfinished and roughly squared blocks to establish foundations and rising walls: dense laminated gypsum known as *marmara*, a variety of dark, coarse-grained saccharoidal gypsum, and selenite gypsum with translucent bladed folia (Pantazis 1967; B. Gomez in Todd 1987: 3-4; Wright 1992: 392-93). Richard Pococke, visiting the island in 1738, noted the quarrying of *marmara* around Larnaca: "They have also in the mountains near that city a very thin marble paving stone, that cuts like chalk with a common saw" (in Cobham 1908: 265-66; Martin 1998: 51). Deposits of *marmara* and saccharoidal gypsum occur about 300 m northeast of Kopetra at *Kafkalies*, which today supplies local producers and the nearby cement factories at Vasiliko and Moni (below, Appendix 6). Extensive post-Roman extraction and erosion have obscured all surface traces of ancient quarrying in this area. Survey of the ridge located several large architectural blocks shaped of sandstone and sandy limestones (sometimes called *pouropetra*), easily worked materials found across the island. This stone was preferred for such large architectural details as lintels and thresholds, as well as decorative moldings. Some of these blocks may have been freshly cut in Roman times, but others appear to have been salvaged from the Late Bronze Age site of *Ayios Dhimitrios*, located across the valley *c.*400 m west of Kopetra. Local fieldstones include rounded basalt, dolomite, and andesite, locally known as *sideropetra*, which probably came from the Vasilikos river-bed.

Cyprus lacks any good source of structural marble, which reached the island during the Roman period through a complex network of suppliers (Bear 1963: 161; Sodini 1989a). A few examples of fine imported stone were noted around the churches, where they served in decorative and non-structural rôles, especially as furniture. White and gray-veined marbles were used for the top surface of several tables at the south church. Small fragments of white, gray, and yellow marbles were cut for the *opus sectile* paving of the north church. Floor and vault mosaics in these two buildings included tesserae of white, yellow, pink, red, blue-gray, and black stone, as well as glass.

Mortar and plaster

Local gypsums and limestones also figured in making mortar, cement, and decorative plaster. For these purposes fine-grained gypsum (*gypsos*) was selected, crushed, and heated to make slaked lime (calcium sulfate hemihydrate). The calcination point is relatively low, *c.*100-130° C, compared with 900° C for limestone (Wright 1985: 373-74). With the addition of water, the mixture yields a light-weight, tenacious slurry that can be combined with various aggregates suitable for construction. Study of selected cement samples from Kopetra identified several different grades of materials, including small to large fragments of gypsum and calcium carbonate set within a gypsum matrix. Examination by P. Goldberg of the *Sirmata* cistern's hydraulic cement lining, for example, revealed particles of clay, chert, chalk, and ceramic. Microscopic and X-ray diffraction analysis of comparable plaster samples from Salamis identified rehydrated hemihydrate residual gypsum with possible anhydrite fragments (Callot 1980: 352-54). A soft secondary limestone known as *havara* was sometimes used for making structural cements too. Calcinated gypsum without the strong aggregate yields a fine plaster that can be easily spread or molded. Comparison of recent gypsum products with Late Bronze Age mortars shows how little the basic technology has changed since prehistory (Wright 1992: 393-94; Malinowski 1998).

Gypsum craftsmanship has a long history in the E Mediterranean in general and in Cyprus in particular. During the Hellenistic period gypsum-based materials became especially popular, perhaps helping to compensate for the poor quality of local stone in monumental construction (Theophrastus, op cit.; Wright 1992: 425). In Roman and early Byzantine times form-cast plaster served as an inexpensive medium for architectural decoration and sculpture.[1] Regional craftsmen were highly regarded for their skilled shaping of molded stucco in fine-grained plaster from the 5th through early 7th c. St. Nilus of Sinai specifically mentions the technique in an early 5th-c. letter admonishing the prefect Olympiodoros not to display in his church "a variety of stuccowork so as to delight the eye in God's house and ... to set up in the nave a thousand crosses and the pictures of different birds and beasts, reptiles and plants" (*PG* 79: 577-80; transl. Mango 1972: 32-33; Karageorghis 1962: 413; Megaw 1974: 69; id. 1976b: 21).

In Cyprus the fragile material is subject to many depositional hazards and does not gracefully tolerate water leaching through porous soils, yet several important Roman examples are known. Architectural plaster of 'early Christian' date has been reported from Gönyeli northwest of Nicosia (Megaw 1953: 137). Excavations at Pyla-*Koutsopetria* on the SE coast have recently uncovered several rooms of a 5th- or 6th-c. house with incised and painted wall-plaster (Christou 1994: 689-91; Hadjisavvas 2000: 692-93). The technique was particularly well suited for church decoration. The small basilica at Marathovouno in N central Cyprus was built and decorated with carved and cast gypsum elements, including fluted columns and molded screens (Papageorghiou 1963). A plaster cornice was found at the Alassa-*Ayia Mavri* basilica in the Kouris valley (Flourentzos 1996: 15 no. 5b, pl. XXV). Excavations at the southwest basilica at Amathus identified molded

1 E.g., Butler 1929: 181; Ovadiah 1970: 207; Downey 1977: 4; Ploug 1985: 161; Wright 1992: 394-96.

gypsum plaques depicting animal chases or hunting scenes (Karageorghis 1962: 412-13, fig. 106a-c; Michaelides 1998: 192 fig. 8). The baptistery *diakonikon* attached to the episcopal basilica at Kourion included a 6th-c. gypsum-plaster cornice painted red, green, and yellow that extended along the walls and transverse arches (Megaw 1976a: 358 fig. 28). Molded gypsum was used extensively in the (early 6th-c.?) rebuilding of the Soloi basilica, where it was favored for Corinthian capitals and other foliage decoration (des Gagniers and Tram Tam Tinh 1985: 94 nos. 57-60, 111 n.109; Megaw 2000 prefers an early 5th-c. date for the building). Cast gypsum moldings and acanthus capitals survive in the later 6th- or early 7th-c. Panagia Angelokistos at Kiti (Karageorghis 1960: 295-97). By far the best preserved group of Cypriot stuccowork comes from the building known as the House of the Oil Press at Salamis. Two parts of this structure, an apsidal hall and an upper room elsewhere in the complex, were embellished with fluted pilasters and dentilated cornices, an animal hunt frieze, and historiated capitals. This elaborate cycle apparently was installed in the late 400s. Its extensive remains offer the best available evidence for understanding Late Roman stuccowork in Cyprus or anywhere in the E Mediterranean (Argoud *et al.* 1980; Callot 1980). The revival or survival of this decorative tradition, unstudied for mediaeval Cyprus, can be seen in the decorative shelf moldings known as *souvantza*, which survive in some traditional buildings on the island (Ionas 1988: 90, 94-97; Rizopoulou-Egoumenidou and Seretis 2000: 427; see also the fine examples at the CAARI building in Nicosia).

Traces of decorative plaster turned up at all three local churches. Recovered fragments range from plain rounded elements to elaborate cornices, including a stepped molding apparently based on one known at Salamis. Of particular importance is a small but complex group of representational images found at the south church. Identified pieces represent baskets, several animals, and the seated Virgin with child. Despite their fragmentary condition, these remarkable pieces compare favorably with the best stucco surviving on the island and probably were made by itinerant artisans.

Timber

Wood played three essential rôles in building Late Roman Kopetra: as an aid during the process of construction, as structural members in upper floors and roofs, and as fuel for making cement, plaster, and rooftiles. Today there is scant physical evidence of its former importance, which only emerges from close study of the architectural remains. Wood boards, for example, were used to construct the formwork lining many foundation trenches, a process most clearly seen at *Sirmata*. Similar shuttering may have been used to stabilize rising walls while the mortar dried; interior timbers may have reinforced some walls as well. Scaffolding was used to give access to upper walls and for centering during the construction of arches and semidomes. Carefully-shaped wood forms played a vital rôle in the initial casting of stucco moldings, which were attached by dowels to the upper walls — a technique clearly evident at the south church. When completed, all three churches were covered by pitched roofs with terracotta tiles supported by sturdy timber frames and decking. Ancillary buildings at *Sirmata* and the residential structures at Areas IV and VI apparently had flat or sloping roofs covered with tiles, *marmara* slabs, or other materials supported by timber beams; at least part of the Area VI building had an upper floor as well. Iron nails presumably coming from these roofs turned up across the site. An iron pivot band found at *Sirmata* documents the use of wood doors in the narthex of the church.

Fragments of charcoal recovered from Kopetra include pine, olive, juniper, walnut, poplar, vines, and the shrubs *Phillyrea* and *Vitex* (Table 3.1). Not all of these species had significant structural potential but many could have been used as fuel.

The densely forested slopes of the Troodos and Kyrenia mountains were well known to classical authors, who esteemed the island's timber resources for shipbuilding in particular (Pliny, *NH* 16.20.3; Amm. Marc. 14.8.14). The island's most important commercial species in Roman times included pine, cypress, cedar, and oak.[2] Extensive quantities of timber, including Aleppo pine, eastern plane, dwarf oak, and alder, were used as internal shoring in the Roman mines at Skouriotissa near Xeros in N Cyprus (Bruce 1937: 650-62). As elsewhere in the Troodos, wood was needed for smelting copper ore near mines in the upper Vasilikos valley. These and other demands must have put tremendous pressure on the island's dwindling woodland resources.

---

2 Christodoulou 1959: 50-51 and 109-13; Thirgood 1987: 70-72; Burnet 1997.

TABLE. 3.1. SUMMARY OF IDENTIFIED BOTANICAL REMAINS
recovered by flotation, after a study by W. O'Brien.

Lot	*Cypressus/ Juniperus*	*Hordeum*	*Juglans*	*Olea*	*Pinus*	*Populus*	*Triticum*	*Vitex*	*Vitis*	*Phillyrea*
I-6					32					
I-7			6						8	
I-18					13					
I-19			3	2	5			7	6	
I-23					3				2	
I-33	1			112	40	1				28
II-27					5					
II-30					7					
II-33			4	2						
IV-6				2	1					
IV-9				2						
IV-10				1	1					
IV-12					1					
IV-15				5						
V-3					3					
VI-4	61	1	8		122		5			
Total	62	1	21	126	233	1	5	7	16	28

Hordeum vulgare ssp. *spontaneum* C. Koch — wild barley)
Juglans regia L. — walnut
Cupressus sempervirens/Juniperus communis — common juniper
Olea europa L. — olive
Pinus halepensis Miller — Aleppo pine
Populus nigra L. — black poplar
Triticum aestivum L. — bread wheat
Vitex agnus — castus L.
Vitis vinifera — grape

Other materials

Little direct evidence survives of the place (no doubt important) of earth and clay in local building. A narrow mudbrick partition spanned the S end of the *Sirmata* narthex, and similar walls probably stood nearby. The residential buildings at Areas IV and VI may well have featured upper walls made of mudbrick or *terre pisé* resting on fieldstone socles. Mud mortar was used to reinforce fieldstone walls across the site. Such unstable materials do not survive well in shallow deposits, however, and are rarely reported in Roman contexts on the island.

Fired bricks never gained much popularity in Roman Cyprus and were not widely used until recently (Christodoulou 1959: 65; Wright 1992: 381). No examples of structural bricks of either square or rectangular shape were noted at Kopetra. By contrast, rooftiles were a prominent feature of the island. Pliny (*NH* 7.56.195) attributes their invention to the mythical Cinyras of Cyprus. Be that as it may, terracotta rooftiles were common at Paphos, Salamis, and other Early Imperial cities.

Fragmentary examples of three distinct tile systems still cover the ground at Kopetra: an elongated tile of curved, almost Laconian shape in a fine red fabric, and two kinds of Corinthian-style tiles made in fine yellow and coarse dark red fabrics, respectively. The fine-fabric tiles were mass-produced elsewhere on the island — the red tiles originating near Paphos and the yellow tiles coming from the lower Mesaoria plain in the east (Rautman *et al.* 1999; below, Appendix 3). The coarse Corinthian-style tiles, while less numerous at the site, were made locally. It is reasonable to assume that most rooftiles were ordered as large groups when individual buildings, particularly churches, were being constructed (below, pp. 53-55). All three types seem to have been used during the late 6th and early 7th c., and the locally made tiles may have continued into the later 7th c. as well. Tile fragments were incorporated in several late, unmortared walls.

Building methods

Methods of construction at Kopetra reflect a village vernacular that was tempered by awareness of urban practices. Rudimentary surveying principles underlie the design of the three churches, which reflect prevailing architectural currents and liturgical needs. The excavated remains show clearly how foundations and walls were built, while arches and roofs can be inferred indirectly and by analogy with better preserved structures on the island. Apart from several architectural innovations introduced at *Sirmata*, it is the decoration of the churches that distinguishes the settlement and attests the artistic aspirations of its inhabitants.

Layout and design

For the most part, buildings were designed within a local tradition that was conditioned by topography and available resources. The relationship of individual structures to the settlement as a whole remains largely unclear. The evidence suggests that in some ways Kopetra may have resembled the relatively compact arrangement of villages long typical of the island.[3] The conspicuous north and south churches stood near the inhabited site's unwalled perimeter. The proximity of two buildings flanking a narrow alley at Area IV implies that open space may have been limited in parts of the village. A low terrace or promontory seems to have been preferred for the siting of all three churches and the Area VI residence. The contrasting plans and features of the two houses imply differences of social status as well as function, with the smaller structure (Area IV) used for agricultural processing and light industry, and the better constructed building (Area VI) littered with a broader variety of artifacts, including fine pottery, glass, and metals.

The design of the churches may also reflect differing levels of patronage and changing social needs. Their common roots in Cypriot architecture is apparent in the choice of the simple aisled basilica plan, the most versatile church form of late antiquity and well established on the island from the 5th c. Unlike the residential buildings and many of the isolated wall sections noted on the surface, all three churches share the same NE orientation. Once the basic decisions — like the size, number, and function of lateral spaces — were made, the design of these buildings emerged over the course of construction. A standard unit of measure is not apparent from the excavated remains. Late Roman builders may have been influenced by the 0.31-m foot known at Antioch, but it is unlikely that this unit was used here any more consistently that it was on the mainland.[4] Building measurements elsewhere might be made either as clear spans or between center lines of features. Interior dimensions were derived from a series of simple proportional relationships among spatial units, which may have been based on a primary dimension such as overall length. Most of these could be established on-site using minimal equipment, primarily wood stakes and string (e.g., Tsafrir 1990; Buchwald 1995). Nothing suggests that abstract geometric principles were employed. A professional *architekton* may have been called to the village to advise on some matters, but most work probably was carried out by local residents.

Foundations

The identified buildings are not especially large and stood on relatively shallow foundations. Relying on the local marl to provide a sturdy platform, builders preferred to cut foundation trenches and rooms out of the bedrock rather than build artificial platforms.[5] This contour-adapting approach resulted in clusters of stepped spaces with varied floor levels reflecting the local topography. At *Sirmata*, the basilica and narthex were excavated into the natural hill to a depth of about 1 m along their N side, while the S aisle and flanking space

---

3 Christodoulou 1959: 63; J. M. Wagstaff in Todd 1987: 8-9; Ionas 1988: 17-39.

4 Cf. Underwood 1948: 64-65; Ovadiah 1970; Schilbach 1970; Restle 1979: 89-135; Hellenkemper 1989: 181-90.

5 For similar trench-built foundations in Cyprus see Argoud *et al.* 1980: 25; Taylor and Megaw 1981: 209-12; du Bouetiez *et al.* 1991: 753-56.

continue all the way to the edge of the mound. The south church similarly was recessed into a low prominence with its S lateral space sited 0.5 m lower, at the level of the surrounding plain. The relatively good condition of both structures results in no small part from their semi-subterranean construction.

Depending on the ground level, walls rested on either shallow foundation courses or the marl itself. Most foundations at *Sirmata* and in Area II consist of a single thin, mortared leveling course of flat, horizontally-laid stones supporting a row of roughly squared gypsum blocks. On average, these foundations lie *c.*0.2-0.3 m below the paved surface. In some cases wood formwork clearly was used within the foundation trench; this has also been documented at Salamis and Amathus. More substantial preparations were needed to support the semidomes. The main apse at *Sirmata* was cut out of the marl, with the back wall resting on a 0.8-m wide foundation course (below, fig. 3.10). In recent years part of the rising wall has shifted off this foundation to reveal a mortared layer of large stones with a smoothed upper surface. A curved line indicating the line of the apse was incised into the top to guide the builders. Small handprints impressed into the surface tell us that in late antiquity, as today, children were irresistibly attracted to play nearby while work was going on.

Rising walls and interior supports

Like the foundations, rising walls were assembled of locally available materials with differing degrees of care. Several approaches to construction can be distinguished within the continuum of local practice. The churches preserve the most solidly built walls, with gypsum and limestone rubble thickly bedded in a mortar cast within wood shuttering. These walls were built in sections that can be distinguished by clear horizontal and vertical seams. Within some walls builders included prefabricated blocks of mortared stone that recalls ashlar construction.[6] These sturdily-mortared stone walls average 0.4-0.5 m thick and were built as both freestanding and partially recessed features. Apse walls, which bore a more substantial load, are somewhat thicker but of similar build.

The same methods were employed for the freestanding cylindrical shafts that formed the nave supports: curved surfaces were shaped by setting small fragments of gypsum and fieldstone in a thick mortar matrix, presumably enclosed by wood formwork, and later covered by one or more layers of plaster. The obvious drawbacks of such features — they would have been difficult to construct and less structurally sound than rectangular piers — make clear that the builders were deliberately imitating stone columns. The colonnades of all three churches were concluded by semicircular wall shafts. These slender rounded strips, 0.4-0.5 m across, were built together with the rising walls and internal piers to articulate the interior space. Located at opposite ends of the main hall, they clearly belonged to the nave colonnades, although in other settings their structural rôle is less certain. In the *Sirmata* narthex, for example, 4 pairs of wall shafts apparently supported transverse arches 3.4 m wide. Elsewhere in Cyprus wall shafts were used primarily to terminate colonnades (e.g., Soloi, Marathovouno, Peyia, Yialousa). Flat shafts apparently supported transverse arches spanning the lateral *katechoumena* at the Kourion episcopal basilica. The wall shaft of space IV at *Sirmata*, however, lacks any clear structural purpose and may simply reflect the popularity of the idea. No such shafts appear at Kopetra outside the three church complexes, nor have they been noted in other secular buildings on the island.

Nave piers and wall shafts probably carried capitals and arcades supporting the upper clerestory wall. Many fragments of plaster Corinthian-inspired capitals were found at Area II, and elsewhere they can be assumed as the conventional means of transition between the cylindrical supporting shaft and the passive, linear mass of the upper wall. Nothing remains of the arcades themselves but their original presence is implied by pier spacing, which ranges from an average of 2.5 m at *Sirmata* to 2.7 m at the south church. Lacking structural marble, local

---

6 Cf. Vann 1989: 243-46 for a similar practice at Carthage.

builders might have considered using timber beams for horizontal architraves, as may have happened at Ayios Philon (Taylor and Megaw 1981: 233; the 2.2-m interval used here is the shortest reported on the island). Yet within its own structural limits, gypsum mortar could have been used to build arches that needed to support only the clerestory and roof. The flexibility of this construction method, still apparent in traditional Cypriot building, could easily have accommodated slight irregularities in the placement of nave supports. In fact, such irregularities appear in most Late Roman buildings on the island.[7] Certainly mortared rubble was used successfully for the much greater semidome spans of all three churches.

A less regular sort of rubble construction that set fieldstones of different sizes in thin beds of either mortar or mud is found in the residential buildings and some secondary church walls. These walls could vary considerably in thickness and quality. The walls of the Area IV residence consist of fieldstones and gypsum fragments that were either dry-laid or set in very little mortar. They do not stand very high and may have been continued by mudbrick. In traditional Cypriot houses mudbrick walls typically rest atop stone foundations, built somewhat thicker than the rising walls, that average 0.6 m high (Christodoulou 1959: 65; Ionas 1988: 145). The secondary partitions at *Sirmata* and Area II also incorporate building spoils, including large fragments of gypsum cement, many with small rounded pebbles, rooftiles, and decorative plaster. Evidence of all-earth construction is less apparent. Mudbricks were used to build a late wall spanning the *Sirmata* narthex and probably were used in the superstructures of many domestic structures. While no longer preserved, terre pisé and rammed earth no doubt met many needs in building houses, stables, hearths, and seasonal structures.

Floors

In contrast to foundations and walls, the greatest variety of floor covering is found at the upper end of the architectural spectrum. As a group, the churches illustrate the hierarchy of materials employed for paving élite buildings in Late Roman Cyprus.[8] Large marble blocks do not appear at the site, but the *opus sectile* paving of the north church's sanctuary was considered almost as prestigious a material. The floor mosaics at the south church occupy the next highest level of patronage and accentuate the most liturgically important parts of the building. The sanctuary mosaic consists of a polychrome geometric panel with tesserae set in a hard cement. A floor mosaic in the S chapel was less well bedded and later covered by a layer of gypsum mortar.

The most common paving method employed carefully-cut *marmara* slabs. Individual blocks were sawn into rectangular panels of regular size averaging 0.05-0.10 m in thickness. These slabs were laid in continuous rows on the leveled marl surface, either with or without a shallow mortar bedding. The well preserved floor of the *Sirmata* basilica shows the thoughtful organization of blocks, with a central axis of large slabs flanked by perpendicularly laid rows of alternately large and small blocks — an arrangement also seen in the narthex of the acropolis basilica at Amathus (Pralong 1994a: 418). Steps, benches, screens, and various kinds of furniture used thin slabs of this cheap and versatile — if not especially enduring — material, which is a main component of traditional building on the island (Christodoulou 1959: 66; Ionas 1988: 141).

Architectural details and decoration

For the most part, Kopetra's buildings were structurally simple and plainly adorned. The lack of marble thresholds with pivot and lock holes, common at Late Roman sites across the E Mediterranean, reflects the paucity of good stone on the island. The narthex doorway at *Sirmata* included two pivot holes set in a threshold made of gypsum cement; the discovery of an iron band illustrates the kind of swinging doors that were used here, probably together with

7 An uneven spacing of supports suggests a horizontal architrave to Taylor and Megaw 1981: 233; and A. Papageorghiou in Aupert 1996: 88.

8 In general, see Megaw 1976b: 4-18.

curtains hung from wood lintels. Elsewhere, doorways may have been closed by wood leaves anchored directly on the flanking wall spurs, without separate jambs. No trace of windows survives among the excavated buildings and no carved mullions have been discovered in the valley. Presumably these would have been narrow arched openings set in the upper walls of both churches and houses to provide light while ensuring the privacy and safety of the occupants. The Aegean preference for large windows, composed in groups or with multiple lights separated by stone mullions, is not known in Cyprus outside of the coastal cities. Thin sheets of *marmara* pierced by multiple drilled holes may have served as window screens.

The three church interiors were embellished to varying degrees by sculptural decoration made of gypsum plaster and stucco. Only a few traces of this were found at *Sirmata* and the north church, but the south church preserved many fragments of a rich sculptural cycle including architectural shafts, capitals, moldings, and representational imagery. The quality of production and range of subjects are directly comparable to the House of the Oil Press at Salamis (Argoud *et al.* 1980; Callot 1980). Study of the Salamis material suggests that in many cases column flutes, wall moldings, and other architectural details were cast in re-usable wood molds and finished in place. At Kopetra such *in situ* stuccowork includes vertical and spirally-fluted column shafts, Corinthian-style capitals, floral patterns, and a distinctive cornice closely resembling one found at Salamis. Finer representational details, including animals and figural elements, may have been pre-cast before installation. The close technical resemblance of the structural plaster and decorative stucco suggests that both techniques were current at Kopetra and probably involved itinerant craftsmen from an urban workshop.

Decoration of the north and south churches was completed by mosaics in the semidome of the main apse and perhaps the upper sanctuary walls. These mosaics survive mainly as colorful loose tesserae, with a number of mortar-bedded fragments preserving various patterns. Wall and vault mosaics were found in churches across the island, although in most cases their locations and subjects are imperfectly known. The documented (if not all surviving) apse programs at Kiti, Livadhia, and Lythrankomi give some sense of the original appearance of the Kopetra mosaics.[9]

Roofs

Tiles provide the main evidence for reconstructing the roofs at Kopetra. Most rooftiles were brought from outside the valley. Presumably ordered in bulk for initial construction, during later repairs they could be used interchangeably on a single building (as also noted at Aliki on Thasos; Sodini and Kolokotsas 1984: 184-86). The churches probably were covered by a series of shallow pitched and outward sloping roofs of continuous or broken slope, with a semi-conical shell over the semidome masonry of the apse. Flat pan tiles probably were laid directly atop timber planking on a mud and straw bedding, while the lighter cover tiles may have been set in place, either with mortar (as at Aliki and Pella) or without. Other buildings probably carried flat earthen surfaces or shed roofs made of tiles or thin gypsum slabs set in a straw and mud mortar on a timber frame, as continued by traditional Cypriot building practices (Ionas 1988: 74-79). Iron nails and wood pegs would have secured the timber framework but do not seem to have been used to attach the tiles themselves. Figure 3.26 below offers one possible solution to the roofing needs of the *Sirmata* complex.

In several cases, run-off from the roofs was directed away from the foundations and into subterranean storage for later use. This implies the presence of an eaves trough or channel along each side of the building feeding one or more vertical drains. At *Sirmata* a downspout at the basilica's NE corner led to a sandstone catch-basin, which drained through a terracotta pipe into the large courtyard cistern. The cistern's size and careful construction reflect the importance of water conservation to the community. At Area II a low channel of mortared stone extended south behind the apse to an unlocated reservoir. At Area VI a covered drain running

9 Megaw 1974: 74-76; 1976b: 22-25; Megaw and Hawkins 1977; Michaelides 1987: 54-57.

through a narrow passage space 4 may have been used for either water storage or waste disposal. The lack of any drain or sign of significant erosion in the Area IV alley suggests the thoroughness with which water was conserved.

Estimated terracotta roofing loads

Roofs are among the most commonly assumed and overlooked parts of the many basilicas built across the Mediterranean in the 5th and 6th c. (Orlandos 1952-54: 386-96). The architectural consistency of the Kopetra churches, which saw innovation primarily in details of liturgical organization and interior decoration, presents few difficulties for understanding how they were covered, leaving more troublesome questions to the realm of secular building. Large numbers of rooftiles were found in all excavation sectors and across the site's surface, and attest three main groups: Laconian-style tiles made in a fine red fabric, small Corinthian-style tiles made in a fine yellow fabric, and large Corinthian-style tiles made in a coarse fabric (below, pp. 177-78). The abundance of the first two kinds of rooftiles at all three churches suggests complex building histories, with different types used for later repairs. Despite some uncertainty, the available evidence permits some rough estimates about the number of tiles originally required by each structure. Calculations based on the average weights of these tiles yield conjectural estimates of the load of the superstructure carried by the buildings.

The church complex at Area I, the only substantially excavated sector at Kopetra, supports the most reliable analysis. The entire building plan is known and the total area can be plausibly reconstructed. The large number of red-fabric rooftiles found at the hillock allows us to assume that these were part of the original scheme, with Corinthian-style tiles added during later repairs. Table 3.2 summarizes the numbers and weights of such tiles at the sector. A slope of 20° is assumed for all pitched roofs, which increases the lateral width (and thus the tiled surface) of individual buildings by *c.*6% (Brodribb 1987: 10). All eaves are given a projecting overhang of 0.25 m. Pan tiles should have been closely set, with any gaps between rows offset by the overlapping of rising tiles. Substantially preserved examples measure 0.70 x 0.34 m and are estimated to have weighed *c.*5 kg; the addition of cover tiles, assumed to weigh one-fourth as much, adds 25% to the total load (so Cato's estimated value of *tegulae* in *Agr.* 14.4). Thus, the red-fabric tile set should weigh *c.*26.25 kg per sq. m. For the sake of simplicity, calculations employ an equal number of pan and cover tiles; one can imagine the extra row of covers was assigned to complete the ridge or fill other gaps in the scheme.

TABLE 3.2. ESTIMATED ROOFTILE LOADS FOR AREA I

Red-fabric tile set:			
0.70 x .034 m pan tile =	0.238 sq. m =	5 kg	
1 sq. m =	4.2 tiles or	21 kg	+25% for cover tiles = 26.25 kg/sq. m
Main basilica:			
width: 10.5 m + 6% = 11.13 m or	16 pan tiles at 0.70 m long		
length: 19.0 m or	56 pan tiles at 0.34 m wide		
16 x 56 = 896 pan tiles	x 5 kg/pan =	4480 kg	+25% for cover tiles = 5600 kg
South lateral space:			
4 x 47 tiles = 188 pan tiles	x 5 kg/pan =	940 kg	+25% for cover tiles =1175 kg
Narthex:			
6 x 45 tiles = 270 pan tiles	x 5 kg/pan =	1350 kg	+25% for cover tiles =1688 kg
Spaces I, III-V:			
4 x 13 tiles = 52 pan tiles			
8 x 63 tiles = 504 pan tiles	556 x 5 kg/pan =	2780 kg	+25% for cover tiles =3475 kg
TOTAL: about 3820 tiles, or			11,938 kg

These assumptions lead one to estimate that the main basilica roof at *Sirmata* required some 896 pan tiles, for a load of 5600 kg. A simple shed roof over the S lateral space involved about 188 pan tiles, with another 270 pan tiles necessary to cover the narthex. At minimum, the church would have needed 1354 pans and the same number of covers, or 2708 tiles in all. This gives a total load in the red-fabric tile set of 8462.5 kg. To these quantities must be added the roofs over the courtyard rooms. The combined areas of spaces I and III-V is about 130 m^2. Applying the same reasoning to these roofs yields a total of 1112 pans and covers, weighing at least 3475 kg. It is likely that as many as 3820 individual tiles weighing almost 12,000 kg were needed to cover the entire complex at Area I.

Similar approximations can be applied to the other two basilicas. Without their complete plans such estimates represent only minimum tile needs, which are derived from the total roof areas rather than from a conjectural reconstruction. (Calculation by area yields a slightly smaller total: e.g., 888 pan tiles for the main hall at *Sirmata* instead of 896 — a difference of less than 1%.) The greater abundance of yellow-fabric Corinthian-style rooftiles at these sectors suggests that these buildings were originally covered with the smaller, heavier tiles. Substantially preserved pans average 0.44 x 0.35-0.40 m in size and weigh *c.*6 kg; the full set with covers would have weighed *c.*45.5 kg per sq. m (Table 3.3). The south church (Area II) with its three-aisle basilica, narthex, and S lateral space, has a minimum roof area of 388 m^2, allowing an overhang of 0.25-m on all sides. This would have required 4700 tiles weighing at least 17,654 kg — over twice the load of the east church at Area I. The known parts of the even larger north church at Area V had a roof area of 563 m^2, which would have needed some 6825 yellow-fabric Corinthian-style tiles weighing well over 25,000 kg.

TABLE 3.3. ESTIMATED ROOFTILE LOADS FOR AREAS II AND V

Yellow-fabric tile set:				
0.44 x 0.375 (avg.) pan tile =	0.165 sq. m =	6 kg		
1 sq. m. =	6.06 tiles or	36.36 kg	+25% for cover tiles =	45.5 kg/sq. m
Area II:				
basilica: 12 x 19 =	228 sq. m			
narthex: 4.25 x 12 =	51 sq. m			
south lateral space: 4.25 x 20.5 =	87 sq. m			
	366 sq. m	+ 6% = 388 sq. m est. total roof area at 20% pitch		
TOTAL:	388 sq. m x 45.5 kg/sq. m =		about 4700 tiles, or	17,654 kg
Area V:				
basilica: 15 x 23.5 =	352.5 sq. m			
narthex: 4.5 x 15 =	67.5 sq. m			
south lateral space: 4.75 x 23.5 =	111.6 sq. m			
	531.6 sq. m	+ 6% = 563 sq. m est. total roof area at 20% pitch		
TOTAL:	563 sq. m x 45.5 kg/sq. m = about 6825 tiles			25,617 kg

One obvious point made by these calculations is the greater efficiency of the red-fabric Laconian-style tile set, which provided more coverage with significantly less weight (26.25 kg *versus* more than 45.5 kg per sq. m) than the yellow-fabric Corinthian-style set. The latter appears on the two larger and earlier churches at the site, and belongs to the most widely used roofing-system of the classical Mediterranean. This conservative tradition is attested across the island and it is unsurprising to find these yellow-fabric tiles manufactured in the region of Salamis, the most thoroughly hellenized of Cypriot cities with a long tradition of monumental building. By contrast, the red-fabric Laconian-style tiles came from the Paphos area and may not have become popular until late antiquity. At Kopetra they appear especially at the late 6th-c. church at *Sirmata* and house(s) near Area VI (above, p. 38); they are present also at the early 7th-c. acropolis basilica at Amathus (Hadjichristophi 1989: 878). It is tempting to see the appeal of these lighter-weight tiles for builders who were repairing structural damage or initiating new work. This advantage seems to have been inherent in the fine-grained terra rossa clays of W Cyprus, however, and did not readily translate into other materials. During the later 6th and 7th c., residents of the Vasilikos valley produced large Corinthian-style tiles averaging 0.56 x 0.48 m and 14-15 kg. The resulting tile set may have exceeded 65 kg per sq. m — half again the load of the yellow-tiles (although still much less than reported loads of over 100 kg per sq. m in early Roman Britain; Brodribb 1987: 11-12). Apart from their strength, the evident advantage of such tiles would seem to be their availability at a time when imported tiles were becoming scarce.

Such speculations, while necessarily approximate, underscore the importance of rooftiles in the life of the village. Over the course of the 6th c., Kopetra's inhabitants imported great quantities of tiles made elsewhere on the island. The dense scatter of tile fragments across the present site indicates that they were commonly used to shelter private houses as well as public buildings. The construction of the three churches alone may have required over 15,000 rooftiles weighing close to 60,000 kg. The vast majority of these tiles would have been carried from their places of manufacture by small coastal ships as far as Zyyi-*Petrini*, and then brought overland by wagon to the site. The care with which these large yet fragile objects were acquired, transported, and then secured in place reflects a major investment of effort and resources for this rural settlement. The complexity and scale of the undertaking were a significant part of its communal identity.

AREA I: A MONASTERY AT *SIRMATA*

Introduction

Sirmata, like the earlier form *Saranda Ayious*, designates the low hill or mound that rises in the SE part of the Kopetra ridge, *c.*200 m west of the Late Roman settlement (LV.20.248; figs. 2.4, 2.7). The toponym appears on the cadastral plan of 1917 and includes fields lying east and south of the hill between the new highway and the older, parallel roadway. The mound, which consists of a limestone and marl core with a thin calcareous soil cover, forms a minor topographic landmark visible to travelers along both the highway and the road leading to Kalavasos and the Vasilikos dam. In the early 20th c., a narrow-gauge railway for transporting gypsum from the nearby quarries at *Kafkalies* curved around the E and S sides of the hill before descending to the river-plain below Kopetra. During the 1980s, the mound became the site of a small asphalt production facility supplying builders of the highway that crossed the valley *c.*100 m to the south. Presumably during this period its periphery was damaged by large-scale earthmoving and a load of tar was dumped on the top. Surrounding fields were left fallow following the events of 1974 through the years of our project.

Today *Sirmata* lies close to the paved road to Kalavasos and the country houses that are being built along it. The mound has a diameter of 30-40 m and rises 6-8 m to reach a maximum elevation of *c.*80 m asl. It was visited on several occasions during the 1970s and 1980s by I. A. Todd as part of the VVP survey (Todd 1979a: 285; id. 1979b: 33). In 1986, McClellan studied the overgrown hill and suggested that architectural remains at the top included a basilica. The site was more systematically surveyed in 1987 and excavated in 1988-89, with additional sondages carried out in 1990.

Area I was excavated as 25 5-m square trenches (fig. 3.1). The first season of work noted much evidence of recent activities. Mechanical equipment had been used to trim back the S and SE margins. A shallow tar-filled pit occupied the NE part of mound. An overgrown, shallow depression near the summit may have been used as a foxhole during the civil unrest of the 1950s. Late Roman features lay close to the mound's modern surface and extended to its eroding perimeter. The best-preserved structural remains included the N and center aisles, narthex, and crypt of a small basilica, all of which had been cut into the hill; remains of a court and surrounding rooms to the north were more fragmentary. Our main objective was to identify and record these surviving features. The relatively shallow stratigraphy usually allowed us to distinguish only a single deposit of fill (Lots I-1, 2, 3, 28) covering the buildings. In some cases, such as the cistern and crypt, we were able to isolate deposits dating to the collapse and brief re-occupation of the complex in about the mid 7th c. (Lots I-6, 7, 23, 32). A few limited sondages below floor levels (e.g., Lots I-5, 20, 31) provide evidence that the basilica was constructed in *c.*600, with the relative chronology of related contexts favoring a slightly earlier date for the beginning of work. The full range of excavated pottery suggests that the area saw some activity in the 5th and 6th c. as well. Preliminary reports of work at *Sirmata* appeared in *Muse* 22 (1988) 54-61 and 23-24 (1989-90) 16-20, and in *RDAC* 1989: 160-66; 1990: 233-36; and 1991: 225-26.

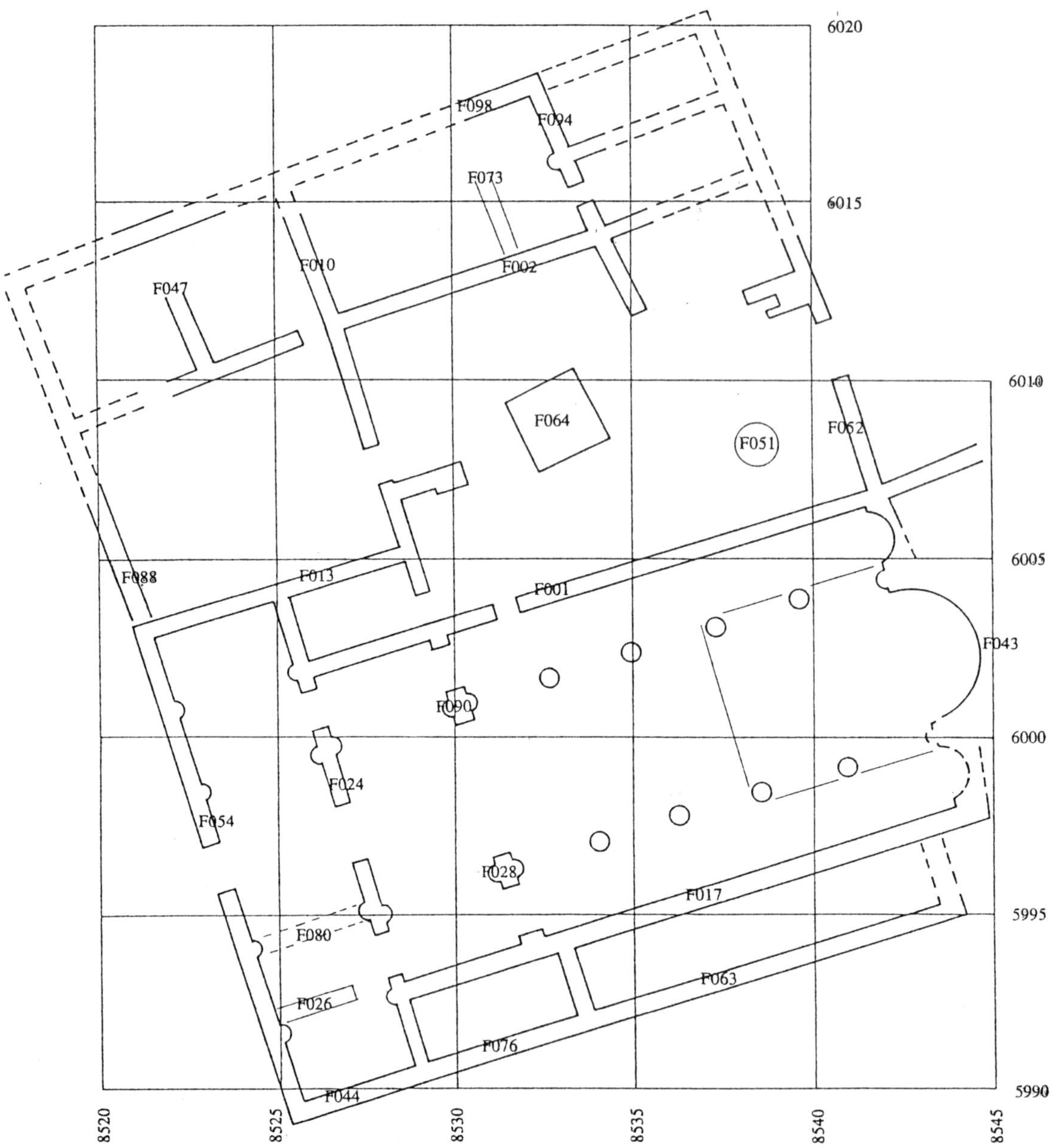

Fig. 3.1. Area I, excavation trench plan.

Architectural features and associated deposits

The *Sirmata* complex presents a compact group of buildings surrounding an open court (figs. 3.2-3.5). The main structure is a three-aisled basilica that occupies the S part of the mound. The court lies along the N flank of the basilica. A squarish foundation stands near the center of the court and a deep cistern is found near its SE corner. Small trapezoidal rooms extend along the other sides of the court. The architectural arrangement and associated finds suggest that the complex was built to house a small monastery that flourished together with the nearby village in the early 7th c.

Basilica

The lower walls, piers, and floor of the basilica survive in relatively good condition and clearly preserve the main parts of its plan (fig. 3.6). The structure consists of a rectangular hall with interior dimensions of *c.*16.2 by 8.8 m, which was divided into three longitudinal aisles. To the east, the central aisle terminates in a broad semicircular apse. The side aisles end in apsidioles or shallow niches set within their E walls. To the west, three doors open off the broad narthex, which projects at both ends beyond the width of the nave. A subterranean crypt occupies the S end of the narthex. A long, narrow structure originally extended along the S flank of the basilica. A single doorway leads from the N aisle to the adjacent court.

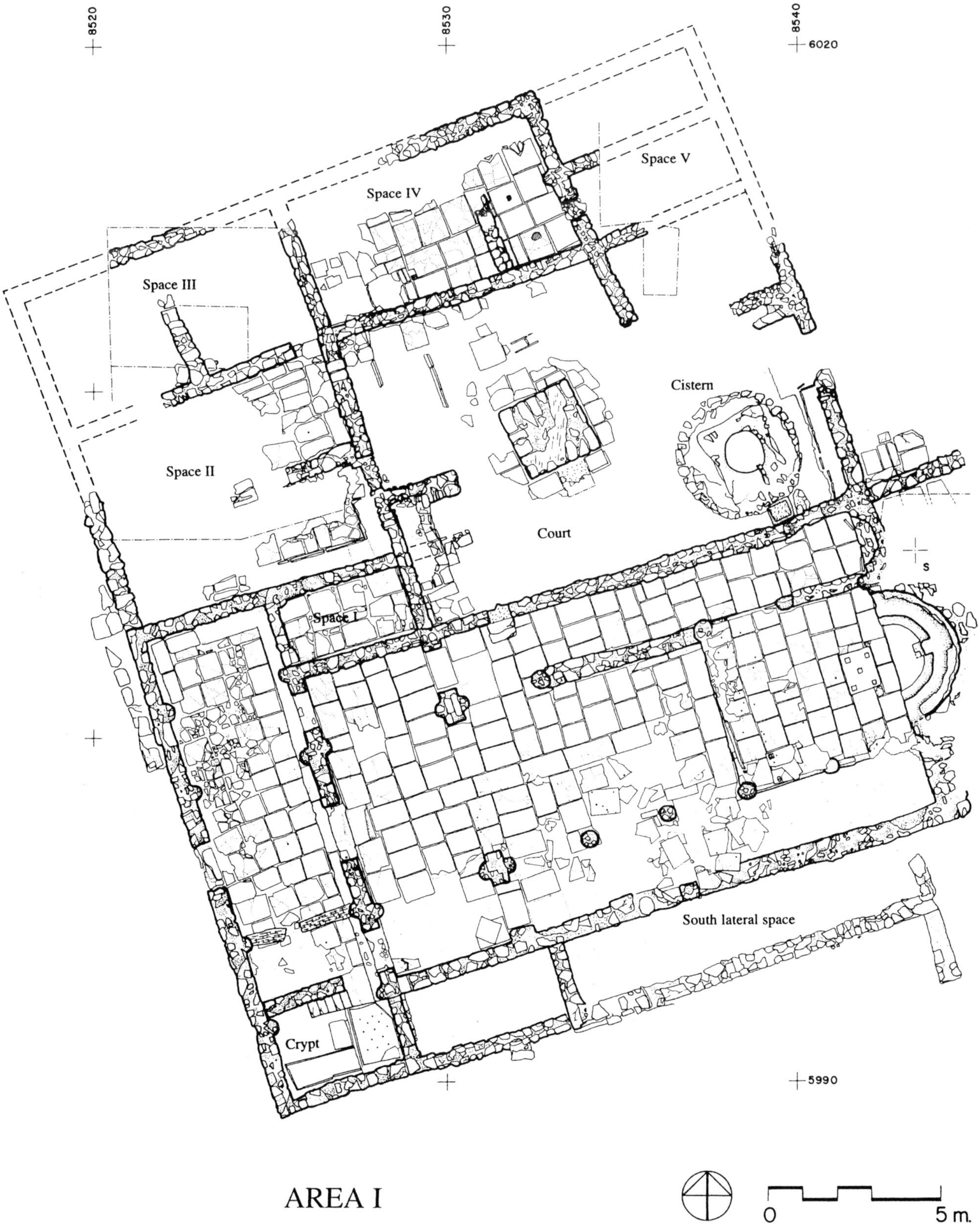

Fig. 3.2. Area I, state plan.

Two colonnades divide the basilica into three longitudinal spaces: a central aisle 4.3-m wide flanked by side aisles 1.8-m wide. These are narrow proportions compared with other Cypriot churches and reflect a cautious approach taken by local builders (below, p. 150). Each colonnade originally consisted of a row of 5 freestanding piers and was concluded by semicircular shafts attached to the E and W walls. The 8 eastern-

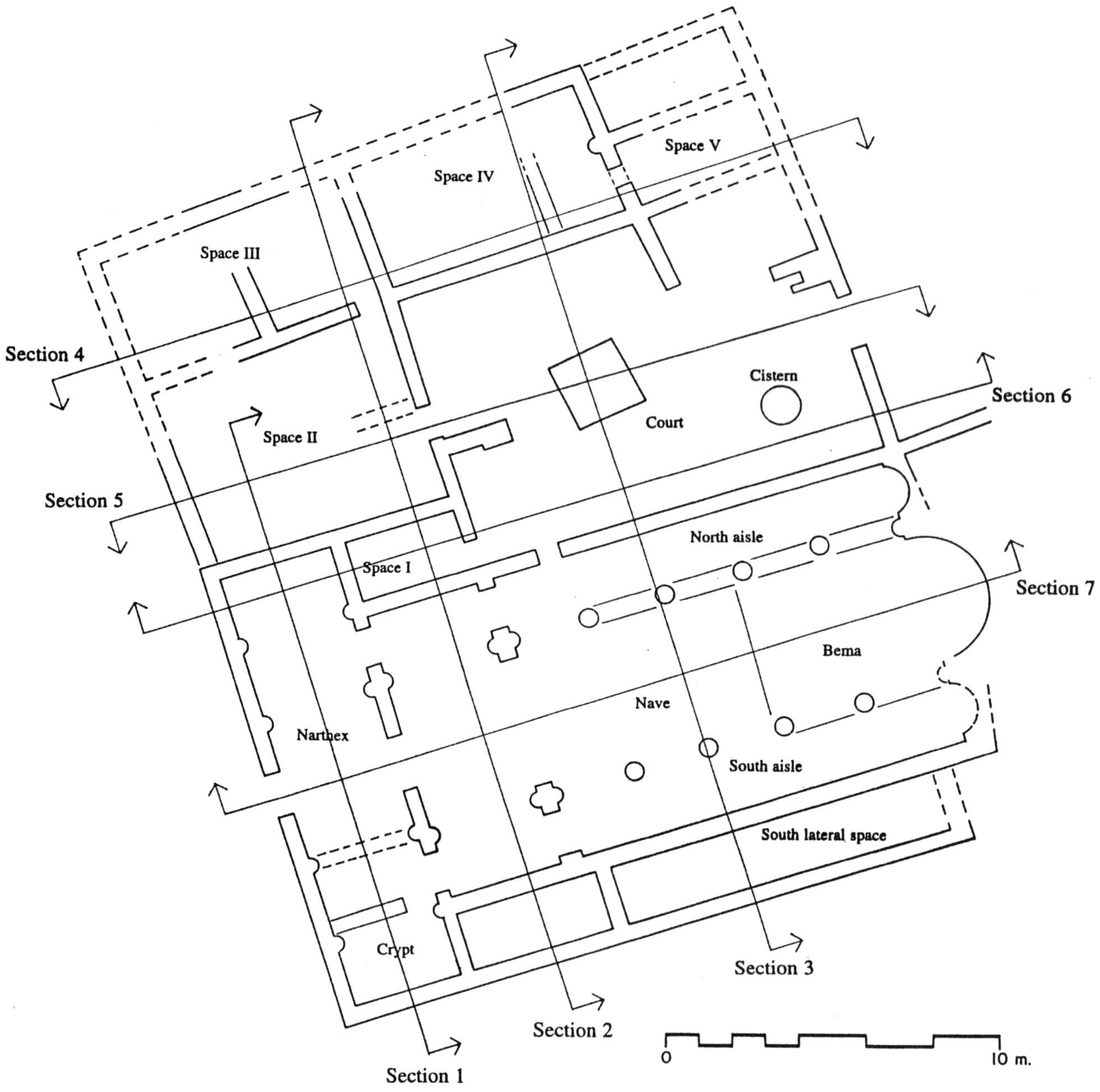

Fig. 3.3. Area I, section plan.

most piers were cylindrical in plan (diam. *c*.0.5 m). Like the walls, they were made of well mortared fieldstone and gypsum fragments covered with one or more thick coats of plaster. Only the third pier of the N colonnade was missing. The rest stand at clear intervals of 1.8 to 2.0 m.

The original appearance of the nave's superstructure is largely conjectural (fig. 3.7). Unfluted piers rose without bases directly from the nave floor to support the upper wall. It is likely that simple capitals marked the transition between piers and superstructure. While no trace of these was recognized during excavation at *Sirmata*, at Area II we recovered several large fragments of Corinthian-derived capitals made of gypsum plaster cast around a mortared rubble core (below, pp. 113-15). The solid construction and relatively consistent spacing of the nave piers imply that they supported a light-weight arcade, although a timber entablature is also possible. Above this level the nave wall probably contained small clerestory windows and was covered by a pitched timber roof with terracotta tiles.

The two westernmost piers stand 3.8 m apart and *c*.3.4 m from the W wall, and when excavated were preserved as high as 0.7 m (Rautman 2001a: fig. 5:2). These piers are rectangular in plan with semicircular shafts facing east and west. Corresponding flat pilasters project from the lateral walls of the nave. The proximity of facing pilasters indicates that the piers stood between three broad doorways opening onto the main hall. This unusual arrangement raises questions about the building's original appearance and use. Taken by

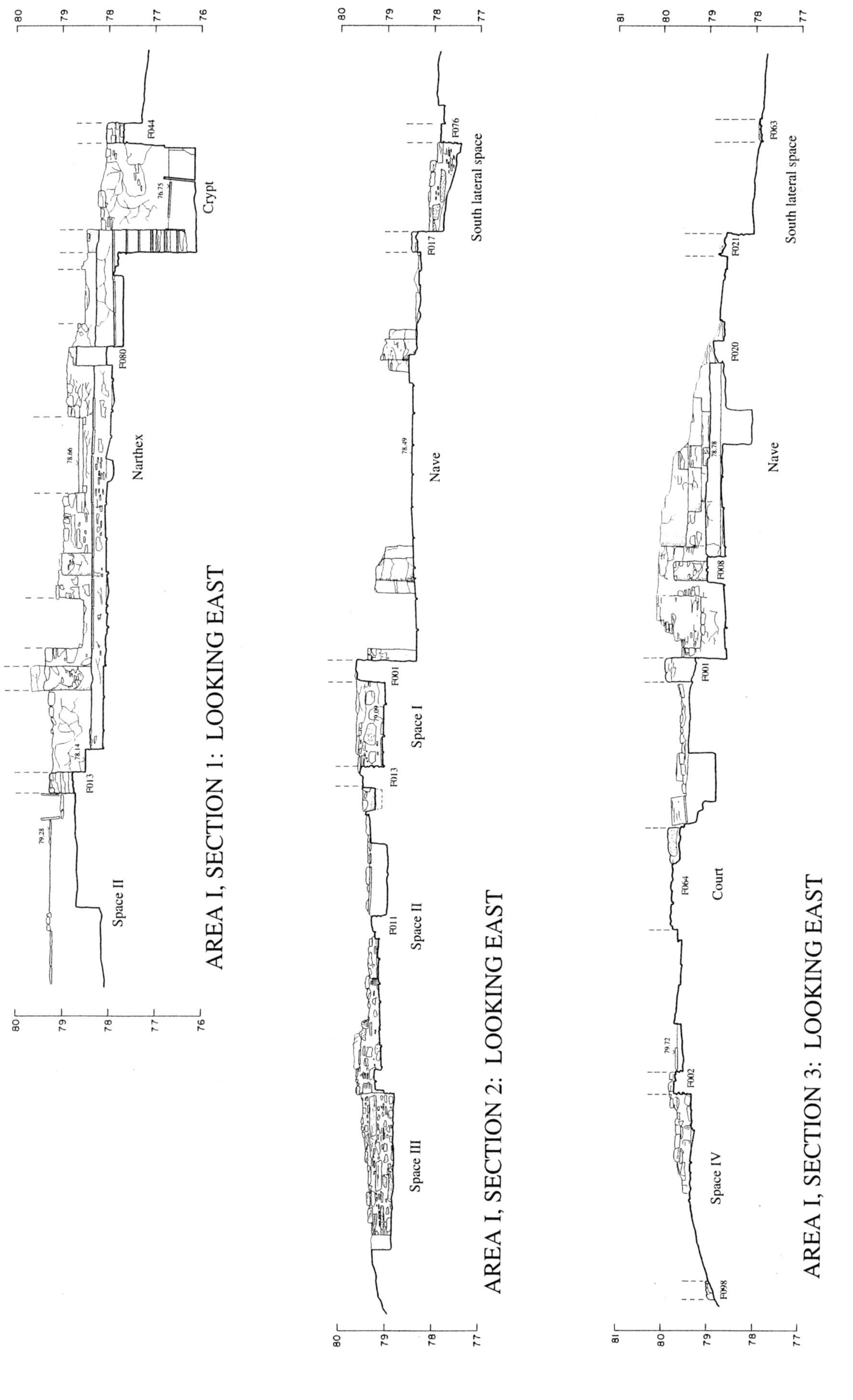

Fig. 3.4. Area I, sections 1-3.

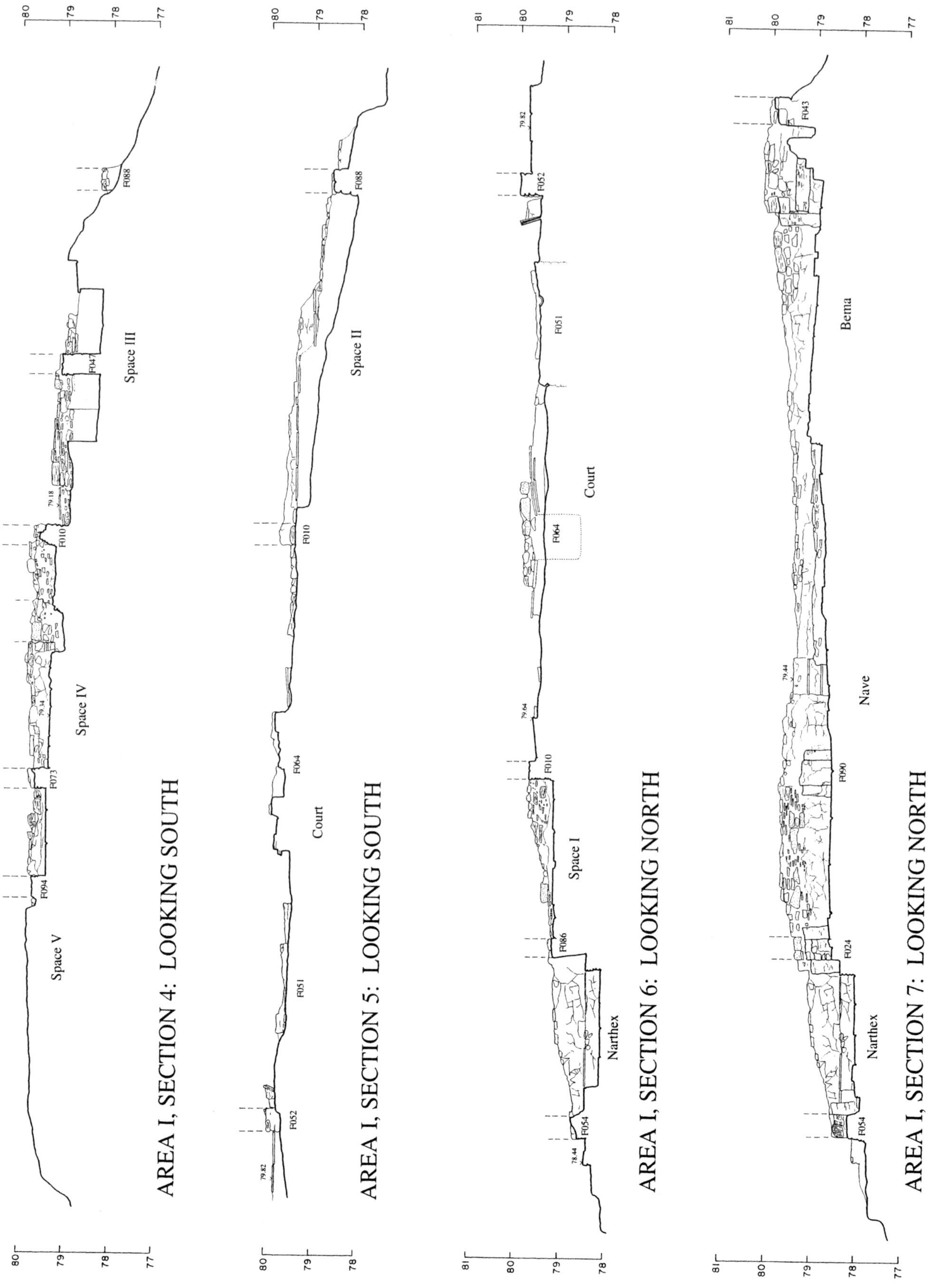

Fig. 3.5. Area I, sections 4-7.

Fig. 3.6. Area I, basilica, view to NE.

themselves, these large freestanding piers might imply the existence of a raised gallery or tower, yet there is no trace in either basilica or narthex of a staircase leading to an upper level. Fragmentary remains in the SW corner of the court could once have belonged to a staircase, but any connection to an upper floor would have been awkward; a gallery should have been directly accessible from the church. At ground level, the presence of broad piers separating wide doorways effectively emphasizes the W end of the nave and provides a transition between narthex and hall. Such an arrangement is otherwise unknown in Cyprus and lacks close parallels elsewhere. Complex piers were used at Kourion, Salamis, and Peyia, but usually to support an outer portico. Only at the E end of the Peyia transept basilica do transverse piers figure in an interior colonnade (Megaw 1960: fig. 36; 1974: 72). Rectilinear nave piers are better known on the mainland, especially in the limestone churches of N Syria. The peculiar emphasis of the W end of the nave by such piers recalls a group of roughly contemporary churches built at el-Anderin in NE Syria (Butler 1929: 80-82, 158-60; Lassus 1947: 232; Grossmann 1973: 39). The arrangement at Kopetra attests the arrival of new architectural ideas, perhaps tempered by some unknown requirements of local monastic practice (Rautman 2001a: 310-13).

Three doorways open from the narthex onto the W end of the nave. The central doorway preserves a lintel with pivot holes for two 0.8-m wide doors that swung inward. A broad iron band found in the vicinity near floor level probably came from one of the door posts. The thresholds of the two side doorway are simple stone slabs without pivot holes.

The basilica floor was covered with flat *marmara* slabs, well preserved in the N and central aisles. Most if not all of these slabs were laid directly on the leveled surface of the mound, without the sub-floor bedding known at Amathus (du Bouetiez *et al.* 1991: 756-59). A single row of 8 gypsum slabs begins at the central doorway and runs east to the raised sanctuary. Fourteen rows of paving slabs, measuring on average 0.6-0.7 x 0.8-0.9 m, are arranged symmetrically about this central axis. These slabs preserve a carefully organized sequence of alternating long and short panels; a similar arrangement appears in the acropolis basilica at Amathus (Pralong 1994a: 418). Some of these floor slabs bear small drilled holes or faintly incised marks. One slab from the eastern nave preserves a series of concentric circles and tangential lines. Some of these marks may relate to the planning of architectural details during construction, although their exact meaning is unclear.[10] A number of other slabs, especially in the W part of the nave, preserve traces of localized burning,

10 Cf. similar lines reported at Resafa by Ulbert 1986: 24, 155, pl. 14.1.

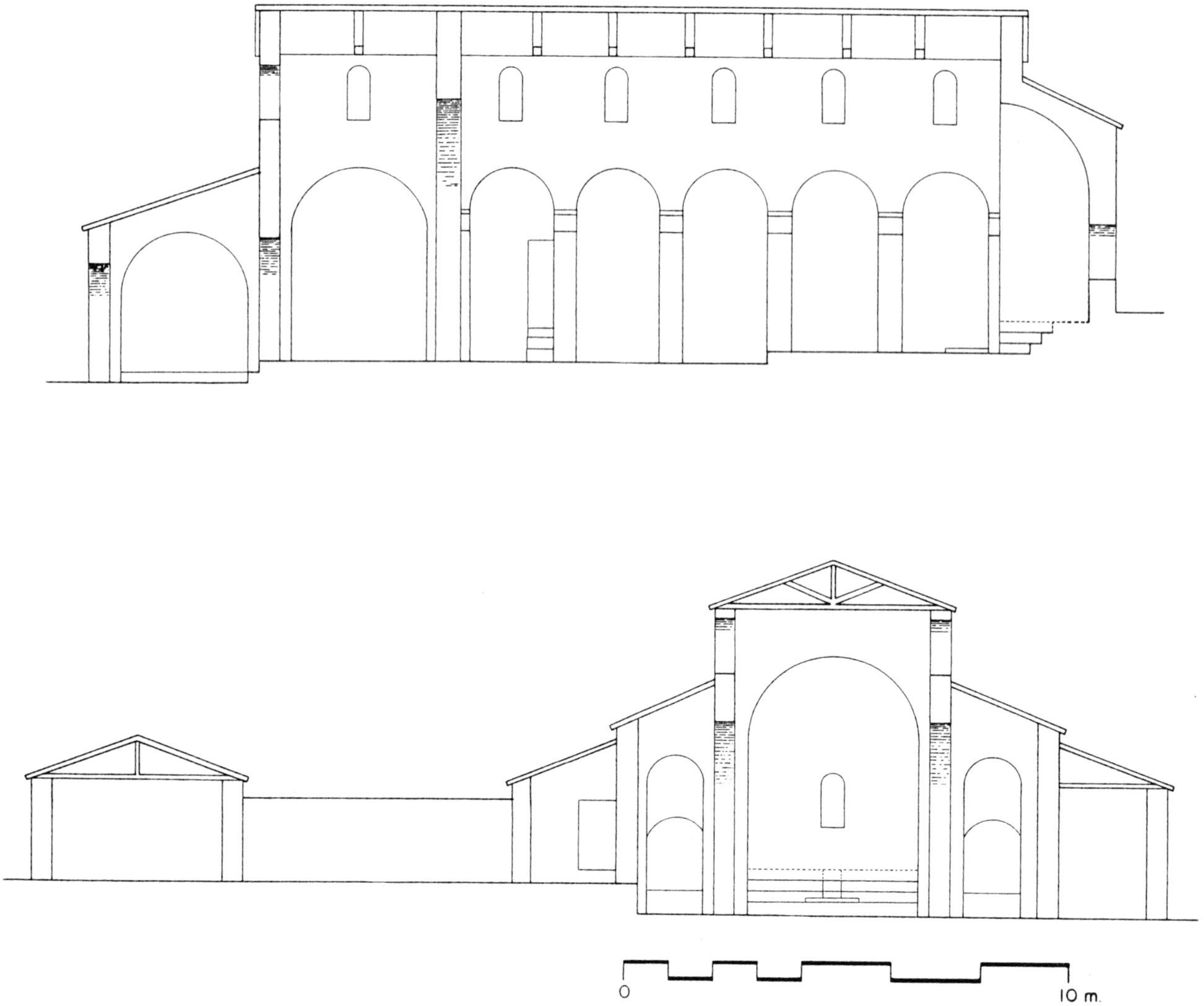

Fig. 3.7. Area I, basilica, reconstructed sections.

perhaps evidence of small fires at the time of the building's collapse or brief re-occupation around the middle of the 7th c. Similar traces of burning were noted in a contemporary context in the acropolis basilica at Amathus (Pralong 1994a: 417).

The raised floor of the *bema* or chancel occupies the two easternmost bays of the central aisle (figs. 3.8-3.9). The lower parts of 4 cylindrical piers were incorporated into a low platform built of mortared gypsum fragments and fieldstones. A molded ledge runs along the perimeter of this platform and may have supported a low barrier or screen. The *bema* floor was paved with 7 transverse rows of gypsum slabs. This kind of raised surface is typical of 6th-c. churches on the island.

The base of the main altar (F027) was incorporated into the *bema* paving immediately in front of the central apse. The gypsum base measures 0.9 x 1.2 m and rises 0.05 m above the surrounding floor, into which it was securely mortared. Five square holes (*c*.0.12 x 0.12 m) were cut near the corners and center of this block in order to support the flat upper table. Fine lines incised on the surface helped guide the carving. The base of a second liturgical table (F042) was found resting on the paving near the S edge of the chancel between the first and second piers. Although this base was not mortared into the floor, its careful placement directly atop the paving suggests it was intentionally installed here, perhaps at a later date. The surviving half of the base preserves two similar support holes. A fragment of one leg (0.30 m long) was found resting in one of the sockets. The roughly worked gypsum shaft is ovoid in section with a square base mortared in place. The fixed location of the main altar is known also at Peyia basilica I and both the southwest and acropolis basilicas at Amathus (Megaw 1960: 348, fig. 26; Pralong 1994a: 424). Secondary tables, perhaps intended for lay offerings, are attested elsewhere on the island but their location generally remains unclear (e.g., Ayios Philon, Kourion, and Amathus).

The main apse extends almost the full width (4.3 m) of the central aisle. Like much of the N and central aisles, the lower apse was excavated into the natural marl of the *Sirmata* hillock; retained by the semicircular

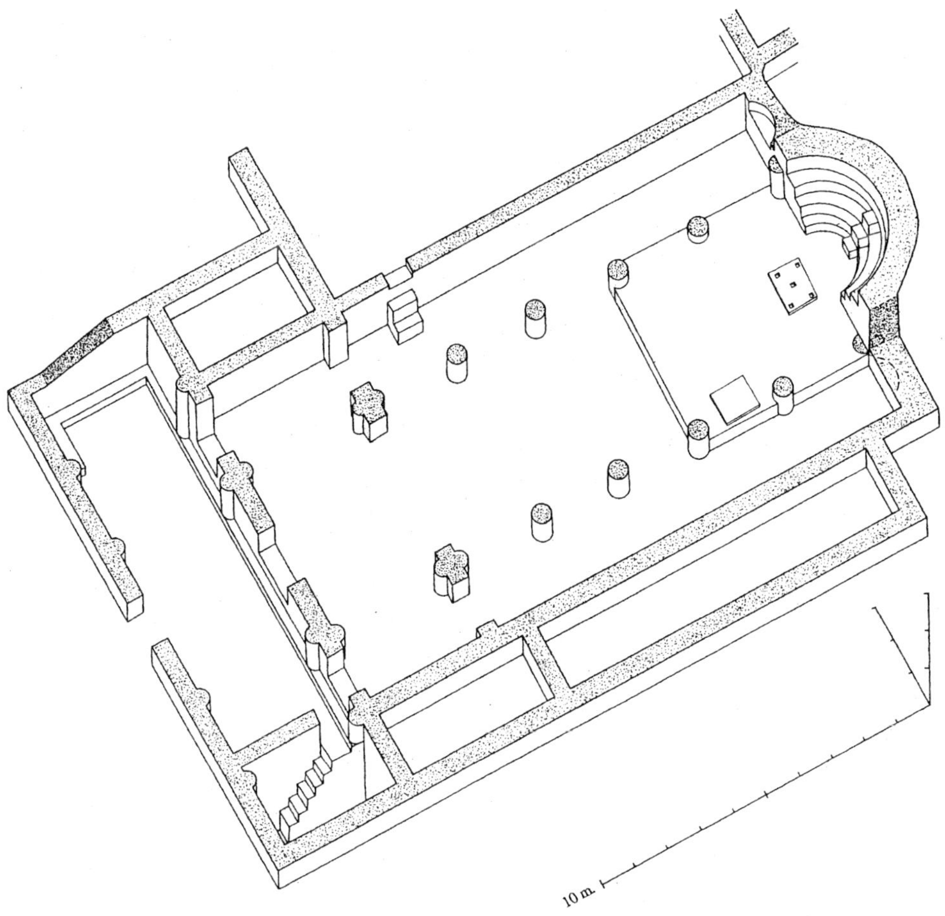

Fig. 3.8. Area I, basilica, isometric view.

Fig. 3.9. Area I, basilica, *bema*, view to S.

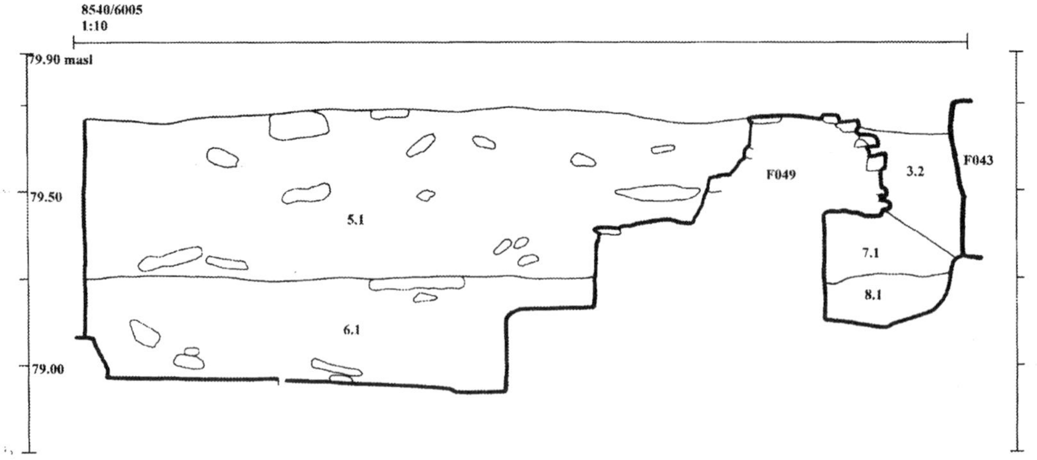

Fig. 3.10. Area I, basilica, *bema*, stratigraphic section at 8540/6004, view to N.

Fig. 3.11. Area I, basilica, S aisle and south lateral space, view to E.

wall, the surrounding mass still shelters the apse floor (fig. 3.5, section 7). A semicircular *synthronon* or clergy bench (F049) fills the main apse. The two lowest steps were built of carefully mortared gypsum fragments with a smooth upper surface; these apparently supported a missing third step made of wood. A small projecting seat lies on the central axis. A narrow trough packed with earth was left between the *synthronon* and the apse wall (fig. 3.10). This may have been intended as a moisture barrier against the hillside or was simply a measure of economy; a similar arrangement appears at the acropolis church at Amathus (Pralong and Saulnier 1986: 885, fig. 14; Pralong 1994a: 425). Small holes drilled at both ends of the second tier may have supported some sort of canopy or screen. Apsidal benches, with or without lower steps, were common features of contemporary churches across the island and in other areas influenced by the architecture of the capital (Papageorghiou 1986: 495).

The N aisle is especially well preserved. The outer wall stands to a height of almost 1.2 m above the paved floor and 0.2 m above the level of the nearby court. This mortared rubble wall varies in width from 0.4 to 0.6 m. Its irregular course bends perceptibly inward toward the east, apparently reflecting the nearby presence of the cistern. It is logical that the cistern would have been built earlier than the basilica, if not necessarily by very much. Intact *marmara* slabs laid in transverse rows pave the floor but do not indicate any internal subdivision. To the west, two gypsum steps rise 0.85 m to reach a doorway 0.65-m wide in the outer wall opening onto the court. The N aisle ends in an semicircular niche set into the E wall at a height of 0.55 m.

The S aisle was built slightly above the natural ground level and has largely succumbed to erosion and recent earthmoving. The surviving foundations consist of a mortared line of fieldstone and gypsum extending from the narthex to the E wall (fig. 3.11). Excavation against the S face of this foundation recovered pottery of the late 6th and early 7th c., including Cypriot Red Slip forms 9A and 9C dishes (Lot I-5). Presumably the S aisle reflected the arrangement of its counterpart and was continuous with an inscribed niche in the E wall.

In their original form both side aisles communicated freely with the central aisle. The surviving piers rest directly on the nave floor without a raised stylobate and show no trace of colonnade screens. The slight disjuncture of the paving rows between the central and N aisles may be the result of repairs made after the colonnade was blocked. At their E end, the aisles were separated from the sanctuary by a low step and probably a freestanding chancel barrier. The purpose of the lateral apsidioles is not altogether clear. Similar inscribed niches appeared in the monumental church of Ayios Epiphanios in Salamis, begun in the late 4th c., and in the 6th c. in the Peyia transept basilica. Such features appear to be compact and economical substitutes for the salient side apses found across the island in the 5th and 6th c. Similar niches probably appeared elsewhere in the countryside, although few rural churches preserve walls much above floor level. Since the *Sirmata* apsidioles clearly stood apart from the defined limits of the *bema*, they may have functioned as lateral chapels.

At a later date the N aisle was separated from the rest of the nave by a wall that occupied the N colonnade. Excavation identified a low screen of uneven thickness (F008) filling the third and fourth intercolumniations and completely replacing the third pier. This partition was built of poorly mortared fieldstone and gypsum and survived to an average height of 0.3 m (fig. 3.5, section 7); it may have continued in mudbrick above this level. Effectively separated from sanctuary and center aisle, the N aisle apparently acted as an independent chapel during this final phase of use, perhaps after the rest of the nave had been abandoned. While occupation details may be unclear, the general sequence appears also in the two other Kopetra churches and elsewhere on the island (e.g., the southeast basilica at Amathus; Christou 1997: 904-5).

Little survives of the basilica's original decoration. The building had neither floor mosaics nor *opus sectile* but was paved entirely with carefully fitted *marmara* slabs. Even the sanctuary, traditionally the most highly decorated part of any church, was covered with this cheap and readily available material, presumably quarried only a few hundred meters away. Colonnade piers and wall shafts would have dominated the interior. These probably carried large if plain capitals cast of gypsum plaster. Plain rounded moldings and a tall crown cornice, attested only by small fragments, evidently lined the upper walls (below, p. 87). All interior surfaces were covered by one or more thick coats of white plaster. Unlike in the other two Kopetra basilicas, no trace was found of mosaics from the upper walls or semidome.

The basilica's interior furnishings may have been similarly modest (below, pp. 84-87). Fragments of two marble table tops found near the modern ground surface (Lot I-1) may once have belonged to the complex, perhaps serving as the main altar and a secondary table. More clearly part of the basilica's original decoration is a set of laminate gypsum panels found in the lower fill near the nave's floor level (Lot I-3). Most of these panels are about 0.15-0.20 m thick and are pierced by small holes drilled at regular intervals. In several cases the perforations are arranged within incised patterns of reticulate grids or semicircular lines. Such panels could either have formed part of an upright screen surrounding the *bema* or have been used to fill windows in the upper nave wall.

Narthex and crypt

The narthex is a broad rectangular space located west of the nave (fig. 3.4, section 1, fig. 3.12). It measures 3.4 m deep by 11.5 m wide, projecting some 2 m beyond the N and S ends of the nave. Three doorways open east onto the nave, while a single doorway 1.3 m wide in the middle of the W wall looked toward the village. The gypsum-paved floor lies about 0.5 m below the nave surface. An intermediate step 0.30-0.35 m wide extends along the full length of the E wall and continues into a slightly deeper masonry bench 0.5 m wide wrapping around the N end of the narthex. At the S end, the floor drops away to a subterranean crypt, accessible by a steep and narrow flight of steps. The narthex floor probably was continued over the crypt by rows of terracotta tiles or gypsum slabs supported on timber beams. Four pairs of semicircular wall shafts articulate the two long narthex walls and subdivide the space into five distinct bays. The two outer pairs of shafts logically lie along the axes of the nave's outer walls. The inner shafts, by contrast, are displaced slightly inward of the nave colonnades, narrowing the width of the central entrance bay to 4.1 m. These facing wall shafts probably supported transverse arches, with or without capitals, spanning the narthex (cf. fig. 3.7). Wall pilasters lining the lateral *katechoumena* of the episcopal basilica at Kourion may have carried similar transverse arches (Megaw 1976a: 346).

At a later date the S end of the narthex was closed off by a slender wall built between the inner pair of facing wall shafts. This partition (F080) was constructed of mudbricks laid directly atop the floor. When excavated, it stood to a height of almost 1 m, but in its original form it must have reached much higher. This is the only intact mudbrick wall at Area I and the best preserved example found at Kopetra. Its construction was no doubt related to the presence of the nearby crypt. By closing off the second bay from the rest of the narthex, this wall created a sort of vestibule to the crypt, which now remained accessible only from the S aisle. Most of the narthex paving survives in good condition, but south of this wall it was found to be considerably eroded, as though exposed to longer use and weathering. This suggests that the crypt and its small ground-level vestibule continued to be used after the basilica had been abandoned.

The crypt occupies the southernmost bay of the narthex. The space (3.4 x 2.4 m) lies 2 m below the narthex. It is accessible by a steep flight of 5 steps built between the S pair of wall pilasters along the crypt's N wall

Fig. 3.12. Area I, basilica, narthex and crypt, view to N.

(fig. 3.4, section 1). The carefully mortared steps are 0.4 m wide and descend 2 m over a distance of only 1.2 m. Sturdy retaining walls define the N and E sides of the crypt, while the S wall shows signs of damage and repair. Excavation outside the S wall found an accumulation of dumped fill including pottery of the Late Bronze Age and early Iron Age, as well as of the late 6th and early 7th c. A.D. (Lot I-8; *RDAC* 1990: 235 fig. 2). The subterranean parts of these walls are well preserved but virtually nothing stands above the outside ground level. Presumably the walls rose the full height of the narthex, with a floor on timber beams extending over the crypt. The location of the steps next to the S aisle's doorway awkwardly interrupts the narthex floor and it would seem preferable to have located the staircase against the S narthex wall. The present arrangement recommends that a hinged door covered the stairs when the crypt was not in use. Located at the S end of the narthex and enclosed on three sides, this upper surface could have functioned as a chapel above the crypt itself.

Two tombs occupy the floor of the crypt (fig. 3.13). The larger and earlier of these (Tomb 1; F036) was set against the E wall. It was built of 4 neatly-cut gypsum slabs that enclose a space measuring 1.7 x 1.1 m and 0.5 m high. The floor consists of a single intact gypsum panel scored by 23 parallel lines and pierced by 13 regularly spaced drilled holes (fig. 3.14). The corners are internally reinforced by quarter-round sections of gypsum plaster which helped support the lid. Several large fragments of the flat cover-slab preserve small drilled holes set within shallow concavities. Excavation of this tomb recovered the generally articulated but

Fig. 3.13. Area I, basilica, crypt floor, view to W.

poorly preserved remains of 4 male adults who had been buried or reinterred here (below, Appendix 5). The second tomb (Tomb 2; F082) was less carefully assembled against the S wall, next to the first. A series of gypsum slabs encloses a narrow space (0.8 x 2.0 m) without a separate floor. This contained the somewhat better preserved and generally articulated remains of three individuals, two male adults and a juvenile aged 9-11 (below, Appendix 5). The contrast in construction between the two features suggests that the second tomb was added to the crypt, probably near the middle of the 7th c.

We noted two distinct periods of collapse during excavation of the *Sirmata* crypt: an initial episode, following which the accumulated fill was leveled near the top of the two tombs, 0.5 m above the original floor; and a second, final filling of the chamber (fig. 3.15). Objects recovered from the earlier occupation and first collapse include a glass flask and 4 lamps (three of glass and one of terracotta) which would have lit the small, underground space during the first half of the 7th c. (Lot I-7). Several iron nails in the fill may come from timber beams that supported the narthex floor. The S wall probably was repaired as part of the clean-up following this first collapse. After this time, both tombs remained accessible and may have received additional burials. The second and final collapse (Lot I-6) is not as closely datable but clearly took place following the re-occupation. Considered together with the construction of the mudbrick wall in the narthex and the colonnade wall in the nave, these events suggest that the crypt continued to be used even after the basilica was abandoned in *c.*650.

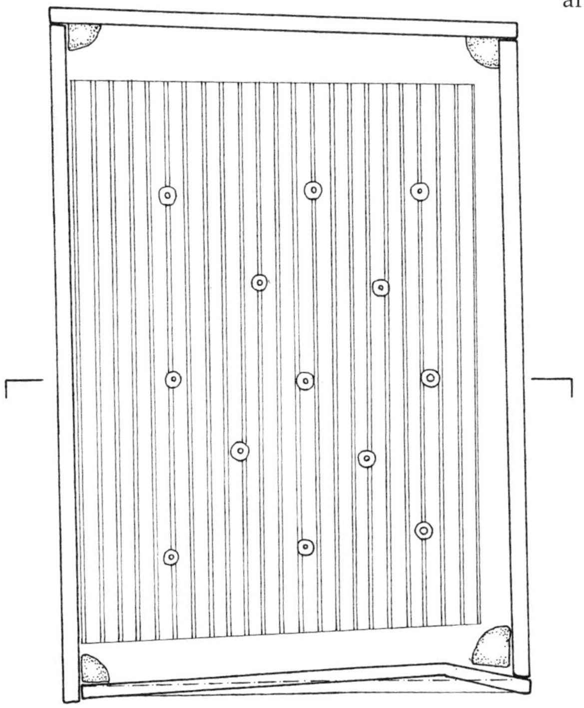

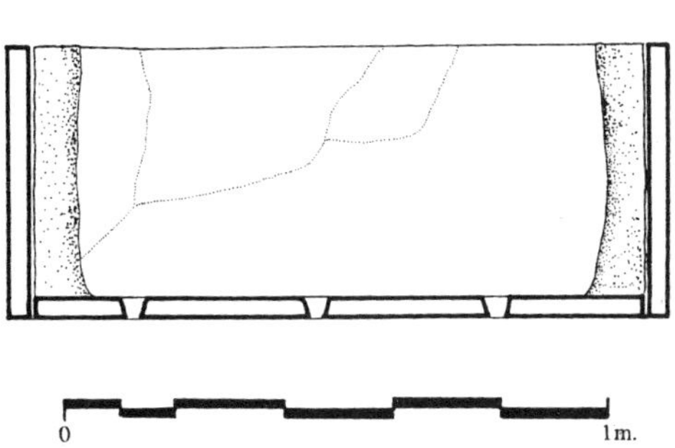

Fig. 3.14. Area I, basilica, crypt, Tomb 1 plan and section.

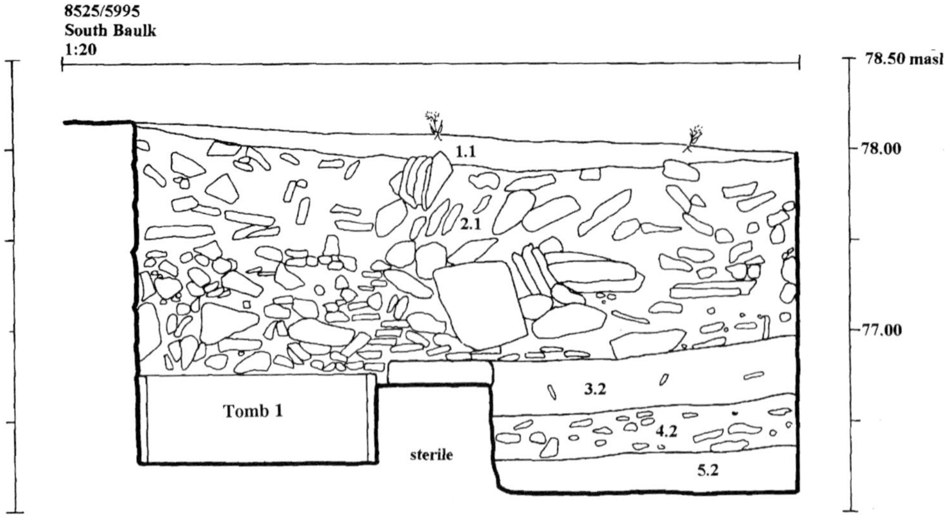

Fig. 3.15. Area I, basilica, crypt, stratigraphic section at 8525/5995, view to S.

The crypt was an important part of the *Sirmata* complex and belonged to its original design. Burials are a regular feature of Cypriot churches but usually appear as either separate mortuary chapels or simple sub-floor graves. At least one burial was cut into the narthex floor of the north church at Kopetra (below, p. 125), and in the southwest basilica at Amathus two simple interments were found in a transitional part of the narthex (A. Papageorghiou in Aupert 1996: 86). At Peyia's basilica II a tomb, perhaps of a church patron, was added to the S end of the narthex in the early 7th c. (Megaw 1955: 45; id. 1974: 70 fig. E). Three graves were installed at opposite ends of the (mediaeval?) narthex added to the basilica at Lysi (Pallas 1977: 299, fig. 199). Lamps and occasionally coins (as at Peyia) are among the most common accompanying objects found (cf. Sodini and Kolokotsas 1984: 227-30). The *Sirmata* crypt is unusual on the island in constituting an original architectural feature that was maintained and expanded over the life of the church, and in reduced form it even outlived the basilica itself.

South lateral spaces

Excavation along the S side of the basilica uncovered a long, eroded foundation that apparently enclosed two lateral spaces. The shallow foundation of mortared stone lies *c.*2 m from and parallel to the basilica and extends 15 m east from the outer narthex wall; it turns north *c.*2 m short of the basilica's E wall (fig. 3.11). The fragmentary remains of a cross wall divide this flanking structure into two parts: a large rectangular room (1.9 x 10.0 m) to the east, and to the west a smaller room (1.9 x 4.3 m). A broad flat stone set next to the W part of this foundation may have supported steps related to an outer doorway. The foundation's W end bonds with the wall of the S crypt, indicating that it was laid out together with the rest of the basilica. It is unlikely that these spaces looked south through an open portico, as has been proposed for other churches. The solid W wall recommends that the outer wall also be understood as a closed plane, perhaps with a door and small windows. Very fragmentary traces of a foundation extend outward from the SE corner of this flanking structure.

The original function of the S lateral spaces, while not certain, seems to have been funerary. The solid wall separating the W room from the narthex precludes its use as a *katechoumenon*, as suggested for similar rooms at Ayios Epiphanios and the episcopal basilica at Kourion (Megaw 1974: 62; Papageorghiou 1986: 494). The eroded remains of a rectangular pier in the S aisle wall may have formed part of a doorway joining the E room with the S aisle. Possibly another door opened directly onto the W end of the S aisle, as seen in the basilica of Area II, and another doorway surely joined the two lateral rooms. The lack of any clear relationship between both the cross and the E wall with the basilica's main features reinforces the likelihood that these rooms functioned independently of the church. The most plausible use is suggested by the discovery of several fragments of a limestone sarcophagus near the SE corner of the basilica, where they had been pushed by earlier bulldozing. The recovered pieces constitute over half of a monolithic box with low feet and internally reinforced corners (fig. 3.16). The reconstructed sarcophagus measures 1.9 x 0.5 m, and stands on 4 low corner feet to a total height of 0.53 m; no sign of a separate lid was recognized. In material and form this sarcophagus closely resembles those used in the S part of the island, especially around Amathus, during the Cypro-Classical period.[11] The largest fragment contained the heavily calcified remains of a double adult bur-

11 Cf. Nicolaou 1976: 168, pl. XIII.3; Hermary 1987: 63-66, nos. 8-25.

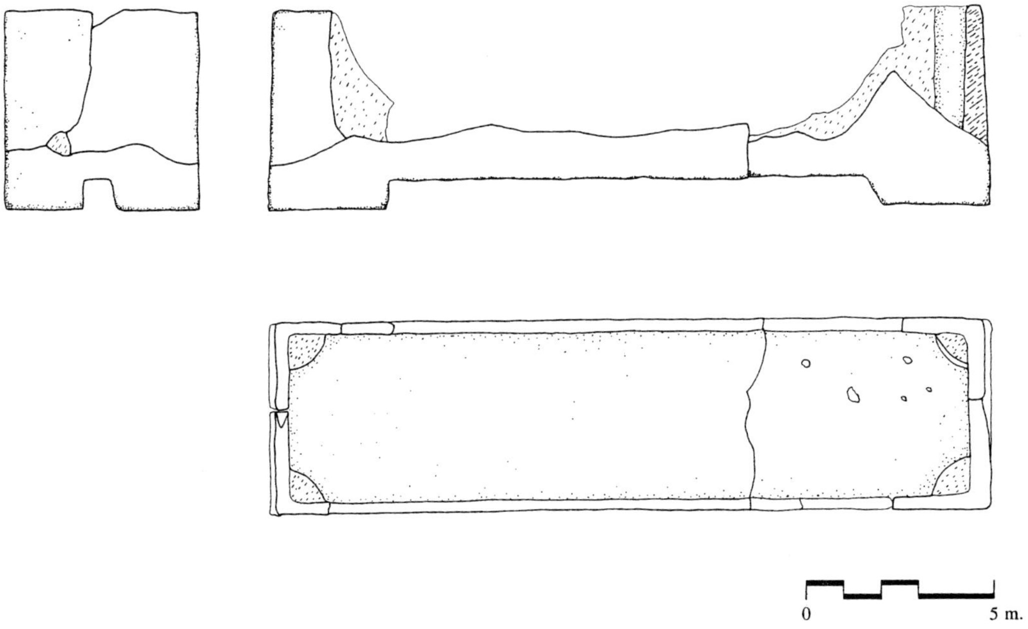

Fig. 3.16. Area I, basilica, sarcophagus from south lateral space.

Fig. 3.17. Area I, court, view to NW.

ial that is roughly contemporary with the church (below, Appendix 5). While the original location of the sarcophagus is uncertain, its discovery near the apse suggests that it may have stood in the E lateral room. Such an arrangement implies that this structure served as a mortuary annexe, as did similar rooms elsewhere on the island.

Court and cistern

The court occupies the highest part of the *Sirmata* hill immediately north of the basilica (figs. 3.2-3.5, 3.17). It has suffered extensive damage and only traces of the original paving and other features survive. Small open spaces or covered rooms originally surrounded the court on three sides. Only the lower walls or foundations are visible today and these vanish altogether toward the mound's crumbling perimeter. The spaces variously opened off the court or communicated with each other. As a group they would have served the domestic needs of this small religious community.

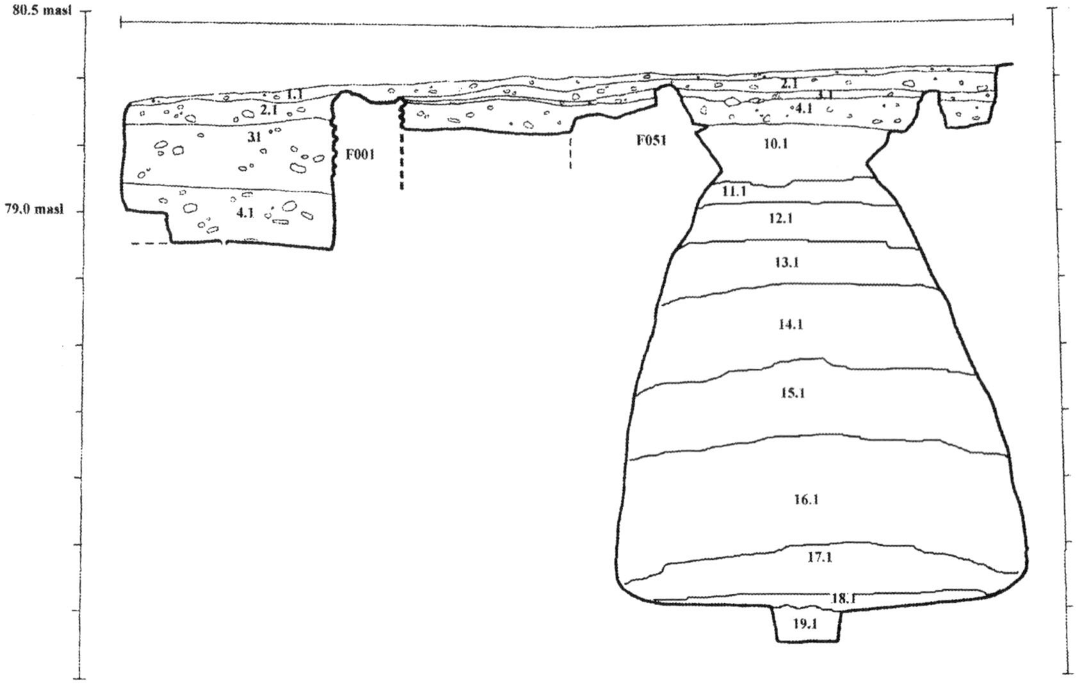

Fig. 3.18. Area I, cistern, stratigraphic section at 8535/6010, view to W.

The court covers an area measuring 8 x 12 m. This broad, open space originally was paved by large gypsum slabs set directly atop the mound surface *c.*1 m above the basilica floor. Isolated fragments of the now uneven surface survive in the SW corner and along the N wall. A sondage excavated against the S face of a large foundation (F064) standing near the center of the court identified two closely superimposed surfaces (F069 and F072) belonging to the original layout and early use of the complex (Lot I-31). Two fragments of handmade cooking pots recovered from below the secondary paving are important for establishing the use of these wares while the monastery was occupied (below, pp. 175-76). A large cistern is located in the court's SE corner, next to the basilica. The incomplete foundations projecting into the court's NE and SW corners are unidentified. Several small bins or troughs were set into the floor of the court during its final phase.

The remains of a large, substantial structure of nearly square plan (F064) stand near the center of the court (figs. 3.4-3.5, sections 3 and 6). This feature consists of a solid mass of large gypsum blocks set in gypsum mortar. It measures *c.*2.2 m on each side and rises from foundations 0.35 m deep to a preserved height of *c.*0.25 m. The structure is not oriented parallel to the surrounding court walls but stands slightly oblique to them. Its original purpose is unclear. The location in the center of a court would be appropriate for some sort of basin or fountain, although no pipe or other water fixture survives (cf. Roux 1998: 53-57). The width and squarish plan (not to mention the paved surrounding floor) are not well suited to most agricultural uses, such as for supporting a press basin for grapes or olives (cf. Callot 1984; Hadjisavvas 1992). Rather, the massive foundation implies the presence of a substantial superstructure that rose above the surrounding rooms. In its original form this may have resembled the more elaborate towers or lookouts known from 6th- and 7th-c. monasteries across the Near East.[12] In their lower parts such features closely resemble early minarets built in Palestine and Syria; however, a minaret is unlikely at Kopetra since the basilica shows no sign of modification for Arab use.[13] Access to such a tower would have required an external ladder, since the 2.2-m square plan leaves little space for interior steps.

The subterranean cistern (F061) occupies the SE corner of the court. The bottle-shaped reservoir was cut to a depth of *c.*3.5 m below the court's surface (fig. 3.18). The bottom has a maximum interior diameter of 3 m and a small settling tank 0.25 m deep occupies the center of the floor. Construction of the cistern was a major undertaking that involved digging a broad cylindrical pit and then reinforcing its sides with a heavily mortared fieldstone and gypsum wall sealed with hard hydraulic cement. The upper wall gradually narrows to a circular opening (1.1 m diameter). A low platform, roughly trapezoidal in plan with slightly concave

---

12 Lassus 1947: 236; Segal 1983: 56 fig. 13; Hirschfeld 1992: 171-76; Biscop 1997: 29-31.

13 Cf. MacAdam 1994: 59-60; for Arab alterations made to the Limeniotissa at Paphos and seaside basilica at Kourion, see Karageorghis 1969: 564-66; Megaw 1986: 513-16; Christou 1996b.

sides, surrounds the cistern mouth at the level of the court. The orientation of this platform echoes the large central foundation (F064), but both depart from the layout of basilica and court, implying the presence of earlier features on the site. A small (0.6 x 0.7 m) sandstone catchbasin was placed between the cistern and the NE corner of basilica. This basin would have been fed by a vertical downspout or wall drain from this corner of the roof (cf. Roux 1998: 21). Three fragmentary sections of terracotta pipe were found leading from the basin to the cistern mouth. The court's paving, with a surface area of almost 100 m^2, presumably directed rainwater in this direction as well. The slight displacement of the basilica's N wall suggests that the cistern was built before the present church.[14]

Perhaps the most important stratigraphic deposit of the Kopetra project was found in the *Sirmata* cistern in 1989. The mouth of the cistern was blocked by an accumulation of fieldstones and rooftiles, stabilized by the characteristic leeching of calcium carbonates into the soil. The upper shaft was filled with a thick layer of fieldstone and gypsum débris. Below this lay a rich assemblage of faunal material, including the remains of a fox, a variety of birds, snakes, rodents, and one or more large equine quadrupeds, all of which had accumulated over an uncertain interval. Careful removal of this débris revealed a remarkable deposit of bones and pottery near the cistern floor (Lot I-32). The skeletal material includes the substantially represented remains of at least two male adults, one (female?) adolescent, three children aged 5-10, one neonate, and two fetal infants (below, Appendix 5). The reasons behind this mass burial remain a matter of lively speculation. No clear sign of physical trauma or critical pathology was noted and the cause of death (presumably shared) is unclear. The larger, circumstantial evidence is more suggestive. The summary disposition of bones in an otherwise clean and functioning cistern constitutes a marked departure from traditional funerary practices and points to a period of dramatic cultural dislocation. The time of the burial can be fixed with some confidence. Diagnostic pottery includes fragments of a Phocean Red Slip bowl form 10A and Cypriot Red Slip forms 8, 9A-C, 10, and 11 (below, fig. 3.23). Considered together with various pieces of coarse pottery and a fragment of a perforated gypsum screen, presumably from the basilica, that were recovered nearby, these fine wares establish a date in the mid 7th c. for the deposit and provide clear evidence that the complex was suddenly abandoned around the time of the Arab campaigns. The accumulation of débris (including the remains of three quadrupeds) in a cistern at Salamis probably reflects the same disruptions (Taylor 1933: 105-7). It may not be possible to determine whether this hasty burial was the direct consequence of an Arab raid on Kopetra or 'collateral damage' incurred during a period of wider lawlessness. Nor can the possibility of plague or other natural disaster be excluded, although the historical sources mention no obvious candidates around this time. The summary burial arrangements and the age-range of the dead — many very young — attest a tragic moment at the close of local habitation.

Excavation of the NE quadrant identified several projecting wall sections defining a small room in this corner of the court. Wall F074 lies roughly parallel to the central foundation and extends 2.2 m south from the N wall. The wall was built of poorly mortared rubble and survives to a maximum height of 0.2 m. A less well preserved section of a mortared rubble wall (F004) projects 1.6 m from the court's E wall. These two walls may once have shaped a small (2.8 x 4.3 m) enclosure in this area.

Several fragmentary features survive in the court's SW corner. The earliest is a foundation that continues the line of the N narthex wall 1.8 m to the east. Only a few stones survive of this feature, which apparently

---

14 The perennial Cypriot concern with water storage is clear from the presence of contemporary wells and cisterns, which often are located near basilicas. At Ayios Kononas, a domestic well 12 m deep was used as late as the 7th c. (Fejfer and Hayes 1995: 67). A well or cistern excavated at Saranda Kolones in Paphos apparently passed out of use around the same time (Megaw 1972: 327-28). Two cisterns, one bottle-shaped, are known near the amphitheater at Paphos (Taylor 1934: 15-16). At Salamis, a large, early Roman cistern with two shafts was rebuilt with unmortared stone in the late 5th or early 6th c. to supply a house or church (Taylor 1933: 107-8). A cistern was installed near the atrium center of the suburban basilica at Kourion in the 6th c. (D. Whittingham in Swiny 1982: 80-85), and a large water tank 7.36 m deep lay on axis before the acropolis basilica at Amathus in the early 7th c. (Pralong 1994a: 438-40; ead. 1994b: 485-90; for another cistern in the W portico, see Pralong and Saulnier 1999: 504-5). A terracotta pipe draining into a well/cistern has been identified in a building adjoining basilica III at Peyia (Christou 1996a: 1094; Bakirtzis 2000). Closer to Kopetra, the contemporary church complex at Maroni-*Petrera* was served by a cistern, *c.*3 m deep and built of mortared rubble (Manning *et al.* 1994: 357-59, pl. XCI.2). The bottle shape found at *Sirmata* also appears in the Aegean (Robinson 1959: pls. 74-75; Felten 1975: 62) and across the Near East (e.g., at Gerasa: Rasson and Seigne 1989: 119 fig. 4; and in general Callot 1984: 79-82; Hirschfeld 1992: 148-61).

Fig. 3.19. Area I, court and west wing, view to NE.

predates the court paving. About 1 m farther north is a parallel wall spur 0.75 m thick (F067) built of unmortared stones and gypsum fragments and projecting 2 m into the court. This spur's neatly squared end and surviving height suggest that it continued above the court's paved surface. A less substantial line of stone (F065) leading 2.3 m south from the spur's midpoint might have enclosed the solid core of a flight of steps to a second storey (similar to Delougaz and Haines 1960: 5, pls. 11-12), yet there is no sign of an upper floor above spaces I and II. The foundations more probably were part of a bench that stood against the W wall of the court. Whatever their intended purpose, they end 1.1 m from the N basilica wall, leaving access to a doorway between the court and space I.

Excavation of the court identified several small rectangular troughs or bins belonging to a final occupation phase. These features vary in size and construction, but usually involve laminate panels or sheets of gypsum set vertically into the court's packed earth surface after the paving slabs had been removed. The gypsum panels average 0.03-0.05 m thick, or about half the thickness of the *marmara* paving blocks. The best preserved of these late features is F053, which was found in the court's SE corner, between the cistern and the E wall. Ten gypsum panels enclose a trough 0.4-m deep, 0.45 m across by 3.2 m long, which was set into the court floor. A smaller related feature (F097), located midway between the central foundation and the N court wall, was assembled of three upright panels buried to a depth of 0.15 m. A patch of burning on the eroded surface to the south suggests that this may once have served as a hearth. Similar but less well preserved troughs were found in the N part of the court and in space II.

West wing

Three distinct spaces lie along the court's W side (figs. 3.2, 3.19). Spaces I and II lie next to the court and space III is located at its NW corner. Space I is a small interior room, 3.5 x 1.9 m in plan, found at the court's SW corner and immediately north of the basilica's deep W bay. Solid walls of mortared rubble stand to the south, west, and north, leaving the room's only access through a 1-m wide opening in the E wall. The well preserved *marmara* floor is about 1.1 m higher than the narthex and 0.6 m higher than the nave paving, but lies about 0.5 m below the court surface (figs. 3.4-3.5, sections 2, 6). Flanked on two sides by the rising walls of basilica and narthex, this small room was illuminated by its court-side door and perhaps a N-facing window. The good condition of both floor and walls indicates that space I was roofed. Sparse finds include table wares (Phocean Red Slip form 10A dish/bowl and a possible Cypriot Red Slip jug), a basin, and a large storage jar (Lots I-11, 12). No other evidence of the room's original function was noted.

Space II is the largest component of the W wing (overall dimensions of 5.6-6.1 x 7.4 m). This trapezoidal area lies immediately north of space I and extends from the court to the line of the basilica's W wall. The outer wall (F088) is known only from eroded foundations, but the lower parts of mortared rubble walls survive on the other three sides. To the south, a carefully built mortared rubble wall (F013), perhaps with a window, separated spaces I and II. On the N side stood a similar wall (F046) with a doorway 0.7 m wide at its E end leading to space III. A doorway 1.0 m wide located near the middle of the long E wall (F010) opened onto the court. This large space may once have been paved, but most of its floor and bedding have eroded along the mound's W slope, leaving gypsum paving only in the NE quadrant (fig. 3.4 sections 1-2; fig. 3.5, section 5). The span exceeds the 4.8-m width of the central aisle and any roof would have required intermediate piers. Lacking such internal supports, space II in its original form apparently was left unroofed.

Important changes were made to space II during its later phases, although its eroded condition obscures most details. The most significant alterations involved blocking the doorway from the court and subdividing the space with an E-W partition wall. The court doorway was filled with a loosely packed screen of unmortared rubble (F029). The partition wall (F011) was similarly built of unmortared fieldstones and gypsum fragments. This wall began immediately north of the court door and projected 2.2 m with a neatly squared end. The remains of a facing wall section 1.0 m farther west may have framed a doorway linking the two halves of the subdivided space. The paving north of the partition is in relatively good condition and suggests that this area was sheltered during this later phase. The less well preserved S half of the space may have served other purposes. A large recessed trough or bin (F070) built along the S and E walls was perhaps used for feeding animals stabled here. Associated late finds include fragments of an African Red Slip form 104C dish and a handmade cooking pot (Lots I-13 and14).

Space III occupies the very eroded NW corner of the complex. This originally comprised a single oblong space measuring roughly 3.6 x 7.8 m in plan. To the east, the room was joined by a narrow doorway to space II to the south and was separated by a mortared rubble wall from the adjacent spaces along the court's N side. Exceptionally for the complex, space III seems to have had only a packed earth floor instead of gypsum paving. Construction and early occupation levels provided a good deposit of material dating from the late 6th and early 7th c. (Lot I-20). Among the diagnostic finds were Phocean Red Slip forms 10A and 10C dishes, a Cypriot Red Slip form 8 dish, thin-walled cooking wares, and at least 16 glass vessels, including bowls, goblets, and lamps. The deposit also contained many shells and some fish bones (below, Appendix 4). Taken with their architectural context underlying a later partition wall (F047), fine wares and beaded-stem lamps suggest a date in the early 7th c. for construction and use of the area.

Like its neighbor to the south, space III was subdivided later by an interior wall (F047). This unmortared rubble feature dates to the early or mid 7th c. and created two rooms of similar size, each measuring about 3.6 x 3.8 m. Questions of access and function remain open.

North wing

The large space IV occupies most of the N wing. The trapezoidal room measures 3.9-4.1 m wide by 7.2-7.4 m long, roughly comparable to the original plan of space III. The N wall is known only by its foundations but the lower parts of the other walls survive. To the west the room was separated from space III by the northward continuation of the long court wall (F010); this section consisted of unmortared gypsum fragments and ultimately collapsed westward into space III. The court wall (F002) to the south was built of fieldstone and gypsum fragments set in mud mortar and stands to a maximum height of 0.3-0.4 m (fig. 3.4, section 3; fig. 3.5, section 4). Irregularities of construction suggest that a doorway of uncertain width once joined the W part of space IV with the court before being blocked in a later phase. The E wall (F094) was carefully built of mortared rubble. Its midpoint is articulated by a semicircular pilaster — the only time that such a shaft is known outside a church context. South of the pilaster a narrow (0.55 m) doorway opened onto the small unexcavated space V; this opening was later blocked as well. Much of the room's original gypsum paving survives in place.

Several important alterations were made to space IV. After the S and E doorways were filled with unmortared rubble, space V may have been accessible only from the north. Perhaps around the same time the room was subdivided by an unmortared rubble wall (F073). This partition stands 2.0 m from the E wall and rises from the gypsum paving. It projects at least 2.3 m from the S wall and survives to a maximum height of 0.3 m. All of these changes seem to have taken place in the early or mid 7th c. while the basilica was still being used.

In a final phase a small oven (F003) was built in the SW corner of space IV (fig. 3.20). The oven was circular in plan with an interior diameter of 1.6 m. The base was constructed of large coarse-fabric rooftiles (e.g., **223**) laid directly atop the gypsum floor. The upper wall consisted of unmortared gypsum and tile fragments,

Fig. 3.20. Area I, north wing, bread oven, view to S.

and partially overlay the collapsed section of the room's W wall (F010). An opening to the north provided access for fuel and oxygen, like domestic ovens noted in late contexts at Salamis (Argoud 1980; Argoud *et al.* 1980: 10, 22). Similar, if more substantial, ovens are known on the mainland.[15] Associated pottery includes plain and cooking wares and three glass vessels (Lots I-22, 23). The oven belongs to a final occupation following the collapse of the basilica around the mid 7th c.

The eroded foundations and walls at the NE corner of the complex were not fully excavated. The E doorway from space IV opened onto the small space V, which measures 2.0 m wide and perhaps 4.5 m long, little larger than space I. A similar space may have stood to the north and communicated with it through an intermediate doorway. No diagnostic object was recovered from these rooms, the arrangement and purpose of which remain unknown.

East wing

The E side of the *Sirmata* mound is the least well preserved. Recent earthmoving destroyed this part of the court and one or more rooms located behind the apse of the basilica. The surviving E wall foundations suggest there was a central doorway, 1.5 m wide, opening from the court. To the south a perpendicular wall (F057) projects 2.8 m east from the NE corner of the basilica. Several gypsum slabs lie on both sides of this wall and indicate that at least two interior spaces occupied the S end of the E wing, one continuing behind the N apse wall to an undetermined length. It is unclear whether other spaces lay farther north.

Pottery and other inventoried artifacts by Lot

Roman pottery from Area I is summarized in Table 3.4.

Lot I-1: Topsoil

Date range: mostly 6th to 7th c.

Catalogued objects:

C4 Dodecanummium, Phocas or early reign of Heraclius, *c.*602-28, Alexandria

6 Cypriot Red Slip form 2?
9 Cypriot Red Slip form 7
18 Cypriot Red Slip form 9A
21 Cypriot Red Slip form 9B
22 Cypriot Red Slip form 9B
28 Cypriot Red Slip form 10?
30 Cypriot Red Slip form 11
47 Phocean Red Slip form 3F
63 Phocean Red Slip form 10C
69 African Red Slip form 97
71 African Red Slip form 101
75 African Red Slip form 105
77 African Red Slip form 105
87 Cypriot Sigillata uncertain form
93 Unidentified fine ware bowl
94 Plain ware A basin
96 Plain ware A basin
99 Plain ware A basin
101 Plain ware A bowl
113 Plain ware B basin
119 Plain ware B jug
121 Plain ware B jug
127 Plain ware D jug

15 E.g., Forsyth and Weitzmann 1973: pl. 22A; Hirschfeld 1992: 85-87; id. 1999: 74-76.

TABLE 3.4. SUMMARY OF ROMAN POTTERY FROM AREA I

Area I	*rim*	*base*	*handle*	*sherd*	*sum*	*weight*	*avg. sherd wt.*
Fine	316	127	7	312	762	12184	15.99
Plain	62	92	36	420	610	11511	18.87
Amphora	236	12	517	6245	7010	184728	26.35
Cook	128	9	83	1618	1838	12670	6.89
Pithos	135	26	26	679	866	95225	109.96
Other	50	12	47	2015	2124	36638	17.25
ROMAN TOTAL	927	278	716	11289	13210	352956	26.72

	rim	*base*	*handle*	*sherd*	*sum*
CRS 1	2				2
CRS 2	19	6		2	27
CRS 3	1				1
CRS 5				2	2
CRS 7	5			2	7
CRS 8	7				7
CRS 9	11	7		8	26
CRS 9A	36	5		9	50
CRS 9B	17	3		4	24
CRS 9C	15	2		4	21
CRS 10	9			3	12
CRS 11	9	6	7	21	43
CRS other	15	31		50	96
CRS TOTAL	146	60	7	105	318
LRC 2	1				1
LRC 3	22	5		7	34
LRC 3C	15	3		3	21
LRC 3D	3				3
LRC 3E	14			5	19
LRC 3F	13	2		2	17
LRC 3G	2				2
LRC 3H	3				3
LRC 5	1				1
LRC 9	4				4
LRC 10	3	1		2	6
LRC 10A	35	2		11	48
LRC 10C	9			5	14
LRC other	5	35		124	164
LRC TOTAL	130	48		159	337
ARS 93	1			1	2
ARS 97	3				3
ARS 101	1				1
ARS 104C	2				2
ARS 105	11	4		3	18
ARS 107	3				3
ARS other	7	6		23	36
ARS TOTAL	28	10		27	65
ERS	2	2		4	8
Other	10	7		17	34
FINE TOTAL	316	127	7	312	762

	rim	*base*	*handle*	*sherd*	*sum*	*weight*
LR1	168	8	398	4457	5031	137865
LR2	6		3	85	94	3860
LR3				2	2	70
LR4	21		22	190	233	6225
LR5/6	5		2	44	51	1250
LR7	2		1	21	24	1670
KAmp1			1	48	49	725
KAmp2	1	1	2	18	22	685
KAmp3			2	14	16	325
KAmp4			8	16	24	1020
KAmp5	1		1	21	23	785
KAmp6			6	60	66	2360
KAmp7			1		1	50
Other	32	3	70	1269	1374	27838
AMPH. TOTAL	236	12	517	6245	7010	184728
Plain A	8	4		12	24	570
Plain B	18	57	29	268	372	4450
Plain C	2	3		3	8	150
Plain D	34	28	7	137	206	6341
PLAIN TOTAL	62	92	36	420	610	11511
Cook A	6		5	26	37	255
Cook C	10		1	15	26	1570
Cook D	112	9	77	1577	1775	10845
COOK TOTAL	128	9	83	1618	1838	12670
Pithos A	17	1	3	79	100	13105
Pithos B	3	1		56	60	7290
Pithos C	13		2	19	34	4820
Pithos D	102	24	21	525	672	70010
PITHOS TOTAL	135	26	26	679	866	95225

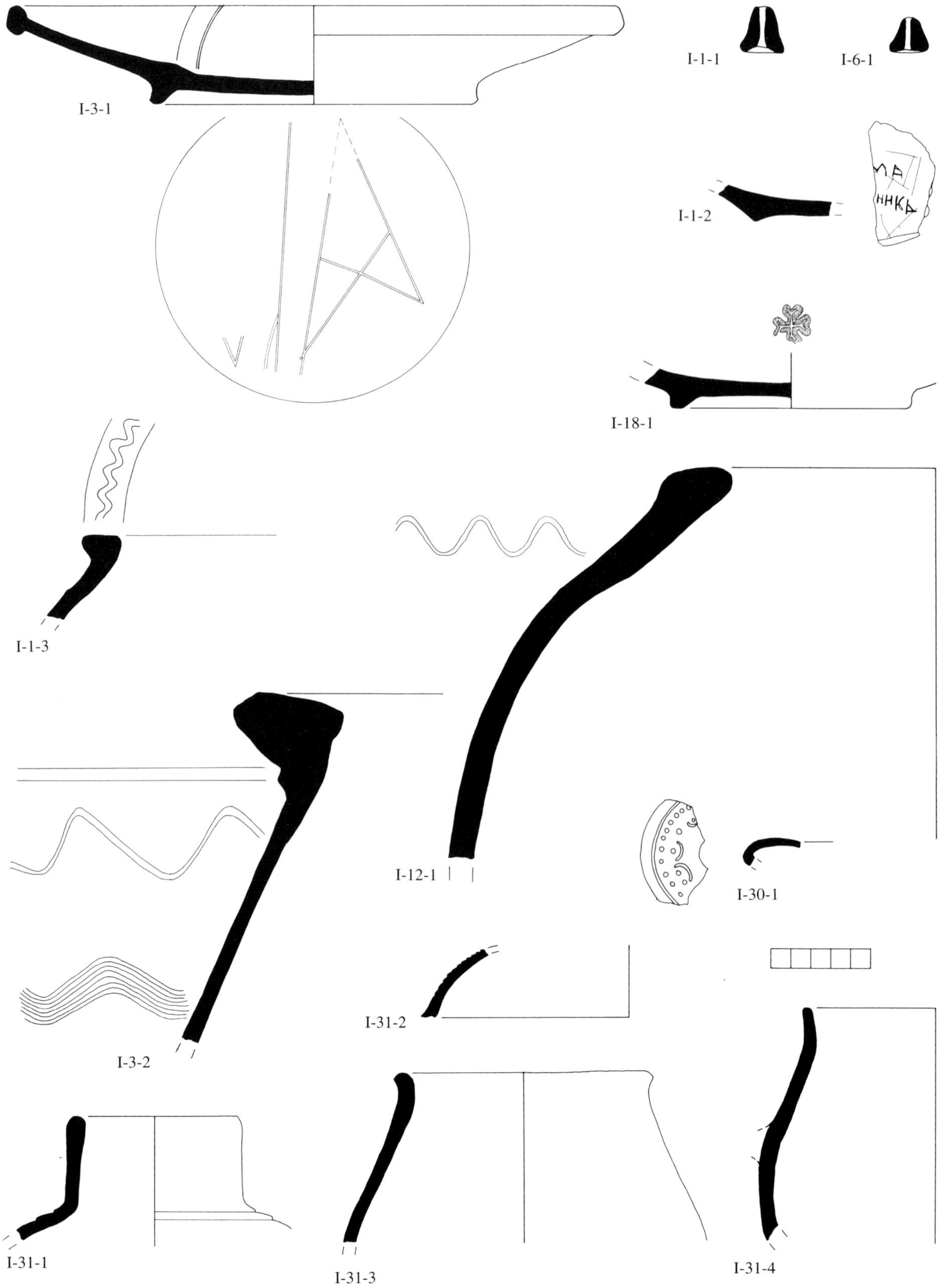

Fig. 3.21. Area I, context pottery.

145 LR2 amphora
146 LR2 amphora
152 LR5/6 amphora
171 Unassigned amphora
178 Cooking ware A lid
190 Cooking ware C pot
208 *Pithos* group A jar
243 Glass bowl?
250 Glass juglet?
251 Glass jug?
253 Glass flask
293 Glass stemmed lamp
294 Glass stemmed lamp
299 Glass hanging lamp
300 Glass hanging lamp?
303 Glass goblet/lamp
305 Glass hanging lamp?

Additional objects:

I-1-1 (fig. 3.21). Conical loom weight or spindle whorl. Max. h. 0.023, w. 0.021. Medium-grained gray fabric (5Y 5/1) with fine dark inclusions. 8520/6005 1.1, KK89-25.

I-1-2 (fig. 3.21). Dish/bowl, Cypriot Red Slip(?), form uncertain. Diam. base uncertain. Medium fine-grained light red fabric (2.5YR 6/6); slip scratched and worn. Floor inscribed:]MA NHKA(?). 8535/6005 1.1, KK88-3.

I-1-3 (fig. 3.21). Storage jar, *pithos* group A. Est. diam. rim 0.20. Medium-grained reddish yellow fabric (5YR 7/6) with large dark inclusions. Small triangular rim with incised wavy line. 8520/6005 1.1.

KK89-21 (not illustrated). Three fragmentary carved bone handles with flat backs, rounded tips with incised bands. 8540/6000 1.1. Cf. Chavane 1975: 48-50, pl. 16; Argoud *et al.* 1980: 45 no. Sal. 7596, pl. XLI.9.

Not inventoried (not illustrated). Fragment of industrial slag with rounded bottom from ceramic(?) crucible. Max. diam. base 0.090. 8525/6005 20.1.

KK89-33 (fig. 3.24.1). Marble bowl.

KK90-8 (fig. 3.24.2). Marble table fragment.

KK89-36 (fig. 3.24.3). Marble table fragment.

KK94-28F-G (fig. 3.24.5). Gypsum screen fragments.

Not inventoried (fig. 3.25.2). Molded plaster wall molding fragment.

Not inventoried (fig. 3.25.3). Molded plaster crown molding fragment.

KK88-21A (fig. 3.25.6). Molded plaster crown molding fragment.

KK88-16 (fig. 3.25.9). Molded plaster pilaster abacus.

KK88-23 (fig. 3.25.11). Molded plaster pilaster capital.

Lot I-2: Basilica, upper collapse

Approximate date: mid 7th c.

Catalogued objects:

35 Cypriot Red Slip unidentified open form
56 Phocean Red Slip form 10A
98 Plain ware A basin
112 Plain ware B basin
114 Plain ware B bowl
123 Plain ware B jug
219 Red-fabric rooftile
307 Glass hanging lamp

Additional objects:

KK94-28H (fig. 3.24.7). Gypsum screen fragment.

Not inventoried (fig. 3.25.1). Molded plaster wall molding fragment.

KK88-15 (fig. 3.25.10). Molded pilaster abacus.

KK88-40. Cypriot Red Slip form 9A, *RDAC* 1989: 165 no. 10, fig. 6.

KK88-41. Cypriot Red Slip form 11, *RDAC* 1989: 165 no. 11, fig. 6.

KK88-43. LR1 amphora, *RDAC* 1989: 165 no. 13, fig. 6.

Lot I-3: Basilica, lower collapse

Approximate date: mid 7th c. Pottery from Lot I-3 is summarized in Table 3.5.

Catalogued objects:

149 LR4 amphora
221 Yellow-fabric rooftile
260 Glass flask
292 Glass stemmed lamp

Additional objects:

I-3-1 (fig. 3.21). Plate, African Red Slip, form 105. Diam. rim 0.31, diam. base 0.162. *c.* 7/8ths represented. Medium fine-grained light red fabric (10R 6/8) with scattered lime, quartz, and fine dark inclusions, occasional medium-size voids on surface. Interior and rim covered with good red slip (near 10R 5/8), worn. Exterior surface paddle smoothed. Incised letters on base. 8520/5995E 3.1, KK89-17.

I-3-2 (fig. 3.21). Storage jar, *pithos* group A. Est. diam. rim 0.34. Coarse-grained light red fabric (2.5YR 5/6-6/6) with abundant lime, quartz, and other dark inclusions. Heavy triangular rim with multiple incised wavy lines on exterior wall. 8525/5995 2.1. Cf. Roux 1998: 48, 64 fig. 48 (Sal. 342) for a similar, substantially intact example of an "amphore 'byzantine'" from a late 7th- or 8th-c. context at the Salamis Campanopetra.

KK94-28A-E (fig. 3.24.4). Gypsum screen fragments.

KK94-28I (fig. 3.24.6). Gypsum screen fragment.

Not inventoried (fig. 3.25.4). Molded plaster wall molding fragment.

Not inventoried (fig. 3.25.5). Molded plaster wall molding fragment.

KK88-45 (fig. 3.25.7). Molded plaster pilaster shaft.

Not inventoried (fig. 3.25.8). Molded plaster pilaster base.

KK88-13 (fig. 3.25.12). Molded plaster figurine fragment. P. h. 0.08, w. 0.076. Fragment suggests lower portion of draped figure seated on ground with right leg crossed in front and left leg bent, similar to earlier Cypriot 'temple boy' figures; incised lines indicate drapery on left leg and back. 8525/6000 4.1.

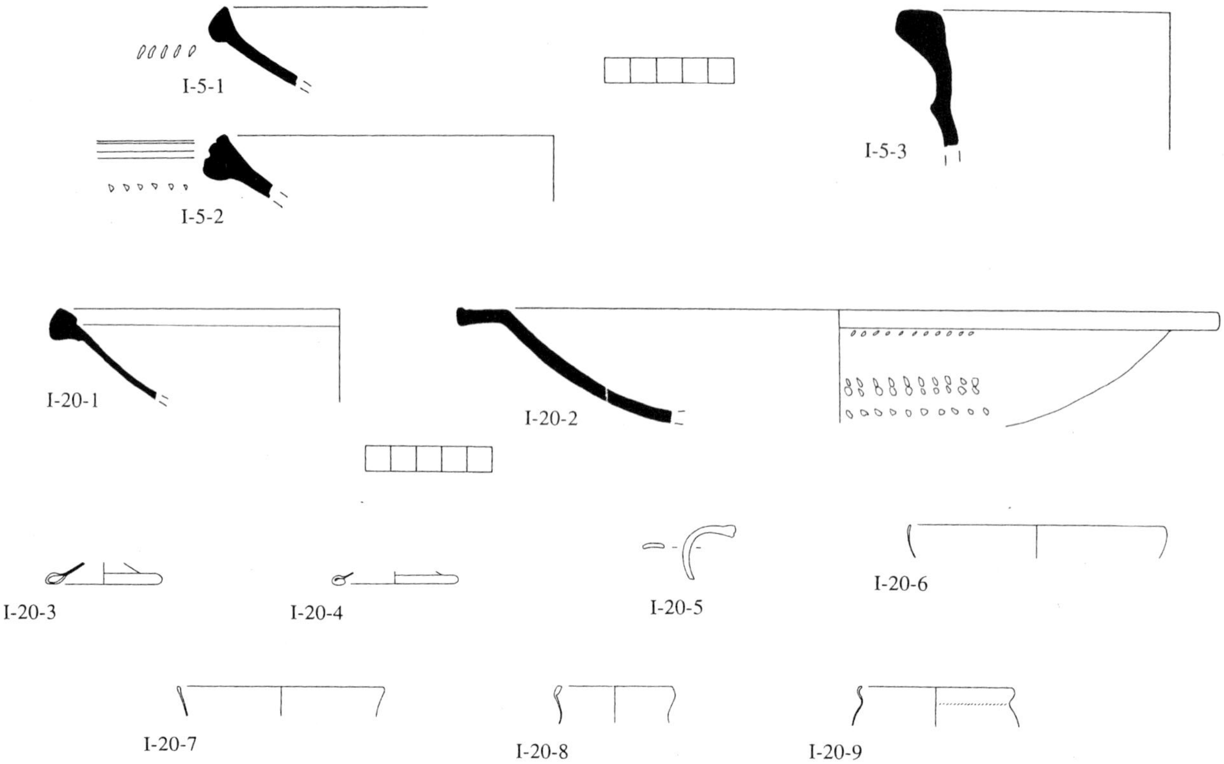

Fig. 3.22. Area I, context pottery, construction.

TABLE 3.5. LOT I-3 POTTERY SUMMARY: BASILICA, LOWER COLLAPSE

Lot I-3		*rim*	*base*	*handle*	*sherd*	*sum*	*weight*
Fine	CRS 2	2				2	40
	CRS 9A	2				2	30
	CRS 9C	1			2	3	50
	CRS 11		1	1	1	3	150
	CRS other	1	4		8	13	250
	LRC 3C	3	1		2	6	80
	LRC other		2		3	5	25
	ARS 105	10	3		3	16	1155
Amphora	LR1	11	1	21	281	314	10745
	LR4	3		3	21	27	480
	KAmp2				5	5	40
	KAmp3			1		1	65
	KAmp4				2	2	30
	KAmp6			4	5	9	795
	Other	4		11	40	55	2325
Plain	B		8		43	51	740
	D	2	4		2	8	185
Cook	A				2	2	20
	C				3	3	200
	D	4		4	88	96	485
Pithos	A				28	28	2655
	B				4	4	295
	C	1			9	10	555
	D	5	1	2	31	39	3615
Other		4		7	162	173	3200
Pre-Roman		4	1	2	12	19	200
Post-Roman					1	1	5
TOTAL		57	26	56	758	897	28415

Lot I-4: Basilica, second-phase use

Approximate date: mid 7th c.

Catalogued object:

58 Phocean Red Slip form 10A

Lot I-5: Basilica, construction

Approximate date: late 6th c. (Cypriot Red Slip form 9c).

Catalogued object:

247 Glass jug

Additional objects (fig. 3.22):

I-5-1. Dish, Cypriot Red Slip, form 9A. Diam. rim uncertain. Fine-grained light red fabric (2.5YR 6/6). Exterior wall decorated with light rouletting and red slip, flaking; exterior rim fired lighter. 8530/5995 3.2.

I-5-2. Dish, Cypriot Red Slip, form 9C. Est. diam. rim 0.26. Fine-grained light red fabric (2.5YR 6/6-6/8). Dish with rouletted wall, heavy rim with two exterior grooves, fired lighter. 8530/5995 3.2.

I-5-3. Basin with heavy rim, plain ware fabric B. Est. diam. rim 0.18. Medium fine-grained light red to reddish yellow fabric (2.5YR 6/6 to 5YR 6/6). Thickened outturned rim with exterior offset. Interior and exterior smoothed, fired very pale brown. 8530/5995 10.2. Cf. **113**.

Not inventoried (not illustrated). Fragment of industrial slag with rounded base from ceramic(?) crucible; top surface partially vitrified. Max. diam. base 0.094. 8530/5995 10.2. Cf. Lot I-28.

TABLE 3.6. LOT I-6 POTTERY SUMMARY: CRYPT, UPPER FILL

Lot I-6		*rim*	*base*	*handle*	*sherd*	*sum*	*weight*
Fine	CRS 9A	1				1	10
	CRS 9C	1				1	85
	CRS 11				1	1	20
	LRC other		2		1	3	25
	ARS 107	1				1	10
	ARS	1	1			2	40
	Other				1	1	5
Amphora	LR1			3	57	60	2645
	LR4				5	5	290
	Other	3			2	5	35
Plain	B				1	1	5
Cook	D			2	26	28	310
Pithos	A	1			2	3	200
	D				1	1	100
Other		3		2	31	36	885
Pre-Roman		1			4	5	40
TOTAL		12	3	7	132	154	4705

Lot I-6: Crypt, upper fill

Approximate date: mid 7th c. (Cypriot Red Slip forms 9A, 9C, 11, African Red Slip form 107). Pottery from Lot I-6 is summarized in Table 3.6.

Catalogued objects:

88 Cypriot Sigillata uncertain form

202 Cooking ware D neck

291 Glass stemmed lamp

255 Glass flask

290 Glass stemmed lamp

302 Glass hanging lamp

306 Glass hanging lamp

Additional objects:

I-6-1 (fig. 3.21). Conical loom weight. Max. h. 0.018, w. 0.020. Medium-grained light brown to gray fabric (2.5Y 6/2) with fine dark inclusions. 8525/5990 6.1, KK89-24.

KK88-1 (not illustrated). Bronze wire handle with single loop preserved. Max. w. 0.055, th. 0.004. 8525/5995 3.2

Lot I-7: Crypt, lower fill

Approximate date: early to mid 7th c.

Catalogued objects:

177 Cooking ware A lid

Additional object:

KK88-28, Terracotta lamp, *RDAC* 1989: 165 no. 15, fig. 7.3.

Lot I-8: Crypt, construction

Date range: Late Bronze Age, early Iron Age, late 6th to early 7th c. A.D.

Catalogued object:

232 Glass plate/bowl

Lot I-9: West of basilica, collapse

Approximate date: early to mid 7th c.

Catalogued objects:

68 African Red Slip form 93

82 African Red Slip form 103/107

Lot I-10: West of basilica, second-phase surface
Approximate date: inconclusive.

Lot I-11: Space I, collapse
Approximate date: mid 7th c.
Catalogued objects:
37 Cypriot Red Slip jug?
110 Plain ware B basin
Additional objects:
KK89-39, Phocean Red Slip form 10A, *RDAC* 1989: 165 no. 9, fig. 6.
KK89-42, LR4 amphora, *RDAC* 1989: 165 no. 12, fig. 6.

Lot I-12: Space I, second-phase use
Approximate date: early to mid 7th c.?
Additional object:
I-12-1 (fig. 3.21). Storage jar, *pithos* group A. Est. diam. rim 0.22. Medium coarse-grained very pale brown fabric (10YR 7/4) with a little lime, abundant small dark inclusions. Thickened rim, incurved wavy line on upper wall. 8525/6005 7.1.

Lot I-13: Space II, collapse
Approximate date: early 7th c.
Catalogued objects:
72 African Red Slip form 104C
236 Glass beaker?

Lot I-14: Space II, second-phase use
Approximate date: mid 7th c.
Catalogued object:
188 Cooking ware C pot (also Lot I-28)

Lot I-15: Space II, construction
Approximate date: inconclusive (late 6th c.?).

Lot I-16: Bench(?), collapse
Approximate date: inconclusive (mid 7th c.?).
Catalogued object:
245 Glass trefoil jug

Lot I-17: Bench(?), construction
Approximate date: inconclusive (early 7th c.?).

Lot I-18: Space III, collapse
Approximate date: mid 7th c.?
Additional object:
I-18-1 (fig. 3.21). Dish, Cypriot Red Slip, form uncertain. Est. diam. base 0.11. Fine-grained light reddish brown to reddish yellow fabric (5YR 6/4 to 7.5YR 6/6) with hard, darker slip (near 2.5YR 4/6). Cross stamp on floor. 8520/6015 2.1, KK89-8. Cf. Hayes 1972: 384 fig. 84.

Lot I-19 Space III, destruction
Approximate date: inconclusive (mid 7th c.?).

TABLE 3.7. LOT I-20 POTTERY SUMMARY: SPACE III, CONSTRUCTION

Lot I-20		*rim*	*base*	*handle*	*sherd*	*sum*	*weight*
Fine	CRS 8	3				3	60
	CRS other	3	1			4	135
	LRC 3C	1				1	15
	LRC 10A	10	2		6	18	415
	LRC 10C	1				1	5
	LRC other		3		20	23	130
	ARS		1		1	2	15
	Other				3	3	20
Amphora	LR1	1		5	288	294	5485
	LR4	2		1	21	24	750
	Other			1	173	174	2685
Plain	A				2	2	10
	B	1		3	18	22	155
	C	1				1	15
	D	2			38	40	435
Cook	A	4			6	10	200
	D	58		13	411	482	2460
Pithos	D	1			12	13	450
Other			1		81	82	400
Pre-Roman		1			5	6	70
TOTAL		89	8	23	1085	1205	13910

Lot I-20: Space III, construction
Approximate date: early 7th c. Pottery from Lot I-20 is summarized in Table 3.7.

Catalogued objects:
59 Phocean Red Slip form 10A
64 Phocean Red Slip form 10C

130 Plain ware D jar/flask
175 Cooking ware A lid
182 Cooking ware A pot
185 Cooking ware A pot
203 Cooking ware D dish
235 Glass bowl?
241 Glass bowl?
265 Glass pattern-molded vessel
266 Glass pattern-molded vessel
283 Glass goblet/lamp
289 Glass goblet/lamp
296 Glass beaded-stem lamp (7th c.)
297 Glass beaded-stem lamp (7th c.)
304 Glass goblet/lamp

Additional objects (fig. 3.22):

I-20-1. Dish, Phocean Red Slip, form 10A. Est. diam. rim 0.22. Fine-grained light red fabric (10R 6/8) with hard, dark slip. 8520/6015 5.1.

I-20-2. Dish, Cypriot Red Slip, form 8. Est. diam. rim 0.26. Fine-grained pink to reddish yellow fabric (5YR 7/4-7/6). Curved, lightly rouletted wall with dark red slip, worn. 8520/6015 5.1, KK94-4.

I-20-3. Glass goblet base. Est. diam. foot 0.045. Clear glass with green-yellow tint and many small bubbles; non-Cypriot? Tubular ring foot. 8520/6015 5.1.

I-20-4. Glass goblet base. Est. diam. foot 0.050. Transparent light blue glass (Fabric 1). Tubular ring foot. 8520/6015 5.2.

I-20-5. Glass handle. P. l. 0.040. Transparent yellowish green glass (Fabric 4) with yellow streaks and many inclusions. Flat strap handle with small tool mark. 8520/6015 5.1.

I-20-6. Glass goblet or lamp rim. Est. diam. rim 0.090. Transparent light blue glass (Fabric 1). Inward-curving, fire-polished rim. 8520/6015 5.1.

I-20-7. Glass goblet or lamp rim. Est. diam. rim 0.080. Transparent light blue glass (Fabric 1). Slightly flaring fire-polished rim. 8520/6015 5.1.

I-20-8. Glass lamp rim. Est. diam. rim 0.045. Transparent light blue glass (Fabric 1). Fire-polished, incurving rim. 8520/6015 5.1.

I-20-9. Glass lamp rim. Est. diam. rim 0.060. Transparent greenish-yellow glass; non-Cypriot? Flat, unpolished rim with flaring body. 8520/6015 5.1.

KK89-4 (not illustrated). Bronze wire hook with small closed loop. Max. l. 0.07, w. 0.022, th. 0.003. 8520/6015 5.1.

Lot I-21: Space IV, collapse

Approximate date: inconclusive (early 7th c.?).

Catalogued object:

240 Glass bowl?

Lot I-22: Space IV, second-phase construction

Approximate date: inconclusive (early 7th c.?).

Catalogued objects:

264 Glass pattern-molded vessel
285 Glass goblet/lamp

Not inventoried (not illustrated). Fragment of bronze wire hook. Max. l. 0.021, th. 0.002.

Lot I-23: Space IV, second-phase use

Approximate date: mid 7th c.?

Catalogued objects:

131 Plain ware D jar/flask
176 Cooking ware A lid
223 Coarse-fabric rooftile
252 Glass flask

Lot I-24: Space IV, construction

Approximate date: inconclusive (late 6th c.?).

Lot I-25: Space V, collapse

Approximate date: inconclusive (mid 7th c.?).

Lot I-26: Space V, second-phase use

Approximate date: inconclusive (mid 7th c.?).

Lot I-27: Space V, construction

Approximate date: inconclusive (late 6th c.?).

Lot I-28: Courtyard, collapse

Approximate date: mid 7th c. Pottery from Lot I-28 is summarized with Lots I-29 and 30 in Table 3.8.

Catalogued objects:

27 Cypriot Red Slip form 10?
55 Phocean Red Slip form 10A?
104 Plain ware A bowl
158 KAmp2 amphora
173 Unassigned amphora
188 Cooking ware C pot (also Lot I-14)
225 Water pipe
242 Glass bowl?
249 Glass juglet

Additional objects (fig. 3.23):

I-28-1. Dish, Cypriot Red Slip, well form? Est. diam. rim 0.28-0.30. Fine-grained light red fabric (2.5YR 6/6) with fine lime. Exterior wall lightly rouletted. 8535/6010 12.1.

I-28-2. Basin, Cypriot Red Slip, form 10. Est. diam. rim 0.34. Fine-grained light red fabric (2.5YR 6/6) with fine lime and quartz. 8535/6010 10.1.

I-28-3. Bowl, African Red Slip, form 97. Est. diam. rim 0.15. Medium-grained red fabric (2.5YR 5/6-5/8) with a little quartz and other fine inclusions. Interior and exterior slipped. Two non-joining sherds presumably from same vessel. 8535/6010 11.1 and 12.1.

I-28-4. Lid, plain fabric A. Est. diam. rim 0.30. Medium coarse-grained very pale brown fabric (10YR 7/4) with abundant lime, quartz, and small gray and red inclusions. 8535/6010 12.1.

I-28-5. Storage jar, *pithos* group B. Diam. rim uncertain. Coarse-grained red fabric (2.5YR 6/6) with medium-size particles of quartz, other dark inclusions; exterior covered with brown slip (7.5YR 5/4). 8535/6010 13.1.

Not inventoried (not illustrated). Iron nail. Max. l. 0.087, th. 0.020. 8345/5935 11.1.

TABLE 3.8. LOTS I-28, 29, 30 POTTERY SUMMARY: COURT, FINAL OCCUPATION AND ABANDONMENT

Lots I-28, 29, 30		*rim*	*base*	*handle*	*sherd*	*sum*	*weight*
Fine	CRS 1	1				1	15
	CRS 2	1	1		2	4	50
	CRS 9A	3	2		3	8	45
	CRS 9C	1				1	65
	CRS 10	2				2	70
	CRS 11		1	2	1	4	120
	CRS other	2	1		5	8	97
	LRC 3	1	1			2	7
	LRC 3C	3				3	35
	LRC 3F	4	1		2	7	70
	LRC 3G	1				1	45
	LRC 10A	1				1	15
	LRC other		1		10	11	20
	ARS 97	2				2	60
	ARS other	1			1	2	10
	Other		1			1	35
Amphora	LR1	13		28	342	383	10980
	LR2	1		1	11	13	350
	LR4	1		3	14	18	555
	LR5/6				2	2	10
	LR7			1	1	2	70
	KAmp2	1			2	3	120
	KAmp5			1	4	5	110
	KAmp6				7	7	185
	Other	1	1	4	206	212	4695
Plain	A	3			1	4	140
	B	1	8		19	28	190
	D	4	2	1	7	14	196
Cook	A	1			3	4	30
	C	4			9	13	420
	D	3		3	121	127	595
Pithos	A	2			9	11	535
	B				9	9	310
	C	1				1	245
	D	7	1	1	55	64	6820
Other		2			94	96	1650
Pre-Roman		2			5	7	255
TOTAL		70	21	45	946	1080	29220

Not inventoried (not illustrated). Two fragments of industrial slag with rounded bottoms from ceramic crucibles. P. h. 0.49, max. diam. base 0.092; p. h. 0.040, max. diam. base 0.093. 8535/6010 12.2. Cf. Lot I-5.

Lot I-29: Courtyard, collapse or second-phase use

Approximate date: mid 7th c. (Cypriot Red Slip form 11; Phocean Red Slip forms 3F, 3G). Pottery from Lot I-29 is summarized with Lots I-28 and 30 in Table 3.8.

Lot I-30: Courtyard, second-phase use

Approximate date: mid 7th c. Pottery from Lot I-30 is summarized with Lots I-28 and 29 in Table 3.8.

Catalogued objects:

117 Plain ware B jug

132 Plain ware D jar/cup

Additional object:

I-30-1 (fig. 3.21). Moldmade terracotta lamp. Est. diam. rim 0.075. Medium-grained reddish yellow fabric (7.5YR

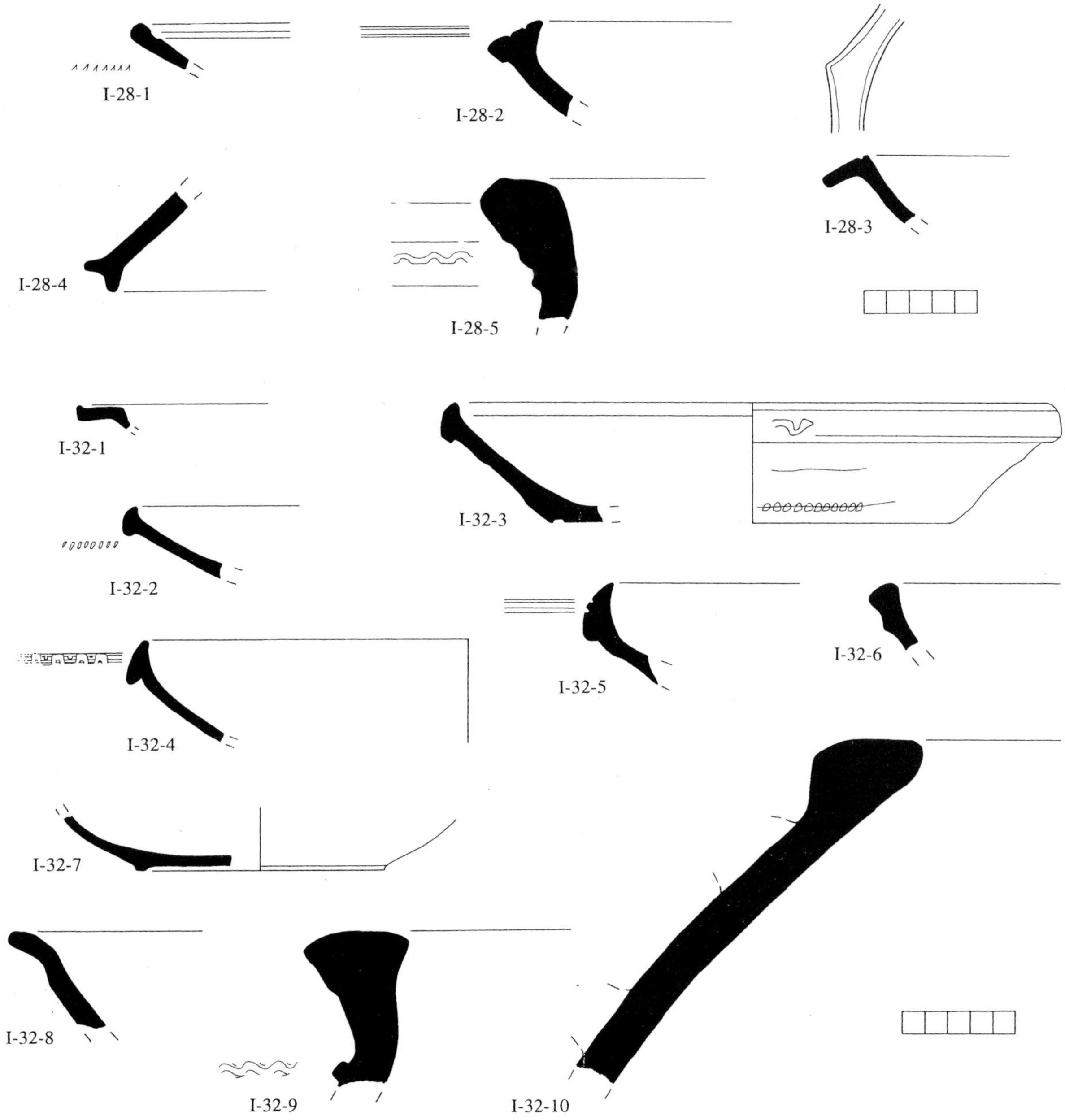

Fig. 3.23. Area I, context pottery, destruction and abandonment.

7/6) with fine lime, black and red inclusions. Circular body with impressed dots. 8530/6010 2.2. Cf. Vessberg 1953: 128, type 20, pl. III.25; Oziol 1977: 279-86 nos. 842-78, pls. 46-48.

Lot I-31: Courtyard, construction

Approximate date: early 7th c.

Catalogued object:

261 Glass flask

Additional objects (fig. 3.21):

I-31-1. LR5 amphora. Est. diam. rim 0.08. Medium-grained light red to reddish yellow fabric (2.5YR 6/6 to 5YR 6/6) with small lime and quartz particles. 8525/6010P 2.1.

I-31-2. Lid, cooking ware group A. Est. diam. rim 0.20. Medium-grained red fabric (10R 5/6) with small quartz particles; interior dark gray, exterior finely ridged, blackened. 8525/6010P 2.1.

I-31-3. Handmade pot, cooking ware group C. Est. diam. rim 0.12. Coarse-grained reddish brown fabric (5YR 4/3-5/3) with many dark inclusions. Globular pot with outturned rim. 8525/6010P 2.1.

I-31-4. Handmade pot, cooking ware group C. Est. diam. rim 0.13. Coarse-grained yellowish red fabric (5YR 5/6) with many dark inclusions. 8525/6010P 2.1.

Lot I-32: Cistern abandonment

Approximate date: mid 7th c. Roman pottery from Lot I-32 is summarized in Table 3.9.

Catalogued object:

227 Glass plate

Additional objects (fig. 3.23):

I-32-1. Dish, Cypriot Red Slip, form 8. Diam. rim uncertain. Medium fine-grained reddish yellow to light brown fabric (5YR 6/6 to 7.5YR 6/4), with soft texture and dull surface. 8535/6010 15.1.

TABLE 3.9. LOT I-32 POTTERY SUMMARY: CISTERN ABANDONMENT

Lot I-32		*rim*	*base*	*handle*	*sherd*	*sum*	*weight*
Fine	CRS 3	1				1	20
	CRS 8	1				1	5
	CRS 9A	1				1	20
	CRS 9B	2	2		2	6	100
	CRS 9C	3	2		1	6	120
	CRS 10	4				4	65
	CRS 11	1		1		2	95
	CRS other				1	1	40
	LRC 10A	2			1	3	55
	LRC other	2				2	55
	ARS		1			1	5
	Other				1	1	5
Amphora	LR1	9		11	41	61	2560
	LR4			1		1	85
	KAmp6				7	7	240
	Other	1		2	9	12	585
Plain	A	1				1	30
	B		1			1	30
	D	1	2		3	6	345
Cook	A			1	1	2	5
	D			1	4	5	130
Pithos	A	1				1	50
	B				2	2	265
	C	2				2	320
	D	4	3	2	5	14	5760
Other					15	15	140
Pre-Roman				1	1	2	205
TOTAL		36	11	20	94	161	11335

I-32-2. Dish, Cypriot Red Slip, form 9A. Est. diam. rim 0.20-0.24. Fine-grained light red fabric (2.5YR 6/6) with a little lime; interior slipped, flaking. Rim fired lighter. 8535/6010 15.1.

I-32-3. Dish, Cypriot Red Slip, form 9B. Est. diam. rim 0.26, est. diam. base 0.18. Fine-grained light red fabric (2.5YR 6/6) with a little lime. Exterior wall roughly finished with incised wavy line on rim, covered with hard red slip, pitted. 8535/6010 15.1, KK93-4.

I-32-4. Dish, Cypriot Red Slip, form 9C. Est. diam. rim 0.28. Fine-grained light red fabric (2.5YR 6/6). Exterior rim grooved, with lightly incised wavy line, covered with red slip, flaking. 8535/6010 15.1.

I-32-5. Dish, Cypriot Red Slip, form 9C. Diam. rim uncertain. Fine-grained light reddish brown fabric (5YR 6/4). 8535/6010 15.1.

I-32-6. Basin, Cypriot Red Slip, form 11. Est. diam. rim 0.30. Medium-grained reddish yellow fabric (5YR 6/6) with fine lime and occasional voids; dull red slip. 8535/6010 15.1.

I-32-7. Dish, Phocean Red Slip, form 3? Est. diam. base 0.20. Dark reddish brown fabric (5YR 5/3) with finely speckled surface and a few small voids, hard fired. 8535/6010 15.1.

I-32-8. Basin? Plain ware fabric A. Diam. rim uncertain. Reddish brown fabric (5YR 5/4) with a little lime and many medium dark inclusions. 8535/6010 15.1.

I-32-9. Storage jar, *pithos* group A. Diam. rim uncertain. Coarse-grained light red fabric (2.5YR 6/6) with abundant lime, quartz, and dark inclusions. 8535/6010 15.1.

I-32-10. Storage jar, *pithos* group D. Est. diam. rim 0.30. Coarse-grained pink fabric (2.5YR 7/4) with abundant lime and dark inclusions. 8535/6010 15.1.

KK89-28 (fig. 3.24.8). Gypsum screen fragment.

Lot I-33: East of basilica, collapse

Approximate date: inconclusive (mid 7th c.?).

Lot I-34: South of basilica, collapse

Approximate date: inconclusive (mid 7th c.?).

Liturgical furnishings (fig. 3.24)

A small stone bowl found near the present ground surface in the vicinity of the court's W wing need not have been used

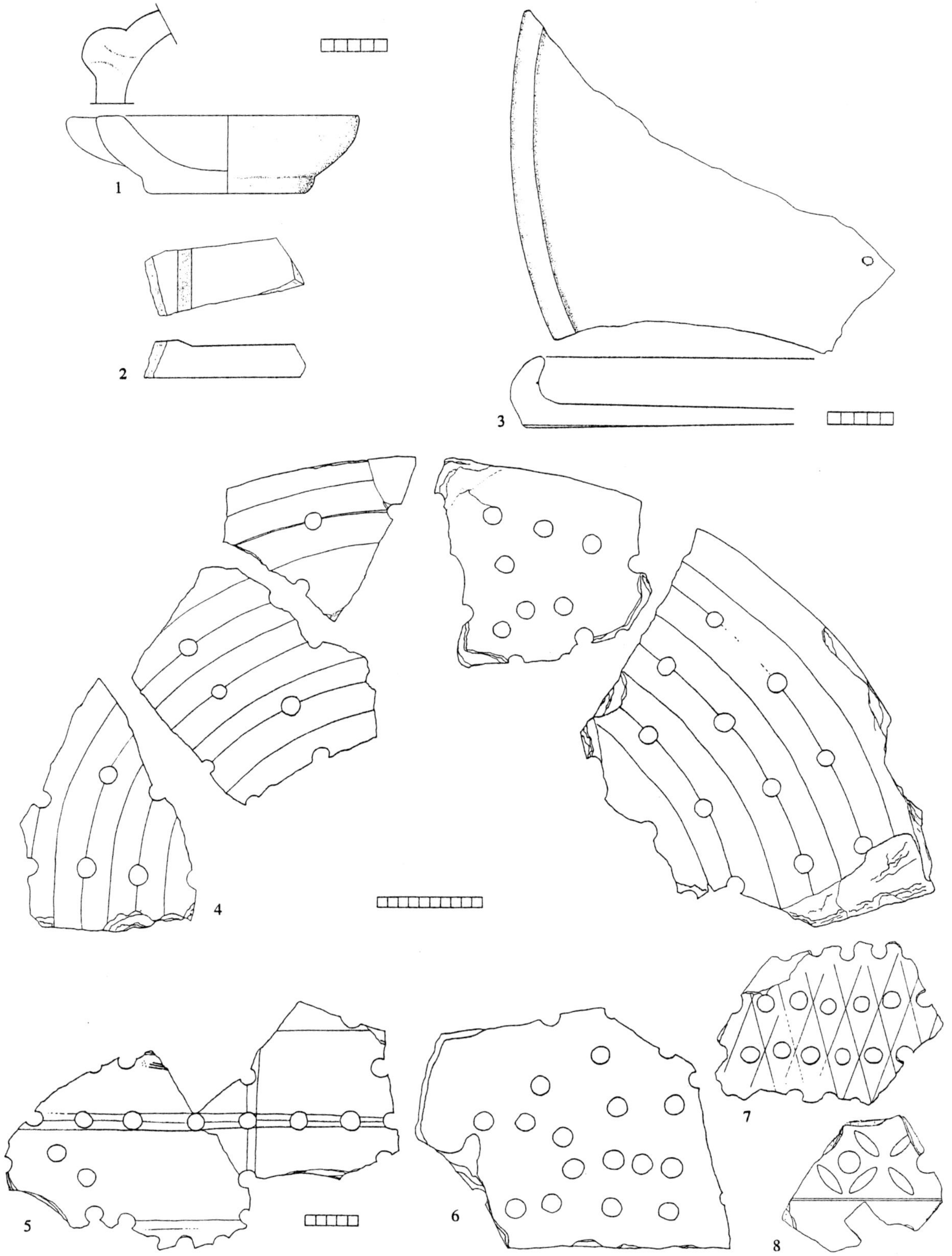

Fig. 3.24. Area I, liturgical and architectural furnishings.

within the church itself. More likely furnishing the basilica were two fragments of marble tables: part of the raised border from a rectangular table, and a large piece of a semicircular table with incurving rim. The rectangular table fragment might have come from either of the sanctuary tables; by contrast, rounded table tops usually were employed for other purposes (Loverance 1990; Chalkia 1991). Like the bowl, both of these fragments came from late levels and may have been moved during post-Roman salvaging.

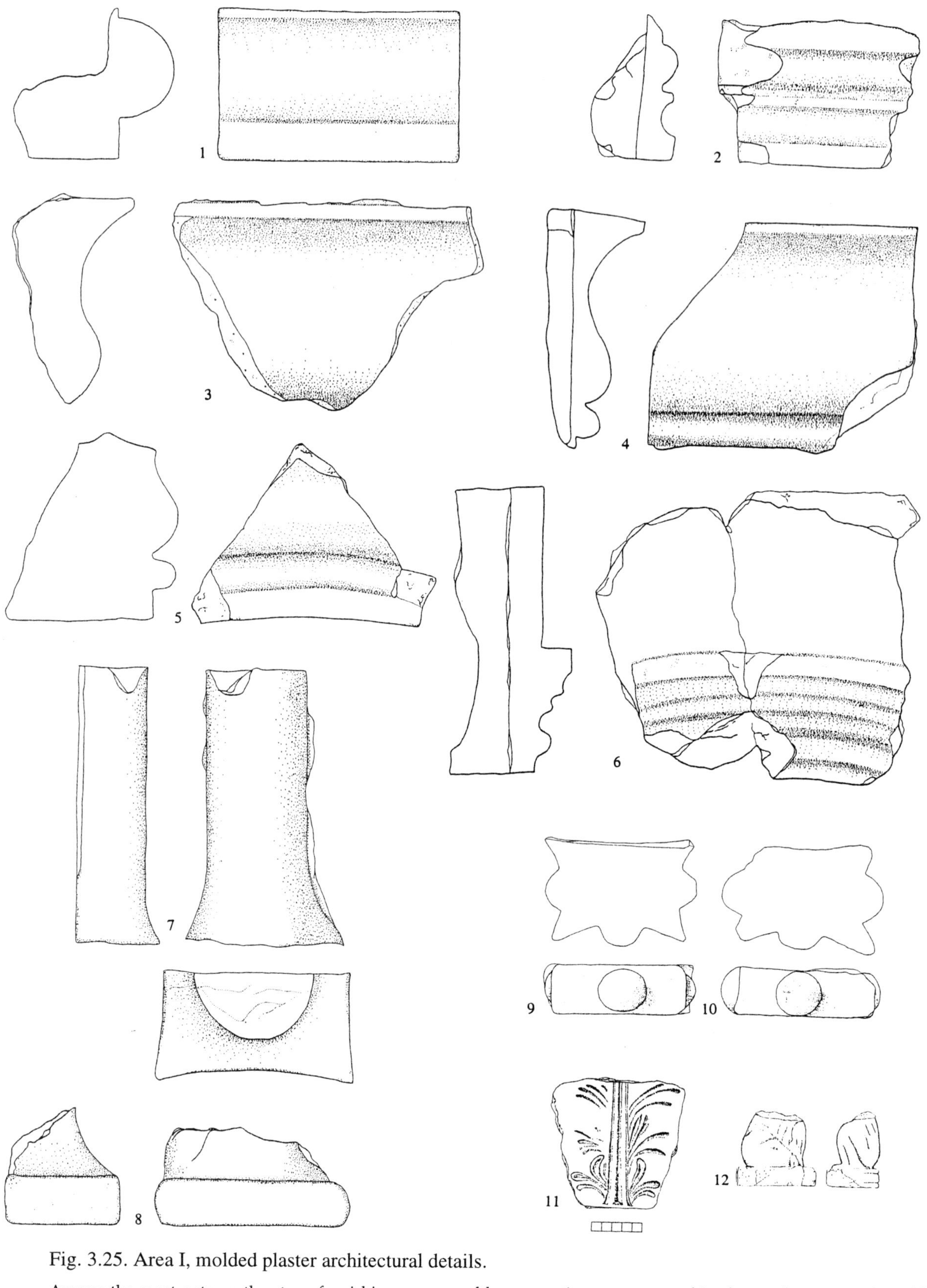

Fig. 3.25. Area I, molded plaster architectural details.

Among the most noteworthy stone furnishings recovered by excavation were many thin sheets of gypsum pierced by multiple holes (diam. 0.015-0.020 m). In some cases lightly incised lines were used to guide the drilling of these holes. Some of the slabs may have functioned as screens enclosing the chancel area. Several of the larger slabs have curved outer surfaces, suggesting that they were used as window screens; this might be envisioned as a modest version of the window screens found at the Salamis Campanopetra and on the mainland (cf. Butler 1929: 243-44; Sodini and Kolokotsas

1984: 118 n.14; Roux 1998: 21, 25 fig. 11). Most examples were found at floor level of the nave and in the overlying fill (Lots I-1 to 3).

Fig. 3.24.1. Marble bowl. Est. diam. rim 0.21; est. diam. base 0.14; max. h. 0.05. Small bowl with projecting rim lugs, approximately half preserved. Surface, Lot I-1, 8520/6010N 1.1, KK89-33. Cf. Chavane 1975: 13-14 nos. 2-3. pls. 1, 57; Rodziewicz 1984: nos. 346, 350-51, pls. 69-70; Kingsley and Raveh 1996: 62 no. ST01, fig. 42, pl. 61.

Fig. 3.24.2. Fragment of a rectangular table with raised border in medium fine-grained white marble. Upper surface smooth, underside roughly finished. P. l. 0.048, w. 0.117, th. 0.026-0.029. Lot I-1, 8525/6015 1.1, KK90-8.

Fig. 3.24.3. Fragment of a (semi)circular table surface with flat bottom and curving rim in fine-grained gray-veined white marble. A small drilled hole in the floor with an iron pin attests an ancient repair. Est. diam. rim 0.90; h. 0.055, th. 0.018. Surface, Lot I-1, 8525/6015E 1.1, KK89-36. Cf. Loverance 1990: 229-31, figs. 17-18; Chalkia 1991: 47-53, type E; Acconci 1998: 497 nos. 75-78.

Fig. 3.24.4. Five fragments of perforated gypsum screen with incised semicircular lines, pierced by drilled holes (0.015-0.020-m diam.). Total reconstructed width of panel *c.*1 m; th. 0.018-0.022. Nave lower fill, Lot I-3, 8530/6000 3.1 and 3.2, KK94-28A-E.

Fig. 3.24.5. Two joining fragments of perforated screen with incised reticulate lines, pierced by multiple drilled holes of diam. 0.015-m; th. 0.018-0.022. Surface, Lot I-1, SG18A, KK94-28F-G.

Fig. 3.24.6. Fragment of perforated gypsum screen. Max. dimensions 0.33 x 0.25, th. 0.023-0.028. Nave lower fill, Lot I-3, 8530/6000 3.1, KK94-28I.

Fig. 3.24.7. Fragment of perforated gypsum screen with 4 rows of drilled holes set within an incised diagonal grid. Max. dimensions 0.16 x 0.22; th. 0.014-0.019. Basilica upper fill, Lot I-2, 8535/6000 2.1, KK94-28H.

Fig. 3.24.8. Fragment of perforated gypsum screen with drilled and square(?) holes set within an incised reticulate pattern. Max. dimensions 0.13 x 0.15; th. 0.047. Cistern, Lot I-32, 8535/6010 16.1, KK89-28.

Architectural decoration

Excavation of the nave's lower levels recovered a number of fragmentary architectural elements made of molded gypsum plaster. The most basic forms include short, straight sections of a semicircular molding (diam. *c.*0.10 m) that projects from a flush surface. These simple rounded shafts may have emphasized structural lines of the building by running around doorways or windows or along the upper wall. Other distinctive fragments present a cyma recta molding 0.23 m tall that probably came from the upper walls of the central aisle; the presence of two curved fragments suggests that this crown molding may have extended around the face of the apse too. A number of smaller objects, including a low base, a flat pilaster capital and an appropriately sized abacus, appear better suited for colonnettes or chancel screen moldings. A single worn fragment (Lot I-3) may depict a seated figure. Taken as a group, the *Sirmata* plaster represents a few basic forms of simple profile. The limited variety suggests that the building's original appearance was relatively plain, in clear contrast to the more elaborate decoration of the south church (below, p. 111).

Fig. 3.25.1. Rounded wall molding flanked by two flat surfaces. P. h. 0.155, l. 0.24. Basilica upper collapse, Lot I-2, 8535/6000 2.1, not inventoried.

Fig. 3.25.2. Wall molding or pilaster base with hollow and rounded elements. P. h. 0.15, l. 0.20. Surface, Lot I-1, SG18C, not inventoried. Cf. Papageorghiou 1963: fig. 5.

Fig. 3.25.3. Crown wall molding. P. h. 0.22, l. 0.31. Surface, Lot I-1, not inventoried.

fig. 3.25.4. Crown wall molding with cyma recta. P. h. 0.24, l. 0.262. Basilica lower collapse, Lot I-3, 8530/6000 3.1, not inventoried. Cf. Callot 1980: figs. 8 and 22b.

Fig. 3.25.5. Curved wall crown molding; iron nail embedded in lower part of molding. P. h. 0.19, l. 0.24. Nave lower fill, Lot I-3, 8535/6000 3.1, not inventoried.

Fig. 3.25.6. Curved wall molding with hollow and rounded elements. P. h. 0.29, l. 0.30. Surface, Lot I-1, KK88-21A.

Fig. 3.25.7. Slender pilaster shaft, flaring toward base. P. l. 0.28, w. 0.10. Basilica lower collapse, Lot I-3, 8530/6000 3.1, KK88-45.

Fig. 3.25.8. Base for slender pilaster shaft. P. h. 0.13, h. base 0.05, w. 0.195. Nave lower collapse, Lot I-3, 8535/6000 3.1, not inventoried.

Fig. 3.25.9. Abacus for pilaster capital, as KK88-15. Front and side edges curve inward and meet at sharp corners; central boss on front and sides. Max. h. 0.05, w. 0.15. Surface, Lot I-1, 8540/6000 1.1, KK88-16.

Fig. 3.25.10. Abacus for pilaster capital, as KK88-16. Max. h. 0.05, w. 0.16. Basilica upper collapse, Lot I-2, 8535/6000 2.1, KK88-15.

Fig. 3.25.11. Pilaster capital with vertical acanthus leaves. P. h. 0.135, w. 0.133. Surface, Lot I-1, 8535/6015 1.1, KK88-23. Cf. Callot 1980: fig. 4 (Salamis); des Gagniers and Tran Tam Tinh 1985: fig. 194 (Soloi); Pralong and Saulnier 1987: fig. 38 (Amathus).

Graphic reconstruction of the buildings at *Sirmata* (figs. 3.7, 3.26)

The proposed reconstruction of the *Sirmata* complex is based on excavated features and knowledge of contemporary building practices in the region.[16] Most of the basilica's plan is relatively clear, with some walls

---

16 Cf. Callot 1980: 344; Sodini and Kolokotsas 1984: 249-51; Hirschfeld 1992; A. Pralong and J.-M. Saulnier

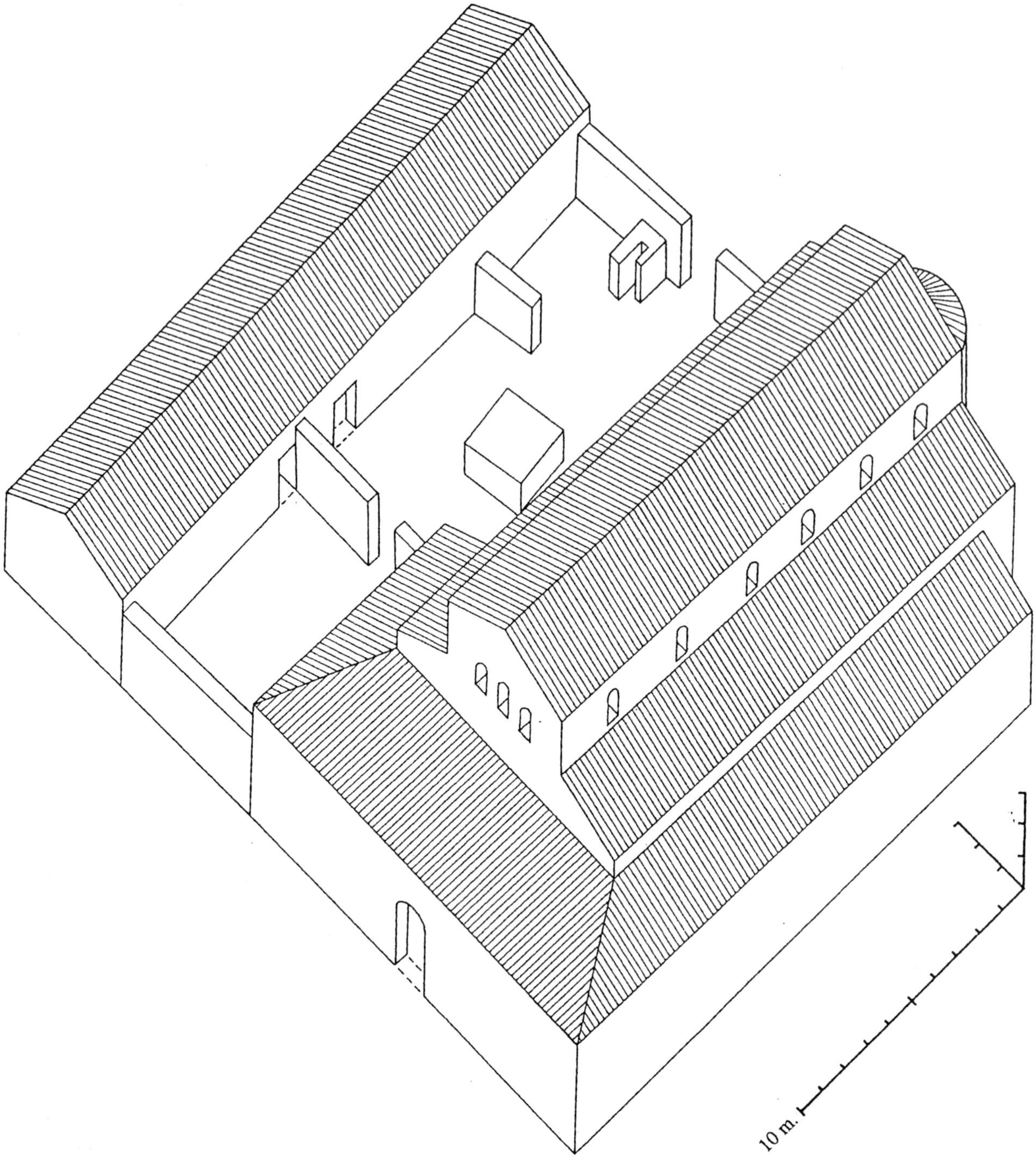

Fig. 3.26. Area I, isometric reconstruction.

walls standing as high as 1.5 m. Other parts of the complex, including the court and the N building, are known by floors, foundations, or lower walls, which in some cases preserve evidence of doorways. The NW and NE corners of the complex have been restored on the basis of adjacent walls. Less well understood features of the court, like the central foundation, are left as low solid forms.

The basilica presents relatively few design problems. Despite many irregularities of plan, the uniform construction of foundations, walls, and piers indicates that basilica, narthex, and lateral spaces were built as an integrated whole. The 4 cylindrical piers of the nave colonnade are reconstructed with simple capitals to support an arcade and clerestory wall to a height of 7 m (fig. 3.7). The two westernmost piers pose interesting questions. Their distance (3.4 m) from the W wall raises the unlikely possibility of high arches extending into the clerestory. In the reconstruction this problem is resolved by omitting the capitals and maintaining the 4.5-m height of the nave arcade. The piers probably carried a high transverse arch across the nave, here restored to match the height of the apse, as well as across both side aisles; the result is an emphasized W bay that remains closely associated with the nave. Clerestory windows in the W wall, had they existed, would have made the W nave bay the most brightly lit part of the church. An upper floor above this space seems unlikely for reasons of access and roofing. More convincing evidence of a narthex gallery survives at the acropolis basilica at Amathus, where a staircase was located in the N end of the narthex (Pralong 1994a: 434). Like the W nave bay, the *Sirmata* narthex is reconstructed with transverse arches but without capitals. A unified system of pitched roofs covers the apse, nave, and S aisles. A continuous outward-sloping shed covers the narthex, S lateral space, and space I.

The court appears as an integral component of the monastery plan. The substantial N wing, comprising spaces III, IV, and V, is treated as a single trapezoidal structure with a long pitched roof, although the irregular walls suggest that these spaces may actually have been roofed in separate sections. Space II is left as an unroofed space opening off the central court. Freestanding walls with outer doorways were probably as common in antiquity as they are in villages today and would have been capped by a single row of rooftiles. Other structures built in and along the E side of the court are not sufficiently clear to be reconstructed.

The elevated viewpoint of the reconstruction emphasizes the rooftiles that at one point covered most of the complex (fig. 3.26). Apart from the two open courts, all structures were presumably covered by sloping roofs with terracotta tiles, perhaps supplemented by thin sheets of gypsum. The average size and approximate weight of the tiles are known and the roofed areas can be roughly estimated (above, p. 53). Assuming an average slope of 20°, the roof of the basilica, including narthex and S lateral spaces, may have used some 2,700 pan and cover tiles weighing close to 8,500 kg. The total load of the complex may have exceeded 3,800 tiles, or 12,000 kg.

The purpose of the reconstruction is to offer a plausible impression of how the *Sirmata* complex appeared in the early 7th c. I have tried to use the simplest building forms and design options for which there is evidence. Other solutions are possible.

Chronological summary and significance

The monastery at *Sirmata* was one of the most conspicuous architectural features of the Vasilikos valley at the turn of the 7th c. The tall plastered walls of the basilica would have been familiar to travelers along nearby roads as well as inhabitants of the area. Opening to the west, the main doors of the church looked toward the nearby village, even as the lives of its occupants remained centered within the complex. The location close to yet clearly apart from the village reflects the spirit of early Christian monasticism, which often sought to retain its independence of settled life. More pragmatic factors may also have played a part: the monastery's foundation may represent a rational economic investment by relocating onto previously unexploited land a group of monks, displaced by simmering tensions on the mainland or otherwise drawn by the agricultural promise of the valley.[17]

While working at *Sirmata* we noted indefinite yet recurring hints of earlier activities in the area. The mound is substantially of natural origin, but a deep sondage at the SW corner found pottery of Classical, Archaic, and even Late Bronze Age date. More directly relevant to late antiquity is the presence of 5th- and 6th-c. pottery in upper fills. This distribution occurs to some extent across the ridge but is especially apparent here in the strong representation of Phocean Red Slip form 3 bowls. Although for the most part lacking stratigraphically secure contexts, this material might derive from earlier activities at this prominent location, as implied also by anomalies in the orientation of architectural features in the court.

The construction in *c.*600 of the small hill-top monastery marked a turning point in the area's history. The three-aisled basilica without galleries was the most common church plan in the E Mediterranean at this time, yet within this basic formula the *Sirmata* church presents several distinctive features. Like many other rural churches, the basilica was built almost entirely of locally available materials, primarily fieldstone and gypsum set in gypsum mortar. Its liturgical organization offers our clearest evidence of rural Cypriot practices, with two tables set on a raised *bema* before the apse with *synthronon*, and lateral apsidioles standing apart from the sanctuary. The nave's overall proportions are exceptionally long and narrow compared with other churches on the island (below, p. 150). The unusual piers of the W nave reflect an innovative solution to local needs and may have drawn upon mainland models, possibly conveyed by new arrivals from Syria. The narthex's wall-pilasters, which probably carried transverse arches, are known at Kourion but not elsewhere in the Cypriot countryside (Megaw 1976a: 346). The narthex crypt, clearly intended from the beginning but unparalleled on the island, recalls similar arrangements in Palestine and Syria, where burials

---

in Aupert 1996: 136 fig. 58; Biscop 1997; Roux 1998.

17 Cf. Villeneuve 1985: 118-21; Biscop 1997: 44-45.

often are associated with cults of saints and martyrs.[18] The presence of a long flanking space that may have been used as a mortuary annex is well known in Cyprus. These burials, like others in the area, probably honored members of the local community. Decoration of the building was minimal.

The court is closely related to the church. The combination of basilica and court in a compact, squarish plan is typical of small monasteries in Palestine and Syria.[19] Enclosed on all sides and partially shaded by high church walls, this open space served as a functional center and meeting place for local inhabitants. The central foundation may have supported a low tower that offered a lookout toward the coast and up the valley. The courtyard cistern was a not-uncommon feature of island basilicas, other examples being known at Amathus and Kourion. Tucked into the court's SE corner and sheltered by the rising walls of the basilica, the *Sirmata* cistern was a well designed response to the perennial need for water. Surrounding spaces met multiple needs. The large W space may have served as an interior court before being subdivided and partially roofed. Rooms to the north may have been used as *kellia* or cells, or perhaps as a *trapeza* or refectory. The lost E wing probably served similar domestic purposes. All of these secondary spaces seem to have been single-storeyed and covered by flat or pitched roofs with terracotta tiles. Together with the basilica they form a compact and well integrated ensemble with a closed, defensive appearance.

The *Sirmata* complex was established as a single undertaking near the end of the 6th c., with some work continuing into the early 7th c. The builders may have incorporated or worked around earlier features on the hill, but the nature of any such remains is unclear. Similar building materials and techniques were employed throughout the complex and survive best in the semi-subterranean parts of the basilica. Several significant changes occurred in the first half of the 7th c., apparently after the building had suffered some damage: a sturdy wall filled the basilica's N colonnade to create a separate chapel, and the court paving was raised and repaired. Unmortared partitions were added to spaces II, III, and IV (cf. Roux 1998: 47 for similar partitions at the Campanopetra). The summary burial of 9 adults, children, and infants in the cistern took place around the middle of the 7th c. While such expedience was known on other dire occasions (e.g., during times of earthquake and plague), it is reasonable to link the assemblage with the widespread social upheaval caused by Arab campaigns on the island. Human and faunal remains made the cistern unusable as surely as did the overlying building débris. This dramatic break in occupation was followed by clear signs of architectural collapse and a reduced level of activity: a series of small troughs, bins, and hearths was installed in the central and inner courts, and a circular bread oven was built of salvaged rooftiles in space IV. The basilica's devotional function was maintained in the crypt, which was accessible through a small vestibule set amid the ruins of the narthex. The re-organization of these tombs, now including multiple interments, resembles the re-use of the narthex tomb in basilica II at Peyia for multiple burials in the later 7th c. (Megaw 1955: 45). The scarcity of later finds suggests that this resumed activity was short-lived, however, and within a few years the mound and surrounding area were abandoned.

This sequence encapsulates the fortunes of the Vasilikos valley — and many coastal parts of Cyprus — during late antiquity. The growth of rural settlement appears in the founding of this small monastic center, perhaps prompted by new arrivals and probably with the support of local landowners. Built shortly before or around 600, the *Sirmata* basilica is one of the latest pre-mediaeval churches known in the area and a close contemporary of the acropolis basilica at Amathus. The monastery's well-being is demonstrated by its carefully built structures and the abundance of fine pottery and glass, and was presumably based on a combination of local farming and donations of valley residents. Its occupation was brought to an abrupt end in one of the island's most vividly preserved moments of mid-century crisis. The ruined complex provided brief shelter for the remaining inhabitants, who re-occupied some of the rooms, built a makeshift oven in one of them, stabled animals in the court, and repaired access to the crypt. With other, more pressing needs to be addressed, the focus of local concern shifted from traditional clerical liturgies to tending for a short while the memories of earlier residents — perhaps the *Saranda Ayioi* — of the valley.

AREA II: THE SOUTH CHURCH

Introduction

Area II lies near the S perimeter of the Late Roman settlement, *c.*200 m west of *Sirmata* (fig. 2.4). Initial survey of the area noted a low, overgrown mound on the lower ridge lying at the intersection of two terrace

18 Lassus 1947: 169-80; Sodini 1986; Tsafrir 1988: 48; Ruggieri 1991: 178-79; cf. Papageorghiou 1985: 322-24.

19 Lassus 1947; Villeneuve 1985: 118-21; Ruggieri 1991: 174-81; Hirschfeld 1992; Biscop 1997: 37-40.

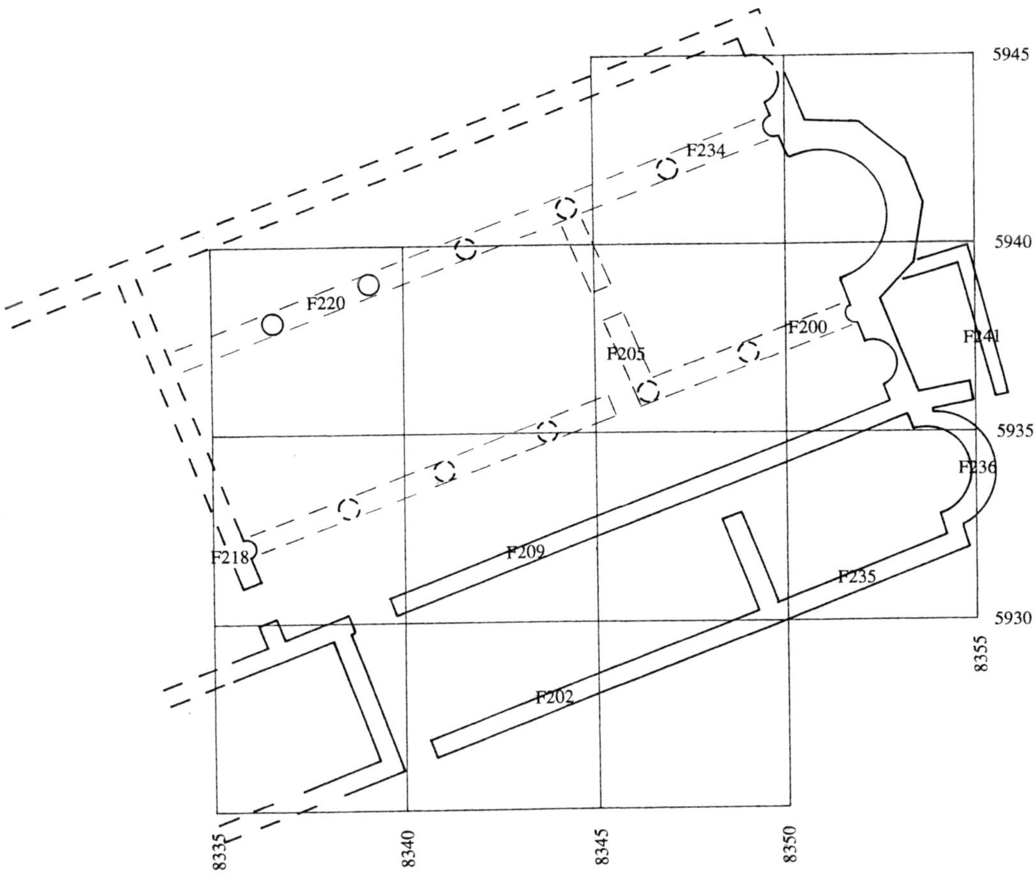

Fig. 3.27. Area II, plan of excavation trench.

walls separating three cultivated fields, numbered 255, 256/1, and 261/1 on the LV.20 cadastral survey map (fig. 2.8). Before excavation, the mound surface appeared continuous with terrain to the north and west but stood as much as 1.5 m above fields to east and south. Approximately 30 m to the southwest the ground begins to slope down toward the level of the river plain. The natural topography has been much altered by construction of the new coastal highway and, before that, a railcart line from the nearby gypsum quarries. The sloping grade of this narrow-gauge railway is clear on aerial photographs, the cadastral map, and recent topographic surveys: it curved around *Sirmata* and passed 30 m south of Area II before descending to the river plain (plots 256/2 and 262/2 on fig. 2.8). The presence of Late Roman sherds on the lower slope, however, suggests that the defile is substantially natural and in late antiquity offered direct approach from the valley floor. East and south of Area II the flat terrain opens toward *Sirmata* and the coast. Survey of the surrounding fields identified a marked drop in the quantity and variety of surface finds to the west, south, and east (above, pp. 32-33). This suggests that Area II stood at the lower edge of the settlement and formed a prominent landmark for visitors coming from the coast.

The VVP survey first observed that the Area II mound belongs to the substantial Late Roman site noted at Kopetra (Todd 1979a: 284; id. 1979b: 32). The presence of intact building remains was demonstrated in 1986 by the excavation of a deep irrigation trench along the W edge of the mound. This encountered several floors and mortared rubble walls that were recorded before backfilling; associated pottery included Late Roman wares as well as a Chalcolithic deposit that appears related to the large site at *Ayious*, some 50 m to the south (Todd and Croft forthcoming). Study of the surface remains in 1987 confirmed the presence of substantial architecture at the sector and encouraged us to undertake excavations from 1989 through 1991.

Work at Area II was limited by existing property boundaries and other practical considerations. Six 5-m trenches opened atop the mound quickly identified the main features of another basilica, including the colonnade walls and three apses. During the two following summers we exposed the rest of the central and S aisles, most of the S lateral space, and features located behind the apse wall (figs. 3.27-30). The N aisle continues into a cultivated field and was not available for study; extensive earthmoving on this property may have disturbed earlier features. The irrigation pipeline cuts through the vicinity of the narthex, which was not explored either. An eroded wall fragment and a small section of paving located *c.*30 m to the west may belong to a nearby building. Excavation near the center of the mound, within the central aisle of the basilica, located a broad pit of post-Roman date that may reflect the quarrying of building material (Lot II-2). Progress

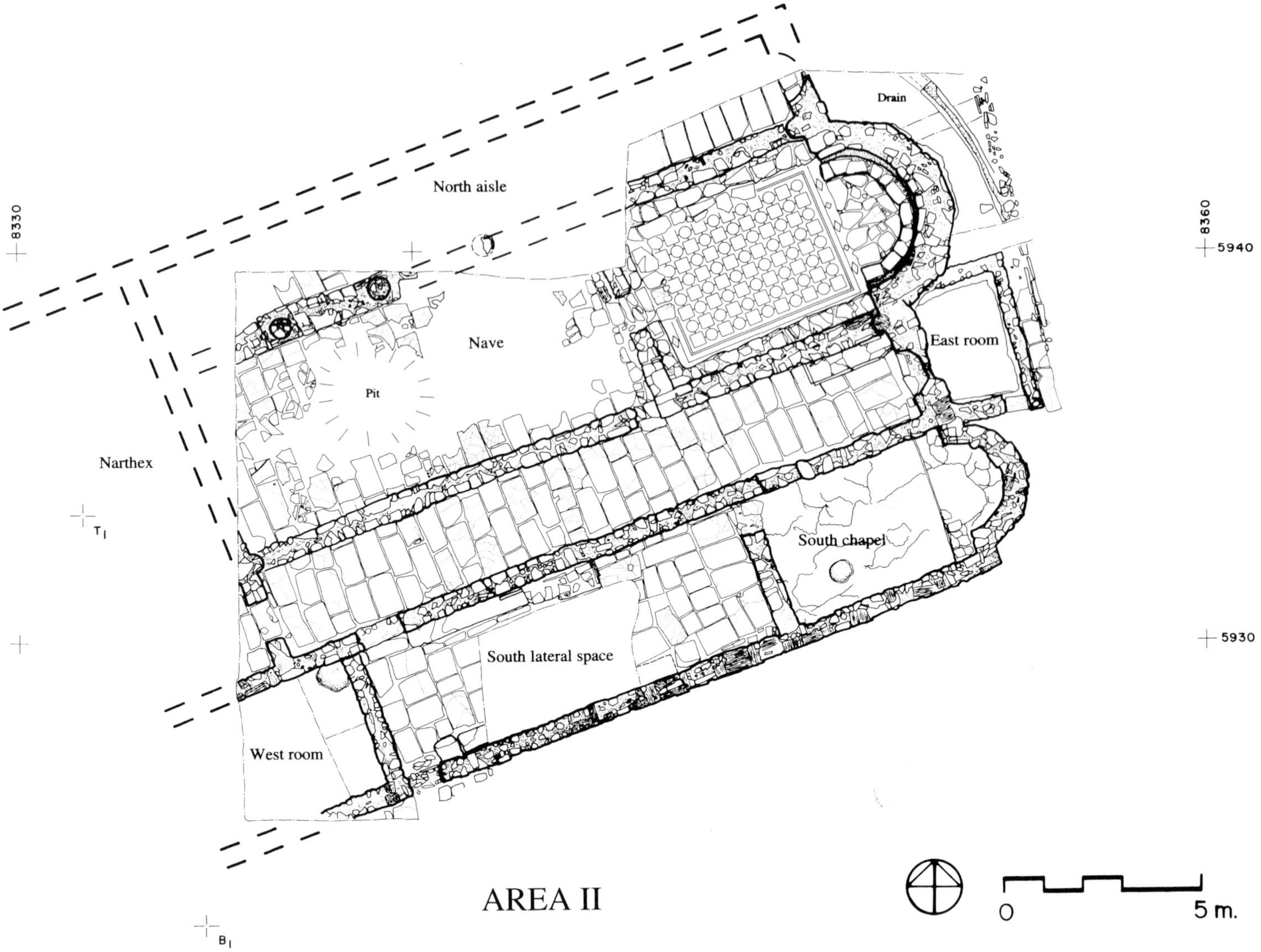

Fig. 3.28. Area II, state plan.

in the S parts of the basilica was slowed by the discovery of a large amount of gypsum plaster sculpture that required special attention in recovery and cleaning; a representative section of the collapsed late wall (L209), which contained much of this sculpture, was left in place. Many fragments of bedded mosaic found in the E trenches also demanded close attention. Several sondages below intact floor levels yielded meager but important evidence documenting the early history of the building (e.g., Lots II-28, 35). Preliminary reports of excavations at Area II appeared in *Muse* 23-24 (1989-90) 20-25 and 25 (1991) 10-13, and in *RDAC* 1990: 236-38; 1991: 226-35; and 1994: 289-95.

Architectural features and associated deposits

Area II remains incompletely excavated and its occupation history is only partially understood. Major building features include a three-aisled basilica and narthex with a long, subdivided space lying along the S side (figs. 3.28-30). The presence of other unexcavated walls in the vicinity indicates that this south church was continuous with the main settlement. While the architectural features are themselves interesting, special attention is due the building's mosaic and stucco decoration, which forms a unique contribution.

Basilica and narthex

The lower walls of the south church are well preserved and permit the reconstruction of its general plan (figs. 3.31-33). The three-aisled nave has an interior length of 17.0 m and width of *c.*10.5 m. To the east a broad apse faces onto the central aisle. Both side aisles end in shallow niches inscribed in the E wall. The unexcavated narthex lies west of the nave. A 3.5-m wide lateral space extends along the S flank of nave and narthex. A small trapezoidal room built against the apse wall east of the S aisle completes the known parts of the complex.

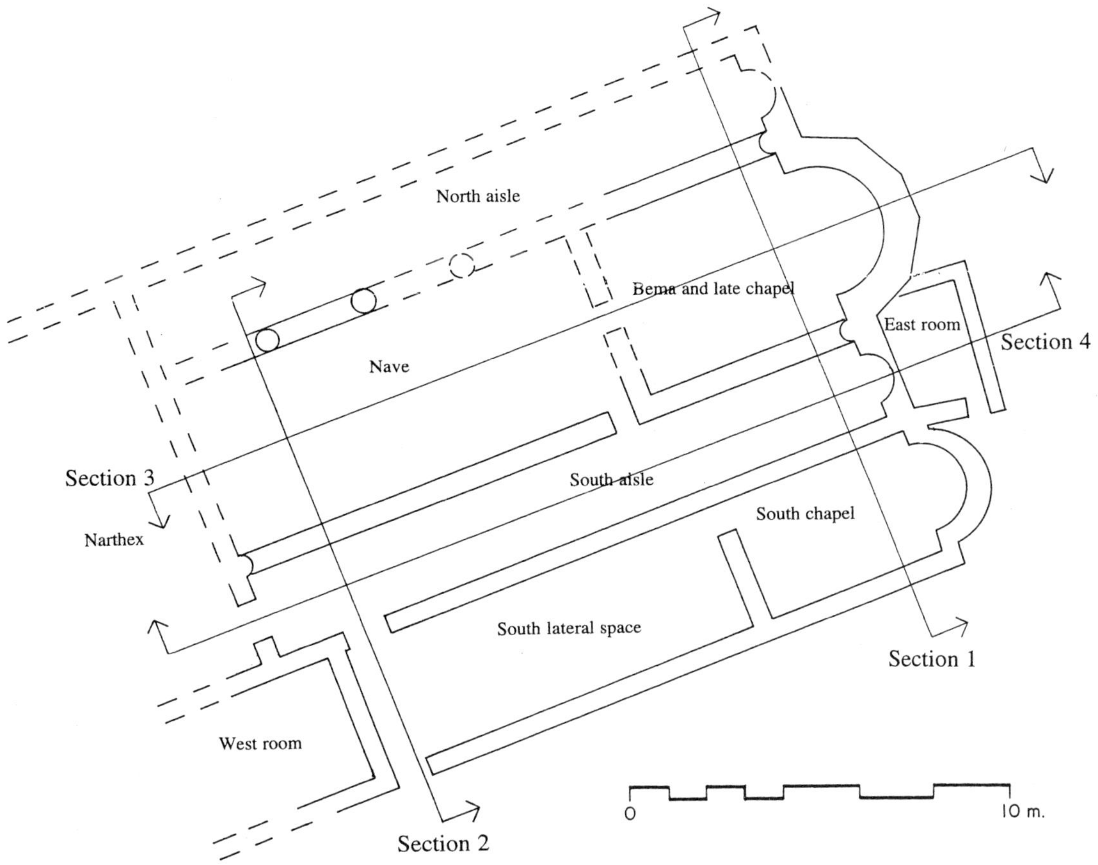

Fig. 3.29. Area II, section plan.

In its original form the nave was subdivided into three aisles by two rows of columns — or, more correctly, cylindrical masonry piers. The width of the central aisle is *c.*4.8 m. The well preserved floor of the S aisle is 2.3 m wide and a symmetrically corresponding aisle can be assumed to the north. Allowing 0.5 m for each colonnade, the total width of the nave would have reached about 10.5 m. Foundations and rising walls were built of fieldstones and gypsum fragments set in gypsum mortar, as seen also at *Sirmata,* and in many cases were assembled with the aid of wood formwork. At one point the N colonnade was partially blocked by a mortared rubble screen set between piers. A less durable wall made of gypsum fragments bedded in mud mortar replaced the S colonnade during a later phase, probably around the middle of the 7th c. (fig. 3.30, sections 3-4).

The lower parts of three piers of the N colonnade survive in place. The two W (excavated) piers were cylindrical in plan and were built of mortared fieldstone and gypsum fragments covered with a thick coat of plaster. Unlike the *Sirmata* piers, which lacked any sort of bottom molding or vertical fluting, these two piers rested on low squarish bases set at a distance of 2.15 m. The westernmost pier stands *c.*2.5 m from the projected line of the nave's W wall. The top of a third (unexcavated) pier is visible at ground level about 2.35 m farther east; its center stands almost exactly at the mid point of the hall, 8.5 m from both E and W walls. The 17-m length of the nave allows space for 5 piers set at 2.2- to 2.5-m intervals. Semicircular shafts attached to the E and W walls originally concluded both colonnades. The recovery of many plaster fragments with vertical and diagonal fluting illustrates the lively appearance of the nave. These fluted piers and pilasters carried capitals made of gypsum plaster molded around a rubble core — fully rounded capitals for the freestanding piers, half-capitals for the wall shafts (cf. Roux 1998: 100-8). Scattered acanthus fragments attest the presence of Corinthian-derived ornament throughout the building (below, p. 113). The wide if somewhat irregular spacing of supports suggests that they carried a light-weight arcade with upper nave wall and pitched roof. A timber entablature, while less likely, cannot be ruled out. Windows were glazed with rectangular glass panes, of which several large fragments were recovered (e.g., Lot II-12). No pierced window or chancel screen fragment like those found at *Sirmata* was noted at Area II.

Slabs of gypsum originally covered all three aisles. This paving is mostly lost in the nave but survives in much of the S aisle (fig. 3.33). Here individual slabs were set in 27 even rows running from north to south, beginning at the W end and continuing to the E wall, where 4 perpendicularly laid slabs conclude the pattern. Most of these paving slabs are *c.*1.1 x 0.55 m in size. Interrupted only by the line of the S colonnade, this

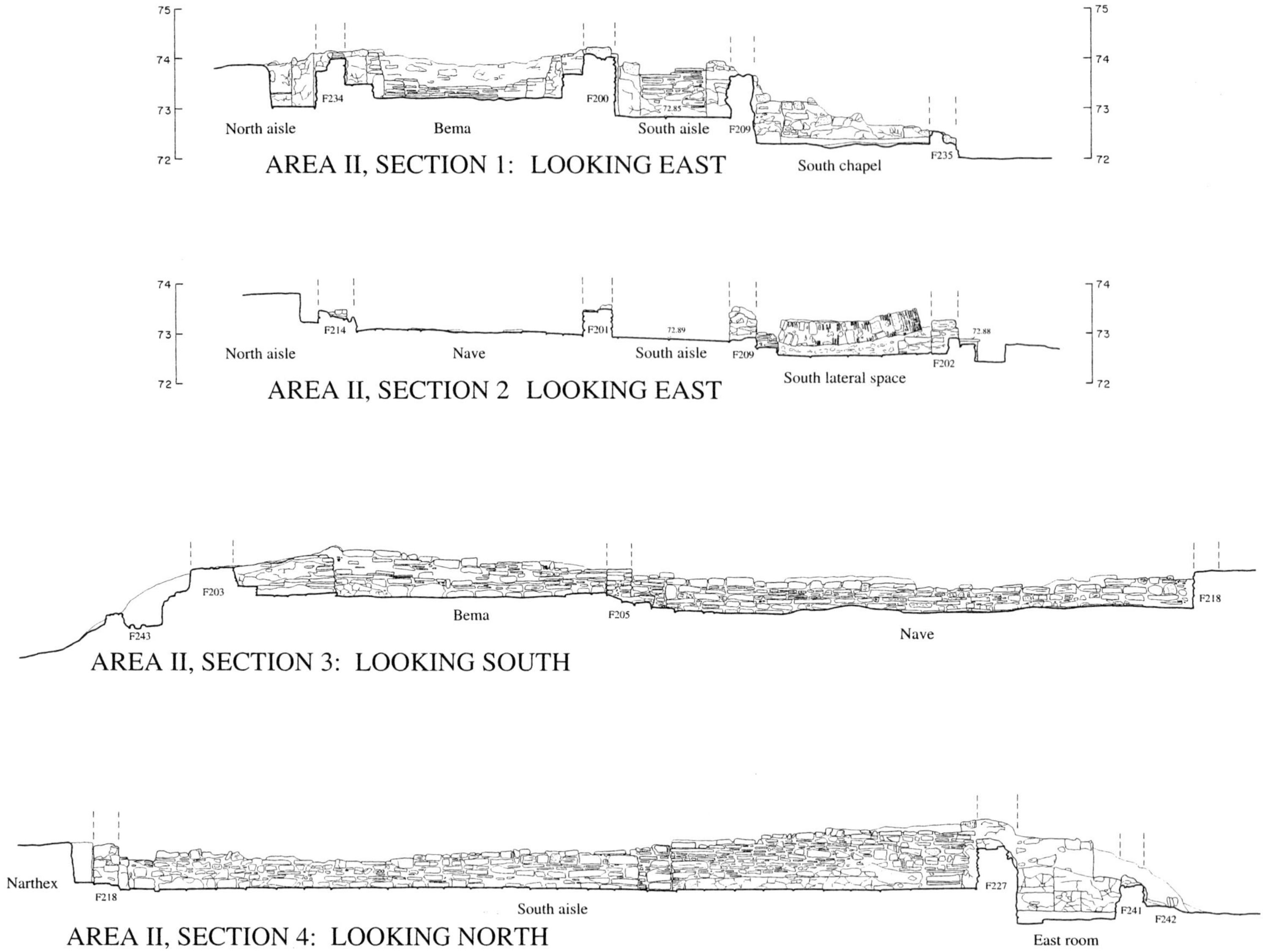

Fig. 3.30. Area II, sections 1-4.

arrangement apparently continued into the central aisle where the floor is less well preserved. Two small sections of a similar surface were identified at opposite ends of the N aisle. In all three aisles the paved floor lies at about the same level (fig. 3.30, sections 1-2). A sondage below the central aisle revealed that the gypsum slabs were laid directly atop the marl bedrock, probably in the second half of the 6th c. (Lot II-35). The later history of the central aisle included the accumulation of building débris atop this paved surface accompanied by intermittent burning (Lot II-20). A thick layer of stone and gypsum noted here (Lots II-3, 19) and across the complex represents the collapse of the roof and nave walls around the middle of the 7th c.

The raised *bema* or chancel platform occupies the E end of the central aisle (fig. 3.30, section 1; fig. 3.34). This surface rises *c.*0.4 m above the level of the nave and is covered by a floor mosaic measuring at least 5.03 m long by 3.66 m wide. Assuming that the nave piers were set at *c.*2.4-m intervals, the floor mosaic would have occupied the first two bays of the central aisle and so defined the limits of the original *bema*. The mosaic consists of polychrome stone tesserae pressed into a pink cement bedding that rests on a cobbled foundation. A single panel (3.3 x 4.4-m) of interlacing circles and squares is surrounded by a border 0.36 m wide of twisted cables (fig. 3.35). Tessera colors include white, yellowish-white, pink, light bluish-gray, black, and red. The closest stylistic parallels for the mosaic belong to the second quarter of the 6th c. (below, p. 117). Later damage to the floor was repaired around the mid 7th c. when the *bema* was re-organized as an independent chapel with low benches lining the walls. The collapse of the semidome and upper walls further battered but ultimately preserved the worn surface.

Fig. 3.31. Area II, view to W.

Fig. 3.32. Area II, basilica, view to N.

Fig. 3.33. Area II, nave, S aisle, and south lateral space, view to E.

Fig. 3.34. Area II, *bema* and late chapel, view to E.

The main apse lies beyond the *bema* to the east. The apse wall was built of mortared fieldstone and gypsum and stands to a maximum height of 0.8 m (fig. 3.30, sections 1, 3; figs. 3.31, 3.34). The curved interior surface is enclosed within an outer shell that presents 5 faceted planes. In its original form the interior diameter was *c.*3.5 m. The upper wall and semidome probably were made of mortared stone and gypsum fragments; pieces of rooftile may have been included as well. Following an episode of structural damage, all traces of the area's original furnishings were removed and the apse wall was reinforced, with its interior span reduced to 3.2 m. About this time a low bench was built of mortared gypsum fragments against the back wall. In its final state the apse floor was a sturdy but uneven surface of irregularly shaped gypsum slabs.

While the plan of the south church presents few surprises, its decoration appears unusually ambitious for a rural village. The focus was the mosaic in the semidome. Excavation recovered a large quantity of tesserae together with both large and small fragments of intact mosaic (below, p. 143). The tesserae, which were made of stone, glass, and gold foil, were cut in a number of small, mostly trapezoidal shapes. Over 20 colors can be distinguished among the surviving pieces, and others may be obscured by erosion and calcification. The subject-matter remains a topic of imaginative speculation but probably included figures, landscape details, and geometric ornament; a non-representational apse mosaic in Cyprus at this time would be exceptional (Michaelides 1987: 54-57. The early 5th-c. apse mosaic in the episcopal basilica at Kourion may have been aniconic; see Megaw 1976a: 23). Some fragments represent repeated curving patterns resembling drapery folds, while other pieces suggest jewelry and floral patterns.

It is uncertain how long the apse mosaic remained in place. The bema's re-organization into an independent chapel suggests that the semidome masonry survived the destruction (by fire?) of the timber-roofed nave, but it is not clear how much of the mosaic was left standing. The preponderance of decorative details instead of recognizable figural passages among the identified fragments implies that the central area collapsed earlier and was removed, leaving in place only the lower border. The later history of the Livadhia and Lythrankomi churches reminds us that elsewhere in Cyprus apse mosaics, even in fragmentary form, continued to participate in decorative church programs.[20]

The stucco decoration constitutes a more striking ensemble, if for no other reason than its survival. Recovered fragments, fortuitously preserved by their re-use in later walls, demonstrate that an elaborate scheme was intended for the nave (below, p. 111). Colonnades included freestanding piers and wall shafts

20 Megaw 1974: 73-76; id. 1976b: 22-27; Michaelides 1987: 54-57.

Fig. 3.35. Area II, *bema*, floor mosaic (J. Ravenhurst).

with vertically and diagonally fluted shafts crowned by large acanthus capitals. A distinctive cornice with notched corbels and rounded moldings ran along the walls above this level and perhaps continued into the arcade as well. A smaller cornice of similar design may have surrounded the main door from the narthex or the apse. Sanctuary furnishings may have included a chancel screen with small molded details, but not the pierced panels seen at *Sirmata*. The nave decoration was completed by several representational pieces, includ-

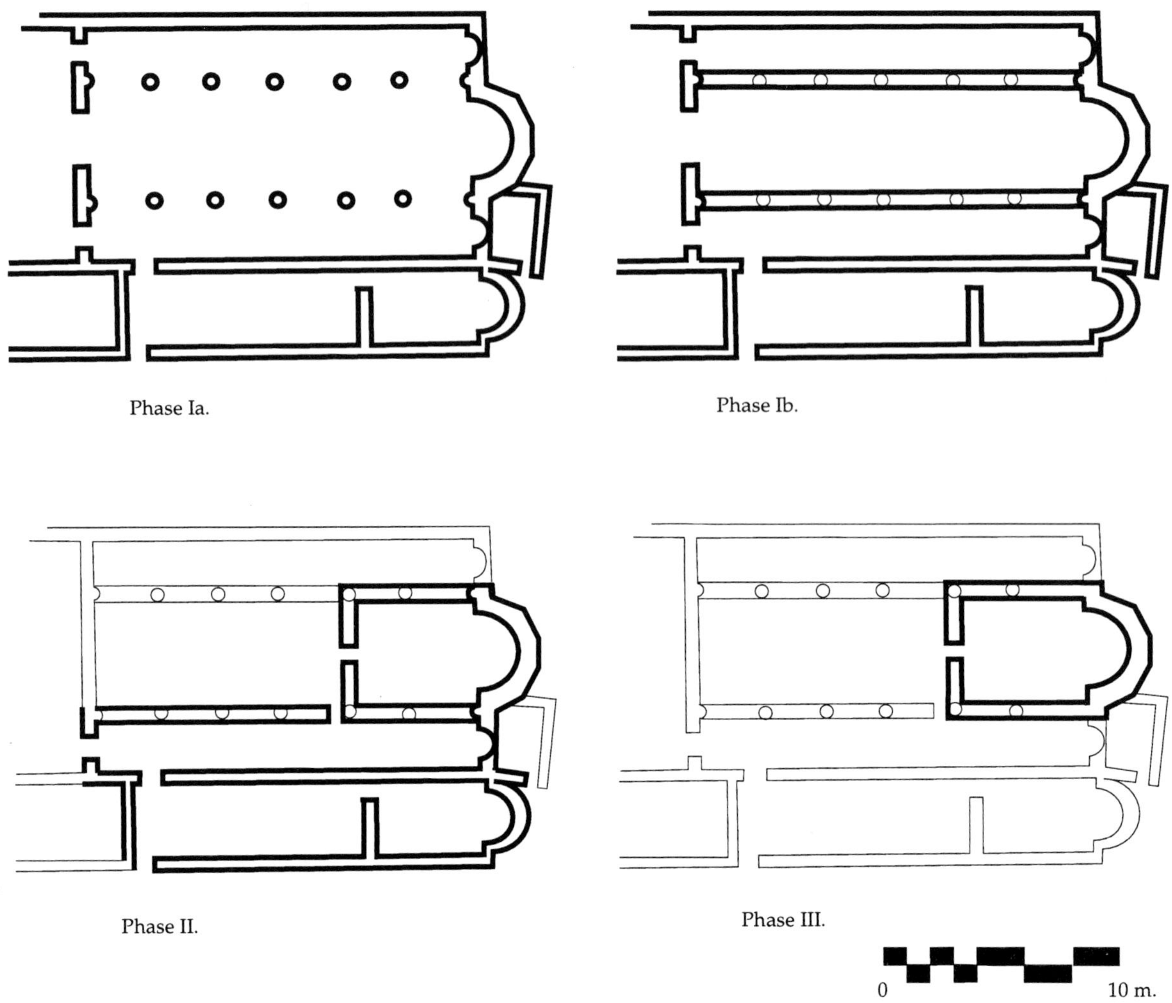

Fig. 3.36. Area II, main occupation phases.

ing a large quadruped and two eagles that apparently perched on the upper walls. Of particular interest are two rectangular panels (0.18-23 m tall by 0.14-16 m wide). One represents an altar or throne set under a column-supported canopy; the other depicts the seated Virgin with child (below, fig. 3.45). The fine detailing and similar scale of the two panels suggest that both were intended to be seen at close hand, perhaps functioning as devotional objects displayed on wood stands at floor level.

Gypsum plaster sculpture was an important decorative medium in Late Roman Cyprus. In church decoration it appears both at rural sites like Alassa-*Ayia Mavri* and Marathovouno, and in large cities like Soloi (Papageorghiou 1963; des Gagniers and Tran Tam Tinh 1985; Flourentzos 1996: 15). In its variety and happy survival, the south church program constitutes an ecclesiastical equivalent of the House of the Oil Press at Salamis — the best preserved late-antique stucco assemblage on the island, if not in the whole E Mediterranean. Closely related moldings were identified at Salamis, which also had a major lower and minor upper order attached to the walls of two rooms (Argoud *et al.* 1980; Callot 1980). At Salamis the zoomorphic decoration occupies a frieze filled with hunting scenes; a frieze (0.10 m thick) with animals is known at the southwest basilica at Amathus as well (Karageorghis 1962: 412-13; Megaw 1976b: 21). The large quadruped and paired eagles are unparalleled on the island and look beyond its shores to mainland sculpture. Most significantly, the two representational panels are unique survivals of devotional objects translated into a distinctively Cypriot medium. Their presence attests both the religious importance of the south church and Kopetra's awareness of wider cultural currents of the 6th c.

At a later date, the *bema* and apse were rebuilt as a small, independent chapel by adding lateral walls with low benches (figs. 3.34, 3.36, phase II; cf. fig. 3.46). The walls were built of unmortared fieldstones and gypsum fragments and replaced the first two pairs of columns flanking the sanctuary, leaving a broad axial doorway as the only access to the chapel. Benches (F204, 206, 238, and 239) were constructed of the same materials directly atop the mosaic floor to a height of 0.5 m (fig. 3.30, section 3); the poorly preserved remains suggest that they continued along the W wall spurs as well. The lower apse wall was reinforced and the floor

Fig. 3.37. Area II, limestone funerary *cippus*.

repaved at the same time. Recovery of large mosaic fragments here indicates that much of the semidome with its mosaic remained standing in this final phase.

A limestone *cippus* was found lying on this late surface (Lot II-12), where it apparently had been used to support an altar surface. This early Roman funerary marker (fig. 3.37; KK89-34) is of standard cylindrical form with simple moldings. The shaft has a diameter of 0.17 m, and rises from a base 0.09 m high to an offset, chamfered top 0.095 m high, for a total height of 0.565 m. It is inscribed with 4 lines of Greek letters 0.028-0.033-m high, partially obscured by plaster, which can be restored to read: [Δ]ημήτριο[ς Δ]ημητρίου [χρησ]τέ [χαίρ]ε. Limestone *cippi* of this sort constitute a distinctive feature of S central Cyprus. Most known examples come from the coastal plain between Kourion and Kition, where they served as funerary monuments and property markers for well-to-do Cypriot landholders in the early Roman period (Mitford 1980: 1318-20, 1374-75; Nicolaou 1989 and 1991). At least 8 other *cippi* have been recovered from the Vasilikos valley: two examples from Mari-*Kopetra*, two intact and three fragmentary examples from Kopetra-*Yirtomylos* in the upper valley, and one example from the river-bed near Kalavasos (Flourentzos 1988: 235-36; Hadjisavvas 1988: 113-15; Todd forthcoming). The presence of this monument at Kopetra may attest a local family that once owned property nearby. As an altar support it was simply a convenient spoil that could be pressed into new service.

None of these important structural changes can be closely dated on stratigraphic grounds. Material recovered from the sanctuary's collapse includes handmade pottery and a follis of Heraclius issued in 629/30 (**C8**; Lots II-12, 13), but these finds provide only a rough *post quem* for the chapel's abandonment. While it is possible that the complex was re-organized in the 630s, the limited extent and makeshift nature of this project are better seen as a response to the mid-century turmoil dramatically evident at *Sirmata*. The construction of a small chapel amid the ruins of a larger complex is a characteristic response of the times that has been noted at Ayios Philon, Polis, Paphos, Amathus (southwest basilica and Ayios Tychonos), Lysi, and elsewhere. The lateral benches are a more unusual feature with uncertain origins and may anticipate the appearance of the walled *bema* at Lythrankomi in the late 7th c. (Megaw and Hawkins 1977: 32-33). Roman *cippi* have been discovered in several Cypriot churches. A fragmentary cippus was found on the nave floor of the basilica at Alassa-*Ayia Mavri* (Flourentzos 1996: 6, 15 no. 6b, pl. XXV). At Tamassos an early Roman cippus was re-used as an altar support (Buchholz 1985: 267-68, pl. IIh). A group of 5 *cippi* found in the acropolis basilica at Amathus may have been used for similar purposes about the same time (Pralong and Saulnier 1987: 747; Pralong 1994a: 417). At Kopetra the *bema* chapel, like the rest of the Area II complex, was reorganized *c.*650, saw a final collapse, and was abandoned at some point in the later 7th c.

Both of the side aisles end in shallow niches or apsidioles recessed in the E wall. The S niche measures 1.2 m across and is 0.6 m deep. Its floor originally lay at the level of the aisle paving. The lower 0.8 m of this niche was filled later with carefully-mortared gypsum rubble and covered with plaster. The raised top surface of the S niche betrays no sign of its original function. The corresponding niche (0.6 m deep) in the N aisle was only partially exposed. It also began at the aisle's paved surface and later was blocked to a height of 0.25 m. The masonry of both niches attests the careful mortaring of fieldstone and gypsum fragments to define smooth planar surfaces.

The collapse of the superstructure filled both aisles around the middle of the 7th c. To judge from the small part that was excavated, the N aisle seems to have been abandoned from this time (Lots II-14, 21 and 22).

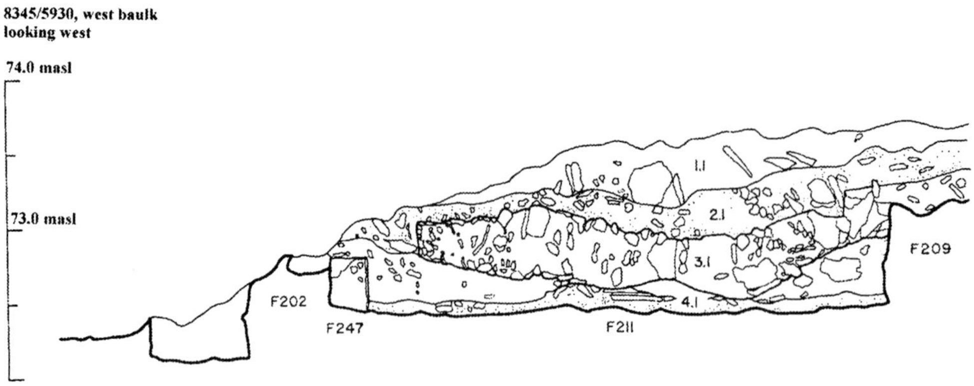

Fig. 3.38. Area II, south lateral space, stratigraphic section at 8345/5930, view to W.

Fig. 3.39. Area II, south aisle, Tomb 3, south at top.

Débris in the S aisle, by contrast, was cleared away and the space became a long hall flanked on the one side by the rubble wall that replaced the S colonnade (F201), and on the other by the basilica's S outer wall (F209; fig. 3.30, sections 3-4). Both of these walls were unmortared and included in their fabric architectural spoils from the original church. A doorway 0.6 m wide in the N wall, later blocked, led to the open space in front of the *bema* chapel; the earlier doors to the narthex and S lateral space appear to have remained open as well (fig. 3.36, phase II). The original paving of the S aisle continued to function as the surface of this newly defined space.

The subsequent collapse of these rebuilt walls covered most of the complex (fig. 3.38). In the S aisle alone this débris was leveled and a packed earth surface was established at a height of 0.2 m above the paving. A gypsum table surface, rectangular (0.91 x 0.54 m) in shape with 5 recessed holes for legs, was found propped against the E wall. The most important feature of this final occupation is the construction of a tomb in the S aisle's NE corner (Tomb 3, F226; fig. 3.39). The tomb consists of three heavy gypsum slabs set in the collapsed débris at the E end of the N wall. The narrow, irregular space contained the articulated skeletal remains of two male adults (below, Appendix 5). Excavation of the raised earth surface (Lot II-7) recovered fragments of a Cypriot Red Slip form 11 basin, a Phocean Red Slip form 10B bowl, and three glass vessels, which together provide a general *post quem* of *c.*600. Parallel deposits suggest that the surface above this débris actually dates after 650: the S colonnade wall rests directly on the original paving, and the lower collapse in the three adjacent spaces (Lots II-11, 13, 16) includes 7th-c. material. The general arrangement and sequence resembles the installation of late tombs in the central and S aisles of basilicas at Polis and Salamis (Childs 1988: 127-28, fig. 5; Roux 1998: 152-57). The upper collapse of the S aisle (Lot II-6) can thus be dated to the second half of the 7th c.

The unexcavated narthex apparently extends the full width of the three-aisled nave. The S narthex wall continues without interruption the line of the S aisle's outer wall and seems to have been built together with it. A doorway 1.0 m wide joins narthex and S aisle. The doorway has carefully squared jambs of mortared rubble and a low, worn threshold that lacks evidence of pivots or door. A similar opening can be assumed for the N side of the building, while a somewhat wider doorway, probably with doors, would have opened onto the central aisle. A single paving slab found *in situ* before the S doorway suggests that the narthex was paved with gypsum at the same level as the basilica. The absence of any later blocking of the doorway means that the narthex shared in the re-occupation of the complex in the mid 7th c.

South lateral spaces

An elongated space 3.5-m wide lies along the S side of the basilica, at a level about 0.5 m below the church itself (fig. 3.33). This long space was divided into at least three separate rooms.

To the east stands the S chapel, an apsidal room (*c.*5.0 m by 3.5 m). The broad semicircular apse projects beyond the E wall of the S aisle with its curving outer surface forming a prominent feature of the plan. The N side of the apse lies slightly behind the basilica's SE corner, with which it does not bond very well. Despite the somewhat eccentric orientation of the chapel apse, shared construction details indicate that it was built around the same time as the basilica. The apse wall of the chapel consists of carefully mortared rubble and stands to a maximum height of 0.9 m (fig. 3.30, section 1; *RDAC* 1991: pl. LXI.2). A layer of loose white, pink, and black stone tesserae found at floor level within the apse attests the original presence of a floor mosaic. Most of the tesserae are relatively large stone cubes that were bedded in a layer of pink mortar (below, p. 118). This mosaic was limited to the apse and did not continue into the rest of the chapel. Associated finds include a glass hanging lamp and a large storage jar (Lot II-11). Like the adjacent aisle, the S chapel also saw an initial disturbance, following which the eroded mosaic surface was covered with a plaster floor and the flanking walls were repaired. The room was abandoned following a subsequent collapse in the later 7th c. (Lot II-10).

The second unit of the S lateral space consists of a single room (10.1 x 3.5 m). At the E end a doorway 0.8 m wide next to the S aisle wall joins this large room with the S chapel; the original presence of another doorway or niche is obscured by its poor state of preservation. Farther west a single raised step leads north through a doorway 1.1 m wide to the basilica's S aisle, which stands 0.5 m higher. A doorway 0.8 m wide opens in the S wall. This exterior doorway might have offered indirect access to the basilica but its narrow width points to incidental use, perhaps only to enter the chapel. In a later phase this doorway was filled with unmortared rubble. This room was paved with a well preserved gypsum floor at the same level as the chapel. Low masonry benches (F246 to the north, F247 and 254 to the south) stood against opposite walls of the room, suggesting that it served as a vestibule preceding the chapel itself. As in the S chapel, this space saw two moments of collapse (Lots II-8, 9), between which the N wall (L209) was rebuilt with architectural spoils to a height of at least 3.25 m (fig. 3.38). The upper level of collapse included several storage vessels and glass wares of the 7th c.

The third flanking unit is the W room, a space of uncertain length and function lying south of the narthex. The uninterrupted lines of its walls indicate that this space was planned along with the rest of the church complex, yet it does not appear to have been accessible from either the narthex or the rest of the S lateral space; perhaps it faced onto a nearby street or plaza. Excavation of the W room identified no paving but only a succession of packed earth surfaces. The lowest surface (Lot II-29) produced no closely datable finds. The floor deposit and lower collapse, however, included fragments of an African Red Slip form 109 dish, a handmade cooking pot, and a glass bracelet (Lots II-27, 28), which demonstrate that the W room remained open into the 7th c.

East room

The final identified part of the complex is the E room, a small interior space built against the E face of the basilica between the two salient apses (figs. 3.31 and 3.40). The room is trapezoidal in plan and measures *c.*3.0 x 2.0 m. To north, east, and south it is defined by walls 0.4-0.5 m thick built of mortared rubble that apparently bond with the basilica. A doorway 0.6 m wide at the SE corner offers the only access. The packed earth floor lies 1.0 m below the level of the sanctuary (fig. 3.30, section 4). The stratigraphy of the space reinforces the chronology proposed for the basilica. A sondage below the floor (Lot II-18) found a fragment of

Fig. 3.40. Area II, east room, view to N.

a Cypriot Red Slip form 2 bowl, which broadly supports the mid 6th-c. construction date of the complex. More abundant finds from the floor level and lower collapse include much fine pottery, with fragments of bowls (Cypriot Red Slip form 9A; Phocean Red Slip form 3F), basins (Cypriot Red Slip forms 7, 11), and a small fusiform unguentarium (Lot II-16). This concentration of fine wares suggests that the E room may have been used for dining and other domestic purposes in the first half of the 7th c., perhaps by the attendant clergy. It is unclear whether the E room was repaired and re-occupied in *c.*650 before its final collapse (Lot II-15) and abandonment.

Pottery and other inventoried artifacts by Lot

Roman pottery from Area II is summarized in Table 3.10.

Lot II-1: Topsoil

Date range: mostly late 6th to 7th c.

Catalogued objects:

C1 AE3, Arcadius, 395-401, Constantinople

C11 Follis, Constans II, 642/43, Constantinople?

45 Phocean Red Slip form 3F

73 African Red Slip form 104C

74 African Red Slip form 105

90 Cypriot Sigillata bowl

102 Plain ware A dish/bowl

140 Plain ware D saucer lid

154 LR7 amphora

160 KAmp2 amphora

216 *Pithos* group D jar

248 Glass juglet?

Additional objects:

KK94-25 (fig. 3.43.6). Plaster molding with letters.

KK91-47 (fig. 3.43.7). Plaster molding with letters.

KK90-26 (fig. 3.43.8). Plaster molding with geometric decoration.

Not inventoried (fig. 3.43.9). Plaster column shaft fragment with vertical fluting.

KK88-7 (fig. 3.44.13). Sandstone capital.

KK91-41 (fig. 3.45.23). Plaster capital(?) fragment.

KK90-41 (fig. 3.45.24). Plaster capital fragment.

Lot II-2: Surface pit in center of basilica

Approximate date: post-mediaeval.

Catalogued objects:

C9 Half-follis, Heraclius, 629/30, Constantinople?

C13 Silver denier, Henry II or Hugh IV, *c.*1285-1359, Cyprus

41 Phocean Red Slip form 3D

215 *Pithos* group D jar

Additional objects:

II-2-1 (fig. 3.41). Small handmade bowl. Est. diam. rim 0.09. Coarse-grained brown to pale brown fabric (10YR 5/3-6/3) with abundant lime, quartz, angular dark inclusions to 0.002, blackened by firing or use. Thick wall with plain rim; single root of pinched, pierced handle. *RDAC* 1994: no. 12, fig. 4. 8340/5935 2.2. Cf. **II-12-1**, **II-13-1**.

KK90-40 (fig. 3.42.1). Marble table fragment.

Not inventoried (fig. 3.43.11). Plaster column shaft fragment with spiral and vertical fluting.

Not inventoried (fig. 3.43.12). Plaster column shaft fragment with spiral fluting.

Not inventoried (not illustrated). Diorite pounder. Max. w. 0.086. 8340/5935 2.2.

TABLE 3.10. SUMMARY OF ROMAN POTTERY FROM AREA II

Area II	*rim*	*base*	*handle*	*sherd*	*sum*	*weight*	*avg. sherd wt.*
Fine	149	89		128	366	6885	18.81
Plain	68	39	21	284	412	8040	19.51
Amphora	96	9	303	3015	3423	85950	25.11
Cook	45	5	49	511	610	6205	10.17
Pithos	64	3	6	257	330	54700	165.76
Other	13	5	12	844	874	12595	14.41
ROMAN TOTAL	435	150	391	5039	6015	174375	28.99

	rim	*base*	*handle*	*sherd*	*sum*
CRS 1	3	1			4
CRS 2	25	4		6	35
CRS 6	1				1
CRS 7	2				2
CRS 8	1				1
CRS 9	2	1		5	8
CRS 9A	15	5		2	22
CRS 9B	8	2		3	13
CRS 9C	12	1		1	14
CRS 10	5			1	6
CRS 11	8	4		17	29
CRS other	6	41		47	94
CRS TOTAL	88	59		82	229
LRC 3	4	7		2	13
LRC 3B	1				1
LRC 3C	2				2
LRC 3D	3				3
LRC 3E	11			1	12
LRC 3F	9			4	13
LRC 3G					
LRC 3H	1				1
LRC 6	1				1
LRC 8		1			1
LRC 10	2	1		1	4
LRC 10A	6				6
LRC 10B	2				2
LRC 10C	1			1	2
LRC other		14		23	37
LRC TOTAL	43	23		32	98
ARS 99C	1				1
ARS 104	2				2
ARS 104C	1				1
ARS 105	5	2		2	9
ARS 106	1				1
ARS 107	1				1
ARS 109	2				2
ARS other		3		5	8
ARS TOTAL	13	5		7	25
Other	5	2		7	14
FINE TOTAL	149	89		128	366

	rim	*base*	*handle*	*sherd*	*sum*	*weight*
LR1	58	4	199	1808	2069	52695
LR2	4		7	183	194	4940
LR4	17	1	18	173	209	4490
LR5/6	4	1	9	207	221	3975
LR7	1	1	3	64	69	1360
KAmp1				38	38	740
KAmp2	3	1	21	73	98	3750
KAmp3			1	1	2	190
KAmp4	2		17	80	99	3175
KAmp5	1		3	126	130	2595
KAmp7				2	2	65
Other	6	1	25	260	292	7975
AMPHORA TOTAL	96	9	303	3015	3423	85950
Plain A	7	1		42	50	780
Plain B	13	21	18	138	190	2380
Plain C				5	5	225
Plain D	48	17	3	99	167	4655
PLAIN TOTAL	68	39	21	284	412	8040
Cook A	7		5	56	68	605
Cook B	2			23	25	100
Cook C	8	4	1	60	73	2470
Cook D	28	1	43	372	444	3030
COOK TOTAL	45	5	49	511	610	6205
Pithos A	12		1	9	22	4710
Pithos B	7	2	4	80	93	11765
Pithos C	18			53	71	19435
Pithos D	27	1	1	115	144	18790
PITHOS TOTAL	64	3	6	257	330	54700

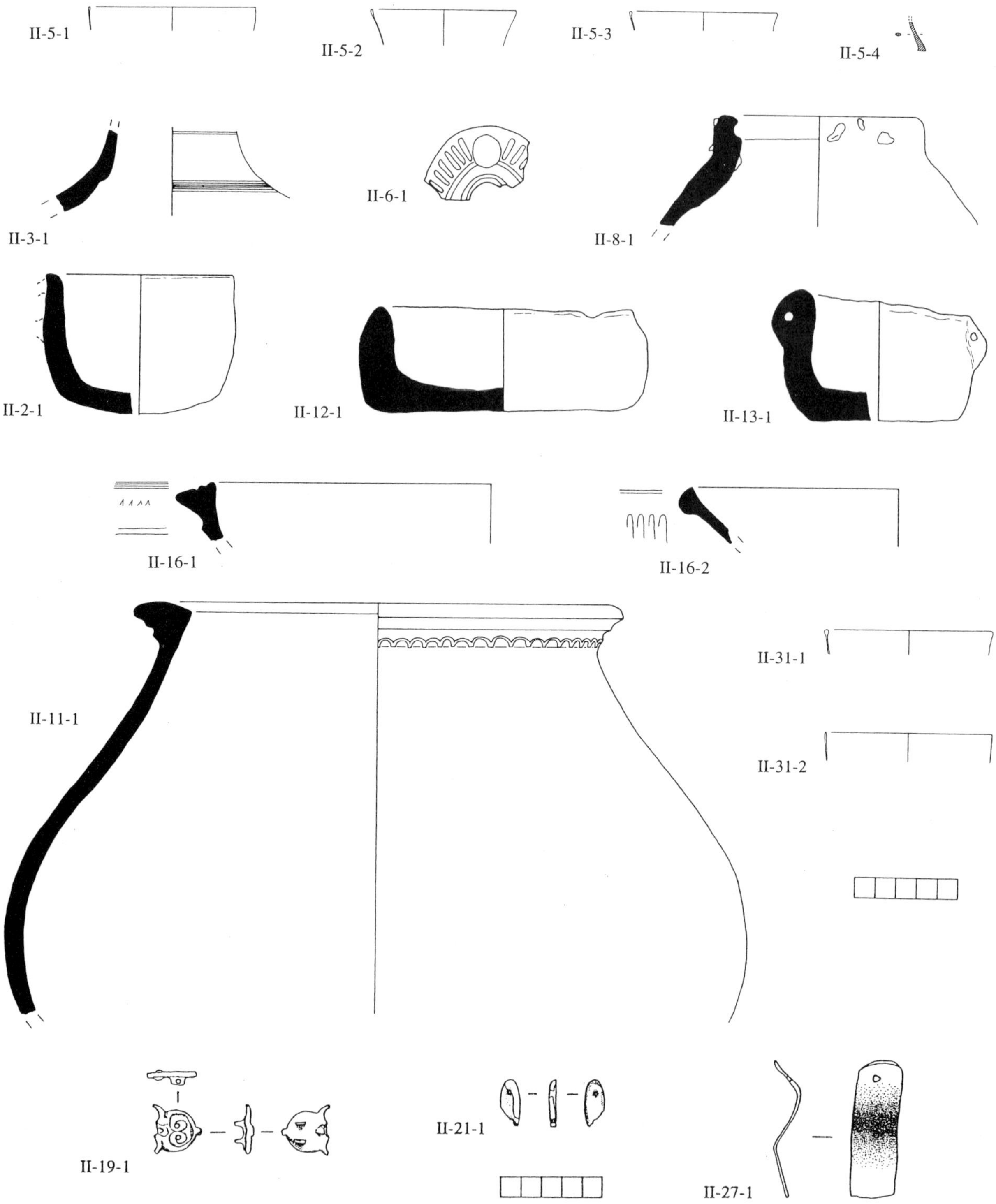

Fig. 3.41. Area II, context pottery.

Lot II-3: Basilica, upper collapse, disturbed
Approximate date: mid 7th c.
Catalogued objects:

C3 Decanummium, Justinian I, 558/59, Nicomedia
C12 Follis, Constans II, 659/60, Constantinople
7 Cypriot Red Slip form 2
20 Cypriot Red Slip form 9A (also Lot II-9)
34 Cypriot Red Slip well form
50 Phocean Red Slip form 3F?
162 KAmp3
281 Glass bowl/goblet/lamp

Additional objects:

II-3-1 (fig. 3.41). Juglet, plain ware B. Medium fine-grained reddish yellow fabric (5YR 7/6) with a little lime and fine mica. Interior and exterior self-slipped, fired pink (7.5YR 8/4); horizontal combed decoration on neck. 8345/5945E 2.1.

See also **II-12-1**.
KK90-39 (fig. 3.42.2). Marble table fragment, with monogram.
Not inventoried (fig. 3.42.4). Marble table fragment.
Not inventoried (fig. 3.43.10). Plaster column shaft with vertical fluting.

Lot II-4: South of basilica, collapse
Approximate date: inconclusive.

Lot II-5: South of basilica, exterior floor deposit
Approximate date: 7th c.?
Catalogued object:
17 Cypriot Red Slip form 9A
Additional objects (fig. 3.41):
II-5-1. Glass goblet or lamp rim. Est. diam. rim 0.080. Transparent light green glass (Fabric 2). Fire-polished rim. 8340/5930 3.2, KK90-48.
II-5-2. Glass goblet or lamp rim. Est. diam. rim 0.070. Transparent light blue glass (Fabric 1). Fire-polished rim. 8340/5930 3.2, KK90-49.
II-5-3. Glass goblet or lamp rim. Est. diam. rim 0.070. Transparent light blue glass (Fabric 1). Fire-polished rim. 8340/5930 3.2, KK90-50.
II-5-4. Glass handle. P. l. 0.018. Dark blue translucent glass with some angular black inclusions and many bubbles; non-Cypriot. Small, oval strap handle. 8340/5930 3.2, KK90-51.

Lot II-6: South aisle, upper collapse
Approximate date: third quarter 7th c.?
Catalogued object:
187 Cooking ware B pot
Additional objects:
II-6-1 (fig. 3.41). Moldmade lamp. Soft textured very pale brown fabric (10YR 7/4-8/4) with dark gray, red, and black inclusions. Circular body, raised rays on shoulder with plain knob handle. 8335/5940S 2.1.
See also **II-12-1**.
KK90-29 (fig. 3.43.5). Plaster molding with scrollwork.
KK89-38A (fig. 3.44.14). Plaster Corinthian capital.
KK90-1A (fig. 3.44.16). Plaster capital fragment with floral patterns.
KK90-1B (fig. 3.44.17). Plaster capital fragment with floral patterns.
KK90-19 (fig. 3.44.18). Plaster capital fragment with rosette and scrollwork.
KK89-35 (fig. 3.44.21). Plaster capital fragment.
KK90-45 (fig. 3.44.22). Plaster capital fragment.
KK91-42 (fig. 3.45.25). Plaster basket relief.
KK91-43 (fig. 3.45.26). Plaster basket relief.
KK91-44 (fig. 3.45.27). Plaster baskets relief.
KK89-15 (fig. 3.45.28). Plaster capital fragment with standing bird.
KK91-45 (fig. 3.45.29). Plaster eagle relief.
KK90-18 (fig. 3.45.32). Plaster relief with shrine.
KK90-9 (fig. 3.45.33). Plaster relief with Virgin and child.

Lot II-7: South aisle, lower collapse
Approximate date: early/mid 7th c. (Cypriot Red Slip form 11, Phocean Red Slip form 10B).
Catalogued objects:
234 Glass bowl?
237 Glass beaker?
284 Glass goblet/lamp
Additional object:
KK90-20 (fig. 3.44.20). Pilaster capital fragment with volute.
Not inventoried (not illustrated). Gypsum table surface.

Lot II-8: South lateral space, upper collapse
Approximate date: mid 7th c.?
Catalogued objects:
36 Cypriot Red Slip form jug/pitcher
126 Plain ware B jug
275 Glass stemmed goblet
Additional objects:
II-8-1 (fig. 3.41). LR4 amphora. Est. diam. rim 0.09. Medium-grained brown fabric (7.5YR 5/4) with scattered lime and quartz. *RDAC* 1994: no. 10, fig. 4. 8345/5935 5.1, KK94-9.
KK90-21A-C (fig. 3.42.7). Marble colonnette or table leg (also Lots II-10, 14).
KK90-11 (fig. 3.44.19). Plaster capital fragment with volute.
KK90-46 (fig. 3.45.31). Plaster quadruped figure.

Lot II-9: South lateral space, lower collapse
Approximate date: early to mid 7th c. Pottery from Lot II-9 is summarized in Table 3.11.
Catalogued objects:
20 Cypriot Red Slip form 9A (also Lot II-3)
231 Glass bowl
Additional object:
KK90-44 (fig. 3.42.6). Marble table fragment.

Lot II-10: South chapel, upper collapse
Approximate date: inconclusive (mid 7th c.?).
Catalogued object:
150 LR4 amphora
Additional objects:
KK90-21A-C (fig. 3.42.7). Marble colonnette or table leg (also Lots II-8, 14).
KK90-13C (fig. 3.43.2). Plaster cornice fragment.
KK90-13A (fig. 3.43.3). Plaster cornice fragment.
See also **II-11-1**.

Lot II-11: South chapel, lower collapse
Approximate date: mid 7th c.?
Catalogued object:
298 Glass hanging lamp
Additional objects:
II-11-1 (fig. 3.41). Storage jar, *pithos* group C. Est. diam. rim 0.21. Coarse-grained red fabric (2.5YR 5/6) with abundant lime, quartz, and medium black inclusions.

TABLE 3.11. LOT II-9 POTTERY SUMMARY: SOUTH LATERAL SPACE, LOWER COLLAPSE

Lot II-9		*rim*	*base*	*handle*	*sherd*	*total*	*weight*
Fine	CRS 2	2				2	330
	CRS 9A	1				1	20
	CRS 9B	1				1	30
Amphora	LR1			1	14	15	275
	LR2				1	1	170
	LR5/6				1	1	10
	KAmp2				1	1	5
	KAmp5				105	105	1730
Cook	D			1	1	2	25
Pithos	B				5	5	1455
	C	3			36	39	8055
Other			1		17	18	285
Pre-Roman				1	1	2	10
TOTAL		7	1	3	182	193	12400

Curved wall with heavy triangular rim, below which runs a single row of impressed decoration. Exterior surface smoothed, covered with darker red slip; rim blackened by use. 8345/5935E 3.1 and 4.1; also Lot II-10.

KK90-22A-B (fig. 3.42.3). Marble table fragment (also Lot II-12).

KK90-15A-B (fig. 3.42.8). Gypsum table leg fragments.

KK90-12 (fig. 3.43.4). Plaster molding fragment.

Lot II-12: Bema, upper collapse

Approximate date: mid 7th c.

Catalogued objects:

128 Plain ware D jug

312 Glass window pane

Additional objects:

II-12-1 (fig. 3.41). Small handmade bowl. Est. diam. rim 0.09. Coarse-grained grayish brown fabric (about 10YR 5/2) with abundant lime, quartz, and other small inclusions; blackened by firing or use. Thick floor and wall with plain rim. 8345/5945 3.2; also Lots II-3 and II-6. Cf. **II-2-1**. See also **II-13-1**.

KK90-22A-B (fig. 3.42.3). Marble table fragment (also Lot II-11).

KK89.34 (fig. 3.37). Limestone funerary *cippus*, *RDAC* 1990: 236-38, pl. L.4.

KK90-25 (fig. 3.44.15). Plaster capital fragment.

TABLE 3.12. LOT II-13 POTTERY SUMMARY: BEMA, LOWER COLLAPSE

Lot II-13		*rim*	*base*	*handle*	*sherd*	*total*	*weight*
Fine	CRS 11	1			2	3	25
	CRS other				1	1	40
	LRC				2	2	15
	ARS 104	2				2	15
	ARS 105	1				1	20
Amphora	LR1			2	17	19	390
	LR2	1			5	6	75
	LR4				3	3	35
	LR5/6				9	9	165
	LR7				4	4	95
	KAmp4				10	10	85
	Other				1	1	15
Plain	B				9	9	90
Cook	A				2	2	5
	D				34	34	140
Other					9	9	150
Pre-Roman		1			2	3	20
TOTAL		6		2	110	118	1380

TABLE 3.13. LOT II-16 POTTERY SUMMARY: EAST ROOM, LOWER COLLAPSE

Lot II-16		*rim*	*base*	*handle*	*sherd*	*total*	*weight*
Fine	CRS 7	1				1	25
	CRS 9A	2				2	25
	CRS 11	1			2	3	30
	LRC 3F	1	1			2	20
Amphora	LR1	1			30	31	355
	LR2				2	2	40
	LR4				11	11	140
	LR5/6				2	2	20
	KAmp2				4	4	25
	KAmp4				1	1	10
	Other				1	1	10
Plain	B				3	3	15
	D	1				1	20
Cook	D	1		1	14	16	40
Pithos	B				1	1	50
Other				1	72	73	520
Pre-Roman		1			7	8	45
TOTAL		9	1	2	150	162	1400

Lot II-13: Bema, lower collapse

Approximate date: mid 7th c. Pottery from Lot II-13 is summarized in Table 3.12.

Catalogued objects:

C8 Follis, Heraclius, 629/30, Constantinople

274 Glass stemmed goblet

Additional objects:

II-13-1 (fig. 3.41). Small handmade bowl. Est. diam. rim 0.10. Coarse-grained brown to grayish brown fabric (10YR 5/3 to 2.5Y 5/2) with abundant lime, quartz, and other small inclusions; blackened by firing or use. Thick floor and wall with plain rim; preserves three (of originally 4) vertically pinched handles with pierced holes. 8350/5945S 5.1; also Lot II-12. Cf. **II-2-1**, **II-12-1**.

Not inventoried (not illustrated). Chipped lithic of fine orange-brown chert, retouched along cutting edge. 8345/5945 4.2.

Lot II-14: North aisle, E end, upper collapse

Approximate date: mid 7th c.

Catalogued object:

189 Cooking ware C pot

Additional objects:

KK90-43 (fig. 3.42.5). Marble table fragment.

KK90-21A-C (fig. 3.42.7). Marble colonnette or table leg (also Lots II-8, 10).

Lot II-15: East room, upper collapse

Approximate date: mid 7th c.

Catalogued objects:

38 Cypriot Red Slip form 6

49 Phocean Red Slip form 3F?

143 LR1 amphora

Lot II-16: East room, lower collapse

Approximate date: early to mid 7th c. (Cypriot Red Slip forms 9A, 11, Phocean Red Slip form 3F). Pottery from Lot II-16 is summarized in Table 3.13.

Catalogued object:

137 Plain ware D fusiform unguentarium

Additional objects (fig. 3.41):

II-16-1. Basin, Cypriot Red Slip form 7. Est. diam. rim 0.28. Medium-grained light reddish brown fabric (2.5YR 6/4). Small triangular rim with two grooves and angular exterior offset; faint rouletting and worn red slip on exterior wall. *RDAC* 1994: 293 no. 1, fig. 4. 8350/5940 8.1.

II-16-2. Dish, Cypriot Red Slip form 9A. Est. diam. rim 0.20. Fine-grained light red fabric (2.5YR 6/6) with scattered lime. Flaring wall rouletted; mottled red slip, fired off-white on exterior rim. *RDAC* 1994: 293 no. 3, fig. 4. 8350/5940 10.1.

Lot II-17: East of basilica, upper collapse

Approximate date: inconclusive (mid/late 7th c.?).

Catalogued object:

256 Glass flask

Lot II-18: East room, first-phase construction

Approximate date: mid 6th c. (Cypriot Red Slip form 2). Pottery from Lot II-18 is summarized in Table 3.14.

Lot II-19: Center aisle, collapse

Approximate date: early to mid 7th c.?

Catalogued objects:

167 Unassigned amphora

230 Glass bowl

282 Glass goblet/lamp

TABLE 3.14. LOT II-18 POTTERY SUMMARY: EAST ROOM, CONSTRUCTION

Lot II-18		*rim*	*base*	*handle*	*sherd*	*total*	*weight*
Fine	CRS 2	4			2	6	55
Amphora	LR1			1	20	21	255
	LR2				5	5	45
	LR4				6	6	55
	KAmp2	1		1	4	6	60
	KAmp5				1	1	35
	Other	1			1	2	105
Plain	B		1			1	5
	D			1	2	3	25
Cook	A	1			7	8	15
	D			1		1	10
Pithos	B		1		3	4	215
	D				3	3	150
Other		1			10	11	85
Pre-Roman		4		26	6	36	355
TOTAL		12	2	30	70	114	1470

288 Glass goblet/lamp
310 Glass hanging lamp
Additional objects:

II-19-1 (fig. 3.41). Bronze belt buckle of 'Syracuse' type. Max. l. 0.023, w. 0.025. Solid heart-shaped plate with rounded tip, decorated with scrolling floral motif; two fastening loops on back. *RDAC* 1994: 293 no. 15, fig. 4. 8340/5940E 4.1, KK91-20. Cf. Chavane 1975: 162-63 no. 466, pls. 46, 69; Argoud *et al.* 1980: 43 no. Sal. 6575, pl. XLI.3; Russell 1982: 139 type 7, fig. 7 nos. 14-16.

KK91-51 (fig. 3.43.1). Plaster cornice fragment.

Lot II-20: Center aisle, W end, burning above lowest collapse
Approximate date: inconclusive (mid 7th c.?).

Lot II-21: North aisle, W end, collapse
Approximate date: inconclusive (mid 7th c.?).
Additional object:

II-21-1 (fig. 3.41). Fragmentary bone applique(?), elongated oval in shape with flat back and rounded front, pierced at both ends by small drilled holes. P. l. 0.023, w. 0.012. 8335/5930 4.1, KK91-35.

Lot II-22: North aisle, E end, lower collapse
Approximate date: inconclusive (mid 7th c.?).

Lot II-23: Sanctuary, bench F239
Approximate date: inconclusive (mid 7th c.?).

Lot II-24: South aisle, Tomb 3 F226
Approximate date: inconclusive (mid 7th c.? Phocean Red Slip form 3).

Lot II-25: East of basilica, lower collapse
Approximate date: inconclusive (mid 7th c.?).

Lot II-26: East of basilica, construction level of drain F243
Approximate date: mid 7th c.
Catalogued object:
C10 Follis, Heraclius, 631-41, mint uncertain
Additional object:

Not inventoried (not illustrated). Fragment of thin bronze strip with one broader, slightly rounded end, pierced (for nail?). Max. l. 0.024, w. 0.017, th. 0.001. 8350/5945 6.1.

Lot II-27: West room, lower collapse
Approximate date: mid 7th c.
Catalogued objects:
83 African Red Slip form 109 (also Lot II-28)
197 Cooking ware C pot (also Lot II-28)
314 Glass bracelet?
Additional object:

II-27-1 (fig. 3.41). Short iron strap, bent into S-shape, with one end pierced (for nail?). Max. l. 0.068, w. 0.023. KK91-29, 8335/5930 3.1.

Lot II-28: West room, floor deposit
Approximate date: early 7th c.
Catalogued objects:
83 African Red Slip form 109 (also Lot II-27)
197 Cooking ware C pot (also Lot II-27)

Lot II-29: South lateral space, W wall foundation deposit
Approximate date: inconclusive (6th c.?).

Lot II-30: Chalcolithic pits
Approximate date: Chalcolithic.

Lot II-31: South lateral space, S bench F254
Approximate date: inconclusive (late 6th/early 7th c.).
Catalogued object:
309 Glass hanging lamp
Additional objects (fig. 3.41):

II-31-1. Glass goblet or lamp rim. Est. diam. rim 0.080. Transparent light green glass (Fabric 2) with angular black inclusions. Fire-polished rim. 8335/5930E 4.2.

II-31-2. Glass goblet or lamp rim. Est. diam. rim 0.080. Transparent light green glass (Fabric 2). Fire-polished rim. 8335/5930E 4.2.

Lot II-32: South lateral space, fallen wall F209
Approximate date: inconclusive (mid/late 7th c.?).
Additional object:
KK91-46 (fig. 3.45.30). Plaster eagle fragment.

Lot II-33: Center aisle, blocked doorway F250
Approximate date: inconclusive (mid/late 7th c.?).

Lit II-34: Center aisle, second-phase surface
Approximate date: 7th c. (Cypriot Red Slip form 9B).
Catalogued objects:
267 Glass pattern-molded vessel
301 Glass wick-tube?

Lot II-35: Center aisle, packing below paved floor
Approximate date: inconclusive (mid 6th c.?).
Catalogued object:
287 Glass goblet/lamp

Liturgical furnishings

Fragments of several liturgical tables were recovered at Area II. Identified pieces come from at least one rectangular table surface in gypsum and as many as 5 in marble. This gives an impression of the number and variety of tables present in the 6th-c. church, even though little can be said about their former location and use. The presence of these rather small pieces in late contexts suggests that some may have been used as building material during the reconstruction of the mid 7th c.; alternatively, they may simply be survivors of later salvaging at the site. The scarcity of marble in rural Cyprus implies that such examples would have been prized by later inhabitants of the area (see examples listed by Roux 1973).

The rectangular gypsum table and corresponding leg fragments may have belonged to the main altar of the church, or perhaps a secondary surface like that at *Sirmata*. The smoothed, flat surface measures 0.93 x 0.55 m, with a maximum thickness of 0.08 m. Five nearly square (0.11 x 0.12 m) holes were cut in the underside to an average depth of 0.05 m. This gypsum slab was discovered leaning against the E wall of the S aisle. Two joining fragments of a corresponding support leg came from the lower collapse of the S chapel, together with a marble table fragment. This raises the possibility that a similar table once stood before the S chapel apse.

The 7 marble fragments belong to at least 5 different tables (fig. 3.42 nos. 1-6). This is a generous but not implausible number of tables to have equipped the building (cf. pieces of at least 7 rectangular and 5 sigma tables found at the Mount Nebo basilica and monastery; Acconci 1998: 478). All have simple molded borders surrounding a recessed rectangular panel, as would be appropriate for either an altar or offering table, although other non-liturgical uses also are possible. All appear to have straight or sloping outer edges; only one example has a slightly concave edge resembling some of the tables from the Kourion episcopal basilica.[21] This suggests that marble surfaces with the same plain border were used for both altars and offering tables, as has been noted at Kourion. One fragment came from the E end of the N aisle; another was found in the S lateral space. Two joining pieces from the S chapel's lower collapse and the upper collapse of the sanctuary show that both spaces remained open in the mid 7th c. Two other fragments were found in disturbed contexts in the nave. Three joining fragments of a tapering marble colonnette were recovered in the upper collapse of the S chapel, where they may have been used as one of several altar supports. The presence of so many table fragments in this room supports its use as a chapel during its final phase.

Fig. 3.42.1. Fragment of a rectangular table with raised border in fine to medium-grained white marble. P. l. 0.175, w. 0.140, th. 0.026-0.054. Surface pit, Lot II-2, 8335/5940S 2.1, KK90-40.

Fig. 3.42.2. Fragment of a rectangular table with raised border in medium fine-grained gray-veined white marble. P. l. 0.279 m, w. 0.108 m, th. 0.038. Monogram (apparently reading 'Menelalou') and graffito on reverse. Upper nave collapse, Lot II-3, 8350/5945 4.1, KK90-39. *RDAC* 1991: 233 fig. 4, pl. LXII.1.

21 Loverance 1990: 229; Chalkia 1991: 54-55; Acconci 1998: 489.

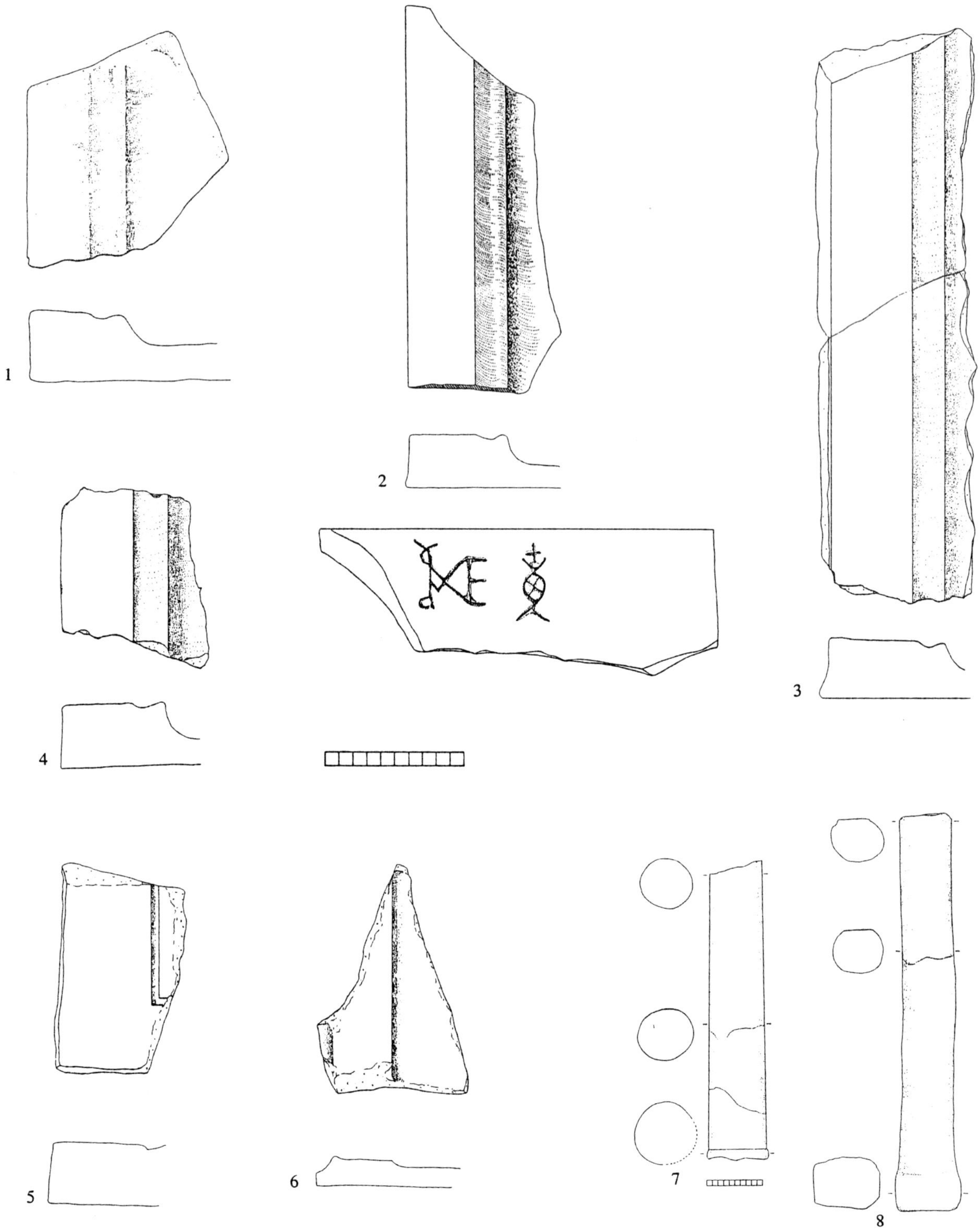

Fig. 3.42. Area II, stone liturgical furnishings.

Fig. 3.42.3. Two joining fragments of a rectangular table with raised border in medium-grained gray-veined white marble. P. l. 0.42, w. 0.115, th. 0.041. Rim and floor polished, underside roughly smoothed. South chapel lower collapse, Lot II-11; *bema* upper collapse, Lot II-12; 8345/5935E 4.1, 8345/5940E 3.1; KK90-22A-B. For similar tables see Roux 1973; Patrich 1988a: 12-28 nos. 57-59; Loverance 1990: 229, figs. 15-16 (episcopal basilica at Kourion); Chalkia 1991: 54-55, type F; Acconci 1998: 489 no. 56, with further examples.

Fig. 3.42.4. Fragment of a rectangular table with raised border in fine-grained gray-veined white marble. P. l. 0.132, w. 0.15, th. 0.018-0.046. Basilica upper collapse, Lot II-3, 8335/5930E 2.1, not inventoried.

Fig. 3.42.5. Fragment of a rectangular table with raised border in fine-grained gray-veined white marble. P. l. 0.015, w. 0.085, th. 0.023-0.043. N aisle E end upper collapse, Lot II-14, 8345/5943 3.1, KK90-43.

Fig. 3.42.6. Fragment of a rectangular table with raised border. P. l. 0.170, w. 0.110, th. 0.014-0.023. Medium to fine-grained gray-veined white marble. S lateral space lower collapse, Lot II-9, 8340/5930 3.1, KK90-44.

Fig. 3.42.7. Three joining sections of colonnette or table leg in fine to medium-grained gray-veined white marble. Total h. 0.55, diam. shaft 0.09-0.10. Tapering shaft rises from rounded base molding to broken upper surface. S lateral space upper collapse, Lot II-8; S chapel upper collapse, Lot II-10; and N aisle upper collapse, Lot II-14; 8545/5935 4.1, 8345/5935E 3.1, 8345/5945 5.1; KK90-21A, B, and C. Cf. Sodini and Kolokotsas 1984: 192-93 figs. 155-56; Patrich 1988a: 127 no. 54 (l. 0.30, diam. 0.08-0.09); Loverance 1990: 237 fig. 29; Acconci 1998: 477-81, 509-11.

Fig. 3.42.8. Two joining sections of table leg with ovoid shaft rising from rectangular base. P. l. 0.72; diam. shaft 0.08-0.09. Fine-grained gypsum. S chapel lower collapse, Lot II-11, 8350/5935 6.1, KK90-15A and B.

One of the marble table fragments carries on the underside a carefully incised monogram and accompanying graffito. The two figures lie next to each other along the border's edge with the outer margin at their top. The monogram is of the box-type commonly used in the 5th and 6th c. (cf. Grierson 1982: 33). The constituent letters can be resolved as 'Menelaou', a name known in Hellenistic Cyprus but not otherwise attested in Roman times (Fraser and Matthews 1987: 307). The nearby graffito seems to combine a cross, chalice, and fish into a single composite figure. Both appear to have been incised at the same time.

A number of inscriptions have been reported on related tables of the period. Most examples concern a dedicatory text incised on the upper molding, such as the invocation of 'Kasiseos and Victor, son of Stephanos' on a table from Avdat in the Negev (Negev 1978: 116-17 no. 32; cf. a more fragmentary example in Saller 1941: 269 inscription no. XVII, pl. 121.2; Acconci 1998: 493-95 no. 68). Inscriptions on the underside of such tables tend to be more abbreviated and frequently take the form of monograms. A table from the cathedral at Pella is inscribed 'ΖΩΤ' (perhaps for 'Zotikos'; Smith and Day 1989: 137 text 100, pl. 35 B-C). Two unrelated table fragments found at Mount Nebo bear box-type monograms on their reverse, which have been read as 'Petros' ('Protos'?) and 'Nax(i?)ou' (Saller 1941: 269 inscription no. XVIII, pl. 121.3-4; Acconci 1998: 489-93 no. 59 and 63). A box-type monogram appears on the back of a table from the episcopal basilica at Kourion (no. CB1916; Megaw 1976a: 358; Loverance 1990: 229). Such marks have been discussed as identifying either the donor of a table or a craftsman or owner of the shop in which it was made. The variety of marks probably reflects a range of customs among different regions. Dedicatory inscriptions appear on the upper surface but the reverse location of a text does not preclude its signifying a donor. Many of these monograms are neatly shaped and placed near the border, as would be appropriate for a patron recording a pious gift. While many such tables must have been offered to churches, relatively few bear inscriptions at all. At Kopetra the appearance of a carefully cut monogram in conjunction with a Christological grafitto reinforces the impression that it refers to the table's donor.

Architectural decoration

The decoration of the south church constitutes a remarkable ensemble of Late Roman stuccowork. The technique's popularity in late antiquity is attested by both literary sources and excavated remains, with the decoration of the Kourion and Soloi basilicas and the House of the Oil Press at Salamis offering the best comparanda. At Kopetra, most of the decorative plaster elements were recovered in Lots II-6 and 8, which include the late walls (especially the S aisle wall L209) that collapsed into the S aisle and S lateral space. Their concentration amid the late building débris and scarcity from other parts of the church indicate that many pieces owe their survival to re-use as *spolia* in unmortared walls, which protected unexposed surfaces. The original location of individual pieces remains uncertain, but it seems likely that most of the decoration was installed in the 6th-c. nave.

A selection of the better preserved architectural fragments is presented here, together with the representational pieces.

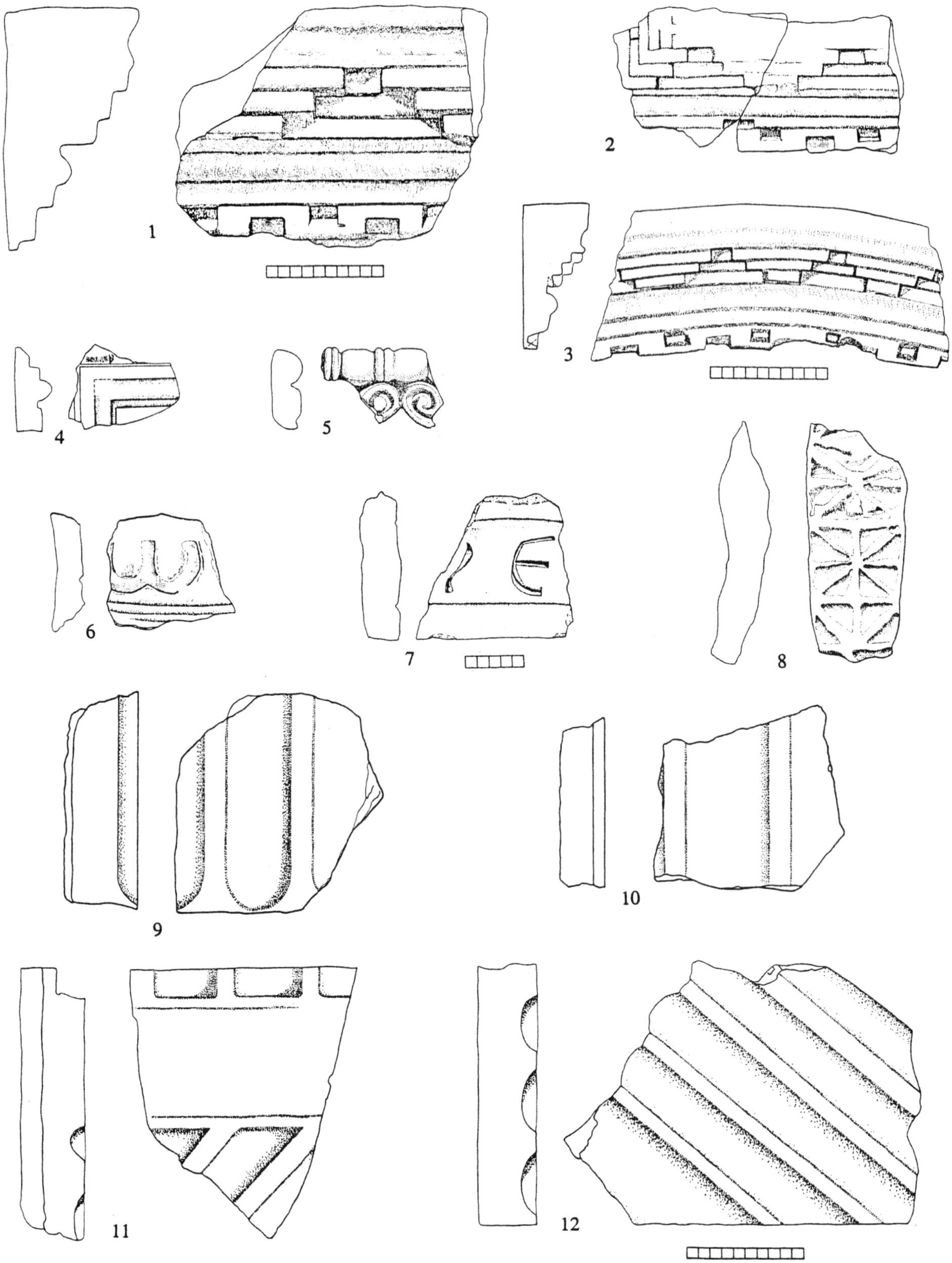

Fig. 3.43. Area II, molded plaster architectural details.

Nave moldings and cornices

Much of the south church's decoration involved moldings and cornices that articulated the building's structural lines. Excavation recovered only a few plain rounded moldings like those found at *Sirmata*, but this scarcity may be due to the later reconstruction of the complex. Better attested is a distinctive cornice that presents a complex profile of a series of small alternating notches, three stepped corbels set between round and hollow moldings, and a crowning cyma recta molding. The scheme appears in two different sizes: the larger cornice stands over 0.25 m in height with an interval of *c*.0.18 m, while the smaller cornice is *c*.0.14 m high with an interval of 0.9-0.11 m. The irregular spacing of elements suggests that details were carved by hand after the stucco had partially dried. Excavated examples include straight and curved sections. One fragment of the smaller cornice turns upward at a right angle, presumably continuing into a broad arch surrounding the narthex door or main apse. Plaster architectural moldings are known elsewhere in Cyprus. A tall but simple cornice with traces of red, green, and yellow pigment was found in the baptistery *diaconicon* of the episcopal basilica at Kourion (Megaw 1976a: 358, fig. 28). More closely related is a cornice that also appears in two sizes at the House of the Oil Press, the decoration of which has been dated to the 5th c. (Argoud *et al.* 1980; Callot 1980). The formal resemblance of these two monuments, despite their different dates, suggests that this craft tradition was relatively conservative and perpetuated by teams of artisans who traveled across the island.

Fig. 3.43.1. Fragment of large horizontal cornice consisting of a row of alternating notches, hollow and rounded moldings, and three rows of stepped fascia or projecting corbels, crowned by a cyma recta. P. h. 0.23, l. 0.27. Center aisle collapse, Lot II-19, 8340/5940E 5.1, KK91-51. Cf. fig. 3.54:5 (KK91-49, from Area V); Argoud *et al.* 1980: pls. XXIVc, XXVI-XXVII; Callot 1980: 361 fig. 8; Roux 1998: 29, 34 fig. 17a-b (Salamis).

Fig. 3.43.2. Two joining fragments of small horizontal cornice with perpendicular corner rising at left, probably marking the springing of an arch. P. h. 0.125, l. 0.25. S chapel upper collapse, Lot II-10, 8350/5935, 5.1, KK90-13C. Cf. Callot 1980: 360 fig. 7; Roux 1998: 34 fig. 17b.

Fig. 3.43.3. Fragment of similar small curved cornice. P. h. 0.13, l. 0.31, th. 0.014-0.057. S chapel upper collapse, Lot II-10, 8350/5935, 5.1, KK90-13A. *RDAC* 1991: 232-33, pl. LXII.2. Cf. Argoud *et al.* 1980: pl. XXVa; Callot 1980: 360 fig. 7.

Fig. 3.43.4. Fragment of small molding with round and hollow elements. P. h. 0.072, l. 0.094. S chapel lower collapse, Lot II-11, 8350/5935 6.1, KK90-12.

Fig. 3.43.5. Fragment of molding with bead-and-reel above scrollwork. P. h. 0.068, l. 0.105. S aisle upper collapse, Lot II-6, 8345/5940S 2.1, KK90-29.

Fig. 3.43.6. Fragment of molding with letters (omega? mu?). P. h. 0.102, w. 0.11. Surface, Lot II-1, 8340/5935E 1.1, KK94-25.

Fig. 3.43.7. Fragment of molding with letters (rho? epsilon). P. h. 0.132, l. 0.127. Surface, Lot II-1, 8340/5935E 1.1, KK91-47.

Fig. 3.43.8. Fragment of molding with narrow band of geometric relief decoration. P. h. 0.087, w. 0.215. Surface, Lot II-1, 8340/5930 1.1, KK90-26.

Column shafts and capitals

A number of fluted elements belong to the wall shafts and cylindrical piers of the nave arcade. Most of these pieces are flat and carry shallow vertical flutes 0.05-0.06 m across. Several examples retain a pronounced curvature in horizontal section where they wrapped around the core of a rising shaft. Fragments of diagonal fluting attest the liveliness of the church's interior and the continuity of an earlier Cypriot fashion (Benson 1956). Spirally-fluted marble columns are known in Kourion's suburban basilica and at Polis.

The nave capitals were made of both sandstone and molded plaster. Several of the 10 original capitals survived in sufficiently large pieces to suggest the grand scale of the order. The best surviving example is a composite Corinthian capital with an original height of over 0.6 m that presents simple volutes rising from an acanthus-wrapped base. Another large fragment (which disintegrated shortly after excavation) included a lattice-like basket pattern in its lower parts, similar to a very worn sandstone capital. Several other fragments bearing foliage patterns and geometric ornament probably came from the nave colonnade as well.

A few fragments belong to a smaller scale of architecture and attest to a minor decorative order within this larger framework. Like the nave's main order, these identified pieces include undercut lattice and acanthus patterns.

Fig. 3.43.9. Fragment of column shaft with vertical fluting. Flat arrises 0.018 wide, 0.056 apart. Fragment slightly curved in section; back scored with light diagonal ridges. P. h. 0.19, w. 0.18. Surface, Lot II-1, 8340/5935E 1.1, not inventoried. Cf. fig. 3.54.6 (Area V).

Fig. 3.43.10. Fragment of column shaft with vertical fluting. Flat arrises 0.018 wide, 0.062 apart. P. h. 0.164, w. 0.162. Upper collapse, disturbed, Lot II-3, 8350/5940 3.2, not inventoried.

Fig. 3.43.11. Fragment of column shaft with flat fascia separating spiral and vertical flutes. P. h. 0.24, w. 0.195. Surface pit, Lot II-2, 8335/5935 2.1, not inventoried.

Fig. 3.43.12. Fragment of column shaft with spiral fluting. Flat arrises 0.012-0.018 wide, 0.038-0.042 apart. Fragment slightly curved in section; back scored with light diagonal ridges. P. h. 0.23; w. 0.305. Surface pit, Lot II-2, 8335/5935 2.1, not inventoried.

Fig. 3.44.13. Sandstone capital with flaring bell supporting rectangular abacus. Faint traces of diagonal reticulate decoration survive on outer face. P. h. 0.26, w. 0.33. Surface, Lot II-1, KK88-7.

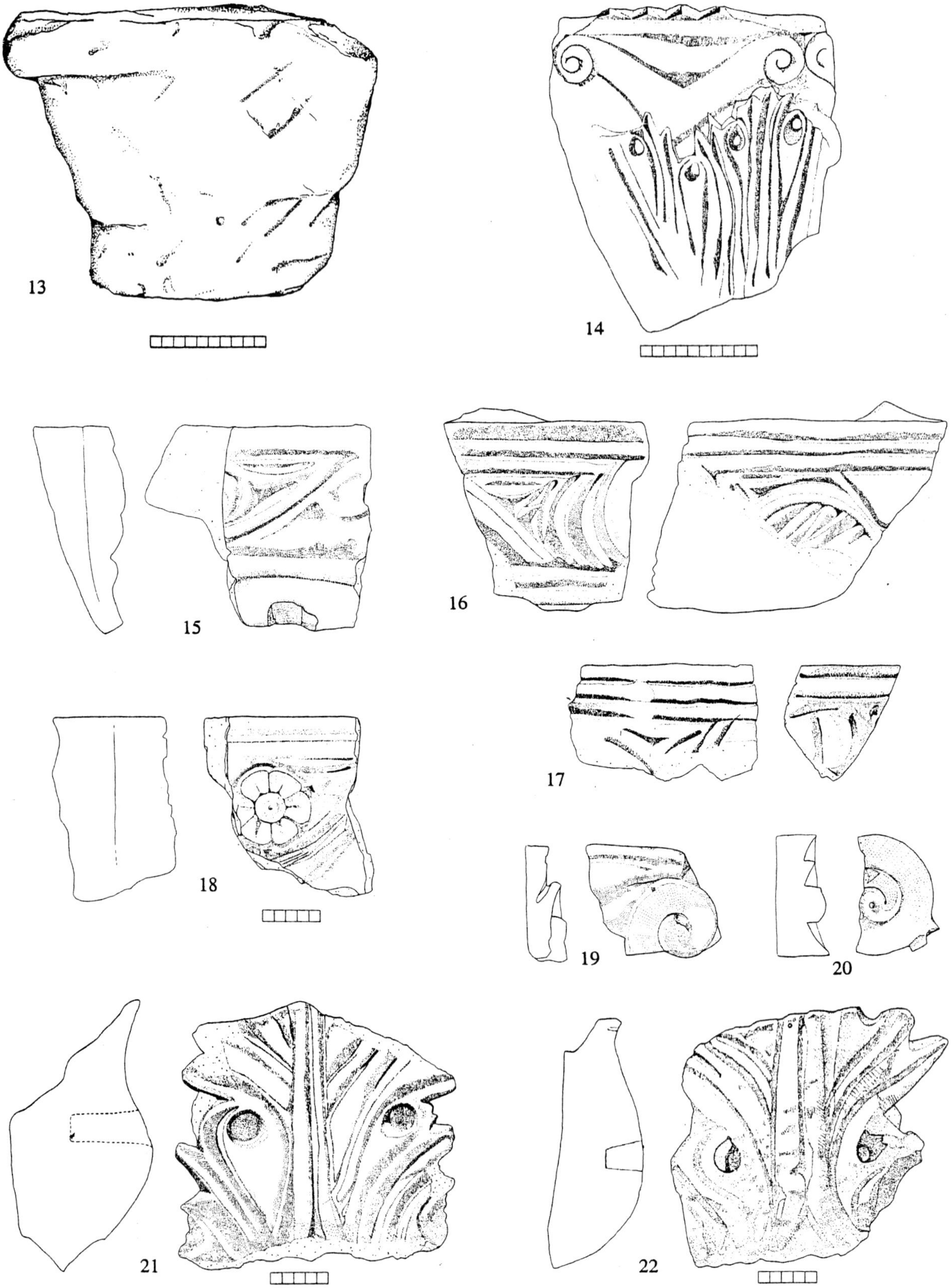

Fig. 3.44. Area II, stone and molded plaster architectural details.

Fig. 3.44.14. Composite Corinthian capital with acanthus leaves, volutes, and inset triangles in abacus; interior surface concave. P. h. 0.58, w. 0.49. S aisle upper collapse, Lot II-6, 8335/5935 3.2, KK89-38A. *Muse* 23-24 (1989-90) 23 fig. 12; *JRA* 5 (1992) 270 fig. 5. Cf. Megaw 1974: figs. 14 (Lythrankomi), 15 (Ayios Philon); Megaw and Hawkins 1977: 30-31, figs. 16-19; des Gagniers and Tran Tam Tinh 1985: 94 nos. 57-60, figs. 193-97 (Soloi).

Fig. 3.44.15. Capital(?) fragment with incised floral patterns. P. h. 0.175, l. 0.194. Sanctuary upper collapse, Lot II-12, 8345/5945 3.2, KK90-25.

Fig. 3.44.16. Capital fragment with three upper fasciae separated by triangular grooves; below, incised floral patterns on adjacent faces. Top surface flat with square hole (0.04-m). P. h. 0.18, l. 0.226, th. 0.16. S aisle upper collapse, Lot II-6, 8340/5935 3.1, KK90-1A.

Fig. 3.44.17. Capital fragment with three fasciae separated by triangular grooves; below, incised floral patterns on adjacent surfaces. P. h. 0.10, l. 0.16. S aisle upper collapse, Lot II-6, 8340/5935 3.1, KK90-1B.

Fig. 3.44.18. Capital fragment with rosette and scrollwork, upper fasciae separated by triangular groove. P. h. 0.166, w. 0.15. S aisle upper collapse, Lot II-6, 8345/5940 4.2, KK90-19. Cf. Callot 1980: figs. 9 and 23e (Salamis).

Fig. 3.44.19. Capital fragment with volute. P. h. 0.105, w. 0.068. S lateral space upper collapse, Lot II-8, 8345/5935 4.1, KK90-11.

Fig. 3.44.20. Capital fragment with volute. P. h. 0.098, l. 0.115. S aisle lower collapse, Lot II-7, 8340/5935 4.1, KK90-20.

Fig. 3.44.21. Fragment of capital with upwardly flaring acanthus leaves flanked by lower incurving leaves and deep circular holes. P. h. 0.232, w. 0.24. S aisle upper collapse, Lot II-6, 8445/5935 3.2, KK89-35. Cf. des Gagniers and Tran Tam Tinh 1985: fig. 195 (Soloi).

Fig. 3.44.22. Capital fragment with upwardly flaring acanthus leaves. P. h. 0.23, w. 0.217. S aisle upper collapse, Lot II-6, 8345/5940S 2.1, KK90-45.

Fig. 3.45.23. Capital(?) fragment with acanthus decoration. P. h. 0.091, l. 0.074. Surface, Lot II-1, 8335/5930E 1.1, KK91-41.

Fig. 3.45.24. Pilaster capital fragment with deeply undercut latticework. P. h. 0.13, l. 0.113. Surface, Lot II-1, 8335/5935 1.1, KK90-41.

Representational sculpture

The representational images form the high point of the program. A bird in profile amid foliage decorates one small capital. Several small, flat pieces seem to depict woven baskets, arranged both singly and in pairs. The largest identifiable element was a free-standing quadruped, perhaps a donkey or horse. The surviving fragment extends from the back of the head to the shanks and measures 0.43 m long; with dowelled head and legs its original length may have reached 0.6 m. The large figure is fully rounded and smoothly finished. It presumably stood on its legs, perhaps with the help of a wall bracket. Also recovered were parts of two large birds, no doubt eagles, whose powerful, upright chests are covered with sharp, jagged feathers. Broad, perhaps outstretched wings were attached to both figures. These were not fully rounded but apparently anchored by wood dowels to the upper wall. A pair of small relief panels completes the known decoration of the interior. One panel depicts a gabled shrine with two fully rounded columns (now lost) flanking a small altar, tabernacle, or *hetoimasia*. The second panel, of similar size, represents the Virgin sitting on a wicker chair and holding the Christ child in her lap. The pair is depicted in a reasonably naturalistic three-quarter view. Both figures are covered by drapery that falls in heavy, angular folds. The subject reflects the rising popularity of the *Theotokos* — and by extension the cultural influence of Constantinople — during the 6th c. Its only parallels in Cyprus occur in monumental mosaic (Michaelides 1987: 54-57; id. 1998: 223-25). The compact form, smooth edges, and absence of back attachments suggest that these two panels were supported on portable stands within the church.

Fig. 3.45.25. Relief of basket with three rows of tall curving, incised triangles crowned by diagonal rope pattern; above, angular loaves(?). P. h. 0.122, l. 0.104. S aisle upper collapse, Lot II-6, 8345/5935 10.1, KK91-42.

Fig. 3.45.26. Relief of similar basket with multiple rows of horizontally overlapping scales crowned by diagonal rope pattern; above, angular loaves(?). P. h. 0.124, l. 0.097. S aisle upper collapse. Lot II-6, 8345/5935 10.1, KK91-43.

Fig. 3.45.27. Relief of two similar baskets; eroded surface. P. h. 0.164, l. 0.24. S aisle upper collapse, Lot II-6, 8345/5935 10.1, KK91-44.

Fig. 3.45.28. Fragment of small capital with fan-shaped oval leaves flanking a standing bird with rounded body. P. h. 0.12, w. 0.14. S aisle upper collapse, Lot II-6, 8335/5935 3.2, KK89-15.

Fig. 3.45.29. Relief of eagle with swelling chest and powerful legs covered by finely articulated overlapping feather pattern; missing head and feet. Back smoothed, with square dowel holes in top and bottom. P. h. 0.282, l. 0.142. S aisle upper collapse, Lot II-6, 8345/5935 10.1, KK91-45. *RDAC* 1994: pl. LXXXI.1. Cf. Downey 1977: 137-39 nos. 163-68, esp. no. 164, pl. XXXVIII (in stucco at Dura Europos). A smaller relief eagle in marble was found at Soloi; des Gagniers and Tran Tam Tinh 1985: 95 no. 75, fig. 186.

Fig. 3.45.30. Smaller relief fragment of a similar eagle. P. h. 0.15, w. 0.13. Collapsed wall F209, Lot II-32, 8340/5940E 3.1, KK91-46.

Fig. 3.45.31. Two joining fragments from the torso of a three-dimensional quadruped with extended front and hind legs; parts of the left ear survive on the head. At both ends are three dowel holds for attaching head and

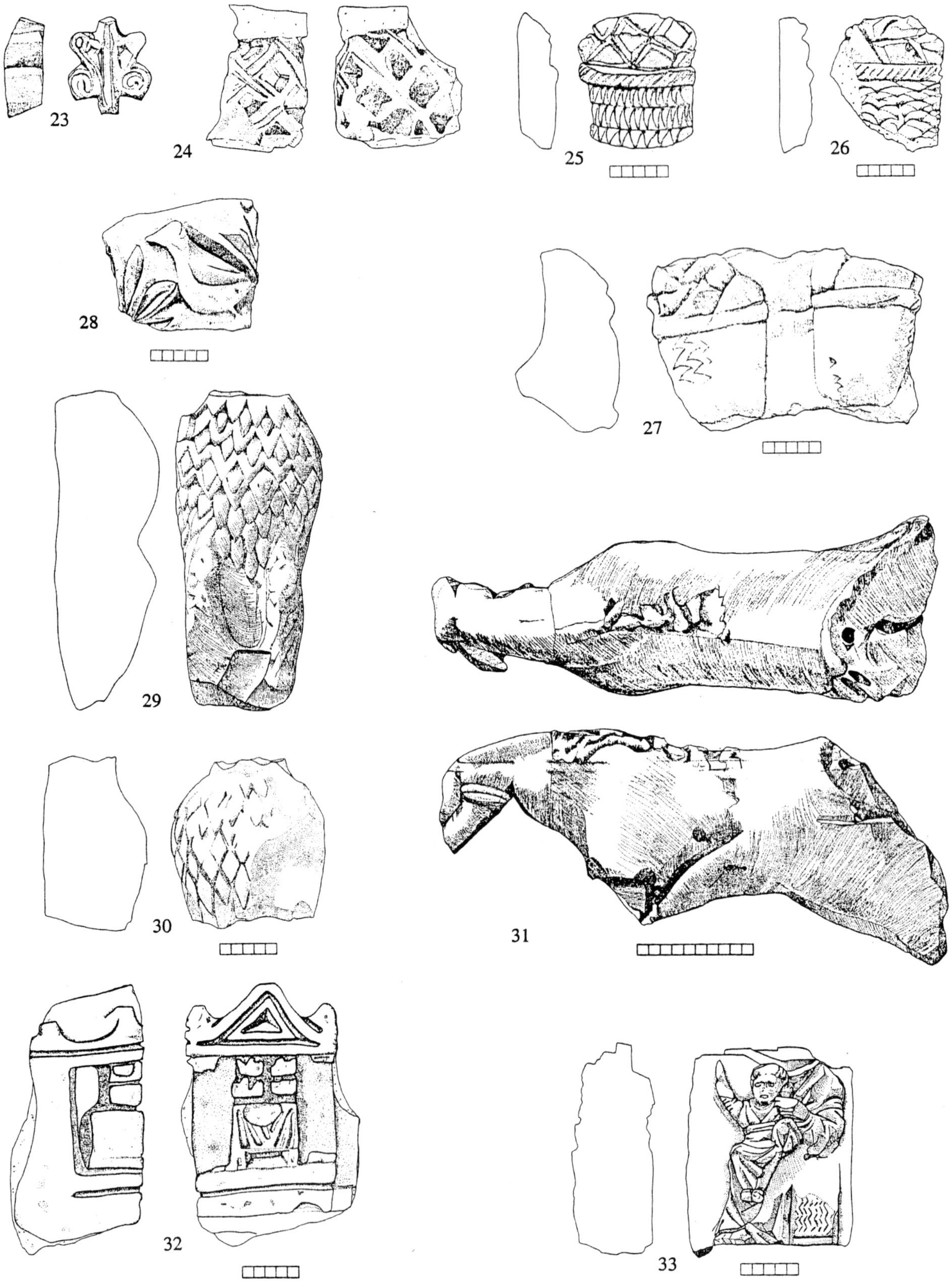

Fig. 3.45. Area II, molded plaster architectural details.

hind legs. P. l. 0.43, h. 0.23, w. 0.16. S lateral space upper collapse, Lot II-8, 8345/5935 3.1, KK90-46.

Fig. 3.45.32. Relief of small shrine with altar on raised platform flanked by columns (now lost) supporting gabled roof with corner palmettes. Altar rests on two legs and is covered by cloth with incised lines and two sets of stacked objects (loaves?). Back surface uneven. P. h. 0.235, w. 0.16, th. 0.121. S aisle upper collapse, Lot II-6, 8345/5940S 2.1, KK90-18. Cf. a similar if more monumental shrine at Alahan *c.*500; Gough 1985: 125, fig. 57, pl. 60.

Fig. 3.45.33. Relief of Virgin and Christ child in fine-grained white plaster, worn and encrusted. The large figure of Mary (lacking head) is seated on chair or bench covered with incised zig-zag patterns, turned to the left with both feet emerging from beneath a long cloak. She points with her left hand to the heavily draped Christ child, who is presented frontally on her lap and points upward with his right hand; the missing left hand may have held a scroll. Back surface slightly recessed, unfinished. P. h. 0.182, w. 0.144, th. 0.07. S aisle upper collapse, Lot II-6, 8345/5940 4.2, KK90-9. *Muse* 23-24 (1989-90) 24 fig. 13; *RDAC* 1991: 233-35, fig. 5, pl. LXII.3; *JRA* 5 (1992) 270 fig. 6.

Floor mosaics (by L. Benson and M. Rautman)

The mosaic floor that occupies the E end of the central aisle presumably formed part of the original decoration of the south church. Today the N and S edges are obscured by the mid 7th-c. benches, but the mosaic's preserved length of 5.03 m suggests that it reached to the second pair of nave supports (fig. 3.34). This would have distinguished the *bema* from the rest of the nave, which was paved at a lower level with plain gypsum slabs. A layer of small cobblestones provides a leveling course for the mosaic and was covered by a setting bed consisting of a pink lime cement with small clay, chert, and ceramic inclusions. Commonly represented colors include white, yellowish-white, pink, light bluish-gray, black, and red. All tesserae are cut stone and average 1.0-1.4 cm in size and 2.8 g in weight, with black tesserae tending to be somewhat smaller (Table 3.15).

TABLE 3.15. AREA II, SANCTUARY FLOOR MOSAIC, COLORS REPRESENTED AMONG A RANDOM SAMPLE OF LOOSE TESSERAE
(including colors present in bedded mosaic but not in loose tesserae)

Color	*count*	*% count*	*wt.*	*% wt.*	*avg. wt.*
White	775	48.0	2195	48.4	2.83
Pink	444	27.5	1245	27.4	2.80
Light bluish-gray	289	17.8	885	19.5	3.06
Black	109	6.7	215	4.7	1.97
Red					
Yellowish-white					
TOTAL	1617	100	4540	100	2.81

The mosaic consists of purely geometric motifs (fig. 3.35). Two border patterns frame the main decorative zone, which is dominated by a cable framework of alternating and interlaced straight squares and circles. The outer border (0.22 m wide) uses white, black, red, and pink tesserae. A band of alternating lozenges and pitched squares is set against a background of white tesserae, 5 on the ends and 7 on the sides.[22] The lozenges and pitched squares are outlined in black and filled with nested bands of red, pink, and white around a central black tessera. The inner border (0.14-m wide) is a two-strand twist pattern set against a black ground. Each strand consists of three rows of tesserae: first, light bluish-gray, white, and yellowish-white; and second, red, pink, and white. Single white tesserae fill the central space between the strands. Three rows of white tesserae separate the inner border from the main design field. Tessera density for both borders is 15-16 per 5-cm square.

The decoration of the main field consists of alternating and interlocked circles and squares arranged in 11 E-W rows and 8 N-S rows, measuring 4.25 by 2.88 m. The center of each circle is filled with one of at least three basic patterns: a cross defined by 4 triangles, two concentric circles with a dot center, or two concentric circles overlain by a cross-like motif.[23] Each square zone is filled with one of at least 4 possible patterns: diagonals, pairs of interlaced oval rings set at right-angles to one another, chevrons, and wavy lines. The diagonals, chevrons, and wavy lines simulate marble paving stones. All of the identified colors were used for the main decorative zone as well as in various combinations, creating an impression of great variety within a simple repetitive pattern.

The best stylistic parallels for the *bema* mosaic date to the second quarter of the 6th c. The rectangular field filled with interlacing or looped polychrome cable-patterns is characteristic of E Mediterranean floor-

22 Cf., for Antioch, Levi 1947: pl. CII; for Aphrodisias, Campbell 1991: 8-9, 36 fig. 18E.

23 For the latter compare Peyia basilica I in Michaelides 1987: no. 59, pl. XXXVI.

mosaics of the 6th c. Interlacing circles are common on the mainland.[24] The combination of circles with ovals and squares constitutes a variant of this basic system[25] and soon reached Cyprus (Megaw 1974: 72; Michaelides 1988: 138-43; id. 1989: 272-92). Mosaics with interlaced circles and diagonally placed squares appear as early as the (early 6th-c.?) floor of the baptistery *diaconikon* at Kourion (Megaw 1976a: figs. 9 and 14), but the combination of orthogonal (not diagonally placed) squares and circles within the cable framework is not yet known elsewhere on the island. The closest parallels are on the mainland. Circles and squares appear in alternation (and filled with Solomon's knots) at Gerasa in the W nave of the mortuary church, which dates after the middle of the 6th c. (Kraeling 1938: 336, pl. LXXVIIc). Interlaced orthogonal squares and circles also are found in the lower pavement of the north chapel at Kafr Kama, dated to the second quarter of the 6th c., where the figures were left essentially undecorated (Ovadiah and Ovadiah 1987: 88 no. 139; pl. C1.4 and fig. J2). In some of these cases, it is possible to detect the influence of *opus sectile* underlying such strict organization of a repetitive scheme (Donceel-Voûte 1995: 93). These similarities broadly agree with the stratigraphic evidence and support a date near the middle of the 6th c. for the building and decoration of the south church.

Much less can be said about the mosaic of the S chapel, which survives only as loose tesserae scattered on a plaster surface. In its original form this small mosaic filled the semicircular floor of the apse. Tesserae are all stone and include three colors: white, pink, and black, as well as a number of smoothed dark pebbles. Individual pieces are roughly cubic, measure on average 1.0-1.5 cm on each side, and weigh 3 g (Table 3.16). White and pink tesserae greatly outnumber the dark ones and no doubt made up the light background for a simple geometric pattern. The mosaic had eroded beyond repair when the chapel was rebuilt in the mid 7th c.

TABLE 3.16. AREA II, SOUTH LATERAL CHAPEL FLOOR MOSAIC, COLORS REPRESENTED AMONG A RANDOM SAMPLE OF LOOSE TESSERAE

Color	*count*	*% count*	*wt.*	*% wt.*	*avg. wt.*
White	622	70.1	1915	72.5	3.08
Pink	260	29.3	715	27.1	2.75
Black pebble	5	0.6	10	0.4	2.00
TOTAL	887	100	2640	100	2.98

The wide distribution of mosaics in Cyprus reflects the popularity of the technique in paving, organizing, and embellishing public and private spaces. Presumably Cypriot workshops were organized like their better documented counterparts on the mainland, venturing from their urban base into the *chora* for specific commissions. Modest examples of floor mosaics, some including figural images, have been found in the countryside at villa-related baths at Alassa, Kouklia, and Mansoura. More extensive but non-representational mosaics survive in the small inland churches at Alassa-*Ayia Mavri*, Trimithos, Tamassos, and Yialousa-*Ayia Trias*, where all three aisles were paved with an elaborate geometric program. As in the cities, these rural projects span a broad range of material, design, quality, and style, reflecting on each occasion the universal variables of craftsmanship and patronage.

Chronological summary and significance

Standing on the S perimeter of the inhabited site, the south church was a key landmark for Late Roman travelers approaching Kopetra from either the lower river plain or the ridge road. The rising mass of the nave was embraced by lower spaces on at least three sides, and other village buildings stood nearby. The building is the largest structure known on this part of the ridge and in late antiquity constituted a visual anchor for area residents.

The main doors of the south church no doubt looked toward the track that rose from the river plain to the southwest. Eroded foundations nearby suggest that the narthex may have been preceded by a court or portico, onto which the W room also opened. A small door on the S flank admitted the visitor to a long, bench-lined vestibule before continuing into the chapel or aisle. Such structures commonly flanked Cypriot churches at this time, with the sunny S side often preferred for chapels. At nearby Amathus, chapels lay along the S side of both the southwest and acropolis basilicas, and similar arrangements are known at Yialousa and Polis. Facing benches were equally popular at Amathus and elsewhere on the island.

24 E.g., the early 6th-c. House of the Phoenix at Antioch; Levi 1947: 351-55, pl. CXXXV.

25 E.g., the early 6th-c. House of Aion; Levi 1947: 355-56, pl. CXXXVI; Campbell 1988: 57-59 and 93 fig. IVA24c, pl. 172.

The projecting apse of the S chapel formed an important part of the E façade, despite the presence of the small E room. Similar projecting side apses belong to lateral chapels at Yialousa and Amathus (southwest and acropolis basilicas; and later at Lysi), with N apsidal chapels found at Kourion (suburban basilica) and Peyia (basilica I). Small rooms stood behind the apse at the great basilicas at Amathus, Kourion, and Salamis, as well as in smaller churches like the suburban basilica at Kourion. The dominant feature of the E façade, however, was the central apse, which rose in a tall polygonal shell, presumably pierced by small windows. The externally faceted apse is usually regarded as a hallmark of Constantinopolitan builders that is found in areas under the cultural influence of the capital (Delvoye 1972: 19; Megaw 1974: 71; Papageorghiou 1986: 493). In Cyprus the polygonal apse is known as early as the 5th c. at the Kourion episcopal basilica and the Paphos Limeniotissa. By the 6th c., the form had caught on across the island, with late examples built at Peyia and the Amathus acropolis. The combination of polygonal and rounded apse forms in the same building, while less common, occurs also at Amathus, Kourion, and Polis.

The south church fits comfortably among the smaller basilicas built in Cyprus during the 6th c. (below, p. 147). The total enclosed area approximates contemporary buildings like the Ayios Kononas, Athienou, and Kourion suburban basilicas, although its nave is both larger and narrow than these. In fact, like the two other churches at Kopetra, the south church has some of the most elongated proportions known on the island. The sanctuary design resembles the *Sirmata* basilica, with the polygonal apse shell reflecting indirect contact with the metropolitan mainstream; in both cases, side aisles ended in simple inscribed niches and stood outside the sanctuary. The latter included a raised *bema* with a mosaic floor that was laid by itinerant craftsmen, who brought with them a few simple patterns known elsewhere in the E Mediterranean. Other liturgical furnishings included several marble tables, one bearing the monogram of a possible patron, which stood in the *bema* and S chapel.

The apse mosaic constitutes an important rural example of a technique once thought restricted to large urban centers. In addition to documented ensembles at Kiti, Livadhia, and Lythrankomi, wall- and vault-mosaics are known at Kourion, and glass tesserae have been reported from many smaller sites. The Kopetra mosaic probably was installed by specialists who were called to work as the church neared completion. Its fragmentary condition does not obscure the original range of colors and patterns (below, p. 144).

Rivaling the apse mosaic was the sculptural stucco on the upper walls. Fluted pilaster shafts, capitals, and wall-moldings were complemented by images of animals, a small shrine, and religious figures. The technique relied on local materials and methods, but the absence of comparable stuccowork in the area suggests that for this too specialized craftsmen were summoned from elsewhere. A molded hunting frieze was found in the S lateral space of the southwest basilica at Amathus, yet closer technical and stylistic connections exist with the House of the Oil Press at Salamis. The late 5th-c. date of the Salamis stucco demonstrates the conservative nature of Cypriot craftsmen, who probably formed mobile bands that worked along the coast. Considered together with traces of plaster decoration identified at churches at Kiti, Marathovouno, Soloi, and elsewhere, Kopetra offers the best available evidence of the *gypsiplasia* that filled late-antique Cypriot churches.

The information at hand indicates that the basilica, S lateral spaces, and E room belong to a single building program (above, fig. 3.36, phase Ia). Stratigraphic evidence combined with stylistic parallels suggests that this took place around the middle of the 6th c. At that time the three aisles were separated by columns or cylindrical piers crowned with molded gypsum capitals, above which rose the upper nave wall and timber roof. The splendidly decorated building soon required repairs, however: one or both colonnades were reinforced (phase Ib) before the nave collapsed towards the middle of the 7th c.

The local response is significant, for the south church was not deserted but re-organized as a more compact religious precinct (fig. 3.36, phase II, fig. 3.46). The N aisle was abandoned, but the lower central aisle was cleared and left as an unroofed court. The earlier sanctuary, its apse still standing, became an independent chapel with flanking walls, low benches, and a doorway facing west. The S wall was rebuilt with materials salvaged from the earlier church, including many pieces of its stucco decoration. A parallel, unmortared wall replaced the S colonnade and created an elongated room in the S aisle stretching from the E niche to the narthex door; to the north, a doorway led to the sanctuary chapel, while another side opening led to the S lateral space and chapel. Both narthex and W room apparently continued in use as well. While details are not entirely clear, this re-occupation encompassed 4 or 5 rooms within the damaged complex. Walls were reconstructed or built anew directly atop earlier floors, which were repaired and used again. The reduced occupation of an earlier church resembles the sequence noted locally at *Sirmata* and elsewhere on the island,[26] where churches suffered damage around the middle of the 7th c. The reconstruction of just the

---

26 E.g., Polis, Ayios Kononas, Paphos, Soloi, Ayios Philon, Salamis, and Amathus.

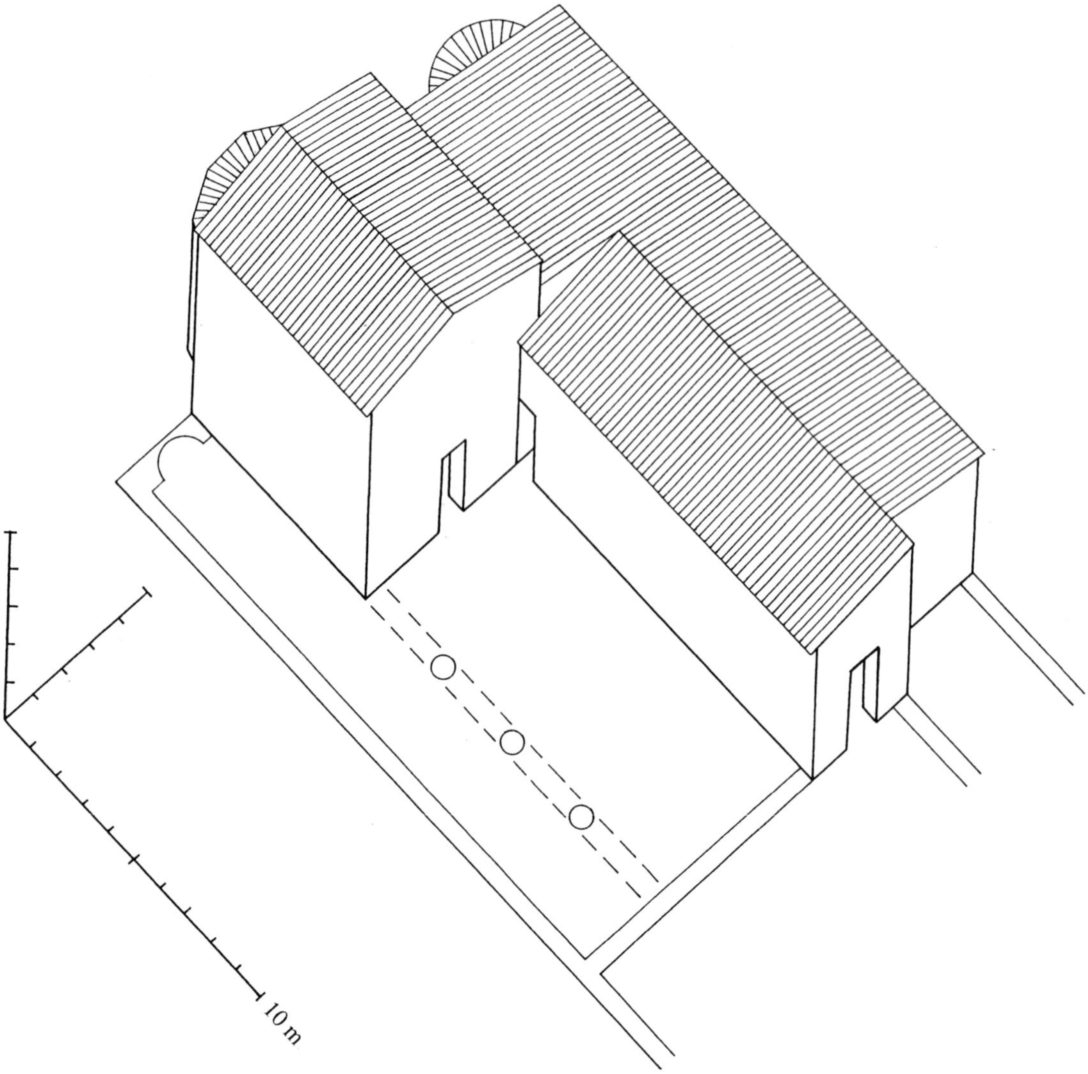

Fig. 3.46. Area II, isometric reconstruction of phase II structures.

bema area as an independent chapel is seen also at Ayios Epiphanios in Salamis and the southeast basilica at Amathus (Jeffery 1928: 345; Christou 1997: 904-5) as well as in the Aegean.[27] The re-organized complex at Kopetra was not used long before another collapse brought down the semidome and the walls of the S aisle. The final recorded activity involved leveling the débris in the S aisle and building a tomb with twin burials against the N wall (fig. 3.36, phase III).

These later phases cannot be dated solely on internal grounds but require reference to the entire site. Extensive repairs cleared the re-occupied spaces to their original floor levels and left behind little fresh diagnostic material. Indeed, by focusing on the stratigraphic record of a single building, it is possible to argue that the complex was rebuilt early in the 7th c. and destroyed during the Arab campaigns of 649-50. Such an interpretation, however, is at odds with our broader assessment of the site. Finds from survey and excavation clearly document the village's prosperity during the early 7th c., a level of general well-being that is inconsistent with limited re-occupation of an important church. Rather, this late activity implies a moment of cultural dislocation like that seen at *Sirmata* (above, pp 90-91). The selective re-occupation of these two neighboring churches suggests that both were damaged and re-organized *c.*650. The discovery of handmade cooking pots with small hanging lamps in late levels at Area II documents the community's increasing reliance on locally produced pottery at this time. The follis of Constans II (**C12**, issued 659/660) recovered from the upper débris suggests that these small, unsteady buildings survived into the third quarter of the 7th c. Similar to the final phase at *Sirmata*, the last commemoration of this religious precinct was the small tomb built for a double burial amid the ruins of the S aisle, roughly contemporary with late burials at nearby Amathus (Prokopiou 1995 and 1996). After centuries of expanding their use of the lower valley's resources, local inhabitants left the ridge behind in favor of other lifeways better suited to their changing world.

27 E.g., Chersonesos and Frankokastello on Crete; Pallas 1979-80: 85 fig. 23, 93 fig. 32.

Fig. 3.47. Area V, view to W (1991).

AREA V: THE NORTH CHURCH

Introduction

Area V occupies a low, flat terrace on the upper Kopetra ridge, *c.*220 m north of Area II and 60 m from Area IV. The sector lies within a single field, numbered 222 on the LV.20 cadastral map, along whose N side runs the 1986 irrigation pipeline (figs. 2.4 and 2.8). To west and northwest the terrain rises gently to the bluff overlooking the Vasilikos river plain. To the south and especially east the ground drops away 2-3 m. Rubble retaining walls on these sides are apparently of recent date; they contain many rooftile fragments and much roughly squared stone that presumably came from early buildings in the area. Preliminary reconnaissance by the VVP survey was followed by systematic sampling of the area in 1987 and 1988, which observed that the quantity of Late Roman sherds, rooftiles, and other building débris declines sharply as one moves farther north and east (above, p. 32). This distribution suggests that Area V lies near the NE edge of the inhabited site, and in late antiquity offered the first glimpse of the village from the upper valley.

During the 1989 and 1990 field seasons, we noted that much building débris was being turned up by seasonal ploughing in the area. We recovered several cut gypsum and sandstone blocks, including three large pieces with elegant decorative moldings not known elsewhere at the site (above, pp. 30-32). Other surface finds — a marble table fragment, a few pieces of *opus sectile*, and many rooftiles and glass tesserae — pointed to the presence of a church. A short section of a mortared rubble wall oriented slightly north of east was visible along the field's N scarp; cleaning revealed the feature to be 0.6 m thick and to extend over 4 m. During the winter of 1990-91, a small grove of olives was planted in the field, bringing to light additional material and endangering the architectural remains.

Suspecting a major building, we gained the co-operation of the landowner and carried out a brief exploratory campaign in 1991. The presence of delicate olive saplings constrained investigation and forced us to work in isolated trenches. Guided as much by the presence of these new plantings and their irrigation tubing as by visible archaeological features, we opened three 5-m square trenches in different parts of the field (fig. 3.47). These first trenches located a small section of curved masonry at the E edge of the terrace, and farther west two wall-sections lying at right-angles to the visible N wall. Two more sections of intersecting wall fragments appeared in a fourth trench near the SW edge of the terrace. The E trench, when expanded, revealed part of a broad semicircular apse and most of a smaller adjacent apse to the south. The similar elevation and construction of these features suggested that the remains all belong to the same Late Roman structure, whose details could be clarified by reference to more fully excavated buildings. Unfortunately, we lacked time to explore further this large and obviously important structure. The limited architectural evidence can be graphically summarized as belonging to a basilica with three aisles and at least one flanking space, similar

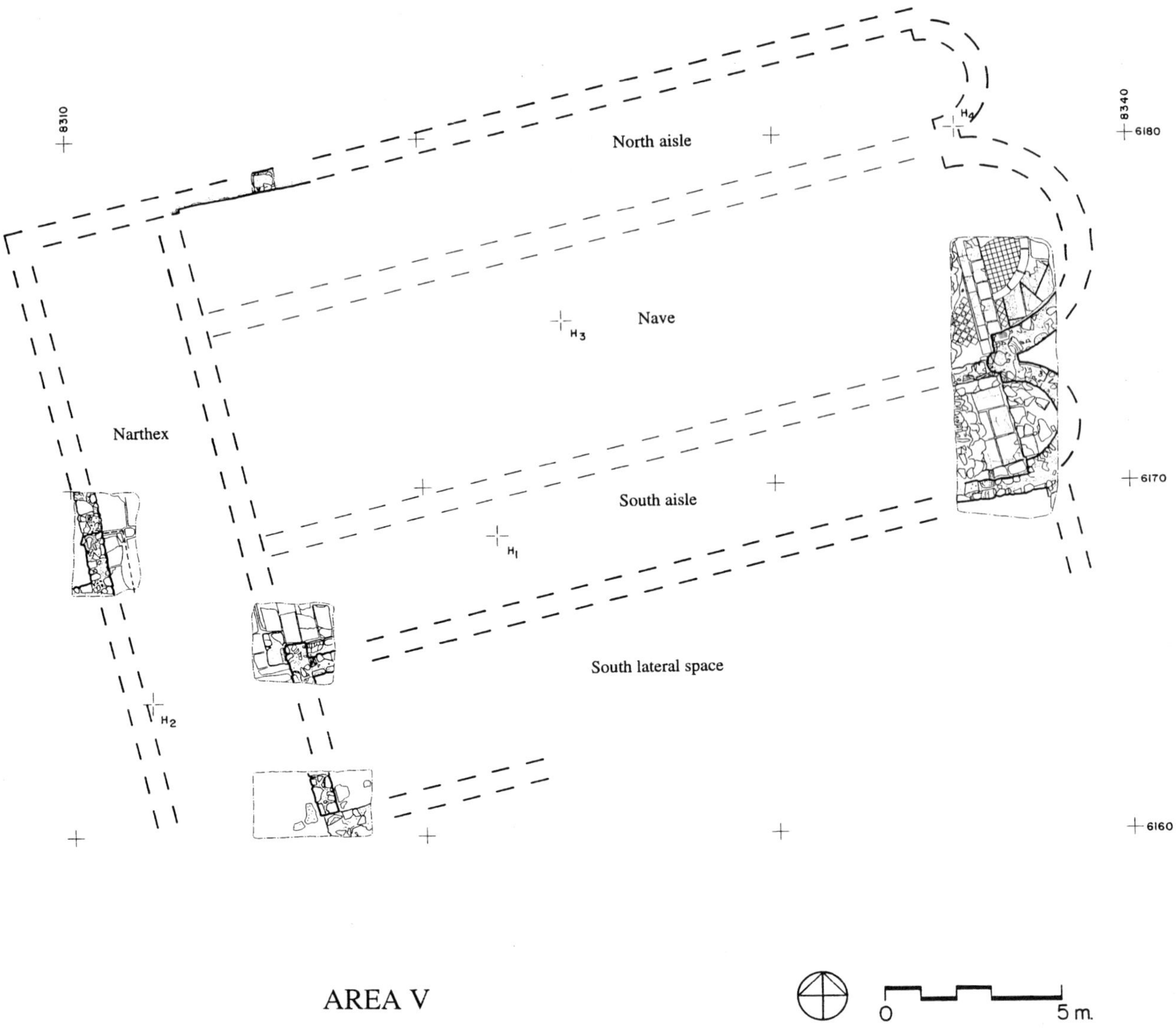

Fig. 3.48. Area V, state plan.

to the east and south churches (Areas I and II). Stratigraphic information and stylistic comparanda suggest the original appearance and approximate date of this north church.[28]

Architectural features and associated deposits

The north church can be discussed only in general terms. The evidence at hand establishes the original purpose, size, and plan of the structure and illustrates some of its decorative details. Comparison with other churches confirms our provisional date for its construction. This was the earliest and largest of the known churches at Kopetra, a three-aisled basilica with a narthex and a long space lying along its S flank (fig. 3.48). Much remains uncertain about the structure, yet its identification significantly enlarges our understanding of local habitation.

The core of the complex was a three-aisled hall measuring *c.*21 m long by 13 m wide. Discovery of the sanctuary established the location and arrangement of the building's E end. The fragmentary wall-section visible in the field's N scarp evidently belongs to the outer wall of the N aisle. The three W trenches identified short sections of perpendicular and intersecting walls lying 1-2 m below present ground level *c.*20 m southwest of the sanctuary. These seem to include the SW corners of both the S aisle and a wide S lateral space, as well as the S jamb of the main outer door of a deep narthex. Most of these walls were made of field-stone and gypsum fragments carefully bedded in thick mortar and covered with one or more coats of white plaster. *Marmara* slabs apparently paved nave and narthex but were not found in the exposed corner of the

28 The excavations were noted in *Muse* 25 (1991) 16-17 and in *RDAC* 1994: 299-301.

Fig. 3.49. Area V, basilica, central and S apse, view to E.

S lateral space. The reconstructed plan is not without problems. Slight deviations in wall orientation may have resulted from our difficulty surveying deep features in small, isolated trenches. The original appearance of the basilica's W wall is more puzzling, with a slight projection in the N wall lying just west of its anticipated line (adjusted in fig. 3.48). The westernmost trench suggests a wide but not implausible outer doorway for the narthex and other structures standing before the church.

The sanctuary is the most clearly understood part of the building. A total area of 24 m^2 near the E edge of the Area V terrace was excavated to the level of the interior floor. These two joined trenches (8335/6173, 8335/6177) exposed substantial sections of two adjacent curved walls belonging to the central and S side apses (fig. 3.49; *RDAC* 1994: pl. LXXXII.1). The apse walls are freestanding and rounded both internally and externally — a form well-established in Cyprus by the early 6th c. but not seen elsewhere at Kopetra (below, p. 151). The carefully built wall (0.8 m thick) of the central apse stands to an average height of 1.0 m and has an estimated diameter of 5.0 m. The S apse wall is 0.6 m thick and has an interior diameter of 2.3 m. A short section of the S lateral wall, relatively poorly preserved and perhaps shifted off its foundation, indicates that the aisle had a width of *c.*3 m. A rounded pilaster articulates the wall between the two apses, and establishes the form and location of the S colonnade. Reconstructed symmetrically, this pilaster fixes the width of the central aisle at 6 m. The length of the hall could have been spanned by 7 columns arranged at 2.6-m intervals.

The *bema* and central apse are paved with *opus sectile* — the only instance of this prestigious floor covering seen at Kopetra. The small exposed part of the *bema* floor presents a grid of large octagons alternating with tiny diagonally-set squares. A slightly raised curb marks the chord of the apse, beyond which lies a central semicircular panel of *opus sectile* with diagonally placed squares alternating with horizontal rows of smaller squares surrounded by a marble border (fig. 3.50). This panel is surrounded by an arc 0.9-1.0 m wide of closely-fitted gypsum slabs, with a strip of *opus sectile* adjoining the curb. The use of gypsum as an outer frame for the *opus sectile* is surprising and without close parallel on the island. The floor's generally good condition indicates that this modest outer zone was intended from the start, however, and probably was concealed beneath a wood *synthronon*. Individual patterns of the central zone are familiar from other Cypriot buildings, especially the churches of nearby Amathus. While not closely datable, this kind of *opus sectile* was especially popular during the 6th c. (below, p. 155).

The sanctuary was covered by a substantial layer of collapsed building débris (fig. 3.51). Removal of this layer from the sanctuary revealed thousands of loose tesserae from the semidome mosaic of the central apse (Lot V-2). Few fragments of bedded mosaic were found at Area V, but the extent and range of tesserae attest the original decoration of the upper walls (below, p. 146). Sparse diagnostic finds include pottery (e.g., Cypriot Red Slip form 8 dish/bowl) dating to the late 6th or early 7th c.

The S aisle was paved with gypsum slabs at a level slightly below the floor of the central aisle. At a later date, the lower part of the S apse was filled with roughly-laid unmortared rubble, preserved to a height of *c.*1 m above floor level. A thick coat of plaster applied to the side apse wall apparently belongs to this modification. Around the same time an unmortared rubble wall 0.45-0.5 m thick replaced all or part of the S colonnade, as also happened at the south church. An unmortared step or low bench was built against this and

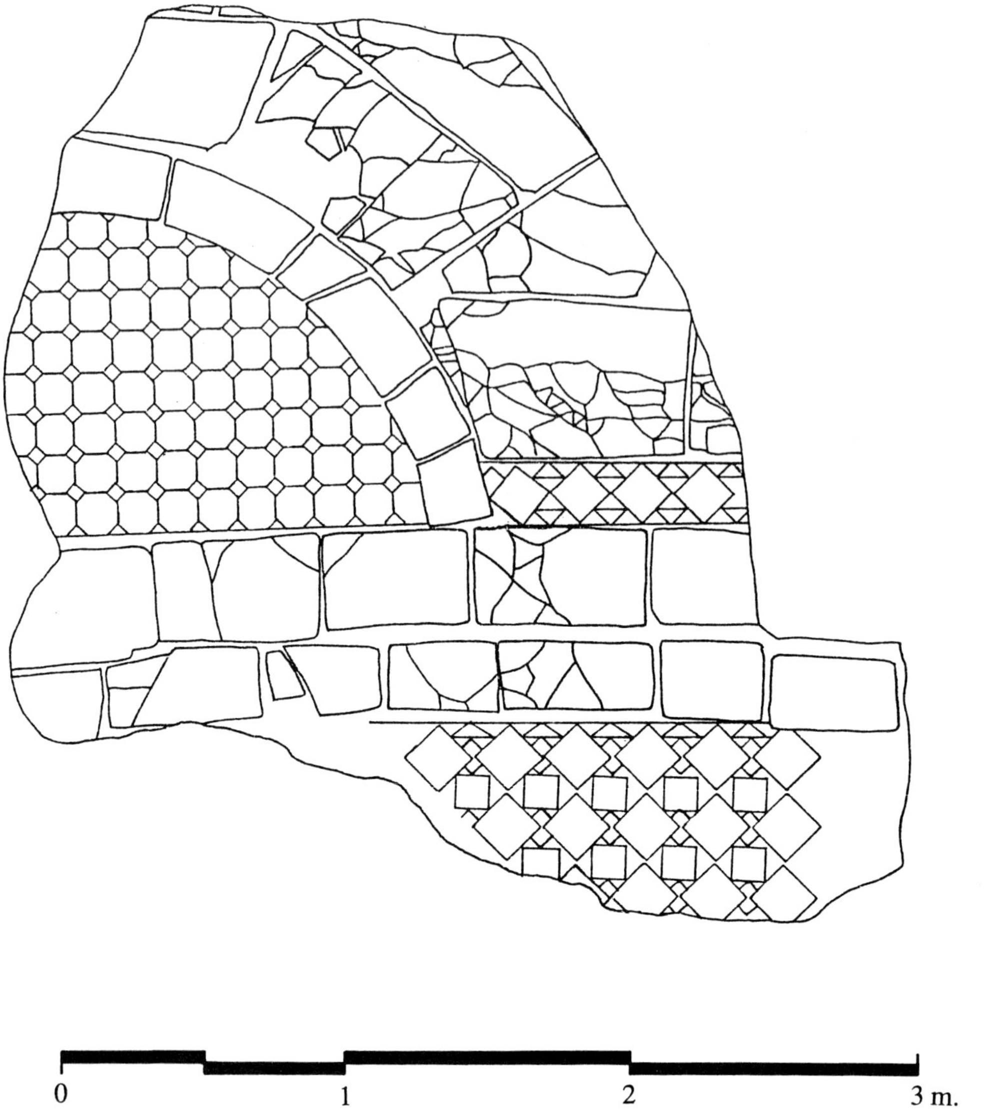

Fig. 3.50. Area V, *opus sectile* floor of central apse (J. Ravenhurst).

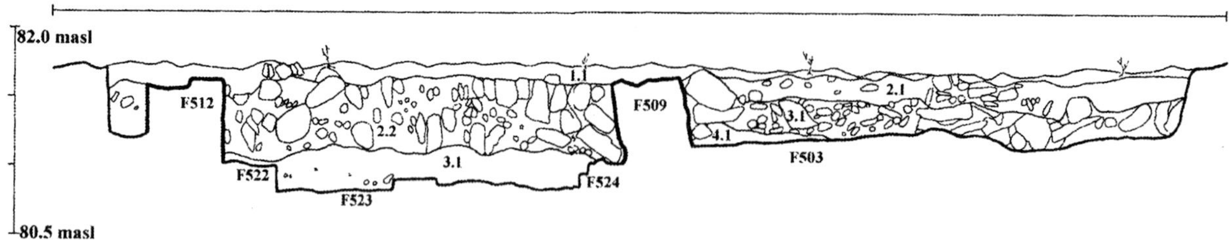

Fig. 3.51. Area V, sanctuary, stratigraphic section at 8335/6173-6177, view to W.

the facing S wall. Objects associated with this late activity include several fine table vessels (e.g., Cypriot Red Slip form 11 basin, African Red Slip form 107 bowl, and a small glass bowl) dating to the early 7th c. (Lot V-4). Other pottery from this phase is summarized in *RDAC* 1994: 302 Table 3.

The W end of the S aisle was identified by one of the three small trenches opened on the opposite side of the Area V terrace (8315/6167). One sturdily-mortared rubble wall appears to be the S wall of the basilica (fig. 3.52). To the west, this wall bonds with a perpendicular spur that projects north by 0.5 m and marks the S jamb of a side narthex door. A low masonry bench built of mortared gypsum fragments begins at this corner and extends along the S wall. Carefully-fitted gypsum slabs belong to the original floor of the S aisle. A large block of gypsum marks the threshold, without trace of pivots, joining the S aisle with the narthex. A massive layer of collapsed débris extended from the S aisle into the narthex (Lot V-3). Context finds include three glass

Fig. 3.52. Area V, SW corner of basilica with bench, view to W.

Fig. 3.53. Area V, burial before central narthex door, view to N.

objects and a large fragment of a handmade cooking pot. The mere presence of the late cooking pot need not imply that a major change took place in how the building was used during this late phase, but it does suggest that the basilica had been repaired and stood largely intact through the mid 7th c.

The narthex lies immediately to the west, its floor paved at the same level as the S aisle. The intervening wall was later reinforced by an abutting pier built directly atop the narthex paving. A sondage through the narthex floor in front of the threshold of the S aisle located not foundations but a sub-floor burial (Tomb 4; F520) lying 0.75 m below the paved surface. The burial occupied a shallow recess (1.5 x 0.4 m in plan) (fig. 3.53; *RDAC* 1994: pl. LXXXII.2). Excavation of this small space found no diagnostic finds but only the very poorly preserved remains of an adult of undetermined sex (below, Appendix 5). Difficulties of access prevented us from fully exploring the burial and determining whether it dates to the initial construction of the

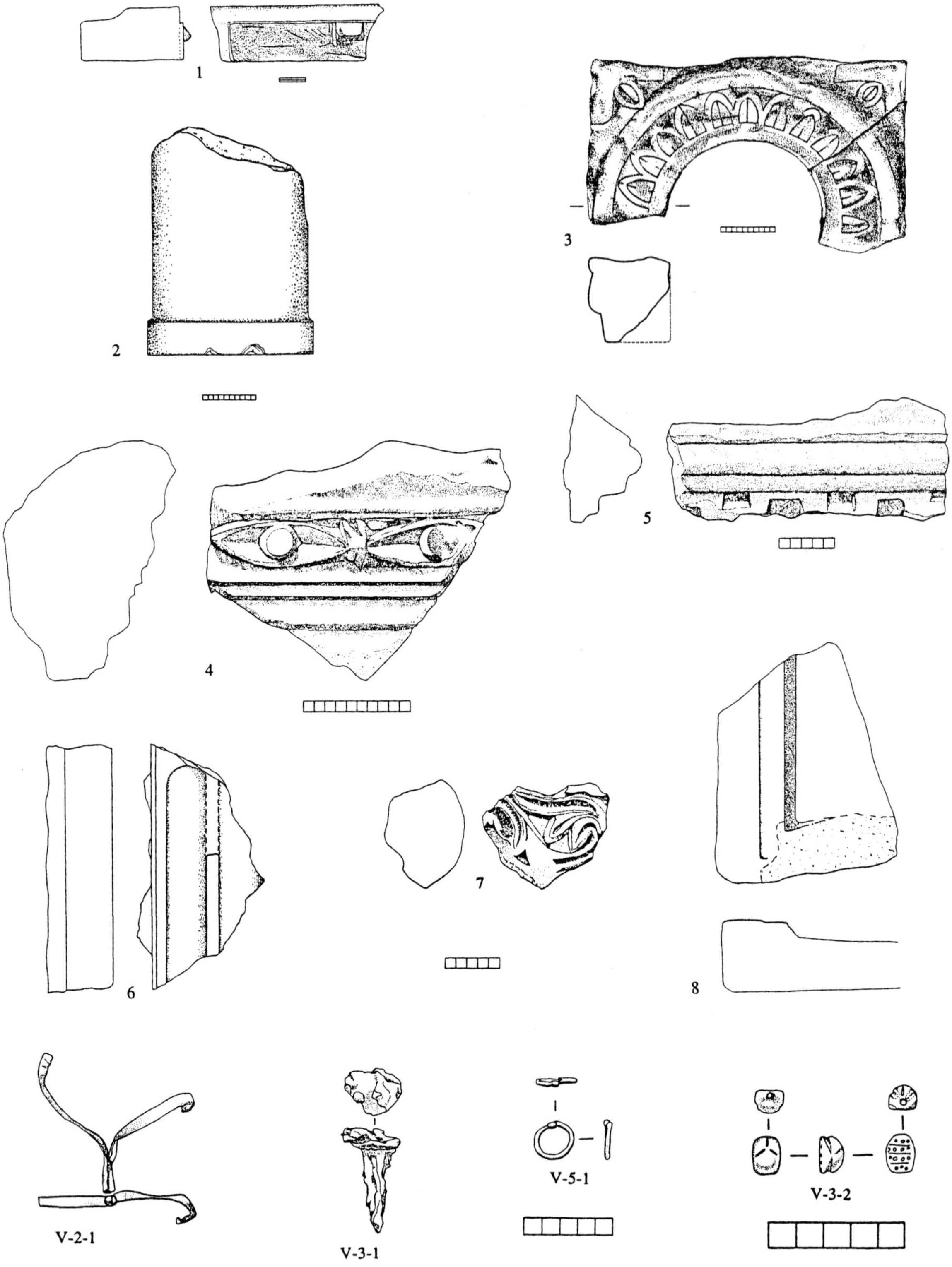

Fig. 3.54. Area V, stone, molded plaster, and metal artifacts.

basilica or a later modification. In either case, it was installed before the narthex pier (F517) was added to the basilica's SW corner.

A short section of the facing narthex wall appeared in another trench located *c*.5 m to the northwest (8310/6170). Excavation here revealed a parallel wall of mortared gypsum rubble that stood 4.2 m away. No trace was found of the rounded pilasters seen at *Sirmata*. A substantial masonry bench runs along the E face of this outer wall, similar to the one at the W end of the S aisle. Gypsum slabs cover the floor. Both wall and bench stop near the basilica's central axis and apparently mark the S edge of a broad main doorway (original width 3.4 m, excluding jambs) in the outer wall. On the W side of this wall a projecting spur of uncertain function continues beyond the limits of excavation, implying that other structures stood in front of the narthex. During a later phase, the main doorway was narrowed or blocked with a screen of unmortared rubble. A small bronze coin, probably a pentanummium of Justinian I or Justin II (**C2**), was found in the lower fill near the W narthex wall (Lot V-3). The area was covered in about the mid 7th c. by the collapse of the upper walls and roof.

The superstructure is an essay in speculation. The semicircular wall-pilaster separating the two apses offers direct evidence for the nave arcades, as does the fragmentary marble pilaster shaft (fig. 3.54.2) found in the area; the late colonnade wall, however, obscures any trace of the stylobate. In their original form the two colonnades probably consisted of cylindrical piers of mortared rubble similar to those at the south and east churches. The scarcity of decorative stucco raises the possibility that some marble columns were used, although few fragments of architectural marble are known at Kopetra, and in Cyprus structural marble is generally limited to coastal cities. The only recovered remnants of plaster decoration come from the area of the narthex. The capitals probably carried the upper wall on arcades.

The perpendicular wall separating nave from narthex also extends slightly to the south, where its continuation was picked up by a final trench (8315/6162). This wall corresponds to a parallel wall reaching out from the S apse and suggests that a 4-m wide lateral space lay along this side of the basilica. Similar flanking spaces at *Sirmata* and at Area II may have functioned as chapels or mortuary annexes. This trench alone identified an eroded earth surface instead of a paved floor. The poor condition of walls and occupation levels suggests that this part of the building was not maintained as long as the nave and narthex.

Some of the objects recovered from the cultivated surface of Area V and its vicinity can be plausibly associated with the north church (Lot V-1). The many Corinthian-style rooftiles littering the area no doubt came from the roof of this large building, which may have required almost 7000 tiles (above, p. 54). Other surface finds include three large blocks of gypsum and sandstone. Two of the latter include decorative moldings that may have surrounded windows or other features in the upper walls. Several additional blocks, including a floral capital and two relief slabs, were found in the general area and may have been part of the building (above, pp. 30-32; figs. 2.12 nos. 4-6). Other surface finds include a single rim fragment from a marble table and various *opus sectile* fragments that probably came from the *bema* floor.

Pottery and other inventoried artifacts by Lot

Roman pottery from Area V is summarized in Table 3.17.

Lot V-1: Topsoil

Date range: mostly 6th to 7th c. (Cypriot Red Slip forms 2, 9A, 9C, 11; Phocean Red Slip forms 3E, 10A, 10B).

Catalogued objects:

169 Unassigned amphora

229 Glass bowl

263 Glass flask

Additional objects:

Not inventoried. African Red Slip form 104C(?). *RDAC* 1994: 301 no. 22, fig. 8.

Not inventoried. Plain ware A bowl. *RDAC* 1994: 301 no. 24, fig. 8.

Fig. 3.54.1. Rectangular sandstone block with drafted margins and raised lifting boss. P. l. 0.64, h. 0.22, w. 0.41. Surface, not inventoried.

Fig. 3.54.3. Hemispherical sandstone arch with egg-and-dart or radiating leaf molding; projecting leaves in corner spandrels. Max. w. 0.59, h. 0.37, th. 0.15, interior w. of opening 0.28. Surface, KK88-26A and B.

Fig. 3.54.4. Fragment of sandstone molding with 3 fasciae, horizontal leaves with raised round centers, and a projecting hollow. P. l. 0.27; h. 0.23, th. 0.14. Surface, KK91-59.

Fig. 3.54.8. Fragment from the corner rim of a rectangular marble table. Coarse-grained, gray-veined marble. P. l. 0.23, w. 0.165, th. 0.045-0.07. Surface, 8315/6167 1.1, KK91-53.

Lot V-2: Basilica, eastern collapse

Approximate date: mid 7th c. (Cypriot Red Slip form 8).

Additional objects:

Fig. 3.54.2. Large fragment of marble pilaster shaft with rounded base. Medium-grained, gray-veined marble, smoothly finished; back roughly picked. P. h. 0.43, w. base 0.31. 8335/6173 2.1, KK91-54.

Fig. 3.54.5. Fragment of large horizontal plaster cornice with row of alternating notches and rounded molding. Max. h. 0.12, l. 0.26. 8335/6173 2.1, KK91-49. Cf. fig. 3.43.1 (KK 91-51 from Area II).

V-2-1 (fig. 3.54). Copper alloy wick-holder with rectangular strip twisted in middle to form short tube with two outwardly curving projections to attach to glass lamp rim. Max. l. 0.065, w. 0.070, diam. tube 0.006. 8335/6177 3.1, KK91-22. Cf. Catling and Dikigoropoulos 1970: 51 no. 19; Chavane 1975: 40 no. 114; Taylor and Megaw 1981: fig. 48.9; Giudice *et al.* 1999: 286 no. 15, fig. 12.7.

Lot V-3: Basilica, western collapse

Approximate date: mid 7th c.?

Catalogued objects:

TABLE 3.17. SUMMARY OF ROMAN POTTERY FROM AREA V

Area V	*rim*	*base*	*handle*	*sherd*	*sum*	*weight*	*avg. sherd wt*
Fine	15	4	2	10	31	650	20.97
Plain	4	4	2	18	28	975	34.82
Amphora		1	8	102	111	2535	22.84
Cook	4		3	30	37	440	11.89
Pithos	4	2	1	20	27	8615	319.07
Other	2			40	42	310	7.38
ROMAN TOTAL	29	11	16	220	276	13525	49.00
	rim	*base*	*handle*	*sherd*	*sum*		
CRS 2	1	2			3		
CRS 8	1			1	2		
CRS 9A	3				3		
CRS 9C	1				1		
CRS 11			2	2	4		
CRS other	1	2		2	5		
CRS TOTAL	7	4	2	5	18		
LRC 3E	1				1		
LRC 10	2				2		
LRC 10A	1				1		
LRC 10C	1				1		
LRC other	1			4	5		
LRC TOTAL	6			4	10		
ARS 107	1				1		
ARS other	1			1	2		
ARS TOTAL	2			1	3		
FINE TOTAL	15	4	2	10	31		
	rim	*base*	*handle*	*sherd*	*sum*	*weight*	
LR1			6	64	70	1525	
LR2				10	10	200	
LR4				4	4	75	
LR5/6				5	5	40	
LR7				3	3	30	
KAmp2			1	6	7	240	
KAmp5			1	1	3	245	
Other		1		9	9	180	
AMPHORA TOTAL		1	8	102	111	2535	
Plain A	2	1			3	280	
Plain B	1	1	1	3	6	95	
Plain C				3	3	35	
Plain D	1	2	1	12	16	565	
PLAIN TOTAL	4	4	2	18	28	975	
Cook A				4	4	20	
Cook C	1				1	165	
Cook D	3		3	26	32	255	
COOK TOTAL	4		3	30	37	440	
Pithos B	2	1		4	7	2045	
Pithos C	1				1	380	
Pithos D	1	1	1	16	19	6190	
PITHOS TOTAL	4	2	1	20	27	8615	

C2 Pentanummium(?), Justinian I or Justin II, 527-578, mint uncertain

239 Glass bowl?

279 Glass stemmed goblet

308 Glass hanging lamp

Additional objects:

Not inventoried. Plain ware D bowl. *RDAC* 1994: 301 no. 23, fig. 8.

Not inventoried. Cooking ware C pot. *RDAC* 1994: 301 no. 26, fig. 8.

KK91-31 (not illustrated). Small fragment of iron buckle(?), badly corroded. Max. l. 0.037, w. 0.024. 8315/6167 3.2.

KK91-33 (not illustrated). Small iron nail, corroded. Max. l. 0.064. 8315/6167 3.2.

Fig. 3.54.6. Fragment of column shaft with vertical fluting. Flat arrises 0.012 wide, 0.037 apart. P. h. 0.24, w. 0.12. 8310/6170 2.1, not inventoried. Cf. fig. 3.43.9 (Area II).

Fig. 3.54.7. Small fragment of plaster capital with floral patterns; traces of light green pigment. P. h. 0.11, w. 0.115. 8310/6170 2.2, KK91-40. Cf. Megaw 1976a: fig. 17 (Kourion).

V-3-2 (fig. 3.54). Black stone scarab of Archaic date, pierced. The reverse is decorated with 4 registers of shallow, drilled holes separated by incised lines. L. 0.013, w. 0.010. 8315/6162 3.1, KK91-34. Cf. Clerc 1991: 1-50 for scarabs and related seals at Amathus, mostly from 7th- and 6th-c. B.C. tombs.

Lot V-4: Basilica, second phase

Approximate date: early 7th c. (Cypriot Red Slip form 11, African Red Slip form 107).

Catalogued object:

238 Glass bowl?

Lot V-5: Basilica, first phase

Approximate date: inconclusive (6th c.?).

Additional object:

KK91-26 (not illustrated). Copper alloy ring with simple band, round in section, bent into circular shape; one end slightly thickened at juncture. Diam. 0.023, th. 0.004. 8280/6055 4.1. Cf. Chavane 1975: 149-50, esp. no. 432, pl. 44.

The *opus sectile* floor

The paving of the sanctuary with *opus sectile* reinforces one's impression of the local importance of the north church and the status of its community. The technique apparently was used throughout the main apse as well as the raised *bema*, probably extending as far as the second nave piers, for a total area of some 30-40 m^2 (fig. 3.49). This would clearly have distinguished the sanctuary from the lower central aisle, had the latter been surfaced with gypsum as at the south and east churches. The use of a limited range of simple geometric shapes reflects a measure of economy.

The *opus sectile* tradition flourished across the E Mediterranean during late antiquity and may have reached its peak of popularity in the first half of the 6th c. (Donceel-Voûte 1995: 93). The lack of a good local supply of marble prevented Cypriot builders from employing it on more than an experimental basis before the 4th c., when significant marble imports first reached the island (Megaw 1976b: 4-9; Sodini 1989a; Michaelides 1993). Among its earliest uses were renovations of the Salamis theater (early 4th c.?) and gymnasium baths (*c.*431). The technique blossomed during the 5th and 6th c., when it appeared in urban public buildings in many coastal cities. Among identified pavements in the island's interior are the Tryphotes basilica in Nicosia, the pilgrimage centers of Ayios Herakleidios at Tamassos and Ayios Spyridon at Trimithos, and rural churches at Athienou, Lysi, and Sygkrasi (Michaelides 1993: fig. 19 for a distribution map; Hadjichristophi 1997). The context of known examples emphasizes the élite nature of the technique, which was featured primarily in churches and townhouses. In churches, *opus sectile* was a convenient way to emphasize sanctuaries, chapels, baptisteries, and important ancillary rooms. It was favored for apse floors, like the N apse at Ayios Epiphanios and the central apse of the acropolis basilica at Amathus (Michaelides 1993: fig. 12; Pralong 1991; ead. 1994a: 424-25, fig. 7). The unusual outer frame seen at Kopetra re-appears in the Middle Byzantine *katholikon* of Ayios Chrysostomos at Koutsovendis (Michaelides 1993: fig. 27).

At least three distinct patterns appear at the north church. A grid of large, diagonally-laid squares, between which lie smaller, oblique squares, was used for the *bema* (fig. 3.50). Two sizes of small triangles fill the voids and gently focus the eye toward the apse. The apse border consists of a simplified pattern of large, diagonally-laid yellow squares with smaller yellow and black triangles. The center of the apse floor is occupied by a semicircular panel with yellow octagons, with alternating short and long sides, and small black squares set at the corners.

These basic patterns occur across the island as well as on the mainland and allow little chronological refinement. Large and small alternating squares with small triangles appear at the Paphos Limeniotissa and the Tryphotes basilica in Nicosia. Alternating octagons and squares are more widely seen at Amathus, Salamis, Kourion, Trimithos, Nicosia, Tamassos, Soloi, and Episkopi, ranging in date from the early 5th c. through the mid or even late 7th c. (Michaelides 1993; Hadjichristophi 2000). Similar examples are found along the Syrian coastlands, an area with which Cypriot artists shared close ties. Interestingly, the builders of Kopetra's north church did not employ the most popular shapes used *c.*600 at the nearby acropolis basilica at Amathus, where a broad range of patterns included variously shaped hexagons with straight and concave sides (Pralong 1991; ead. 1994a: 421-23). The mingling of small fragments of different materials of varying quality — marble, schist, limestone, and terracotta — seen at Kourion, Amathus, and elsewhere may reflect their late date, limited resources, or other factors surrounding their commission.

Chronological summary and significance

The north church was the earliest and grandest of the three identified basilicas at Kopetra. Located near the NE edge of the inhabited ridge, the site today is covered by a flourishing olive grove and betrays little sign of its former importance. The major architectural features are fairly well preserved, thanks to their large scale, relative inaccessibility, and heavy accumulation of overburden. All these factors discouraged our excavation of the building, yet it deserves more than a footnote in the island's architectural history.

The reconstructed plan relies on both comparisons with the south church, however incompletely known, and the somewhat formulaic planning of 6th-c. basilicas, which admittedly are better understood in cities than in the countryside. The north church was a large, three-aisled affair measuring roughly 21 x 13 m and enclosing an area of perhaps 280 m^2. The broad central aisle had a free span of almost 6 m and probably was flanked by 7 pairs of cylindrical piers set at intervals of *c.*2.6 m. Walls and piers were constructed of mortared gypsum and supported a timber roof covered by terracotta tiles. A deep narthex preceded the nave and a long flanking space lay along its S side. In most respects the plan is characteristic of churches built across the island, especially in rural areas, during the 5th and 6th c. (below, p. 149). Similarities among the three Kopetra basilicas suggest that later builders looked to this building as a local model.

Other features distinguish the north church from its companions. Most importantly, only in this building do projecting apses instead of inscribed niches face the side aisles. All three apses, moreover, are semicircular in plan and lack the polygonal shell widely used by the mid 6th c. Among the best known mainland examples of salient semicircular apses is the pilgrimage church at Qalat Siman (Butler 1929: 97-105). The form was known earlier in Palestine, but during the 5th c. was more commonly employed in Cyprus;[29] it has even been suggested that such Cypriot churches may in some way have inspired the Syrian builders (Roux 1998: 241-42). Closer to home, three salient semicircular apses appear in the monumental basilica B at Soloi and the Salamis Campanopetra, and at smaller scale in Kourion's suburban basilica. It may be significant that most of these buildings are located in N or central Cyprus and date from the 5th or early 6th c. An early 6th-c. foundation for the north Kopetra church is supported by the *opus sectile* paving of *bema* and central apse — the only example of the technique anywhere in the Vasilikos valley. Colorful glass mosaics in the semidome completed what is known of the sanctuary decoration. The rest of the nave surely was ornamented in some way and the paucity of recovered stucco hints that marble, later salvaged from the site, may also have played a rôle.

The early 6th-c. date proposed for the building agrees with the chronological distribution of pottery at the site. Its location on the upper ridge implies that this may have been the earliest part of the Late Roman settlement, which over time spread south towards Area II (above, p. 37). Subsequent modifications resemble those noted at *Sirmata* and Area II. At least one burial was installed below the narthex paving, immediately in front of the nave door. The S colonnade was at least partially replaced by a rubble wall, either stabilizing a weakened structure or subdividing the nave for other reasons. The floor of the S apse was raised almost 1.0 m above the floor by a rubble packing, and flanking steps or low benches were added to the S aisle's walls. These alterations took place in the late 6th and early 7th c. The basilica was maintained until its superstructure collapsed, probably *c.*650.

The north church was built during the early years of the village, at a time of population and economic growth. By the mid 500s, contact with the Aegean was increasingly evident in the quantities of Phocean Red Slip pottery and amphoras that reached the site. Other Cypriot churches provided the builders with the basic plan for the basilica, the scale of which reflects a significant investment of local resources. Constructed mainly of local materials, the north church saw specialized teams of craftsmen arrive to install the *opus sectile* floor, wall mosaics, and stucco sculpture. However modest by urban standards, in a rural context these measures constituted a monumental initiative whose results shaped the lives of later generations in the valley.

---

29 E.g., Aphendrika Asomatoi, Ayios Philon, Yialousa-*Ayia Trias*, Lambousa, and Lysi.

Fig. 3.55. Area IV, view to N.

AREAS IV AND VI: TWO RESIDENTIAL BUILDINGS

Introduction

Most of our excavation at Kopetra was driven by the need to document the exposed and threatened remains of large public buildings in Areas I, II, and V. During the 1991 season, we carried out limited work in three other sectors in order to broaden our perspective of the site. The choice of excavation areas was guided in part by systematic survey of the ridge but also by practical concerns of access and permission. The absence of activity levels or architectural features at Area III, 75 m east of Area II, indicates that this broad, flat expanse lies beyond the SE limits of settlement (above, p. 43). In exploring the central ridge at Areas IV and VI, by contrast, we found the remains of several other buildings belonging to two distinct residential quarters. Similar domestic structures must cover much of the ridge.

Area IV occupies a field lying *c.*160 m north of Area II and 60 m south of Area V (LV.20.219; figs. 2.4 and 2.8). Excavation for the irrigation pipeline in 1986 encountered floors and walls of several buildings in the vicinity. The following year we systematically surveyed the area, recovering pottery and a large stone weight from an agricultural press. Five square trenches opened south of the pipeline located habitation levels immediately below the present ground surface. The poorly preserved remains apparently belong to two buildings separated by a narrow alleyway. Area VI is situated atop a rocky escarpment located *c.*60 m southwest of Area IV. Surface collection noted a variety of artifacts, including many sherds, rooftiles, mortared stones, and other building débris. Excavation of a pair of 5-m square trenches, later expanded and joined, revealed three or more spaces belonging to a well-built residential complex. The two structures present contrasting approaches to siting, spatial organization, wall construction, and occupation. Excavations were reported briefly in *Muse* 25 (1991) 13-15 and *RDAC* 1994: 296-99 and 301-6.

Area IV: Architectural features and associated deposits

The meager architectural remains of Area IV are known by 5 trenches oriented diagonally to the survey grid and identified as A-E (figs. 3.55-3.57). Walls generally were built of lightly mortared or unmortared rubble and stand to a maximum height of 0.3-0.4 m. Floors are either packed earth or paved with gypsum slabs. Taken as a whole, these structures are among the least substantial at the site. The discovery of stone grinders and press weights on the surface suggests that some agricultural processing took place nearby.

Two long walls run from west to east through the S part of the sector to define the edges of an irregular alley (Trs. C and D). The excavated part of this corridor ranges in width from 1.2 to 1.5 m as it passes between two separate buildings. To the east, the alley either forks or widens into a broad open area. The unroofed alley presents a succession of hard-packed earth surfaces that accumulated over the 6th and early 7th c. (Lots IV-15 and 16).

The unexcavated structure 2 lies south of the alley. Identified wall fragments were built of mortared gypsum and to the west form the edges of a doorway 0.7 m wide without threshold. The associated floor of this covered space is of packed earth.

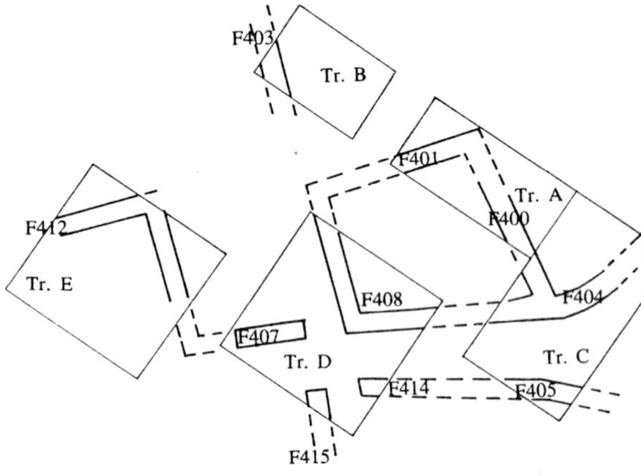

Fig. 3.56. Area IV, trench plan.

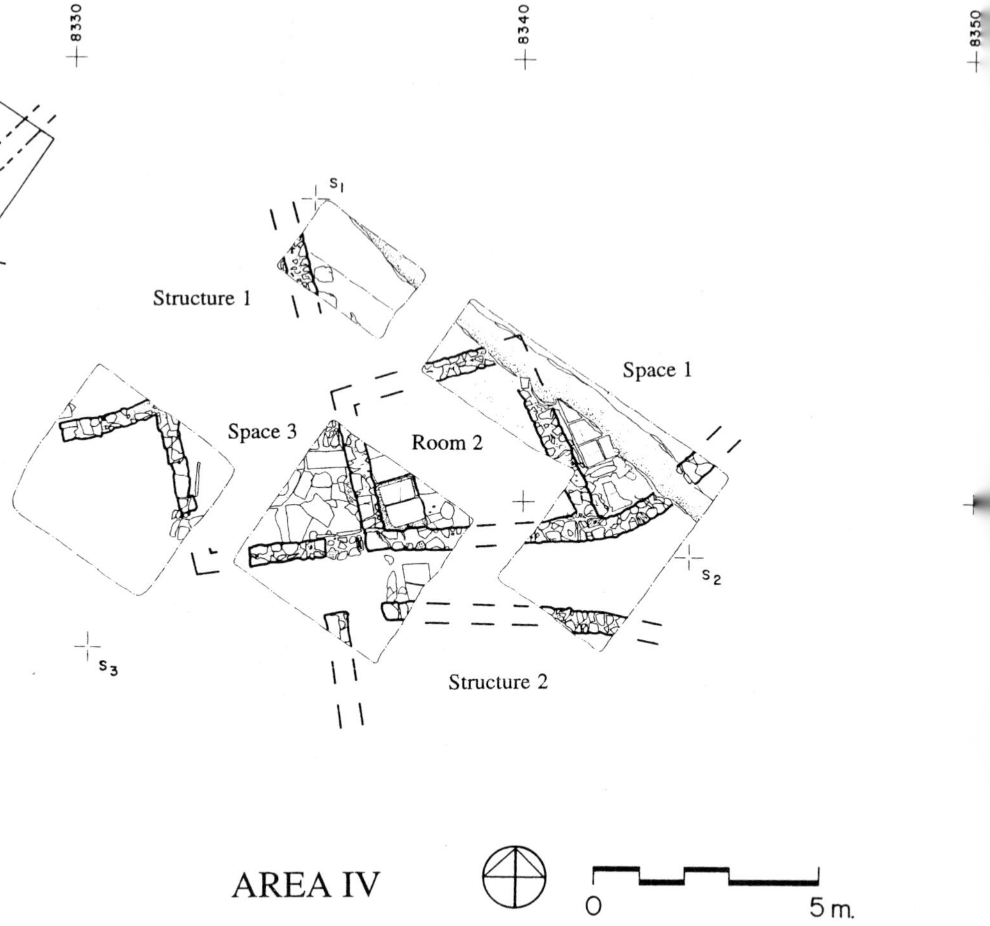

Fig. 3.57. Area IV, state plan.

Structure 1 lies north of the alley. Here we identified several walls belonging to at least three and as many as 6 small spaces, none of which was completely cleared. The two best-understood spaces, 2 and 3, are roughly trapezoidal in plan and lie next to the alley. Space 3 looks onto the alley through a doorway 0.9 m wide located directly opposite the doorway to structure 2 (Trs. D and E). The space is *c.*3.5 m wide and continues north beyond the limit of excavation, giving it an interior area of at least 13 m^2. As an entryway, space 3 may have been left partially unroofed. A layer of gypsum slabs, much disturbed and worn, covers the floor. The relatively slight walls consist of rubble gypsum and fieldstone set in a mud mortar; they average 0.4-0.5 m thick. The doorway jambs are neatly squared with larger stones. The doorway itself lacks any threshold and was blocked with rubble fill during a later phase, when the gypsum floor was covered with earth (Lot IV-10; *RDAC* 1994: pl. LXXXI.3). Building débris filled the room at some point in the 7th c. (Lot IV-9).

Room 2 lies immediately east of space 3 (Trs. A, C, and D). This irregularly shaped room measures 3.5-4.2 x 3.0-3.8 m. No doorway was identified but it may have been accessible from the north. A small basin (1.0 x 0.8 m) of uncertain function was set in the SW corner of the room (Tr. D). The basin is lined with plaster and drains through a narrow opening in the S wall into the alley (fig. 3.58). Next to the basin lie several closely-fitted gypsum slabs, indicating that this interior room was originally paved. Fragmentary cuttings and signs of wear on this surface, together with pressing equipment in the area, suggest that the basin may have served for processing agricultural products. No diagnostic artifact was recovered (Lots IV-6, 7, 8).

Space 1 lies immediately east of room 2 at the apparent corner of the alley (Trs. A and C). The irrigation pipeline cut a swathe 0.7 m wide diagonally through this space, extending northwest from the alley (fig. 3.59). Despite this disturbance, the SW corner of space 1 preserved a series of levels probably dating to the 6th and 7th c. (Lots IV-3, 4, 5). A layer of charcoal and ash located between surfaces may belong to a moment

Fig. 3.58. Area IV, room 2 with basin (left) and space 3 (right), view to S

Fig. 3.59. Area IV, stratigraphic section at Tr. A-C, view to W.

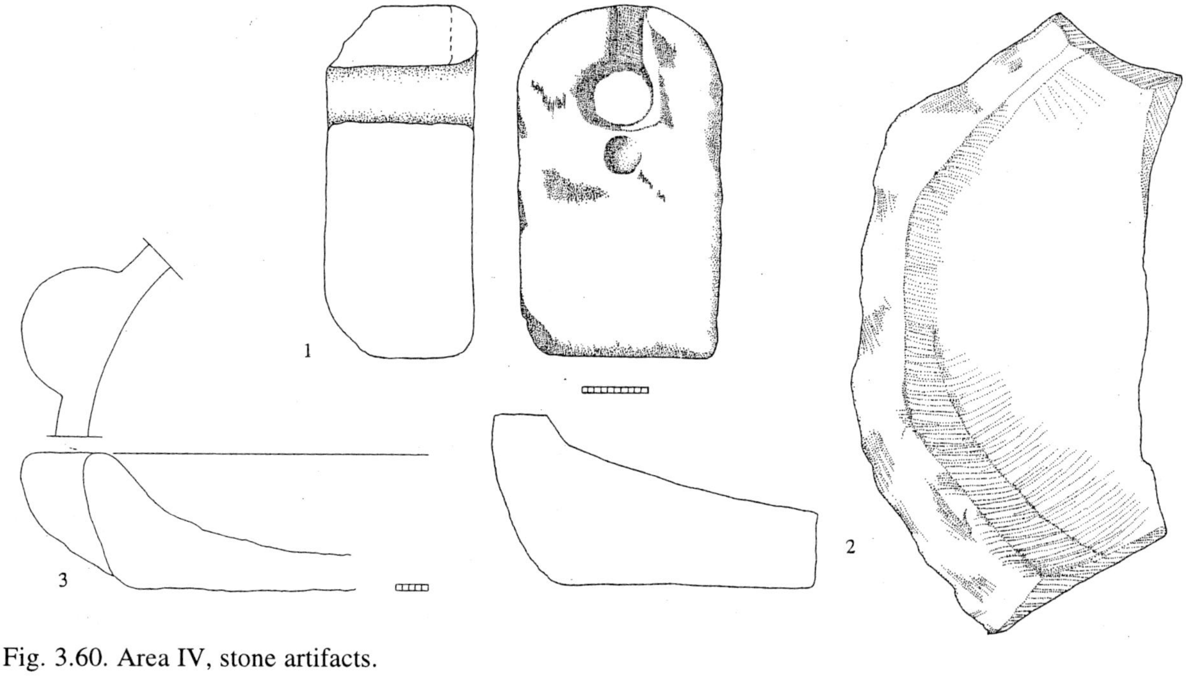

Fig. 3.60. Area IV, stone artifacts.

of destruction. Fragments of a handmade cooking pot recovered from the latest levels, perhaps associated with a small hearth in the SW corner, suggest it was still being used around the mid 7th c. (Lot IV-2). Scant remains indicate the presence of three other spaces (Trs. B, E; Lots IV-11, 12, and 13).

Few diagnostic artifacts were found in these irregularly organized spaces. Despite a scattering of fine wares on the surface, very few pieces were found in occupation levels. Excavated pottery was dominated by amphoras, which made up over half of the finds (Table 3.18; *RDAC* 1994: 298 Table 2). More helpful was the surface discovery of two stone press weights and part of a stone crushing basin (fig. 3.60 nos. 1-2). A large fragment of another shallow stone bowl or crushing basin (fig. 3.60 no. 3) was found built into the alley wall of structure 1. These large objects, together with several ground stone implements and the preponderance of storage jars (amphoras, *pithoi*), confirm the utilitarian character of the buildings, whose occupants apparently engaged in small-scale industry and processing of field crops.

Area IV: Inventoried artifacts by Lot

Roman pottery from Area IV is summarized in Table 3.18.

Lot IV-1: Topsoil

Date range: mostly 6th to 7th c.

Catalogued objects:

5 Cypriot Red Slip form 1/2

184 Cooking ware A pot

246 Glass juglet

276 Glass goblet?

Additional objects:

Fig. 3.60.1. Press weight. Oblong rectangular sandstone block with rounded upper end. P. l. 0.54, w. 0.30, th. 0.23. A hole (diam. 0.10 m), recessed to accommodate suspension cords, pierces the upper end. Surface; left in field. Cf. Hadjisavvas 1992: 7-16, 60, type 1(a). *RDAC* 1994: 297, pl. LXXXI.2.

Not inventoried (not illustrated). Press weight. Elongated calcarenite fragment preserving part of round hole at one end. P. l. 1.05. Surface; left in field.

Fig. 3.60.2. Crushing basin. P. l. 0.94, w. 0.48. Approximately half of a broad, shallow calcarenite basin with an original diameter of perhaps 1.2 m. Crudely hollowed bowl; back and sides unfinished. Surface; left in field. *RDAC* 1994: 297, pl. LXXX.2.

See also fig. 2.12.3.

Lot IV-2: Space 1, collapse

Approximate date: mid 7th c.

Catalogued object:

196 Cooking ware C pot

Additional object:

Not inventoried. Plain ware A bowl. Tr. C 2.1. *RDAC* 1994: 297-99 no. 18, fig. 6.

Diorite pounder (not illustrated). Max. w. 0.114. Tr. C 2.1, KK94-38.

Lot IV-3: Space 1, second-phase use

Approximate date: inconclusive (7th c.?).

Lot IV-4: Space 1, first-phase use

Approximate date: inconclusive (late 6th/early 7th c.?).

Lot IV-5: Space 1, below paved floor

Approximate date: inconclusive.

Additional object:

Not inventoried (not illustrated). Large iron nail. Max. l. 0.13, th. 0.014. Tr. C 6.2.

Lot IV-6: Room 2, collapse

Approximate date: inconclusive (7th c.?).

Lot IV-7: Room 2, first-phase floor

Approximate date: inconclusive (7th c.?).

Lot IV-8: Room 2, below first phase

Approximate date: inconclusive (late 6th/early 7th c.?).

Lot IV-9: Space 3, collapse

Approximate date: inconclusive (7th c.?).

Additional object:

Not inventoried. *Pithos* group A jar. Tr. D 3.2. *RDAC* 1994: 299 no. 21, fig. 6.

Lot IV-10: Space 3, second-phase use

Approx. date: early 7th c. (Cypriot Red Slip form 9C).

Lot IV-11: Unidentified W space, collapse

Approximate date: inconclusive (mid 7th c.?).

Lot IV-12: Unidentified NE space, collapse

Approximate date: inconclusive (mid 7th c.?)

Catalogued object:

183 Cooking ware A pot (also Lot IV-13)

Lot IV-13: Unidentified NE space, below paved floor

Approximate date: inconclusive (7th c.?).

Catalogued object:

183 Cooking ware A pot (also Lot IV-12)

Additional object:

Diorite pounder (not illustrated). Max. w. 0.098. Tr. B 4.1, KK94-42.

Lot IV-14: Alley, collapse

Approximate date: inconclusive (7th c.?).

Lot IV-15: Alley, upper surface

Approximate date: early to mid 7th c. (Cypriot Red Slip form 9A).

Catalogued object:

286 Glass goblet/lamp

Lot IV-16: Alley, lower surface

Approx. date: early 7th c. (Cypriot Red Slip form 9C).

Additional object:

Not inventoried. Cypriot Red Slip form 9A. Tr. C 4.1. *RDAC* 1994: 297 no. 16, fig. 6.

TABLE 3.18. SUMMARY OF ROMAN POTTERY FROM AREA IV

Area IV	*rim*	*base*	*handle*	*sherd*	*sum*	*weight*	*avg. sherd wt.*
Fine	11	1		8	20	525	26.25
Plain	5	2	1	38	46	1595	34.67
Amphora	9	1	46	536	592	15785	26.67
Cook	23		10	126	159	1415	8.90
Pithos	20	3	2	142	167	15255	91.35
Other		3	2	57	62	980	15.81
ROMAN TOTAL	68	10	61	907	1046	35555	33.99
	rim	*base*	*handle*	*sherd*	*sum*		
CRS 2	1				1		
CRS 9A	2				2		
CRS 9C	4				4		
CRS 10	1				1		
CRS other		1		4	5		
CRS TOTAL	8	1		4	13		
LRC other	1			4	5		
ARS 104	1				1		
Other	1				1		
FINE TOTAL	11	1		8	20		
	rim	*base*	*handle*	*sherd*	*sum*	*weight*	
LR1	8		39	328	375	10380	
LR2	1		3	13	17	915	
LR3				1	1	10	
LR4				10	10	300	
LR5/6				54	54	960	
LR7		1	1	15	17	690	
KAmp1				6	6	75	
KAmp2			1	19	20	370	
KAmp4				1	1	40	
KAmp5				10	10	240	
Other			2	79	81	1805	
AMPHORA TOTAL	9	1	46	536	592	15785	
Plain A	1				1	5	
Plain B		1		3	4	40	
Plain C				1	1	10	
Plain D	4	1	1	34	40	1540	
PLAIN TOTAL	5	2	1	38	46	1595	
Cook A	3		3	5	11	170	
Cook C	1		1	6	8	430	
Cook D	19		6	115	140	815	
Cook total	23		10	126	159	1415	
Pithos A	4				4	1605	
Pithos B	6	2		15	23	5730	
Pithos C	1			2	3	615	
Pithos D	9	1	2	125	137	7305	
PITHOS TOTAL	20	3	2	142	167	15255	

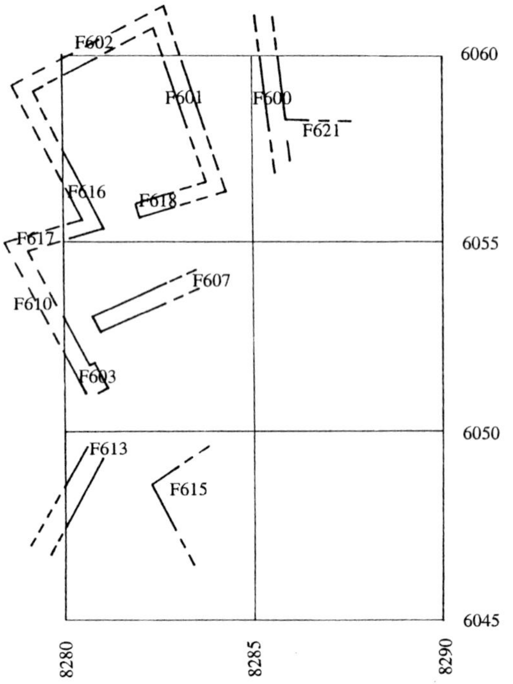

Fig. 3.61. Area VI, trench plan.

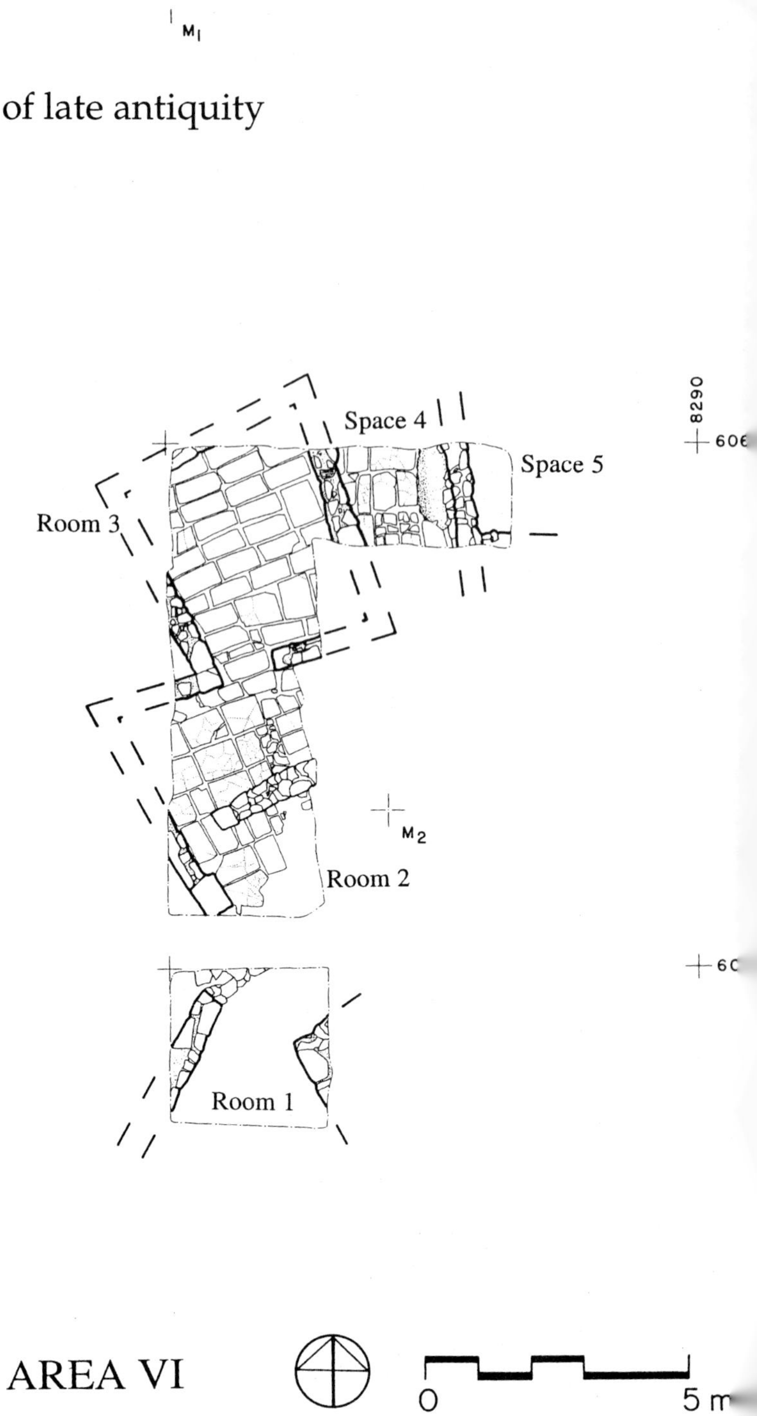

Fig. 3.62. Area VI, state plan.

Area VI: Architectural features and associated deposits

Located at a higher level *c.*60 m to the southwest, the more substantial remains of Area VI embody an altogether different kind of habitation (figs. 3.61-3.64). Survey of this area noted a broad variety of material, including abundant fine wares and amphoras as well as building débris. Trial excavation of two 5-m trenches found well preserved walls just below the ploughzone; these trenches were expanded and joined to expose a total of *c.*43 m^2 of a multi-level building complex. Walls generally were carefully built of mortared gypsum and fieldstone and surrounded paved rooms. Most of these rooms saw two main periods of use before the superstructure collapsed around the mid 7th c. (figs. 3.65-3.66).

Room 1 lies at the S edge of the sector, where a 5-m trench located two converging walls (8280/6050). The well-built E wall, while mostly embedded in the E scarp, apparently turns northeast to form the S edge of room 2. The oblique orientation of the W wall (0.5 m thick) suggests that this may have been a later addition that eventually joined the W wall of room 2. Only the upper walls were exposed in this trench and no clear surface was reached.

A doorway 1.5 m wide opens from room 1 onto the SW corner of room 2, a large trapezoidal space lying immediately to the north (8280/6055). Three of this room's surrounding walls are known from the identified

Fig. 3.63. Area VI, view to N.

Fig. 3.64. Area VI, rooms 2 and 3, view to E.

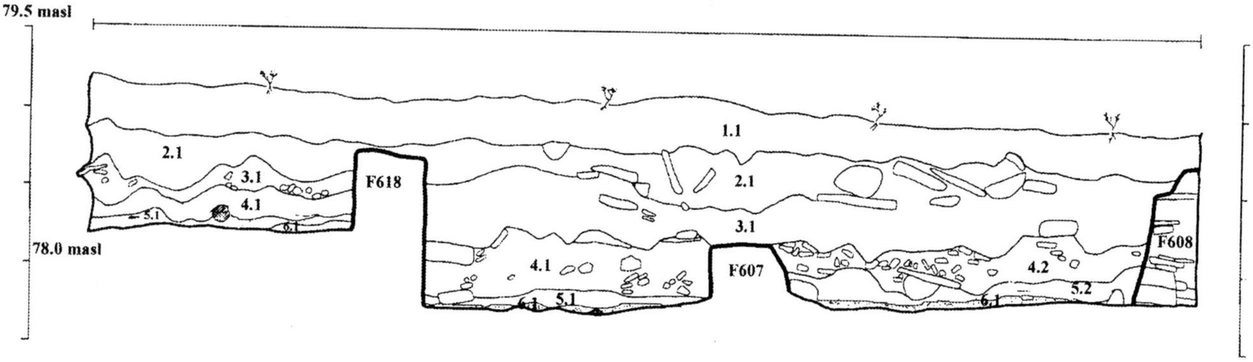

Fig. 3.65. Area VI, stratigraphic section at 8280/6058-6060, view to E.

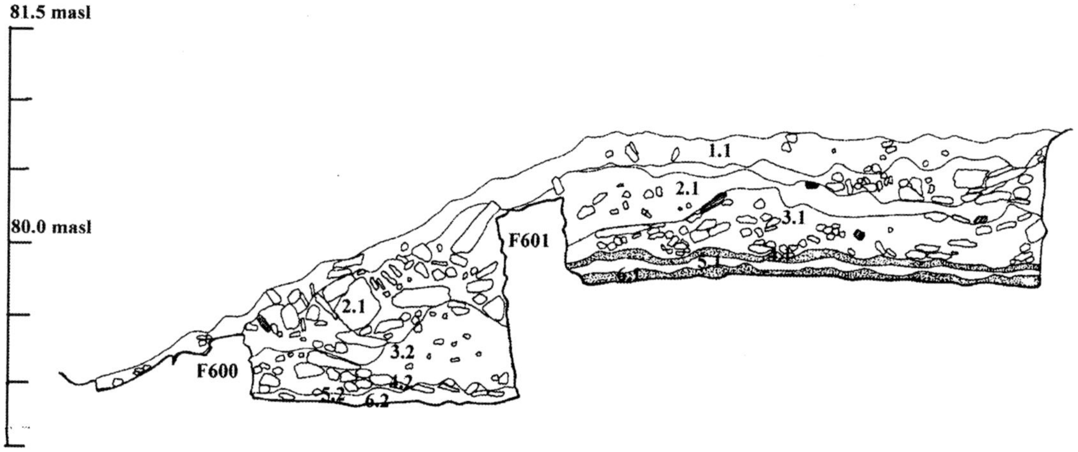

Fig. 3.66. Area VI, stratigraphic section at 8280/6060, view to S.

remains, which establish a maximum length of 6.5 m and a minimum width of 4.5 m, for an enclosed area of perhaps 30 m^2. The space was paved with gypsum slabs, which are better preserved in the N half. Traces of a low bench, consisting of flat gypsum slabs set atop the leveled marl, were found against the W wall. The large area and scarcity of rooftiles in the fill suggest that room 2 may have been an unroofed court.

Room 2 was modified on at least one occasion. The clearest evidence of its late use is the construction of a flimsy rubble wall, 0.4-0.5-m thick, directly atop the gypsum floor. The partition extends across the room leaving a passage 0.7 m wide at its W end. Fragments of a Cypriot Red Slip dish (form 9) recovered near floor level (Lots VI-10, 15) indicate that the room was open in the late 6th or early 7th c. The collapse of the building's superstructure apparently included part of an upper floor above the adjacent room 3. This was accompanied by widespread burning, with several ashy layers containing the remains of charred walnut beams. A good deposit of mid 7th-c. material (Lot VI-5) can be associated with this destruction. Among the recovered artifacts are a follis of Heraclius datable to 629/630 (**C7**), fragments of a Cypriot Red Slip dish (form 9B), several glass vessels including a hexagonal bottle (**271**), various plain table wares, and a large storage jar.

Room 3 lies immediately to the north and faces onto room 2 through a doorway 1.0 m wide without a separate threshold (8280/6058, 8280/6060). The southward aspect looking onto an open court resembles the preferred arrangement of traditional Cypriot houses, and would have taken advantage of the sun and afternoon sea-breeze from the lower valley (Christodoulou 1959: 66; Ionas 1988). This trapezoidal space measures 4.0 m long by 3.0 m wide, for a total area of *c.*12 m^2. Surrounding walls were carefully built of mortared gypsum fragments (average width 0.5 m) and stand over 1 m high; the collapsed superstructure indicates that gypsum and fieldstone construction continued into an upper room to a height of at least 3 m. This may have resembled the use of stone as high as second-storey window-sills in some traditional island houses, with upper walls built of mudbricks and wood beams (Sinos 1984: 335-37). Room 3 was carefully paved with gypsum slabs, laid in uneven rows extending from east to west, at a level slightly above the surface of room 2. Two levels of collapse suggest that an upper storey stood above room 3 as late as the mid 7th c.

Excavation of room 3 noted one or two levels of burning (Lots VI-13, 14) close to its paved surface. The lower level of the ensuing collapse (Lot VI-11) includes objects presumably coming from room 3 itself, such as two Cypriot Red Slip dishes (forms 9B, 9C), 4 glass vessels, and various plain wares. The upper level of architectural débris (Lot VI-6; *RDAC* 1994: pl. LXXXIII.2) included an uneven layer of gypsum slabs apparently from an upper storey; this also spread into the N part of room 2 and is continuous with Lot VI-5 (e.g., **271**). This context includes another follis of Heraclius (**C5**, issued 611-613), more glass, a ceramic mortarium (**103**), and two examples of handmade cooking pots (**193**, **195**). Taken together, these deposits date the collapse of the most substantial part of this complex to the middle of the 7th c.

Along the E side of room 3 the ground drops away sharply to the level of the lower field (8280/6060). Excavation of a step trench across this slope identified space 4, a narrow area with a paved surface lying *c.*1 m below the floor of room 3. A short section of another N-S wall was found immediately to the east. Running parallel with the N-S escarpment, these walls belong to a narrow corridor stretching along the E edge of rooms 2 and 3. The presence of a gypsum surface and a shallow sub-floor drain next to the E wall suggests that this was an interior passageway that stood in the shadow of a raised terrace to the west. At least one more space, identified on fig. 3.62 as space 5, flanked this low corridor to the east.

The construction and early use of space 4, like the rest of the complex, remain poorly understood (Lots VI-17 and 18). Evidence of secondary occupation (Lot VI-16) includes small fragments of two African Red Slip bowls (forms 93 and 107) datable to the late 6th or early 7th c. Two Cypriot Red Slip dishes (form 9C, well form), an African Red Slip bowl (form 105), and several table vessels of glass and unslipped pottery were found among débris associated with the room's mid 7th-c. collapse (Lot VI-12). The presence of another handmade cooking pot (**194**) within the upper collapse (Lot VI-7) suggests that some of this material was once used above room 3.

Area VI: Pottery and other inventoried artifacts by lot

Roman pottery from Area VI is summarized in Table 3.19.

Lot VI-1: Topsoil

Date range: mostly 6th-7th c.

Catalogued object:

106 Plain ware A jug

Lot VI-2: Upper collapse, disturbed

Approximate date: 7th c.?

Catalogued object:

C6 Follis, Heraclius, 612/13, Cyzicus

Additional object:

Diorite pounder/mortar (not illustrated). Max. w. 0.115. 8280/6050 2.1, KK94-44.

TABLE 3.19. SUMMARY OF ROMAN POTTERY FROM AREA VI

Area VI	*rim*	*base*	*handle*	*sherd*	*sum*	*weight*	*avg. sherd wt.*
Fine	25	11		15	51	1200	23.53
Plain	24	25	8	176	233	6945	29.81
Amphora	63	3	78	1923	2067	69710	33.73
Cook	33		12	254	299	6470	21.64
Pithos	14	4		113	131	20355	155.38
Other		1		119	120	1910	15.92
ROMAN TOTAL	159	44	98	2600	2901	106590	36.74
	rim	*base*	*handle*	*sherd*	*sum*		
CRS 3	1				1		
CRS 9		2		1	3		
CRS 9A	1				1		
CRS 9B	3	2			5		
CRS 9C	6	1		1	8		
CRS 11	1				1		
CRS other	1	2		7	10		
CRS total	13	7		9	29		
LRC 3	1				1		
LRC 3F	3				3		
LRC 3G	1				1		
LRC 10	4	2			6		
LRC other				5	5		
LRC total	9	2		5	16		
ARS 105	1				1		
ARS 107	1				1		
ARS other	1	2		1	4		
ARS TOTAL	3	2		1	6		
FINE TOTAL	25	11		15	51		
	rim	*base*	*handle*	*sherd*	*sum*	*weight*	
LR1	50	3	55	1456	1564	51425	
LR2				8	8	155	
LR4	5		12	205	222	8925	
LR5/6	6		3	131	140	5110	
LR7				5	5	165	
KAmp1				4	4	200	
KAmp2	1		2	28	31	1105	
KAmp5				5	5	85	
Other	1		6	81	88	2540	
AMPHORA TOTAL	63	3	78	1923	2067	69710	
Plain A	4	3		15	22	520	
Plain B	12	5	1	93	111	2215	
Plain C				1	1	10	
Plain D	8	17	7	67	99	4200	
PLAIN TOTAL	24	25	8	176	233	6945	
Cook A	1			22	23	160	
Cook C	22		5	79	106	4840	
Cook D	10		7	153	170	1470	
COOK TOTAL	33		12	254	299	6470	
Pithos A	2			5	7	1605	
Pithos B	4			27	31	4340	
Pithos C	3	1		32	36	6310	
Pithos D	5	3		49	57	8100	
PITHOS TOTAL	14	4		113	131	20355	

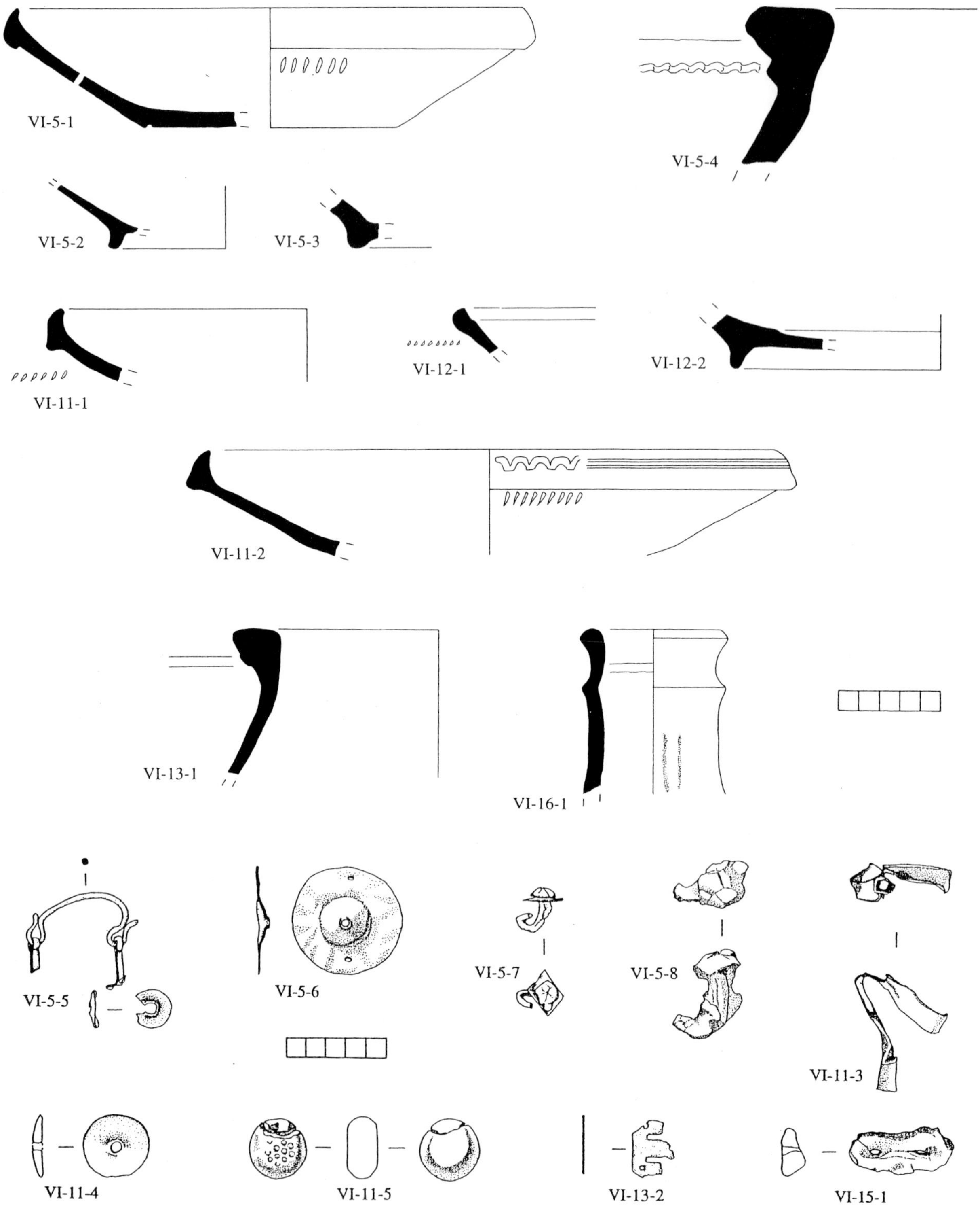

Fig. 3.67. Area VI, context artifacts.

Lot VI-3: Upper collapse

Approximate date: 7th c.?

Catalogued objects:

186 Cooking ware A pot

311 Glass window pane

Lot VI-4: Room 1, upper collapse

Approximate date: mid 7th c. (Cypriot Red Slip form 9A; Phocean Red Slip form 3F).

Additional objects:

Not inventoried (not illustrated). Diorite pounder. Max. w. 0.116. 8280/6050 3.1.

Not inventoried (not illustrated). Two fragments of small iron spatula(?) with slender handle, flat oval bowl with slightly raised edge; badly corroded. Max. l. 0.045, w. 0.019; max. l. 0.033, w. 0.010. 8280/6050 3.1.

Lot VI-5: Room 2, upper collapse

Approximate date: mid 7th c. (Cypriot Red Slip form 9B).

Catalogued objects:

C7 Follis, Heraclius, 629/630, Constantinople
95 Plain ware A basin (also Lot VI-10)
120 Plain ware B jug
136 Plain ware D amphoriskos
144 LR1 amphora
259 Glass flask
271 Glass hexagonal bottle (also Lots VI-6 and 10)
277 Glass stemmed goblet

Additional objects (fig. 3.67):

VI-5-1. Dish, Cypriot Red Slip form 9B. Est. diam. rim 0.25; est. diam. base 0.13. Fine-grained light red fabric (2.5YR 6/6) with a little lime. Exterior wall rouletted, slipped; rim fired off-white. 8280/6055 4.1, KK93-3.

VI-5-2. Small jar/jug, plain ware B. Est. diam. base 0.11. Medium-grained light red fabric (2.5YR 6/6) with a little lime. 8280/6055 4.1.

VI-5-3. Jar/jug, plain ware D. Est. diam. base 0.13. Medium-grained reddish yellow fabric (7.5YR 7/4-7/6) with lime, quartz, and a little mica. 8280/6055 4.1.

VI-5-4. Storage jar, *pithos* group C. Est. diam. rim 0.27. Coarse-grained light red fabric (2.5YR 5/6-6/6) with brown exterior surface; abundant lime, quartz, and other dark inclusions. Heavy triangular rim with a single band of impressed decoration around neck. 8280/6055 4.1.

VI-5-5. Bronze wire handle with attached anchors. Handle round in section, looped at both ends. Found together with small discoid handle-guard(?). Max. diam. 0.055. 8280/6055 4.1, KK91-24. *RDAC* 1994: 306 no. 41, fig. 10. Cf. Chavane 1975: 34 no. 101, pl. 12.

VI-5-6. Bronze handle-guard with conical center, pierced; two smaller nail holes on flange. Diam. 0.055. 8280/6055 4.1, KK91-27. *RDAC* 1994: 306 no. 42, fig. 10.

VI-5-7. Small iron nail, square in section, perforating a small square of bronze. Max. l. 0.033, w. 0.018. 8280/6055 4.1, KK91-28.

VI-5-8. Small iron nail. Max. l. 0.035, th. 0.020. 8280/6055 4.1, KK91-32.

Lot VI-6: Room 3, upper collapse

Approximate date: mid 7th c. (Cypriot Red Slip form 9C).

Catalogued objects:

C5 Follis, Heraclius, 611-613, Nicomedia
103 Plain ware A mortarium
142 LR1 amphora
193 Cooking ware C pot (also Lot VI-7)
194 Cooking ware C pot (also Lot VI-7)
195 Cooking ware C pot
270 Glass bottle
271 Glass hexagonal bottle (also Lots VI-5, 10)
273 Glass stemmed goblet

Additional objects:

Not inventoried (not illustrated). Numerous fragments of vesicular basalt. 8280/6060 3.1.

Lot VI-7: Space 4, upper collapse

Approximate date: mid 7th c. (Cypriot Red Slip forms 9B and 9C).

Catalogued objects:

26 Cypriot Red Slip form 9C
193 Cooking ware C pot (also Lot VI-6)
194 Cooking ware C pot (also Lot VI-6)

Lot VI-8: Space 5, upper collapse

Approximate date: inconclusive (mid 7th c.?).

Lot VI-9: Room 1, lower collapse

Approximate date: early to mid 7th c.

Catalogued objects:

233 Glass bowl
244 Glass bowl

Lot VI-10: Room 2, burning above second-phase surface

Approximate date: mid 7th c.?

Catalogued objects:

95 Plain ware A basin (also Lot VI-5)
135 Plain ware D pitcher
271 Glass hexagonal bottle (also Lots VI-5 and 6)

Lot VI-11: Room 3, lower collapse

Approximate date: mid 7th c.

Catalogued objects:

129 Plain ware D jar
134 Plain ware D bowl
153 LR5/6 amphora
198 Cooking ware D pot
257 Glass flask
258 Glass flask
269 Glass bottle
295 Glass stemmed lamp

Additional objects (fig. 3.67):

VI-11-1. Dish, Cypriot Red Slip form 9B. Est. diam. rim 0.24. Fine-grained light red fabric (2.5YR 6/6) with scattered lime. Interior slip streaked; exterior wall and rim fired off-white. 8280/6058 4.1. *RDAC* 1994: 303 no. 30, fig. 10.

VI-11-2. Dish, Cypriot Red Slip form 9C. Est. diam. rim 0.28. Fine-grained light reddish brown fabric (5YR 6/4) with scattered lime. Thickened vertical rim with two grooves and incised short wavy line. 8280/6058 4.1, KK93-9.

VI-11-3. Fragment of bronze wick-holder preserving tube and single suspension arm. Max. l. 0.060, w. 0.045. 8280/6058 4.1, KK91-21. Cf. **V-2-1**.

VI-11-4. Pierced gypsum disk with drilled hole at center; spindle whorl or loom weight(?). Diam. 0.032, max. th. 0.005. 8280/6060 4.1, KK91-37.

VI-11-5. Gypsum plaster token with faint raised dots. Diam. 0.029, th. 0.025. 8280/6058 4.1, KK91-38.

Not inventoried (not illustrated). Numerous fragments of vesicular basalt. 8280/6058 4.1.

Lot VI-12: Space 4, lower collapse

Approximate date: mid 7th c. (Cypriot Red Slip form 9C).

Catalogued objects:

107 Plain ware A jug

108 Plain ware A jug

109 Plain ware A jug

116 Plain ware B dish

124 Plain ware B jug

254 Glass flask

272 Glass stemmed goblet

280 Glass stemmed goblet

Additional objects (fig. 3.67):

VI-12-1. Dish, Cypriot Red Slip well form. Diam. rim uncertain. Medium-grained light red fabric (2.5YR 6/6) with scattered lime, small voids; faint exterior rouletting. *RDAC* 1994: 303 no. 28, fig. 10. 8280/6060 4.2.

VI-12-2. Dish, African Red Slip 105. Est. diam. base 0.20. Medium-grained red fabric (2.5YR 6/8) with fine lime and quartz to 0.002. Hard red slip (2.5YR 5/6) on floor. 8280/6060 4.2.

Lot VI-13: Room 3, upper burning

Approximate date: inconclusive (mid 7th c.?).

Catalogued objects:

228 Glass unguentarium

268 Glass bottle

Additional objects (fig. 3.67):

VI-13-1. Storage jar, *pithos* group D. Est. diam. rim 0.18. Coarse-grained reddish brown fabric (about 5YR 4/3) with abundant lime, quartz, other dark inclusions. Curved wall with triangular rim. 8280/6058 5.1.

VI-13-2. Flat bronze attachment with 2 small rectangular perforations; traces of 3 nailholes survive. P. l. 0.029, w. 0.021, th. 0.001. 8280/6058 5.1, KK91-23.

Lot VI-14: Room 3, lower burning

Approximate date: inconclusive (mid 7th c.?).

Lot VI-15: Room 2, second-phase surface

Approximate date: early 7th c. (Cypriot Red Slip form 9).

Additional object (fig. 3.67):

VI-15-1. Small flattened iron loop, perhaps from a chain; badly corroded. 8280/6055 5.2, KK91-30.

Lot VI-16: Space 4, second-phase surface

Approximate date: early 7th c. (African Red Slip form 107).

Catalogued object:

67 African Red Slip 93

Additional object (fig. 3.67):

VI-16-1. LR1 amphora. Est. diam. rim 0.06. Medium-grained light red fabric (2.5YR 6.6) with darker yellow exterior surface, abundant lime, quartz, and other small inclusions. Dark red slip applied to rim and neck. 8280/6060 5.1.

Lot VI-17: Space 4, first-phase use

Approximate date: inconclusive.

Lot VI-18: Space 4, first-phase floor

Approximate date: inconclusive.

Chronological summary and significance

The building remains at Areas IV and VI offer contrasting views of residential life near the middle of the village at Kopetra. Area IV evidently served a number of utilitarian purposes — agricultural, industrial, and residential — during the late 6th and early 7th c. Identified features occupy a flat area on the central ridge. Slender walls enclose small, irregularly-shaped spaces that opened onto a narrow alley. The presence of medium-size stone weights and pressing beds suggests that these buildings were also the scene of grape or olive processing, and perhaps the manufacture of domestic crafts (cf. Hadjisavvas 1988: 111-20; id. 1992). By contrast, Area VI was occupied by a more monumental structure with a suite of sturdy rooms arranged on multiple levels. These spaces were used over several generations, with repairs and modifications respecting the original paved floors. Plentiful pottery and several coins attest the late date of activities. Fine ceramic and glass wares suggest that the building's occupants may have held special status in the community. The terraced arrangement of small spaces would be appropriate for a private residence, perhaps of a local landowner.

These poorly understood buildings belong to a vernacular tradition that reached across Cyprus and the E Mediterranean, surviving from late antiquity[30] until fairly recent times.[31] Terrain and geomorphology strongly influenced the siting and organization of simple structures. Using cheap, locally-available materials, builders set up small clusters of trapezoidal spaces combining covered rooms with open courts. Stone walls were founded directly atop the local marl, sometimes retaining bedrock as footing for steps or benches. Rising walls were more regular and carefully assembled at Area VI; both buildings may have used mudbrick in their upper parts. Rooms were closed by wood doors anchored in flanking wall spurs without special thresholds

30 E.g., Catling 1972: 6-9; Christou 1994: 689-91; Fejfer 1995: 78-86; Hirschfeld 1997; Toumazou *et al.* 1998.

31 Christodoulou 1959: 64-69; Sinos 1984: 335-37; Ionas 1988; Aurenche *et al.* 1993.

or jambs, and often were paved with gypsum slabs. Interior rooms were roughly 12-13 m^2 in area, with courts being somewhat larger. Clear spans measured at least 3.0-3.5 m, similar to traditional Cypriot building practice since the Middle Ages.[32] Upper rooms had gypsum floors and looked onto interior courts and across nearby alleys. Roofs were made of packed earth, flat gypsum panels, or terracotta tiles supported by timber beams, and were gently sloped if not actually pitched. Both buildings were located within the settlement's perimeter and offered no obvious provisions for animals. Evidence of household production at Area IV suggests a kind of economic output by one family that was not apparent for their neighbors at Area VI.

The occupants themselves remain largely unknown. The Area IV building comprised at least three rooms with an average area of over 13 m^2; most of the rooms at Area VI are similar. Presumably a single family occupied each residence. For comparative purposes it can be noted that in 1946 Cypriot village populations averaged 2.08 persons per room (significantly greater than the 1.52 persons per room observed in towns), with a median household size of 3.69 persons. Of rural households, 37.4% occupied a single-room dwelling, 35.8% lived in two rooms, 16.1% lived in three rooms, and 10.7% occupied 4 or more rooms, often with animals stabled nearby (Christodoulou 1959: 64). Such data, despite their obvious limitations, illustrate the modest well-being enjoyed by at least some of the residents of Late Roman Kopetra.

The later history of the buildings at Areas IV and VI follows the sequence met in the churches. Apparently built in the 6th c., all were continuously occupied and saw occasional repairs, subdivisions, and renovations extending into the early 7th c. Like the churches, these residential structures were badly damaged *c.*650, in some cases accompanied by fire, and their walls and roofs collapsed. The presence of a few handmade cooking vessels amid the débris at Areas IV and VI indicates that these areas continued to be inhabited as late as the eve of the Arab campaigns. Lacking clear signs of subsequent activity, this part of the site was left undisturbed by those villagers who remained.

THE APSE MOSAICS (by L. Benson and M. Rautman)

Excavation at Areas II and V recovered substantial evidence of fine mosaics from the superstructures of these two churches. At both sectors tesserae were found in greatest quantity near floor level in the vicinity of the sanctuary, within and immediately in front of the apse. Most tesserae were loosely scattered within the soil matrix, but a number of mortared fragments with embedded tesserae were preserved as well. The limited distribution of mosaics within each sector and the clearly preserved curvature of the larger fragments suggest that they originally belonged to the decoration of the central apses.

The extensive exposure of the south church (Area II) produced *c.*600 fragments of mosaics. While most preserved only a few tesserae in their mortar bedding, it is clear that a significant part of the original apse mosaic (diameter almost 3.6 m) was missing from the collapsed débris. The mosaic's original appearance is unknowable, yet its remains illustrate many technical aspects of Cypriot production.

The matrix of the south church's apse mosaic consists of the local gypsum plaster applied in two main layers: the primary underlayer and the setting bed. The underlayer (occasionally comprising two distinct strata) consists of a rather coarse-grained, yellowish gypsum plaster that was applied directly to the masonry surface. This averages 4-5 cm thick and probably was anchored by iron or wood pegs set in mortar. Chopped straw and grass, attested by impressions left in many fragments, helped solidify the underlayer and lessen its mass.[33] By contrast, the outer setting bed was made of a fine-grained and dense white plaster. This was applied in a relatively uniform layer 1.7-1.9 cm thick into which tesserae were directly set. Some bedding fragments have a plain finished edge that meets the tesselated surface at an oblique angle.

The wet surface of the setting bed was painted with broad areas of color approximating the motifs to be filled with tesserae. Some of the preserved fragments show a limited range of colors: primarily yellow, light to medium green, light red, brownish red, and light purple.[34] Individual tesserae were gently pressed into the soft painted plaster. Some areas reveal special care in the precise shaping and close placement of tesserae, but in other, less carefully-rendered sections the painted plaster appears plainly. The combined effect of paint and widely spaced tesserae would have been most appropriate for broad expanses of background in which the

32 Sinos 1986: 521-22 and 533; Ionas 1988: 47-53.

33 Cf. Megaw and Hawkins 1977: 132-36. No crushed brick or pottery was observed in this preparatory coating, as noted at Saraçhane; Harrison and Gill 1986: 183.

34 Cf. the range at Lythrankomi and Saraçhane; Megaw and Hawkins 1977: 132; Harrison and Gill 1986: 183-84.

paint formed part of the finished scheme. Some fragments preserve a painted surface 2 cm wide with bevelled edge; they probably formed part of the apse border.

Individual tesserae were cut of glass and stone, the latter comprising *c.*12% of the total at the south church. Glass tesserae are either translucent or opaque. Most pieces are trapezoidal or rectangular on their largest side, but less regular shapes were used to fill irregular design spaces. Glass tesserae were consistently smaller in size (on average 0.8 x 0.9 x 0.6 cm, weighing 0.3-0.7 g), while stone pieces tended to be slightly larger (1.0 x 0.8 x 0.65 cm, and 0.7-1.0 g).

Over 20 colors can be distinguished among the tesserae from Area II and the original range was probably broader.[35] Some of the glass tesserae have suffered partial oxidation and decay, a process that has altered or completely obscured their original colors. This deterioration may have been encouraged by the rather poor, bubbly quality of the glass used. The colors summarized in Table 3.20 occur in sufficient quantities to identify them as close to their original appearance. Translucent glass tesserae are yellow-amber, green, pink, light blue, and clear. Some of the translucent yellow-amber and clear tesserae have a thin layer of gold foil just under the upper exposed surface; no silver-capped tesserae were noted. Opaque glass tesserae include blue, light blue, greenish-blue, yellow, greenish-yellow, green yellowish-green, orange, red, light purple, and gray-blue. Stone tesserae are white, pink, orange, gray-brown, yellowish-white, and grayish-white. None of the white stone tesserae shows any sign of applied paint.[36]

TABLE 3.20. AREA II, APSE MOSAIC, COLORS REPRESENTED
among a random sample of loose tesserae (including colors present in bedded fragments)

Material	*color*	*count*	*% count*	*wt.*	*% wt.*	*avg. wt.*
Glass/translucent	all	406	10.7	210	12.9	0.52
Glass/foil	gold	389	10.2	130	8.0	0.33
Glass/opaque	blue	1533	40.2	425	26.1	0.28
	light blue	292	7.7	95	5.8	0.33
	greenish-blue	281	7.4	135	8.3	0.48
	yellow	178	4.7	105	6.4	0.60
	greenish-yellow	117	3.1	50	3.1	0.43
	green	90	2.4	45	2.8	0.50
	red	42	1.1	30	1.8	0.71
	yellowish-green	20	0.5	15	0.9	0.75
	orange	5	0.1	5	0.3	1.00
	gray-blue					
	light purple					
Stone	white	225	5.9	210	12.9	0.93
	pink	119	3.1	90	5.5	0.76
	light orange	91	2.4	60	3.7	0.66
	gray-brown	23	0.6	25	1.5	1.09
	yellowish-white					
	grayish-white					
TOTAL		3811	100.1	1630	100.0	0.43

The sequence of laying tesserae appears most clearly in the (apparently) representational fragments. Outline tesserae were laid first and the motif was filled with colored tesserae. The background was completed last, often in widening arcs of tesserae surrounding the primary forms. In most cases tesserae were set with their surface parallel to the plaster bed. Occasionally gold-capped tesserae were laid at an angle of *c.*20° to take full advantage of their reflective qualities.

The subject of the south church mosaic remains unclear. The mosaic probably included figures; while some fragments suggest drapery, no examples were noted of the fine detail and coloring normally found in human features.[37] Most of the larger fragments suggest floral and geometric motifs that may have formed part of the lower border.

---

35 At least 48 colors are attested at Lythrankomi; Megaw and Hawkins 1977: 136.

36 Cf. Megaw and Hawkins 1977: 133 and n.604.

37 Cf. 3(?) fragments of faces identified at Saraçhane in Harrison and Gill 1986: 184-85.

Fig. 3.68. Area II, mosaic fragment.

Fig. 3.70. Area II, mosaic fragment.

Fig. 3.69. Area II, mosaic fragment.

Fig. 3.71. Area II, mosaic fragment.

Identified vegetal patterns include grasses, leaves, stems, and flowers. The most common floral motif consists of blossoms formed by opaque pink, white and red tesserae outlined in blue. The curvilinear forms defined by blue outline are filled with broad areas of graduated colors. In general, these tesserae are neatly cut and closely set, with about 36 tesserae fitting into a 5-cm square. One small fragment displays a more finely detailed blossom that was delicately modeled in greenish-blue, white, pink, and red tesserae, all tiny and carefully cut, although the setting left much plaster visible between them.[38] Stems, leaves, and grasses are clearly associated with the floral motifs on a number of fragments. Vines or perhaps reeds may be represented by narrow wavy bands of opaque blue and light blue tesserae that split and fan in curving arcs.

Other motifs can be suggested. Some fragments seem to represent simple rectilinear border patterns, or perhaps long straight drapery passages. Circular motifs appear in other fragments.[39] On one fragment a circle of opaque blue is inscribed within a square outlined in opaque blue tesserae, with blue and translucent tesserae filling the spandrels. The center is greenish-blue; alternating rays (probably 8) of greenish-blue and translucent tesserae (probably originally with gold caps) extend outward. The diameter of the circle is 13.5 cm and about 40 tesserae occupy a 5-cm square. The same motif also employs a different color scheme, with a blue and white circle, light blue rays, and pink and red spandrels.

Two of the largest intact fragments from Area II depict objects set against a dark variegated background of blue, gray-blue, greenish-blue, and light purple (figs. 3.68-3.69). The flaring form on the larger fragment suggests the arm of a cross or perhaps the trunk of a palm tree.[40] A related fragment may represent a pinecone or palm frond in darkened yellowish-green tesserae (fig. 3.70). About 34 tesserae appear within a 5-cm square.

38 Cf. similar blossoms at the earlier basilica at Soloi and the borders at Kiti and Lythrankomi.

39 Cf. Harrison and Gill 1986: 188 nos. 41-44.

40 Cf. Megaw and Hawkins 1977: 53-54.

A single small fragment includes 3 pendant tear-drop forms, which may depict tassels, jewels, or some other hanging ornament (fig. 3.71). The design is rendered in opaque blue, light blue, white, yellowish-green, and gold foil tesserae at a density of *c*.50 per 5-cm square. The white stone drops are surrounded by blue contours, and seem to hang from blue cords upon light blue fabric.

Excavation of the north church (Area V) was limited in scope and recovered a smaller quantity of mosaics. Loose tesserae and small embedded fragments were abundant in the exposed parts of the sanctuary, and the preserved curvature of the larger fragments attests their original location in the 5-m wide central apse. In all essential respects, this mosaic resembles the slightly smaller and later mosaic of the south church. Two distinct layers of gypsum plaster were used for the bedding, which was painted before tesserae were laid. Tesserae were cut of glass and stone, the latter accounting for only 6% of the total. The opaque, translucent, and gold-capped glass tesserae are of the same poor, bubbly quality and are indistinguishable from those at the south church. Opaque glass tesserae represent a similar range of colors, lacking only the vibrant greenish-blue (Table 3.21). The color range of translucent glass tesserae is similar to the south church. Stone tesserae include the same white, and pink shades, but grayish-white, light orange, and gray-brown are absent. Average sizes are comparable.

TABLE 3.21. AREA V, APSE MOSAIC, COLORS REPRESENTED
among a random sample of loose tesserae

Material	*color*	*count*	*% count*	*wt.*	*% wt.*	*avg. wt.*
Glass/translucent	all	342	9.3	180	11.1	0.53
Glass/foil	gold	233	6.3	80	5.0	0.34
Glass/opaque	blue	1901	51.5	695	43.0	0.37
	yellow	250	6.8	150	9.3	0.60
	green	210	5.7	85	5.3	0.40
	red	202	5.5	120	7.4	0.59
	greenish yellow	112	3.0	40	2.5	0.36
	yellowish green	101	2.7	50	3.1	0.50
	gray-blue	66	1.8	30	1.9	0.45
	light blue	45	1.2	20	1.2	0.44
	light purple	16	0.4	5	0.3	0.31
	orange	4	0.1	5	0.3	1.25
Stone	white	170	4.6	130	8.0	0.76
	pink	40	1.1	25	1.5	0.63
TOTAL		3692	100.0	1615	99.9	0.44

Similar rectilinear borders, vegetal motifs, and geometric patterns appear among the very fragmentary mosaics from the north church. Rectilinear border-pieces consist of alternating straight rows of single-color tesserae. The color range differentiates three kinds of borders, of which the most common is dominated by opaque green, yellowish-green, and greenish-yellow tesserae laid *c*.33 per 5-cm square. Swelling acanthus-like forms in opaque green, white, yellowish-green, greenish-yellow, and greenish-blue tesserae can be detected in several fragments, closely set with up to 45 tesserae per 5-cm square (fig. 3.72). At least two floral patterns are clearly represented in addition to grasses and stems. In one case, greenish stems with leaves support delicate red flowers. Red tesserae outline the paired flower lobes and opaque blue define the leaves, which are filled with opaque green and translucent tesserae. The precise workmanship recalls the lower border of the Kiti apse (Michaelides 1987: pl. XXVI). Another floral motif represents a flame-like white flower outlined by opaque blue tesserae (fig. 3.73). Additional flowers seem to be present in other smaller fragments. Geometric motifs feature circles, interlocked circles, and inscribed crosses in various color schemes at densities of *c*.31 tesserae per 5-cm square (fig. 3.74). One fine fragment shows the flaring arm of an opaque purple cross outlined by small opaque blue tesserae.

These mosaics attest the presence at Kopetra of a consistent artistic tradition during the 6th c. The two churches are separated in date by at least one and perhaps two generations, yet material and technical affinities suggest that both were decorated by individuals of the same training or workshop. Equipped with tesserae and copybooks and perhaps working only seasonally, these craftsmen were probably based in Kourion, Amathus, or Salamis, and were called to aspiring towns on specific occasions. The motifs identified at Kopetra attest the consistent use of distinct border zones, vegetal and floral motifs, and geometric patterns with a preference for circular and inscribed-cross forms. The appearance of these patterns, together with the prominence of figured compositions in other 6th-c. churches, makes it likely that both churches represented fig-

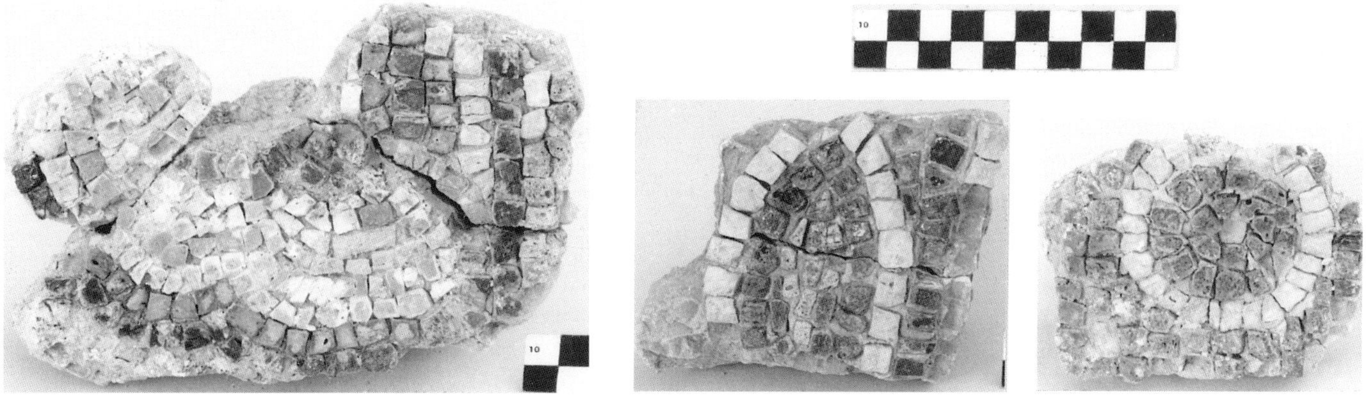

Figs. 3.72-3.74. Area V, mosaic fragments.

ures as well. Indeed, the appearance of the Virgin in the three documented apse ensembles on Cyprus implies that she also appeared at Kopetra, echoing the small plaster image found at the south church (above, p. 117). Like the iconography, the diffusion of the glass mosaic technique into the Cypriot countryside may be seen as reflecting the spread of metropolitan culture across the eastern provinces.

THE CHURCHES OF THE CYPRIOT *CHORA*

The three churches identified at Kopetra were among the most enduring cultural features of the Vasilikos valley both in late antiquity and during our recent exploration of the site. This confirms the special place that religious buildings occupied in the classical landscape. The basilicas were among the largest and most substantial structures built in the valley. They were prominently situated, occupied key points in and around the settlement. Presumably founded by area residents and maintained by their descendants, these buildings remain the most tangible expressions of a significant and continuing investment of wealth that was generated locally during the 6th and early 7th c.

Considered as a group, the churches document the architectural evolution of an island village. The large north church was founded on the upper ridge during the settlement's initial expansion in the early 6th c. Carefully assembled of local materials, its sanctuary decorated with an *opus sectile* floor and vault mosaics, this building established an enduring precedent for later generations. Around the middle of the century a second, slightly smaller basilica was built near the lower edge of the market town. The south church emulates its neighbor yet reflects recent developments in E Mediterranean architecture and decoration. These two closely related structures were actively involved in the daily affairs of local inhabitants. By contrast, the east church built at *Sirmata* marks a monastic departure around the end of the century. Its modest scale enclosed barely half the area of the north church, which may reflect the fact that the basilica formed part of a larger ensemble that included a court with surrounding rooms, as well as other rural assets. All of these buildings were maintained and repaired through the first half of the 7th c., but suffered serious damage around the time of the Arab campaigns. The south and east churches saw modest repairs, in both cases care being taken to preserve the memories of deceased residents, yet soon were left behind as inhabitants relocated elsewhere.

It is difficult to say how representative this picture is of other parts of Cyprus. Literary sources are reticent in discussing rural affairs, and vernacular building traditions have received little sustained attention (Sinos 1984; id. 1986: 520-21; Ionas 1988). Basilicas certainly were erected across the island and many of the 80-100 known examples stood in villages (fig. 3.75; Hadjichristophi 1998; Michaelides 1998: 195). Despite their former importance, very few have been systematically studied; most are isolated ruins, accidentally discovered, cursorily excavated, and briefly reported. Outside the large cities of Soloi, Paphos, Kourion, Amathus, and Salamis, it is only at Aphendrika, Peyia, and perhaps Lapithos and Morphou that local building traditions can be traced in more than a single structure.[41] Further information is avail-

41 Megaw 1946; id. 1958: 34; id. 1960; Pallas 1977: 267-306; Papageorghiou 1993: 43.

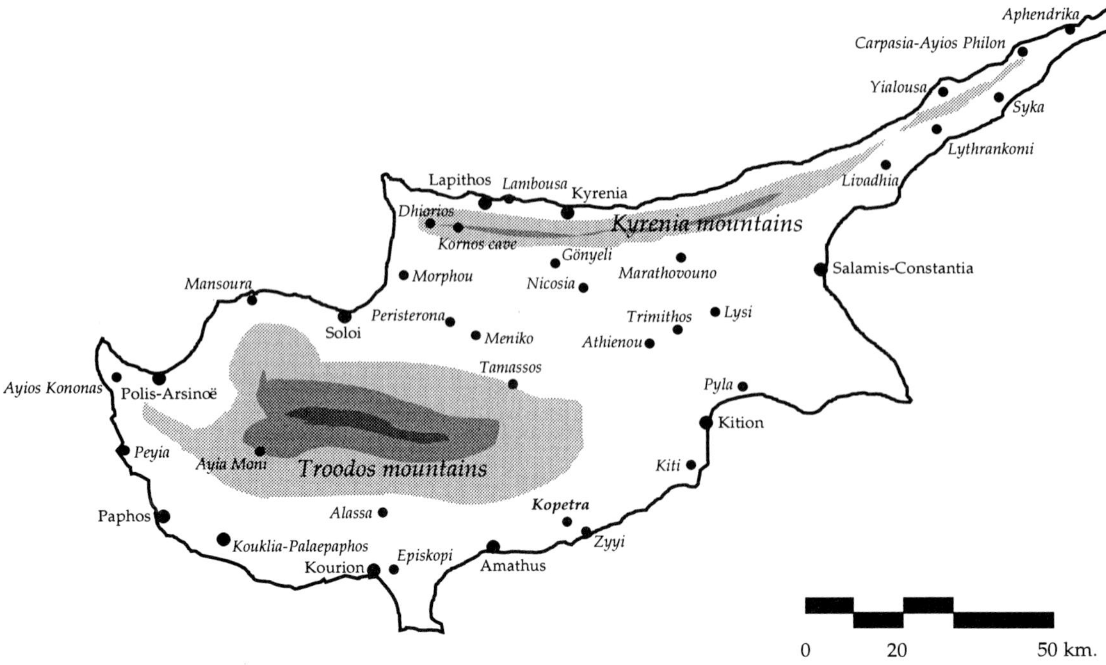

Fig. 3.75. Late Roman Cyprus, with selected urban and secondary settlements.

able from the mainland, although the relationship of that very different landscape to Cyprus remains unclear (below, p. 256). In Syria and Palestine, multiple churches were not uncommon at settlements like Umm el-Jimal, Rihab, and Khirbat al-Samra.[42]

Kopetra provides important information for understanding the spatial relationship of churches and settlement on the island. The north and south churches were situated at opposite ends of the village, while the *Sirmata* complex stood slightly apart from it. Despite their scattered locations, all three basilicas are oriented east by northeast (above, fig. 2.4). Certain villages on the mainland are known to share this arrangement of churches.[43] Such peripheral distribution often seems to reflect a community's growth over time, additional churches being built to serve new neighborhoods as they developed. Instances of divergent orientation among local churches usually can be attributed to specific topographic factors. No other rural Cypriot site has been explored on a comparable scale. The solitary basilica at Ayios Kononas joined a small gathering of houses in the Akamas in the late 6th c. (Fejfer 1995: 73-86). At coastal Peyia-*Ayios Yeoryios*, three churches and a baptistery were built in the 6th and early 7th c. as part of an ecclesiastical quarter that also contained a bath; however, the actual extent of settlement remains unclear.[44] At Kopetra the spread of three churches across the ridge reflects the special rôle such buildings played in rural life.

The main approach to the Kopetra churches was from the west. Today, open fields lying in front of both the north and south churches imply that these areas were unobstructed, or at least not substantially developed. Traces of walls and paving noted slightly west of the south church may belong to a portico facing onto a court or plaza. Elsewhere, axial forecourts were built as an effective means of emphasizing one's arrival at public and private buildings. Well-established at cities and religious centers across the Mediterranean, forecourts or atria appear in Cyprus in urban houses and churches at Soloi, Paphos, Kourion, Amathus, and Salamis.[45] Courtyard cisterns are found near the midpoint of the central axis of the Kourion suburban basilica and the acropolis basilica at Amathus; other water features are so located at the

42 E.g., Lassus 1947; Gatier 1994: 17-24; de Vries 1998.

43 E.g., Tchalenko 1953-58: vol. II; Tate 1992.

44 Megaw 1955: 45; 1960; Pallas 1977: 275-80; Papageorghiou 1993: 36; Christou 1994: 689; id. 1995: 836; Bakirtzis 1995, 2000; Hadjisavvas 1998: 967.

45 Orlandos 1952-54: vol. I, 98-110; Delvoye 1972: 18-19; Papageorghiou 1986: 492-93.

Paphos Chrysopolitissa and the Salamis Campanopetra. Axially arranged courts appear outside major cities at Ayios Philon, Yialousa, and Peyia basilica I. In town and country alike, one normally entered these courts from the west by a single doorway and then continued to the narthex and nave. Despite the occasional presence of narrow lateral doorways, the W façade offered the primary access to the interior.

All of the Kopetra churches had a narthex, which ranged in depth from 3.4 m at *Sirmata* to 4.3 m at the north church. All seem to have been paved and opened through three doorways onto the nave; flanking benches and a central outer door were found at *Sirmata* and the north church. At *Sirmata* the narthex is known to have extended beyond the width of the nave, was subdivided by interior wall pilasters carrying transverse arches, and included a crypt at its S end. The narthex was an important feature of Cypriot church planning.[46] Usually a single outer door led to a simple hall spanning the basilica's W end, with side doors leading north and south to other rooms; in all known cases, three doorways opened onto the nave. Interior wall shafts outside the nave have not been noted elsewhere in rural Cyprus, perhaps because of their poor preservation, although shallow pilasters survive in the lateral *katechoumena* of the episcopal basilica at Kourion (Megaw 1976a: 346). Most Cypriot narthexes would have been covered by a westward sloping roof, with or without hipped corners.

Builders at Kopetra employed the type of church plan most commonly used in Cyprus and across the E Mediterranean during the 5th through 7th c. The three-aisled buildings vary in area from over 270 m^2 at the north church to less than 150 m^2 at *Sirmata*. These dimensions reflect the range of rural Cypriot churches, with the north church constituting one of the island's larger village examples and the *Sirmata* basilica one of the smallest (Table 3.22). In terms of their length, width, and total area, the Kopetra churches became smaller during the 6th c. This progression may be fortuitous or it may reflect changing interests, slowing population growth, or dwindling resources for church building. A similar trend toward smaller buildings over the same interval can be seen among the three main basilicas at Peyia.

TABLE 3.22. INTERIOR DIMENSIONS, PROPORTIONS, AND INTERCOLUMNIAL INTERVALS OF SELECTED CYPRIOT BASILICAS, RANKED BY OVERALL PROPORTIONS (L : W)

Church	*date*	*length*	*width*	*total area*	*L:W*	*W nave*	*L:W nave*	*W:W nave*	*cols.*	*intercolum.*
Lysi	6/7 c.	12.5	11.8	148	1.06	5.5	2.27	2.15	4?	2.5?
Ayios Kononas	l 6 c.	14.3	12.4	177	1.15	6.1	2.34	2.03	4	2.9
Sykha Panayia	6 c.	12.3	10.2	125	1.21	4.3	2.86	2.37	4	2.5
Marathovouno	5/6 c.	17.3	14.2	246	1.22	6.6	2.62	2.15	5	2.9
Peyia basilica II	l 6 c.	16.8	13.8	232	1.22	5.2	3.23	2.65	5	2.8
Yialousa-*Ayia Trias*	5 c.	17.3	13.6	235	1.27	6.2	2.79	2.19	5	2.9
Peyia basilica III	e 7 c.	14.5	11.2	162	1.29	4.5	3.22	2.49	4	2.9
Ayios Philon	e 5 c.	17.6	13.4	236	1.31	5.9	2.98	2.27	7?	2.2 ?
Aphendrika Asomatoi	5 c.	15.0	11.1	167	1.35	4.8	3.13	2.31	5	2.5
Aphendrika Panayia	6 c.	22.2	15.9	353	1.40	7.2	3.08	2.21	7	2.8
Peyia basilica I	e 6 c.	27.8	19.3	537	1.44	7.2	3.86	2.68	8	3.1
Kourion suburban basilica	l 5/e 6 c.	16.1	10.7	172	1.50	4.5	3.58	2.38	5?	2.7 ?
Athienou-*Yiorkous*	5/6 c.	16.6	11.0	183	1.51	?	?	?	5?	2.8 ?
Kopetra north church	**e 6 c.**	**21.0**	**13.0**	**273**	**1.62**	**6.5**	**3.23**	**2.00**	**7?**	**2.6 ?**
Kopetra south church	**m 6 c.**	**17.0**	**10.5**	**179**	**1.62**	**5.3**	**3.21**	**1.98**	**5**	**2.8**
Kopetra east church	**l 6 c.**	**16.2**	**8.8**	**143**	**1.84**	**4.3**	**3.38**	**2.05**	**5**	**2.5**
Average		17.2	12.6	223	1.38	5.6	3.05	2.26	5	2.8

The process of design relied less on principles of abstract geometry than on local topography and resources. While surveying Kopetra's churches we noted many planning irregularities.

46 Absent only at Lysi in E central Cyprus; Karageorghis 1964: 374-76; Pallas 1977: 299, fig. 199.

Inconsistent dimensions were found in doorways, walls, and major architectural features, which argues against the use of a consistent foot or similar module. This disregard for prevailing units of measure applies to other Cypriot churches as well. A foot of 0.315 m has been proposed for basilica B at Soloi and the Salamis Campanopetra, two large churches that no doubt were laid out by trained architects.[47] Architectural modules may have been employed more often on the mainland but even here the evidence is inconclusive.[48] As in S Asia Minor, Palestine and elsewhere, church planning in the Cypriot countryside seems to have been a progressive undertaking that began by establishing a single long wall, and derived from it secondary dimensions in an approximate way.

Despite the uncertainty of individual measurements, the Kopetra churches in some respects exhibit a distinctive approach to planning. This is most clearly seen in the total proportions of the nave. The north and south churches are of very different overall size, yet for both buildings the ratio of length to width is 1.62. The proportions of the *Sirmata* basilica reach 1.84, thanks to the unusual arrangement of the W end. Few churches on the mainland exhibit such long and narrow overall proportions.[49] These ratios stand at the upper limit of contemporary Cypriot church building. Table 3.22 summarizes the approximate dimensions and proportions of 16 basilicas built outside the main cities from the 5th to early 7th c. Within this group Kopetra's churches appear to be about average in total area, which ranges from 125 m^2 to 537 m^2 with an average of 223 m^2. Proportional relationships of length to width vary from *c.*1.1 to 1.5, with an average of 1.30 when excluding Kopetra's (1.38 when including them). Simply put, Kopetra preserves some of the most elongated plans known on the island.

The three churches are related by other proportional relationships as well. The ratio of length to width of the central aisle varies from 3.21 : 1 at the south church to 3.38 at *Sirmata*, compared with an average of 3.05 : 1 for all churches included in Table 3.22. This preference for a narrow central aisle is shared by the three Peyia churches and the suburban basilica at Kourion. The internal nave ratios at Kopetra are almost uniformly 2.00, with a nearly perfect 1 : 2 : 1 relationship prevailing among the widths of the three aisles. The Peyia churches, by contrast, reflect a very different tradition, with an average of 1 : 2.6 : 1. Kopetra's builders clearly preferred long and narrow interior spaces.

This tendency may be related to the arrangement of interior nave supports. The east and south church colonnades consisted of 5 pairs of mortared rubble piers set at average interaxial spacings of 2.5 and 2.8 m, although in both cases supports actually were placed at closer, less even intervals. The 7 conjectured members of the north church colonnade would have stood *c.*2.6 m apart. The number of nave supports among contemporary rural basilicas on the island ranges from 4 at the Sykha Panayia, Ayios Kononas, and Peyia basilica III to 7 at Ayios Philon and 8 at Peyia basilica I. Logically enough, these numbers vary in direct relationship with the total length of the nave. The intercolumnar intervals within this group are not well documented but exhibit less consistency than one might expect. The exceptionally narrow 2.2-m spacing reported at Ayios Philon, for example, has been explained as necessary to support a timber architrave and upper gallery (Taylor and Megaw 1981: 233). Galleries also have been proposed at Yialousa, the suburban basilica at Kourion, and Peyia basilica I, which exhibit intercolumniations of 2.7 to 3.1 m (Papageorghiou 1986: 493). Usually there is scant evidence to distinguish between the use of an interior architrave or arcade. Most Cypriot examples fit within the range of 2.13-3.50 m for contemporary arcades in N Syria, but those were built of very different materials (Lassus 1947: 73-74). The clear use of mortared rubble to define windows, semidomes, and arcades in a number of Roman and later buildings in Cyprus suggests that arcades frequently were employed. Since there is no evidence of a gallery at Kopetra, the relatively close spacing seen here apparently reflects the cautiousness of local builders, who no doubt were aware of the

47 Des Gagniers and Tran Tam Tinh 1985: 48-49, 99 n.7; Roux 1998: 19.

48 Underwood 1948; Restle 1979: 89-135; Hellenkemper 1989: 181-90; Tsafrir 1990.

49 Cf. Ovadiah 1970: 203-4; Buchwald 1995: Table 3; Hill 1996.

hazards of using mortared rubble piers instead of monolithic columns. The Marathovouno church, where similar gypsum rubble piers stood at 2.9-m intervals, may be considered the exception that proves the rule: the basilica was repaired at least twice and may not have survived into the 7th c.[50] In both cases builders chose to stick with the cylindrical pier form, despite its evident limitations, in order to preserve the formal vocabulary of classical public life.

The sanctuary constitutes the liturgical focus of any church and its design reflects both available resources and intentions for use. Several important features appear in all three churches at Kopetra: a broad central apse with flanking apses or inscribed apsidioles in the side aisles, and a raised *bema* occupying the E end of the central aisle, further emphasized by special paving and wall mosaics at the north and south churches. Minor differences in design and decoration within this basic formula may reflect changing architectural taste as well as scale, funding, and audience. The triapsidal plan of the north church is first met in Cyprus at the early churches at Ayios Philon, Aphendrika, Lambousa, and Yialousa. Most of the urban basilicas built in the later 5th and 6th c. (e.g., at Soloi [although Megaw 2000 now proposes an early 5th-c. date for basilica B], Polis, Paphos, Kourion, Amathus, and Salamis) have fully-defined triapsidal plans, several incorporating polygonal exterior walls. This is especially true at Peyia, which was strongly influenced by nearby Paphos and frequent contact with Constantinople (Delvoye 1972: 20; Bakirtzis 1995). The considerable prestige of the new pilgrimage church at Qalat Siman may have been a factor in the continuing popularity of rounded apse forms on the island (Roux 1998: 241-42). Closer at hand, the three semicircular apses of the southeast basilica at Amathus, perhaps built in the later 5th c. as the city's cathedral, would have offered a monumental prototype for the Kopetra north church (E. Prokopiou in Aupert 1996: 162-64). The appearance of the triapsidal plan at Kopetra shows the plan's rural diffusion in the 6th c.

The inscribed lateral apsidioles seen at the south and east churches can be understood as a related insular development dating back to the great church of Ayios Epiphanios in Salamis. In the 6th c., the use of flanking apsidioles may have been an economical substitute for salient apses that was especially popular in the countryside. Rural basilicas, while often poorly preserved, usually exhibit straight aisle walls that are sufficiently thick to have held such features. The walls of the Peyia transept basilica preserve apsidioles like those seen at Kopetra; the side aisles at Marathovouno, Athienou-*Yiorkous*, and Ayios Kononas end in straight walls that may have contained similar niches. Interestingly, these are not the smallest of rural basilicas (cf. Table 3.22). By employing apsidioles as a substitute for free-standing side apses, Kopetra's builders may have followed a common rural recourse.

The raised *bema* floor is known across the island. In the north and south churches this part of the sanctuary is further emphasized by a shift from gypsum paving to *opus sectile* or mosaic. This hierarchical differentiation appears more clearly in urban than rural basilicas. The presence of a low chancel screen surrounding the *bema*, likely if not certain at *Sirmata* and the north church, is known elsewhere in the countryside. Floor cuttings at Yialousa, Marathovouno, and the acropolis basilica at Amathus indicate the placement of sanctuary barriers. Marble or limestone screen fragments carved with decorative patterns, broadly similar to those recovered by the Kopetra survey, have been found at Ayios Philon, Ayios Kononas, Athienou, Marathovouno, and Tamassos.[51]

At Kopetra the total sanctuary area appears to be a function of its intercolumnar spacing. In reaching the second set of nave columns the *bema* includes *c.*24 m^2 at *Sirmata* and 29 m^2 at the south church, or 16-17% of the total nave area. In the great basilicas of Soloi, Kourion, and Salamis, the raised sanctuary floors project well into the nave and reach as far as the third or fourth columns. A local model for the Kopetra arrangement may have been the southwest

50 Karageorghis 1963: 385-86; Pallas 1977: 299-301; Papageorghiou 1963: 101; cf. id. 1993: 49.

51 Papageorghiou 1963; Bakirtzis 1976; Taylor and Megaw 1981: 235; Fejfer 1995: 83.

basilica at Amathus, where the *bema* reaches the second pair of columns and was paved with *opus sectile*. At Peyia, the *bema* fills the first two intercolumniations of basilica I but stops short of the second set of nave columns in the smaller basilicas II and III; in all three cases, screens extended laterally to include the ends of the side aisles as well. The *bema* similarly stops midway between the first and second columns of the nave arcade at Yialousa and Marathovouno but remains limited to the central aisle. When viewed in this context, the Kopetra churches seem to preserve a consistent local tradition amid the variety of contemporary practice.

The lateral expansion of the chancel noted at Peyia reflects important liturgical changes that reached Cyprus during the 6th c. In basilicas I-III, the chancel screen projected sideways from the last column of the nave arcade. Evidence of this lateral extension includes a raised floor surface, change of paving, and cuttings for the chancel screen. Elsewhere, the extended chancel appears almost exclusively at coastal sites, including the great basilicas at Soloi, Paphos, Kourion, and Salamis, and (among smaller churches) the suburban basilica at Kourion and the acropolis basilica at Amathus. Traces of a partition inserted at the end of the Marathovouno N aisle may belong to either a side chancel or a separate chapel (Papageorghiou 1963: 91). Early studies sought to understand this arrangement as a result of liturgical reforms instituted under Justin II (565-578), but more recent investigations have looked to other sources.[52] In 6th-c. Palestine and Syria the spread of the extended chancel apparently reflects the growing cult of martyrs.[53] Its rarity — if not absence — in rural Cyprus suggests that the idea was slow to reach beyond the coastal cities, owing to either a lack of available relics or a preference for other forms of commemoration.

The semicircular *synthronon* is among the most important sanctuary furnishings known at Kopetra. The arrangements at *Sirmata* are the best preserved, with two stepped surfaces and a projecting axial seat solidly built against the apse wall. At the north church, the apse paving indicates the presence of a moveable clergy bench, probably built of wood against the back wall. At the south church, a rubble bench may have replaced a similar *synthronon* when the complex was rebuilt. These examples indicate that apsidal clergy benches were more common in the *chora* than other preserved examples suggest. Originating perhaps in Constantinople in the 5th c., the *synthronon* has been identified as a characteristic of metropolitan-influenced church building in the 6th c.[54] Semicircular clergy benches of more or less elaborate form have been identified in a large number of churches across Cilicia, Isauria, Syria, and Palestine, ranging from a simple foundation for a wood seat to multiple steps and usually reflecting the size of the structure.[55] In the 6th c., *synthronoi* built of solid masonry appeared in the great churches of Soloi, Kourion, and Salamis and as additions or new foundations at smaller churches at Peyia, Kourion, Amathus, Ayia Moni, Kiti, Meniko, Aphendrika, Ayios Philon, and Lapithos. The emphasized axial seat found at *Sirmata* is one of the best preserved examples of the so-called 'bishop's throne' in Cyprus; its presence in many rural mainland churches, like its absence from the island's probable cathedrals, shows that it does not necessarily carry special episcopal status (Duval 1994: 188-89). The apparent lack of masonry benches at Kopetra's north and south churches suggests that wood *synthronoi* may sometimes have been preferred in the countryside. The simple apsidal bench installed at the south church in the mid 7th c. is characteristic of subsequent Byzantine architecture, even as the image of the multi-tiered *synthronon* is maintained in later painting (Lafontaine-Dosogne 1993: 192).

One or more tables stood in each of Kopetra's basilicas, although their placement is not always clear. At *Sirmata*, the main altar stood atop a permanent base immediately before the apse, with a secondary table for lay offerings set at the S side of the *bema*. The well-preserved

---

52 Freshfield 1873; cf. Mathews 1971: 162.

53 Delvoye 1972: 20; Smith and Day 1989: 88-90; Sodini 1989b: 353; Duval 1994: 162-63.

54 Orlandos 1952-54: vol. II, 489-509; Mathews 1971: 109.

55 Duval 1994: 188-91; Hill 1996: 22.

opus sectile paving of the north church's apse suggests that the altar was located farther forward, near the middle of the *bema*. The mosaic floor at the south church shows no sign of a permanent altar base in the *bema*; an independent altar probably stood in the S chapel as well. This apparent inconsistency suggests some uncertainty about how and where the altar should be installed. Permanent altar bases are well known in the Aegean and on the Syro-Palestine mainland, where they have been identified as characteristic of the mid 6th through mid 7th c.[56] Only a few examples have been found in Cyprus. In addition to *Sirmata*, fixed altar bases have been identified in the southwest basilica at Amathus and Peyia basilica I; in all three buildings the table stood well in front of the apse in the E part of the *bema*. In most other cases, the floor is insufficiently preserved to establish the original arrangement. Perhaps some of these altars consisted of a wood or stone surface mounted on a moveable wood frame, in the manner of dining tables, and were placed without regard to the sanctuary paving (Pallas 1979-80: 49). The patchy evidence reveals the lack of a fixed insular tradition, in town as well as country.

The altar itself usually consisted of a simple rectangular slab of stone mounted on a pedestal or 4 or 5 legs at a height of *c.*1 m (cf. Orlandos 1952-54: vol. II, 444-52). One such gypsum surface was found at the south church together with various pieces of marble tables that stood, like the altar, without a permanent base. A single border fragment was recovered at the north church. Apart from a circular tray found at *Sirmata*, all of the Kopetra examples apparently came from undecorated rectangular tables.[57] The usual assumption is that liturgical altars and lateral tables were rectangular in shape, while sigmoidal tables could be used for other purposes in ecclesiastical annexes.[58] In domestic contexts, tables had varied uses and could be rectangular, sigma-shaped, or semicircular; unfortunately, the shape is not always apparent from small fragments. Throughout most of the countryside marble tables may have been limited to churches and villas.[59]

The three churches at Kopetra, however incompletely understood, offer the best available evidence for reconstructing the liturgy in the Cypriot countryside. In most respects, rural practices probably reflected rituals of the urban basilicas, which in the 6th c. were guided by the autocephalous archbishop in Salamis-Constantia. Three doorways opened from the narthex onto the nave, whose ceremonial functioning focused on the E end of the central aisle. The altar stood on a raised *bema* before the apse, allowing sufficient space for the officiating priest to stand between *synthronon* and altar, facing the congregation. One or more secondary tables may have stood elsewhere in the *bema* — at *Sirmata*, a second table was placed next to the S aisle — perhaps to accommodate the readings or receive offerings from the congregation.[60] Side aisles terminated in apses or wall niches, which remained outside the chancel limits. The

---

56 Orlandos 1952-54: vol. II, 438-44; Sodini and Kolokotsas 1984: 17-19; Duval 1994: 169-74; Hill 1996: 27; L. Habas in Hirschfeld 1999: 122-23.

57 Similar tables are found, if not always published, across Cyprus and the E Mediterranean (in general, see Chalkia 1991). The episcopal basilica at Kourion produced an especially large number of marble fragments belonging to tables, supports, and other furnishings (Loverance 1990). Two fragments of rectangular tables and two pieces of curved tables were found at the acropolis basilica at Amathus (Pralong 1994a: 452). Excavations at Ayios Philon identified fragments of both an altar and a secondary offering table (Taylor and Megaw 1981: 235, pls. XL.10, XLI.3a). A catalogue of lunate or sigma-shaped tables found in Cyprus would include published examples from Peyia, Soloi, Lapithos, and the Akrotiri peninsula, in addition to some 35 pieces recovered in secular and religious contexts at Salamis (Roux 1973: 181-96; Argoud *et al.* 1980: 35; Bakirtzis 2000: 159, photo 9). Among rural churches, undecorated marble table fragments have been reported at Athienou-*Yiorkous* and Alassa-*Ayia Mavri* (Bakirtzis 1976: 264, fig. 2, pl. XLIII.5; Flourentzos 1996: 15 no. 2b, pl. XXV).

58 Sodini and Kolokotsas 1984: 203-6; Acconci 1998: 477-78.

59 In several cases *cippi* found in basilicas may have served as table supports (e.g., at Alassa, Amathus, Kopetra, and Tamassos.

60 Pallas 1979-80: 40-55; cf. Donceel-Voutê 1988: 524.

purpose of these lateral apses remains uncertain, but their liturgical independence of the *bema* suggests they may have served as small chapels. By *c.*600, all of these side apses had been partially filled with masonry, providing the worshipper with a shallow, table-high surface for the display of relics or devotional images. Elsewhere in Cyprus, the chancel could be expanded laterally to absorb such flanking apses into a fully developed tripartite sanctuary, as became standard in later Byzantine architecture. This development is clearly documented by the three Peyia churches and in coastal cities such as Soloi, Paphos, Kourion, and Salamis. Apart perhaps from Marathovouno, the idea of the lateral chancel may not have spread as readily into the countryside in Cyprus as it did during the later 6th c. on the mainland, where it is associated with the cult of relics.[61] The continued independence of side apses at Kopetra may reflect a conservative aspect of the rural liturgy that continued to afford direct access to locally-meaningful commemorative spaces.

An interest in additional devotional areas may underlie the popularity of lateral chapels and related rooms. Independent secondary spaces lay along the S flank of all three Kopetra churches and were clearly separated from both nave and narthex. At the south church, these lateral spaces included side benches and an apsidal chapel accessible by a single doorway from the lower side aisle. Lateral spaces with benches were common features of Cypriot churches.[62] In rural Cyprus, lateral spaces are smaller and often stand far from the sanctuary; these are better understood as chapels or mortuary annexes (e.g., Yialousa, Ayios Philon, the suburban basilica at Kourion, and Peyia basilica I). Most of these chapels end in a projecting apse, either semicircular or polygonal. As seen at Kopetra, in smaller churches a simple inscribed wall-niche may have served instead of salient apses. The seeming inconsistency of these chapels may in many cases be the result of later additions.

Burials took place in all of the Kopetra churches and may have been a common feature of the countryside. At least one burial was set into the narthex floor at the north church. At *Sirmata*, a recessed crypt with two tombs lay below the narthex and a sarcophagus apparently occupied the S lateral space. The renovation of this crypt and the addition of a late tomb at the south church attest the local importance of enclosed burials through the mid 7th c. Burial within churches was regarded as a distinct honor across the E Mediterranean in late antiquity, with both urban and rural examples known in Syria and Palestine.[63] Presumed burial arrangements of several early saints played an important rôle in reshaping the religious topography of the island.[64] As at Kopetra, burials were normally limited to the narthex and flanking rooms (Sodini and Kolokotsas 1984: 223-25).

---

61 J. W. Crowfoot in Kraeling 1938: 181-83; Sodini 1989b: 349-53; Duval 1994: 164.

62 Among early examples are the symmetrical halls usually identified as *katechoumena* at Ayios Epiphanios at Salamis and the Kourion episcopal basilica (Megaw 1976a: 340 and 363), while later examples at Paphos, Kourion, and Amathus include corridors leading to other rooms.

63 Lassus 1947: 230-32; Sodini and Kolokotsas 1984: 222-23; Sodini 1986; Ruggieri 1991: 178-79; Hirschfeld 1992: 130-43.

64 Barnabas and Epiphanios were buried in mortuary chapels near Salamis, Heracleidios within his church at Tamassos, Philon in his church complex at Carpasia, and Tychon at one time occupied a church at Amathus (Karageorghis 1976: 888-91; Taylor and Megaw 1981; Papageorghiou 1986: 495-96; E. Prokopiou in Aupert 1996: 153-60; Falkenhausen 1999). The presence of a stone-lined tomb and reliquary at the Salamis Campanopetra reflects contact with the cult of relics, which spread outward from Palestine in the 6th c. and reached at least the coast of Cyprus (Papageorghiou 1985: 322-24; Roux 1998: 148-51). Closer to Kopetra, a small reliquary in the shape of a sarcophagus has recently been discovered at the southeast basilica at Amathus (Hadjisavvas 1998: 672). Less celebrated burials are known among some of the island's smaller churches, including the suburban basilica at Kourion, the southwest basilica at Amathus, Aphendrika Panayia, and at Marathovouno (Papageorghiou 1963; id. 1986: 496; id. in Aupert 1996: 84-88). At Peyia a (female) patron may have occupied a tomb set into the narthex of basilica II in the early 7th c. (Megaw 1955: 45).

Church floors at Kopetra reflect the variety of interior decoration techniques known on the island, ranging from locally available stone to fine polychrome mosaics (Megaw 1976b; Hadjichristophi 2000). Cut gypsum slabs were an inexpensive substitute for imported marble to pave urban basilicas and country chapels alike. The isolated appearance of floor mosaics suggests that these probably were made by itinerant craftsmen summoned to work on specific commissions in rural villas and towns.[65] The two panels in Kopetra's south church constitute an interesting example of a minor ecclesiastical commission. Apart from the Alassa and Mansoura baths and Peyia churches, all of these mosaics seem to be non-representational. Their stylistic range, despite some uncertainty about dates, broadly corresponds with mainland developments (Megaw 1985b; Michaelides 1989: 284-90). *Opus sectile*, the most prestigious of available paving techniques, appears in the countryside at Tamassos, Trimithos, Nicosia, Lysi, and Episkopi-*Serayia*.[66] Its presence at Kopetra, if truly limited to the *bema* of the north church, is unusual among rural churches on the island.

Traveling craft specialists probably worked in tandem with local villagers to decorate upper walls. Apse- and wall-mosaics were installed by urban workshops that ventured into the countryside for specific commissions, as at Kopetra, Kiti, Livadhia, and Lythrankomi. The decoration of the north and south churches confirms the likelihood that apse mosaics commonly were set up at the same churches that had mosaic or *opus sectile* floors, perhaps even by the same teams of craftsmen; by contrast, none of these materials appears at *Sirmata*. The stucco decoration seen at Kopetra also must have been more widespread than surviving examples suggest, both across Cyprus and on the mainland. Amathus, Soloi, and Salamis preserve most of the comparanda; more fragmentary examples are known at Gönyeli, Kiti, and Marathovouno. The surviving sculpture from the south church, unique in both its extent and subject-matter, probably was made by a team of craftsmen brought from a coastal city for the occasion.

Built over the span of 3 or 4 generations, the churches of Kopetra conspicuously mark the physical, economic, and cultural parameters of a forgotten village. Motive forces underlying their foundation are unknown but may reflect the interests of an emerging rural élite that controlled sub-regional production and exchange in the 6th c. The location here of two parish churches and a minor monastery constitutes a major religious focus for the Vasilikos valley, the resources of which were invested in their construction, decoration, and upkeep. Considered together, these structures document the existence of a small, church-oriented settlement similar to those found across the Near East.

Kopetra's diverse resource base, with broad coastal plain, reliable if accentuated patterns of rainfall, adequate building stone, and upland forests and mineral reserves, may be taken as representative of much of the *chora*. Survey and excavation indicate that local settlement flourished during the 6th and early 7th c. as part of a prosperity that reached across much of the island. Two basilicas, presumably begun at the initiative of leading village families, were erected by local workmen with experienced artisans summoned from the coast to complete their decoration. The slightly later church at *Sirmata* was built with an unusual plan as part of an independent monastic complex, reflecting a measure of innovation that was possible within the valley. As a group, these churches embody the social, religious, and architectural aspirations of a village of modest affluence, a place of limited resources that nevertheless shared in the cultural currents of the day. Their special contribution is to document the evolution of building traditions in a small community, and to suggest how much elsewhere has been lost.

---

65 Examples of secular mosaics have been found in varied rural contexts, including an unknown (3rd-c.?) building near Kouklia and two baths, apparently belonging to 4th- to 5th-c. villas, at Alassa and Mansoura (Maier 1985: 24-25, pl. 12 nos. 3-5; Michaelides 1987: 37-38 and 45 nos. 40-41 and 51). Outside the coastal cities mosaics decorated churches at Alassa, Peyia, Yialousa, and Nicosia-*Bedestan*, as well as the important shrines of Ayios Herakleidios at Tamassos and Ayios Spyridon at Trimithos (Megaw 1976b: 9-18; Michaelides 1988).

66 Megaw 1976b: 4-9; Michaelides 1993; Hadjichristophi 2000.

4
Coins

Fourteen coins could be identified and dated among the assorted discoid metal objects found during survey and excavation at Kopetra. Most of the identified coins are bronze (copper alloy) issues of later Roman (4th- to 5th-c.) and early Byzantine (6th- to 7th-c.) date, and pertain directly to the site's occupation. Not included here are several obscure coins probably dating to the 4th to 6th c. as well as a few 6th- and early 7th-c. coins, said to have been found in the vicinity, that were shown to us while we were working in the valley. A slight mediaeval presence is represented by a silver denier of Henry II found in upper levels at Area II. A single early 20th-c. Ottoman issue and several late 20th-c. Cypriot coins, not discussed here, were picked up in the S part of the survey area.

The potential of coins to provide clear information concerning their date and place of origin qualifies them as a uniquely important part of the archaeological record. Their primary historical contribution is twofold: to help date specific excavation contexts, and to document commercial and political links between the valley and the wider Mediterranean world. Individual coins considered singly tell us little, but as a group they form an essential part of our understanding of this small settlement.

The dozen identified pre-mediaeval coins were drawn from 4 of the 5 main excavation sectors: 7 from Area II, 3 from Area VI, and one each from Areas I and V. The majority (9) were found in or near the basilicas, as might be expected from the emphasis of excavation; the disparity in number between the east (Area I) and south (Area II) churches, however, remains unexplained. Three coins came from the terraced residence at Area VI but none was found at the more modest Area IV complex. Few coins were recovered in stratigraphically secure contexts; in fact, some of the best preserved examples came from surface levels. The most significant contexts at Area II include the lower collapse of the *bema* (Lot II-13, **C8**) and construction of a drain (Lot II-26, **C10**). At Area VI both **C5** and **C7** were found amid the débris of adjacent rooms (Lots VI-5 and 6). All sectors produced contemporary pottery, confirming their occupation during the 6th and early 7th c.

The coins provide more helpful testimony when considered as a group. Apart from a single issue of Arcadius, the pre-mediaeval site is represented by 11 datable coins ranging from Justinian I to Constans II. When distributed by date, this series culminates in the early 7th c., specifically during the early reign of Heraclius (fig. 4.1; note that including approximate attributions would slightly increase the recorded 5th- and 6th-c. totals). Most (7) issues are folles, with the largest number (5?) coming from Constantinople. This picture of economic growth clearly resembles the more abundant evidence of fine pottery, which preserves a strong Aegean presence into the early 600s (below, pp. 208-9). The architectural form and decorative vocabulary of the three churches fit well within this 6th-c. milieu. Coins, pottery, and buildings also provide slight but important signs of activity lingering into the third quarter of the 7th c., immediately following the Arab campaigns. The subsequent absence of all three kinds of evidence supports the impression of a dramatically reduced level of monetary activity in the lower valley through the Middle Ages.

Numismatic evidence has played an important rôle in understanding events on Cyprus during the 7th c. It appears that the island saw a steady increase in the supply of coins during the early 600s. Many bronze issues of Heraclius and Constans II have turned up by accident and through excavation. Most of these have come from cities and coastal areas, especially as part of hoards concealed during times of economic or political stress.

The largest number allegedly constituted a cache of copper coins, discovered in the mid 19th c., containing 509 issues of Constans II. Substantial hoards of gold solidi of Heraclius and Constans II have been reported from Soloi, Mandres near Famagusta, and Larnaca shore (Dikigoropoulos 1940-48: 96 nn.9-20; id. 1956: 255-60; Megaw 1951: 260; id. 1953: 137). Such considerable deposits of wealth, taken together with the famous silver

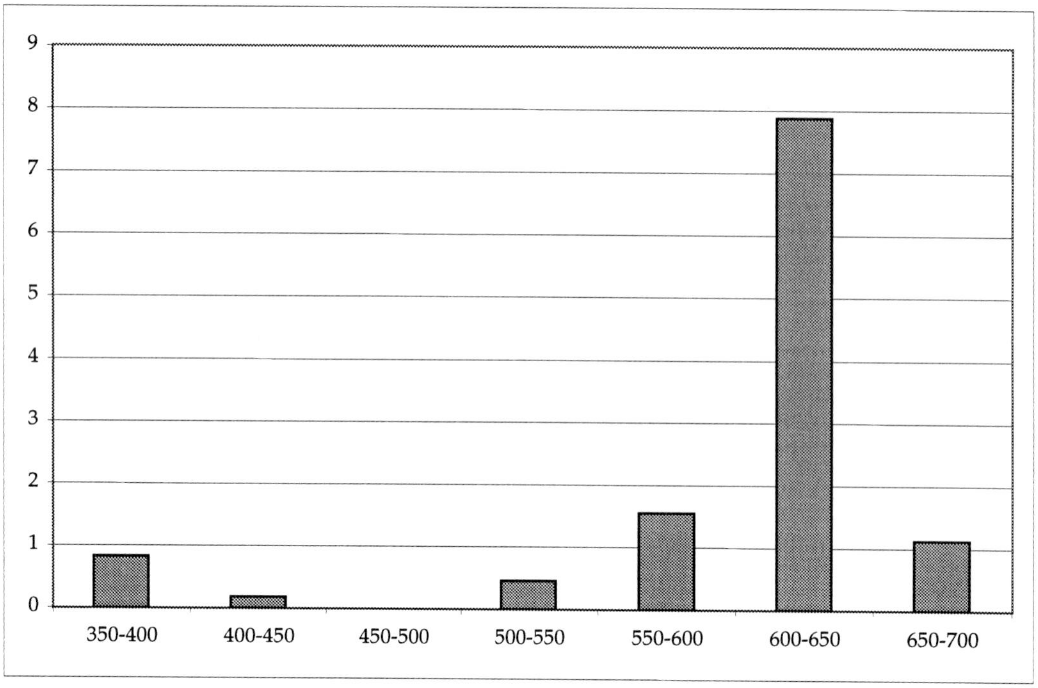

Fig. 4.1. Chronological distribution of datable Late Roman and Early Byzantine coins at Kopetra, apportioned by half-century.

TABLE 4.1. MID-6th to MID-7th-c. COINS REPORTED FROM SELECTED EXCAVATIONS IN CYPRUS

Site	*Justinian I/ Justin II*	*Tiberius II/ M. Tiberius*	*Phocas/ Heraclius*	*Heraclius*	*Constans II*
Paphos, Odeion		K K	M?	M M M M M M M M M M M M M M M M K K K K I I I I I	M M M M M M M M M M M M M M M M M M M M? M? K K K K
Kourion, Univ. of Pennsylvania expedition	M M M M K K K I I I I E E E	M M M M M M K K I I X	M K	M M M M M M M M M K L I	M M M M M M
Carpasia-Ayios Philon	E			M M M E E	M M M M M M M M M M M? M? hoard: 15M
Paphos, Garrison's Camp	M			M M M M IB	M M I I
Paphos, House of Dionysos	E?			M K?	
Kopetra	I E		I	M M M M M M K	M M
Maroni-*Petrera*				M M M M M M K	M M
Alassa-*Ayia Mavri*		M		M M M M	

treasure found at Karavas, near Lapithos, reflect important if isolated moments of insecurity around the time of Arab assaults on the island. Examples recovered by controlled excavation offer broader comparanda (Table 4.1). Urban centers naturally are the best represented. The 7th c., especially the reigns of Heraclius and Constans II, are well represented among coins found at Saranda Kolones (Paphos) (Megaw 1972: 339). Excavation of the odeion at Paphos recovered a large number of 7th-c. coins falling off sharply during the reign of Constans II; up to 17 of these may actually post-date the Arab campaigns (Nicolaou 1990: 193-204). The University of Pennsylvania expedition to Kourion found a generous series of early Byzantine coins extending into the 660s (Cox 1959: 78-82). Issues of Constans II were the latest Byzantine coins to be found in quantity by the short-lived Lyon expedition at Salamis (Helly 1973: 200). Late occupation levels at the Ayios Philon church complex yielded 18 identifiable coins of this period, plus a hoard of 15 folles of Constans II (Taylor and Megaw 1981: 219 and 228-30). Two coins of Maurice Tiberius and a follis of Phocas were found near the basilica at Soloi (des Gagniers and Tran Tam Tinh 1985: 89-91). In Paphos two Heraclian coins came from the House of Dionysos, and 5 issues of Heraclius and 4 of Constans II have been found so far at *Toumballos* (Nicolaou 1990: 92-93; Giudice *et al.* 1993: 307; iid. 1994: 261; iid. 1998: 197-98; iid. 2000: 281). Early 7th-c. coins are commonly recovered if less thoroughly reported in rural contexts. Work in the Kouris valley at Alassa-*Ayia Mavri*, a small basilica comparable in some ways to Kopetra, recovered a follis of Maurice Tiberius and 4 more of Heraclius; at least three of these were minted in Constantinople (Flourentzos 1996: 16-19). Excavations at the Maroni-*Petrera* basilica, not far from Kopetra, found at least 8 (and perhaps 10) coins datable to 625-650; their distribution closely resembles those at Kopetra (M. J. Ponting in Manning *et al.* 1994: 364-65; iid. 2002: 60-63).

Such evidence indicates that the supply of coinage to Cyprus, like many parts of the late empire, increased during the reigns of Heraclius and Constans II. Coins appear to have circulated widely on the island. Most reported examples are folles — the largest and best preserved bronze coins then in use. Despite its dwindling availability, some fractional coinage appears in the cities and even at villages like Kopetra, although the frequency with which such coins were used in rural marketplaces is unclear. Constantinople became increasingly prominent as a minting authority with the loss of Alexandria and shutting down of other mints in the 7th c. (Grierson 1982: 105-6; Hendy 1985: 417-21). Internal and external factors effectively curtailed supply to the province around mid century. Monetary reforms implemented by Constans II around 655 may have played a part, for relatively few folles were minted after 658 and subsequent coinage appears scarce everywhere (Yannopoulos 1983; Hendy 1985: 640-45; Morrisson 1986: 149-53 and 158-61). Of greater consequence was the disruption of traditional paths of Mediterranean exchange by the Arab campaigns, an event clearly preserved by the broader archaeological record (below, pp. 260-61). The short-lived countermarking of folles, probably carried out at Constantia under Constantine IV, can be interpreted as one symptom of the sharply reduced supply of coin to the island as well as continuing local demand (Dikigoropoulos 1940-48: 98-99; Grierson 1982: 121; Yannopoulos 1983). The scarcity of 8th- and 9th-c. coins in both town and country suggests that exchange during this period was carried out by other means, probably on a barter or in-kind basis. As elsewhere along the Byzantine periphery, Cypriots presumably adopted more self-sufficient strategies and developed networks of local exchange that relied less on externally supplied currency. Coins seem to have played only a minor rôle in their daily lives before the arrival of the Latins in the late 12th c. The denier of Henry II from Area II is typical of many Crusader coins that have turned up across the island, and foreshadows its growing integration into the economies of western Europe (Metcalf 1995; A. Destrooper-Georgiades in Prokopiou 1997b: 319-21).

Catalogue

C1 (fig. 4.2). AE3, Arcadius, 395-401, Constantinople.
Obv.: Bust r. (pearl diadem) DNARCADI VSPFAV[G].
Rev.: Emperor crowned by Victory. VIRTVS EXERCI[TI]. In ex., CONS[.
Cf. Grierson and Mays 1992: 124 nos. 218-22.
Lot II-1, 8340/5930 1.1, KK90-37.

C2 (fig. 4.2). Pentanummium(?), Justinian I or Justin II, 527-78, mint uncertain.
Obv.: Bust r.
Rev.: **V**.
Cf. Bellinger 1966: 177 no. 327; 192 no. 370.2; 259 nos. 208-9.
Lot V-3, 8315/6170 4.1, KK91-13.

C3 (fig. 4.2). Decanummium, Justinian I, 558/59, Nicomedia.
Obv.: Justinian, bust r. with diadem, cuirass, and *paludamentum*. Fragmentary inscription]IN[ ]ANV[ ]PP.
Rev.: **I** surmounted by cross. To l., ANNO; to r., XXXII; in ex., NIK.
Cf. Bellinger 1966: 123 no. 157.
Lot II-3, 8335/5930 2.4, KK91-15.

C4 (fig. 4.2). Dodecanummium, Phocas or early reign of Heraclius, *c.*602-28, Alexandria.
Obv.: Bust, obscure.
Rev.: **IB**. Between, cross; in ex., [A]LE[Ξ.
Cf. Grierson 1968: I, 192-95 nos. 105-6, cf. 336-37 no. 191.

Fig. 4.2. Coins: C1-5, 7-13.

RDAC 1989: 165 no. 14.
Lot I-1, surface, KK88-2.

C5 (fig. 4.2). Follis, Heraclius, 611-13, Nicomedia.
Obv.: Heraclius, bust with short beard, facing, wearing cuirass, *paludamentum*, and helmet with *pendilia*; in r. hand, gl. cr. Fragmentary inscription DNhR[ACLI...] (?).
Rev.: **M**. Beneath, A. To l., ANNO; to r., I[; in ex., NIKO. Overstruck.
Class 1; cf. Grierson 1968: I, 315-16 nos. 153a, 155a.
Lot VI-6, 8280/6050 3.1, KK91-14.

C6 (not illustrated). Follis, Heraclius, 612/13, Cyzicus.
Obv.: To l., Heraclius, and to r., Heraclius Constantine, both standing.
Rev.: **M**. To l., [ANN]O; to r. III (?); in ex., KYZ.
Class 2; cf. Grierson 1968: I, 325 no. 175.
Lot VI-2, 8280/6060 2.1, KK91-3.

C7 (fig. 4.2). Follis, Heraclius, 629/30, Constantinople.
Obv.: Heraclius standing, facing, wearing military dress and crown; in r. hand, long cross; l. hand on hip. To r., Heraclius Constantine standing, in r. hand gl. cross. To l. Rh (monogram).
Rev.: **M**. Beneath, A. To l., [AN]NO; to r., XX (?); in ex., CO[N].
Class 5; cf. Grierson 1968: I, 295 no. 105a.
Lot VI-5, 8280/6055 4.1, KK91-4.

C8 (fig. 4.2). Follis, Heraclius, 629/30, Constantinople.
Obv.: To left, Heraclius standing, wearing crown with cross; in r. hand, long cross, l. hand on hip. To r., Heraclius Constantine standing, wearing crown with cross; in r. hand, gl. cr. Between heads, cross.
Rev.: **M**. To l., ANNO; to r., XX; in ex., CON. Beneath, B.
Class 5; cf. Grierson 1968: I, 295-96 nos. 105b.1-3.
Lot II-13, 8345/5940 4.1, KK89-13.

C9 (fig. 4.2). Half-follis, Heraclius, 629/30, Constantinople?
Obv: To l., Heraclius standing, wearing military dress and crown with cross, holding large cross in r. hand. To r., Heraclius Constantine standing, wearing *chlamys* and crown with cross, in r. hand gl. cross. Between heads, cross.

Rev.: **K**. Above, cross; to l. [A]NNO; to r., XX. Beneath, Δ (?). Overstruck.
Class 5a; cf. Grierson 1968: I, 303 no. 118d.2, cf. no. 19c.
Lot II-2, 8335/5940 2.1, KK89-11.

C10 (fig. 4.2). Follis, Heraclius, 631-41, mint uncertain, clipped.
Obv.: In center, Heraclius with long beard, wearing military dress and crown with cross, holding long cross. To r., Heraclius Constantine; to l., Heraclonas.
Rev.: **M**. Above, christogram; to l., A]NNO; to r., XX (?); in ex., illegible.
Class 6; cf. Grierson 1968: I, 305-6 nos. 125-27.
Lot II-26, 8350/5945 6.1, KK90-33.

C11 (fig. 4.2). Follis, Constans II, 642/43, Constantinople?
Obv.: Constans standing, facing, wearing *chlamys* and crown; in r. hand, long cross; in l. hand gl., cr.
Rev.: **m**. Above, [A]NA; to l., [O]ΦA; in ex., to l., B.
Class 2; cf. Grierson 1968: II, 445 no. 61b.
Lot II-1, 8335/5940 1.1, KK89-12.

C12 (fig. 4.2). Follis, Constans II, 659/60, Constantinople.
Obv.: Constans standing, facing, in r. hand, long cross. To l., I over Q (?). To r., **M** over obscure *officina* mark; above, cross.
Rev.: Heraclius, Constantine IV, and Tiberius standing, facing, each wearing *chlamys* and crown with cross, holding gl. cross in r. hand. In field r., B.
Class 9; cf. Grierson 1968: II, 455 no. 82c.3.
Lot II-3, 8335/5930 2.3, KK91-7.

C13 (fig. 4.2). Silver denier, Henry II (1285-1324) or Hugh IV (1324-1359), Cyprus.
Obv.: Cross]:REI[.
Rev.: Lion of Cyprus, IR]L'M ED' Ch[IPR'].
Cf. Schlumberger 1878: 193-94 nos. 23, 26, pl. VI; des Gagniers and Tran Tam Tinh 1985: 89-90 nos. 24-25, 30, 32; Metcalf 1995: 323-26, 331-32; Giudice *et al.* 1998: 198 nos. A10, A11.
Lot II-2, 8335/5940S 2.1, KK89-30.

TABLE 5.1. SUMMARY OF ALL POTTERY RECOVERED AT KOPETRA, BY AREA AND PERIOD

Count	*Chal.* %	*Chal.* *no.*	*Br. Age* %	*Br. Age* *no.*	*EIA* %	*EIA* *no.*	*Cl.-H.* %	*Cl.-H.* *no.*	*Oth. Pre-Rom* %	*Oth. Pre-Rom* *no.*	*Roman* %	*Roman* *no.*	*Post-R.* %	*Post-R.* *no.*	*Total* %	*Total* *no.*
Survey	1.4	109	0.2	19	3.2	247	0.2	14	1.5	115	92.5	7170	1.0	75	23.3	7749
Area I	0.1	20	1.8	259	1.9	264	0.1	17	2.4	345	93.6	13210	0.0	3	42.5	14118
Area II	2.7	170	0.2	13	0.9	59	0.3	18	0.4	23	95.3	6015	0.3	16	19.0	6314
Area III	0.4	3			1.5	8			0.3	2	98.3	746			2.3	759
Area IV	0.2	2	0.1	1	1.0	11	0.1	1	0.5	5	98.1	1046			3.2	1066
Area V	0.3	1			6.3	19	1.8	6	1.0	3	90.1	274	0.3	1	0.9	304
Area VI	0.0	1			0.3	8	0.2	6	0.1	3	99.3	2901	0.0	1	8.8	2920
TOTAL	0.9	306	0.9	292	1.9	616	0.2	62	1.5	496	94.4	31362	0.3	96	100.0	33230

Weight	*Chal.* %	*Chal.* g	*Br. Age* %	*Br. Age* g	*EIA* %	*EIA* g	*Cl.-H.* %	*Cl.-H.* g	*Oth. Pre-Rom* %	*Oth. Pre-Rom* g	*Roman* %	*Roman* g	*Post-R.* %	*Post-R.* g	*Total* %	*Total* g
Survey	0.6	2440	0.1	485	5.8	23785	0.1	275	0.9	3630	92.2	377570	0.4	1470	36.7	409655
Area I	0.1	290	0.4	1371	1.3	4640	0.0	80	0.8	2780	97.5	352956	0.0	20	32.4	362137
Area II	1.0	1780	0.1	210	0.7	1300	0.2	385	0.2	355	97.4	174375	0.3	545	16.0	178950
Area III	0.5	30			1.6	90			0.4	25	97.5	5570			0.5	5715
Area IV	0.1	20	0.0	15	0.5	190	0.1	20	1.1	415	98.2	35555			3.2	36215
Area V	0.0	5			14.1	2470	4.9	845	1.7	300	78.7	13525	0.2	40	1.5	17185
Area VI	0.0	10			0.1	95	0.1	125	0.1	80	99.7	106590	0.0	30	9.6	106930
TOTAL	0.4	4575	0.2	2081	2.9	32570	0.2	1730	0.7	7585	95.5	1066141	0.2	2105	100.0	1116787

TABLE 5.2. SUMMARY OF ALL ROMAN POTTERY RECOVERED AT KOPETRA, BY AREA AND FUNCTIONAL CATEGORY

Count	*Fine* %	*Fine* no.	*Plain* %	*Plain* no.	*Amph.* %	*Amph.* no.	*Cook* %	*Cook* no.	*Pithos* %	*Pithos* no.	*Other* %	*Other* no.	*Total* %	*Total* no.
Survey	12.3	879	2.1	149	53.3	3825	6.9	494	11.3	812	14.1	1011	22.8	7170
Area I	5.8	762	4.6	610	53.1	7010	13.9	1838	6.6	866	16.2	2124	42.1	13210
Area II	6.1	366	6.8	412	56.9	3423	10.1	610	5.5	330	14.5	874	19.2	6015
Area III	8.8	65	3.8	28	41.6	310	10.6	79	1.9	14	33.5	250	2.4	746
Area IV	1.9	20	4.4	46	56.6	592	15.2	159	16.0	167	5.9	62	3.3	1046
Area V	11.3	31	9.5	26	40.5	111	13.5	37	9.9	27	15.3	42	1.0	274
Area VI	1.8	51	8.0	233	71.3	2067	10.3	299	4.5	131	4.1	120	9.2	2901
TOTAL	6.9	2174	4.8	1504	55.3	17338	11.2	3516	7.5	2347	14.3	4483	100.0	31362

Weight	*Fine* %	*Fine* g	*Plain* %	*Plain* g	*Amph.* %	*Amph.* g	*Cook* %	*Cook* g	*Pithos* %	*Pithos* g	*Other* %	*Other* g	*Total* %	*Total* g
Survey	4.4	16565	1.4	5360	44.5	168235	1.6	5845	43.4	163540	4.8	18025	35.4	377570
Area I	3.5	12184	3.3	11511	52.3	184728	3.6	12670	27.0	95225	10.4	36638	33.1	352956
Area II	3.9	6885	4.6	8040	49.3	85950	3.6	6205	31.4	54700	7.2	12595	16.4	174375
Area III	6.3	350	4.7	260	56.6	3155	4.9	275	6.5	360	21.0	1170	0.5	5570
Area IV	1.5	525	4.5	1595	44.4	15785	4.0	1415	42.9	15255	2.8	980	3.3	35555
Area V	4.8	650	7.2	975	18.7	2535	3.3	440	63.7	8615	2.3	310	1.3	13525
Area VI	1.1	1200	6.5	6945	65.4	69710	6.1	6470	19.1	20355	1.8	1910	10.0	106590
TOTAL	3.6	38359	3.3	34686	49.7	530098	3.1	33320	33.6	358050	6.7	71628	100.0	1066141

5
Roman and late Roman ceramics

"Nothing here but kitchen things," he said, with a little laugh for the insignificance of kitchen things.
Susan Glaspell, "A jury of her peers" (1918)

Introduction

The pottery from Kopetra reflects much of the long history of human habitation in the Vasilikos valley. Chalcolithic sherds attest the proximity of early prehistoric settlement on the W and S parts of the ridge. Scattered Late Bronze Age wares may come from either the large complex at *Ayios Dhimitrios* across the valley or contemporary burials at *Mangia* to the northeast. Iron Age pottery occurs across the site and is especially prominent near the adjacent *Mangia* ridge. By contrast, Classical, Hellenistic, and early Roman material was observed no more frequently than it has been in many parts of the valley. The predominance of 5th- through 7th-c. pottery indicates that the settlement at Kopetra was probably established and certainly flourished during this period (Table 5.1).

The material discussed in this chapter was assembled by informal reconnaissance, systematic surface survey, and controlled excavation. Apart from stray surface finds, all ceramics were processed by survey unit or excavation basket. Objects were taken to the project's *apotheke* in Kalavasos to be washed and dried. Sherds were sorted by wares and recorded by count and weight. The fragmentary nature of finds from the first season discouraged efforts to estimate vessel equivalents. In most cases the minimum sherd size for recording was 1 cm^2 of finished surface area and 5 g in weight. Contents of individual baskets (the primary unit of excavation) were noted on forms for entry into the expedition data base. Following the close of excavation, the records of individual baskets were combined into deposits and, following further study, into stratigraphic Lots. Virtually all of the excavated pottery is included in the summary tables above in chapt. 3 (Tables 3.4, 3.10, 3.17-3.19). The bulk of this material came from Areas I and II, which offer the most reliable assemblages for quantified study.

The main purpose of this chapter is to provide an overview of the ceramics used at Kopetra during late antiquity (Table 5.2). Functional categories, shapes, and fabrics are reviewed in this introduction. The catalogue presents a selection of vessels that illustrate the variety of fabrics and forms found between 1986 and 1992. Additional examples are included with the stratigraphic discussion of individual sectors. The pottery is organized by function and fabric, beginning with fine table vessels and continuing through plain wares, amphoras, cooking wares, and storage jars or *pithoi;* as a rule, open vessels precede closed shapes. Examples of the main types of rooftiles and water pipe appear at the end of the catalogue. Parallels cited are limited to less familiar forms, with priority given to other examples from Cyprus. Where evidence permits, an approximate date-range is suggested for the occurrence of a form in the E Mediterranean. The conclusion explores the significance of the assemblage. Pre-Roman pottery is summarized with discussion of the Kopetra area survey. The very few ceramic lamps are discussed with their respective deposits in chapt. 3. All published finds were deposited at the Larnaca District Archaeological Museum by June 1995, when most of the catalogue was completed. In a few cases further research has raised alternative identifications to those implied by the catalogue sequence, and these are discussed in the individual entries.

Fine wares

The fine table wares provide a framework of datable material reaching across the Kopetra ridge. Most of the pottery came from levels of collapse or abandonment dating to the mid to late 7th c. Excavation identified few closed deposits and none that included datable coins. The fine wares bear the primary responsibility for site phasing but offer little new evidence for assessing published chronologies (Table 5.3).

Fine wares account for 12.3% by count (4.4% by weight) of the survey material, with an average sherd weight of almost 19 g. At Areas I and II they comprise *c.*6% by count (3.7% by weight) of all pottery, with an

TABLE 5.3. SUMMARY OF ALL ROMAN FINE WARES, BY AREA AND WEIGHT

Count	*Survey* %	*Survey* *no.*	*Area I* %	*Area I* *no.*	*Area II* %	*Area II* *no.*	*Area III* %	*Area III* *no.*	*Area IV* %	*Area IV* *no.*	*Area V* %	*Area V* *no.*	*Area VI* %	*Area VI* *no.*	*Total* %	*Total* *no.*
CRS	56.0	492	41.7	318	62.6	229	43.1	28	65.0	13	58.1	18	56.9	29	51.8	1127
LRC	33.6	295	44.2	337	26.8	98	52.3	34	25.0	5	32.3	10	31.4	16	36.6	795
ARS	4.6	40	8.5	65	6.8	25	4.6	3	5.0	1	9.7	3	11.8	6	6.6	143
ERS	1.7	15	1.1	8											1.1	23
Other	4.2	37	4.5	34	3.8	14			5.0	1					4.0	86
Percent	100.0		100.0		100.0		100.0		100.0		100.0		100.0			
TOTAL		879		762		366		65		20		31		51	100.0	2174
Weight	*Survey* %	*Survey* *g.*	*Area I* %	*Area I* *g.*	*Area II* %	*Area II* *g.*	*Area III* %	*Area III* *g.*	*Area IV* %	*Area IV* *g.*	*Area V* %	*Area V* *g.*	*Area VI* %	*Area VI* *g.*	*Total* %	*Total* *g.*
CRS	67.2	11125	56.0	6817	70.7	4870	37.1	130	82.9	435	75.4	490	70.4	845	64.4	24712
LRC	24.5	4065	26.3	3202	18.0	1240	60.0	210	12.4	65	21.5	140	17.5	210	23.8	9132
ARS	4.4	725	13.7	1665	8.9	610	2.9	10	2.9	15	3.1	20	12.1	145	8.3	3190
ERS	1.2	200	0.6	75											0.7	275
Other	2.7	450	3.5	425	2.4	165			1.9	10					2.7	1050
Percent	100.0		100.0		100.0		100.0		100.0		100.0		100.0			
Total		16565		12184		6885		350		525		650		1200	100.0	38359

Avg. Sh. Wt.	*CRS no.*	*CRS wt.*	*CRS avg. wt.*	*LRC no.*	*LRC wt.*	*LRC avg. wt.*	*ARS no.*	*ARS wt.*	*ARS avg. wt.*	*misc. no.*	*misc. wt.*	*misc. avg. wt.*	*Total*	*Total wt.*	*Avg. sh. wt.*
Survey	492	11125	22.6	295	4065	13.8	40	725	18.1	52	650	12.5	879	16565	18.9
Area I	318	6817	21.4	334	3202	9.6	65	1665	25.6	42	500	11.9	762	12184	16.0
Area II	229	4870	21.3	98	1240	12.3	25	610	24.4	14	165	11.8	366	6885	18.8
Area III	28	130	4.6	34	210	6.2	3	10	3.3				65	350	5.4
Area IV	13	435	33.5	5	65	13.0	1	15	15.0	1	10	10.0	20	525	26.3
Area V	18	490	27.2	10	140	14.0	3	20	6.7				31	650	21.0
Area VI	29	845	29.1	16	210	13.1	6	145	24.7				51	1200	23.5
Site	1127	24712	21.9	792	9132	11.5	143	3190	22.3	109	1325	12.2	2174	38359	17.6

average weight of 16-19 g. At Area V, where the basilica's sanctuary makes up a larger portion of the total excavated area, they account for 11.3% by count (4.8% by weight) of the total, with an average weight of 21 g. The residential buildings in Areas IV and VI yielded fewer but generally larger sherds (*c.*1.8% by count, 1.3% by weight), with an average weight of 23-26 g. Cypriot Red Slip, Phocean Red Slip, and African Red Slip wares are well attested in the primary forms proposed by Hayes (1972). A few examples of Egyptian Red Slip and residual sigillata also were noted.

Cypriot Red Slip (CRS)

The most common fine ware at Kopetra is Cypriot Red Slip. It appears in the standard fabric and forms identified by Hayes (1972), whose suggestion of a Cypriot provenance is supported by distribution patterns and compositional study.[1] The fabric is uniformly fine grained. It has few visible inclusions apart from scattered fine particles and occasional large lumps of lime that erupted during firing and pit the surface. The appearance of lime in all forms suggests that a uniform clay source was employed and clay preparation was minimal. The fired clay has a hard texture and ranges in color from light reddish brown or light red to reddish yellow (2.5YR 6/4-6/6 to 5YR 6/4-7/6). A number of over-fired vessels extend the darker end of the spectrum to a distinctive maroon or purple. Refiring of test specimens from Paphos has found that original kiln temperatures reached 900-1000° C (M. Daszkiewicz and J. Raabe in Meyza 1995: 184). Inner surfaces and rims usually are carefully smoothed and covered with a slightly darker slip that often flakes in large patches. Outer walls are more summarily finished. Kiln stacking is reflected in the off-white or smoky black discoloration of the outer rims of many dishes.

---

1 Rautman *et al.* 1993; Gomez *et al.* 1995; Meyza 1995 and 2000; Schneider 2000: 533-34.

Cypriot Red Slip ware includes both shallow dishes and deep basins with sharply ridged walls, and is presented by the forms established by Hayes. A few examples of the early forms 1, 2, and 3 appear across the site, with the form 2 shallow dish the best represented (**1-7**). The form 8 dish/bowl with flat ledge rim is equally common among the survey pottery (**13-15**). The form 9 broad dish, the later 6th- and 7th-c. continuation of form 2, is the most frequently reported shape and accounts for almost half of all identified examples (**16-26**). The plain rim and low foot of form 9A represent the most common version, although the larger and more elaborate forms 9B and 9C are strongly represented. The few examples of cross-stamped floors probably belong to this shape (e.g., **21**). Of the three types of basins (forms 7, 10, and 11), the deeply-ridged and undecorated form 11 is the most common (**9-12, 27-31**). Other recorded shapes include several examples of the 'well form' first noted at Anemurium — a broad, shallow dish with rounded offset rim (**32-34**). An example of the rare form 6 dish/bowl (or domed lid) was recovered at Area II (**38**). A handful of sherds belong to closed shapes, apparently including a small pitcher (**36-37**). Unslipped vessels of this or a closely related fabric are discussed with plain ware group B.

The chronological scheme set out by Hayes is accepted with minor changes. Recent proposals have been made, especially on the basis of work at Jalame (Palestine) and Paphos, to push back the initial production of some vessel shapes, particularly forms 1-2 and 7-9, into the 5th c. or even earlier.[2] Few stratified deposits were identified at Jalame and the site's chronological problems have been discussed elsewhere (e.g., Hayes 1998b: 11-12; id. 2001b: 278; Meyza 2000). Excavations conducted in Paphos, by contrast, typically encounter those problems associated with the frequent damage and prolonged occupation of a complex urban site. The situation is complicated by an expanding corpus of published examples, including a number of shapes variously (but not always consistently) described as hybrid, transitional, or variant. Refinement of Hayes' original sequence may be long overdue, but the stratified evidence of most E Mediterranean sites still broadly supports his proposed chronology. We identified few good deposits to add to this discussion, yet the distribution of forms — both from sealed contexts and for Kopetra as a whole — agrees with the range of coins found at the site.

Cypriot Red Slip has been found across the coastal Near East from Cilicia to Egypt, with further examples reported in Cyrenaica and the Aegean, including Constantinople (Hayes 1972: 385-86; Meyza 1995: 187 pl. 2 for a recent distribution map). It is the dominant Late Roman fine ware in Cyprus, with the greatest formal variety noted in the vicinity of Paphos (Lund 1993: 111-13; Meyza 1995 and 2000). About a dozen main forms are present at Kopetra, where Cypriot Red Slip accounts for over half of all fine ware among the survey data and at most excavation sectors; only at Areas I and III is it surpassed by Phocean Red Slip. The date-range for the ware at Kopetra extends from the late 4th- to 5th-c. form 1 through the late 6th- to 7th-c. forms 9B/C, 10 and 11; most identifiable shapes belong to the 7th c. The average sherd size is *c.*21 g at Areas I and II, 23 g in the survey, and a little larger (27-33 g) at Areas IV, V, and VI. This can be compared to an average Cypriot Red Slip sherd weight of 25 g observed at Tell Keisan (Palestine) (Landgraf 1980: 66).

Phocean Red Slip/Late Roman C (LRC)

The second best-represented kind of fine pottery is Phocean Red Slip, still widely known as Late Roman C ware. Its main production area can be localized in the vicinity of Phocea (Eski Foça) on the W coast of Asia Minor.[3] A number of other regional centers apparently produced similar shapes using distinct local clays (e.g., variants of form 3 were made at Sardis; Rautman 1995b: 42), but these were not so widely distributed. The ware appears at Kopetra in its standard fabric and most popular shapes. The clay is normally fine grained and includes varying amounts of lime and occasional fine particles of mica or quartz. The hard-fired fabric is consistently light red in color (10R 6/6-6/8 to 2.5YR 6/6-6/8). Firing conditions apparently account for infrequent variations to red (10R 5/6-5/8) or reddish yellow (5YR 7/8). Inner surfaces and rims usually are carefully smoothed, while bases and outer walls often are scored by turning marks. The outer rims of some dishes of form 3 bear fine rouletting and more frequently are fired off-white or blackened. Several stamped floors preserve crosses and other images (**51-54**).

Apart from a few examples of the form 5 dish with horizontal rim, most identifiable vessels belong to the dish/bowl of form 3 and its successor form 10. Of the earlier examples the best-represented shapes are forms 3D, 3E, and 3F, which occur in differing proportions among the excavation sectors (**41-51**). These small dishes are distinguished primarily by their rims, which became shorter and broader during the 5th and 6th c.; all three variants occasionally carry rouletted decoration and stamped floors (Mackensen 1991; Vaag 2001). The small, unrouletted version of form 3F also was noted at Area II. The late 6th- to 7th-c. dish/bowl of form

---

2 E.g., Johnson 1988: 154; Meyza 1995 and 2000; Rowe 1998; id. 1999: 277.

3 Hayes 1980a: lix; Mayet and Picon 1986; Schneider 2000: 533.

10 is characterized by a heavy, squarish or flattened rim without exterior rouletting (**55-64**). Its great popularity at Kopetra indicates that the ware continued to reach the site during the first half of the 7th c. Finds from Areas I and VI suggest that Phocean Red Slip imports may actually have increased at this time and among the survey data almost half of all such sherds belong to this late shape. The heavy knobbed or square rim form 10A is the most common Phocean Red Slip vessel found at the site and comprises about a third of all identified examples recovered by the survey. While the rounded rims of forms 10B and 10C cannot always be distinguished, the flattened, elongated rim of form 10C, a 7th-c. shape, is well represented at Area I and in the survey. No example of the ware departs significantly from Hayes' original classification. A few aspects of his chronology have been refined by Mackensen (1991). Datable forms at Kopetra generally agree with other fine wares and coins from the site.

Phocean Red Slip was widely distributed across the E Mediterranean between the late 4th and 7th c. (Hayes 1972: 368-69; Abadie-Reynal 1989). Some 16 shapes were identified at Kopetra, where it accounts for about a third by count (24% by weight) of all fine wares, with an average sherd weighing *c.*11.5 g. The ware is best represented at Areas I and III, where it makes up 44% and 52% by count (26% and 60% by weight) of the fine wares. Here the low average sherd-weights of 9.6 g and 6.2 g suggest that some of the material may have come from redeposited fills. A similarly small average weight of 7.9 g was noted for Phocean Red Slip at Tell Keisan (Landgraf 1980: 66).

African Red Slip (ARS)

African Red Slip ware constitutes a small but important part of the assemblage, thanks to its known origin in Tunisia and developed typological study.[4] The fabric at Kopetra appears typical of the ware's later production phases: it is generally coarse grained with noticeable lime and quartz inclusions. The hard-textured body is consistently light red in color (10R 6/8 to 2.5YR 6/8). Inner surfaces are usually carefully smoothed and coated with a hard red slip, which is frequently pitted by erupting particles of lime.

The forms and chronological sequence presented by Hayes (1972 and 1980a) in some cases have been adjusted following suggestions offered by Fulford and Peacock (1984), Mackensen (1993), and Lund (1995). The 56 sherds of identifiable shape found at Kopetra broadly agree with the dates offered by the other fine pottery and document a small but steady supply to the site.

African Red Slip traveled widely across the late empire and is found throughout the E Mediterranean. Ten distinct forms were identified at Kopetra, where the ware accounts for 6.6% by count (8.3% by weight) of all fine pottery. The thick, durable walls yield an average sherd size of *c.*18 g in the survey and 25 g at Areas I, II, and VI. Among the earlier examples are forms 67, 93, and 97, bowls dating to the late 5th and mid 6th c. (**65-69**). Most identifiable vessels belong to the 6th- and early 7th-c. forms 104 through the dish/plate 107, which account for 79% and 93% by count of the ware at Areas I and II, respectively (**72-82**). The most commonly recognized shape is the broad dish with heavy rim form 105. A few examples of the spiral-burnished dish form 109 (late 6th to late 7th c.) conclude the series (**83**).

Egyptian Red Slip (ERS)

Several fabrics were distinguished among the Egyptian Red Slip series, which was produced at various sites.[5] Only a few examples of Egyptian Red Slip wares were recorded at Area I, confirming the general scarcity noted by the Kopetra and VVP surveys — and for that matter elsewhere on the island.[6] This is surprising in view of Egypt's geographic proximity to Cyprus and may reflect its limited distribution in this direction. Recognized examples at Kopetra present a soft texture and light body ranging in color from light reddish brown to brown or pink (5YR 6/4 to 7.5YR 5/4-7/4). The clay has a soft, dull appearance and contains many dark inclusions. The slip is flat dark red and often flakes badly. The handful of recorded forms includes simple out-turned rims with lightly punched or rouletted ornament (**84-86**).

Other fine wares

Residual sigillata and other unidentified red fabrics make up less than 5% of the fine wares. Recognized forms include small bowls of Cypriot Sigillata and Eastern Sigillatas A and perhaps B (**87-93**). The paucity of identified fine table vessels and other ceramics from the 1st through 4th c. suggests only intermittent activity before the 5th c. (see also below, p. 208).

---

4 Hayes 1972; Peacock, Bejaoui, and Ben Lazreg 1990; Mackensen 1993 and 1998; Lund 1995; Reynolds 1995; Taylor and Robinson 1996.

5 Hayes 1972: 387-401; Rodziewicz 1976; Egloff 1977; Ballet and Picon 1987.

6 Cf. Hayes 1972: 395-97; id. 1980b; Lund 1993; Manning *et al.* 2002: 42.

Plain wares

Kopetra's plain pottery encompasses a number of unslipped vessels and basins of evident domestic use. Previous reports of Cypriot excavations have not distinguished consistently among Roman plain wares and offer only a prelude to their future systematic study. The material was too fragmentary to establish individual wares, which in the case of small pieces sometimes can be confused with amphoras. While it is assumed on the basis of other finds that most examples are Late Roman in date, some may be slightly earlier. Sherds of similar fabrics and shapes were assigned to 4 categories (Table 5.4).

TABLE 5.4. SUMMARY OF ALL ROMAN PLAIN AND COOKING WARES AND *PITHOI*, BY AREA AND WEIGHT

Count	*Survey* %	*Survey* no.	*Area I* %	*Area I* no.	*Area II* %	*Area II* no.	*Area III* %	*Area III* no.	*Area IV* %.	*Area IV* no.	*Area V* %	*Area V* no.	*Area VI* %	*Area VI* no.	*TOTAL* %	*TOTAL* no.
Plain A	7.4	11	3.9	24	12.1	50	10.7	3	2.2	1	11.5	3	9.4	22	7.6	114
Plain B	54.4	81	61.0	372	46.1	190	82.1	23	8.7	4	23.1	6	47.6	111	52.3	787
Plain C			1.3	8	1.2	5			2.2	1	11.5	3	0.4	1	1.2	18
Plain D	38.3	57	33.8	206	40.5	167	7.1	2	87.0	40	53.9	14	42.5	99	38.9	585
TOTAL	100.0	149	100.0	610	100.0	412	100.0	28	100.0	46	100.0	26	100.0	233	100.0	1504
Cook A	9.3	46	2.0	37	11.1	68			6.9	11	10.8	4	7.7	23	5.4	189
Cook B	0.4	2			4.1	25									0.8	27
Cook C	1.0	5	1.4	26	12.0	73			5.0	8	2.7	1	35.5	106	6.2	219
Cook D	89.3	441	96.6	1775	72.8	444	100.0	79	88.1	140	86.5	32	56.9	170	87.6	3081
TOTAL	100.0	494	100.0	1838	100.0	610	100.0	79	100.0	159	100.0	37	100.0	299	100.0	3516
Pithos A	10.3	84	11.6	100	6.7	22			2.4	4			5.3	7	9.3	217
Pithos B	9.0	73	6.9	60	28.2	93	57.1	8	13.8	23	25.9	7	23.7	31	12.6	295
Pithos C	6.2	50	3.9	34	21.5	71	7.1	1	1.8	3	3.7	1	27.5	36	8.4	196
Pithos D	74.5	605	77.6	672	43.6	144	35.7	5	82.0	137	70.4	19	43.5	57	69.8	1639
TOTAL	100.0	812	100.0	866	100.0	330	100.0	14	100.0	167	100.0	27	100.0	131	100.0	2347
Weight	*Survey* %	*Survey* g	*Area I* %	*Area I* g	*Area II* %	*Area II* g	*Area III* %	*Area III* g	*Area IV* %	*Area IV* g	*Area V* %	*Area V* g	*Area VI* %	*Area VI* g	*TOTAL* %	*TOTAL* g
Plain A	8.7	465	5.0	570	9.7	780	30.8	80	0.3	5	28.7	280	7.5	520	7.8	2700
Plain B	24.2	1295	38.7	4450	29.6	2380	59.6	155	2.5	40	9.7	95	31.9	2215	30.7	10630
Plain C			1.3	150	2.8	225			0.6	10	3.6	35	0.1	10	1.2	430
Plain D	67.2	3600	55.1	6341	57.9	4655	9.6	25	96.6	1540	58.0	565	60.5	4200	60.3	20926
TOTAL	100.0	5360	100.0	11511	100.0	8040	100.0	260	100.0	1595	100.0	975	100.0	6945	100.0	34686
Cook A	10.0	585	2.0	255	9.8	605			12.0	170	4.6	20	2.5	160	5.4	1795
Cook B	0.5	30			1.6	100									0.4	130
Cook C	4.7	275	12.4	1570	39.8	2470			30.4	430	37.5	165	74.8	4840	29.3	9750
Cook D	84.8	4955	85.6	10845	48.8	3030	100.0	275	57.6	815	58.0	255	22.7	1470	65.0	21645
TOTAL	100.0	5845	100.0	12670	100.0	6205	100.0	275	100.0	1415	100.0	440	100.0	6470	100.0	33320
Pithos A	9.5	15450	13.8	13105	8.6	4710			10.5	1605			7.9	1605	10.2	36475
Pithos B	9.2	15055	7.7	7290	21.5	11765	33.3	120	37.6	5730	23.7	2045	21.3	4340	12.9	46345
Pithos C	6.7	10920	5.1	4820	35.5	19435	23.6	85	4.0	615	4.4	380	31.0	6310	11.9	42565
Pithos D	74.7	122115	73.5	70010	34.4	18790	43.1	155	47.9	7305	71.9	6190	39.8	8100	65.0	232665
TOTAL	100.0	163540	100.0	95225	100.0	54700	100.0	360	100.0	15255	100.0	8615	100.0	20355	100.0	358050

Group A

Plain ware vessels made in several heavy, dense fabrics belong to this category. These coarse-grained clays have many medium to large lime, quartz, and other inclusions that give the outer surface a rough, gritty texture. The color of the fired clay ranges from light red (2.5YR 6/6) to yellowish red and light reddish brown (7.5YR 7/4-7/6 to 10YR 6/4-7/3). Group A vessels are mostly basins with straight walls and simple flattened rims (**94-99**). Other examples include unslipped kitchen vessels and heavy flat lids (**100-109**). Up to 8% of Kopetra's plain pottery belongs to this category, whose provenance remains undetermined.

Group B

This category includes a narrow range of light-bodied, fine-grained fabrics that carry few inclusions apart from scattered particles or small lumps of lime. The fired clay varies from light red to very pale brown and pink in color (5YR 6/6-7/8 to 7.5YR 7/4-8/4), resembling the lighter end of the Cypriot Red Slip spectrum; small sherds can be difficult to distinguish from worn examples of fine pottery. Compositional analysis of group B sherds confirms the close relationship of the two wares (below, Appendix 3). The largest vessels of this category are broad, open bowls and basins with straight walls (**110-16**). Most often the fabric is found in small jugs or pitchers that rise from a ring base to a plain vertical rim with a narrow strap handle (**117-26**). Such vessels generally were wet-smoothed before firing, giving outer walls a uniform, buff appearance. Related examples identified as unslipped versions of Cypriot Red Slip have been reported on the island (e.g., at Paphos: Meyza 2000: 515). Group B fabrics are the most common of the classified plain wares, accounting for about half of the total by count (30% by weight).

Group C

Examples of these fabrics are distinguished by their light body and conspicuously micaceous surface, which suggests a source in Asia Minor. Members of this group belong mostly to small closed vessels. The few identified examples came primarily from Areas I and II.

Group D

All other fabrics appear under this heading in the Tables. Among the standard shapes is a small spherical cup that rises from a flat or gently rounded base through a lightly ridged wall to end in a plain vertical rim (**130-32**); in one case two small strap handles attach to the rim. The medium-grained yellowish red fabric (2.5YR 5/6-5YR 5/6) contains fine particles of lime and quartz, a little gold mica, and many small dark inclusions. Other examples are more poorly preserved. Broadly similar shapes are known in Palestine and Syria.[7]

Amphoras

Amphoras account for almost half by count of the Roman and Late Roman pottery at Kopetra. Roughly two-thirds of all amphora sherds belong to the type of panel-ridged vessel known as LR1, which appears at the site in several different fabrics reflecting multiple production centers in Cilicia, Syria, and Cyprus. Other recognized amphora types were imported from Gaza (LR4), Palestine (LR5/6), Egypt (LR7), Syria (KAmp2), the Aegean coastlands (LR2, 3, and perhaps KAmp1), N Africa (KAmp5), and other unidentified sources. Altogether 13 types in various fabrics were distinguished in recording. The quantified data are conditioned by the limits of excavation — especially at Areas III-V, where the recovery of multiple fragments of individual vessels has a significant effect on the summary tables (Table 5.5). As at other sites, small body sherds could not always be distinguished from similar plain wares.

LR1

This class of amphora describes a sandy-textured cylindrical vessel with a distinctive panel-ridged body (**142-44**). The thin wall rises from a rounded base to a broad shoulder with a tall cylindrical neck and plain vertical rim. The wall is covered with a characteristic pattern of horizontal ridges that appear closely set toward top and bottom but more widely spaced at the vessel's slightly pinched mid-section and shoulder. Two heavy rolled handles with deep lengthwise grooves are joined by roughly splayed attachments to neck and shoulder. As noted elsewhere, there is some evidence at Kopetra for distinguishing larger and smaller versions of the basic form. The height of most examples known from other sites is *c.*0.4-0.5 m; estimated capacities range widely from less than 6 to over 25 liters.[8] Considerable variation also exists in the height and proportions of the neck, the set of the handles, and the rim form. Red and brown cursive dipinti and other markings occasionally appear on the necks and shoulders. Few if any examples at Kopetra preserve traces of a pitch lining.

LR1 amphoras appear to have been made at several E Mediterranean locations and usually are associated with the production of olive oil and sometimes wine, primarily from the early 5th through mid 7th c.[9] Such

---

7 E.g., Peleg 1989: 76-77; Sodini and Villeneuve 1992: 199-202.

8 Egloff 1977: 112; Bass 1982: 155-63; van Alfen 1996: 203-7.

9 Riley 1979: 215; Rossiter and Freed 1991: 158-59; van Alfen 1996: 208-9; Arthur and Oren 1998: 201-3; Decker 2001: 76-80.

TABLE 5.5. SUMMARY OF ALL ROMAN AMPHORAS, BY AREA AND WEIGHT

Count	*Survey* %	*Survey* no.	*Area I* %	*Area I* no.	*Area II* %	*Area II* no.	*Area III* %	*Area III* no.	*Area IV* %	*Area IV* no.	*Area V* %	*Area V* no.	*Area VI* %	*Area VI* no.	*Total* %	*Total* no.
LR1	69.9	2673	71.8	5031	60.4	2069	69.7	216	63.3	375	63.1	70	75.7	1564	69.2	11998
LR2	0.2	9	1.3	94	5.7	194			2.9	17	9.0	10	0.4	8	1.9	332
LR3	0.0	1	0.0	2					0.2	1					0.0	4
LR4	0.7	27	3.3	233	6.1	209	4.8	15	1.7	10	3.6	4	10.7	222	4.2	720
LR5/6	0.3	10	0.7	51	6.5	221	4.2	13	9.1	54	4.5	5	6.8	140	2.9	494
LR7	0.0	1	0.3	24	2.0	69	0.3	1	2.9	17	2.7	3	0.2	5	0.7	120
KAmp1	0.8	30	0.7	49	1.1	38			1.0	6			0.1	4	0.7	127
KAmp2	3.9	148	0.3	22	2.9	98	6.8	21	3.4	20	6.3	7	1.5	31	2.0	347
KAmp3	0.5	19	0.2	16	0.1	2									0.2	37
KAmp4	0.7	27	0.3	24	2.9	99	2.9	9	0.2	1					0.9	160
KAmp5	0.3	13	0.3	23	3.8	130	1.0	3	1.7	10	2.7	3	0.2	5	1.1	187
KAmp6	0.9	33	0.9	66											0.6	99
KAmp7	0.2	7	0.0	1	0.1	2									0.1	10
Other	21.6	827	19.6	1374	8.5	292	10.3	32	13.7	81	8.1	9	4.3	88	15.6	2703
TOTAL	100.0	3825	100.0	7010	100.0	3423	100.0	310	100.0	592	100.0	111	100.0	2067	100.0	17338
LR1(1)	12.3	470	7.5	528	7.6	261	0.3	1	13.7	81	5.4	6	50.6	1045	13.7	2392
LR1(2)	36.5	1397	28.9	2026	13.3	456	11.3	35	16.4	97	18	20	2.7	56	23.6	4087
LR1(3)	20.1	770	22.7	1591	15.9	544	16.5	51	9.6	57	16.2	18	8.7	180	18.5	3211
LR1(5)	0.9	36	12.6	886	23.6	808	41.6	129	23.6	140	23.4	26	13.7	283	13.3	2308
LR1 all	69.6	2673	71.8	5031	60.4	2069	69.7	216	63.3	375	63.1	70	75.7	1564	69.2	11998

Weight	*Survey* %	*Survey* g	*Area I* %	*Area I* g	*Area II* %	*Area II* g	*Area III* %	*Area III* g	*Area IV* %	*Area IV* g	*Area V* %	*Area V* g	*Area VI* %	*Area VI* g	*Total* %	*Total* g
LR1	74.9	126010	74.6	137865	61.3	52695	74.8	2360	65.8	10380	60.2	1525	73.8	51425	72.1	382260
LR2	0.1	235	2.1	3860	5.8	4940			5.8	915	7.9	200	0.2	155	1.9	10305
LR3	0.0	60	0.0	70					0.1	10					0.0	140
LR4	0.9	1550	3.4	6225	5.2	4490	6.0	190	1.9	300	3.0	75	12.8	8925	2.4	12830
LR5/6	0.3	500	0.7	1250	4.6	3975	3.3	105	6.1	960	1.6	40	7.3	5110	2.3	11940
LR7	0.1	100	0.9	1670	1.6	1360	0.3	10	4.4	690	1.2	30	0.2	165	0.4	2355
KAmp1	0.4	715	0.4	725	0.9	740			0.5	75			0.3	200	0.5	2455
KAmp2	4.0	6760	0.4	685	4.4	3750	6.5	205	2.3	370	9.5	240	1.6	1105	2.5	13115
KAmp3	0.5	820	0.2	325	0.2	190									0.3	1335
KAmp4	0.6	930	0.6	1020	3.7	3175	2.9	90	0.3	40					2.7	14180
KAmp5	0.6	1075	0.4	785	3.0	2595	1.0	30	1.5	240	9.7	245	0.1	85	1.0	5055
KAmp6	1.2	2085	1.3	2360											0.8	4445
KAmp7	0.2	325	0.0	50	0.1	65									0.1	440
Other	16.1	27070	15.1	27838	9.3	7975	5.2	165	11.4	1805	7.1	180	3.6	2540	13.1	69243
TOTAL	100.0	168235	100.0	184728	100.0	85950	100.0	3155	100.0	15785	100.0	2535	100.0	69710	100.0	530098
LR1(1)	14.1	23795	8.7	16115	7.6	6565	0.3	10	18.0	2850	10.3	260	49.6	34560	15.9	84155
LR1(2)	33.2	55840	31.6	58340	13.3	11400	9.7	305	15.8	2500	11.8	300	3.9	2730	24.8	131415
LR1(3)	26.1	43980	22.6	41800	19.9	17080	29.0	915	12.3	1935	10.1	255	8.7	6075	21.2	112040
LR1(5)	1.4	2395	11.7	21610	20.5	17650	35.8	1130	19.6	3095	28.0	710	11.6	8060	10.3	54650
LR1 all	74.9	126010	74.6	137865	61.3	52695	74.8	2360	65.8	10380	60.2	1525	73.8	51425	72.1	382260

vessels are regularly reported in multiple fabrics (Riley 1979: 212; Williams 1989: 95; Lund 1993: 130). Kiln sites have been posited (if not always demonstrated) along the Cilician and Syrian coastlines, as well as in

Cyprus itself.[10] The fabrics most often found at Kopetra are designated LR1(1), LR1(2), and LR1(3) in the summary tables; fabric LR1(5) includes all other or uncertain sherds.

LR1(1) amphoras are readily distinguished by their dull color and gritty surface. The fired fabric extends through a wide range of subdued tones from light brown or pink (10YR 7/4 to 7.5YR 7/4) to a dull pale yellow, light gray, or dingy white (2.5Y 8/2 to 5Y 7/2-8/2). The clay is relatively smooth in texture but appears loaded with many medium to large red, green, and black inclusions that give the surface a rough, almost rasp-like texture. Many sherds leave jagged breaks and tend to laminate and splinter; the generally dull surface texture suggests low firing temperatures. Thin-section analysis of representative specimens identified a fine-grained marly clay groundmass with basic rock fragments and abundant pyroxene inclusions that may have been added as a temper. Some examples exhibit a hypocrystalline groundmass with distinctive round rock fragments and grains of clinopyroxene and olivine, reminiscent of peridotite, or wehrlite (Rautman *et al.* 1999: 379). Thin-section and compositional study of the fabric reveals close affinities with clays found in the S central part of Cyprus, and suggests that most LR1(1) amphoras were manufactured in this area. The fabric appears close to the 'Cypriot version' of the LR1 form identified at Kourion by Hayes (forthcoming), where it is especially common in 7th-c. levels; it may also occur at Yassi Ada (van Alfen 1996: 195-96 type IV). At Kopetra the fabric constitutes *c.*7.5% by count of all amphoras at Areas I and II, and 12.3% by count of the survey amphoras. A single example of a low stand was identified in the same fabric (**174**).

LR1(2) is the most commonly encountered amphora fabric at Kopetra and accounts for about one-third of all LR1 sherds from the site. This sandy-textured fabric was fired to a light red to reddish yellow core (2.5YR 6/6 to 7.5YR 6/6-7/7), with a lighter reddish yellow surface (5YR 7/6-7/8). The surface is speckled with many fine particles of lime and altered pyroxenes that appear as small red, green, gray, and black inclusions. Large quartz lumps and even small chips of pottery (in one case a fragment of Eastern Sigillata A) are occasionally found in the body. Individual sherds have a crisp, brittle texture that breaks with sharp edges. Thin-section analysis found the fine-grained bioclastic groundmass to contain recrystallized patches, occasional chert and quartz grains, discrete foraminifera (microfossils), micritic clasts and drusy replacements, fine clinopyroxenes, and altered amphiboles. Larger inclusions are calcareous constituents and common pyroxenes, which also have been identified in examples from other sites.[11] Compositional study noted a close relationship between examples of LR1(2) and LR1(3), which probably originated in the same region. Similar fabrics have been reported throughout the E Mediterranean and apparently were produced at multiple locations in Cilicia and Syria.[12]

LR1(3) is a similar sandy-textured fabric that generally makes up 15-20% of all amphoras at the site. The medium-grained fabric varies in section from reddish yellow to very pale brown (5YR 6/6 to 10YR 7/3-7/4), while the surface is a lighter pale yellow (about 2.5YR 8/4). Fine lime, quartz, and dark red inclusions give an evenly speckled section but are less visible on the finished surface, which usually takes on a worn, mottled appearance lacking the crisply variegated surface of LR1(2). Breaks tend to be uneven and rough, but without jagged splintering. Thin-section study identified a fine-grained marly clay groundmass containing neomorphic patches of micrite and discrete foraminifera. Among the larger inclusions are altered basic rock fragments and pyroxene (Rautman *et al.* 1999: 379). The chemical resemblance of LR1(2) and LR1(3) specimens indicates that the two fabrics are closely related and probably were produced over the same region. The chronological relationship between the two variants remains unclear.

LR1(5) includes all examples of this shape that could not be assigned to one of the above groups.

LR1 amphoras in various fabrics and a range of sizes were widely distributed across the Mediterranean between the 5th and mid 7th c. (Martini and Steckner 1993: 197-98 fig. 46 for a distribution map). While very common in Constantinople, Cilicia, Syria, Cyprus, and Cyrenaica (Riley 1979: 212-15; Hayes 1992: 63-64), the type is less well represented in Palestine.[13] It is the most frequently reported amphora in Cyprus.[14] The

---

10 Ballet and Picon 1987: 24; Empereur and Picon 1988 and 1989; Touma 1989: 873; Michaelides 1998: 236-37; Demesticha 2000; Manning *et al.* 2000; Demesticha and Michaelides 2001.

11 Peacock and Williams 1986: 185-87; Williams 1987: 237; Rautman *et al.* 1999: 379.

12 Riley 1979: 212-15; Peacock and Williams 1986: 185-87; Empereur and Picon 1988: 38; iid. 1989: 242; Touma 1989: 873; id. 2001: 50.

13 Riley 1975: 33; Tubb 1986: 55-56; Johnson 1988: 212; Oleson *et al.* 1994: 15; Kingsley 1999: 270.

14 There are published examples from Cape Andreas (Green 1973: 161, figs. 21-22; Taylor and Megaw 1981: 221 nos. 362 and 387-89; Parker 1992a: 107-8), Cape Kiti (Engvig and Åström 1975: fig. 22 no. S-

lack of consistency in published forms and fabric descriptions reflects considerable variation among production centers, which usually requires laboratory analysis to ascertain (below, Appendix 3; Empereur and Picon 1989: 242; Rautman *et al.* 1999). Many of the examples found in Cyprus appear to be in the standard fabrics LR1(2) and LR1(3), which originated on the mainland. Cypriot LR1(1) fabric amphoras may be among those reported at Cape Andreas, Salamis, Dhiorios, Ayios Philon, Ayios Kononas, and Kourion. Empereur and Picon (1988; iid. 1989: 242; Touma 1989: 873; id. 2001: 50) suggest that LR1 amphoras were produced at Amathus and Kourion. A recently excavated kiln site at Paphos yielded examples of LR1 fabric amphoras (Demesticha 2000; Demesticha and Michaelides 2001). Another kiln (for the smaller version LR1a) may have been located near the Vasilikos river outlet at Zyyi-*Petrini* (Manning *et al.* 2000).

LR2

This amphora type designates a distinctive thick-walled globular vessel that rises from a rounded base with small knobbed toe to a broad shoulder (**145-47**). The neck rises to a plain rounded rim or (more often) flares outward. Heavy rolled handles join the upper shoulder and neck. Shoulder and upper body are scored by closely-set deep, horizontal grooves; the wavy patterns noted elsewhere in later 6th- and early 7th-c. contexts do not appear regularly at Kopetra.[15] Complete examples from other sites stand 0.45-0.55 m in height and have an average capacity of 30-40 liters (Bass 1982: 157-63). At Kopetra the fabric is typically medium-grained and ranges in color from red to light reddish brown (10R 6/6 to 2.5YR 6/4-6/6), tending to be a little darker (about 2.5YR 5/2-6/2) on the outer surface. The fabric carries much mica and lime particles as large as 0.003 m; the surface is usually pitted by numerous irregular voids. Observed variations in fabric and manufacture as well as distribution patterns suggest that amphoras of this type were produced at several places around the Aegean and Black Sea.[16] Cypriot production seems unlikely (cf. Hautumm 1981: 46; Abadie-Reynal 1989: 157).

LR2 amphoras were produced primarily between the late 4th and early 7th c. and apparently carried both oil and wine (Karagiorgou 2001: 146-47). They appear across the Mediterranean but are not frequently found in the Near East (Riley 1979: 218; Hautumm 1981: 30-45). LR2 amphoras occasionally are reported in Cyprus,[17] but are not common among the surface finds from the Vasilikos valley survey. At Kopetra the greatest concentration of LR2 amphoras was noted at Area II, where they comprise over 5% of all amphoras from the sector. At Area I they account for only 1-2% of the total.

LR3

The thin wall of this elongated amphora type rises steeply from a narrow base to an ovoid body with broad shoulder, a slender neck, and thickened rim. One or two looped handles join the upper shoulder and neck. Complete examples from other sites average 0.4-0.7 m in height with a capacity of 10-12 liters.[18] The fabric is distinctively fine grained and includes abundant mica; at other sites the fabrics appear gray, reddish brown, and red. Petrographic study suggests an origin in western Asia Minor. A resinous interior coating noted on many examples indicates that LR3 amphoras were commonly used to transport wine, although evidence for olive oil is also known.[19] These 'micaceous water jars' were distributed across the Mediterranean from early Roman times down through the 6th c., but are less commonly found in the Near East (Riley 1975: 3). Among the few examples reported from Cyprus is a vessel from the N necropolis at Kition

---

20c, fig. 28 no. S-30c; McCaslin 1978: figs. 247-48 N9018, fig. 258 N2029; Engvig and Beichmann 1984: 182 nos. S-100c to 105c, figs. 3-8), Salamis (Diederichs 1980b: 55 nos. 211-35), Dhiorios (Catling 1972: 32 no. P319, 44 no. P266), Kornos (Catling and Dikigoropoulos 1970: 47 no. 4), Paphos (Daszewski 1970: 141, pl. XXXIII:5; Megaw 1971: 131 and 146, fig. 5 no. 22; Giudice *et al.* 1999: 286-91 nos. 18, 24 and 35, figs. 3b.5, 3c.1 and 3d.1), Peyia-*Ayios Yeoryios* (Bakirtzis 2000: 165 photo 1), Alassa-*Ayia Mavri* (Flourentzos 1996: 18 nos. 42-43, p. 20 no. 95, p. 24), Kourion (Leonard 1987: 108 fig. 61b; Hayes forthcoming), Amathus (Empereur 1985: 989 fig. 36; Touma 1989: 873; id. 2001: 50), and elsewhere along the S coast (Morris and Peatfield 1987: 210-11, nos. K109, TS117-120, Lund 1993: 130-32; K. Jacobsen in Sørensen *et al.* 1998: 359; Manning *et al.* 2002: 42).

15 Cf. Bass 1982: 159-60; Abadie-Reynal and Sodini 1992: 56; Hayes 1992: 66.

16 Riley 1979: 217-19; Megaw and Jones 1983: 246; Peacock and Williams 1986: 182-84; Martini and Steckner 1993: 197-98 fig. 46 for a distribution map; Karagiorgou 2001.

17 Engvig and Åström 1975: fig. 41 no. S-58c; Taylor and Megaw 1981: 221 no. 369, fig. 43; des Gagniers and Tran Tam Tinh 1985: 98 nos. 96a-c, figs. 229-31; Manning *et al.* 2002: 42.

18 Robinson 1959: 15; Egloff 1977: 116; Rautman 1995b: 64-66.

19 Riley 1979: 183-86, 229-30; Peacock and Williams 1986: 188-90; Oleson *et al.* 1994: 16.

(Nicolaou 1976: 261, pl. XXXIII: 2). A few sherds also are known at Maroni-*Petrera* (Manning *et al.* 2002: 42). Only 4 fragmentary examples were noted at Kopetra.

LR4

Several varieties of thick-walled cylindrical vessels belong to this amphora type (**148-50**). The straight wall rises from a rounded or conical base and narrows to a relatively wide mouth; rims tend to be short and rounded, occasionally curving slightly outward. Short, crudely formed handles define tight loops attached to opposite points on the shoulder, which frequently is scored by deep horizontal grooves. Irregular clay blobs often were smeared across the roughly finished surface, especially around the mouth and splayed handle attachments. Complete specimens from other sites range up to 0.85 m in height with an estimated capacity of 16 to 26.5 liters.[20] The fabric at Kopetra is dull and medium grained, ranging in color from reddish yellow to light red (5YR 6/6 to 2.5YR 6/8) on the surface to a gray interior and core. Fine mica, medium to large particles of lime and quartz, and occasional shell fragments occur throughout the body. Petrographic analysis and distribution patterns suggest an origin in the vicinity of Ashkelon and Gaza, but the vessels may have been produced elsewhere as well; at least 4 fabrics have been distinguished.[21] Drawing on a tradition that may go back to the 1st c. A.D., most amphoras of this type date from the 4th through 7th c. Earlier examples seem to be shorter and more carefully manufactured; the large, crudely finished vessels found at Kopetra belong to the later phases of production.[22] The principal contents were wine, including the renowned white wines of Roman Gaza, and less frequently olive oil.[23] Gaza amphoras are well known throughout the E Mediterranean (Kingsley 2001: fig. 3.4 for a recent distribution map). In Cyprus they have been reported at Kourion (Williams 1987: 236-37; Hayes forthcoming), Peyia-*Ayios Yeoryios* (Bakirtzis 1996: 159, fig. 10), Paphos (Giudice *et al.* 1999: 286 no. 17, fig. 3b.4), and around Palaepaphos (Lund 1993: 132-33). They appear at Zyyi-*Petrini*, and at Maroni-*Petrera* account for *c.*10% of all amphoras by weight (Manning *et al.* 2000: 251; iid. 2002: 42). While not well represented in the Kopetra survey, LR4 amphoras account for 3.3% and 6.1% by count of the amphoras excavated at Areas I and II, respectively.

LR5/6

This amphora type, the so-called Palestinian bag amphora or baggy jar, consists of a broad vessel with a rounded bottom and wide waist (**151-53**). The relatively thick wall rises through sloping shoulders to a short neck with vertical rim. Paired handles form small loops on the upper shoulder. Light ridging covers the outer wall, narrowing to a finely spaced, shallow grooving on the upper shoulder. Complete examples from other sites average slightly less than 0.5 m in height, with an estimated capacity of 20-26.5 liters (Egloff 1977: 117-18; Kingsley 2001: 50). Elsewhere, amphoras of this form have been noted in red and gray fabrics (designated LR5 and LR6, respectively) but only the red version was consistently identified at Kopetra. The sandy-textured, medium-grained fabric averages reddish yellow (5YR 7/6) with a pinkish surface; the body is finely speckled with gray, red, green, and black inclusions as well as larger particles of quartz. Petrographic analysis and distribution patterns suggest that the most common fabrics originated in Palestine.[24] Vessels of this shape may also have been produced at other locales in Egypt and the Near East;[25] even Amathus may have produced its own version (Touma 2001: 50). This was a multi-purpose domestic container which, when pressed into commercial use, often contained wine (Johnson 1988: 214; Kingsley 2001: 49-51). LR5 and LR6 amphoras constitute a late phase in the production of storage jars in Palestine extending from at least the 2nd c. B.C. into Islamic times. Excavated examples in the E Mediterranean date primarily to the 4th through 7th c. (Kingsley 2001: fig. 3.4 for a recent distribution map). One might expect Cyprus, given its location, to have received large quantities of this type of amphora, even though it has been infrequently reported on the island.[26] Examples from mid and late 7th-c. levels at Saranda Kolones, Kourion, and other late sites may be of Umayyad date (Hayes forthcoming; cf. Sodini and Villeneuve 1992: 197-99). At Kopetra the vessel type is well represented at Areas II, IV, and VI, where it accounts for 5-10% of all amphoras.

---

20 Egloff 1977: 116-17; Kingsley 2001: 49.

21 Riley 1979: 219-23; Schuring 1984: 172-74; Peacock and Williams 1986: 196-99; Tubb 1986: 51-55; Blakeley 1988: 35-38; Empereur and Picon 1989: 243; Majcherek 1995: 164-65.

22 Zemer 1977: 61; Majcherek 1992: 106-9; id. 1995: 168-69.

23 Riley 1979: 219-23; Mayerson 1985; Whitehouse *et al.* 1985: 203; Johnson 1988: 211-12; Kingsley 2001: 49-55; for other possibilities cf. Majcherek 1995: 163 n.6.

24 Zemer 1977: 66-69; Johnson 1986: 589-91; Peacock and Williams 1986: 191-92; Oleson *et al.* 1994: 16.

25 Empereur and Picon 1989: 243; iid. 1998: 7.

26 Touma 1989: 873; Lund 1993: 135; K. Jacobsen in Sørensen *et al.* 1998: 357; Giudice *et al.* 1999: 284 no. 10 [seemingly misidentified], fig. 3a.9; Manning *et al.* 2000: 251; iid. 2002: 42.

LR7

Both shape and fabric distinguish this type of amphora (**154**). The vessel rises from a solid spike through a cylindrical body and narrows to a short neck with a plain, rounded rim. The outer wall usually bears broad spiral ridges extending from base to shoulder. Two thick, rolled handles are attached to shoulder and neck, which appears increasingly taller in 6th- and 7th-c. examples. Intact examples at other sites include a smaller (0.6-0.7 m high with a capacity of 5-6 liters) and larger series (0.85-1.0 m high with a capacity of *c.*16 liters; Egloff 1977: 114-16). The medium coarse-grained fabric is dark reddish brown to brown in color (7.5YR 4/4-5/4) and often has a darker core. Large flecks of gold mica and scattered medium-size particles of lime are visible in the body. The fired fabric retains a dull, dense quality with a surface that abrades easily. The distinctive fabric indicates a source in the Nile valley, especially in the vicinity of Sheik Abada (Antinoopolis), Ashmunein (Hermopolis Magna), and Zawyet el-Maïetin in central Egypt.[27] A resinous interior coating is often observed and the principal contents presumably were wine. Significant quantities of LR7 amphoras have been reported in 4th- to 7th-c. contexts from Egypt as far west as Carthage,[28] but they are rarely mentioned in Cypriot excavation reports (perhaps Diederichs 1980b: 55 nos. 207-9, pl. 20; Manning *et al.* 2002: 42). At Kopetra a few sherds appeared in each excavation sector, and at Area II they total 2% by count of all amphoras.

Other classified amphoras

Seven other kinds of amphoras (KAmp1-7) were distinguished at Kopetra. Three of these (KAmp 1, 2, and 7) can be associated with complete examples from other sites; KAmp 3-6 designate other fabrics that belong to amphora-like containers of uncertain shape. Most types comprise less than 1% of all amphoras and are of uncertain origin.

KAmp1

This amphora type comprises an ovoid vessel that rises from a rounded base to a conical neck and flattened rim (**155-57**). Two high arching handles join the upper shoulder and neck. The exterior wall may be lightly ridged and occasionally bears multiple bands of fine horizontal grooving near the shoulder. The vessel most closely resembles Benghazi LR13 (Riley 1979: 231-32) and Saraçhane amphora types 36 and 37; it may be a late version related to LR2 (cf. Hayes 1992: 71, cf. amphora types 10 and 29). At Kopetra such amphoras appear in two clearly different fabrics. KAmp1(1) is coarse grained and reddish yellow to pale brown in color (7.5YR 6/6 to 10YR 8/3). The body is densely littered with lime and other dark inclusions, which give the interior surface a distinctive gritty texture. In many specimens the inclusions resemble those found in local coarse wares of early Iron Age date and suggest that KAmp1(1) may be a Cypriot version of an imported Late Roman type (cf. Hayes 1980b: 379). KAmp1(2) is medium grained, light red to reddish yellow (2.5YR 6/6 to 5YR 7/6), often with a dark gray core, and contains abundant lime and fine mica particles; a thin, very pale brown wash (10YR 8/3) covers the exterior of several examples. Thin-section specimens exhibit a fine-grained marly clay groundmass recalling the fabric of LR1(3) sherds, but compositional analysis suggests a possible origin in central Cyprus (Rautman *et al.* 1999: 380, 383-85). Such amphoras are best known in the standard fabric primarily from Benghazi, Yassi Ada, and Istanbul, and may have originated in the E Aegean or Black Sea area.[29] Reported examples in Cyprus include Ayios Philon (Taylor and Megaw 1981: 221 no. 372, fig. 4), the Kioni anchorage in the Akamas (Leonard 1995a: 145-46 no. B3-11, fig. 34), Paphos (Megaw 1971: 131-32 no. 22; id. 1972: 328; Giudice *et al.* 1999: 291 no. 37, fig. 3d.2), Kourion (Hayes forthcoming), and Amathus, where two different fabrics may have been produced (Empereur and Verlinden 1987: 16 fig. 12; Touma 1989: 872-73 figs. 28-29; id. 2001: 51). Similar sherds were found in association with the LR1 kiln site at Paphos (Demesticha and Michaelides 2001). Both fabrics occur infrequently at Kopetra.

KAmp2

This amphora type is distinguished primarily by its fabric (**158-61**). The hard, medium-grained fabric fires strong light red (2.5YR 6/6), often with a gray core (10YR 6/3), and is filled with medium-size angular black inclusions with a little quartz or mica. The fine-grained, red groundmass contains a moderate amount of quartz silt and subordinate amounts of carbonate material, as well as detrital clinopyroxene and tremolite. Larger mineral inclusions are subhedral clinopyroxenes and chloritised basic rock fragments, with

27 Peacock and Williams 1986: 204-5; Ballet and Picon 1987: 36-38; Empereur and Picon 1989: 244-46; Ballet *et al.* 1991: 134-40.

28 Egloff 1977: 114-16; Riley 1979: 225; Majcherek 1992: 105; Reynolds 1995: 180-83.

29 Riley 1979: 231-32; Bass 1982: 157-60; Hayes 1992: 71.

occasional grains of polycrystalline metamorphic quartz. Compositional analysis of 11 examples revealed a well-defined chemical profile that is clearly differentiated from most Cypriot ceramic groups and more probably originated in N Syria (Rautman *et al.* 1999: 380 and 385). Not all parts of this vessel type are known at Kopetra. The base consists of a solid toe with a straight, steeply rising wall. The only identified rim fragment is roughly triangular in shape with an exterior offset. The handle is ovoid in section and attaches to the curving shoulder. Most examples were unevenly potted and roughly finished.

In fabric and form, KAmp2 resembles a reported type of middle Roman or Late Roman amphora with solid toe, carrot-shaped body, wide shoulder, and tall neck that is known from Tarsus and near Tyre.[30] Similar amphoras have been reported along the coast of Cilicia and Syria, including in 5th- and 6th-c. levels at Antioch, and Seleucia-Pieria has been proposed as a production site.[31] A related amphora reportedly from Kition appeared in the Cesnola Collection (di Cesnola 1894: II, 5, pl. CXLV no. 1076). Other apparent Cypriot examples come from Kourion (Hayes forthcoming), 7th-c. levels at Ayios Philon (Taylor and Megaw 1981: 245 nos. 465-67, fig. 61), and perhaps Dhiorios (Catling 1972: fig. 11 P67, fig. 33 no. P232). While not often encountered during excavation, KAmp2 amphoras constitute 4% of all amphoras from the survey.

KAmp3

This amphora type is known only by its fabric and rim form (**162**). The fabric has a medium-grained, sandy texture and is usually reddish yellow in color (7.5YR 7/4-7/6), with fine lime particles and other inclusions. The vertical neck ends in a plain rim with a diameter of *c.*0.06 m and a simple rolled lip. At Kopetra examples of this amphora type came mainly from the survey and excavations at Area I.

KAmp4

This fabric varies from a dull pink to greenish gray in color and is easily abraded. The body is densely filled with many small to medium-size dark inclusions resembling those of amphora LR1(1), presumably reflecting a Cypriot origin. Body sherds resemble LR1 type amphoras but generally lack the distinctive panel ridging. Most examples came from Area II.

KAmp5

Amphoras of apparent N African manufacture are included under this heading (**163-66**). Fabrics are generally medium grained and strong light red in color (10R 6/8 to 2.5YR 6/8-6/4), often with a darker core, and include particles of lime as large as 0.003 m. Exterior surfaces are smoothed and occasionally preserve traces of a light greenish or pale yellow saline wash (close to 5Y 8/3). Bases tend to be heavy and rounded, while rims resemble those published elsewhere through the 7th c. (e.g., Riley 1979: 198-205 and 225-28). N African amphoras are not commonly reported from Cyprus.[32] Most Kopetra examples came from Area II.

KAmp6

The thick-walled fabric of this poorly understood amphora type is distinguished by a large number of small quartz particles appearing near the surface. The exterior wall is lightly ridged and is covered by a slightly lighter wash. At Kopetra, examples of this amphora type were identified only by the survey and at Area I.

KAmp7

Several examples of the middle Roman 'hollow foot' amphora were noted by the survey. The vessel type is distinguished by its high ring base, tall conical neck, and elongated, sharply arched handles.[33] At Kopetra the hard-textured fabric is usually a strong red in color (2.5YR 5/8-6/8) with thick strap handles fired to a darker core. Fine dark inclusions and medium-size particles of quartz fill the body. Such amphoras appear in two different fabrics and have been identified primarily in 3rd- and 4th-c. contexts; the distribution of known examples suggests an origin in the E Mediterranean.[34] Cypriot examples have been identified at Ayios Philon (Taylor and Megaw 1981: 248 no. 483, fig. 61), Salamis (Diederichs 1980b: 57 nos. 265-67, pl. 21), and Paphos (Archaeological Museum); the vessel in the Cesnola Collection is said to come from Dhali (di Cesnola 1894: II, 5, pl. CXLIV no. 1071).

---

30 Jones 1950: 278 no. 831, figs. 166 and 209; Chollot 1973: 148, fig. 3, pl. I.5; Zemer 1977: 49 no. 40.

31 Taylor and Megaw 1981: 244; Empereur and Picon 1989: 232, figs. 9-10.

32 E.g., Lund 1993: 128-30; Leonard 1995a: 142-43; Manning *et al.* 2002: 42-43.

33 Riley 1979: 189-92; Peacock and Williams 1986: 193-95.

34 Riley 1979: 191-92, fig. 35; Empereur and Picon 1989: 233; Panella 1986: 626 fig. 25 for a distribution map; Majcherek 1993: 218.

Unassigned amphoras

A few less common amphoras were noted but not systematically quantified (**167-73**). These include such distinctive earlier Roman forms as the bifid or double-barrel horned handles of Aegean (sub-Koan?) amphoras. A single example was noted of a stand made in local fabric (**174**). Most of the unassigned amphoras came from surface contexts.

Cooking wares

The cooking wares from Kopetra belong to a variety of Cypriot, Palestinian, and Anatolian fabrics. The integrity of regional ceramic traditions in Hellenistic and early Roman times gradually gave way in late antiquity to a limited number of shapes shared among neighboring areas. As was the case along the coastal mainland, Cypriot potters employed a variety of clays and preparation methods and were influenced by contemporary forms. Cooking wares are grouped into categories of form as well as fabric (Table 5.4).

Group A

This category comprises one or more hard red fabrics (about 10R 5/8 to 2.5YR 5/6) used to make thin-walled vessels with finely-ridged exterior surfaces (**175-86**). Three forms are common at Kopetra: a shallow conical lid with a knob or narrow strap handles; a deep pot with flattish bottom and tall straight wall rising to a simple flattened rim with paired horizontal handles; and a globular pot with vertically thickened rim and flat strap handles. The fabric may also have been used for pitchers, although no good example was identified. Group A cooking wares are well known in Palestine;[35] similar vessels have been reported from the E Mediterranean coastlands (e.g., Williams 1989: 70-71). At Kopetra they are best represented among the survey and Area II data, where they account for up to 10% of the cooking wares.

Group B

This relatively coarse-grained reddish brown fabric (5YR 5/3-5/4) contains small particles of lime and quartz, but is distinguished by the large golden mica flecks on the surface (**187**). At Kopetra the fabric appears in a globular pot with out-turned rim and broad, lightly-ridged strap handles. Both fabric and form point to a source in Asia Minor. Similar examples have been reported at Kourion (Hayes 1980b: 378; Swiny 1982: 184). At Kopetra group B cooking wares were found almost exclusively at Area II.

Group C

The most distinctive cooking ware at the site is a variable, coarse-grained brown fabric (7.5YR 6/4 to 10YR 6/4, and darker) with many large, irregular inclusions (**188-97**). Such fabrics were used for several types of wheelmade and handmade vessels found in the latest levels. In two types of shallow cooking dish or casserole the thick wall rises from a rounded bottom to a plain rim, turned either out or in, below which are attached horizontal handles (**188-92**). These dishes have estimated rim diameters of 0.20-0.23 m and apparently were made on a slow turntable, perhaps after the model of other mass-produced, wheel-ridged cooking wares (cf. Catling 1972). A type of handmade shallow dish with smoothed, flaring wall but no rim apparently was used as both a cooking surface and a lid (**193-94**). The most commonly noted shape is a handmade globular pot with a maximum diameter of *c.*0.20 m, an out-turned vertical rim, and a pair of heavy, rolled handles attached to neck and shoulder (**195-97).** The same coarse fabric and non-wheel technique also were used to make three small bowl-shaped lamps excavated at Area II (**II-2-1, II-12-1, II-13-1**). Laboratory analysis of 11 sherds identified a chemical similarity with the large, locally made Corinthian-style rooftiles and *pithoi* (Rautman *et al.* 1993: 259-60). The thick walls and coarse, heavily-tempered fabric appear well suited to the thermal stress posed by repeated exposure to fire (Woods 1986). The non-standardized shapes and simple manufacture suggest such vessels originated in the Vasilikos valley and probably were made at the neighborhood or even the household level (Rautman 1998: 96-97).

Altogether more than 200 sherds of cooking ware group C were noted across the site, especially at Areas II and VI. The thick walls yield a very large average sherd-size of 44.5 g. Wheelmade dishes or casseroles with out-turned rims were recovered from late levels at Areas I and II, while the in-turned-rim form appeared only among the survey finds. Fragments of the handmade dish or lid came from levels of collapse at Area VI. The most widely noted form was the handmade globular pot, which turned up at Areas I, II, IV, and VI. The discovery of two examples (**I-31-3** and **I-31-4**) beneath a late paved floor at Area I indicates that such vessels

35 E.g., Delougaz and Haines 1960; Adan-Bayewitz 1986; Johnson 1988; Peleg 1989; Magness 1993: 211-15.

were made as early as the first or second quarter of the 7th c. Elsewhere their presence at or near floor level demonstrates that coarse-fabric cooking vessels were used at the time of the site's abandonment (*c.*650). The discovery of such pots in the latest occupation levels at Area II suggests that they continued to be used during the complex's re-occupation in the third quarter of the 7th c. Similar handmade cooking vessels have been noted in late contexts at nearby Maroni-*Petrera* (Manning *et al.* 1994: 367; iid. 2002: 52), Salamis (Diederichs 1980b: no. 303, pl. 25), and in the abandonment débris of the Kourion basilica, which dates to the late 7th or early 8th c. (Megaw 1986: 511-12, fig. 8b; Hayes forthcoming). The appearance of these local forms at Kopetra already in the first half of the 7th c. suggests that the production of Dhiorios and other specialized pottery centers was being supplemented to some extent by valley residents (Rautman 1998: 89).

Group D

Several other cooking wares appear in distinctive Cypriot shapes (**198-203**). Our early efforts to differentiate local fabrics soon gave way to Hayes' (1991: 81) assessment of the variability of Cypriot cooking fabrics. Cooking vessels no doubt were produced at a number of island locations using locally available clays. The best known series comes from the pottery-works near Dhiorios in N Cyprus; two standard cooking pots were produced in a hard brick-red fabric during the 6th and 7th c. at *Mersineri* (Catling 1972). Identifiable Dhiorios-type pots are not often found at Kopetra, where the most frequently noted vessel is a deep cooking pot with hollow, in-turned rim and a finely-ridged outer wall (**198-200**). The fabric is usually light red (2.5YR 6/6-6/8) and includes much fine lime, quartz, and other dark particles. Variations in shape and fabric probably reflect different places of manufacture in Cyprus and perhaps Palestine as well (Oleson *et al.* 1994: 38; Bakirtzis 1996: 153-57); however, compositional analysis of 5 specimens suggests a general correspondence with other Cypriot red wares. Similar examples have been reported at Kourion (Hayes forthcoming), Paphos (Giudice *et al.* 1999: 284 no. 12, fig. 3a.10), Dhiorios (Catling 1972: fig. 16 no. P421, fig. 27 no. P185), and Salamis (Catling and Dikigoropoulos 1970: fig. 3 no. 14, fig. 7 nos. 7-8; Diederichs 1980b: 45 no. 165, 62 no. 304).

Pithoi

Large storage jars or *dolia* are classified as *pithoi*. Such vessels are readily distinguished from other plain wares by their coarse fabric, 0.02- to 0.03-m thick walls built up in sections, heavy rims, and characteristic decoration; their bulky size precludes use for the table or transport. The clay of most examples closely resembles the coarse-fabric Corinthian-style rooftiles known in the area, and small fragments are indeed hard to differentiate. Vessels found at Kopetra belong to a long tradition of local *pithos* manufacture and use. Excavation of the Late Bronze Age complex at *Ayios Dhimitrios* produced great numbers of the unwieldy storage vessels, which apparently were produced in the vicinity by residents or itinerant craftsmen (Keswani 1989: 12-18). Similarities of fabric and function suggest that related clay sources, and perhaps methods of manufacture, were used in these very different periods. Compositional analysis of Late Roman *pithoi* reveals a close relationship with other locally produced ceramics (Rautman *et al.* 1993: 259-60). Such a picture of manufacture and use on the sub-regional level probably applies to other parts of Cyprus as well (London 1991; Ionas 1998). The Kopetra examples illustrate the formal variety of this late phase of local production.

Pithos fragments are conspicuous surface features of the valley. Thick walls and heavy rims designed to survive hard domestic use also effectively withstand surface ploughing and weathering. Despite their abundance there is little direct dating evidence for such vessels. *Pithoi* are well known at Late Bronze Age sites and *pitharia* continue to be made at several places on the island.[36] Roman-era vessels have been less well studied, with most published examples coming from Dhiorios and Ayios Philon in the north (Catling 1972; Taylor and Megaw 1981), and Kourion, Alassa-*Ayia Mavri*, and Maroni-*Petrera* in the south (Leonard 1987; Flourentzos 1996: 25-27; Manning *et al.* 2002: 54-55). These large pots generally share similar shapes and decorative patterns. The stout form, heavy rim, and incised wavy lines are known in Anatolia and the Aegean as well.[37] The multiple horizontal bands of relief cording may have been intended to reinforce or conceal the junctures of wall sections of these large, generally handmade vessels. The presence of abundant fragments at rural habitation sites confirms that *pithoi* played an important rôle in the processing and storage of grain, oil, wine, and other agricultural products. It is assumed that most of the *pithoi* found on the surface at Kopetra belong to the time of the village's 6th- to 7th-c. *floruit*. Many of the standard fabrics, forms, and decorative motives also appear in excavated contexts and in some cases can be assigned to specific

36 Keswani 1989: 17-18 n.1; London *et al.* 1990; Ionas 1998: 124-31; id. 2000: 50-54.

37 E.g., Boardman 1989: 109-10, nos. 244-61 for examples from Chian Emporio, mostly dating to the first half of the 7th c.; Devos *et al.* 1999 for examples at Pessinus in Phrygia.

occupation phases. Closely related examples found at Maroni-*Petrera* belong to the same chronological span (Manning *et al.* 2002: 54-55). At Salamis related examples have been identified in contexts dating to the later 7th and 8th c. (Roux 1998: 48). Some of the Kopetra *pithoi*, especially examples from Areas I and II, may date to the final occupation phase following the disruptions of the mid 7th c.

All *pithoi* from Kopetra share the same basic fabric and were grouped by rim shape and surface decoration (Table 5.4). The fabric is generally dense and coarse grained with many large inclusions, including chert, limestone, and medium to large igneous particles; it does not vary consistently with form or decoration. Groups A through C include the most distinctive kinds of decoration noted at the site.

Group A

This category includes large vessels with an upward or inward sloping shoulder that ends in a heavy triangular rim (**204-208**). The exterior wall below the rim is decorated with incised wavy-line patterns, usually single but sometimes double, which are occasionally punctuated by impressed dots. Group members account for *c.*10% of all *pithoi* found by the survey and at Area I.

Group B

This group designates a dark red or brown fabric with a dark brown slip covering the outer wall (**209**). Lightly incised or pinched decoration sometimes appears together with the slipped surface. Group B includes *c.*9% of all *pithoi* from the survey; it accounts for about a quarter of all *pithoi* excavated at Areas II, V, and VI.

Group C

Pithoi of this group feature single or multiple bands of finger-molded corded decoration, which usually surround the neck below the triangular rim (**210-13**). At Areas II and VI such vessels constitute about a quarter of all *pithoi*, but elsewhere they are much less common.

Group D

All other heavy vessels are included under this heading (**214-17**). The rims present much variation that often does not accord with the decorative forms of Groups A, B, and C. These pots usually rested on a flat disc base with a diameter of 0.12-0.20 m. Most had heavy rolled handles, and in some cases thick lugs were attached to the rim.

Rooftiles and water pipes

Bricks, rooftiles, and water pipes constitute an important (if often overlooked) part of any ceramic environment.[38] Structural brick was not widely used in Roman Cyprus and is absent at Kopetra, where thin sheets of gypsum and limestone were readily available to builders (above, pp. 45-46). By contrast, rooftiles remain abundant on the surface. Three primary types were distinguished by shape, size, and fabric. A series of long, narrow pan and cover tiles of curved section appears in a fine red fabric; these were identified for convenience as Laconian-style (without implying any relation to early Greek roofs; cf. Sodini and Kolokotsas 1984: 184-86). Large, flat pan tiles (*tegulae*) appear in a dark, coarse fabric, while smaller pan tiles and ridged cover tiles (*imbrices*) were made in a light yellow fabric. These flat tiles with their pitched covers continue the Corinthian-style roofing system, which spread across the E Mediterranean in antiquity and became widespread in Cyprus in Classical and Hellenistic times (Salles 1983: 110-12; Wright 1992: 383-84). The possibility of other kinds of rooftiles is suggested by a few fragmentary pieces. The widespread distribution of these three main types suggests that they were used in different kinds of structures and sometimes together on the same building, perhaps as a result of later repairs. Individual forms are not closely datable, but the large Corinthian-style rooftiles appear to have been among the latest used at the site. Many kinds of Roman rooftiles have been reported at Kourion (Huffstot 1987; Leonard 1987), Amathus (Hadjichristophi 1989), and Ayios Philon (Taylor and Megaw 1981), and are readily apparent elsewhere on the island and the coastal mainland (Wright 1992: 383-84 and 498-500).

The narrow Laconian-style tile has a slightly curved pan surrounded by a broad raised rim on three sides (**219-20**). On many examples the floor is lightly inscribed with the letters ΛΕ or ΛΕC. Nearly intact examples measure *c.*0.70 x 0.34 m and weigh roughly 5 kg. Curved cover tiles with an average thickness of 0.08-0.10 m protected the joint between adjacent pan tiles. Pans and covers were made in a consistently fine-grained red to

---

38 McWhirr 1979; Landgraf 1980: 83-84; Tomber 1987.

dark red fabric (about 2.5YR 5/6-6/6) with small particles of lime but few other inclusions. Compositional analysis of 30 examples established their close relationship with Cypriot Red Slip pottery; they appear to be the products of related workshops located in W Cyprus (below, Appendix 3; Rautman *et al.* 1993: 260-61; Gomez *et al.* 1996). Similar rooftiles with identical letter-forms have been reported at the early 7th-c. acropolis basilica at Amathus (Hadjichristophi 1989: 878, type IV, fig. 36), and can be seen at other sites including Ayios Kononas, Peyia, Paphos, Kourion, and Pyla. An intact example in the Cesnola Collection is attributed to Kition or Kourion (di Cesnola 1894: II, 5, pl. CXLII no. 1058; cf. Myres 1914: 306 no. 1853). This basic tile form has been identified in other fabrics across the Near East and Aegean.[39]

The second standard type is a small, carefully-made Corinthian-style pan tile with a ridged cover tile (**221-22**). The flat pan has broad raised borders on two sides, with a transverse rounded molding located toward the upper edge. Nearly complete examples measure *c.*0.44 x 0.35-0.40 m and weigh about 6 kg. Many cover tiles have a raised lower border. Several cover tiles preserve a small raised cross on the outer surface. Pan and cover tiles were made of the same fine-grained yellow fabric that ranges in color from light pink (5YR 7/4 to 7.5YR 7/4) to very pale brown (10YR 7/3). Scattered small igneous and limestone inclusions appear in many examples. Compositional study of yellow-fabric rooftiles indicates that they were produced in workshops operating in the lower Mesaoria plain, probably near Salamis (below, Appendix 3; Rautman *et al.* 1999: 382-83), where rooftiles of similar size and shape in a fabric described as greenish yellow were used to cover Roman buildings (Argoud *et al.* 1980: 36; Roux 1998: 21). The same kind of tile is common also at Amathus (Hadjichristophi 1989: 877 type II, fig. 34). Such Corinthian-style rooftiles apparently were important objects of trade, for they figure prominently among multiple Late Roman shipwrecks and spillages noted at Cape Andreas, around which ships leaving Salamis would have sailed *en route* to N Cyprus, Cilicia, and the Aegean.[40] Rooftiles and related building materials have been noted at other shipwrecks across the Mediterranean (Tomber 1987; Parker 1992b: 16-18; Oleson *et al.* 1994: 63).

The third type consists of a large Corinthian-style tile set (**223-24**). Complete examples of the flat pan tiles measure *c.*0.56 x 0.48 m and weigh 14 to 15 kg. The broad, flat surface is surrounded on three sides by a heavy squared border. Several examples preserve lightly impressed lines and wavy patterns on their floors. A number of cover tiles of plain, angled section with similarly thick sides apparently belongs to this set, although half-round covers may also have been used. All of these heavy tiles share a coarse-grained fabric, typically light brown in color (5YR 5/6 to 7.5YR 6/4) but often darker, with many small to medium-size igneous inclusions. The fabric and large size suggest that these tiles were produced in the Vasilikos region, probably by small rural operations (below, Appendix 3; Peacock 1979: 6; Rautman *et al.* 1993: 259-60). Local manufacture of large Corinthian-style rooftiles may have been influenced by the popularity of the form at Amathus, where it appears in a different fabric (Hadjichristophi 1989: 888 type III, fig. 35). Corinthian-style tiles of uncertain fabric also are known at Ayios Philon (Taylor and Megaw 1981: 231-32, fig. 51), Kourion (Huffstot 1987: 263-99; Leonard 1987: 114-15, fig. 66), and Alassa-*Ayia Mavri* (Flourentzos 1996: 15 no. 17b, pl. XXVIII). Similar rooftiles found at the Salamis Campanopetra may belong to repairs of the great church carried out in the late 6th or 7th c. (Roux 1998: 21, 26 fig. 12a). Corinthian-style rooftiles may well have been made near villages across the E Mediterranean, wherever local clays were available (e.g., Rossiter and Freed 1991: 151).

Rooftiles in the Corinthian tradition continued to be made in Cyprus into the mid 20th c. A workshop at Kornos village in the central part of the island produced pan tiles (*keramidi epipedo*) measuring 0.275 x 0.19 m in size. These were used with cover tiles (*keramidi kholetroto*) of curved section ranging from 0.36 to 0.45 m in length (Ionas 1998: 41). In the early 20th c. rooftiles were being manufactured in the vicinity of Famagusta and Limassol (Ionas 1988: 143; id. 2000: 133-35).

The only examples of terracotta water pipe found at Kopetra belong to a short conduit that drained rainwater into the cistern at Area I. Fragmentary pieces suggest that these pipe segments (e.g., **225**) had an original diameter of 0.14-0.18 m and were at least 0.37 m long. The fabric is pale yellow to pink (2.5Y 7/4 to 7.5YR 7/4) and consists of a bioclastic, calcareous groundmass with relatively large, angular to round dark red-brown altered basic rock fragments. Thin-section samples revealed other constituents including occasional orthopyroxene, clinopyroxene, and weathered plagioclase. Compositional analysis of 5 examples noted a close relationship with LR1(1) amphoras and Chalcolithic pottery from the Vasilikos valley, which points to a probable production zone in SW and S central Cyprus (below, Appendix 3; Rautman *et al.* 1999: 380-83). Water pipe fragments in a different fabric have been found in the upper Vasilikos valley (Todd

39 E.g., Smith and Day 1989: 40, pl. 28 for similar letters; Sodini and Kolokotsas 1984: 184-86.
40 Green 1973: 153 site 12, fig. 9; 161-64 site 14, figs. 24-25; Parker 1992a: 107-8.

forthcoming). Cylindrical pipes were used at Kition and Salamis in Classical and Hellenistic times[41] and in later antiquity appeared across the island.[42] A few examples have been noted at Ayios Kononas.

Format of the catalogue and tables

Each catalogue entry identifies excavated pottery by Lot and deposit numbers. Unstratified sherds are assigned cadastral plot (LV.20) or survey grid (SG) numbers, or are noted as general surface finds (K-gen). Materials salvaged from the 1986 irrigation pipeline excavation are located approximately within each trench (e.g., K86-Tr. B 35-40). Site inventory (KK) numbers are included for objects registered with the Department of Antiquities. Fabric descriptions employ the standard Munsell soil color charts. Inclusions are characterized as small (<1 mm), medium (1-2 mm) or large (>2 mm across). Comparanda generally are limited to Cyprus and its immediate neighbors.

The tables summarize the pottery by sector and ware. Both sherd counts and weights are given together with their percentages. Tables 5.1-5.2 are arranged to show the variation of individual categories among different sectors. Tables 5.3-5.5 analyze the composition of each sector's pottery as well as of the site as a whole. Pottery from individual sectors as well as selected Lots is detailed in chapt. 3. Average sherd weights are provided for the fine wares in Table 5.3 and can be derived from the presented data for the other wares. Percentages and averages are given to a single significant decimal place to avoid distraction, which occasionally leaves small rounding errors in the totals.

---

41 Nicolaou 1976: 149-52; Argoud *et al.* 1980: 36; Salles 1983: 107-10; id. 1993.

42 Bruce 1937: 663, fig. 367; Last 1975: 39-72; Leonard 1987: 115, distinguishing 5 fabrics; Petit *et al.* 1996: 182.

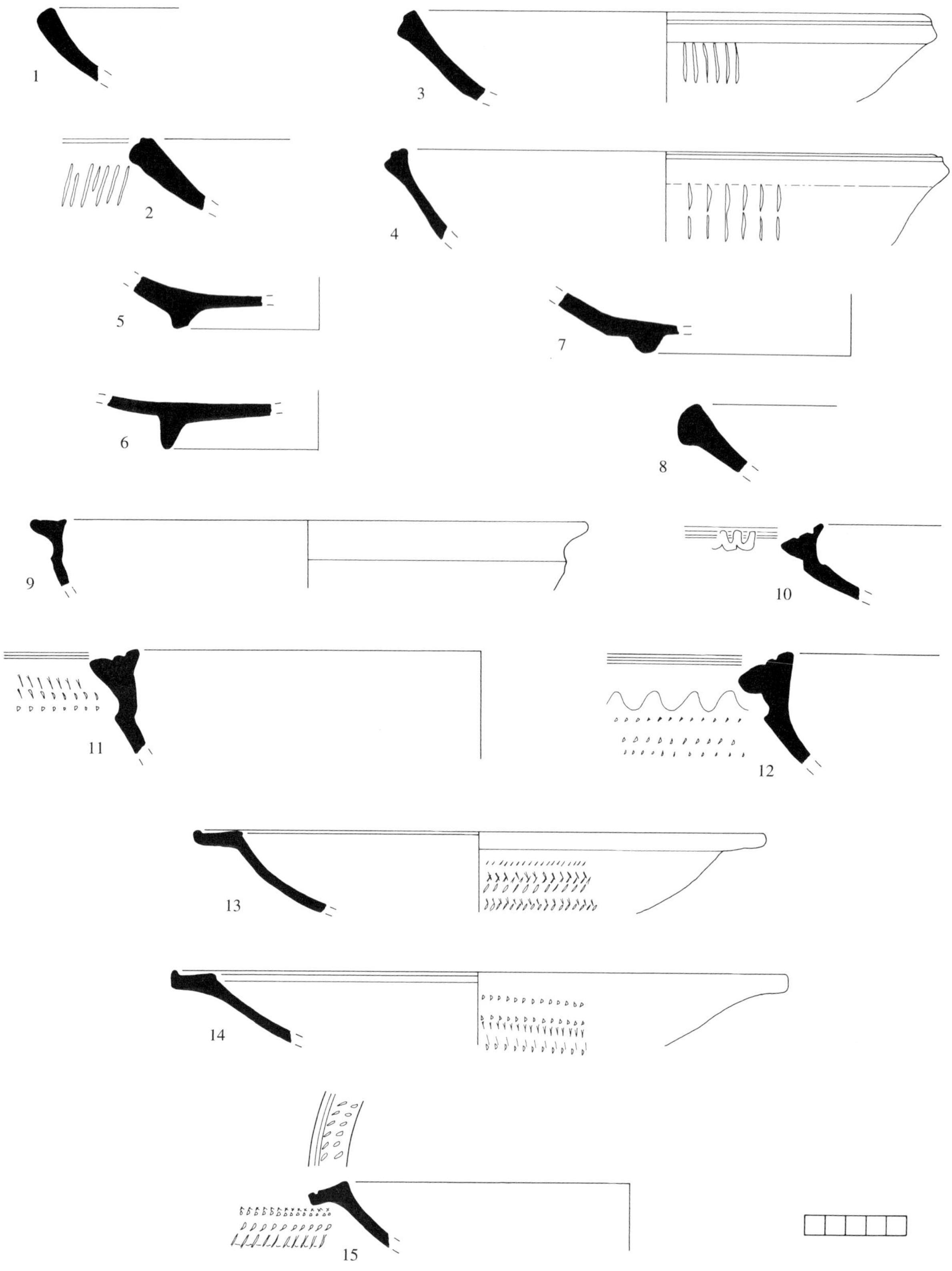

Fig. 5.1. Fine pottery: Cypriot Red Slip.

Catalogue

Fine ware

Cypriot Red Slip ware

1. Dish, form 1. Diam. rim uncertain. Fine-grained light red fabric (2.5YR 6/6) with scattered lime. Thick wall and plain rim. Interior well slipped; exterior slip worn, rim fired lighter. SG64.
Approximate date of form *c.*375-475; Hayes 1972: 373; id. 1980a: 528.

2. Dish, form 2. Diam. rim uncertain. Medium-grained reddish yellow fabric (5YR 7/6) with scattered lime and fine mica. Plain rim with two grooves. Interior slip worn; exterior crudely rouletted. SG42A.
Approximate date of form *c.*450-550; Hayes 1972: 375; Meyza 2000: 519.

3. Dish, form 2. Est. diam. rim 0.25. Fine-grained reddish yellow fabric (5YR 7/6) with gray core (5Y 5/1). Interior covered with dark red slip, worn; exterior covered with rouletting and slipped, worn. K-gen, KK93-1.

4. Dish, form 2. Est. diam. rim 0.26. Medium fine-grained light red fabric (2.5YR 6/6) with scattered fine lime. Dish with rouletted wall, thickened rim with grooved top; worn slip. K-gen, KK94-5.

5. Dish, form 1 or 2. Est. diam. base 0.15. Medium-grained light red fabric (2.5YR 6/6) with scattered lime. Low angular foot. Lot IV-1, Tr. C 1.1. *RDAC* 1994: 297 no. 17, fig. 6.

6. Dish, form 2? Est. diam. base 0.15. Medium fine-grained very pale brown fabric (10YR 7/4) with scattered lime. Interior covered with patchy brown slip; exterior good light red slip (to 2.5YR 6/6). Lot I-1, 8525/5995 1.1.

7. Dish, form 2. Est. diam. base 0.20. Medium-grained light red fabric (2.5YR 5/4-6/6), with scattered lime; unslipped. Lot II-3, 8350/5945 2.2.

8. Dish, form 2/9. Est. diam. rim 0.32. Medium-grained light reddish brown to reddish yellow fabric (2.5YR 6/4 to 5YR 7/6) with scattered lime, mica, medium-size voids. Flaring wall with heavy rounded rim. Interior and exterior slipped, worn; exterior rim fired lighter. SG69.
Cf. Hayes 1972: 375 no. 13, fig. 80 (mid 6th c.?).

9. Basin, form 7, small version. Est. diam. rim 0.24. Fine-grained reddish yellow fabric (5YR 6/8) with scattered lime, mica. Exterior rouletted; interior and exterior covered with mottled slip, dripped and finger-marked. Lot I-1, 8530/6000E 1.1.
Approximate date of form *c.*550-625; Hayes 1972: 379; Meyza 2000: 521.

10. Basin, form 7, small version. Est. diam. rim 0.25. Fine-grained reddish yellow fabric (5YR 6/6-7/6) with fine lime. Interior smoothed and covered with good red slip; exterior wall scored by dragged grits. Top of rim and upper wall fired lighter. K-gen.

11. Basin, form 7, large version. Est. diam. rim 0.34. Medium-grained light reddish brown to light red fabric (2.5YR 6/4-6/6) with darker core, small lime particles. Interior covered with mottled red slip; exterior faintly rouletted, worn. Top of rim fired off-white, flaking. K-gen.

12. Basin, form 7, large version. Est. diam. rim 0.34. Medium-grained reddish yellow fabric (5YR 7/6) with scattered lime, small dark grits, and fine mica. Interior and exterior rouletted, decorated with incised wavy line, and covered with dark red slip, pitted and eroded. Top of rim fired darker. SG16.

13. Dish/bowl, form 8. Est. diam. rim 0.30. Fine-grained light red fabric (2.5YR 6/6) with slightly darker core, lime particles to 0.002, scattered voids, some large and elongated. Roughly potted wall and rim; exterior wall rouletted; interior and exterior slipped. K86-Tr. G 80-90.
Approximate date of form *c.*575-625; Hayes 1980a: 528.

14. Dish/bowl, form 8. Est. diam. rim 0.28. Medium fine-grained light red fabric (2.5YR 6/6) with darker core, lime, dark inclusions, large voids. Exterior wall covered with fine rouletting, eroded slip. K86-Tr. B 35-40.

15. Dish/bowl, form 8. Est. diam. rim. 0.28. Medium fine-grained reddish yellow fabric (5YR 6/6) with scattered lime and mica. Exterior wall and top of rim rouletted; interior and exterior slipped, worn. SG50A.

16. Dish, form 9A. Est. diam. rim 0.14. Fine-grained pink fabric (2.5YR 6/6) with fine scattered lime and many voids. Roughly finished; interior and exterior slipped, exterior rim fired lighter. K86-Tr. G 80-90.
Approximate date of form *c.*550-600; Hayes 1972: 382. For the earlier phases of the shape and its relation to forms 1-2, see Hayes 1985: 194; Meyza 2000: 511-12.

17. Dish, form 9A. Est. diam. rim 0.24. Fine-grained light red fabric (2.5YR 6/6-6/8) with scattered fine lime. Dish with flat grooved base, flaring rouletted wall, thickened rim with convex outer face. Roughly potted; exterior wall rouletted, covered with mottled red slip, fired off-white on exterior rim. Lot II-5, 8340/5935 3.1, KK93-2. *RDAC* 1994: 293 no. 2, fig. 4.

18. Dish, form 9A. Est. diam. rim 0.21. Fine-grained light red fabric (2.5 YR 6/6-6/8) with scattered lime. Dish with flat base, flaring wall with thickened rim. Interior slip worn; exterior wall scored by dragged grits, well slipped; exterior rim fired lighter. Lot I-1, surface.

19. Dish, form 9A. Est. diam. rim 0.24. Medium fine-grained reddish yellow fabric (5YR 6/6-7/6). Interior slip eroded; exterior wall scored by dragged grits. K-gen.

20. Dish, form 9A. Est. diam. rim 0.30. Approximately half preserved. Fine-grained reddish yellow fabric (5YR 6/6) with slightly darker core, scattered fine lime. Interior smoothed and well slipped; exterior wall roughly tooled, slipped; exterior rim mottled in firing. Lots II-3 and 9, 8340/5930 3.1, 8350/5940 5.2.

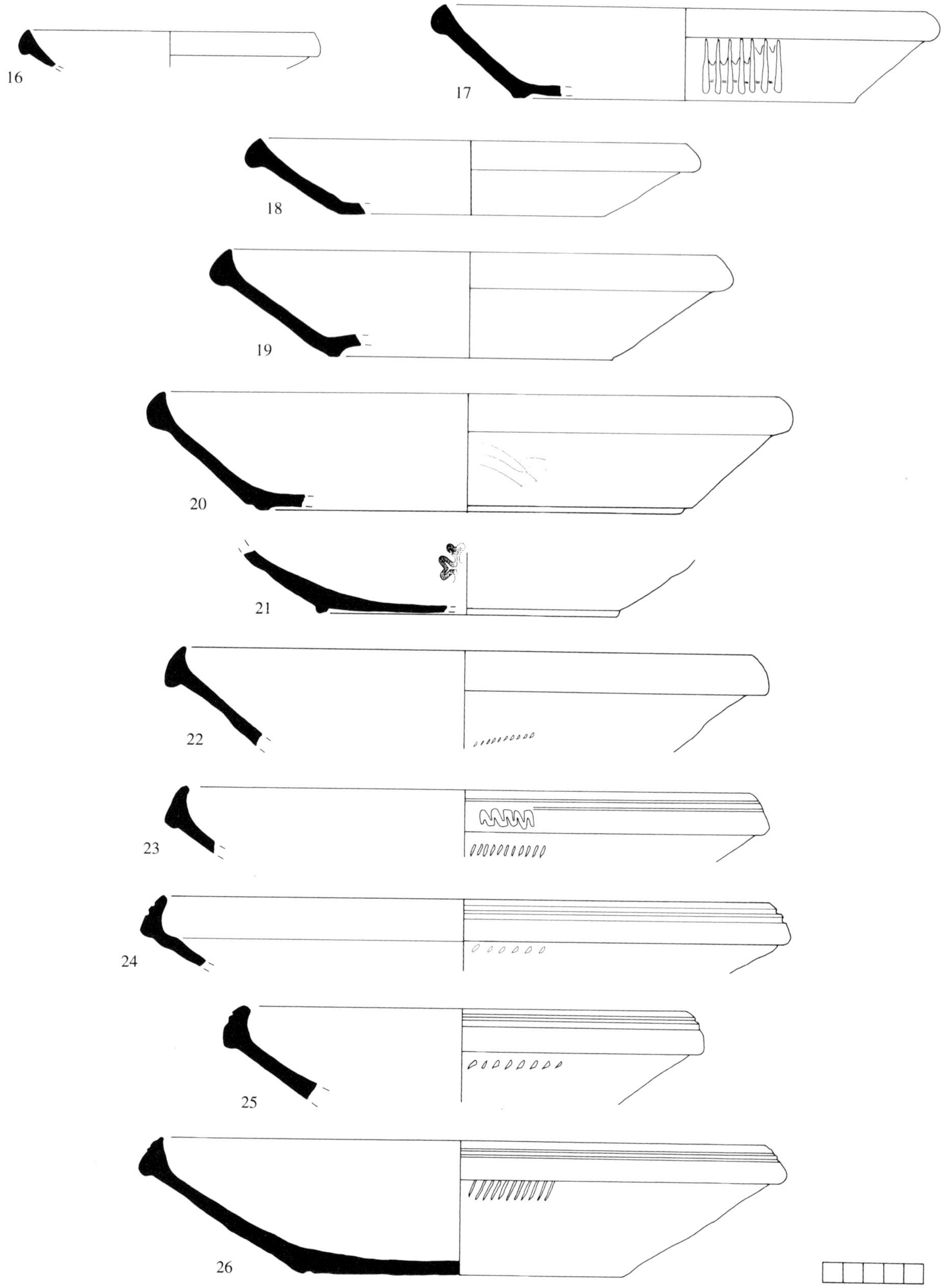

Fig. 5.2. Fine pottery: Cypriot Red Slip.

21. Dish, form 9A/B. Est. diam. base 0.15. Low ledge-foot with cross stamp on floor. Transitional example of normally unstamped form 9A. Lot I-1, 8520/6005 1.1.
See **I-18-1** for another Cypriot Red Slip cross stamp. Cf. Hayes 1972: 384 fig. 84k, cf. 382; Diederichs 1980a for other stamped dishes of this type at Salamis.

22. Dish, form 9B. Est. diam. rim 0.28. Medium fine-grained light red fabric (2.5YR 6/4-6/6) with scattered lime. Interior and exterior covered with dark red slip; exterior wall lightly rouletted, rim fired off-white. Lot I-1, 8525/5995 1.1.
Approximate date of form *c.*580/600-700 (Hayes 1972: 382) or perhaps a little earlier (Egloff 1977: 36, 77 no. 25, pl. 108 [deposits M and N, *c.*550-570]).

23. Dish, form 9C. Est. diam. rim 0.28. Fine-grained light reddish brown fabric (5YR 6/4) with scattered lime to 0.003. Interior and exterior covered with good slip; exterior wall rouletted, rim grooved and incised with wavy line, fired lighter. K-gen, KK93-8.
Approximate date of form *c.*580/600-700; Hayes 1972: 382.

24. Dish, form 9C. Est. diam. rim 0.30. Medium fine-grained light red fabric (2.5YR 5/6-6/6) with scattered lime and mica. Interior smoothed and slipped; exterior wall roughly finished, slipped, rim fired lighter. K-gen.

25. Dish, form 9C. Est. diam. rim 0.22. Medium fine-grained light red fabric (2.5YR 6/6) with scattered lime. Interior and exterior well slipped; exterior rim fired lighter. K-gen, KK93-6.

26. Dish, form 9C. Est. diam. rim 0.30; Est. diam. base 0.16. Fine-grained light red to pink fabric (2.5YR 6/6 to 5YR 7/4) with scattered fine lime. Interior smoothed and slipped; exterior unevenly smoothed leaving finger-marks, rouletted and slipped, rim fired lighter. Lot VI-7, 8280/6060 3.2, KK93-10.

27. Basin, form 10? Est. diam. rim 0.26. Medium fine-grained light red fabric (2.5YR 6/6) with scattered lime. Exterior rim fired lighter. Lot I-28, 8525/6010 2.1, KK93-7.
Approximate date of form *c.*625-675; Hayes 1972: 383; Meyza 2000: 521-24.

28. Basin, form 10? Diam. rim uncertain. Medium fine-grained light red fabric (5YR 7/6) with scattered lime. Roughly potted and summarily slipped. Lot I-1, 8540/6000 1.1.

29. Basin, form 11. Est. diam. rim 0.30. Medium-grained light red fabric (10R 6/6 to 2.5YR 6/6) with scattered lime. Basin with straight wall and plain thickened rim, horizontal rolled handle attached to upper wall. Roughly smoothed and slipped. SG57, KK94-6.
Approximate date of form *c.*550-650+; Hayes 1972: 383.

30. Basin, form 11. Est. diam. rim 0.34. Medium-grained light red fabric (2.5YR 6/6) with scattered lime to 0.003. Interior smoothed, exterior ridged with mottled slip. Lot I-1, 8535/6010 1.1, KK94-7.

31. Basin, form 11. Est. diam. base 0.28. Medium-grained light red fabric (5YR 7/6) with scattered lime. Roughly finished and slipped. SG64, KK94-8.

32. Dish, well form. Est. diam. rim 0.30. Fine-grained reddish yellow fabric (5YR 6/6-7/6) with scattered lime particles and several large voids. Broad dish with plain rim offset by two interior grooves; exterior wall rouletted; interior and exterior wall covered with flaking red slip. K86-Tr. G 80-90, KK94-1.
Approximate date of form *c.*600-700; Williams 1989: 34-35 nos. 191-94, fig. 15; cf. Catling 1972: 9, fig. 5 no. P95; and further Meyza 2000: 515-17, fig. 5.

33. Dish, well form. Est. diam. rim 0.30. Fine-grained light red fabric (2.5YR 6/8) with little lime and rare fine mica. Broad dish with flaring wall and rounded rim offset on interior; exterior wall rouletted; interior and exterior covered with mottled red slip. K-gen, KK94-2.

34. Dish, well form. Est. diam. rim 0.28. Fine-grained reddish yellow fabric (5YR 6/6-7/6) with scattered lime. Exterior wall densely rouletted; interior and exterior wall slipped, flaking. Lot II-3, 8345/5945E 2.1, KK94-3. *RDAC* 1994: 293 no. 4, fig. 4.

35. Unidentified open form. Est. diam. base 0.07. Medium coarse-grained pink fabric (7.5YR 7/4) with scattered lime, dark angular inclusions. Interior surface slipped, flaking; exterior slipped. Lot I-2, 8535/6000 2.1.

36. Jug/pitcher. Est. diam. rim 0.08. Medium-grained red to reddish yellow fabric (2.5YR 5/6 to 5YR 6/8). Plain vertical rim with broad strap handle. Good red slip, streaked and worn at top of rim. Lot II-8, 8345/5935 3.1.
Cf. Catling and Dikigoropoulos 1970: 46 no. 1, fig. 3, pl. XXX (Kornos cave deposit, now dated *c.*643/44); Catling 1972: fig. 36 no. P329 (mid 7th c.); Hayes 1972: 383-84 (Nicosia-*Ypsilantis* well site).

37. Jug? Diam. base uncertain. Medium-grained light red fabric (2.5YR 6/6). String-cut base, roughly finished. Lot I-11, 8525/6005 5.1.

38. Dish/bowl, form 6. Est. diam. rim 0.26. Fine-grained reddish brown fabric (5YR 5/3-5/4) with scattered fine lime. Curved wall with flattened surface and slight interior hook; exterior wall decorated with two horizontal grooves and rouletting. Interior and exterior covered with worn slip, fired dark gray. Lot II-15, 8350/5940 6.1. *RDAC* 1994: 293 no. 5, fig. 4.
Cf. Waagé 1948: 53 no. 960, fig. 53 (center right), pl. XI. Hayes 1972: 377 suggests a 6th-c. date for the shape; Williams 1989: 37 no. 212, fig. 17 prefers a 4th-c. date for a domed lid found in a 6th- to 7th-c. context (Group B3); Meyza 2000: 521. The form is rare in either case.

Phocean Red Slip (Late Roman C) ware

39. Dish, form 2A. Est. diam. rim 0.24. Medium fine-grained light red fabric (10R 6/6-6/8) with fine lime, dark inclusions. Broad flaring rim with interior offset. Hard red slip. SG15.
Approximate date of form *c.*375-425/50; cf. Waagé 1948:

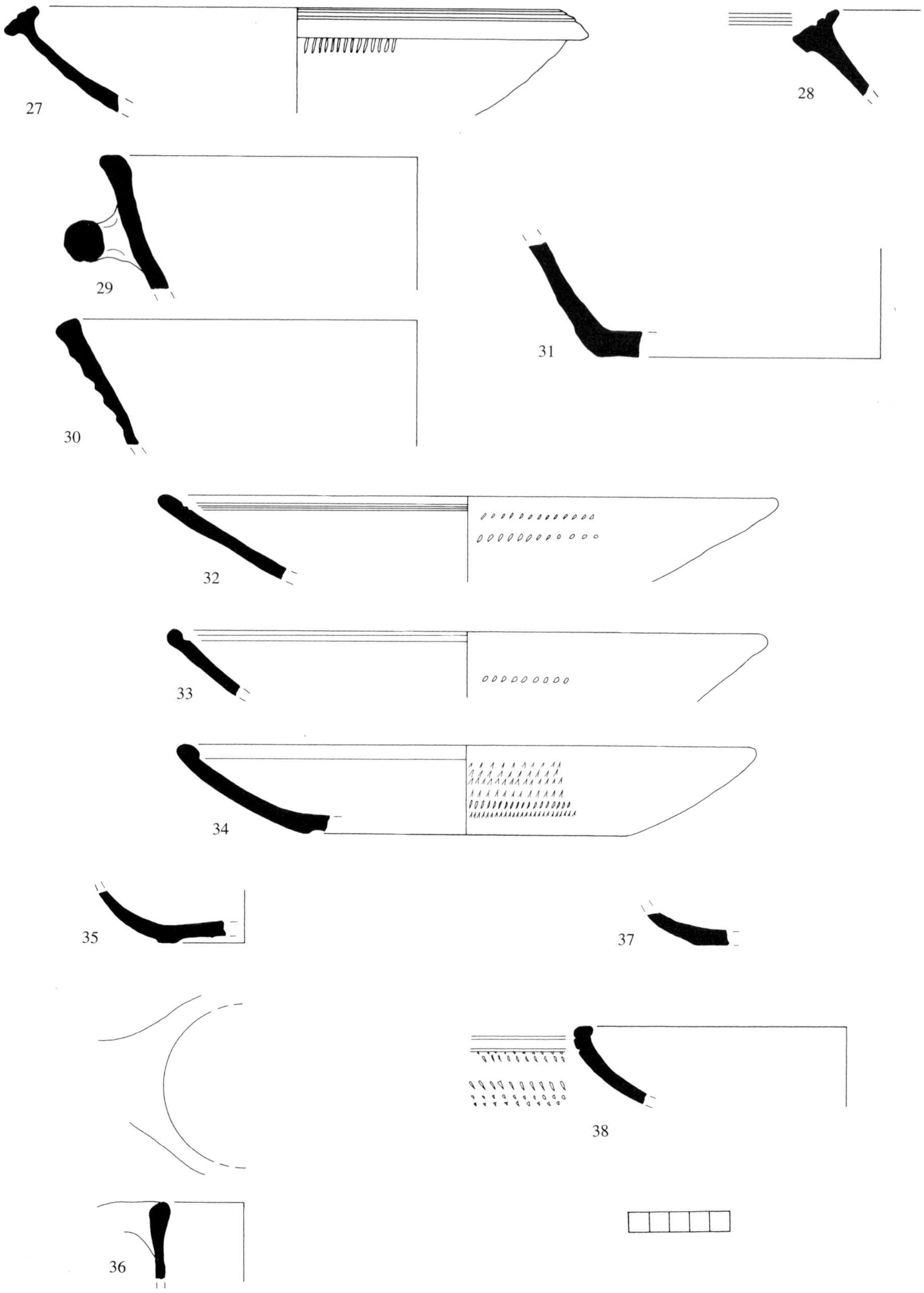

Fig. 5.3. Fine pottery: Cypriot Red Slip.

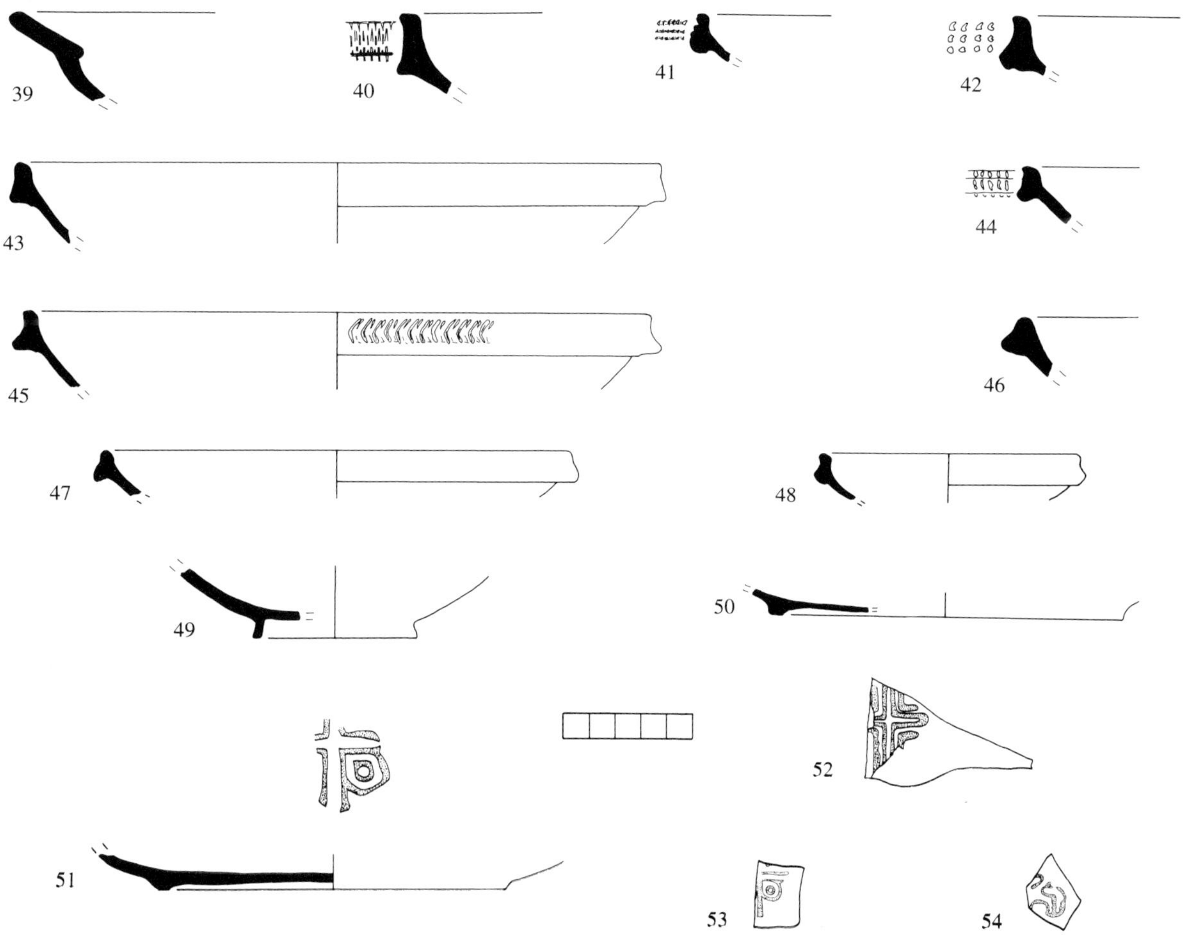

Fig. 5.4. Fine pottery: Phocean Red Slip.

52 no. 910, pl. X; Hayes 1972: 328-29; Williams 1989: 47.

40. Dish, form 3B. Diam. rim uncertain. Fine-grained light red fabric (2.5YR 6/6). Vertical rim with fine rouletting. Red/orange slip interior. K-gen.
Approximate date of form *c.*425-500; Hayes 1972: 337; Mackensen 1984: 92.

41. Dish, form 3D. Est. diam. rim 0.20. Fine-grained red fabric (10R 5/6), finely speckled purplish appearance. Lot II-2, 8335/5935 3.1.
Approximate date of form *c.*425-500; Hayes 1972: 337-38; Mackensen 1984: 89.

42. Dish, form 3E. Est. diam. rim 0.30. Medium-grained light red fabric (2.5YR 6/8). Exterior rim rouletted, fired off-white. K-gen.
Approximate date of form *c.*475-525; Hayes 1972: 337-38; Mackensen 1984: 89.

43. Dish, form 3E. Est. diam. rim 0.24. Fine-grained light red fabric (10R 6/8). Exterior rim plain. K-gen.

44. Dish, form 3F. Est. diam. rim 0.24. Fine-grained light red fabric (10R 5/6) with scattered fine lime. Exterior rim rouletted. K-gen.
Approximate date of form *c.*500-575; Hayes 1972: 338.

45. Dish, form 3F. Est. diam. rim 0.24. Fine-grained light red fabric (10R 6/8) with fine scattered lime. Vertical rim with exterior rouletting; lower rim fired darker red. Lot II-1, 8335/5935 1.1. *RDAC* 1994: 293 no. 6, fig. 4.

46. Dish, form 3H. Est. diam. rim 0.24. Fine-grained red fabric (10R 6/8). LV.20 223/1.
Approximate date of form *c.*500-600; Hayes 1972: 338.

47. Dish, form 3F, small version. Est. diam. rim 0.18. Fine-grained light red fabric (10R 6/6) with fine lime. Exterior rim blackened. Lot I-1, 8525/6010 1.1.

48. Dish, form 3F, small version. Est. diam. rim 0.10. Fine-grained light red fabric (10R 6/8) with fine lime. Exterior rim fired lighter. SG33.

49. Dish, form 3F? base, small version. Est. diam. base 0.06. Fine-grained light red fabric (2.5YR 6/6) with fine lime, speckled section. Interior smoothed, covered with dark red slip; exterior paddle smoothed, pitted. Lot II-15, 8350/5940 5.1.

50. Dish, form 3F? base. Est. diam. base 0.13. Fine-grained light red fabric (10R 6/6). Interior floor paddle smoothed. Lot II-3, 8350/5940 3.2.

51. Dish, form 3F? base. Est. diam. base 0.14. Fine-grained weak red to red fabric (10R5/4-5/6). Cross stamp. K-gen, KK91-56.

52. Dish, form 3? base. Fine-grained light red fabric (10R 6/6). Cross stamp. K-gen.

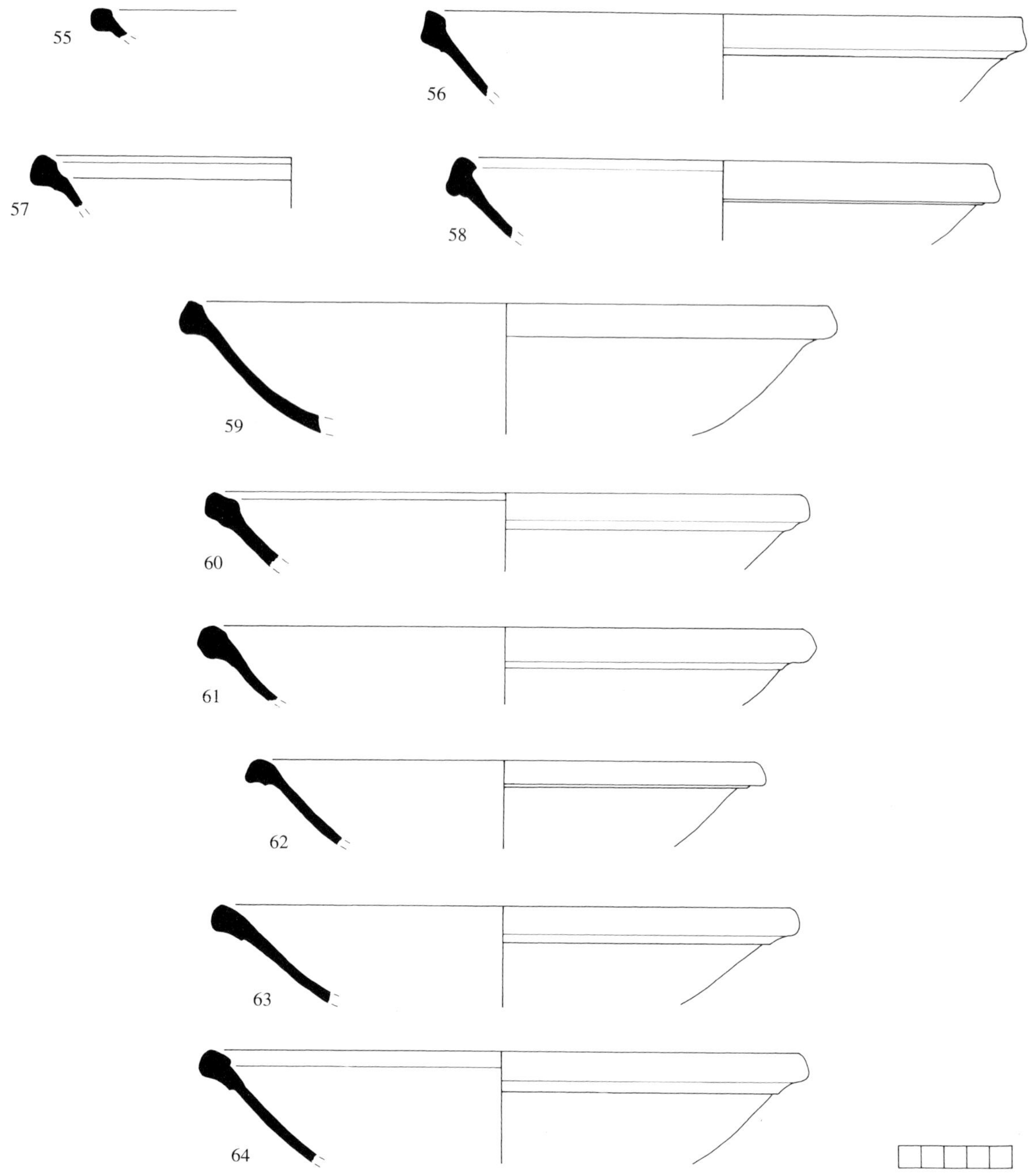

Fig. 5.5. Fine pottery: Phocean Red Slip.

53. Dish, form 3? base. Fine-grained light red fabric (10R 6/6). Cross stamp. K-gen.

54. Dish, form 3? base. Fine-grained light red fabric (10R 6/6). Donkey stamp. SG56.

55. Dish, form 10A? Est. diam. rim 0.20. Medium-grained light red fabric (2.5YR 7/8) of soft texture. Small bowl with square rim. Rim lighter. Lot I-28, 8525/6010 2.1. Approximate date of form *c.*575-625; Hayes 1972: 345-46; Mackensen 1984: 44.

56. Dish, form 10A. Est. diam. rim 0.26. Medium fine-grained red to light red fabric (10R 5/6-6/6) with scattered fine lime. Exterior rim light gray. Lot I-2, 8540/6005 3.1.

57. Dish, form 10A. Est. diam. rim 0.22. Medium-grained light red fabric (2.5YR 6/8) with scattered fine lime, pitted. K-gen.

58. Dish, form 10A. Est. diam. rim 0.24. Fine-grained red fabric (2.5YR 5/6). Heavy squarish rim, fired darker red. Lot I-4, 8530/6000 4.1.

59. Dish, form 10A. Est. diam. rim 0.28. Fine-grained light red fabric (2.5YR 6/6-6/8) with scattered lime, fine mica. Evenly fired. Lot I-20, 8520/6015 5.1.

60. Dish, form 10A. Est. diam. rim 0.26. Fine-grained light red fabric (10R 6/8) with fine scattered lime. Entire exterior wall and rim fired dark gray. SG41.

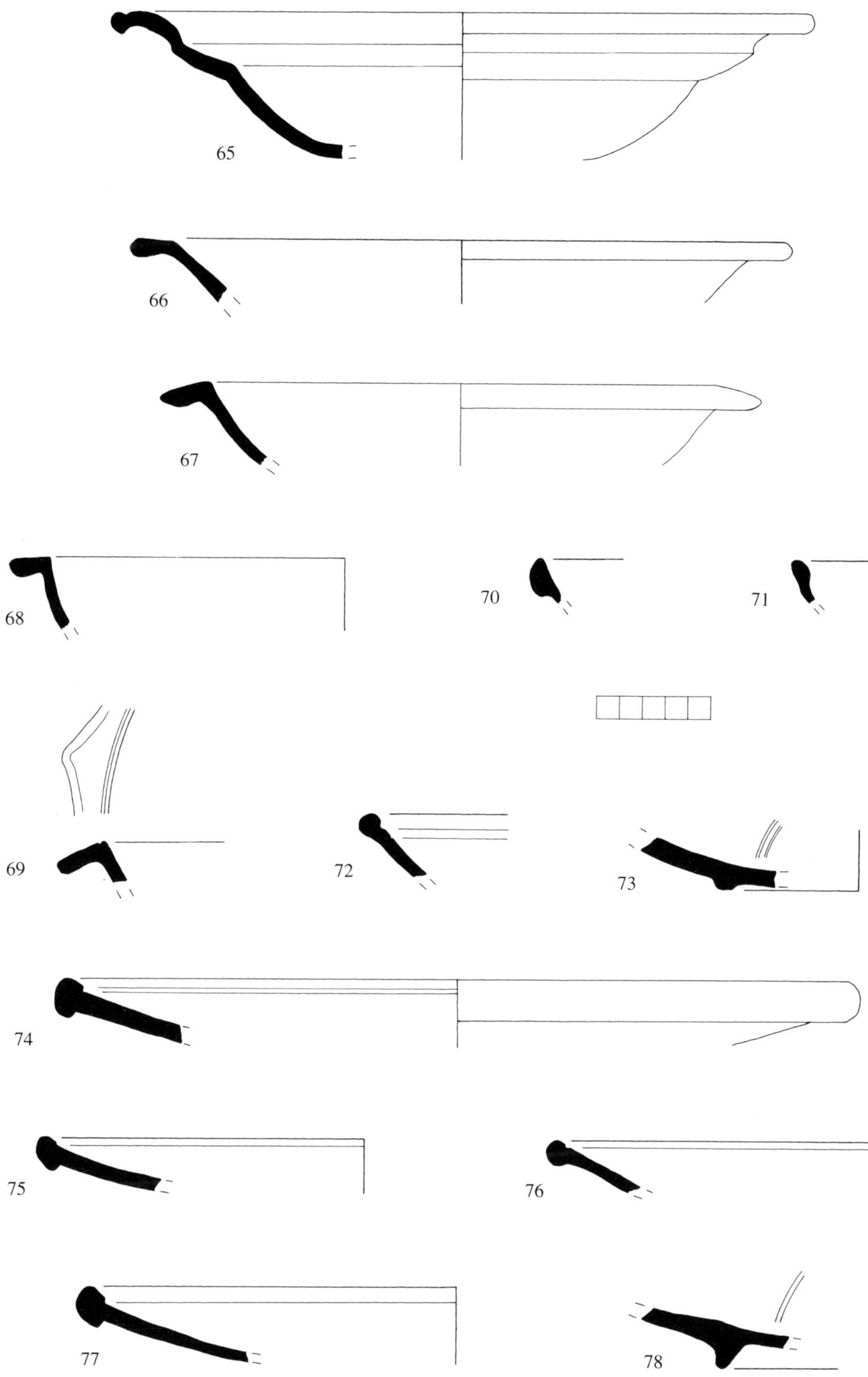

Fig. 5.6. Fine pottery: African Red Slip.

61. Dish, form 10A. Est. diam. rim 0.26. Fine-grained light red fabric (2.5YR 6/8) with fine scattered lime. Exterior rim paddle smoothed, fired off-white. K86-Tr. B 35-40.

62. Dish, form 10B. Est. diam. rim 0.22. Fine-grained light red fabric (10R 6/6 to 2.5YR 6/6) with fine speckled section. Exterior wall scored by small voids and dragged grits; exterior rim mottled in firing. SG54.
Approximate date of form *c.*570-early 7th c.; Hayes 1972: 345-46; Mackensen 1984: 44.

63. Dish, form 10C. Est. diam. rim 0.25. Fine-grained light red fabric (10R 6/8). Exterior wall scored by dragged grits; exterior rim blackened. Lot I-1, 8540/6010 1.1.
Approximate date of form early 7th c. to *c.*675; Hayes

1972: 345-46; Mackensen 1984: 44.

64. Dish, form 10C. Est. diam. rim 0.26. Fine-grained red to light red fabric (2.5YR 5/8-6/8) with finely speckled surface. Lot I-20, 8520/6015 2.2 and 5.1.

African Red Slip ware

65. Bowl, form 67. Est. diam. rim 0.30. Medium-grained light red fabric (2.5YR 6/6-6/8) with scattered lime and quartz. Hard dark red slip on interior, worn. K-gen.
Approximate date of form *c.*360-470; Hayes 1972: 116; Lund 1995: 504-6.

66. Bowl, form 93B. Est. diam. rim 0.28. Medium coarse-grained light red fabric (2.5YR 6/8) with fine quartz and other dark inclusions. Good slip on interior wall and exterior of rim, pitted. K-gen.
Approximate date of form *c.*475-550; Hayes 1972: 147-48; Mackensen 1993: 413-14; Lund 1995: 523.

67. Bowl, form 93? Est. diam. rim 0.22. Medium coarse-grained reddish yellow fabric (5YR 5/6-6/6) with fine lime, medium quartz, and other dark grits. Interior and exterior rim slipped. Lot VI-16, 8280/6060 5.2.

68. Bowl, form 93. Est. diam. rim 0.26. Medium-grained light red fabric (2.5YR 6/8) with a little lime, quartz; interior smoothed, slipped. Repair hole and lead clamp on rim. Lot I-9, 8520/5995 2.1.

69. Bowl, form 97. Est. diam. rim 0.15. Medium-grained light red fabric (10R 6/8) with widely scattered quartz. Smooth, hard light red slip interior and exterior. Lot I-1, 8535/6005 1.1.
Approximate date of form mid 5th to mid 6th c.; Hayes 1972: 151; Fulford and Peacock 1984: 69; Lund 1995: 525-26.

70. Bowl, form 99. Diam. rim uncertain. Medium-grained light red fabric with little quartz. Smooth, hard light red slip interior and exterior rim. SG42.
Approximate date of form mid 5th c. to early 7th c.; Hayes 1980a: 515-16; Fulford and Peacock 1984: 71; Mackensen 1993: 415-17; Lund 1995: 526-28.

71. Footed dish, form 101. Diam. rim uncertain. Medium-grained light red fabric (2.5YR 6/8) with scattered quartz. Lot I-1, 8535/6010 1.1.
Approximate date of form mid 6th to late 7th c.; Hayes 1972: 156; id. 1980a: 486; Fulford and Peacock 1984: 71; Lund 1995: 530-31; Reynolds 1995: 152.

72. Dish/bowl, form 104C. Diam. rim uncertain. Medium coarse-grained light red fabric (2.5YR 6/8) with scattered quartz, smooth, hard red slip. Lot I-13, 8525/6010 2.2.
Approximate date of form *c.*550-625; Hayes 1972: 166; Fulford and Peacock 1984: 73-74; Mackensen 1993: 429; Lund 1995: 536-37.

73. Dish/bowl, form 104C. Est. diam. base 0.11. Medium coarse-grained light red fabric (10R 6/8 to 2.5YR 6/8) with scattered lime and quartz, pitted. Low foot, sloping floor with two concentric grooves. Lot II-1, 8340/5935N 1.1. *RDAC* 1994: 293 no. 8, fig. 4.

74. Plate, form 105. Est. diam. rim 0.34. Medium coarse-grained light red fabric (10R 6/8 to 2.5YR 6/8) with scattered lime and quartz. Good interior slip with traces of spiral brushwork. Lot II-1, 8340/5940 1.1. *RDAC* 1994: 293 no. 7, fig. 4.
Approximate date of form *c.*550-650; Hayes 1972: 169; Fulford and Peacock 1984: 74; Lund 1995: 537-38.

75. Plate, form 105. Est. diam. rim 0.28. Medium coarse-grained light red fabric (2.5YR 6/8 to 5YR 7/8) with darker core, abundant lime and quartz. Interior and exterior eroded. Lot I-1, 8525/5995 1.1.

76. Plate, form 104C. Est. diam. rim 0.29. Medium coarse-grained light red fabric (2.5YR 6/8) with finely speckled surface. Good dark slip interior, smoothed. K-gen.

77. Plate, form 105. Est. diam. rim 0.33. Medium-grained light red fabric (10R 6/8 to 2.5YR 6/6-6/8) with scattered lime and quartz. Good hard red slip interior, smoothed. Lot I-1, 8535/6010 1.1.
See **I-3-1** for a nearly complete example of the form.

78. Plate, form 105? Est. diam. base 0.18. Medium-grained light red fabric (2.5YR 6/6-6/8) with scattered lime and quartz. Interior covered with good red slip. SG68.

79. Plate, form 106. Est. diam. rim 0.30. Medium coarse-grained light red fabric (10R 6/8 to 2.5YR 6/8) with scattered lime. Surface eroded. SG4A.
Approximate date of form *c.*525-650; Hayes 1972: 171; Fulford and Peacock 1984: 74; Williams 1989: 43; Lund 1995: 538-39.

80. Bowl, form 107. Est. diam. rim 0.30. Medium-grained light red fabric (10R 6/8 to 2.5YR 6/8) with fine lime, quartz, and other dark inclusions. Good interior red slip, slightly pitted; exterior smoothed. Repair hole on rim. K-gen.
Approximate date of form *c.*550-675; Hayes 1972: 171; Fulford and Peacock 1984: 74-75; Mackensen 1993: 425; Lund 1995: 540.

81. Dish/bowl, form 103/107? Est. diam. base 0.12. Medium coarse-grained light red fabric (2.5YR 6/8) with abundant lime and quartz. Interior slipped, pitted. Low ring base. SG8.

82. Dish/bowl, form 103/107. Est. diam. base 0.12. Medium coarse-grained light red fabric (2.5YR 6/8) with abundant lime and quartz. Low ring base. Lot I-9, 8520/6015 3.1.

83. Dish, form 109. Est. diam. rim 0.26. Medium-grained red to light red fabric (2.5YR 5/6-6/6) with fine lime, quartz, and other dark inclusions. Straight wall with slight interior groove. Interior slipped, lightly spiral-burnished, eroded; upper exterior wall slipped. Lots II-27 and 28, 8335/5930 3.1 and 4.1.
Approximate date of form late 6th to late 7th c.; Hayes 1980a: 517; Fulford and Peacock 1984: 75; Lund 1995: 541.

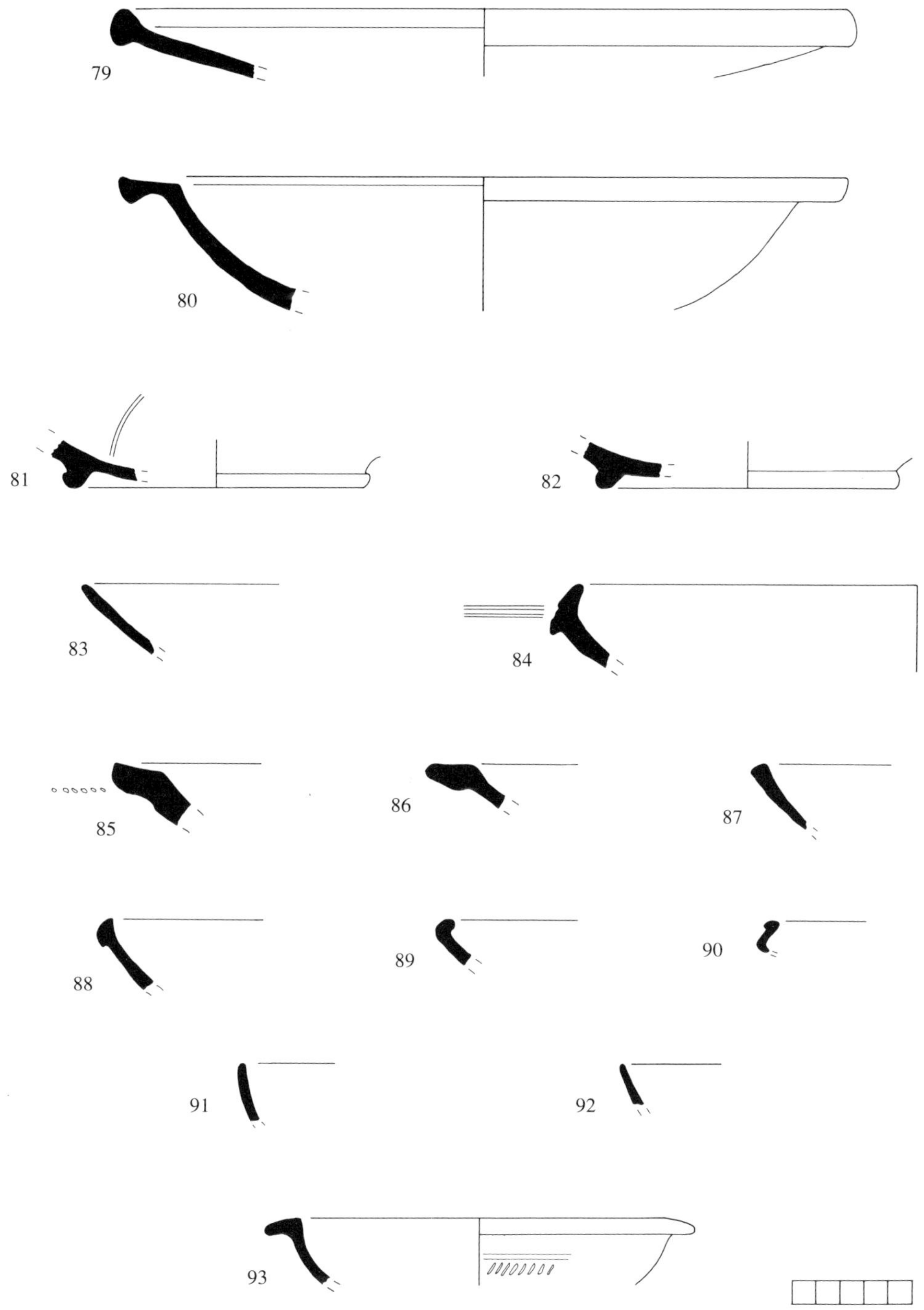

Fig. 5.7. Fine pottery: African Red Slip and other wares.

Egyptian Red Slip wares

84. Bowl, Egyptian Red Slip B? Est. diam. rim 0.28. Coarse, loose-grained light reddish brown to brown fabric (5YR 6/4 to 7.5YR 5/4) with lime particles to 0.004, silver and gold mica flecks, and large irregular voids. Sloping wall with vertical in-turned rim, exterior overhang with two grooves. Interior and exterior covered with thick red/orange slip, cracked and flaking. SG5A.

85. Dish/bowl. Diam. rim uncertain. Dull-textured pink to very pale brown fabric (7.5YR 7/4 to 10YR 7/4) with small dark inclusions. Thick out-turned rim, flattened on top, with slight exterior offset and row of lightly impressed dots. Dull dark red slip interior and exterior, flaking. K86-Tr. G 80-90.

86. Dish/bowl. Diam. rim uncertain. Dull-textured pink to very pale brown fabric (7.5YR 7/4 to 10YR 7/4) with small dark inclusions. Flattened, out-turned rim. Dull red slip (2.5YR 5/6) interior and exterior. K86-Tr. G 80-90.

Cypriot Sigillata

87. Bowl. Diam. rim uncertain. Fine-grained light reddish brown fabric (2.5YR 6/4). Flaring wall with thickened rim.

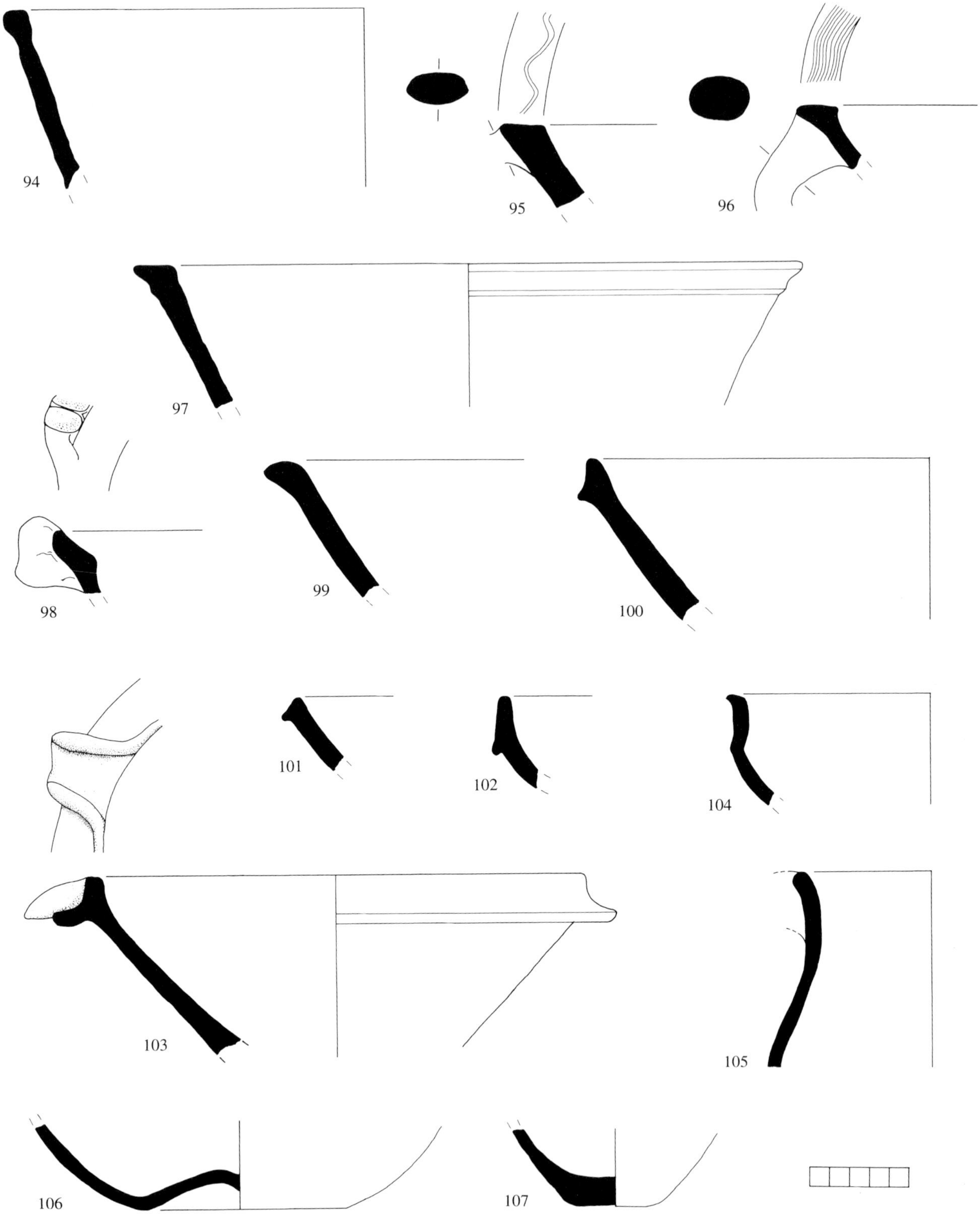

Fig. 5.8. Plain pottery.

Lot I-1, 8530/6005 1.1.
Cf. Hayes 1991: 44 form P29, fig. XIX (*c.*A.D. 100-150+).

88. Dish. Diam. rim uncertain. Medium-grained light reddish brown (2.5YR 6/4). Flaring wall with vertical thickened rim, exterior overhang. Interior slipped; exterior finely smoothed, covered with dark red to brown slip, rim fired dark brown/gray. Lot I-6, 8525/5995 2.1.
Cf. Robinson 1959: 41 no. G174, pl. 67; Hayes 1991: 40 form P11, fig. XVIII (*c.*A.D. 50-150).

89. Dish. Diam. rim uncertain. Medium fine-grained light red fabric (2.5YR 6/6) with clean break. Flaring convex wall with incurved rim. Exterior fired light red. SG71.
Cf. Hayes 1991: 40-41 form P12, fig. XVIII, 189 fig. LXVI nos. 23-24 (*c*.50-150 A.D.).

90. Small carinated bowl with out-turned rim. Diam. rim uncertain. Fine-grained light reddish brown fabric (2.5YR 6/4), shading to purple, with good hard slip. Lot II-1, surface.
Hayes 1967: 70 form 7B; Hayes 1991: 42-43 form P22B, fig. XIX (late 1st-2nd c.). Cf. Williams 1989: 37 no. 213, fig. 17, who prefers a domed lid in early Cypriot Red Slip.

Other fine wares

91. Bowl, Eastern Sigillata B? Est. diam. rim 0.10. Fine-grained light red to reddish yellow fabric (2.5YR 6/8 to 5YR 7/8) with fine lime, scattered mica. Small dish with straight wall, slipped. SG1.

92. Bowl, Eastern Sigillata B? Diam. rim uncertain. Medium-grained light red fabric (2.5YR 6/6). Small dish with straight flaring wall. Interior and exterior covered with good red slip. SG31.

93. Bowl. Est. diam. rim 0.15. Fine-grained reddish yellow fabric (7.5YR 7/6) with fine lime and mica. Flaring wall with horizontal out-turned rim, slight groove. Exterior wall bears light rouletting. Interior and exterior covered with light red slip (near 2.5YR 6/8), streaked. Lot I-1, 8530/6015 1.1.

Plain wares

Group A

94. Basin with knobbed rim. Est. diam. rim 0.34. Coarse-grained light reddish yellow fabric (about 5YR 7/6) with abundant lime, quartz and other dark inclusions; grainy texture with pink surface. Flaring wall with knobbed rim; interior lightly ridged. Lot I-1, 8530/6015S 1.1.

95. Basin with flattened rim. Est. diam. rim 0.38. Coarse-grained light red to pink fabric (7.5YR 7/4) with large particles of lime, quartz, and many other dark inclusions. Thick flaring wall with flattened out-turned rim, combed lines on top; thick rolled handle attached to rim. Lots VI-5 and 10, 8280/6055 4.1 and 8280/6058 4.2.
Cf. Manning *et al.* 2000: fig. 13.d.

96. Basin with flattened rim. Diam. rim uncertain. Coarse-grained reddish yellow to yellow fabric (7.5YR 7/6 to 10YR 7/6) with abundant lime, quartz, and red, gray, and black inclusions. Flaring wall with flattened out-turned rim, combed wavy lines on top; thick rolled handle attached to rim and upper wall. Lot I-1, 8535/6010 1.1.
Cf. Hayes forthcoming, from the episcopal basilica at Kourion.

97. Basin with flattened rim. Est. diam. rim 0.28. Same fabric as **96**. K86-Tr. B 45-50.

98. Basin with out-turned rim. Est. diam. rim 0.40. Coarse-grained red fabric (2.5YR 5/6-5/8) with darker core, abundant lime, quartz, and many dark angular inclusions. Out-turned rim with broad handle with impressed fingermarks. Lot I-2, 8530/6005 3.1.

99. Basin. Est. diam. rim 0.38. Medium coarse-grained yellowish red fabric (5YR 5/6) with lime, quartz, and other dark inclusions. Flaring wall with rounded rim. Lot I-1, 8530/5995 1.1.

100. Bowl with flanged rim. Est. diam. rim 0.34. Coarse-grained light red fabric (2.5YR 6/6) with gray core; grainy texture with abundant lime, quartz, and red, green, and black inclusions. SG15.
Cf. Catling 1972: 33 fig. 20 no. P229, 67 fig. 38 no. P220A (7th c.).

101. Bowl with flanged rim. Est. diam. rim 0.27. Coarse-grained reddish yellow fabric (5YR 7/6 to 7.5YR 7/6) with scattered lime and fine to medium-size inclusions. Lot I-1, 8525/5995 1.1.

102. Dish/bowl. Diam. rim uncertain. Coarse-grained pink to reddish yellow fabric (5YR 7/4-7/6) with gray core; grainy texture with scattered lime, quartz, many dark inclusions, and a little mica. Interior surface wet smoothed, eroded. Lot II-1, 8340/5930 1.1.

103. Mortarium, *c.* seven-eighths preserved. Diam. rim 0.24. Medium-grained light red fabric (2.5YR 6/6) with darker core, many small red, gray, and quartz-like inclusions, and scattered lime. Exterior wall lightly ridged, covered with mottled wash (about 10YR 8/2 to 2.5Y 8/2). Interior surface worn, encrusted, but without large interior grits. Lot VI-6, 8280/6060 3.1, KK91-55.
Cf. Catling 1972: 72 fig. 40 nos. P578-79.

104. Bowl with vertical rim. Est. diam. rim 0.20. Coarse-grained light red fabric (2.5YR 6/6) with quartz and many fine to medium-size inclusions; smoothed. Vertical rim with slight carination, out-turned lip. Lot I-28, 8525/6010E 2.1.

105. Jug? Est. diam. rim 0.13. Coarse-grained pink to light reddish brown fabric (5YR 6/4-7/4) with many particles of lime and other large inclusions that give a raspy surface. Incurving wall with out-turned rounded rim; handle root. K-gen. Cf. **106**.

106. Jug. Est. diam. base 0.10. Coarse-grained pinkish fabric (5YR 7/4) with many particles of lime and red, green, and gray inclusions that give a raspy surface; heavily encrusted. Recessed button base. Lot VI-1 surface.
Cf. **105**. For the recessed base see Catling and Dikigoropoulos 1970: 47-48 nos. 5-10, fig. 3, 56 nos. 9-13, fig. 7 (mid 7th c.); Taylor and Megaw 1981: 221 no. 384, fig. 45 (7th c.); Bass 1982: 171-72 nos. P24-27, fig. 8-12 (early 7th c.); Tushingham 1985: 324, fig. 32 no. 32; Hayes 2001a: 447 no. B43, fig. 8 (early 7th c.).

107. Small jug. Est. diam. base 0.05. Coarse-grained light red fabric (2.5YR 6/6) with abundant lime, many medium to large inclusions. Lot VI-12, 8280/6060 3.1.

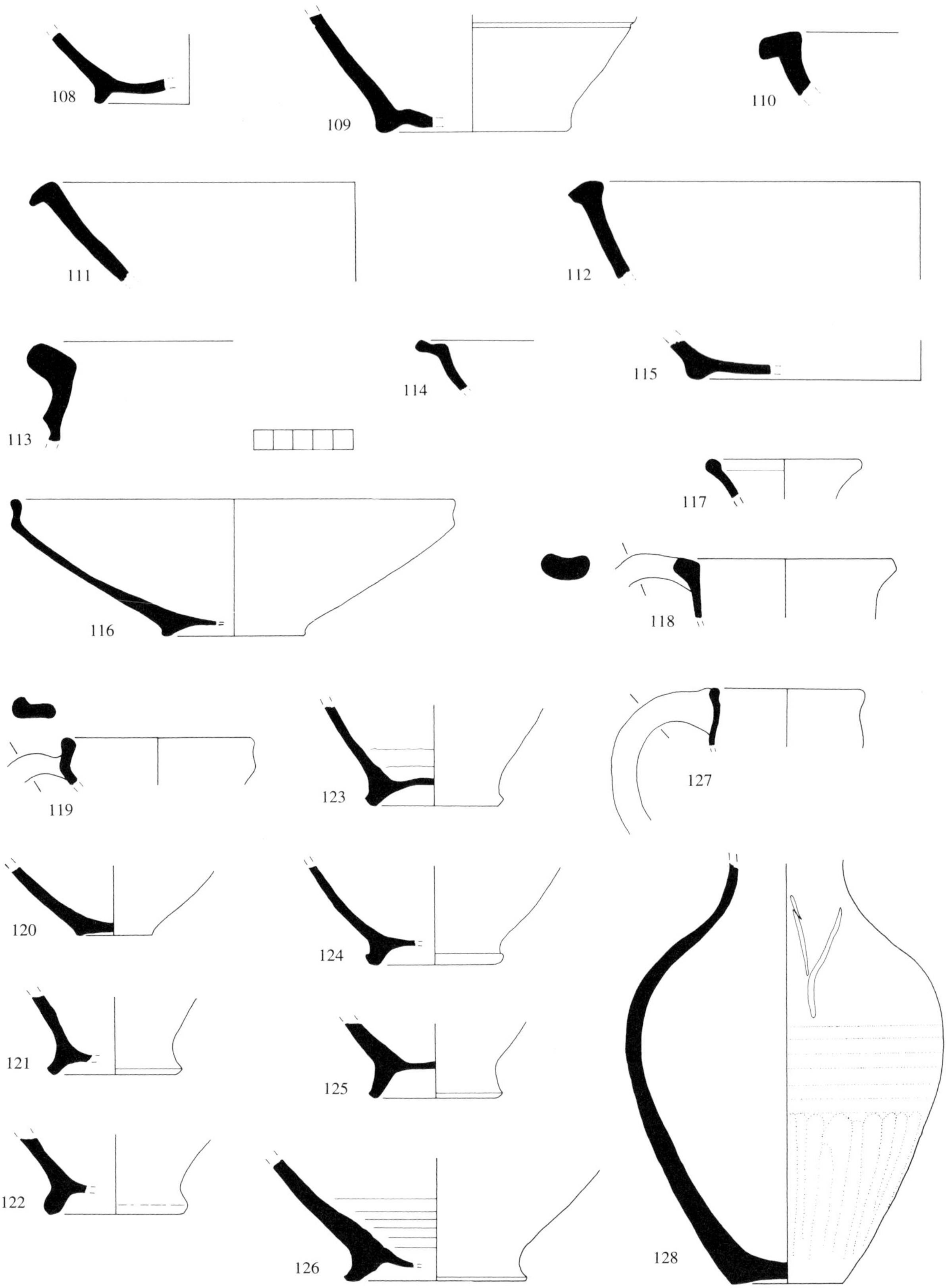

Fig. 5.9. Plain pottery.

108. Jug. Est. diam. base 0.09. Coarse-grained reddish yellow fabric (5YR 6/6) with abundant lime, quartz, and other dark inclusions, partially smoothed on reddish yellow surface (7.5YR 7/6). Low ring base. Lot VI-12, 8280/6060 4.2.

109. Jug. Est. diam. base 0.09. Coarse-grained pink to reddish yellow fabric (5YR 7/4-7/6) with medium size particles lime and abundant green, gray, and black inclusions (to 0.005), especially on exterior surface. Lot VI-12, 8280/6060 4.2. *RDAC* 1994: 306 no. 33, fig. 10.
Cf. Catling and Dikigoropoulos 1970: 54 nos. 9-13, fig. 7 for similar bases from the Salamis bench deposit (mid 7th c.).

Group B

110. Basin with out-turned rim. Est. diam. rim 0.32. Medium fine-grained pink fabric (7.5YR 7/4). Interior and exterior smoothed and self-slipped, surface fired very pale brown (10YR 8/3-8/4). Lot I-11, 8525/6005 5.1.

111. Basin with downturned rim. Est. diam. rim 0.30. Light red fabric (2.5YR 7/6) with scattered lime. Interior and exterior smoothed, self-slipped; surface fired very pale brown (near 10YR 7/4-8/6). SG18D.

112. Basin with thickened rim. Est. diam. rim 0.32. Light red fabric with few inclusions. Interior fired light red; exterior smoothed, self-slipped; surface fired very pale brown (near 10YR 7/4-8/4). Lot I-2, 8525/6005S 2.1.

113. Basin with heavy rim. Diam. rim uncertain. Light reddish yellow fabric (5YR 7/6-7/8) with few inclusions but fine mica. Thickened out-turned rim with pronounced exterior offset. Interior and exterior fired very pale brown (10YR 8/3). Lot I-1, 8530/6015 1.1.
Cf. **I-5-3**. Perhaps related to Cypriot Red Slip form 7 (mid 6th to early 7th c.); cf. **9-12**.

114. Small bowl with out-turned rim. Diam. rim uncertain. Medium fine-grained light red fabric (5YR 7/6) with scattered lime and occasional large voids. Interior light red, exterior reddish yellow (7.5YR 7/4-7/6). Lot I-2, 8535/6005 2.1.

115. Bowl with ring base. Est. diam. base 0.22. Medium fine-grained pink fabric (7.5YR 7/4) with scattered lime. Interior smoothed and self-slipped; exterior reddish yellow (5YR 7/4-7/6), scored by dragged grits. SG17A.

116. Dish with vertical rim and ring base. Est. diam. rim 0.22, base 0.07. Medium fine-grained reddish yellow fabric (5YR 6/6-7/6) with scattered lime, fine mica, a few voids. Flaring wall rises from low ring base to vertical carinated rim. Interior smoothed, flaking; exterior lower wall scored by a few dragged grits, evenly fired light red with smooth soft texture, flaking. Lot VI-12, 8280/6060 4.2.
Cf. Oleson *et al.* 1994: 53 no. RG43, fig. 16 for the shape in a fine fabric.

117. Jug. Est. diam. rim 0.06. Medium fine-grained reddish yellow fabric (5YR 7/6) with very pale brown surface. Out-turned thickened rim. Lot I-30, 8525/6015 4.1.

118. Jug. Est. diam. rim 0.10. Medium fine-grained reddish yellow fabric (5YR 7/6) with very pale brown surface (10YR 7/3). Exterior roughly finished with small clay blobs on surface. Out-turned thickened rim with broad strap handle. SG3.

119. Jug. Est. diam. rim 0.09. Same fabric as **118**. Incurved vertical rim with grooved strap handle. Lot I-1, 8535/6005 1.1.

120. Jug with recessed base. Est. diam. base 0.038. Medium-grained pale yellow fabric (2.5YR 8/4) with sparse lime and few inclusions. Lot VI-5, 8280/6055 4.1. *RDAC* 1994: 303 no. 31, fig. 10.

121. Jug with ring base. Est. diam. base 0.06. Medium fine-grained reddish yellow fabric (5YR 7/6-7/8) with scattered lime and a few large voids. Interior lightly ridged; exterior smoothed, fired very pale brown (10YR 7/3-7/4). Lot I-1, 8530/6010S 1.1.
Cf. **116, 122-25**; Diederichs 1980b: 54 nos. 202-4, pl. 19.

122. Jug with ring base. Est. diam. base 0.065. Medium fine-grained reddish yellow fabric (5YR 6/6-7/6) with scattered fine lime. K-gen.

123. Jug with ring base. Est. diam. rim 0.06. Medium fine-grained reddish yellow fabric (5YR 6/6-7/6) with scattered lime. Interior lightly ridged; exterior smoothed, mottled very pale brown (10YR 8/4). Lot I-2, 8525/6005 5.2.

124. Jug with ring base. Est. diam. base 0.06. Fine-grained very pale brown fabric (10YR 7/3-7/4) with fine lime, sparse mica. Thin curved wall rises from ring base; interior lightly ridged; exterior smoothed, lightly scored. Lot VI-12, 8280/6060 4.2. *RDAC* 1994: 303-6 no. 32, fig. 10.

125. Jug with high ring base. Est. diam. base 0.06. Fine-grained pink fabric (7.5YR 7/4-8/4) with few inclusions. Interior smoothed; exterior smoothed and cleanly finished, fired pale yellow (2.5YR 8/4 to 10YR 8/4). SG13A.

126. Jug with ring base. Est. diam. base 0.08. Fine-grained light red fabric (2.5YR 6/6) with scattered fine lime and quartz, a few fine gold mica flecks. Interior lightly ridged; exterior and base very pale brown (10YR 7/4), carefully smoothed with a few dragged grits. Lot II-8, 8345/5935 3.1.

Group C

No examples catalogued.

Group D

127. Jug. Est. diam. rim 0.07. Medium fine-grained reddish yellow fabric (7.5YR 7/4-7/6) with medium-size particles lime, red, green, and gray inclusions. Vertical plain rim with rounded strap handle. Lot I-1, 8520/6005 1.1.

128. Jug with slightly concave base in 22 joining sherds. Diam. base 0.055. Medium-grained pink to reddish yellow fabric (5YR 7/4-7/6) with abundant lime to 0.004, quartz, and other small red and dark inclusions. Steep wall rises from thick flat base through rounded shoulder and narrow neck. Interior ridged; exterior roughly finished, mid body horizontally paddle-smoothed, lower body smoothed vertically, soft surface texture. Y-shaped graffito incised on upper shoulder. Lot II-12, 8350/5945S 3.1.

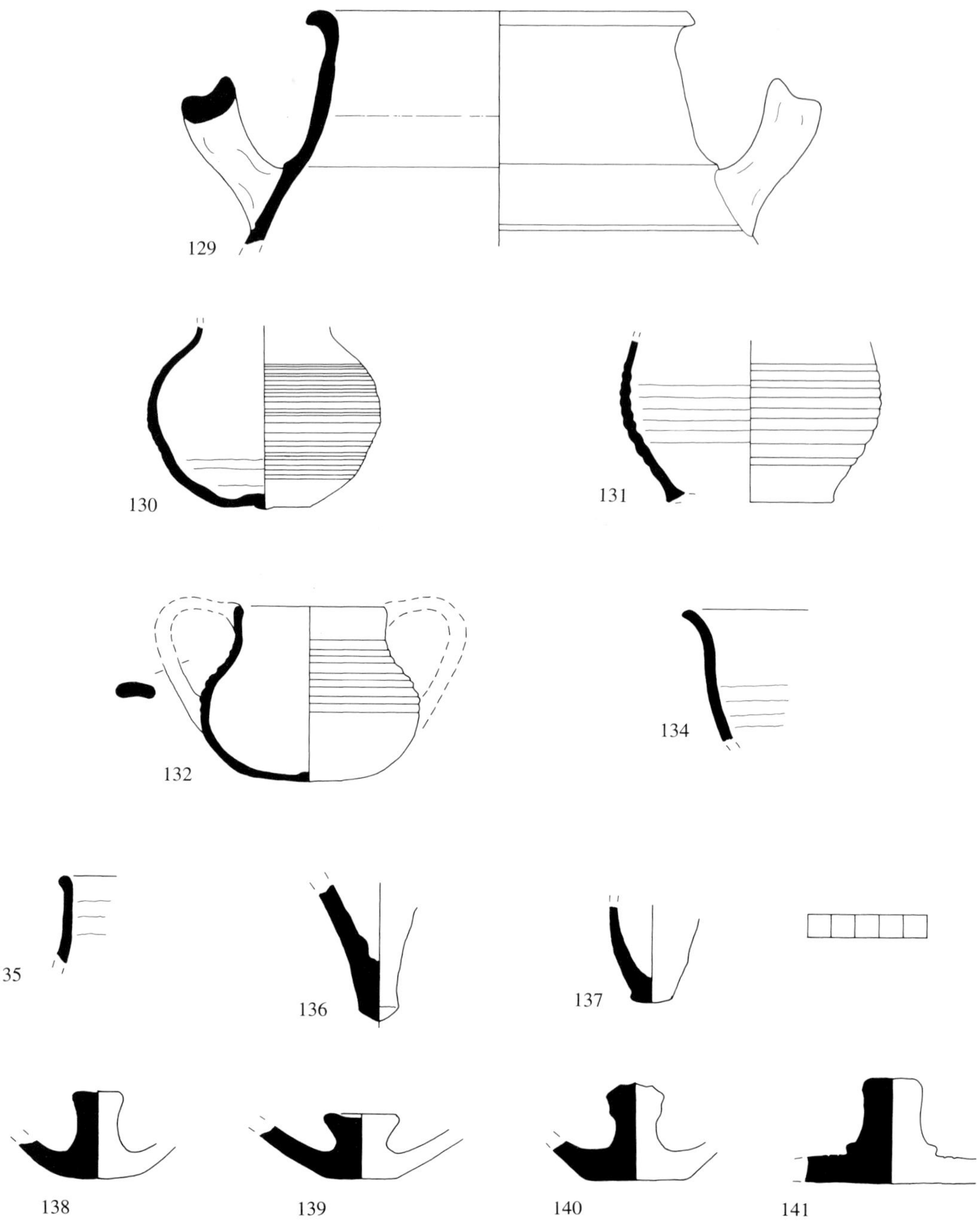

Fig. 5.10. Plain pottery.

Piriform jugs with flat or slightly concave bases appear frequently in 6th- and early 7th-c. contexts: Robinson 1959: 114 nos. M321-22, pl. 31 (early 6th c.), 121-22, pl. 35 (Group N, 7th c.); Catling 1972: 9 fig. 5 nos. P105, P157 (mid/late 7th c.); Riley 1979: 395; Bass 1982: 168-69; Boardman 1989: 103 nos. 185-90, fig. 32 (mid 7th c.; N.B. pl. 22 misnumbered).

129. Wide-mouth jar in 8 sherds. Diam. rim 0.15-0.17. Medium fine-grained light red fabric (2.5YR 6/6) with fine lime and small to medium-size dark inclusions. Large jar with tall wide neck and rounded, out-turned rim. Paired strap handles with broad central groove, horizontally attached and curving upward from shoulder. Interior summarily finished, often flaking; exterior well smoothed, fired a little lighter. Lot VI-11, 8280/6058 4.1.

130. Small jar/flask in 9 sherds. Est. max. diam. 0.10. Medium coarse-grained light red fabric (2.5YR 6/6) with fine lime, quartz, and small dark particles. Spherical wall rises from button base to narrow neck. Interior surface mottled light brown; exterior wall ridged, covered with dark gray/black slip, worn. Lot I-20, 8520/6015 5.1.

131. Small jar/flask in 4 sherds. Est. diam. base 0.07; max. diam. 0.11. Medium-grained light red fabric (2.5YR 6/6) with lime in fine particles and a few large inclusions and a few dark inclusions. Disc base(?) with spherical wall. Exterior wall ridged. Lot I-23, 8520/6015 5.1.

Cf. Catling 1972: 9 fig. 5 no. P158 (mid/late 7th c.); Peleg

1989: 76-77 no. 3, fig. 57 (stratum IV, *c.*650-750); Hayes 2001a: 447 B30, fig. 7 (early 7th c.).

132. Small jar/cup in 11 sherds. Est. diam. rim 0.06; max. diam. 0.09. Medium-grained red to light red fabric (2.5YR 5/6-6/6) with many small quartz particles and other inclusions, gold mica flecks; texture soft and flaking. Exterior lightly ridged, covered with dull light red slip, worn. Lot I-30, 8530/6010 2.2.
Cf. slightly larger jars in Rasson and Seigne 1989: 140 nos. 35-36, fig. 10:3-4 (level 3, 7th-8th c.).

[**133.** Unassigned.]

134. Small bowl with out-turned rim. Est. diam. rim. 0.06. Soft-textured pink fabric (7.5YR 7/4) with small lime particles and other fine inclusions. Interior lightly ridged; exterior smoothed. Lot VI-11, 8280/6058 4.1.

135. Pitcher with trefoil neck. Est. diam. rim 0.03-0.04. Medium-grained pink fabric (7.5YR 7/4) with fine lime, quartz, and other dark inclusions. Lot VI-10, 8280/6058 4.2.

136. Amphoriskos base. Max h. 0.06. Medium-grained very pale brown fabric (10YR 8/4) with fine lime, red and gray inclusions. Exterior smoothed. Lot VI-5, 8280/6055 4.1.

137. Fusiform unguentarium or amphoriskos base. Max. h. 0.04. Medium-grained bright light-red fabric (2.5YR 6/8) with much fine gold mica. Interior lightly ridged; exterior smoothed. Lot II-16, 8350/5940 8.1.
For discussion of the general type see Riley 1979: 363; Hayes 1992: 8-9; for an example from Paphos see id. 1991: 209 no. 10, fig. LXXII.

138. Saucer lid. Coarse-grained pink to reddish yellow fabric (5YR 7/4-7/6) with medium to large particles of lime and other dark inclusions. SG10.
Cf. in general **139-40;** Adan-Bayewitz 1986: 106-7, fig. 3 nos. 14-15 ('amphora lids'); Williams 1989: 74-75 nos. 434-40, figs. 40-41; Boardman 1989: 110 nos. 262-64, fig. 42 (mid 7th c.); Flourentzos 1996: 17 no. 10, pl. XXXI; Hayes 2001a: 447 no. B28, fig. 7 (early 7th c.).

139. Saucer lid. Medium-grained reddish yellow fabric (5YR 6/6) with scattered lime and other dark inclusions. Exterior surfaces smoothed and covered with off-white saline wash. SG71.

140. Saucer lid. Coarse-grained light red fabric (2.5YR 6/6) with medium-size particles of lime, quartz and other dark inclusions. Lot II-1, 8345/5930S 1.1.

141. Saucer lid. Coarse-grained very pale brown fabric (10YR 7/3-7/4) with medium to large particles of lime and other dark inclusions. K86-Tr. B 0-5.

Amphoras

LR1

142. Amphora. Diam. rim 0.085. Medium-grained very pale brown fabric (10YR 7/3-7/4) with abundant lime, quartz, and red, green, gray, and black inclusions that give the surface a sandy texture (fabric LR1[1]). Lot VI-6, 8280/6060 3.1. *RDAC* 1994: 306 no. 35, fig. 10.
Cf. Diederichs 1980b: 55 nos. 211-12, pls. 19-20; Hayes 1980b: fig. 15.

143. Amphora. Diam. rim 0.050. Medium-grained pink to very pale brown fabric (7.5YR 7/4 to 10YR 7/4) with fine lime, quartz, and many medium to large red, gray, and black inclusions (fabric LR1[1]). Panel-ridged amphora with narrow neck. Lot II-15, 8350/5940 5.1, KK93-14. *RDAC* 1994: 293 no. 9, fig. 4.
Cf. Williams 1989: 96 no. 565, fig. 57.

144. Amphora. Diam. rim 0.085-0.09. Medium-grained pink to reddish yellow fabric (5YR 7/4-7/6 to 7.5YR 7/4-8/4) with fine lime and many small red and black inclusions (fabric LR1[2]). Lot VI-5, 8280/6055 4.1, KK93-13.

LR2

145. Amphora. Est. diam. rim 0.07. Medium fine-grained light reddish brown fabric (2.5YR 6/4), exterior a little darker (2.5Y 5/2-6/2), interior shading red to purple (10R 6/6), with scattered lime and abundant mica. Lot I-1, 8530/6015 1.1.

146. Amphora. Est. diam. rim 0.09. Medium-grained light red fabric (2.5YR 6/6) with lime, fine mica, and many irregular voids. Lot I-1, 8520/6010N 1.1.

147. Amphora. Est. diam. rim 0.08. Medium-grained light reddish brown fabric (5YR 6/4) with fine lime and mica. K-gen.

LR3

No examples catalogued.

LR4

148. Amphora. Est. diam. rim 0.10. Medium-grained light red to reddish yellow fabric (2.5YR 6/8 to 5YR 7/8) with gray core and scattered lime and quartz. Plain rounded rim. K-gen, KK94-10.

149. Amphora. Est. diam. rim 0.10. Medium-grained reddish yellow fabric (5YR 6/6) with abundant lime and quartz. Exterior wall roughly ridged. Lot I-3, 8525/6000S 3.1.

150. Amphora. Est. diam. base 0.034. Medium-grained reddish yellow fabric (5YR 6/6) with scattered lime and quartz. Interior floor bears excess clay; exterior lightly ridged. Lot II-10, 8350/5935 5.1.
For the conical, flat-bottomed base cf. Keay 1984: 278 no. E/GB/E.58 fig. 122 no. 10, fig. 123 no. 3 (type LIVB); Oleson *et al.* 1994: 18 A29, fig. 4.

LR5/6

151. Amphora. Est. diam. rim 0.09. Sandy-textured light reddish yellow fabric (5YR 7/6) with pink surface, scattered fine quartz, mica, and other dark inclusions, irregular voids. Grooved upper shoulder, vertical rim. K-gen, KK94-12.

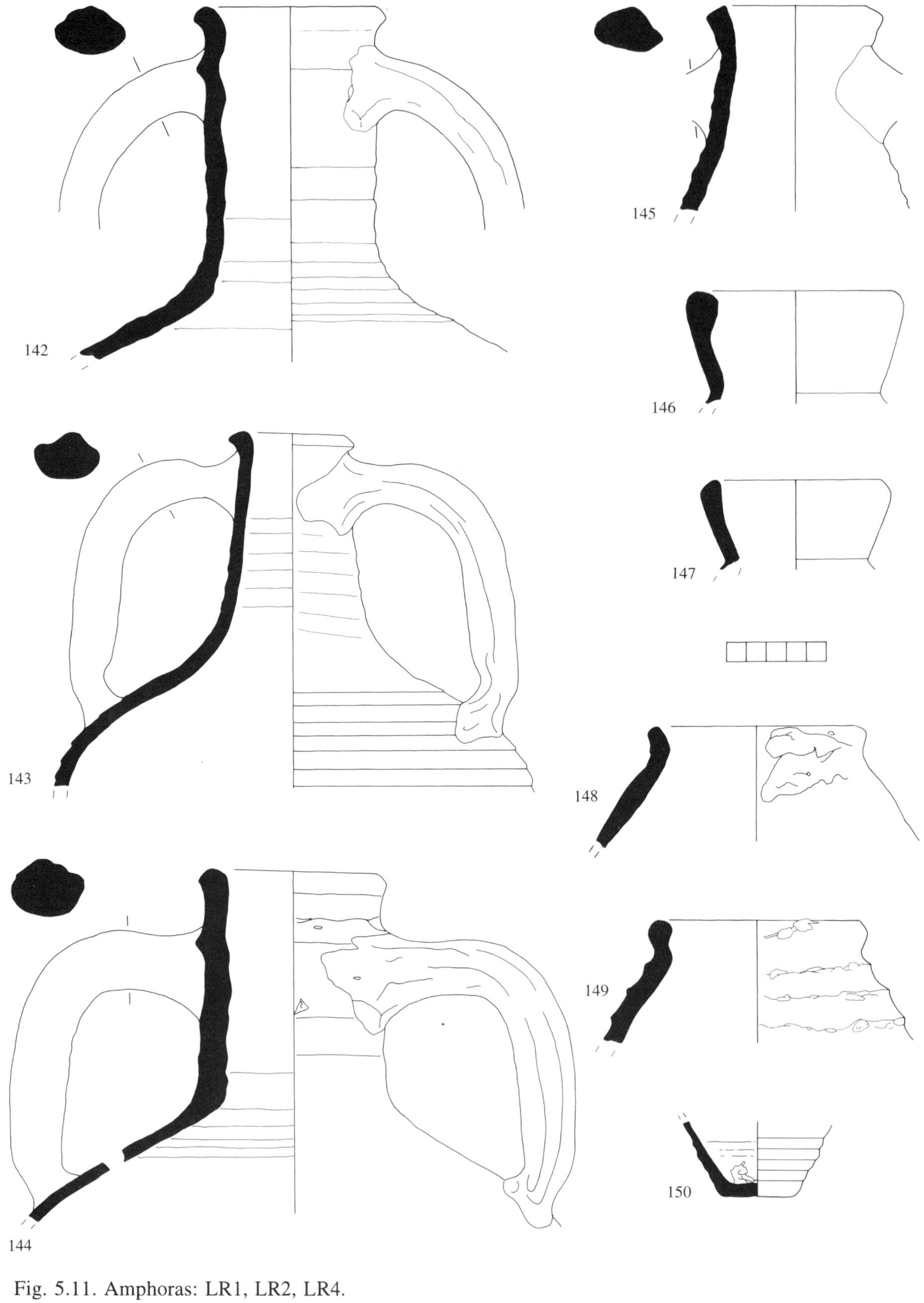

Fig. 5.11. Amphoras: LR1, LR2, LR4.

152. Amphora. Est. diam. rim 0.09. Sandy-textured fabric as **151**. Lot I-1, 8530/6010E and 6015E 1.1.

153. Amphora. Est. diam. rim 0.07. Sandy-textured red fabric (10R 5/6) with fine lime and other dark inclusions. Lot VI-11, 8280/6060 4.1, KK94-13.

LR7

154. Amphora toe. Max. l. 0.105. Medium coarse-grained brown fabric (7.5YR 5/4) with darker core, lime, quartz,

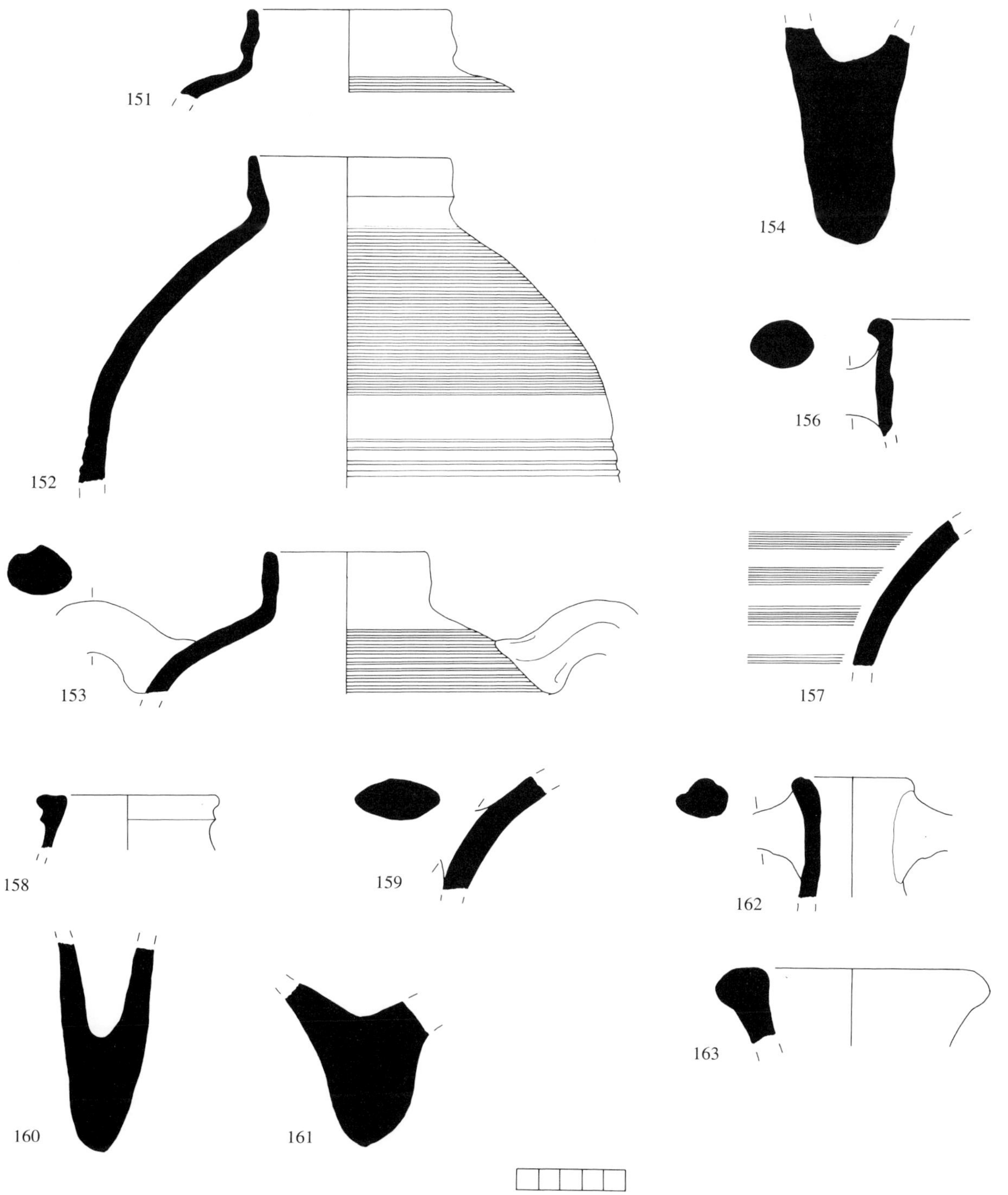

Fig. 5.12. Amphoras: LR5/6, 7, minor forms.

and large golden mica flecks. Surface eroded. Lot II-1, 8315/5920 1.1.

155. Amphora, fragment of wall (not illustrated). Medium-grained reddish brown fabric (5YR 5/4 to 7.5YR 5/4) on exterior, shading to yellowish brown (10YR 5/6) on interior, with lime, quartz, and large golden mica flecks. Exterior covered with broad, well-defined ridges at 0.02-m intervals. K-gen.

KAmp1

156. Amphora. Diam. rim uncertain but *c*.0.01. Medium fine-grained very pale brown fabric (10YR 7/4) with fine lime and mica. Interior smoothed; exterior surface a little lighter to very pale brown (10YR 8/4). Plain rounded rim with rolled handle. The fabric appears a little finer than other examples, with bands of horizontal combing. SG41A.

157. Amphora, fragment of wall. Medium-grained reddish yellow fabric (7.5YR 6/6) with fine lime, quartz, and many small to medium-size black inclusions (fabric KAmp1/1). Thick wall with multiple bands of combed horizontal decoration. SG4.

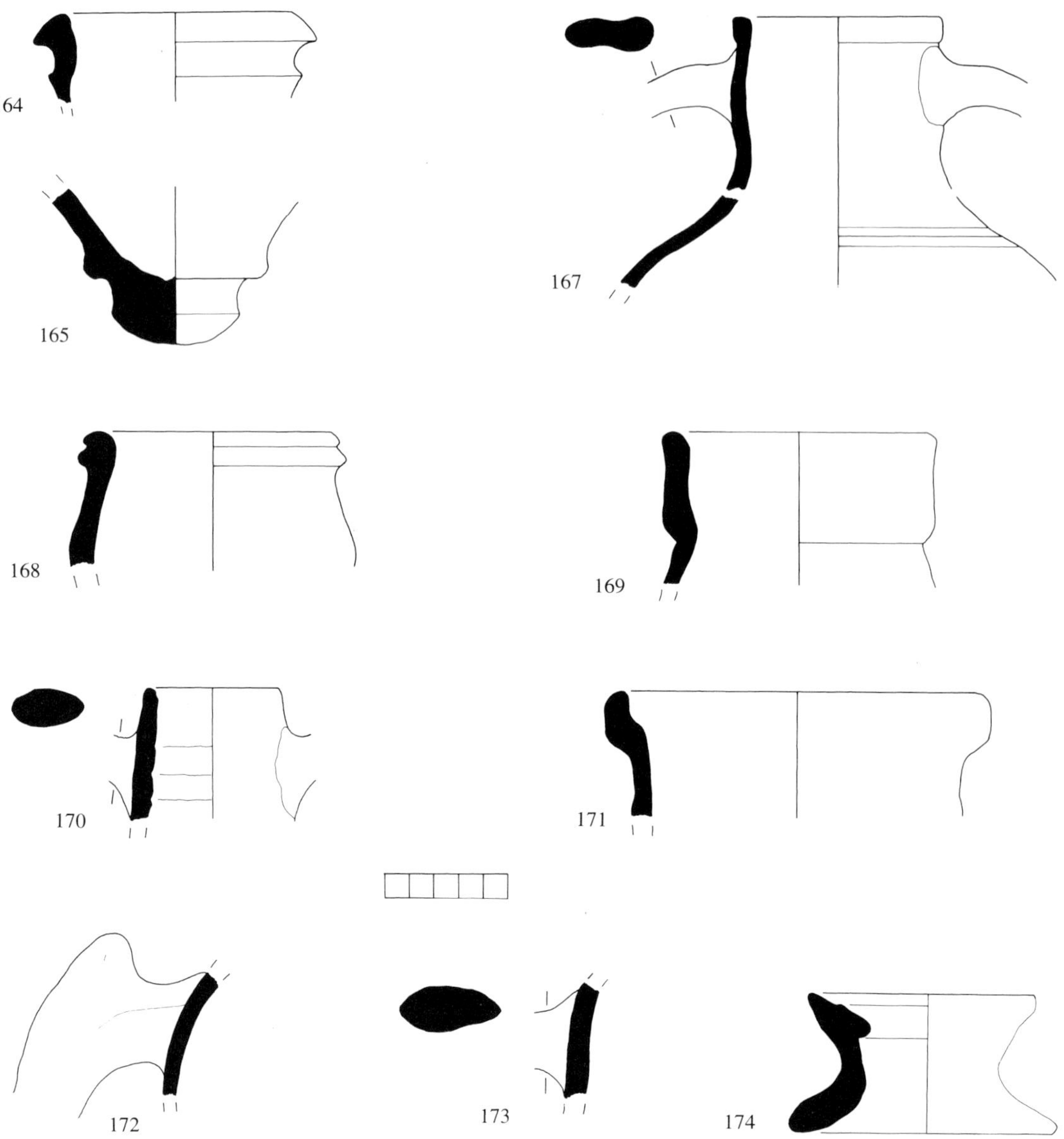

Fig. 5.13. Amphoras: minor forms.

KAmp2

158. Amphora. Est. diam. rim 0.06. Medium coarse-grained pink to light red fabric (2.5YR 6/6) with large angular black inclusions. Lot I-28, 8540/6010 3.1.
Cf. Taylor and Megaw 1981: 245 nos. 465-66, fig. 61.

159. Amphora, fragment of wall with handle. Medium-grained light red fabric (2.5YR 6/6) with gray to grayish brown core (10YR 6/3), densely speckled with quartz to 0.002, mica, and many medium to large red and black inclusions. Ovoid-section handle. SG42.

160. Amphora toe. Max. h. 0.10. Medium-grained light red fabric (2.5YR 6/6) with large angular black inclusions. Lot II-1, surface.
Cf. Taylor and Megaw 1981: 245 no. 467, fig. 61.

161. Amphora toe. Max. h. 0.08. Same fabric as **159**. K-gen.

KAmp3

162. Amphora. Est. diam. rim 0.05. Medium coarse-grained reddish yellow fabric (7.5YR 7/4-7/6) with fine lime and other inclusions, including small particles of quartz or mica. Lot II-3, 8345/5945 2.1.

KAmp4

No examples catalogued.

KAmp5

163. Amphora. Est. diam. rim 0.10. Medium-grained light red fabric (2.5YR 6/8 to 5YR 6/8) with small particles of lime, quartz, and other dark inclusions. Rounded rim, smoothed. SG42.

164. Amphora. Est. diam. rim 0.09. Medium-grained pink to reddish yellow fabric (5YR 7/6) with scattered lime and quartz; smooth break. Soft, smooth texture with traces of a light exterior wash. K86-Tr. B 20-25.
Cf. Riley 1979: 225-26 nos. 360-61, fig. 92 (deposit 142, mid 6th c.).

165. Amphora. Low rounded foot gently offset from rising wall. Medium coarse-grained orange to light red fabric (2.5YR 6/8 to 10R 6/8) with darker core, lime and quartz to 0.003, and a few dark inclusions. Rounded base with exterior offset. SG65.
Cf. Riley 1979: 234 no. 391, fig. 96 (deposit 137, mid 6th c.); Keay 1984: 338-39, figs. 157-59 (type LXII var. A, Tunisian).

166. Amphora toe (not illustrated). Max. h. 0.12. Medium coarse-grained light red fabric (10R 6/8 to 2.5YR 6/8) with scattered lime. Exterior smoothed, covered with pale yellow wash (about 5Y 8/3). SG64A.

KAmp6

No examples catalogued.

KAmp7

No examples catalogued.

Unassigned amphoras

167. Amphora. Est. diam. rim 0.08. Medium-grained reddish yellow fabric (about 5YR 7/6) with lime, quartz, and other dark inclusions. Exterior lightly ridged, fired light reddish brown (5YR 6/4). Tall neck with plain vertical rim, paired strap handles attached to upper neck. Lot II-19, 8340/5940 4.1.

168. Amphora. Est. diam. rim 0.09. Medium-grained light red fabric (2.5YR 6/6) with scattered lime, medium-size quartz particles, and gray and red inclusions; uneven break. K-gen.

169. Amphora. Est. diam. rim 0.10. Medium-grained pink fabric (7.5YR 7/4) with scattered lime and quartz, dark red and gray inclusions, and a little mica. Vertical rim with exterior offset; exterior covered with light gray to white slip or saline wash (2.5YR 7/2-8/3). Lot V-1, 8315/6162 2.3. *RDAC* 1994: 301 no. 25, fig. 8.

170. Amphora. Est. diam. rim 0.05. Medium-grained strong red fabric (2.5YR 6/4-6/8 in section, brighter at surface), with scattered lime, fine mica, and a few small dark red inclusions and fine voids. Interior and exterior lightly ridged, covered with matte black slip. Ovoid-section strap handle. SG42.

171. Amphora. Est. diam. rim 0.14. Medium-grained light red fabric (3.5YR 6/6-6/8) with scattered lime, fine mica, and dark red inclusions; uneven break. Lot I-1, 8540/6000 1.1.

172. Amphora. Fragment of wall with handle. Medium-grained pale yellow fabric (2.5Y 7/4-8/4) with small dark inclusions; eroded surface. Horn handle. SG26.
Cf. Riley 1979: 147-48 (Early Roman); Peacock and Williams 1986: 102-8.

173. Amphora. Fragment of wall with handle. Medium-grained hard orange to red fabric (2.5YR 5/8-6/8) with fine red and gray inclusions and quartz to 0.004. Ovoid-section handle. Lot I-28, 8525/6010E 2.1.

174. Amphora stand. Est. diam. base 0.10. Coarse-grained light red fabric (2.5YR 6/6) with a greenish exterior surface, scattered lime, red, gray, and black inclusions, especially dense on upper surface. SG15.
Cf. Catling 1972: 11 fig. 7; Riley 1979: 353-54 nos. 959-65, fig. 128 (Middle Roman); Williams 1989: 103; Manning *et al.* 2000: fig. 13.f.

Cooking wares

Group A

175. Lid with knob handle in two non-joining sections. Est. diam. rim 0.23. Medium coarse-grained red fabric (2.5YR 5/6) with dark brown core, lime, quartz, mica, and medium-size gray inclusions. Broad shallow lid with knob handle. Interior and exterior lightly ridged. Lot I-20, 8520/6015 5.1.
Cf. Adan-Bayewitz 1986: 108-9, fig. 4 nos. 8-10; Peleg 1989: 71.

176. Lid with knob handle. Est. diam. rim 0.22. Medium coarse-grained red fabric (2.5YR 5/4-5/6) with lime and quartz. Interior smoothed, mottled orange/red; exterior sharply ridged. Knob handle pierced. Lot I-23, 8525/6015 3.3.
Cf. Adan-Bayewitz 1986: 108-9 illus. 115-16, fig. 4 nos. 8-9.

177. Lid, handle missing. Est. diam. rim 0.22. Medium coarse-grained light red fabric (2.5YR 6/6) with lime and quartz. Exterior sharply ridged, mottled dark gray. Lot I-7, 8525/5995 4.2.

178. Lid. Est. diam. rim 0.24. Medium-grained red fabric (10R 5/8 to 2.5YR 5/8) with small particles of lime, quartz, and a little mica. Exterior smoothed. Lot I-1, 8590/6000 1.1.
Cf. Williams 1989: 74 no. 433, fig. 40.

179. Lid. Est. diam. rim 0.20. Medium-grained light red fabric (2.5YR 6/6) with small particles of lime, quartz, mica, and other dark inclusions. Exterior smoothed. K-gen.

180. Lid. Est. diam. rim. 0.20. Medium coarse-grained light reddish brown fabric (5YR 6/4) with gray core, mottled surfaces. Interior smoothed; exterior ridged. K-gen.

181. Lid handle. Medium-grained red fabric (2.5YR 5/6) with fine lime and quartz. SG5A.
Cf. Taylor and Megaw 1981: 221 no. 379, fig. 44 (7th c.); Williams 1989: 73 no. 426, fig. 40.

182. Deep pot. Est. diam. rim 0.25. Medium coarse-grained light red fabric (2.5YR 6/8) with lime, quartz, and other dark inclusions. Straight flaring wall with flattened vertical rim. Paired roll handles, horizontally attached below rim. Interior smoothed; exterior wall ridged. Lot I-20, 8520/6015 5.1.
Cf. Adan-Bayewitz 1986: 107, fig. 3 no. 21; Peleg 1989: 65-72.

183. Shallow pot in 10 sherds. Est. diam. rim 0.17. Medium coarse-grained fabric with fine lime, quartz, and mica;

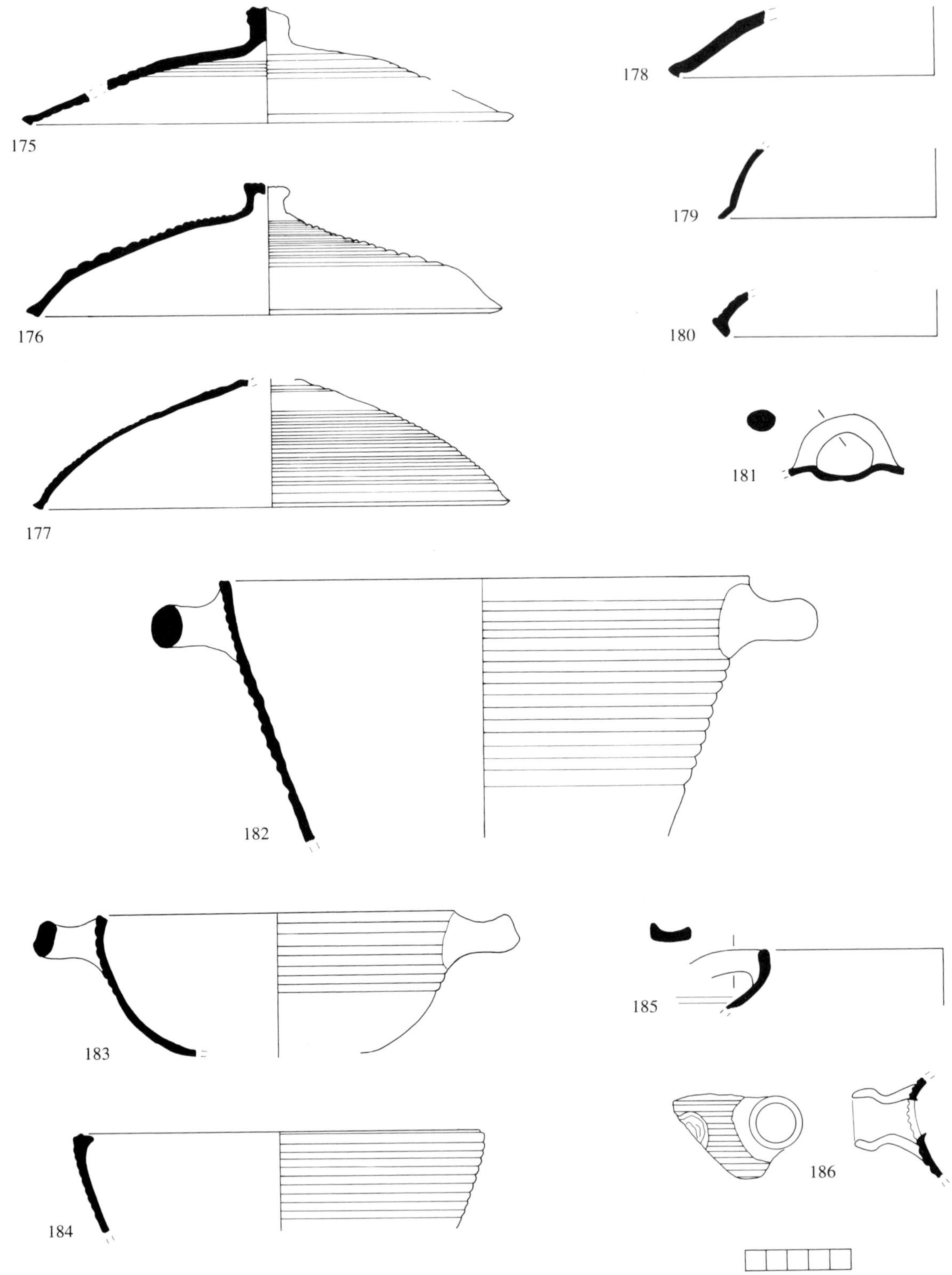

Fig. 5.14. Cooking pottery.

blackened by use to dark reddish brown (about 5YR 3/2-4/2). Thin wall rises to flattened, slightly in-turned rim. Paired handles attached below rim. Interior smoothed; upper exterior wall ridged. Lots IV-12 and 13, Tr. B 3.1 and 4.1. *RDAC* 1994: 299 no. 19, fig. 6.

Cf. Tushingham 1985: 321, fig. 30 no. 30; Williams 1989: 70 no. 412, fig. 38.

184. Shallow pot. Est. diam. rim 0.19. Medium coarse-grained light red fabric (2.5YR 6/6) with small lime, quartz, and mica particles. Thin wall rises to thickened in-

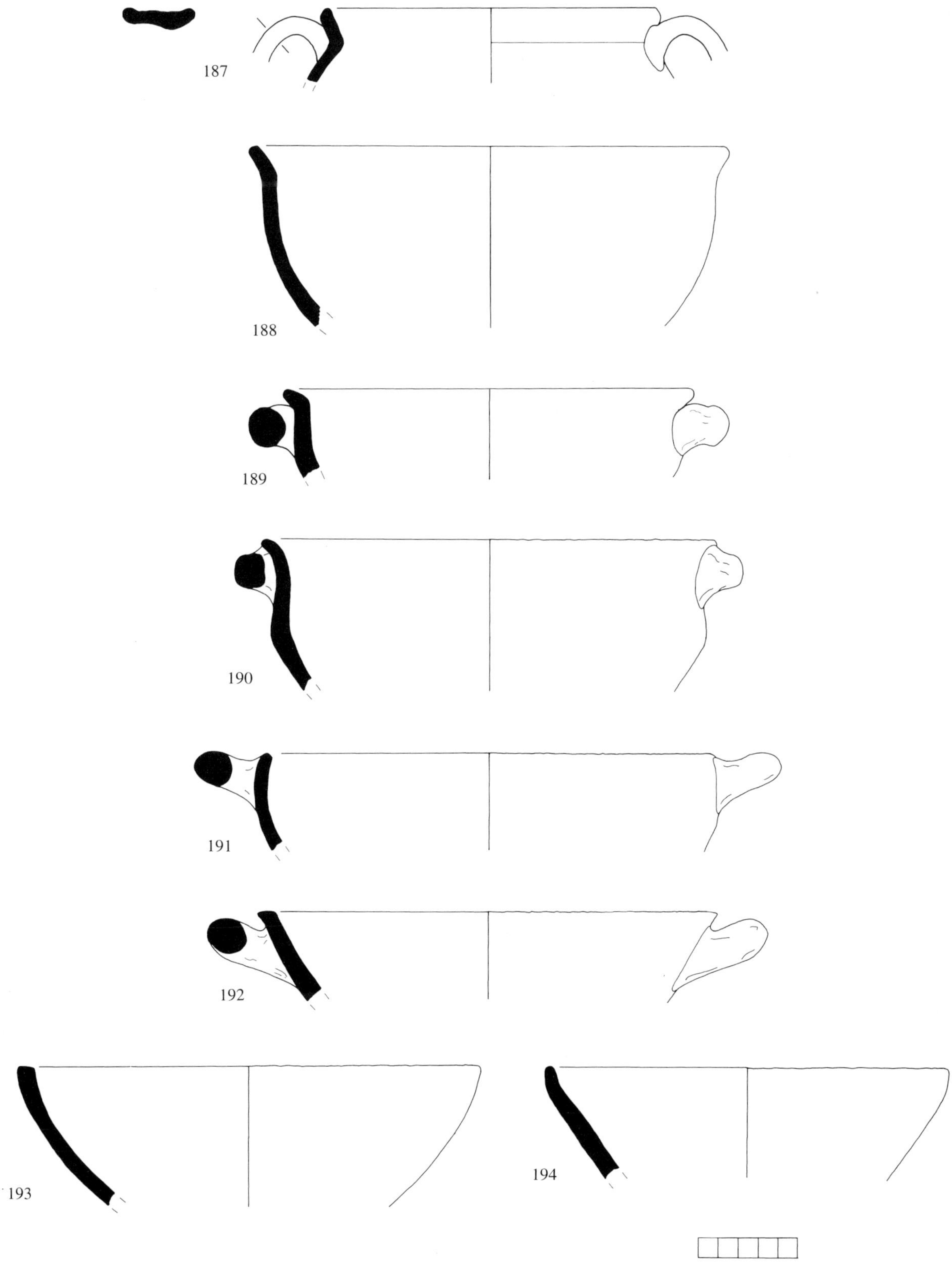

Fig. 5.15. Cooking pottery.

turned rim. Interior smoothed; exterior wall ridged. Lot IV-1, Tr. C 1.1.

Cf. Taylor and Megaw 1981: 245 no. 468, fig. 60.

185. Cooking pot. Est. diam. rim 0.17. Medium-grained red fabric (2.5YR 4/8-5/8) with abundant lime and fine quartz. Plain vertical rim with strap handle. Lot I-20, 8520/6015 5.2.

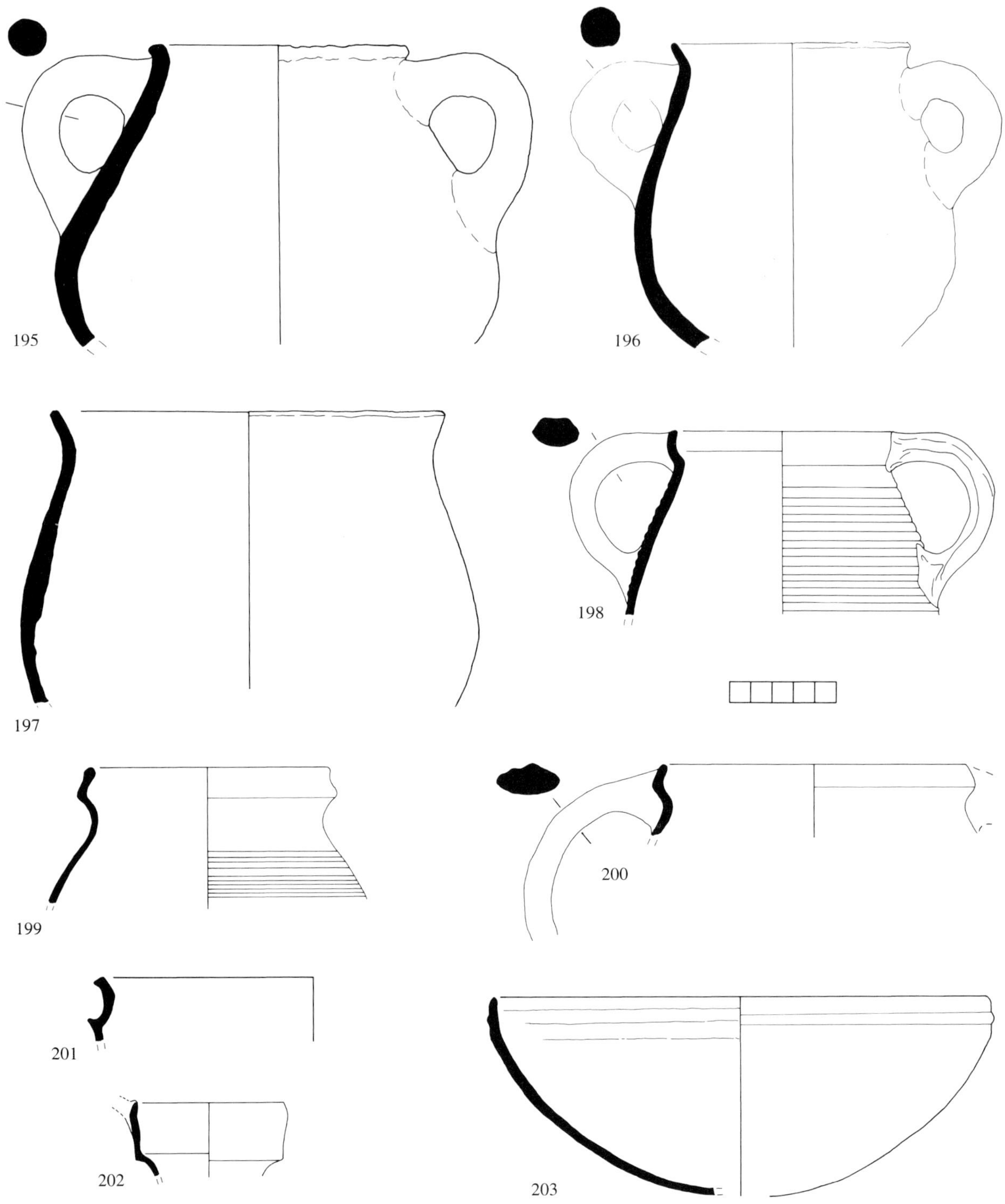

Fig. 5.16. Cooking pottery.

186. Cooking pot with spout. Diam. spout 0.024. Medium-grained red fabric (2.5YR 5/6) with small lime and quartz particles. Thin incurved wall with horizontal spout, handle root. Exterior finely ridged. Lot VI-3, 8280/6058 3.1.

Group B

187. Cooking pot. Est. diam. rim 0.16. Medium-grained reddish brown fabric (5YR 5/3-5/4) with small lime and quartz particles and abundant gold mica on surface; mostly smudged by use. High out-turned rim with broad strap handle. Lot II-6, 8345/5935 3.1.
Cf. Hayes 1980b: fig. 10; id. 1992: 55-57; e.g., fig. 79 no. 109 (deposit 50, 8th c.).

Group C

188. Cooking pot. Est. diam. rim 0.23. Medium coarse-grained red fabric (2.5YR 5/8-6/8) with darker core, fine lime, quartz, and small to medium-size dark inclusions. Thick wheelmade wall rises to plain, out-turned rim. Interior and exterior roughly smoothed, scored by dragged grits. Lots I-14 and 28, 8525/6010E 2.1 and 8528/6010S 3.1.

189. Cooking pot. Est. diam. rim 0.20. Coarse-grained reddish brown fabric (7.5YR 5/4) with lime, quartz, and many large angular inclusions. Thick wheelmade carinated wall rises to plain, out-turned rim. Undulating rolled handle, horizontally attached below rim. Lot II-14, 8345/5945 3.1. Rautman 1998: fig. 4.1.

190. Cooking pot. Est. diam. rim 0.22. Coarse-grained red fabric (2.5YR 5/6) with lime, quartz, and many small dark inclusions. Thick wheelmade carinated wall rises to plain out-turned rim. Rolled handle, squarish in section, horizontally attached below rim. Lot I-1, 8520/6000 1.1. Rautman 1998: fig. 4.2.

191. Handmade cooking dish. Est. diam. rim 0.22. Coarse-grained light brown fabric (7.5YR 6/4-7/4) with lime, quartz, and many dark inclusions. Shallow dish with slightly incurving wall and plain rim. Rolled handle horizontally attached at rim. K-gen, KK94-14. Rautman 1998: fig. 4.3.

192. Handmade cooking dish. Est. diam. rim 0.22. Coarse-grained light yellowish brown fabric (10YR 6/4) with scattered lime, quartz, and many dark inclusions. Handmade shallow dish with plain rim. Rolled handle horizontally attached below rim. SG77, KK94-15. Rautman 1998: fig. 4.4.

193. Handmade cooking dish. Est. diam. rim 0.22. Coarse-grained light brown fabric (7.5YR 6/4) with lime, quartz, and many dark inclusions. Shallow dish with sloping wall and plain vertical rim; lacking handles. Lots VI-6 and 7, 8280/6060 3.1 and 3.2, KK94-16. Rautman 1998: fig. 4.5.

194. Handmade cooking dish. Est. diam. rim 0.22. Coarse-grained light brown fabric (7.5YR 6/4) with lime, quartz, and many dark inclusions. Shallow dish with sloping wall and plain vertical rim; lacking handles. Lots VI-6 and 7, 8280/6060 3.1 and 3.2, KK94-17. *RDAC* 1994: 306 no. 37, fig. 10; Rautman 1998: fig. 4.6.
Cf. Adan-Bayewitz 1986: 108, 127 fig. 4 no. 7 for a similar, unevenly-made shape.

195. Handmade cooking pot with vertical handles. Est. diam. rim 0.12. Coarse-grained reddish brown fabric (5YR 5/4-6/4) with lime, quartz, and many dark inclusions. Globular pot with out-turned rim, vertical rolled handle. Lot VI-6, 8280/6060 3.1, KK93-12. *RDAC* 1994: 306 no. 38, fig. 10; Rautman 1998: fig. 4.7.
Cf. Megaw 1986: 512 fig. 8b (CB3984/1; 8th c.).

196. Handmade cooking pot. Diam. rim uncertain. Coarse-grained dark brown fabric (7.5YR 4/4 to 10YR 4/3) with gray core, lime, quartz, and many medium-size dark inclusions. Thick incurving wall with plain vertical rim; lacking handles. Lot IV-2, Tr. C 2.1. *RDAC* 1994: 299 no. 20, fig. 6.

197. Handmade cooking pot. Est. diam. rim 0.20. Coarse-grained reddish brown fabric (5YR 5/4) with abundant lime, quartz, and many angular dark inclusions. Globular pot with out-turned rim; lacking handles. Lots II-27 and 28, 8335/5930 3.1 and 4.1, KK94-18. *RDAC* 1994: 293 no. 11, fig. 4; Rautman 1998: fig. 4.8.

Group D

198. Cooking pot. Est. diam. rim 0.10. Coarse-grained red fabric (2.5YR 4/6-5/6) with scattered lime, quartz, and small dark inclusions. Deep pot with concave vertical rim, finely ridged wall; vertical handles rise from mid body to rim. Lot VI-11, 8280/6058 4.1, KK93-11. *RDAC* 1994: 306 no. 36, fig. 10.
Cf. Catling and Dikigoropoulos 1970: 56 nos. 7-8, fig. 7 (mid 7th c.); Catling 1972: 11, fig. 7 no. P96, 45 fig. 27 no. P185; Hayes 1980b: figs. 5-6; Adan-Bayewitz 1986: 108, fig. 4 nos. 3-4; Williams 1989: 69 nos. 406-7, fig. 37.

199. Cooking pot, lacking handles. Est. diam. rim 0.11. Medium-grained light red fabric (2.5YR 6/6-6/8) with scattered fine lime, quartz, and other small dark inclusions. Deep pot with concave vertical rim, finely ridged wall. K-gen.

200. Cooking pot. Est. diam. rim 0.14. Medium-grained light red fabric (2.5YR 6/6) with darker core, medium-size lime, quartz, and other dark inclusions. Deep pot with concave vertical rim, vertical strap handle. K-gen.

201. Cooking pot. Est. diam. rim 0.20. Coarse-grained red fabric (about 10R 5/6) with medium-size lime, quartz, and other dark inclusions. Thin wall rises to convex rim with sharp exterior offset. SG17A.

202. Closed vessel with tall neck. Est. diam. rim 0.04. Medium-grained light red fabric (2.5YR 6/6) with scattered lime and quartz. Vertical wall rises to raised rim with exterior offset; handle root at top of rim. Lot I-6, 8525/5995 2.1.

203. Cooking dish in 28 sherds from at least two vessels. Est. diam. rim 0.23. Medium coarse-grained red fabric (2.5YR 5/6) with a little lime, quartz, and fine mica. Wheelmade shallow bowl with thin wall ends in plain vertical form. Interior irregularly smoothed by hand; exterior deeply scored by dragged grits. Perhaps a lid, although interior residues suggest use as a cooking dish. Lot I-20, 8520/6015 5.1.

Pithoi

Group A

204. Storage jar. Diam. rim uncertain. Coarse-grained very pale brown fabric (10YR 7/4) with lighter exterior, finely speckled with lime and quartz, with medium-size red and gray inclusions. Triangular rim with single row of molded decoration, stamped rosette(s), incised wavy line on upper wall. SG62.

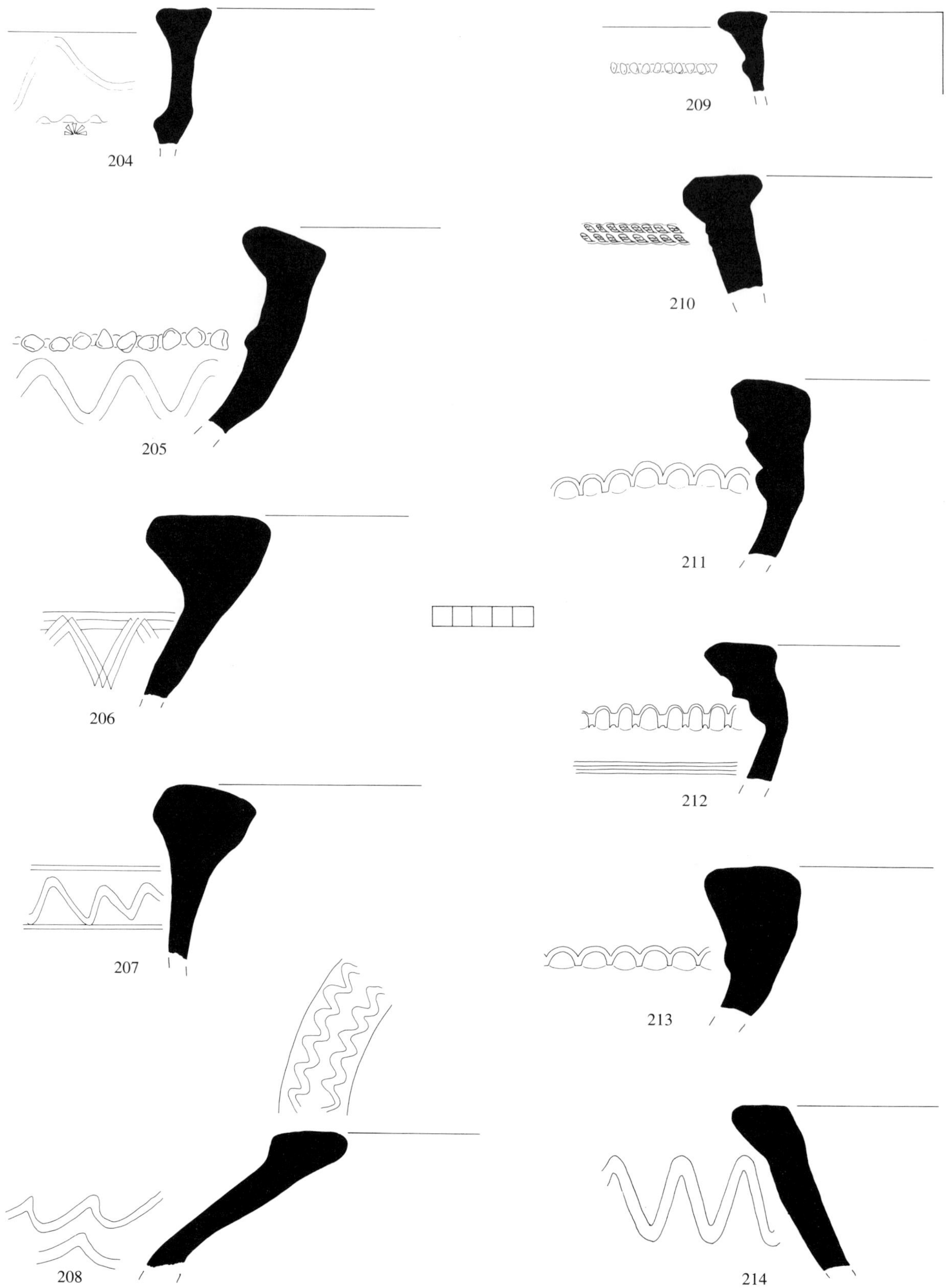

Fig. 5.17. *Pithoi*.

Cf. Devos *et al.* 1999: 104 for other stamps on *pithoi*.

205. Storage jar. Est. diam. rim 0.35. Coarse-grained light red fabric (2.5YR 6/8) with many medium to large inclusions. Thickened out-turned rim with single row of crudely impressed decoration, incised wavy line on upper wall. SG7A, KK93-20.

206. Storage jar. Diam. rim uncertain. Coarse-grained reddish brown fabric (5YR 5/4-6/5) with lime, quartz, and other dark inclusions. Heavy triangular rim with lightly incised horizontal and wavy lines on upper wall. SG31A, KK93-19.

207. Storage jar. Diam. rim uncertain. Coarse-grained light red fabric (2.5YR 6/6) with gray core, with medium-size quartz particles and other inclusions. Heavy triangular rim with incised horizontal and wavy lines on upper wall. SG26.

208. Storage jar. Est. diam. rim 0.24. Coarse-grained reddish yellow fabric (5YR 6/6) with medium-size lime and quartz particles and other dark inclusions. Slightly thickened rim with pairs of incised wavy lines on top of rim and on upper wall. Lot I-1, 8530/6005 surface.

Group B

209. Storage jar. Est. diam. rim 0.18. Coarse-grained light red fabric (10R 6/6) with scattered lime and quartz particles. Triangular rim with single row of impressed decoration on upper wall; top of rim and exterior covered with dark brown to black slip. K-gen.

Group C

210. Storage jar. Diam. rim uncertain. Coarse-grained light red fabric (2.5YR 6/4-6/6) with sparse lime and quartz, scattered black inclusions. Thickened and flattened rim with two bands of impressed corded decoration on upper wall. SG76A.

211. Storage jar. Est. diam. rim 0.30. Coarse-grained light red fabric (2.5YR 6/6) with lime, quartz, and many dark inclusions. Heavy triangular rim with single row of impressed decoration around neck. K-gen, KK94-19.

212. Storage jar. Diam. rim uncertain. Coarse-grained light reddish brown fabric (5YR 5/4 to 7.5YR 6/4) with lime, quartz, and many large angular inclusions. Out-turned triangular rim with stepped profile and single row of impressed decoration around neck. SG56A, KK93-16.

213. Storage jar. Est. diam. rim 0.40. Coarse-grained light red fabric (2.5YR 6/6) with lime, quartz, and many dark inclusions. Heavy triangular rim with single row of impressed decoration around neck. K-gen, KK93-15.

Group D

214. Storage jar. Est. diam. rim 0.40. Coarse-grained reddish yellow fabric (5YR 7/6) with lime, quartz, and many medium-size inclusions. Slightly thickened rim with lightly incised wavy line on upper wall. SG75, KK93-18.

215. Storage jar. Diam. rim uncertain. Coarse-grained light red fabric (2.5YR 6/8) with lime, quartz, and medium-size dark inclusions. Curving wall ends in thickened, out-turned rim; heavy ovoid handle below. Incised horizontal and wavy lines on upper wall. Lot II-2, 8335/5935 2.1 and 3.1.

216. Storage jar. Diam. rim uncertain. Coarse-grained light brown fabric (7.5YR 6/4) with lime, quartz and other dark inclusions. Vertical wall with plain rim joining broad strap handle with incised cross. Lot II-1, 8350/5930 surface.
Cf. Devos *et al.* 1999: 98 fig. 8e for a similar cross on a *pithos* wall.

217. Storage jar. Est. diam. rim 0.30. Coarse-grained pink fabric (5YR 7/4 to 7.5YR 7/4) with many large dark inclusions. Vertical wall with thickened rim. Incised wavy line on top of rim. SG15.
Cf. Williams 1989: 80 no. 471, fig. 45.

218. Storage jar. Diam. rim uncertain. Coarse-grained light reddish brown fabric (5YR 6/3) with lime, quartz, and other dark inclusions. Vertical wall with plain rim joining broad strap handle with impressed finger-marks and stamped palmettes. SG8.

Rooftiles and water pipes

219. Laconian-style rooftile. Max. l. 0.70, w. 0.33. Medium fine-grained light red fabric with small to medium-size particles of lime. Slightly concave section with raised rim. Floor lightly inscribed ΛΕ[C]. Lot I-2, 8525/6000 3.2.
Cf. di Cesnola 1894: II, 5, pl. CXLII no. 1058 (l. *c.*0.635); Myres 1914: 306 no. 1853 (w. *c.*0.32); Hadjichristophi 1989: 878, fig. 36 (type IV).

220. Laconian-style cover tile. Max. l. 0.19, w. 0.13. Same fabric as **218**. K-gen.

221. Corinthian-style rooftile. Max. l. 0.435, w. 0.35. Medium fine-grained yellow fabric (2.5YR 8/6) with occasional small inclusions. Flat section with narrow offset upper ridge, raised side edges, and triangular down-slope flow directors; flat back. Lot I-3, 8535/6000 3.1.
Cf. Argoud *et al.* 1980: 36 (various examples, none illustrated); Taylor and Megaw 1981: 232 fig. 51; Hufstot 1987: 264-65, 190-93 fig. 179 (type X, 1st-4th c.); Hadjichristophi 1989: 877, figs. 33-34 (type II); Roux 1998: 21, 26 fig. 12a-b.

222. Corinthian-style cover tile. Max. l. 0.423, w. 0.105. Same fabric as **220**. Mold-made pitched outer ridge with curved inner surface; raised border at one end. Lot I-2, 8535/6000 2.1.
Cf. Hufstot 1987: 281-89, fig. 195 (1st-4th c.); Roux 1998: 21, 26 fig. 12c.

223. Corinthian-style rooftile. Max. l. 0.55, w. 0.465. Coarse-grained light red to light brown fabric (2.5YR 4/6-5/6) with much lime, quartz, and many medium to large inclusions. Flat section with continuous raised upper and side edges, triangular down-slope flow directors; flat back. Light patterns inscribed on floor. Lot I-23, 8525/6015 3.6.
Cf. Hufstot 1987: 268-71, 294, figs. 185-89 (type Z; one complete example measuring 0.57 x 0.47 m, dated late 1st c.); Hadjichristophi 1989: 878, fig. 35 (type III, although cf. type I fabric); Flourentzos 1996: 15 no. 17b. The size is similar to tiles found at Deir Déhès (0.53 x 0.43 m; J.-L. Biscop in Sodini *et al.* 1980: 210).

224. Corinthian-style cover tile. Max. l. 0.28, w. 0.11. Same fabric as **223**. K-gen.

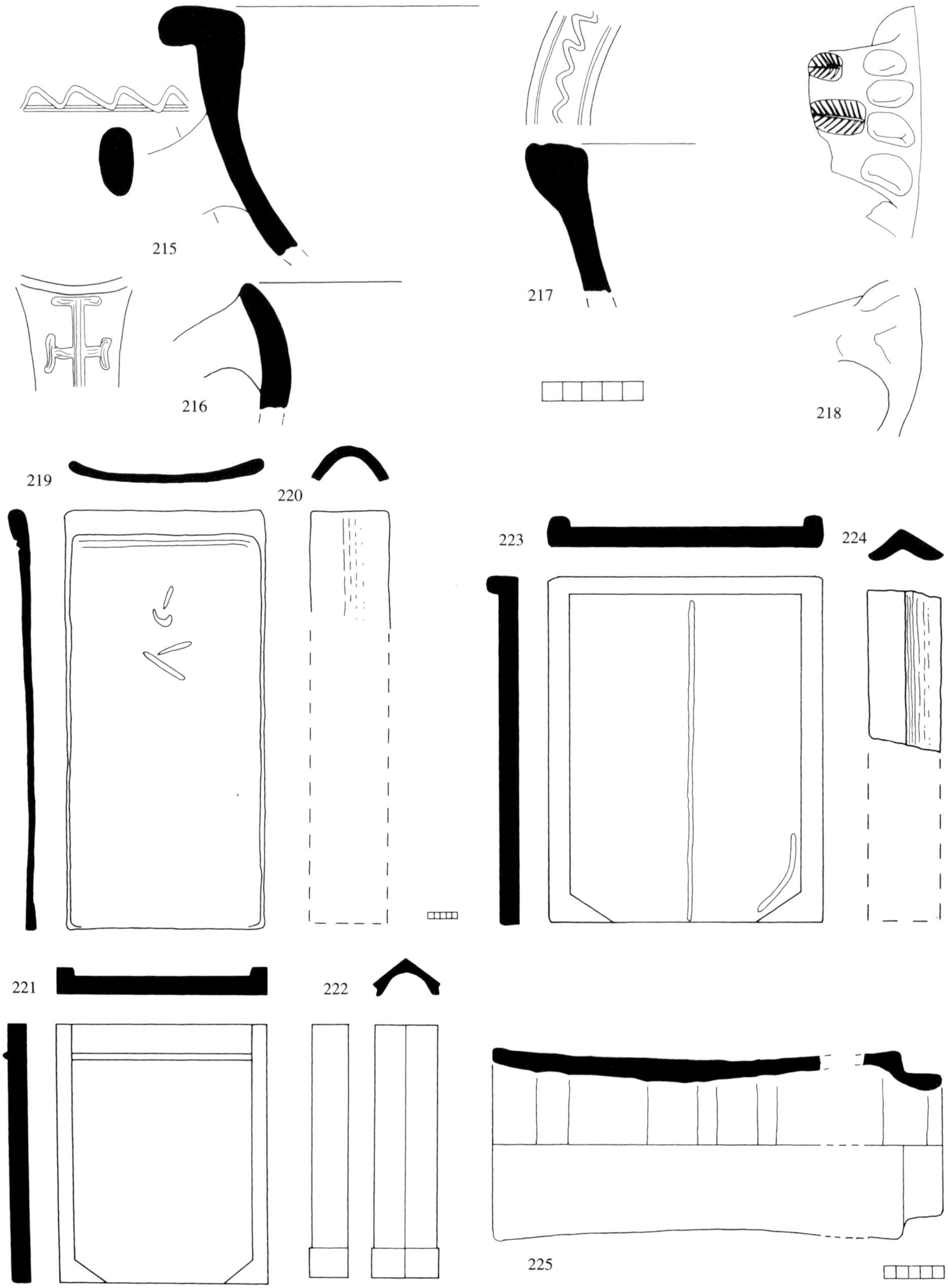

Fig. 5.18. *Pithoi*, rooftiles, waterpipe.

225. Cylindrical pipe section. Est. minimum l. 0.37, max. diam. 0.18. Coarse-grained pale yellow to pink fabric (2.5Y7/4 to 7.5YR 7/4) with large red angular inclusions. Lot I-28.

Cf. Salles 1993: nos. 123-30, figs. 142-49 for Hellenistic pipes from Kition-*Bamboula*; Argoud *et al.* 1980: 36 nos. 2.72.110, 117, 118, 121 for Late Roman Salamis.

The pottery of a small place

The pottery and rooftiles from Kopetra offer a detailed view of one Cypriot village of the late empire. Over the course of 5 field seasons we recorded 33,230 sherds weighing a total of almost 1,117 kg (Table 5.1). The quantity of material, while dwarfed by urban excavations, constitutes a substantial sample for a minor habitation site and provides a wealth of information about rural lifeways. Both imported and local wares are well represented. Abundant rooftiles provide evidence for reconstructing the physical appearance and economic status of this small place.

Understanding how pottery was used locally was one of the main objectives of our project and its thorough documentation a primary goal. Relatively little such material had been published from Cyprus at the time we began work. Apart from Hayes' (1972 and 1980b) studies of Late Roman fine wares, most comparanda came from surveys and excavations carried out much earlier in the N part of the island.[43] Fortunately, we were able to refer to a selection of artifacts that the VVP had gathered over the span of 20 years (Todd forthcoming). The primary groups and much of the formal typology were drawn up in 1987 on the basis of survey finds and were refined using pottery excavated in 1988. The result was a system of recording that worked well for the main imported wares but was less successful for unfamiliar kinds of amphoras and domestic pottery. In retrospect, a streamlined recording system using broader categories might have been just as helpful. The fragmentary condition of most pottery meant that individual shapes could rarely be completed. We also found that regional fabrics varied widely. Our program of compositional analysis, which set selected fabric groups on firmer foundations, was initiated only after excavations had been concluded and most pottery recorded. Results to date indicate that LR1(2) and LR1(3) amphoras came from the same general area (Cilicia and N Syria); therefore from this standpoint they need not have been differentiated (Rautman *et al.* 1993 and 1999). By contrast, we might have paid more attention to quantifying different types of rooftiles.

It is important to acknowledge some of the limitations of this discussion. The study of Late Roman pottery still faces basic problems of chronology, production, and use.[44] Certain familiar vessel types, including fine pottery but especially amphoras and domestic wares, can be dated only approximately. Questions of supply and distribution remain unresolved, and it is not always certain that the time when a ware was manufactured in one part of the Mediterranean corresponds with its availability elsewhere. The range of intended amphora contents and other uses served by pottery require further research. Such cautions pertain especially to the final years of Roman manufacture, for few ceramic forms belong solely to the 7th c. (Hayes 1998a).

The picture presented here also reflects the sampling procedures used at Kopetra. Most of the pottery came from 7 different contexts: the surface survey and 6 excavated sectors. The interpretation of survey material involves special problems, including the tendency of later occupation phases to appear over-represented in the ploughzone.[45] Our collection of surface pottery by both intensive and extensive methods produced similar but not identical results (above, p. 25). The quantity of pottery recovered from individual excavation sectors ranges from less than 6 kg at Area III to over 360 kg at Area I. Only Areas I and II yielded sufficient quantities to support extended statistical discussion, although other sectors are reported in the tables for comparative purposes. A fair amount of variation exists among these data-sets, no doubt reflecting different activities, dates, functions, and levels of patronage. The settlement's small size, its brief habitation span, and the selectiveness of our excavations are other factors that condition the available evidence. Over 60% by count (50% by weight) of all pottery came

---

43 E.g., Catling and Dikigoropoulos 1970; Catling 1972; Diederichs 1980b; Taylor and Megaw 1980.

44 Recently reviewed by Hayes 1998b and 2001b; Sodini 2000.

45 Alcock 1993a: 49-53; Lund 1993: 140.

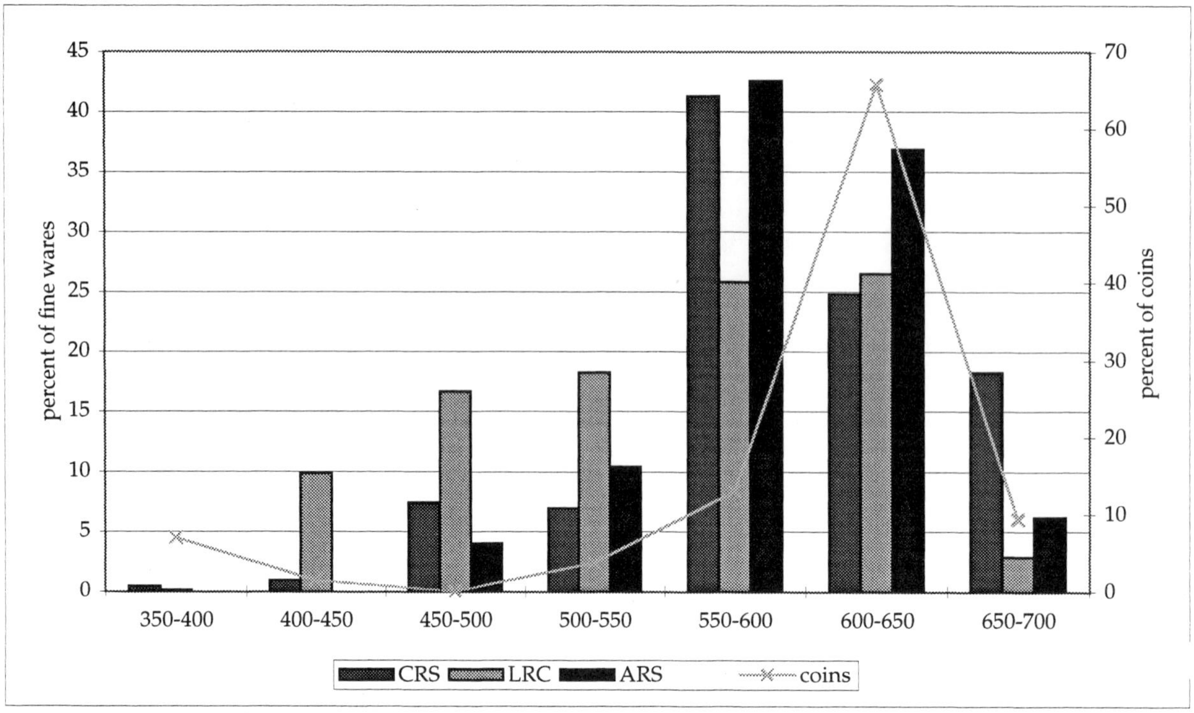

Fig. 5.19. Relative frequency of all identified fine wares (n=1352) and coins (n=12) from Kopetra.

from the three churches (primarily Areas I and II), and it may fairly be asked how representative these contexts are of local economic life. Combining survey and excavation pottery certainly increases the sample size and presumably improves its statistical credibility, but this step necessarily clouds the picture between different parts of the site. In this report the finds generally are aggregated when sketching the broad outlines of pottery use but are differentiated for comparison with other projects.

The pottery suggests that the Kopetra ridge was sparsely inhabited through much of antiquity. Chalcolithic sherds were found in the S part of the survey area and at nearby Area II, while Late Bronze Age finds appear mainly at Area I and in the E part of the site. Most of the early Iron Age pottery was recovered by survey along the settlement's N edge and by excavation in this vicinity at Area V. Little of this early material came from pre-Roman contexts but instead was found in redeposited fills and on the surface. Roman-era material comprises more than 90% of the survey and excavation pottery.

Fine wares establish the short, busy life of the Late Roman village (see also Rautman 2000). The standard table wares of late antiquity — Cypriot, Phocean, and African red-slipped pottery — were relatively common everywhere. The presence of only a few examples of Cypriot Sigillata, Eastern Sigillatas A and B, and Egyptian Red Slip indicates that this was essentially a single-period settlement, without significant local antecedent or successor. It should be noted that early Roman fine pottery is well represented elsewhere in the valley, including the nearby sites of *Ayious* and *Pamboules* (below, p. 239). Fine wares generally comprise less than 10% of all Late Roman pottery at Kopetra. Their strong representation among the survey data results from their selection as diagnostic artifacts by the judgement sample. Interestingly, fine wares occurred least frequently at the two residential sectors (Areas IV and VI), where they make up less than 2% by both count and weight of the total assemblage. Most of the examples presented here came from topsoil or other mixed contexts. While the fine pottery offers little grounds for re-assessing published dates, the chronological distribution broadly agrees with the evidence of most E Mediterranean sites.

Table wares present a picture of rural prosperity. These familiar objects of modest luxury also carry the primary burden of phasing the site's occupation. Figure 5.19 records the relative frequency of all datable fine ware sherds recovered by survey and excavation, together with the dozen identified coins from the site. Early forms reflect little activity before 400, with a

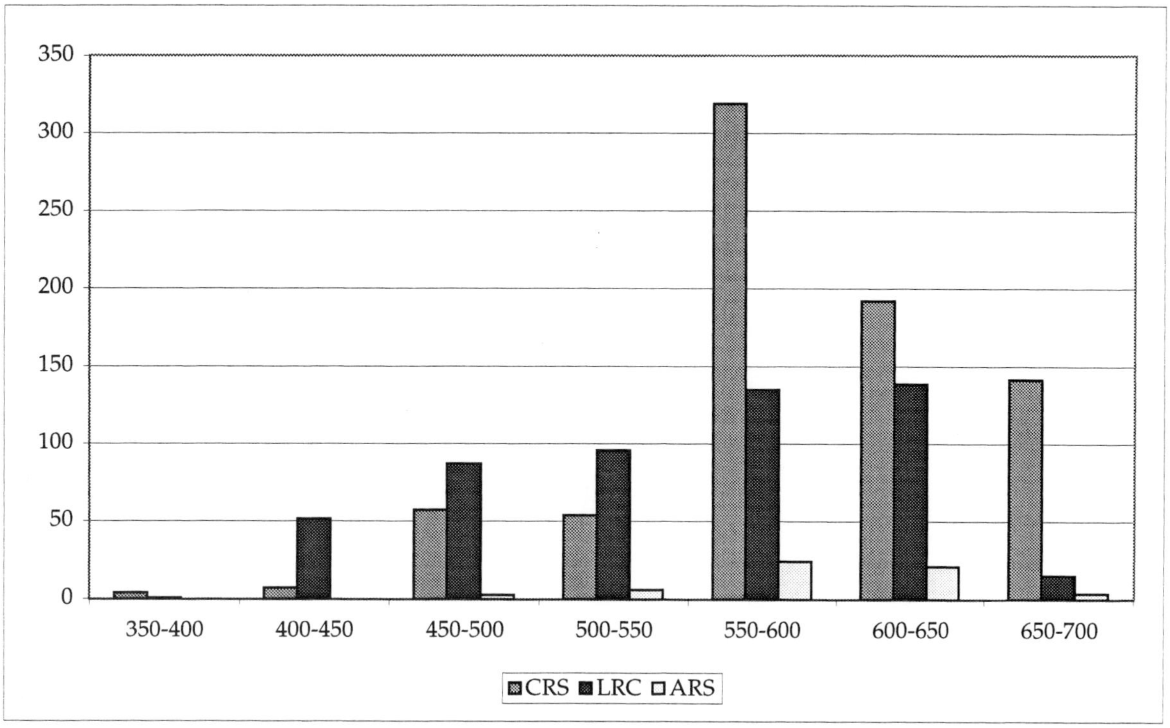

Fig. 5.20. Chronological distribution of all identified fine wares from Kopetra (n=1352).

clear but modest presence emerging over the 5th and early 6th c. Use of fine pottery increased sharply during the later 6th c.; 60-70% of datable forms belong to the years between 550 and 650. This impression recurs elsewhere, with similar patterns within the three main wares observed among both survey and excavation finds. Unsurprisingly, this is the same interval when the three known churches were built. The frequency of coins culminates in the early 600s as well. Quantities of Cypriot Red Slip fell during the early 7th c. and all three wares appear much reduced after 650.

The chronological distribution of identified shapes provides further details. Figure 5.20 reveals little sign of sustained activity before Phocean Red Slip appeared *c.*400. About the middle of the 5th c. Cypriot Red Slip began to arrive in significant quantities, but Phocean Red Slip (especially forms 3C, 3E, and 3F dishes) remained the fine ware of choice for much of the 5th and 6th c. The ware's reliable supply into the early 600s is attested by many examples of the dish form 10. The steady import of Aegean pottery during the late 6th to early 7th c. contrasts with data from some sites but is supported by the other fine wares at Kopetra. Cypriot Red Slip rose to local prominence in the later 500s with the introduction of the form 9A dish and form 11 basin. A small but steady supply of African Red Slip emerged around the middle of the 6th c., probably as part of its renewed distribution following Justinian's reconquest of N Africa.[46] The total amount of fine pottery remained steady during the late 400s and early 500s but increased three-fold in the second half of the 6th c., when the three wares occurred in the approximate ratio of 10 : 5 : 1. The growing availability of fine pottery is directly attributable to the great surge of Cypriot Red Slip, whose domination of the local market continued until the site's abandonment a hundred years later. In general terms, Kopetra participated fully in the island's larger markets and through them reached the wider Roman world.

The end of local habitation is more difficult to establish on ceramic grounds. It is possible that the dates assigned here to some 6th-c. forms should be advanced by a couple of decades, which would imply that pottery use increased more gradually during the years before 550. Since the site's widespread damage *c.*650 would have dampened local demand, many of the vessels assigned to the second half of the 7th c. in fig. 5.20 probably were used earlier as well.

46 Hayes 1972: 463; id. 2001b: 279; Abadie-Reynal 1989: 155-59.

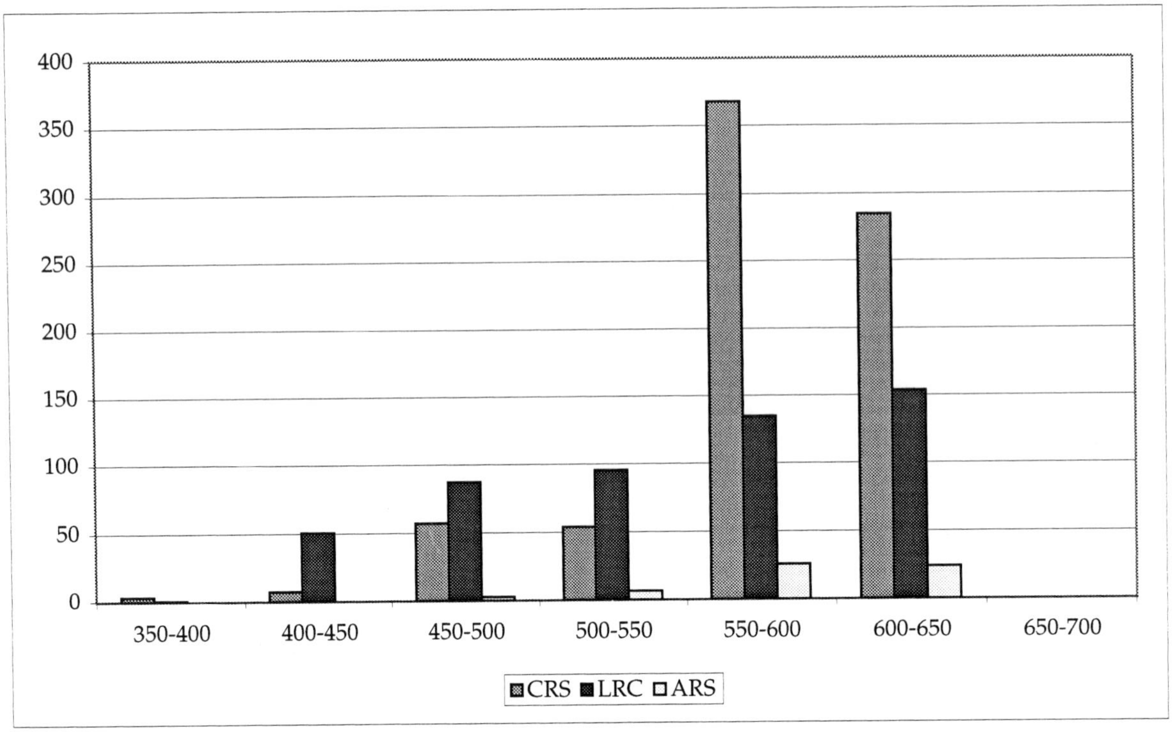

Fig. 5.21. Revised chronological distribution of all identified fine wares from Kopetra (n=1352).

In fact, apart from Areas I and II there is scant evidence of activity at Kopetra after the years of the Arab raids, *c.*649-50. The *Sirmata* cistern deposit (Lot I-32) attests a dramatic break in local habitation that extended across the site. The presence of only a single coin dating after the 640s, an issue of Constans II from 659/60 (**C12**) at Area II , reflects a similarly sharp decline in circulation at Kopetra and across the E Mediterranean. Figure 5.21 illustrates the effect of re-assigning all of Kopetra's 7th-c. fine wares to the first half of the century. This revision is also misleading, however, since it excludes any new arrivals after 650, despite clear signs of limited re-occupation at Areas I and II. Assuming that significant supplies of fine wares stopped arriving in 650, 660, or 675 only underscores the rapid growth of the village and throws its decline into higher relief.

As indices of provincial trade and exchange, Kopetra's fine pottery raises a number of questions concerning the place of Cyprus in the Mediterranean economy. Phocean Red Slip was a key element in the local marketplace from the middle of the 5th c., and only in the last quarter of the 6th c. was it overtaken by the indigenous Cypriot Red Slip. The last quarter of the 6th and first quarter of the 7th c. saw the high point of use of local fine ware, with African Red Slip and Phocean Red Slip accounting for *c.*36-38% of all identified forms. This relatively high proportion of imports at the village level may reflect the prestige of the wares or the mechanisms of their distribution. Like glass and bronze table vessels, fine pottery did not, as a rule, travel as an independent commodity but as one minor (albeit readily documentable) component of bulkier cargoes including grain and building material.[47] In this light both the export of Cypriot pottery and the import of non-Cypriot wares can be seen as reflecting the reciprocal exchange of other goods between different Mediterranean regions. Traffic between the Egyptian granaries and Constantinople, for example, would have offered a ready return route for Phocean Red Slip and other products originating in western Asia Minor. One can imagine that Phocean Red Slip may have posed a viable alternative to Cypriot Red Slip at the seaside markets near Zyyi-*Petrini* or Amathus (below, p. 242). As elsewhere in the E Mediterranean, the small but persistent supply of African Red Slip probably reached Cyprus via Aegean traders.

47 Wickham 1988: 190-92; Reynolds 1995: 127-30; Ward-Perkins 2001: 174.

The plain pottery extends the range of table and kitchen wares used at the site. Like the fine wares, these generally small, unslipped vessels consistently comprise less than 10% of all Late Roman pottery here. Most examples came from Areas I and II, although for unknown reasons they are best proportionally represented at Areas V and VI. The most frequently recorded vessel types are shallow basins and narrow-mouth jugs. Of special interest is a series of small, single-handle jugs that were made in a fabric closely related to Cypriot Red Slip. Together with a few large bowls and related forms, such vessels apparently belong to a line of unslipped domestic wares that were produced along with Cypriot Red Slip and red-fabric rooftiles by large *fabricae* in W Cyprus. Such a possibility raises questions about Cypriot pottery-making in late antiquity. How well organized was the red ware industry? Were the unslipped workshops the same as or simply located close to the fine-ware centers? Does plain ware production chronologically coincide with or extend beyond Cypriot Red Slip? Were unslipped wares significantly cheaper than Cypriot Red Slip? Were they distributed along the same paths as Cypriot Red Slip and red-fabric tiles, or were they intended for a more restricted market? The questions raised at Kopetra can at least draw attention to these vessels elsewhere on the island

Amphoras comprise about half of Kopetra's pottery and offer the best potential for understanding its commercial contacts. The highest proportion came from Area VI, where they account for *c.*70% by count (65% by weight) of the finds. Amphoras are least well represented (at 40% by count, 19% by weight) at Area V, where half of the excavated area lay within the church sanctuary. The 6 primary members of the standard E Mediterranean amphora 'package' are present, together with several less well known types. Assuming that local tastes and customs remained constant, the chronological distribution of these containers should broadly agree with the fine wares.

The local assemblage is dominated by LR1 amphoras, which make up *c.*70% of all transport vessels. Field prospection has shown that these were produced at a number of points along the coasts of Cilicia, Syria, and Cyprus mainly during the 5th through 7th c. The region's geomorphological homogeneity has hindered efforts to differentiate the many fabrics. Laboratory analysis of representative examples demonstrates that at least one fabric, constituting more than 20% of the total, originated on the island, probably in the broad valleys of the lower Mesaoria and S central plains. Two other related fabrics, together accounting for over 60% of the total, were imported from the surrounding coastlands. Various other fabrics may reflect minor manufacturing points in the region. After proportionally distributing the remaining examples, LR1 amphoras from the mainland may be said to have outnumbered Cypriot products about 3 : 1 in the local marketplace.

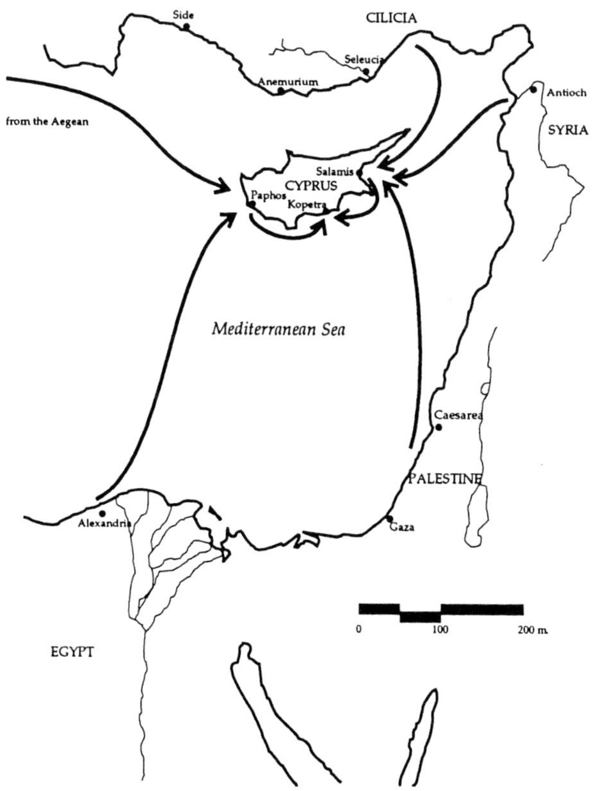

Fig. 5.22. Map of East Mediterranean with sources of major ceramic imports at Kopetra.

This picture is reinforced by smaller numbers of other transport vessels. Non-Cypriot amphoras include LR2 and LR3 from the Aegean, LR4 from Gaza and the S Negev, LR5/6 from Palestine, and LR7 from Egypt. KAmp2 amphoras seem to have originated around Seleucia-Peiria. The few examples of KAmp5 came from N Africa. Five major source-areas thus are represented at

Kopetra. The big suppliers clearly were Cilicia and N Syria, followed by Cyprus itself; the wider Palestinian region appears next. Significantly, all of these regions lie east of Kopetra and most of their amphoras would have passed through the ports at Salamis and Kition. Aegean, N African, and Egyptian amphoras, which arrived mostly via Paphos, are less frequently present (fig. 5.22). Cilicia and Syria thus emerge as the main providers of the village's agricultural imports.

Cooking wares reinforce the regional context of the site. These relatively light-weight, brittle sherds consistently comprise 10-15% by count (3-6% by weight) of the Late Roman pottery, with smaller quantities among the survey data reflecting wear and tear in the ploughzone. Apart from a few examples imported from Asia Minor, most cooking pots apparently came from unidentified Palestinian and Cypriot sources. The contemporary pottery-works at Dhiorios-*Mersineri*, made prominent by accidental discovery and detailed publication, did not supply much of the cooking wares used at Kopetra. The main shape produced at Dhiorios — a finely-ridged globular pot with out-turned rim — is far less popular than other forms that are better known on the mainland and in S Cyprus. The eastern connection appears most clearly in cooking wares found in the domestic spaces at Area I (e.g., Lot 20), and raises the possibility of culinary links with the expanding monastic movement in Palestine.[48] General fabric similarities with red-firing clays on the island probably reflect the output of several manufacturing centers along the S coast. Presumably these mass-produced wares followed the paths of amphora distribution to reach Kopetra.

The emergence of handmade pots in the early and mid 7th c. offers indirect evidence of the declining availability of imported cooking wares. At least 4 basic thick-walled shapes were made in coarse clays from the Vasilikos region. The simple potting, either by hand or on a slow wheel, and non-standard appearance of these vessels suggest that many were made in domestic workshops for use at the household or neighborhood level. As noted for other cultures, both the technique and place of production imply that women were actively involved in making these special wares (Vincentelli 2000: 51-53). Such pots were present in late contexts at Area I (Lots I-14, 28, 31) and were relatively plentiful at Areas II and VI (Lots II-14, 27, 28; VI-6, 7), which indicates they were in common use by mid-century. Their appearance around the time that Cypriot Red Slip was dwindling suggests that they offered a local substitute for vessels from W Cyprus as those became expensive or scarce. The continuing supply of fine Aegean pottery hints that most of the cooking pots they replaced came from Palestinian workshops, whose distribution was disrupted by the Persian and Arab campaigns beginning in the early 600s. Together with contemporary examples from elsewhere in the Vasilikos and Maroni valleys, Amathus, Salamis, and Kourion, these pots represent a ceramic substratum that became important with contracting exchange-routes and the cultural dislocation caused by hostile actions on the island (Rautman 1998: 89).

The abundant *pithoi* found at Kopetra provide special information about village economy and pottery production. The large size of most sherds yields a wide disparity between an average representation of *c*.8% by count and more than 30% by weight of all Late Roman pottery at the site. At 16% by count (43% by weight) *pithos* sherds are best represented at Area IV, where some level of agricultural processing clearly took place. By contrast, except for Area III these large storage vessels are least well attested at the higher-end residence at Area VI. Despite the lack of fully-represented forms and close evidence for dating, a variety of large storage vessels can be attributed to artisans working locally. Compositional analysis of selected examples confirms that most of these bulky vessels were made of valley clays. Moreover, the distinctive variations of rim and shoulder decoration have not often been reported elsewhere.[49] From a functional standpoint such vessels would have been used to store

48 Cf. Peleg 1989: 61-72; Hirschfeld 1992: 99-100; Magness 1993: 211-21; for the architectural context, see Rautman 2001a: 314-16.

49 For examples see Catling 1972; Taylor and Megaw 1981; Leonard 1987; Flourentzos 1996.

large quantities of agricultural products, either dry or liquid. No example was found complete or in an undisturbed context, but the many fragments from Area IV presumably reflect household production and storage (cf. Hadjisavvas 1992: 78-79; Devos *et al.* 1999: 79-81). The abundance of similar sherds at Areas I, II, and V may indicate that at least some of the agricultural surplus was controlled by the Church, either derived from its own land-holdings or received as donations.

Rooftiles are prominent in the Kopetra assemblage. Although not weighed during recording, they clearly formed the major share of ceramic imports in sheer bulk, perhaps equaled only by fully loaded LR1 amphoras.[50] Virtually all rooftiles appear to be Cypriot products. The two most common types were made outside the Vasilikos valley near Paphos and Salamis — the main poles of the island's marketplace through whose ports most goods passed on their way to Kopetra. The red-fabric Laconian-style tiles are closely related to the Cypriot Red Slip industry; they apparently were made in W Cyprus and distributed together with fine and unslipped kitchen wares. Yellow-fabric tiles originated in the lower Mesaoria plain and accompanied LR1 amphoras shipped through the harbor at Salamis-Constantia. The only products of the Vasilikos region were the much larger Corinthian-style tiles, whose coarse fabric appears closely related to the handmade cooking pots and *pithoi*. There is little indication of the production dates or formal development of these tiles. Presumably most imported tiles, like fine pottery, arrived during the late 6th and early 7th c.; in fact, the lion's share probably was destined for the three churches built between 500 and 600 (above, pp. 53-55). It is uncertain whether the local tile-making tradition, less well attested among recorded examples, extends over the entire life of the settlement or, like the handmade cooking pots, emerged only in the 7th c. as other tiles became scarce.

Like fine and cooking pottery, rooftiles constitute not a means of economic transport but the very substance of exchange. The great demand for tiles that accompanied the building of each basilica, no doubt including a generous allowance for breakage, underscores the rôle played by the Church (or its patrons) in ordering commodities on a large scale. Builders of much smaller private houses needed far fewer tiles since they also used gypsum slabs for their roofs. The presence of multiple types at each sector confirms that all three kinds of tiles helped cover the same buildings during at least their latest phases, when the large Corinthian-style tiles apparently were used to replace broken or damaged pieces. A similarly complex picture is seen at the slightly later Amathus acropolis basilica, where both Laconian- and Corinthian-style tiles were employed in its final 7th-c. phase (Hadjichristophi 1989). At both sites larger and heavier rooftiles of apparently local origin may have been used to supplement a dwindling supply from more distant producers.

TABLE 5.6. PROVENANCE OF MAJOR CERAMIC GROUPS AT KOPETRA
(parenthesized wares <1%, bold-face wares >10% of all fine pottery, amphoras, cooking wares, or rooftiles)

W Mediterranean and Aegean	*Egypt*	*SW Cyprus*	*Central Cyprus*	*E Cyprus*	*N Syria*	*Palestine*
LRC	ERS	**CRS**				
ARS						
LR2	(LR7)	**LR1**	**LR1**	**LR1**	**LR1**	LR4
(LR3)		(KAmp1)	(KAmp1)	(KAmp1)	KAmp2	LR5/6
(KAmp5)						
		Cypriot cooking ware?	Handmade cooking ware	Cypriot cooking ware?		Palestinian cooking ware
		Red Tile	**Other Tile**	**Yellow Tile**		

Table 5.6 summarizes the main ceramic wares found at Kopetra by their probable place of origin. Differentiation of their relative quantities (i.e., <1%, 1-10%, and >10% of each function-

50 Cf. Peacock 1979; Landgraf 1980: 88-89; Tomber 1987: 169-71.

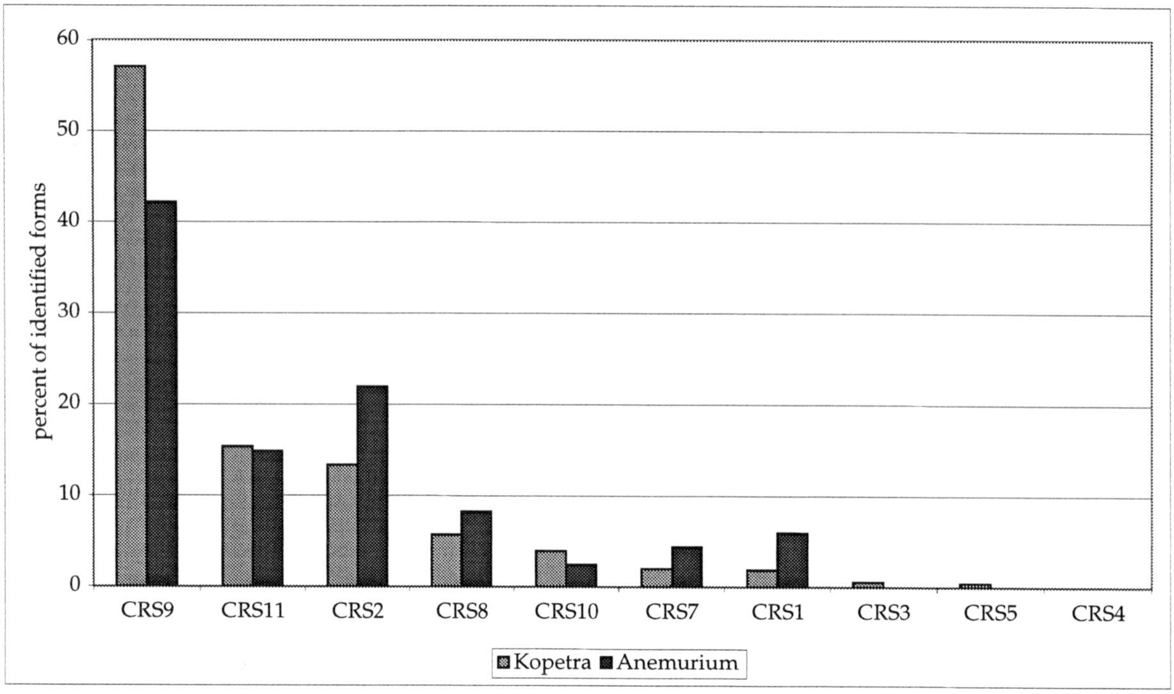

Fig. 5.23. Comparison of identified Cypriot Red Slip forms recovered by survey and excavation at Kopetra (n=773) and Anemurium (n=672).

al category) clarifies the major exchange paths that reached the site from neighboring regions (fig. 5.22). Despite the site's location along the S coastal highway, most commercial traffic would have passed through the lower valley to and from ships anchored off-shore near Zyyi-*Petrini*, close to the Vasilikos river mouth. Presumably these were small craft that sailed along the coast, stopping briefly at local market towns between the major ports of Paphos, Amathus, Kition, and Salamis. The most important products arriving from the W part of the island included Cypriot Red Slip pottery and red-fabric rooftiles. Both were shipped through Paphos-area harbors with other goods newly arrived from the Aegean and Egypt. Ships from Salamis and other ports in E Cyprus carried primarily yellow-fabric rooftiles and LR1 amphoras from the Mesaoria as well as Cilicia and N Syria. Amphoras from Palestine and the Gaza area may also have followed this path. The two cargo routes were supplemented by LR1 and related amphoras manufactured at various sites along the S coast. While some island products clearly dominated the local market, at one time or another a variety of imported pottery and amphora-borne commodities was available here.

This picture of Late Roman pottery use at Kopetra fits comfortably within larger patterns observed at contemporary sites on the island and across the E Mediterranean (below, p. 253). The broad outlines of agreement reflect the workings of a complex exchange-network linking cities and countryside.[51] Detailed information from a growing number of places establishes the wide distribution of major ceramic wares, together with other, larger cargoes, from the later 4th through mid 7th c. Significant departures from prevailing trends reflect the impact of unknown economic, environmental, and political factors.

Further clarification of how pottery was used in late antiquity depends on the presence of quantified data from multiple sites. Relatively little such information is available, however, and in many respects our picture of Kopetra stands by itself. The variety of proposed methods for counting pottery further complicates the prospects for intra-site discussion, and the present range of opinion suggests that direct comparisons among multiple sites may be an option that lies in the distant future.[52] Despite such limitations, the evidence at hand can at least raise questions to guide future research.

---

51 Fulford 1989; Woolf 1992; Tomber 1993; Reynolds 1995; Lund 1996; Kingsley and Decker 2001a.

52 Cf. Orton *et al.* 1993; Tomber 1993; Blakeley 1996.

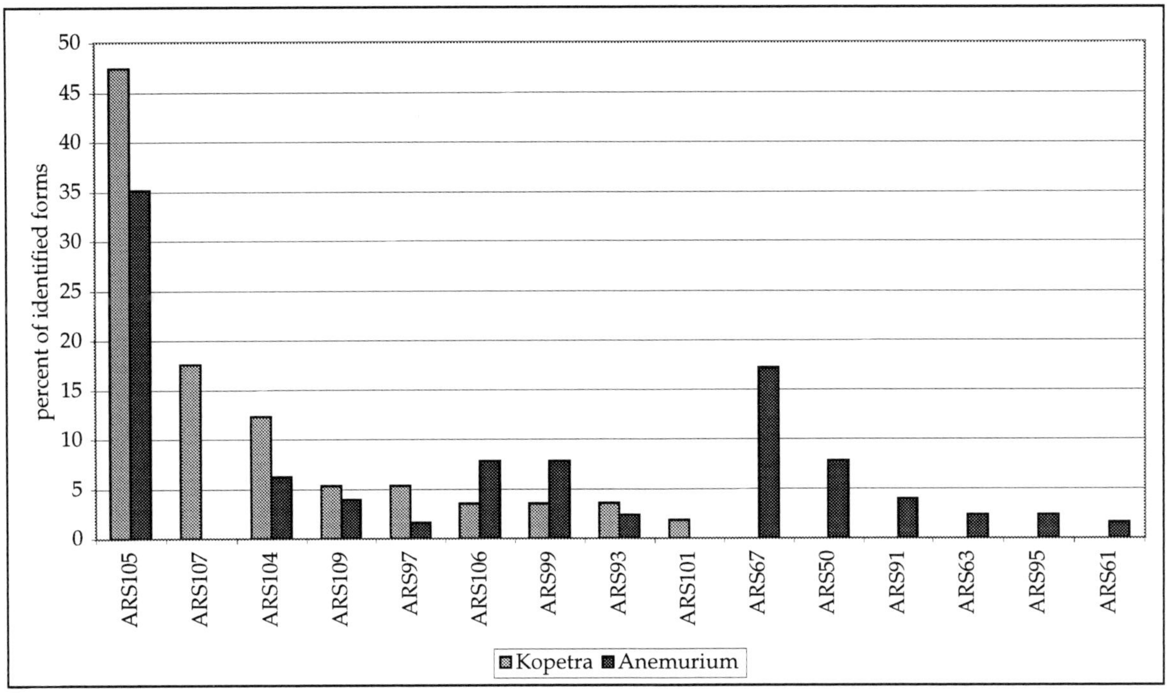

Fig. 5.24. Comparison of identified African Red Slip forms recovered by survey and excavation at Kopetra (n=57) and Anemurium (n=128).

Anemurium provides the best opportunity for comparison. This small city on the Cilician coast flourished during the 5th and 6th c., when a number of public buildings, baths, and churches were built within its walls (Russell 1982; Campbell 1998). Published pottery from the site documents its history and commercial contacts. Imported fine wares reached their peak between 550 and 600 (Williams 1989: 116-17; cf. Lund 1992: fig. 110). The dominance of the local market by Cypriot Red Slip resembles the situation at Kopetra, with forms 9, 11, and 2 accounting for 79-86% of the total at both sites (fig. 5.23). A larger number of shapes is attested at Kopetra (9 forms), although more examples of these forms are known at Anemurium (6 of 7 forms >5%). The supply of African Red Slip reflects similar correspondences and underscores Kopetra's relatively brief, late career (fig. 5.24). Anemurium presents a greater variety of shapes (13 forms) but these examples are spread over a much wider chronological range; about the same number occur frequently (5-6 forms >5%). By contrast, Phocean Red Slip is much more abundant at Kopetra, particularly during the site's latest phase, when form 10 alone constitutes almost half (248 of 522) of all identified examples (compared with only 1 of 154 at Anemurium). This striking contrast points to the existence of close contacts between Cyprus and the Aegean during the late 6th and early 7th c., and stresses the growing importance of economic connections among rural areas. The island's special significance to Constantinople at this time emerges within the wider historical context of the E Mediterranean (below, p. 255).

The future publication of quantified data from other sites will enlarge our understanding of the many rôles pottery played at this level of Late Roman society. For now, the ceramics from Kopetra illustrate the range of goods that could be consumed in one island village, presumably by the families of landowners, farmers, artisans, merchants, and clerics who lived here while working in the valley. Their quantity and variety show that fine table vessels, standardized transport jars, and utilitarian household pots all held an important place in rural life. No less clearly than the churches, these objects attest a level of economic prosperity and social vitality that was based on strong links with other parts of the late empire, and would be transformed during the 7th c.

6

Glass

Murray C. McClellan

Introduction

Glass vessels were ubiquitous in Late Roman Cyprus, where their use rivaled that of fine pottery. Nonetheless, glass vessels of this period have tended to receive only cursory treatment in survey or excavation reports from the island. The present account of the glass vessels from Kopetra and the forthcoming publication of the glass from the Kourion episcopal basilica (Young forthcoming) address this relative neglect.

During survey and excavation at Kopetra all glass fragments were recorded on survey or deposit sheets and brought to the laboratory for analysis. Fragments larger than 0.01 m in length were categorized by fabric and, where possible, by form. The basic terminology used in this discussion has been set out by Harden (1936: 6-24) and Weinberg (1988: xiv-xv). Since all of the glass fragments were significantly decayed and since most were similar in size (ranging from 0.01 to 0.10 m), no attempt was made to weigh the fragments. The catalogue presents a representative selection of all recovered vessel types.

Four major fabrics were discerned among the 942 glass fragments recovered by survey and excavation. The dominant type, Fabric 1, is a transparent light blue glass; rims, bases, and handles often include angular black impurities. Over 700 fragments, or nearly 75% of the total, are composed of Fabric 1. Fabric 2 is a transparent, light green glass that is sometimes streaked with yellow and tends to have angular black impurities; 140 fragments (nearly 15%) are composed of this fabric. Fabric 3, a transparent, greenish-blue glass, and Fabric 4, a transparent, yellowish-green glass, are represented by only 64 (6.8%) and 15 (1.6%) examples, respectively. At least three of the 4 fabrics were used at the same set of manufacturing centers: a Fabric 1 hanging lamp (**298**) has Fabric 2 handles, and another Fabric 1 hanging lamp (**307**) has a Fabric 4 handle. A number of other glass fabrics are sparsely represented at Kopetra. Among these minor fabrics are a colorless glass with a purple, grayish blue, or grayish yellow tinge, a dark green glass, and a transparent dark blue glass. These minor fabrics account for only 29 fragments (3.1%).

It has been argued that glass was produced on Cyprus during the 2nd and 3rd c. A.D. (Vessberg 1956: 216-19) if not from the late 1st c. B.C. (Seefried 1986; McClellan 1984: 326-27; id. 1993: 216). The production of glass objects on Cyprus in the Late Roman period is suggested by discoveries made at Ayios Philon, Soloi, and Kourion. The light blue-green, dark blue, and red glass 'wasters' found behind the baptistery at Ayios Philon were apparently used to produce mosaic tesserae (Taylor and Megaw 1981: 227). Cullet, slag, and wasters have been reported at Soloi (Hayes 1975) and Kourion (Young 1993). The discovery of a late 7th- or 8th-c. deposit of wasters and other glass fragments under the Frankish fort at Saranda Kolones (Paphos) indicates that glass-production on Cyprus did not cease after the mid 7th c. (Megaw 1971: 131, fig. 5.18; id. 1972: 339-40).

Any discussion of glass production on Cyprus must note the fact that the island has no deposits of pure silica sands and the sandstones that do exist have such high levels of iron that they are not suitable for producing glass (Bear 1963: 181-82; Constantinou 1980: 14). Since Cyprus lacks one of the basic ingredients of the soda-lime-silica glass used throughout antiquity, any manufacture of transparent glass on the island depends on the import of material from elsewhere. Raw glass cullet clearly was produced for export at Levantine sites such as Beth Shearim (Brill 1967; Weinberg 1988: 25, 284), where a 9-ton slab of unusable cullet was discovered in a 4th-c. context. In spite of their fragility, some of the glass vessels used in Late Roman Cyprus may have been imported, and it is possible that some were produced by itinerant craftsmen carrying their own recycled glass fragments, a practice apparently attested by the

11th-c. ship wrecked off Serçe Limen in Turkey. Such imported or itinerant-produced glass vessels nonetheless probably formed a small percentage of the Cypriot glass corpus, and it is reasonable to assume that local craftsmen supplied most glass used on the island in this period. Local glass workshops would have had easy access to ample supplies of fuel, as necessary to the production of ancient glass as the basic silica-lime-soda ingredients, and would have incurred less expense and breakage in getting their products to market. There is little reason to doubt that the 4 major fabrics found at Kopetra represent the products of Cypriot workshops.[1]

The chronological range of the Kopetra glass is rather restricted. A few fragments (**226-28**) belong to vessels that can be dated to the first three centuries A.D. A few others (**250** and **251**) may be as early as the 5th c. The remainder belong to forms that were popular from the mid 5th to mid 7th c. With one or two exceptions, it is not possible to assign a narrow chronological limit to the types of glass vessels found at Kopetra, though it is entirely possible that the vast majority belong to the first half of the 7th c. The beaded-stemmed lamp seems to be restricted to the 7th c.; two examples of this type (**296** and **297**) were discovered in the foundation deposit of space III at *Sirmata* and two others were found on the surface near Area II. There is some suggestion that the goblet with flat discoid base (**278-80**) may likewise date to the 7th c.

The vessel forms represented among the glass fragments are all of standard types well known from other E Mediterranean and Near Eastern sites. The most common form was a simple fire-polished rim (**285** and **286**) that belonged to a stemmed goblet or lamp. It is notable that few ceramic cups or lamps were recovered at Kopetra, whose Late Roman inhabitants seemed to have relied on glass vessels for drinking and lighting their churches and houses (cf. Catling 1972: 77-78). Nearly every vessel form among the Kopetra glass corpus, including glass window panes, was represented at the three basilicas as well as at Area VI. One exception is the small flask or bottle (**268-70**) that was found only at Area VI; this form, presumably used for personal anointment, apparently had no rôle in the liturgy of the Church. Few glass fragments were recovered from Area IV, a fact that reinforces the impression of relative poverty in this quarter.

The poorly understood post-depositional history of the glass fragments makes it nearly impossible to suggest exactly where any given vessel may have been used or even where it had been discarded after breakage. One can reasonably assume that most vessels would have been used and discarded somewhere within the sector where they were found. This is especially true for the isolated hillock of *Sirmata*, where it is extremely unlikely that any human or natural agency could have been responsible for bringing fragments up the hill after the complex was abandoned. It is suggestive, therefore, that significant concentrations of glass fragments were recovered on the western portion of Area I, especially in the NW space III. This concentration most likely reflects the discarding of glass fragments after use; it is unlikely that it represents an intentional hoarding of broken glass vessels for recycling such as is attested at Jerash (Baur 1938: 514-515), Khirbat al-Karak (Delougaz and Haines 1960: 49), Caesarea (Peleg and Reich 1992: 158), and elsewhere. The only unequivocal association that can be made between findspot and use is in the Area I crypt (Lot I-7), where a flask (**255**), a stemmed lamp (**290**), and two hanging lamps (**302** and **306**), together with a ceramic lamp (KK88-28), were all part of the tomb's ritual furniture.

Roman glass

Only three fragments of glass found by the survey and in mixed upper levels at *Sirmata* belong to forms that can be dated from the 1st to 3rd c. A.D. The earliest piece (**226**) is actually the weathering crust of a mold-blown vessel, the glass of which has totally decayed. The original vessel was probably a pyxis or a small flask made in the second half of the 1st c. A.D. Vessels with similar patterns of ivy sprays, perhaps produced from the same mold, have been found on Cyprus (Vessberg 1956: 153, fig. 47.18; and an unpublished example, no. D1711, in the Cyprus Museum) and in Syria (British Museum 1913.5-22.19). Unprovenanced examples include a piece in the Corning Museum and two pyxides from the former Constable-Maxwell collection (Constable-Maxwell 1979: 96 and 153-54); vessels made from related molds include a pyxis said to be from Tyre (Matheson 1980: 47-48 no. 124, with other parallels). These mold-blown vessels may have been

---

1 The present investigations have yielded nothing to suggest that glass was produced at Kopetra itself, though given the traces of metalworking found at *Sirmata* it is possible that some of the glass material used at the site was locally produced.

produced in the workshop of Ennion or one of his followers (Harden 1935; id. 1944-45; Calvi 1965; Matheson 1980: 47; Price 1991).

Among the Kopetra glass, only two fragments (**227** and **228**) belong to types dating to the 2nd to 3rd c. One (**227**) is a fragment of a bowl with crimped band decoration. Similar bowls have been found at Aulona in Cyprus (Vessberg 1956: 133, fig. 42:16), at Samaria (Crowfoot 1957: 415, fig. 96.5), Jerash (Meyer 1988: 185, fig. 5 G, H), Jalame (Weinberg 1988: 55 nos. 118-21, fig. 4-16), Sardis (von Saldern 1980: 21-22 nos. 94-101), near Afyon in Turkey (Lightfoot 1989: 36 no. 35), at Tarrha on Crete (Buechner 1960: 112 no. 16), at Corinth (Davidson 1952: 98 nos. 612-13) and elsewhere. The type seems to have been produced in the first half of the 2nd c. A fragment from the lower part of a candlestick unguentarium (**228**) belongs to a type quite common in Cyprus (Vessberg 1956: Type III, 164, fig. 49.20; Webb 1986: 37 no. 113, with further references). This type has generally been assigned to the 2nd to 3rd c. (Harden 1936: type H, 267), though a late 1st-c. date has been suggested (cf. McClellan 1993: 217, n.4).

Late Roman glass

Bowls

Very few bowl shapes can be identified among the Late Roman glass vessels at Kopetra. The three rim fragments of shallow bowls (**229-31**) come from topsoil or collapse deposits excavated at Area II. The wide tubular rims of two of these bowls (**229** and **230**) are reminiscent of plates found in early Byzantine (*c.*324-491) deposits at Jerash (Meyer 1988: 189, fig. 6:J). The added handles of one bowl (**230**) are paralleled by pieces discovered at Jerash (Baur 1938: 528 nos. 34, 36, and 37, fig. 23; Meyer 1988: 212, fig. 12 T) and Sardis (von Saldern 1980: 45, nos. 234-36); the handles may indicate that this vessel was used as a hanging lamp, as Tatton-Brown interprets an example from Carthage (Tatton-Brown 1994: no. 39; cf. also Stern 1985 for examples from Anemurium). These shallow bowls undoubtedly had solid, slightly concave, bottoms (e.g., Baur 1938: Type G, fig. 23), though no such bottoms were recovered at Kopetra. Two fragments (**231** and **232**) are both composed of colorless glass and may well be non-Cypriot in origin. The thin flat base with ring foot (**232**) is similar to a fragment found in a deposit of *c.*491-636 at Jerash (Meyer 1988: 198, fig. 8 T) and to one found at Labraunda (Hellström 1965: 85 no. 22, pls. 30 and 40). Another fragment (**233**), from Area VI, belongs to a common type of deep bowl with pushed-in tubular base ring. The type is known in the 4th c. (Weinberg 1988: 43; Sussman 1976: fig. 4.13), and comparable bases have been found in 5th- to early 7th-c. contexts at Khirbat al-Karak (Delougaz and Haines 1960: pl. 59.18), Caesarea Maritima (Peleg and Reich 1992: fig. 18.7), Shavei Zion (Barag 1967: no. 14), and el-Lejjun (Jones forthcoming: no. 40).

A number of rims found at Kopetra (**234-44**) belong to various open vessels, though in their fragmentary state it is difficult to determine whether they come from bowls, beakers, goblets, or lamps. Other rims that clearly come from goblets and lamps (**281-89, 299, 300, 303,** and **304**) are discussed below. One example (**234**) has the thickened, fire-polished rim seen on goblets and lamps, though its flaring shape makes it more likely that it comes from a bowl or a beaker. Bowls with flaring rims were produced throughout the Roman period and have been found in a 6th-c. context at el-Lejjun (Jones forthcoming: nos. 92-94) and a 7th-c. context at Jerash (Meyer 1988: 206, fig. 10 S). A rim (**235**) from a construction deposit in the NW room of the *Sirmata* complex has a similar outward curve, but it has two very fine wheel-ground grooves on the interior. Such wheel-cut grooves appear on early Roman cast bowls and are found on the exterior of many later blown vessels but are quite unusual on the interior of blown vessels; a similar bowl with out-turned rim and an interior wheel-cut groove was found in a 4th-c. context at Jalame, where it is compared to the so-called Alexandrian bowls of the 2nd c. (Weinberg 1988: 56-57, no. 139). Two other rims (**236** and **237**) have body walls that angle inward and may come from small bowls or beakers. A fragment (**238**) recovered in a second-phase surface from the north church has a particularly thick, solid rim; similar rims have been discovered at Khirbat al-Karak (Delougaz and Haines: pl. 59.7) and Beth Shean (Tzori 1973: fig. 11.4). A fragment of another bowl-shaped vessel (**239**) has a folded-out tubular rim like those from 6th-and 7th-c. contexts at el-Lejjun (Jones forthcoming: nos. 99-101), Saraçhane (Hayes 1992: 403 no. 29), and Carthage (Tatton-Brown 1984: 198, fig. 66.32).

Several rims of small bowls or flasks found at Kopetra are ornamented with added translucent dark blue or brownish purple threads. The use of such ornamental colored glass threads is quite common on 4th- to 7th-c. flasks (cf. Saller 1941: 320-21 nos. 405-14; Barag 1967: nos. 8-9; cf. also below, **253** and **254**). One fragment (**240**), from the N part of the Area I complex, has a broad marvered band of dark blue on the exterior of the rim. A similar bowl was found in an 11th- to 13th-c. context at Saraçhane (Hayes 1992: 405 no. 86); it is more reasonable to assume that the Constantinopolitan example belongs to the 6th to 7th c. than to suggest that this bowl type continued to be produced into the second millennium. From the *Sirmata* crypt region was recovered a rim fragment (**243**) with several partially marvered threads of a brownish purple glass, a pattern which is also paralleled on a piece in a late context at Saraçhane (Hayes 1992: 405, no. 89). Two other rim fragments from *Sirmata*, one (**241**) from the construction débris in space III and the other (**242**) from the courtyard, have unmarvered dark blue threads on the exterior. Three small, non-joining, fragments found at Area VI (**244**) come from a bowl of translucent, dark blue glass that was certainly imported into Cyprus. While vessels composed of this sort of glass were particularly popular in the early Imperial period (Auth 1975: 153), and it is possible that **244** is much earlier than its deposit might indicate, translucent dark blue was also used for pattern-molded vessels that could not be any earlier than the 4th c. (cf. **266** below).

Jugs and jars

Few fragments from jugs or jars have been recovered at Kopetra. The rim of a trefoil jug (**245**) was found in collapsed débris north of the *Sirmata* basilica; similar vessels have been found at Kourion (Young 1993: fig. 10), Jerash (Baur 1938: 540 no. 82, fig. 18.238; Meyer 1988: 206, fig. 10 A), el-Lejjun (Jones forthcoming: no. 51), Khirbat al-Karak (Delougaz and Haines 1960: pl. 60.1), and Shavei Zion (Barag 1967: fig. 16.20). A tall strap handle (**246**) was found in the domestic structures in Area IV and may have come from a similar trefoil jug (cf. Delougaz and Haines 1960: pl. 60.1). From a deposit associated with the construction of the *Sirmata* basilica was recovered an unusual open loop handle formed from a strap of fused rods (**247**); the shape matches a handle at Khirbat al-Karak (Delougaz and Haines 1960: pl. 60.7). Two short handles attached to tubular rims (**248** and **249**) probably belonged to small jugs or bowls; a similar handle was found at Khirbat al-Karak (Delougaz and Haines 1960: pl. 60.8). A small ring handle with tooled indentations (**250**) may have come from a jar; similar ring handles have been found in 4th-c. contexts in Egypt (Harden 1936: 183 nos. 509-10) and at Jalame (Weinberg 1988: 82 no. 377), and from a later context at Jerash (Baur 1938: 528, no. 42). The trail-wound base (**251**) may have come from either a bowl or a jug and can be paralleled by bases from a number of E and W Mediterranean sites (cf. the comparanda given for examples found at Jalame and at el-Lejjun: Weinberg 1998: 58-59; Jones forthcoming: nos. 49-50). **250** and **251** both come from topsoil levels at Area I and may be as early as the 5th c.

Flasks

The most common closed glass vessel found at Kopetra is a flask with tall conical or cylindrical neck. Flasks of these types, either plain or decorated with applied trails, occur throughout the Mediterranean in contexts ranging from the early 5th through the 7th c. (cf. von Saldern 1980: 71-72, 82-83; Weinberg 1988: 70-71; Meyer 1988: 202, 207; Jones forthcoming: nos. 63-67 and 120-23). Examples of conical-necked flasks with applied decoration, which are especially common in the Syro-Palestinian region (Meyer 1988: 207), have been found in space IV at *Sirmata* (**252** and **253**) and at Area VI (**254**). One (**272**) belongs to a vessel with a rather short neck and is decorated with a single wound thread. The type is apparently rare on Cyprus (Vessberg 1956: 156, fig. 48.20), but similar vessels have been found at Jerash (Baur 1938: 533 no. 60, fig. 63; Meyer 1988: 207, fig. 11 G), Khirbat al-Karak (Delougaz and Haines: pl. 60.5), el-Lejjun (Jones forthcoming: no. 121), Rehovot-in-the-Negev (Patrich 1988b: 139 no. 33), Nazareth (Bagatti 1969: 313 no. 21), Shavei Zion (Barag 1967: no. 5), Labraunda (Hellström 1965: 85, pl. 40.7), and Carthage (Tatton-Brown 1984: 204, no. 71). Two other fragments (**253** and **254**) come from similar flasks and have, in addition to an applied thread composed of the same glass as the vessel, an added decorative thread of translucent blue. This decorative schema can be found on flasks from Saraçhane (Hayes 1992: 403 no. 25), Argos (Aupert 1980: nos. 366-78), Jerash (Baur 1938: 533-34 nos. 59, 61 and 62, fig. 31, with report of 14 similar vessels), and Mount Nebo (Saller 1941: 320-21, pl. 142). A flask with a tall conical neck decorated with irregular blue-green threads was found at the Kourion basilica (Young 1993: fig. 7).

An example of an undecorated flask with a tall conical neck (**255**), discovered in the collapse of the *Sirmata* crypt, is paralleled by pieces from the 5th- to early 7th-c. synagogue at Beth Shean (Zori 1967: fig. 11:4) and from 6th-c. contexts at Saraçhane (Hayes 1992: 403 no. 32) and Sardis (von Saldern 1988: 70-71 no. 480). A fragment of flask with an indented juncture of neck and shoulder (**256**) found in the south church at Kopetra can be compared to flasks from Ayios Philon (Taylor and Megaw 1981: 225 no. 21), Sardis (von Saldern 1980: 69-70 no. 477), Jerash (Meyer 1988: 202, fig. 9 T), el-Lejjun (Jones forthcoming: no. 63), the Mount of Olives (Bagatti and Milik 1958: fig. 33.23), and Jalame (Weinberg 1988: 71 no. 283). Three examples of flasks with narrow cylindrical necks (**257-59**) were recovered at Area VI. One of these flasks (**257**) has a funnel-shaped mouth similar to ones found in a late 6th-c. context at Argos (Aupert 1980: nos. 345-47). Another (**258**) has a short cylindrical neck with a tooled indentation, paralleled by a fragment from an early 8th-c. context at Pella (Smith and Day 1989: 114, pl. 60.5). The third flask (**259**) seems to have come from a vessel with a tall cylindrical neck, such as those found at the House of the Oil Press in Salamis (Argoud *et al.* 1980: 44, pl. XLI.6) and at Khirbat al-Karak (Delougaz and Haines: pl. 59.22).

These flasks would have had depressed or kicked bottoms, such as those found at Saraçhane (Hayes 1992: 402 no. 5), Jerash (Baur 1938: 537 no. 74), Samaria (Crowfoot 1957: fig. 95:4 and 9), Nazareth (Bagatti 1969: 313 nos. 22-23), Shavei Zion (Barag 1967: nos. 11-12), and Beth Shean (Fitzgerald 1931: pl. 39.19 and 25). Two non-joining fragments of a globular flask with a kicked bottom (**260**) were found in the upper levels of collapse near the *Sirmata* crypt and may belong to the neck and rim of a flask (**255**) found in the lower level of the same collapse. A fragment of a similar vessel (**261**) came from a deposit associated with the construction of the *Sirmata* courtyard. A deep kicked bottom (**262**) was found in the settlement area to the north of Area II. From the north church was recovered a fragment (**263**) from the body of a globular flask with a pin-hole indentation on its side.

A number of fragments of vessels with pattern-molded ribbed decoration were found at Kopetra. This technique, which involves the modification by twisting or reblowing of an original mold-blown pattern, has its origins in the 3rd and 4th c. (Stern 1977: 107-10; Weinberg 1988: 79 nos. 346-47), although the discovery of a pattern-molded fragment in an Umayyad context at Jerash (Meyer 1988: 215, fig. 13 V) suggests that its use was prolonged. Three pattern-molded fragments (**264-66**) were found in the rooms to the north of the courtyard of Area I and one fragment (**267**) came from a late surface in the nave of the south church. One of these fragments (**266**) is composed of a translucent, dark blue glass, while another (**267**) is composed of a transparent, dark green glass. Both of these may have been imported into Cyprus. A pattern-molded goblet from Kourion, of "shiny green"glass, similarly has been taken to be an import (Young 1993: 42, fig. 3). The Kopetra pattern-molded fragments are too small to assign to a vessel type with certainty, though pattern-molded flasks were apparently much more common than were pattern-molded goblets.

The rim and neck fragments of three small flasks (**268-70**) were recovered from the structure in Area VI. Small flasks with flat or incurving rim, no doubt used as unguentaria, have a long history stretching back into the early Roman period (Harden 1936: 191-94; Vessberg 1956: 165-66; Weinberg 1988: 73-74). Small flasks with folded-over rims like **268** have been found, among other places, at Jerash (Baur 1938: 543 no. 98; Meyer 1988: 197-98, fig. 8 D-F), the synagogue at Ma'oz Hayyim (Tzaferis 1982: fig. 12.10), and Khirbat al-Karak (Delougaz and Haines: pl. 60.11), while small flasks with cup-like incurving rims as on **269** and **270** can be paralleled at Jerash (Meyer 1988: 203, fig. 10 G) and Labraunda (Hellström 1965: 85 nos. 3-4).

Bottles

Three fragments of a thick, hexagonal mold-blown bottle (**271**) were found scattered across three different deposits of collapse in space 2 and room 3 at Area VI. This bottle was fashioned out of the same Fabric 1 common at Kopetra, although it is unique at the site and unparalleled among published corpora of Late Roman glass. In technique it is related to the 6th- to early 7th-c. series of mold-blown hexagonal 'pilgrim vessels', though it lacks the molded designs characteristic of those Syro-Palestinian products (Barag 1970; id. 1971; Matheson 1980: 129-38). Its context strongly suggests that the bottle was in use in the upper storey of the structure at the time of its collapse.

Stemmed goblets

The most frequently encountered categories of glass artifacts at Kopetra, as at most 5th- through 7th-c. sites, are stemmed goblets, stemmed lamps, and tumbler lamps. To be sure, the survival rate of the thick stems or handles of these types is higher than for fragments from thin-walled vessels, and hence it is more probable that they will enter the archaeological record. These types, moreover, are readily recognizable and thus more likely to be singled out in the field or lab for special comment. Further, since much of the archaeological investigation of the 5th through 7th c. has been directed towards the uncovering of churches, the ecclesiastical functions of goblets and lamps may be in part responsible for their relative frequency among reported glass finds. It seems nonetheless that the goblet and the lamp were particularly popular forms produced by glass workshops of the period. Since in many instances one cannot distinguish among the rims of each of these related types, all rims that may have belonged to either a goblet or a lamp will be discussed as a group (**281-89**).

The stemmed goblet has a long pedigree stretching back into the 4th c., if not earlier (Harden 1936: 167; Isings 1957: 139-40 form 40; von Saldern 1980: 53-56; Meyer 1988: 199-200). By the 6th c., stemmed goblets seem to have replaced beakers as the dominant drinking vessel form at most sites (Jones forthcoming), although goblets may have also functioned as lamps, as the three-handled example from Jerash probably did (Baur 1938: 524 no. 17, fig. 20.376). Broken stems and bases could also have served as stoppers (Sussman 1976: 99, pl. 19.1). Stemmed goblets have been found in 5th- through 7th-c. contexts throughout the Mediterranean and the Near East (cf. the citations in Chavane 1975: 57-59; von Saldern 1980: 54-55 nos. 49-55; Stern 1985: 44-46; Meyer 1988: 199-201; Smith and Day 1989: 110 and 114-15; Hayes 1992: 400; Peleg and Reich 1992: 156 no. 10), and the type seems to continue with little modification into the early second millennium.

At Kopetra there are two basic varieties of stemmed goblets. The first (**272-75**) has a thin stem with a domed base that terminates in a tubular foot. The second variety (**278-80**) has a thick solid stem with a flat, irregular, discoid base. Meyer (1988: 199 and 211) has observed that among the vessels at Jerash the variety with solid stems and flat bases seems to continue into the Umayyad period, while the type with domed bases and tubular feet does not. Similarly, Hayes (1992: 400) suggests that among the Saraçhane goblets those with heavy discoid bases belong to a late phase of his Series I type and date as late as the 8th c. Three examples of goblets with hollow stems and flat discoid bases having tubular feet are recorded at Kourion (Young 1993: 41, fig. 2), one of which was found in a late 7th-c. context. Similar hollow-stemmed goblets with flat bases and tubular feet were recovered in some quantity in the 8th- to 9th-c. glass workshop at Paphos (Megaw 1972: 131 no. 20). Both varieties of stemmed goblets were recovered in a hoard of glass fragments at Ayios Philon that presumably had been collected in the basilica over some period of time (Taylor and Megaw 1981: 227, fig. 45.26-27). Of course, a note of caution must be sounded when making anything more than the most general of comparisons across differing manufacturing traditions. Nonetheless, it appears that the goblets with tall domed bases may have gone out of production before the 7th c.

Of the thin-stemmed variety of goblet, one example from Kopetra (**272**) has a hollow stem closed off at the top by the bowl of the vessel, while another (**273**) is also closed off at the bottom by a pontil scar. A similar goblet is in the collection of the Cyprus Museum (Vessberg 1956: 145, fig. 45.18), and comparable pieces have been found at Salamis (Chavane 1975: 57-59 no. 161), Argos (Aupert 1980: nos. 413-14), Khirbat al-Karak (Delougaz and Haines 1960: pl. 60.22), Nazareth (Bagatti 1969: 313 no. 32), and at the synagogue of Ma'oz Hayyim (Tzaferis 1982: 240, fig. 12.8). A fragmentary stem (**274**) with a deep depression on the underside of its thin, twisted stem may be related to the Series II type identified at Saraçhane, though there is no evidence that the Kopetra foot had been separately formed as was apparently the case with the Constantinopolitan goblets (Hayes 1992, 400 nos. 22-24). A fragment of a thin stem with rounded cup (**275**) can be paralleled by an example found in a 7th-c. context at Jerash (Meyer 1988: 201, fig. 9.7) and by one from an 8th-c. context at Pella (Smith and Day 1989: 114, pl. 60.11). The base of a particularly tall goblet (**276**) seems to be related to the Saraçhane Series I vessels (Hayes 1992: 400 nos. 10, 12 and 16-20), although it may belong to some other type of footed vessel. Similar tall-footed goblets have been recovered at Dhiorios (Catling 1972: 76, fig. 41 G9), Salamis (Chavane 1975: 59 no. 155), Jerash (Baur 1938: 525 no. 22), Beth Shean (Zori 1967: fig. 11.11; Tzori 1973: fig. 11.8), Caesarea Maritima (Peleg and Reich 1992: fig. 18.8), and Carthage (Tatton-Brown 1994: no. 34).

One goblet fragment (**277**) is unique among the pieces recovered from Kopetra in that it has a hollow stem and tubular foot but the stem is thick and has been tooled into a fluted bead shape; similar fluted bead-shaped stems have been found at Ayios Philon (Taylor and Megaw 1981: 227 no. 32) and at Sardis (von Saldern 1980: 54). Examples of goblets with rounded bead stems from Argos (Aupert 1980: no. 412), Aegina (Felten 1975: 73 no. 136), Labraunda (Hellström 1965: 85 nos. 29-30), Sardis (von Saldern 1980: 10, pl. 10 C), and Carthage (Tatton-Brown 1984: 200-1 nos. 41-49) suggest that the type was made in the 5th and 6th c. However, the context of **277**, the collapse of the structure of Area VI, implies that the type was still used during the 7th c.

A nearly complete profile of a thick-stemmed goblet (**278**) was found in the pipeline trench dug at Kopetra in 1986, in a presumed domestic zone north of Area II. It had a fire-polished rim, a rounded, tooled, stem, and a solid disc base like ones found at Dhiorios (Catling 1972: 76, fig. 41:G), Samaria (Crowfoot 1957: 416, fig. 96.11), Khirbat al-Karak (Delougaz and Haines 1960: pl. 60.16-18), Nazareth (Bagatti 1969: 313, no. 29), Shavei Zion (Barag 1967: 67, fig. 16.16), Kefar 'Ara (Sussman 1976: fig. 4.8), and Kursi-Gersesa (Barag 1983: 38, fig. 9.9). A stem of a similar goblet (**279**) was found in the collapse of the W part of the north church. A third solid stem fragment (**280**) was recovered in the débris at Area VI. It was apparently an import and may be related to the type that Hayes suggests may have been made at Carthage (Hayes 1992: 400 nos. 82-83).

The most frequently encountered shape among the glass vessels at Kopetra, as at most Late Roman sites, is the rounded, fire-polished rim (**281-89**). As the restorable profiles of **278** and **290** demonstrate, this rim form was used both on stemmed goblets and on stemmed lamps. It is possible that some of these rims may have belonged to small bowls. Most are nearly vertical, though they range from slightly flaring (**281**) to slightly curved (**289**). Similar rims have been found in 6th- and 7th-c. contexts at el-Lejjun (Jones forthcoming: nos. 95-97), Jerash (Meyer 1988: 206, fig. 10 S-V), Caesarea (Peleg and Reich 1992: 155, fig. 18.35), Rehovot-in-the-Negev (Patrich 1988b: 138 nos. 19-29), Constantinople (Hayes 1992: 202 no. 21), and Carthage (Tatton-Brown 1984: 195, fig. 65.12).

Stemmed lamps

Like the stemmed goblet, stemmed lamps were produced throughout the Mediterranean from the 5th c. onwards (Crowfoot and Harden 1931; Saller 1941: 316-17; Crowfoot 1957: 415; Chavane 1975: 62-64; von

Saldern 1980: Type 3 lamp, 49-51; Meyer 1988: 203-5). The form, with its long narrow toe and spreading cup-shaped body, was designed to be placed within a metal polycandelon (von Saldern 1980: 50; McNicoll *et al.* 1982: pl. 150.2; Hayes 1992: 400, 443 n.3) that was, in turn, suspended by a metal chain. It would seem that stemmed lamps could also be suspended individually, as apparently was the case with a fragment found still within a bronze hanger at the synagogue at Ma'oz Hayyim (Tzaferis 1982: pl. 36 B). Whatever its shape or method of suspension, a lamp would have a wick probably held in place by a bronze holder (cf. Baur 1938: 517), though the discovery at Caesarea of 30 perforated clay discs together with several hundred stemmed lamp fragments suggests such discs may also have been used to keep wicks suspended in the oil (Peleg and Reich 1992: 158-60). Frequently found at churches and synagogues, stemmed lamps have also been found in non-religious contexts, such as at the kiln site of Dhiorios (Catling 1972: 76). At Kopetra, stemmed lamps have been recovered at each of the three basilicas as well as at Area VI.

Two different types of stemmed lamps have been found at Kopetra: lamps with hollow stems and lamps with solid beaded stems. Of the more numerous hollow-stemmed lamps, three separate varieties can be identified. An example of the first variety (**290**) found in the crypt of Area I has a sharply tapering, thin glass stem that terminates in a short, solid knob. Similar lamps have been found at Salamis (Chavane 1975: 66 no. 175), in a 4th- to early 7th-c. context at Sardis (von Saldern 1980: 51 no. 274), in a 5th- to 7th-c. context at Nessana (Harden 1962: 84 no. 51), in a 6th- to 7th-c. context at Beth Shean (Tzori 1973: fig. 11.15), in a late 6th- to early 7th-c. context at Saraçhane (Hayes 1992: 403 nos. 37-38), in the early 7th-c. deposit at the Byzantine wall of Caesarea (Peleg and Reich 1992: 158-59, fig. 20.12-15), in a context of *c.*630-670 at Jerash (Meyer 1988: 203-4, fig. 10 I; cf. also Baur 1938: 521 no. 4, pl. 140), in an early 8th-c. context at Pella (Smith and Day 1989: 114-15, pl. 60.14), and in a late 6th-c. context at Carthage (Tatton-Brown 1994: no. 43). The second variety of hollow-stemmed lamps found at Kopetra (**291-93**) has a broader, nearly cylindrical, stem. Two of the examples of this type from Kopetra (**291** and **292**) have thin-walled stems and are similar to lamps found at Salamis and elsewhere on Cyprus (Chavane 1975: 66 no. 174; Vessberg 1956: 173, fig. 51.12), as well as to examples from el-Lejjun (Jones forthcoming: no. 107), Jerash (Baur 1938: 524 no. 15), Mt. Nebo (Saller 1941: 316, pl. 140.19-21), Rehovot-in-the-Negev (Patrich 1988b: 136 no. 14), Jerusalem (Bagatti and Milik 1958: fig. 35.14), Nessana (Harden 1962: 85 no. 54), Khirbet Shema' (Meyers *et al.* 1976: pl. 8.7.32), Ma'oz Hayyim (Tzaferis 1982: 240, fig. 12.2), Samaria (Crowfoot 1957: 415, fig. 96.6), and Caesarea (Peleg and Reich 1992: 158-59, fig. 20.2-9). The third variety, represented by two examples from Kopetra (**294** and **295**), has an appreciably thicker, more rounded stem and a distinct constriction at the juncture of stem and flaring cup wall. Similar thick-walled, constricted lamps have been found at Soloi (Vessberg 1956: 174, fig. 51:13-14) and Salamis (Chavane 1975: 67, nos. 177-82), and the type may be the precursor of the stemmed lamp type apparently produced in the late 8th- to early 9th-c. glass factory at Paphos (Megaw 1971: 131, fig. 5.18; 1972: 339-40). Saller (1941: 316, pl. 140.22-24) suggested that the thick-walled, constricted lamps found at Mt. Nebo may be later than the cylindrical variety.

Although there is some evidence to suggest that the cylindrical stemmed lamps began to be produced earlier than the other varieties, the Kopetra finds suggest that all three varieties were used in the 7th c. Two examples of the second variety (**291** and **292**) were found in the débris above the *Sirmata* crypt and in all likelihood were hung there together with an example of the first variety (**290**). An example of the third variety (**295**) was found in the lower collapse of room 3 at Area VI, a space that seems to have been in use down to the middle of the 7th c. All three varieties of stemmed lamps are represented in the hoard of fragments found in a jar in room H9, to the south of the Ayios Philon basilica (Taylor and Megaw 1981: 227, fig. 45.34-47); this hoard of glass fragments was presumably deposited in the mid 7th c. and represents the types that were still in use at that time. Similarly, in the Caesarea collection, both tapering and cylindrical stemmed lamps occur in early 7th-c. contexts (Peleg and Reich 1992: 155-58).

Two fragments of lamps with solid beaded stems (**296** and **297**) were recovered from Lot I-20, which is associated with the initial construction of space III at *Sirmata*. Beaded-stemmed lamps are particularly numerous at Jerash and have been found there in Umayyad (A.D. 661-747) contexts, leading Meyer to speculate that the type was first produced later than the initial series of hollow-stemmed lamps (Meyer 1988: 212-13, fig. 13 A-C; cf. also Baur 1938: 519-21 nos. 1-3, with mention of 175 other examples). This supposition is supported by the discovery of beaded-stemmed lamps in 7th-c. contexts at Salamis (Chavane 1975: 64-65 nos. 169-70), and in an early 8th-c. context at Pella (Smith and Day 1989: 114-15, pl. 60.13). No beaded-stemmed lamps were represented in the Ayios Philon hoard, and such lamps are apparently absent at the 6th-c. legionary fortress of el-Lejjun (Jones forthcoming), at the 5th- to 7th-c. North Church at Rehovot-in-the-Negev (Patrich 1988b: 136), and from pre-616 deposits at Sardis (though some of the Sardis fragments assigned to beaded-stemmed goblets may actually belong to lamps; von Saldern 1980: 59 nos. 368-69). Beaded-stemmed lamps have also been found at Mt. Nebo (Saller 1941: 317, pl. 140.28-29, with mention of 9 more),

Beth Shean (Fitzgerald 1931: pl. 39.29; Zori 1967: 162, fig. 11.1-2; Tzori 1973: fig. 11.19), Nazareth (Bagatti 1969: 313 no. 36), Kursi-Gergesa (Barag 1983: 38, fig. 9.10), and the Ma'oz Hayyim synagogue (Tzaferis 1982: 240, fig. 12.1). Beaded-stemmed lamps and goblets continued to be produced into the 11th and 12th c. (Davidson 1952; Hayes 1992: 404 no. 57).

Hanging lamps

Besides the stemmed lamps and perhaps stemmed goblets, bowl-shaped vessels with suspension handles undoubtedly functioned as lamps in the Late Roman period (cf. the reconstruction at Pella of hanging lamps with bronze hangers in Smith and Day 1989: 114-15, fig. 32). Two separate types have been identified among the glass fragments from Kopetra: a tall, tumbler-shaped bowl with handles attached to a tubular rim (**298** and **299**) and a globular bowl with cracked-off rim and with handles attached to the upper body (**302**). In addition to these unequivocal examples of lamps, a number of handles and one base that most probably belonged to hanging lamps are discussed below. Shallow bowls equipped with handles may have also served as lamps (see **230**).

Tumbler-shaped hanging lamps seem to have originated in the late 4th or early 5th c. (Isings 1957: 162 form 134; von Saldern 1980: 46-48, type 2) and continued to be produced into the 12th c. (Davidson 1952: nos. 733-34, fig. 14; Hayes 1992: 401 nos. 56 and 65; for a variant on a stemmed foot from 11th-c. Fustat, cf. Pinder-Wilson and Scanlon 1973: 22, no. 14). Numerous fragments were recovered from the lower collapse in the S chapel in Area II that preserve the complete profile of a tumbler-shaped lamp (**298**); the rim of another was found in the NW corner of the Area I basilica. A similar lamp was reputedly found at Paphos (Fitzwilliam Museum 1978: 54 no. 110a) and an example with applied foot-knobs was recovered from the Campanopetra basilica at Salamis (Chavane 1975: 56 no. 153). A tumbler-shaped hanging lamp found in the débris from the late 8th- to early 9th-c. glass factory at Paphos (Megaw 1971: 131, fig. 5.21; id. 1972: 328) has a similar shape but its mid-body ring handles with long trails link it to the Constantinopolitan series that Hayes dates to the 8th c. (1992: 400 no. 39). Tumbler-shaped lamps have been found in stratum III (A.D. 502-551) at el-Lejjun (Jones forthcoming: nos. 102, 103, 105), at the 5th- to 6th-c. synagogue at Ma'oz Hayyim (Tzaferis 1982: 240, fig. 12.3-7) and the contemporary church at Shavei Zion (Barag 1967: 68, fig. 16.21-22), in the late 5th- to late 7th-c. North Church at Rehovot-in-the-Negev (Patrich 1988b: 134 nos. 1-7), in levels of *c.*630-670 at Jerash (Meyer 1988: 205-6, fig. 10 N-P; cf. also a footed example, Baur 1938: 524 no. 17), in the 6th- to early 7th-c. synagogues at Beth Shean (Zori 1967: fig. 11.9) and Ma'on (Rahmani 1960: fig. 9:1), and in an early 8th-c. level at Pella (Smith and Day 1989: 114, fig. 60.4). Examples have been excavated at Sardis in contexts ranging from the 5th through the early 7th c. (von Saldern 1980: 47-49), at Salona, where they are assigned to the 5th c. (Auth 1975: 166, no. 112, with mention of 6 others), and in 6th-c. contexts at Carthage (Tatton-Brown 1984: 202, no. 57). A rim fragment from a similar lamp (**300**) was found in the same surface deposit as **299**.

Among the bases of "well over 100 tumbler-shaped vessels" found at Siyâgha at Mt. Nebo were 17 that had narrow, hollow wick tubes attached to the center of the inside of the bowl (Saller 1941: 315-16 nos. 1-17). One wick tube (**301**) was discovered on a late surface outside the S chapel of phase II in Area II at Kopetra. Wick tubes have been found in 5th- to 6th-c. contexts at el-Lejjun (Jones forthcoming: no. 104), in a 7th-c. context at Jerash (Meyer 1988: 205, fig. 10 Q), at Samaria (Crowfoot 1957: 418, fig. 99.2-3), at Gezer (Crowfoot and Harden 1931: pl. 28), at the Mount of Olives (Bagatti and Milik 1958: 147, fig. 35.11), at 5th- through early 7th-c. contexts at Nessana (Harden 1962: 84 no. 47), at the North Church at Rehovot-in-the-Negev (Patrich 1988b: 136 nos. 8-12), Beth Shean (Zori 1967: fig. 11:10) and Ma'on (Rahmani 1960: fig. 9.2), in an early 6th-c. context in the Athenian Agora (Frantz 1988: no. G576, pl. 72 b), and in later contexts ranging from the early Islamic up to the present (references in Meyer 1988: 206).

Two fragments (**302**) of a hanging lamp with a globular body and cracked-off rim were found in the lower fill in the *Sirmata* crypt. A rim of a similar vessel (**303**) was located in the topsoil deposit above the same crypt, while the rim of a third globular-bodied lamp (**304**) was encountered in the foundation deposit from room III. Examples of globular-bodied lamps have been found at Jerash (Crowfoot and Harden 1931: pl. 30.41), at the Mount of Olives (Bagatti and Milik 1958: fig. 35.12), and in an early 7th-c. deposit at the city wall of Caesarea (Peleg and Reich 1992: 155, fig. 18.19). Two of the Kopetra globular lamps (**303** and **304**) seem to be imports.

A kicked base (**305**) identical to the base of the tumbler-shaped lamp **298** was found near the lamp fragment **299** and both may have come from the same vessel. Similarly, a handle fragment (**306**) was found in the same deposit as the globular-shaped lamp **302** and both may belong to the same vessel. Other handles that apparently belong to either tumbler-shaped or globular-shaped hanging lamps were found in the narthex at *Sirmata* (**307**), the south church (**309** and **310**), and the north church (**308**). Similar handles are represented in the Ayios Philon glass hoard (Taylor and Megaw 1981: 227 nos. 15-17).

Non-vessels

Nine deposits from Areas II and VI produced fragments of roller-molded window panes. While some parts of the Near East apparently began to produce window panes by the crown glass technique as early as the 4th c. (Harden 1961), roller-molded panes were certainly used at some Near Eastern sites of the 5th through 7th c.: el-Lejjun (Jones forthcoming); Jerash (Meyer 1988: 194-95), Rehovot-in-the-Negev (Patrich 1988b: 140), Samaria (Crowfoot 1957: 421); Shavei Zion (Barag 1967: 69-70). Panes made by roller-molding or by flattening opened cylinders comprised the largest category by weight of glass objects found at Sardis (von Saldern 1980: 91-92) and such panes are known from Carthage (Tatton-Brown 1984: 208). The window glass reported from Ayios Philon appears to be crown glass (Taylor and Megaw 1981: 227). Roller-molded panes, on the other hand, have been excavated at Maroni-*Petrera*. While most of the examples of window panes at Kopetra are composed of Fabric 2 (**311**) or other presumably Cypriot fabrics, one deposit in the collapse of the Area II sanctuary yielded 50 fragments of window panes (**312**), made out of a light blue glass that may have been imported into the island. At Ayios Philon the window glass is described as being "clear, bluish glass, occasionally greenish yellow" (Taylor and Megaw 1981: 227).

Among the corpus of glass from Kopetra is a stray surface find of a lentoid glass token or bezel (**313**). This type of artifact is commonplace in the Roman period and examples from Carthage (Tatton-Brown 1984: 209, no. 116), Sardis (von Saldern 1980: 105 nos. 803-11), and Jerash (Meyer 1988: 195, fig. 7 Z) demonstrate that this type, suitable for gaming pieces or ring stones (or both), continued to be used into the 6th c. A fragment of an unusual glass bracelet formed from fused rods (**314**) was recovered from the lower collapse of the south church; it is composed of a dark brown glass and is certainly an import.

Catalogue

Roman glass

226. Weathering crust from fragment of mold-blown vessel. Max. l. 0.029. Relief pattern of ivy with heart-shaped leaves. Mid to late 1st c. K-gen.

227. Fragment of plate with out-turned rim and crimped band decoration. Est. diam. rim 0.190, p. h. 0.017. Thick tubular rim of colorless glass with purple tinge formed by folding out and down, leaving elongated oval section. Greenish yellow glass trail added to top of rim and tooled into crimped band form. Imported? Late 1st to 3rd c. Lot I-32, 8535/6010 15.1.

228. Base of candlestick unguentarium. Max. h. 0.014. Fabric 1. Convex upper body with indentation at juncture with rounded sides; slightly concave base with oval pontil mark. 2nd to 3rd c. Lot VI-13, 8280/6060 5.1.

Late Roman glass

Bowls

229. Rim of shallow bowl. Est. diam. rim 0.140, max. h. 0.004. Fabric 1 with angular black impurities. Tubular, rim folded out and down. Lot V-1, 8315/6167 1.1.

230. Rim and handle of shallow bowl. Diam. rim uncertain, max. h. 0.012. Fabric 1 with angular black impurities and elongated bubbles. Rim folded out and down, broken off at beginning of vessel wall. Added handle at top of rim, which is deformed where vertical handle was pressed in. Lot II-19, 8335/5940 3.1.

231. Rim of shallow bowl. Est. diam. rim 0.150, max. h. 0.006. Colorless glass with slight purplish tinge. No impurities; small pinprick bubbles. Tubular rim folded up and in. Lot II-9, 8345/5935 6.1.

232. Two non-joining fragments of base of plate or shallow bowl. Est. diam. base 0.040, max. l. 0.022. Colorless glass with grayish yellow tinge; no visible impurities; pinprick bubbles. Flat base with small ring foot formed by added thread. Lot I-8, 8525/5990 10.1.

233. Foot of bowl with kicked base. Est. diam. foot 0.060, max. h. 0.018. Fabric 2. High kicked base with small pin impression on underside; small part of flaring bowl preserved; wide, pushed-in tubular ring foot. Lot VI-9, 8280/6050 4.1.

234. Rim of bowl(?). Est. diam. rim 0.110, max. h. 0.020. Fabric 2 with angular black impurities and elongated bubbles. Slightly flaring, rounded rim. Lot II-7, 8335/5940S 3.1.

235. Three non-joining fragments of rim of bowl(?). Est. diam. rim 0.080, max. h. 0.012. Fabric 1 with angular black impurities. Rounded, fire-polished, slightly flaring rim; two sets of thin wheel-ground grooves on interior of rim. Lot I-20, 8520/6015 5.2.

236. Rim of beaker? Est. diam. rim 0.055, max. h. 0.019. Fabric 1. Rounded, fire-polished, rim; outward flaring body. Lot I-13, 8525/6010 2.2.

237. Rim of beaker? Est. diam. rim 0.060, max. h. 0.015. Fabric 1. Rounded, fire-polished, rim; body flares out from below rim. Lot II-7, 8345/5940S 3.1.

238. Rim of bowl? Est. diam. rim 0.070, max. h. 0.022. Transparent green glass with very few bubbles and some small, rounded black inclusions. Solid, thickened and fire-polished rim. Imported? Lot V-4, 8335/6173 4.1.

239. Rim of bowl? Est. diam. rim 0.070, max. h. 0.014. Fabric 3 with angular black impurities and streaks of yellow. Tubular rim folded out and down; slightly flaring body. Lot V-3, 8315/6167 2.1.

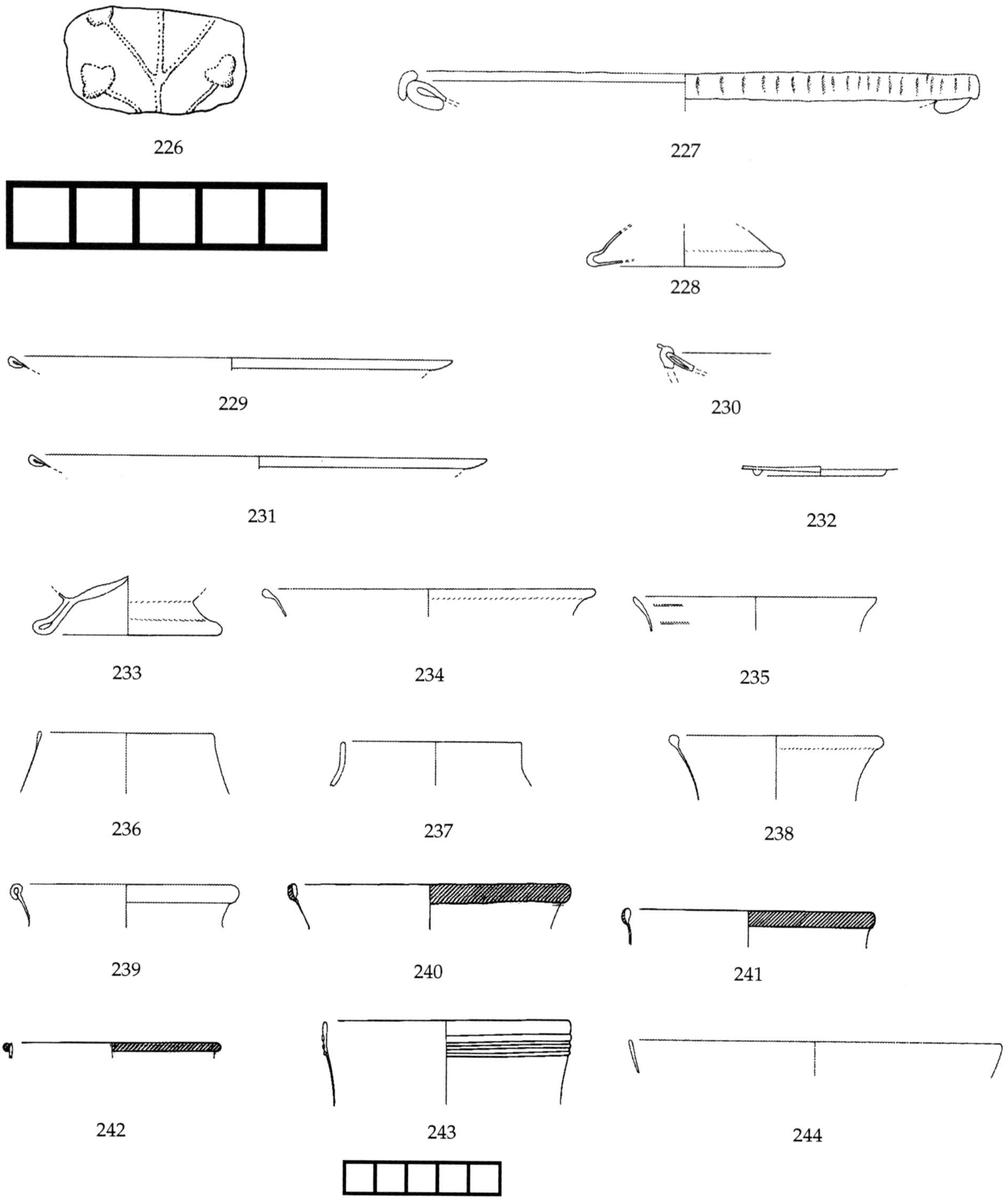

Fig. 6.1. Roman and Late Roman glass: bowls.

240. Four joining fragments of rim of small bowl? Est. diam. rim 0.090, max. h. 0.015. Translucent dark blue glass on rim; body composed of a grayish blue glass; one large angular impurity on rim; pinprick bubbles. Flattened oval rim, folded out and down, with marvered thread of dark blue glass. Imported? Lot I-21, 8525/6015 2.1.

241. Rim of small bowl? Est. diam. rim 0.080, max. h. 0.012. Transparent light blue glass. Rounded, fire-polished, rim; on exterior of rim an added thread of translucent dark blue glass with several small irregular black impurities. Lot I-20, 8520/6015 5.2.

242. Rim of small bowl? Est. diam. rim 0.070, max. h. 0.005. Colorless glass with gray-blue tinge. Rounded, rim-polished rim with added, flattened oval, thread of translucent dark blue; straight-sided walls. Lot I-28, 8535/6010 2.2.

243. Three non-joining fragments of rim of small bowl? Est. diam. rim 0.080, max. h. 0.028. Fabric 1. Rounded, fire-

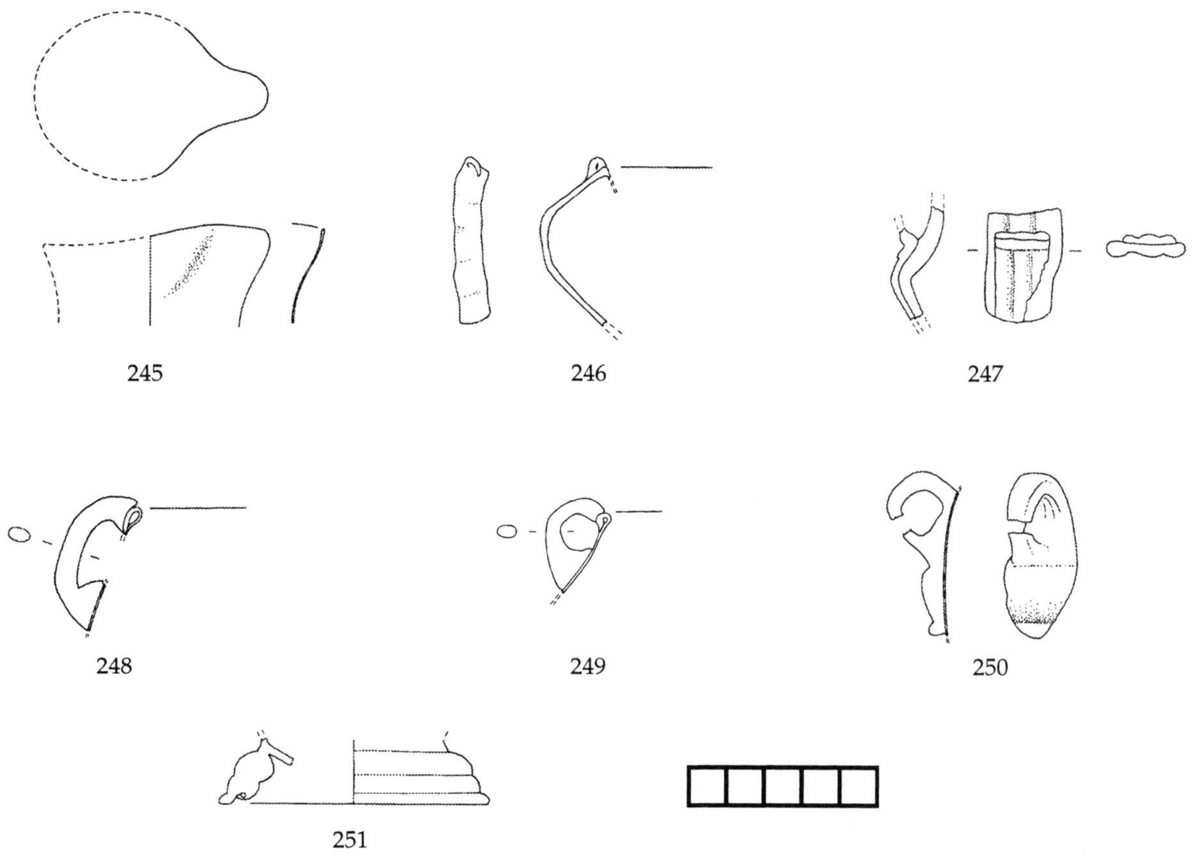

Fig. 6.2. Late Roman glass: jugs and jars.

polished rim; straight-sided body with added translucent brownish purple glass wound around three times and partially marvered in. Lot I-1, 8520/5995 1.1.

244. Three non-joining fragments from rim of bowl. Est. diam. rim 0.120, max. h. 0.011. Dark blue transparent glass with very small spherical bubbles. Smooth, fire-polished rim. Imported? Lot VI-9, 8280/6050 4.1.

Jugs and jars

245. Three non-joining fragments from rim of trefoil jug. Max. h. 0.027. Fabric 1 with elongated bubbles. Rounded, fire-polished rim, pinched into at least three wide spouts. Lot I-16, 8525/6010S 2.1.

246. Handle of juglet. Max. L. 0.044. Fabric 1 with many angular black impurities. Irregularly-shaped strap handle added to thin, rounded rim. Junction with lower body not preserved. Lot IV-1, surface.

247. Handle of jug. Max. h. 0.032. Grayish green glass with many pinprick bubbles. S-shaped handle formed from three fused rods; folded back on itself to form open loop. Lot I-5, 8530/5995 3.1.

248. Rim and handle of juglet? Est. diam. rim 0.030, max. h. 0.027. Fabric 1 with angular black impurities. Tubular rim pulled out and down; flaring neck; added handle from rim to neck. Lot II-1, 8340/5930 1.1.

249. Rim and handle of juglet. Max. h. 0.038. Bright green glass with a few, rounded, black impurities. Oval tubular rim pulled in and down; straight-sided handle applied to upper body and pulled up to rim. Imported? Lot I-28, 8525/6010 2.2.

250. Handle of juglet? Max. h. 0.046. Grayish green glass with many pinprick bubbles. Thick ring handle with two tooled indentations on tail. Lot I-1, 8530/6000 1.1.

251. Wound base of jug? Diam. base 0.070, max. h. 0.018. Green glass. Base formed from coil wound three times. Lot I-1, 8540/6000 1.1.

Flasks

252. Rim and neck of flask. Diam. mouth 0.044, max. h. 0.070. Fabric 1 with angular black impurities. Smooth, slightly thickened rim; short conical neck; sloping shoulders. Trail of same glass dropped on lower neck and wound up to below rim. Lot I-23, 8525/6015 3.3.

253. Rim and neck of flask. Est. diam. rim 0.040, max. h. 0.030. Fabric 1 with angular black impurities. Rounded fire-polished rim; straight-sided neck with added, unmarvered thread of translucent dark blue glass and, below, a very fine Fabric 1 thread wound around. Lot I-1, 8520/6015S 1.1.

254. Rim and neck of flask. Est. diam. rim 0.050, max. h. 0.011. Fabric 1. Rounded, fire-polished, rim; straight-sided neck with a Fabric 1 thread and a translucent light blue thread applied below rim. Lot VI-12, 8280/6060 4.2.

255. Seven fragments from rim and neck of flask. Diam. rim 0.040, max. h. 0.119. Fabric 1 with angular black impurities. Slightly out-turned, rounded fire-polished rim;

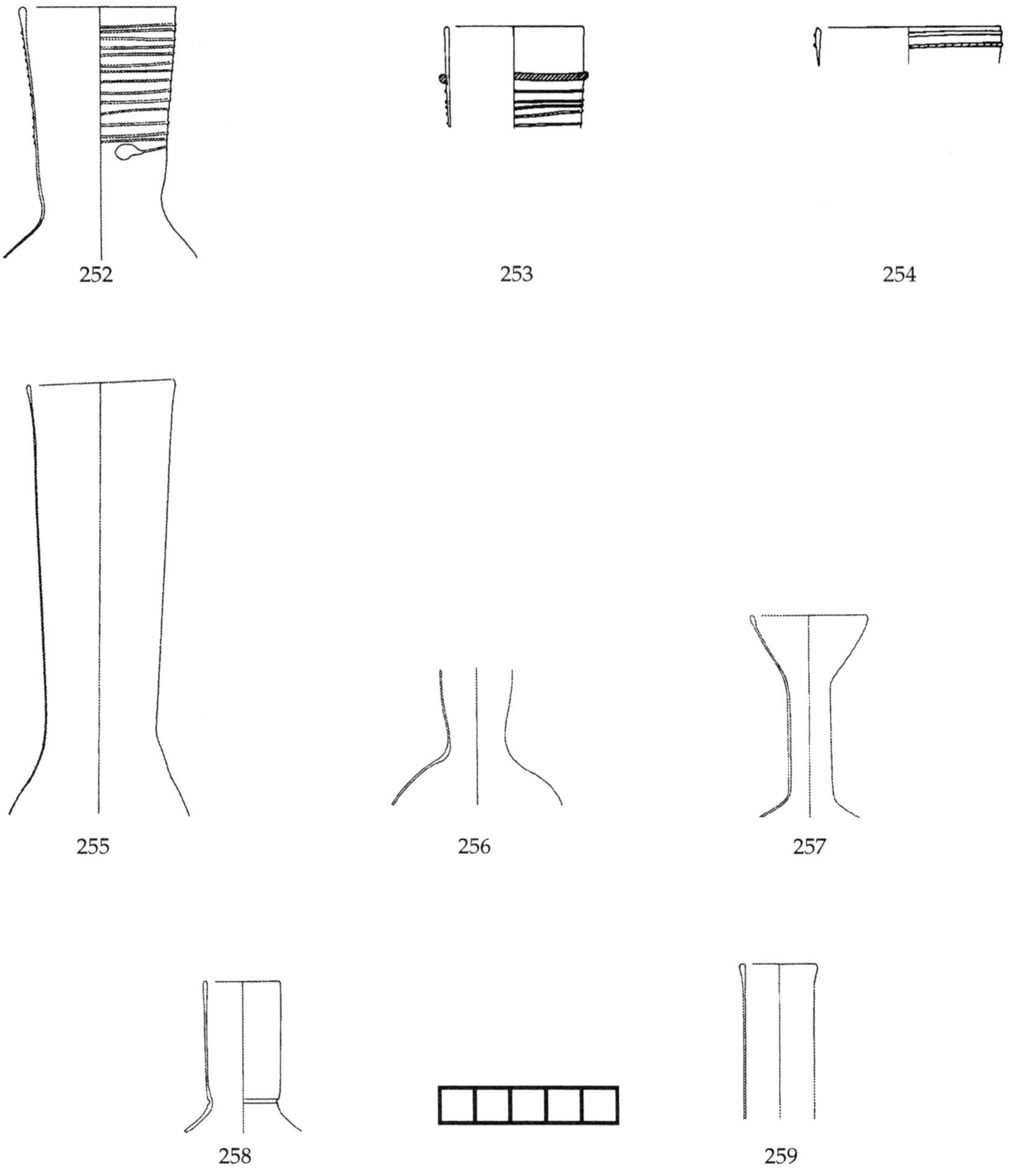

Fig. 6.3. Late Roman glass: flasks.

tall, conical neck; sloping shoulders. Lot I-7, 8520/5995 4.1 and 6.1, KK 88-30. *RDAC* 1989: 166 no. 13 (misprinted for 17), fig. 7.1.

256. Neck and shoulders of flask. Max. h. 0.050. Fabric 1. Slightly flaring neck; rounded shoulders. Lot II-17, 8350/5940 3.2.

257. Rim and neck of flask. Diam. rim 0.033, max. h. 0.060. Fabric 4. Slightly thickened, fire-polished rim; wide flaring mouth and narrow, cylindrical neck; flaring shoulders. Lot VI-11, 8280/6058 4.1. *RDAC* 1994: 306 no. 39, fig. 10.

258. Rim and neck of flask. Est. diam. rim 0.021, max. h. 0.044. Fabric 2 with angular black impurities. Slightly thickened, fire-polished rim; cylindrical neck; slight tooling between neck and sloping shoulder. Lot VI-11, 8280/6058 4.1.

259. Rim and neck of flask. Est. diam. rim 0.020, max. h. 0.046. Fabric 1 with angular black impurities. Narrow, cylindrical neck with slightly thickened fire-polished rim. Lot VI-5, 8280/6055 4.1.
Cf. Baur 1938, 541, no. 89; Delougaz and Haines 1960, pl. 59.22; Hayes 1992, 403, fig. 151.32.

260. Two non-joining fragments from lower body of flask. Est. diam. bottom 0.090. Fabric 1. Globular body; deep kicked bottom; no pontil mark preserved. Lot I-3, 8520/5995E 3.1.

261. Bottom of flask. Est. diam. base 0.090, max. l. 0.071. Fabric 1. Lower part of body wall and portion of kicked bottom. Lot I-31, 8530/6010 3.1.

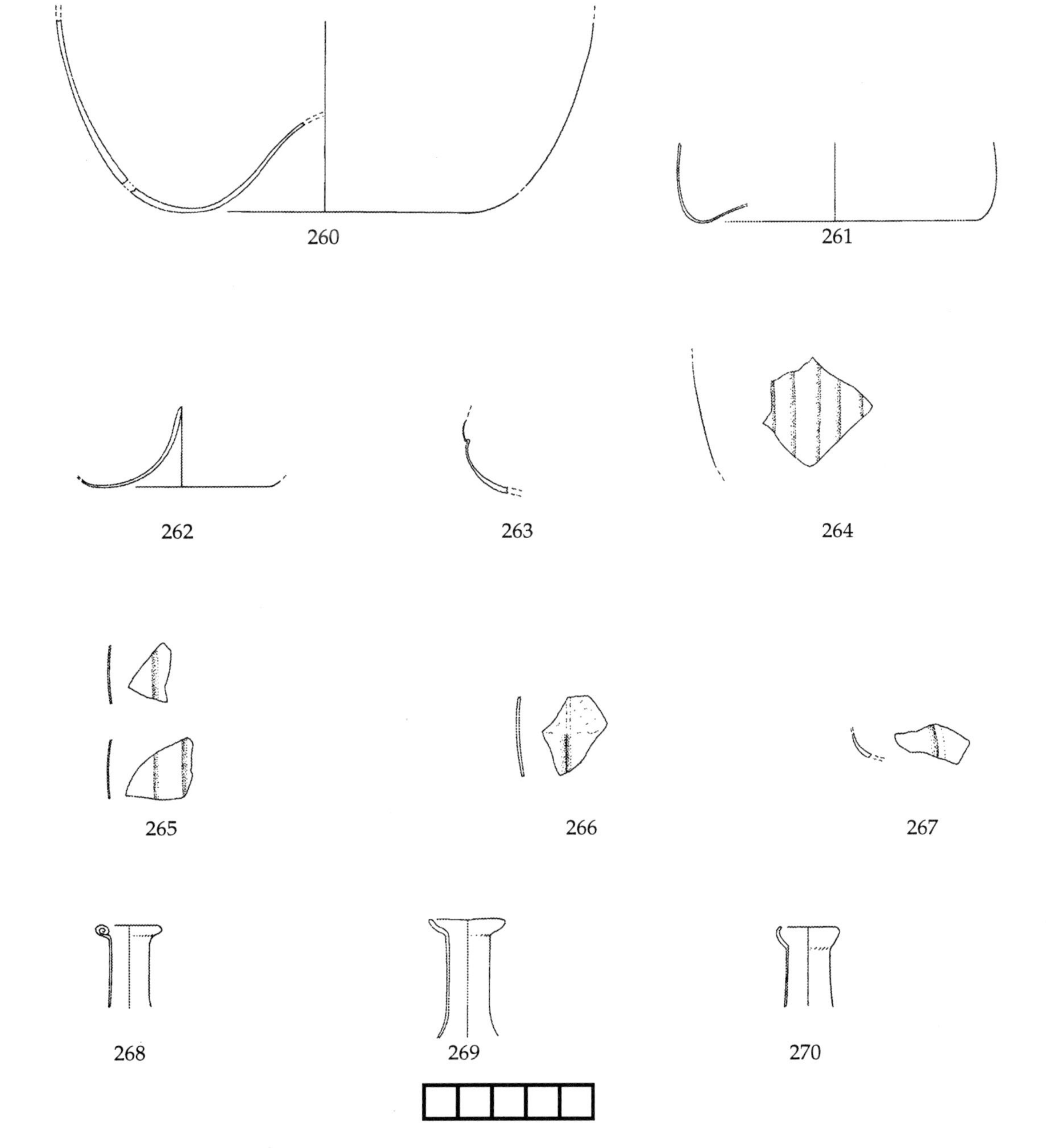

Fig. 6.4. Late Roman glass: flasks.

262. Bottom of flask (?). Est. diam. base 0.060. Fabric 1. Deep kicked bottom; no pontil mark. K86-Tr. B (=SG13).

263. Fragment from lower body of flask. Max. h. 0.042. Fabric 1 with angular black impurities. Globular body; on side a pin-hole indentation. Lot V-1, 8310/6170 1.1.

264. Three non-joining fragments of pattern-molded vessel. Max. h. 0.034. Fabric 1. Rounded, thin-walled vessel with diffused vertical ribbing. Lot I-22, 8525/6015 4.2.

265. Two non-joining fragments from pattern-molded vessel. Max. l. (a) 0.016, (b) 0.019. Fabric 1. Thin-walled vessel with diffused vertical ribbing. Lot I-20, 8520/6015 5.2.

266. Body fragment from pattern-molded vessel. Max. h. 0.025. Translucent dark blue glass. Thin-walled vessel with diffused vertical rib. Imported? Lot I-20, 8520/6015 5.1.

267. Six non-joining fragments of pattern-molded vessel. Max. h. 0.022. Transparent dark green glass with many small to pinprick bubbles and no visible impurities. Traces of at least two diffused vertical ribs. Imported? Lot II-34, 8340/5940 5.1.

Bottles

268. Rim and neck of small bottle. Diam. rim 0.020, max. h. 0.025. Transparent grayish blue glass. Irregular, tubular rim, folded in and flattened; thin, cylindrical neck. Lot VI-13, 8280/6060 5.1.

269. Rim and neck of small bottle. Diam. rim 0.022-0.020, max. h. 0.037. Fabric 1. Very irregular, fire-polished, con-

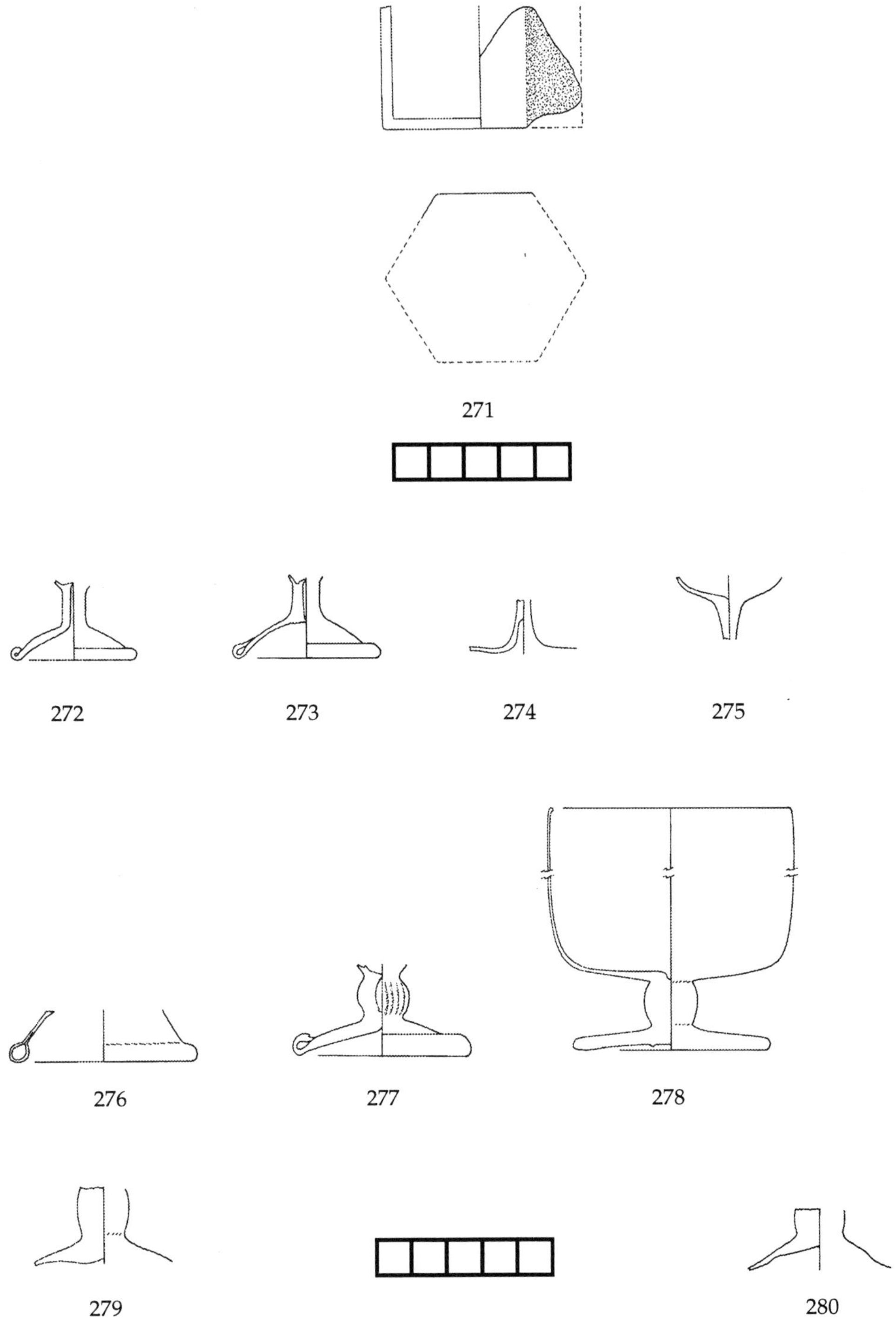

Fig. 6.5. Late Roman glass: bottle and stemmed goblets.

cave rim; cylindrical neck, sloping shoulders. Lot VI-11, 8280/6060 4.1.

270. Rim and neck of small bottle. Diam. rim 0.019, max. h. 0.024. Fabric 1. Irregular, fire-polished, concave rim; slightly flaring neck. Lot VI-6, 8280/6060 3.1.

271. Three non-joining fragments of hexagonal bottle. Max. h. 0.063, th. 0.003-0.0015. Fabric 1. Flat base and flat sides with rounded edges. Lots VI-5, 6, and 10; 8280/6055 4.1, 8280/6060 3.1, and 8280/6058 4.2.

Stemmed goblets

272. Base and stem of stemmed goblet. Diam. base 0.036, diam. stem 0.007, max. h. 0.022. Fabric 3. Hollow stem capped at top; domed base with tubular foot; no pontil mark. Lot VI-12, 8280/6060 4.2.

273. Base and stem of stemmed goblet. Diam. base 0.042, diam. stem 0.008, max. h. 0.024. Fabric 4. Hollow cylindri-

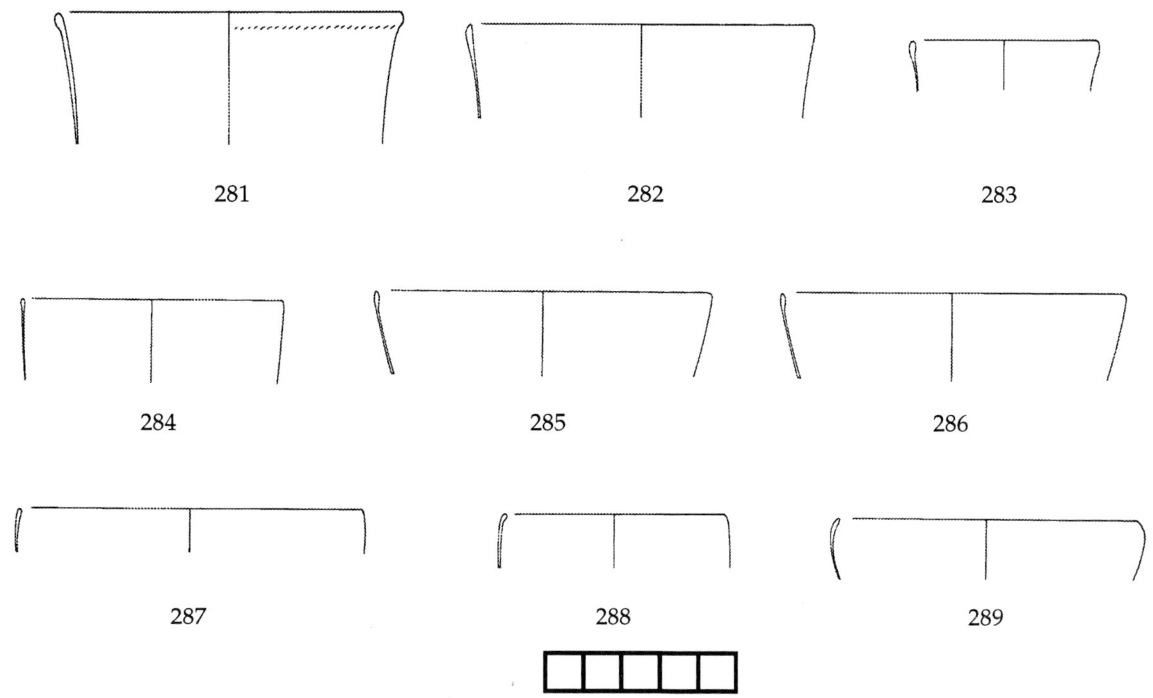

Fig. 6.6. Late Roman glass: goblet/lamp rims.

cal stem capped at top and bottom; domed base with tubular foot; pontil mark. Lot VI-6, 8280/6060 3.1.

274. Base and stem of stemmed goblet. Max. h. 0.015. Fabric 1. Very thin stem with twist marks; deep depression in stem; concave base. Lot II-13, 8345/5940 4.1.

275. Lower body and stem of stemmed goblet. Max. h. 0.019. Fabric 1. Globular body twisted into thin, solid stem. Lot II-8, 8340/5930 2.1.

276. Base of goblet? Diam. base 0.054, max. h. 0.015. Fabric 2. High conical base; thin tubular foot. Surface, Lot IV-1, Tr. B 1.1.

277. Base and stem of stemmed goblet. Diam. base 0.050, max. h. 0.025. Fabric 3. Rounded, thick, hollow, stem with tooled, vertical fluting; flaring base with tubular foot; pontil mark. Lot VI-5, 8280/6055 4.1. *RDAC* 1994: 306 no. 40, fig. 10.

278. Stemmed goblet. Est. diam. rim 0.070, diam. base 0.060, h. 0.065. Fabric 2. Several joining fragments of base, stem, and lower body, and several other non-joining fragments of rim and upper body. Rounded, fire-polished rim; straight-sided body; flat bottom of cup; short solid stem tooled into semi-spherical shape; solid discoid base with irregular edge and pontil mark. K86-Tr. B (=SG13).

279. Stem and base of stemmed goblet. Max. h. 0.023. Fabric 1 with angular black impurities. Fragment of solid stem tooled into semi-spherical shape; concave base. Lot V-3, 8310/6170 4.1.

280. Base and stem of stemmed goblet. Max. h. 0.017. Transparent green glass with no bubbles or impurities. Fragment of solid, semi-spherical, stem; concave base. Imported? Lot VI-12, 8280/6060 4.2.

Goblet/lamp rims

281. Rim of small bowl, goblet, or lamp. Est. diam. rim 0.090. Fabric 2. Slightly flaring, rounded, fire-polished rim; straight-sided body. Lot II-3, 8335/5930 2.1.

282. Rim of goblet or lamp. Est. diam. rim 0.090, max. h. 0.021. Fabric 1. Rounded, fire-polished rim; tapering body. Lot II-19, 8340/5940E 5.1.

283. Rim of goblet or lamp. Est. diam. rim 0.050, max. h. 0.021. Fabric 1. Rounded, fire-polished rim; straight-sided body walls. Lot I-20, 8520/6015 5.2.

284. Rim of goblet or lamp. Est. diam. rim 0.070, max. h. 0.014. Fabric 1. Rounded, fire-polished rim; tapering body. Lot II-7, 8340/5935 4.1.

285. Rim of goblet or lamp. Est. diam. rim 0.090, max. h. 0.023. Fabric 1. Rounded, fire-polished rim; straight-sided body. Lot I-22, 8525/6015 4.2.

286. Rim of goblet or lamp. Est. diam. rim 0.090, max. h. 0.023. Fabric 3. Smooth, slightly incurved, fire-polished rim; tapering body. Rim irregular at one point where bubble had burst. Lot IV-15, Tr. D 3.1.

287. Rim of goblet or lamp. Est. diam. rim 0.090, max. h. 0.012. Fabric 1. Rounded, fire-polished rim. Lot II-35, 8340/5940 6.1.

288. Rim of goblet or lamp. Est. diam. rim 0.060, max. h. 0.016. Fabric 1. Incurving, rounded and fire-polished rim. Lot II-19, 8340/5940E 5.1.

289. Rim of goblet or lamp. Est. diam. rim 0.080, max. h. 0.018. Fabric 1. Incurving, rounded and fire-polished rim. Lot I-20, 8520/6015 5.2.

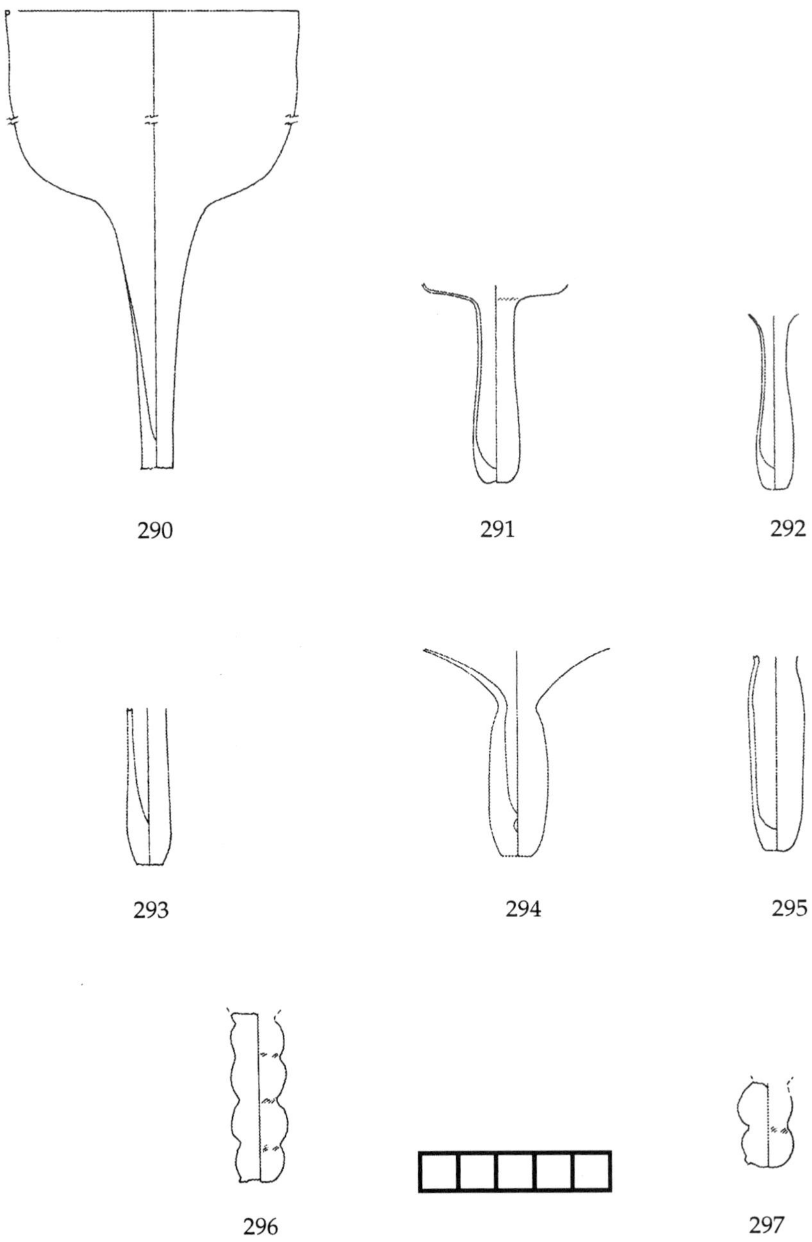

Fig. 6.7. Late Roman glass: stemmed lamps.

Stemmed lamps

290. Forty-three fragments of stemmed lamp. Est. diam. rim 0.080, h. 0.13. Fabric 3 with angular black impurities. Rounded, fire-polished rim; straight-sided body; thin, downward tapering stem; solid toe. Lot I-7, 8525/5995 4.2, 5.1, and 6.1, KK88-29. *RDAC* 1989: 166 no. 16, fig. 7.2.

291. Stem of stemmed lamp. Max. h. 0.055. Fabric 1. Thin, slightly rounded stem; solid toe with pontil mark. Lot I-6, 8525/5990 4.1.

292. Stem of stemmed lamp. Max. h. 0.049. Fabric 1. Thin, slightly rounded stem; solid toe with pontil mark. Lot I-3, 8520/5995E 3.1.

293. Stem of stemmed lamp. Max. h. 0.043. Fabric 3. Thin stem; thick solid toe with pontil mark. Surface, Lot I-1, 8535/5995 1.1.

294. Stem of stemmed lamp. Max. h. 0.062. Fabric 1. Flaring body; constriction at top of thick, rounded stem; thick toe with embedded bubble; pontil mark. Lot I-1, 8540/6005 2.2.

295. Stem of stemmed lamp. Max. h. 0.054. Fabric 2. Constriction at top of rounded stem; thick solid toe with pontil mark. Lot VI-11, 8280/6060 4.1.

296. Fragment of a beaded-stem lamp. Max. h. 0.045. Fabric 1. Solid stemmed with 4, irregular, tooled beads. Circular pontil mark. Lot I-20, 8520/6015 5.2.

297. Fragment of a beaded-stem lamp. Max. h. 0.022. Fabric 1. Solid stem with two, irregular, tooled beads. Circular pontil mark. Lot I-20, 8520/6015 5.2.

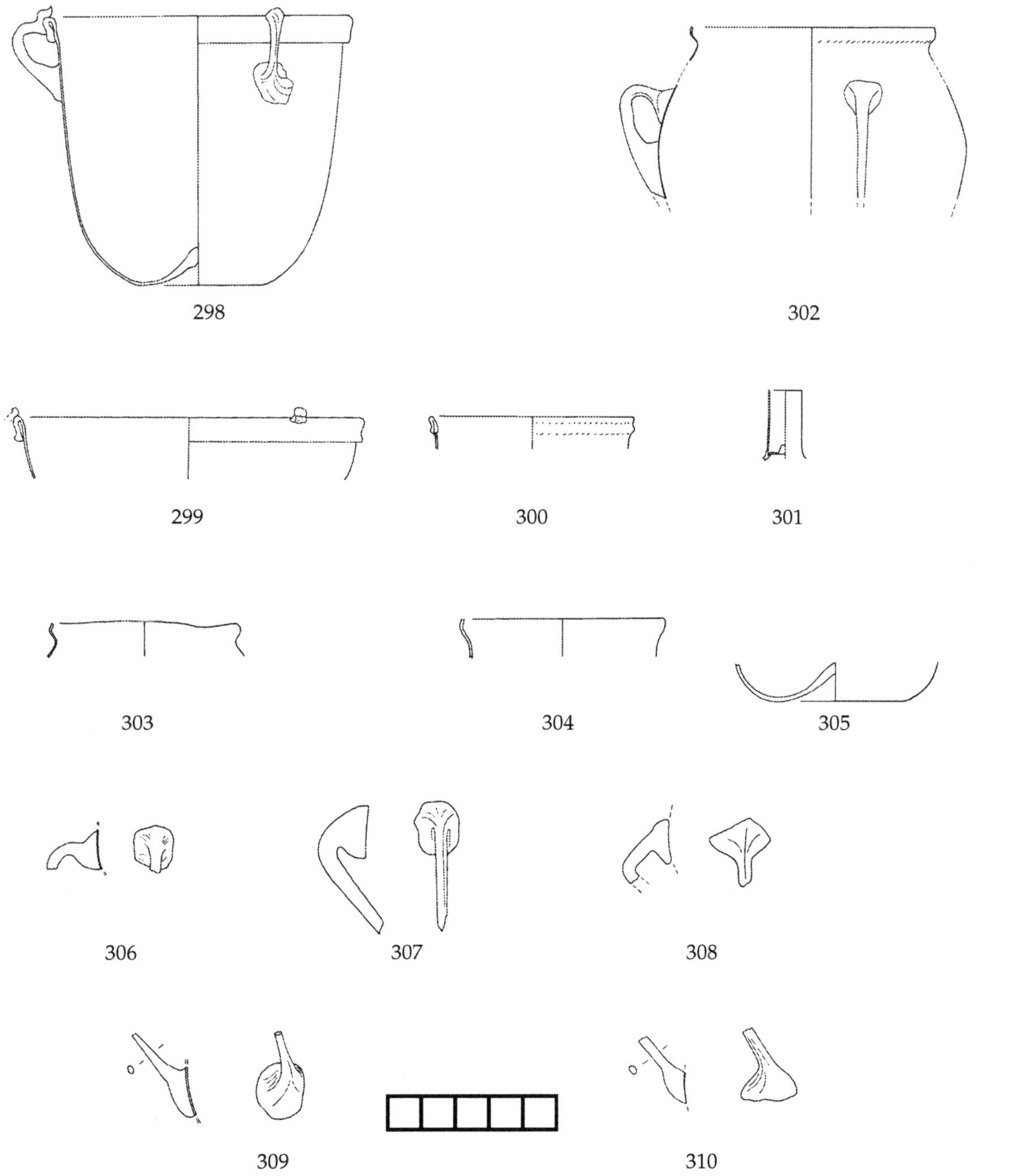

Fig. 6.8. Late Roman glass: hanging lamps.

Hanging lamps

298. Hanging lamp. H. 0.085. Est. diam. rim 0.092. Body of Fabric 1 glass; handles of Fabric 2a with yellow streaks. Tubular rim folded out and down, straight-sided body, and rounded base with slight kick and a ring pontil mark. Three gobs added to upper body and pulled up into thin angular handles attached to rim. Lot II-11, 8350/5935 6.1. *RDAC* 1994: 293 no. 14, fig. 4.

299. Two (non-joining) fragments of hanging lamp. Est. diam. rim 0.10, max. h. 0.019. Fabric 2. Tubular rim folded out and down; trace of small handle; slightly convex body. Lot I-1, 8525/6005 1.1.

300. Rim of hanging lamp? Est. diam. rim 0.060, max. h. 0.010. Fabric 1. Rim folded in and down, straight-sided body. Lot I-1, 8525/6015 1.1.

301. Wick tube? Fabric 2. Thin tube attached to domed bottom of lamp. Lot II-34, 8340/5940 5.1.

302. Two non-joining fragments of hanging lamp. Est. diam. rim 0.070. Fabric 3 with angular black impurities. Cracked-off and unpolished rim; rounded lip; rounded body; gob added to upper body and pulled down into thin angular handle. Lot I-7, 8525/5995 4.2.

303. Rim of goblet or lamp. Est. diam. rim 0.055, max. h. 0.011. Transparent grayish-yellow glass with few pinprick bubbles and no visible impurities. Irregular, wavy, cracked-off and unpolished rim; convex lip; flaring body. Lot I-1, 8520/5995E 1.1.

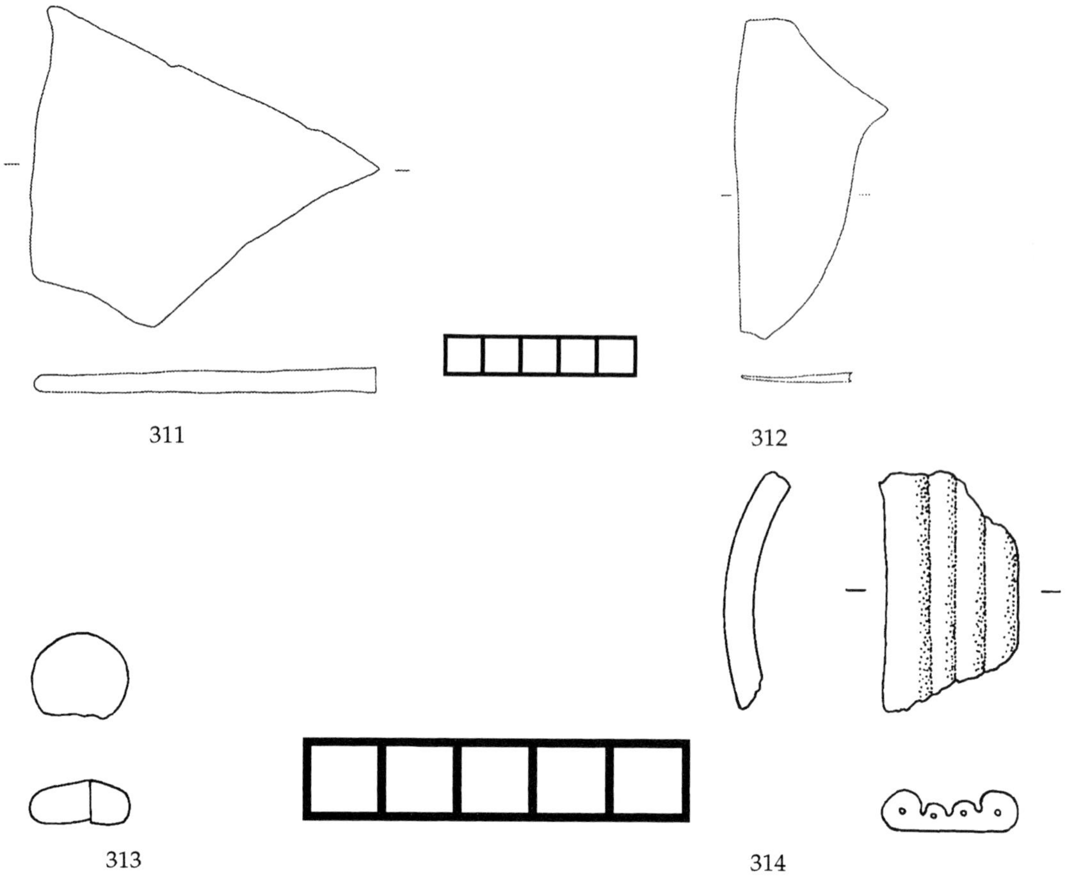

Fig. 6.9. Late Roman glass: non-vessels.

304. Rim of goblet or lamp. Est. diam. rim 0.060, max. h. 0.013. Transparent greenish-yellow glass with few pinprick bubbles and no visible impurities. Cracked-off, unpolished rim; convex lip. Imported? Lot I-20, 8520/6015 5.2.

305. Base of hanging lamp? Est. diam. base 0.040, max. h. 0.012. Fabric 2. Kicked base with pontil mark. Surface, Lot I-1, 8530/6005 1.1.

306. Handle from hanging lamp. Max. l. 0.012. Fabric 3. Gob added to rounded body and pulled down into thin handle. Lot I-7, 8525/5995 4.2.

307. Handle from hanging lamp. Max. l. 0.040. Body in Fabric 1; handle in Fabric 4 with angular black impurities and with streaks of yellow. Gob added to body and pulled down into thin angular handle. Lot I-2, 8525/6000 3.3.

308. Handle from hanging lamp. Max. l. 0.023. Fabric with angular black impurities and with yellow streaks. Gob added to rounded body and pulled down into thin angular handle. Lot V-3, 8315/6167 3.1.

309. Handle from hanging lamp. Max. l. 0.030. Fabric 1. Gob added to rounded body and pulled down into thin angular handle. Lot II-31, 8335/5930E 4.1.

310. Handle from hanging lamp. Max. l. 0.026. Fabric 1 with yellow streaks. Gob added to body and pulled down into thin angular handle. Lot II-19, 8340/5940E 5.1.

Non-vessels

311. Window pane. Max. l. 0.090, th. 0.005-0.007. Fabric 1. Flat, roller-molded sheet tapering to rounded edge. Lot VI-3, 8280/6055 3.1.

312. Fifty fragments (250 g) of window panes. Max. l. 0.088. Light blue glass with many spherical bubbles, some small angular black and a few larger white impurities. Flat, roller-molded sheet tapering to rounded edge. Lot II-12, 8345/5935E 4.1. *RDAC* 1994: 293 no. 13, fig. 4.
Cf. Meyer 1988: 194-95.

313. Token? Diam. 0.030. Fabric 2. Lentoid token or bezel. Surface, K-gen.

314. Two, non-joining, fragments of bracelet? Est. diam. 0.090, max. l. 0.034. Translucent dark brown glass. Bracelet composed of 4 fused rods, each flattened circular in section with a very small hollow. Imported? Lot II-27, 8335/5930 3.1.

7

Kopetra in late antiquity

> I arrive in port on the tenth day
> and see the island, a world not a part of the world,
> for one finds there gathered all the charms of the world ...
> Nikolaos Mouzalon, *Paraitesis*, *c.* 1107-10

A village of the early 7th c.

It is late afternoon as one approaches. The morning ship from Amathus was delayed by rough seas and crosswinds, and only after midday does one finally reach the valley. The noisy bustle of the seaside fades quickly after setting off on the well-worn road along the left bank of the Vasilikos river. Rising gently through a series of broad plateaus, one passes by small hamlets set among glowing fields of wheat, already half harvested, where scattered olive trees provide patches of welcome shade from the early summer sun. An hour's walk brings one across the coastal highway, much traveled yet little wider than the valley track, before climbing the next ridge. Near the top the sea breeze becomes stronger, which tempts one to pause and admire the expansive view of the coast before pressing on.

A diverging track to the left leads to the village at the upper end of the ridge. On the right appears a familiar landmark, a low hill with a small monastery whose freshly plastered walls bask in the afternoon sun. As one draws closer, the raised mound makes the basilica seem even taller than its modest size would suggest. From here one can distinguish individual buildings of the village, a tumble of houses and shops scattered across the undulating terrain. Straight ahead, near the lower outskirts, another church is visible, its patched walls and roof the result of recent repairs. At the settlement's upper end stands a third basilica, an early embodiment of local pride that continues to impress visitors with its large size and careful upkeep. These are the oldest and most imposing buildings known in the valley.

Entering one of these churches offers a refreshing interlude amid the bright, warm day. The outer porch welcomes one into the cool, quiet interior as one passes from the low narthex into the nave, its tall, top-lit space flanked by darkened porticos beyond rows of columns. The stately arrangement reminds one of the streets and colonnades of Amathus, but the subdued ambience achieves a timeless transformation of that busy public world. The decoration gradually emerges from the dimness: mosaics on the floor and in the semidome overlooking the sanctuary, with shadowed reliefs to either side. Pausing before devotional panels along the lower walls, one finds the same vision of eternity presented in churches across the island, in villages no less than cities, and on the mainland. At the same time there are reminders of village ancestors buried here, local inhabitants sanctified by tradition and time, whose commemoration helps one to rejoin family and community and re-affirm one's place in the world.

Dusty paths weave between clusters of low buildings as one walks through the village. Children play where alleys widen and older residents gather in their shaded intervals. The deepest shadows lie below the large terrace houses near the village center, homes of local landowners whose relatives live in the city. Passing by an open doorway one glimpses the inner court where family members sit on side benches and talk as they prepare the evening meal. Nearby buildings are crowded with activity: men and women making baskets and pots, displays of garden produce and household goods, small presses for working grapes and olives. Around the village's periphery one finds low walls enclosing open yards with threshing floors as well as goats and sheep. Within some are squat rounded ovens, carefully built of broken rooftiles for baking bread and evening casserôles; the remains of small hearths for working metal and firing pots lie amid clumps of brush nearby. As one leaves the village these walls gradually give way to simple boundaries marking family gardens, densely planted with vegetables. Most families set out a nearby garden to support themselves, tending them in the cool of morning and late afternoon when not working in more distant fields.

It has been a good spring and the harvest underway may yield more than 200 kg of grain per hectare. Local custom recommends that these fields be left fallow every other year, ploughing under the weeds before seeding in the spring in order to conserve moisture for the next growing season. Household manuring is limited to village gardens, for most fields lie too far flung to benefit from such added nutrients except when grazed by livestock. The effective commute by foot is an hour or two, which in the valley means a distance of c.4-6 km. Half of the fields one sees now lie fallow and are being grazed by goats and sheep.

Close to a hundred families live in the village. A typical household, while always fluctuating in age, sex, and size, includes about 6 members: one older and two younger adults, and two or three children of varied ages. Roughly 15,000 calories are required daily to sustain this group, which must work 6-7 ha to support itself, with additional fields needed to provide fodder for an ass or ox. In some respects children are more efficient producers than working animals, requiring only 2,000-2,500 daily calories to help in the fields and around the house. Grain makes up three-quarters of the nutritional needs of an average family, which consumes about 1,400 kg during the year. Each household additionally may use up to 300 liters of olive oil for food, lighting, washing, and other domestic tasks. Garden vegetables and gathered bulbs, grasses, and vetches supplement this diet, while mountain game and livestock, a rarity, are for special occasions. Other animals depend on agricultural by-products and forage in the vicinity.

Most villagers work in the fields. Some of the younger men have found seasonal employment in the copper mines at Spilios, 4 km to the north and 500 m higher in the valley, although few households can spare the labor away from their crops. Several of the larger families have begun to lease their more distant holdings to other farmers and now pursue the greater, if riskier, profits of trade. A strong market for grain has made it possible to cultivate remote fields and build terraced orchards on the upper slopes. The central location of the settlement within the valley has encouraged its growth as a market town, with local products gathered nearby for transport along the coastal highway and down to the seaside anchorage. At the same time, an intermittent fair has begun to supplement the supply of goods from across the sea. Dishes for the table come from as far as the Aegean and N Africa, while oil is brought from the nearby mainland. A few other foodstuffs arrive in perishable containers. Wine is of secondary importance at this small settlement and is bought mainly by its leading families and churchmen.

The success of this busy activity appears throughout the village — in the abundance of fine pottery, glass, and other imported commodities, but especially in the prominence of its churches. These monuments of local piety, together with the clergy attending them, celebrate generations of hard work and resourcefulness by local residents, whose ancestors lived in the surrounding hills and plain. They have gathered on the ridge in these good times not just for convenience and safety but to form a genuine community, a social microcosm of the outside world and the largest valley settlement in memory. It is a fortunate historical moment when local people have found the promise of the New Rome's empire fulfilled.

The Vasilikos valley in late antiquity

The prosperity met at Kopetra, both on the ground and in poetic construct above, is inexplicable apart from its wider setting. The settlement embodies the tangible benefits that were possible for a small town operating within a provincial Roman countryside. Residents of differing social levels occupied neighboring structures within a continuous architectural framework. Multiple churches promoted a public display of corporate well-being that could be seen across the valley, while a plentiful supply of specialized pottery and glass attests a measure of relative comfort enjoyed in daily life. As the largest period site known in the area, the village represents a level of economic success achieved by mediating production and consumption on a sub-regional scale.

The Vasilikos valley is one of several large catchment systems originating in the eastern Troodos mountains of S central Cyprus. Probably to be identified with Ptolemy's Tetios, the Vasilikos (*Vasilopotamos*) river descends through a rugged landscape today used for summer pasturage, with a few terraced orchards set among its maquis-covered slopes. In the upper valley, slag heaps still mark copper mines that were worked at *Petra* and *Spilios* during the Late Bronze Age, in Classical, Hellenistic, and Roman times, and as recently as the 1970s. About 3 km farther south, just below the present village of Kalavasos, the valley opens onto a sloping limestone shelf whose rich terra rossa soils are planted with cereals, pulses, olives, vines, and carobs — foundations of the local economy in mediaeval and modern times. The river finally reaches the sea at Vasiliko, a toponym that recalls the legendary landing near here of Helena Augusta on her return from the Holy Land. Her donation of a fragment of the True Cross is said still to be preserved in a church at nearby Tochni.[1]

The valley presents a cross-section of the island's geography and history. Over the last 25 years the VVP has established by survey and excavation how early peoples recognized the natural bounty of the area.[2] Systematic reconnaissance has been based on a 20% transect sample of the valley, supplemented by intensive scrutiny of key sites (L. S. Hordynsky and J. J. Johnson in Keller and Rupp 1983: 331-32; Todd forthcoming). By tracing long-term patterns of settlement, the VVP has noted cycles of growth during the Neolithic period (6th millennium B.C.), Late Bronze Age (mid-2nd millennium B.C.), and late antiquity (mid-1st millennium A.D.). The earliest inhabitants apparently were drawn by the area's natural resources to live atop the low mound of *Tenta*, while Chalcolithic farmers gathered on the overlooking ridge at *Ayious* (above, fig. 2.3). In the Late Bronze Age, people farmed and herded flocks on the plain while working the upper valley's copper mines; a large building complex at *Ayios Dhimitrios* apparently served as a sub-regional administrative center for the production of this and other commodities. The rise of the Iron Age kingdom of Amathus coincided with a period of reduced activity in the valley, which may have remained sparsely inhabited through classical times but revived in the late Hellenistic and early Roman periods.

The 1st and 2nd c. A.D. are represented by at least 32 sites visited by the VVP, although the paucity of 3rd- to 4th-c. pottery suggests that many of these were left behind between the 2nd and 4th c. The greater abundance of Late Roman material indicates that close to 70% (23) of these places were again occupied in late antiquity and even grew in size and complexity through the 6th and early 7th c. At least 44 sites are assignable to this period, including seasonal agricultural encampments, isolated presses for grapes and olives, and permanent villages. Almost half of this number (21) were new establishments without clear signs of earlier Roman habitation. Late Roman sites appear widely distributed across the coastal plain, many within ready reach of arable fields (fig. 7.1, a preliminary overview that anticipates Todd's forthcoming report). By contrast, activity areas above modern Kalavasos apparently looked toward terraced orchards and vineyards, with the largest clustering near the mines at *Spilios*. At least 5 sizeable Roman-era sites extend along the W side of the valley leading up to the mines, culminating in the expansive complex at *Spilios* itself (Pantazis 1967; Koucky and Steinberg 1982a and 1982b).

Four places stand out among the Roman-era settlements of the central and lower valley. The largest appears to be Kopetra, which occupies a natural promontory above the river within

1 Hackett 1901: 9, 434; Jeffery 1918: 353; Leontios Makhairas in Dawkins 1932: 6-9.

2 Todd 1979a, 1979b, 1982, 1985, 1987, and 1989; South 1984; South *et al.* 1989.

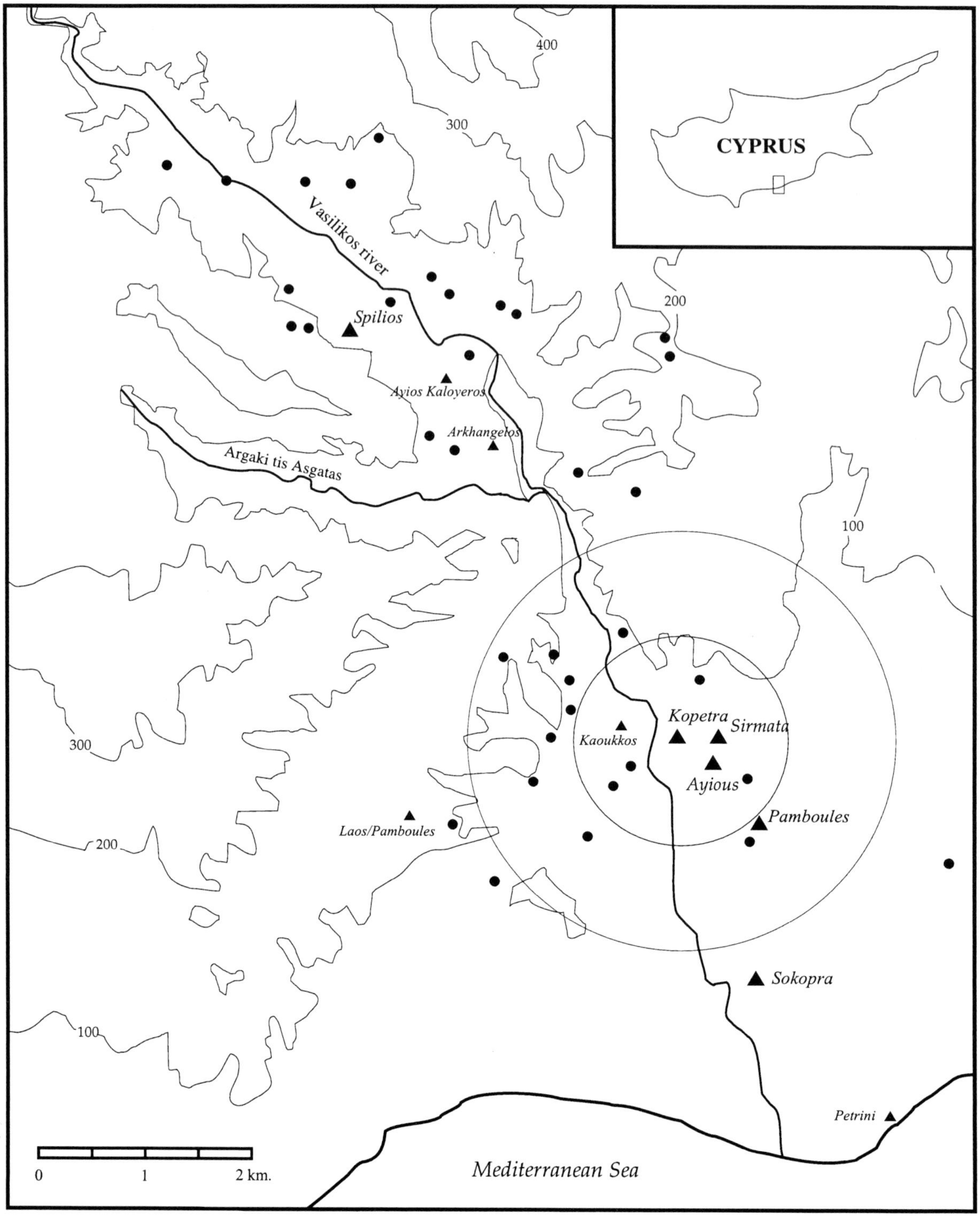

Fig. 7.1. Distribution of primary and secondary Late Roman occupation sites in the Vasilikos valley identified by the VVP (circles indicate 1- and 2-km distance from Kopetra).

sight of both the sea and the upper valley (above, figs. 2.2 and 2.5; fig. 7.2). This nucleated, cluster-type settlement, unwalled but clearly situated with an eye to defense, looks forward in many ways to the siting of traditional Cypriot villages. Often such places have names preserving this sense of potential hazard and offer a vantage point (*anephane*) overlooking the main access route (Christodoulou 1959: 62). Presumably natural springs or shallow aquifers that could be tapped by wells underlie the Kopetra ridge. The Vasilikos river, even before construction of the modern dam, was useful mainly as a source of building material; like other rivers on the island, it typically was either dry or violent and dangerous when in flood. Kopetra's loca-

Fig. 7.2. View from *Kaoukkous* on the Vasilikos river plain, view to SE toward Kopetra, with *Pamboules* to right (2000).

tion would have offered early residents two essential resources: farmland on the adjacent plain and nearby outcrops of good-quality gypsum. The variety of soils within easy walking distance — plateau terra rossas and alluvial deposits in the lower valley — provided complementary possibilities for subsistence farming (below, Appendix 2; Christodoulou 1959: 62; Wagstaff 1988: 66-67). Gypsum lies close to the surface at *Kafkalies, Mangia,* and elsewhere, and the easily-worked building material may have been exported as well. The settlement's central location is well situated for communication with its neighbors. Over a dozen contemporary sites have been identified within a 2-km radius. Moreover, Kopetra lies near the presumed intersection of two important roads: the valley's traditional N-S axis and the coastal highway between Amathus and Kition (cf. Mitford 1980: fig. 1; Bekker-Nielsen 1993: 184). Like the nearby dominant places of the Neolithic and Late Bronze Age, most of these features pre-date Roman times.

Many of these situational advantages also apply to the S part of the ridge at *Ayious* and *Pamboules*. Today the new coastal highway runs directly through *Ayious,* which occupies a natural slope leading down to the river plain (fig. 7.3). The distribution of Roman-era pottery indicates that habitation at *Ayious* was clearly separate from Kopetra to the north, on the one hand, and from the contemporary site at *Pamboules* to the south, on the other (Todd 1979a: 278-81; id. 1979b: 31). Both *Ayious* and *Pamboules* were occupied in early Roman times as well as in the 6th and 7th c. *Pamboules* is especially well sited on the S side of this natural corridor across the valley and enjoys many of the same topographic benefits as Kopetra. The *Pamboules* vicinity was intensively sampled in 1976-78 and 1988 by the VVP, whose main interest was the site's Late Neolithic and Chalcolithic components.[3] The VVP survey also collected a great deal of Late Roman pottery but noted surprisingly little architectural débris (mortared field-stones or rooftiles) in the area. This anomaly clearly distinguishes the site from its larger, nearby counterparts and raises the possibility that habitation was secondary to other activities. Relatively impermanent shelters may have been favored, as would be appropriate for an open-air market or seasonal fair (*panêgyris*) rather than a more developed, permanent place like Kopetra.[4]

---

3 Todd 1979a: 285; id. 1979b: 33; id. 1989: 48-49; Clarke and Todd 1993: 11-14, esp. fig. 1 for the topography of this part of the valley.

4 MacMullen 1970: 333; de Ligt 1993: 38-39; Graf 2001: 230-32.

Fig. 7.3. View from *Pamboules,* view to N to Kopetra and *Ayious* (foreground) (2000).

Fig. 7.4. View from *Sokopra,* view to N to *Pamboules* (2000).

Traces of another prominent settlement appear at *Sokopra*, a low, flat plateau lying along the river channel about 2.5 km below Kopetra, 1.5 km from *Pamboules*, and 1.5 km from the shore (fig. 7.4). Like Kopetra, habitation at *Sokopra* was initially identified by a broad scat-

Fig. 7.5. Zyyi-*Petrini*, view to E (1990).

ter of sherds and building débris extending over an area of at least 2 ha (J. Johnson and L. Hordynsky in Todd 1982: 66). Closer inspection established that this was another year-round village that may have functioned as a sub-regional economic center. *Sokopra* similarly shows little trace of earlier Hellenistic or Roman activity. Residents apparently were attracted here because of its location near the lower river close to its agricultural base, where it served as a natural collection-point for local products as well as rural markets on the surrounding plain. Its distance from Kopetra resembles the spacing of traditional Cypriot villages at 3- to 5-km intervals (Christodoulou 1959: 62).

Sokopra lies only a short walk from the seaside site of Zyyi-*Petrini*, a fourth main point of interest. Pottery of the Late Bronze Age, early Iron Age, and Hellenistic periods has been found by the VVP survey in this coastal vicinity, extending from Tochni-*Lakkous* east toward the present village of Zyyi (Todd forthcoming). Presumably some facilities existed already in the early 4th c. when Helena Augusta reputedly landed near here; her donation of a devotional relic at Tochni, a few km to the northeast, may imply the presence of the nearest substantial church or settlement — or be pure mediaeval invention. Signs of Late Roman activity were noted here by the VVP and have been further explored by the Maroni Valley Archaeological Survey Project (MVASP). The present site lies directly on the water with its S margin eroded by the sea (fig. 7.5). A series of buildings are visible over a distance of 150 m in the S-facing scarp, including walls and floors that stand *c.*1 m above the summer sea-level. A poorly preserved stone-lined feature, measuring at least 1 m high and 0.8 m wide, may belong to a pottery kiln, perhaps for the production of LR1 amphoras (Manning *et al.* 2000). Surface finds extend *c.*50 m inland, for a total estimated extent of 2 ha. Pottery recovered from the area includes a range of Late Roman wares similar to those found elsewhere in the valley and attests activity primarily during the 6th and early 7th c. The seaside setting and period of occupation suggest that *Petrini* was one of many small commercial points along the S coast that prospered as ships anchored offshore to take on and unload their cargoes (see Leonard 1995b: 235 fig. 11 for probable locations). Goods arriving by ship were then transported overland to nearby market centers like *Sokopra*, *Pamboules*, and Kopetra, and thence to smaller sites in the valley.

Clearly Kopetra was not just a farming settlement but a market village with an important rôle to play in the local economy. Established roads led to the site from similar communities in the lower Pentakomo and Maroni valleys, while secondary tracks arrived from *Spilios* and scattered *komai* in the Troodos foothills. The mid-valley location allowed it to act as a sub-regional economic node, a collection point for local products and a redistribution center for imported commodities. Compared with finds from elsewhere in the valley, the great variety of goods attested at Kopetra — rooftiles, fine wares, amphoras, and the foodstuffs they contained — suggests the presence of established markets or seasonal fairs in the vicinity, through which goods passed on their way into the countryside.

Imports

Building materials constitute a large part of these imported materials. Two kinds of rooftiles arrived in quantity: red-fabric Laconian-style tiles made near Paphos in W Cyprus, and yellow-fabric Corinthian-style tiles made in the lower Mesaoria plain to the east. The distribution of these heavy objects is not known beyond the island's shores, which supports the view that building materials figured prominently in short-distance trade in the region (Parker 1992b: 95). Both types of rooftiles were carried by ships along the coast as far as the anchorage at *Petrini*, where they were unloaded for transport to sites within the valley. The expense and inconvenience of overland travel are reflected by their dwindling numbers with distance from the sea, to which Kopetra (located 4 km from the shore) forms a conspicuous exception. Here yellow-fabric tiles are the more abundant, although there is some indication that red-fabric tiles were increasingly used in the later 6th c. (above, pp. 37-38). Large coarse-fabric rooftiles in the Corinthian tradition may have been made earlier in the area but were especially common during the early 7th c.

The next largest group of imported goods consists of amphoras with their contents. Most originated in the E Mediterranean, with LR1 and KAmp2 accounting for some two-thirds of all transport vessels found at Kopetra. The best represented fabrics are LR1(2) and LR1(3), which apparently came from Cilicia and N Syria. The tremendous cultivation of olives in these areas argues in favor of oil as Kopetra's primary import. The Palestine region provided a small but steady supply of LR4 and LR5/6 amphoras carrying wine or other products. These bulky commodities probably followed centuries-old sea-lanes to arrive at the east-facing harbors at Salamis and Kition, with some ships sailing directly to Amathus. LR1(1) amphoras and yellow-fabric rooftiles from the lower Mesaoria would have joined these cargoes aboard ships leaving Salamis on their way along the island's S coast.

Fine wares came almost exclusively from the west. Phocean Red Slip pottery arrived throughout late antiquity, and from the mid 6th c. was joined by increasing quantities of African Red Slip. Traveling in the company of other goods — luxuries, agricultural products, building materials — these wares would have been attractive cargo for ships returning along the grain route to Egypt after unloading their stocks at imperial warehouses on Tenedos in the N Aegean. Since these ships left Egypt fully loaded with grain (and with penalties in place for supplementing cargoes; Sirks 1991: 211), it is understandable that few examples of Egyptian Red Slip and LR7 amphoras reached the valley, even though Cypriot fine wares and amphoras are abundant in Egypt.[5] Most of these goods arrived at ports in W Cyprus, where they were joined by products of the Paphiote hinterland, especially Cypriot Red Slip (which dominated the local market from 550), unslipped tableware, and red-fabric rooftiles. LR1(1) and KAmp1 amphoras would also have been added to ships sailing eastward to Kourion, Amathus, and coastal anchorages like *Petrini*. Seasonal fairs and market towns like Kopetra and *Sokopra* marked the final stage of rural distribution.[6]

Imported ceramics in the valley thus represent several distinct source areas (above Table 5.6; fig. 5.22). Their relative proportions reflect factors of geography as well as value. The distribution of rooftiles, the bulkiest commodity, appears to be the most regionally restricted, the three major types originating in Cyprus and not otherwise known beyond the island. Agricultural supplies came mainly from the E Mediterranean, primarily Cilicia and N Syria,

---

5 Egloff 1977; Ballet 1995; Arthur and Oren 1998.

6 MacMullen 1970; de Ligt 1993: 108-11.

followed by Cyprus itself, with the wider Palestine region ranking third. High-value/low-bulk fine wares from N Africa and the Aegean were the goods that traveled farthest to reach the site. This distribution pattern reflects a logical decline over distance that apparently was tempered by officially sponsored exchange in the form of the grain route between Alexandria and Constantinople. Paths of ecclesiastical, military, and political traffic may have exerted a similar if much smaller effect. Such mechanisms would have assured steady, subsidized contact with the Aegean while suppressing Egyptian imports to the island.

Local production

The presence of market items in the Vasilikos valley — primarily pottery but also glass and coins — provides indirect evidence for local productivity. These goods reflect the reciprocal exchange of products or services originating in the valley. The scale of local production can theoretically be estimated as equal to the quantity of imported goods together with the material surplus that was invested in local building, after subtracting transport and marketing costs as well as rents and profits extracted by landowners. The demands of State and Church surely influenced this exchange, even if their direction and significance remain unclear.[7] Kopetra, as one of the smallest yet most thoroughly investigated period-sites on the island, shows how this dynamic economic environment may have operated during the 6th and early 7th c. Its ceramics represent a variety of goods that were consumed locally, presumably by landowners, artisans, shopkeepers, mineworkers, and farmers who lived in town. Local success at resource exploitation appears clearly in the churches they built and maintained as well as the commodities they consumed. The evident well-being of local inhabitants presupposes their participation in broad networks of exchange that reached across the late empire.

Analysis of the Vasilikos valley's economic output is largely speculative. Literary sources are mostly early, vague, and do not pertain specifically to the area, although they offer important testimony of how the island was viewed from afar (below, p. 255). Survey and excavation evidence is more directly relevant. All of this information, however scarce and uneven, can be combined cautiously with ethnographic information and knowledge of traditional farming patterns to reconstruct the area's productive capacity in late antiquity.[8]

Grapes and olives

Grapes and olives have always numbered among the island's major crops. Cypriot wine was widely regarded in antiquity and during the Byzantine period its production flourished under the protection of St. Tychon. The heavy, sweet-tasting *Commanderia* produced on estates of the Knights Hospitallers was distributed across W Europe following the Second Crusade. Today vines are common features of most villages in S central Cyprus, where trellised leaves provide courtyard shade and grapes are consumed primarily in the home. While small vineyards can be found on the upper slopes, large operations are not common in the Vasilikos or neighboring valleys. Instead, the greatest concentration of vines is in the cooler, higher elevations of the Troodos mountains, which are better suited to their cultivation.[9]

By contrast, oleoculture has long been favored in this part of Cyprus and some quantity of oil was produced here in Roman times. Pliny (*NH* 15.2-6) mentions the range of soils and temperate climate olives need to flourish, and these conditions prevail across much of the E Mediterranean. Byzantine and later sources note that olives were raised in the Mesaoria plain and the vicinity of Limassol.[10] In S central Cyprus the important Late Bronze Age sites of Kalavasos-*Ayios Dhimitrios* and Maroni-*Vournes* were key centers for the production and storage of oil,

---

7 Hendy 1985: 564; van Alfen 1996: 211-12; Sodini 2000: 195-96; Kingsley and Decker 2001b.

8 Christoudoulou 1959; Thirgood 1989; Ionas 1993-94; but note the cautions of Halstead 1987: 77-79.

9 Christodoulou 1959: 152-56 and 170-72; White 1970: 229-46; Malamut 1988: 387-90 and 410-11; Hadjisavvas 1992: 2-4.

10 Christodoulou 1959: 170-73; Malamut 1988: 410-11.

which was an essential part of the island's early economy.[11] Stone basins and weights observed at Kopetra and contemporary sites attest the pressing of olives or grapes on at least a small scale. A large gypsum press weight lies on the river plain just west of Kopetra at Kalavasos-*Kaoukkos*.[12] A more substantial pressing operation discovered at Mari-*Kopetra* in the lower valley indicates a larger scale of production in Hellenistic and Roman times.[13] Similar equipment — large suspension weights and crushing basins of calcarenite stone — was used to process grapes and olives, and indeed may have been used on a seasonal basis for both crops. Yet it seems likely that oil continued to be the more important of the two products in this region. Olives are better suited to the area's warm climate and light calcareous soils. More importantly, oil was an indispensable foodstuff throughout the Roman world. Even though oil, like wine, may not have been distributed in significant quantities by the State, it was essential for the caloric needs of an agricultural workforce.[14] Recent estimates of the annual rate of consumption of olive oil have ranged from 20 to 50 liters (1 liter weighing slightly more than 1 kg) per person during the Roman period, with the lower figure perhaps more typical of the countryside. A village with 500 inhabitants thus may have needed between 10,000 and 25,000 liters each year as food. Oil also was burned as fuel for lamps; assuming a liter of oil lasts about 134 hours, a town of 500 might have required over 1350 liters per year for lighting.[15] To these very rough estimates can be added oil that was used as skin soap, moisturizers, garden fertilizer, insecticides, preservatives, and for other domestic needs. For comparative purposes it can be noted that Roman production in the Segermes valley of Tunisia may have yielded 80 liters of oil per cultivated ha.[16] By this reckoning the inhabitants of Kopetra might have required at least 125 ha planted in olive trees to supply basic needs. Since the olive is prone to biennial harvest, the actual area under cultivation may have ranged from 250 to 600 ha.

Amphoras found in the Vasilikos valley document the demand for these two primary commodities, as well as other goods they may have contained. Most of the standard Late Roman amphora types (LR1-7) are associated with wine, which does not seem to have been locally produced in great quantity. LR1 amphoras, which account for two-thirds of all transport vessels at Kopetra, carried both wine and oil, much of it originating in Cilicia and Syria. Oil may well have been the more important of the two. Amphora types most often associated with wine (LR2-7) are not especially common in the valley and at Kopetra comprise less than 10% of the total. While animal skins, wood barrels, and other non-ceramic containers may have been used, the low representation of these principally wine-bearing vessels implies that (imported) wines were considered something of a luxury in this rural setting, especially since its nutritional value was so modest (*c.*700 calories per liter[17]). By contrast, the abundance of LR1 amphoras from the mainland demonstrates a sustained demand for oil in a region that was otherwise suitable for olive cultivation. Their large numbers attest the benefits of the island's provincial membership by compensating for shortfalls occasioned by accident, drought, or shifts of population. They also suggest that other crops were being produced for the wider market. The most likely alternatives are cereals, especially wheat and barley.

Cereals

Grain occupied a central place in the Roman world and was widely grown for local needs.[18] The major cereal produced for human consumption was wheat, the cornerstone of the 'average

---

11 South 1984; South *et al.* 1989; Cadogan 1992; Hadjisavvas 1992 and 1996; Knapp 1997: 66-67.

12 For the site, see J. J. Johnson and L. Hordynsky in Todd 1982: 66; Todd forthcoming.

13 Hadjisavvas 1988: 113-15; 1992: 34-40; cf. for the mainland Callot 1984; Frankel 1997.

14 Foxhall and Forbes 1982: 68; Sirks 1991: 388-91; Hadjisavvas 1996: 129; Mattingly 1996: 222-23.

15 At one hour per person per day; Mattingly 1996: 224-25.

16 Assuming 2 liters of oil per tree planted at an average density of 40 per ha; P. Ørsted in Ørsted *et al.* 2000: 143-44.

17 Foxhall and Forbes 1982: 68; Mattingly 1996: 223.

18 In general Jasny 1944; Foxhall and Forbes 1982; Garnsey 1988: 49-53; for late antiquity Kaplan 1992: 28-30.

classical diet'. Other grains, including the more deeply rooted dark summer wheat, barley, rye, and millet, were normally raised for the low end of the market, but were also more dependable during a variety of adverse conditions (Rickman 1980: 5-6; Sarpaki 1992: 69). Barley's drought tolerance and shorter ripening season, for example, recommended it for emergency consumption and animal fodder. While acknowledging the methodological problems involved in reconstructing past populations and dietary requirements, one can estimate the average annual consumption of cereals in antiquity at *c.*237 kg per person.[19] In areas where terrain and climate allowed, cereals also were important market crops that under favorable conditions could yield a surplus on a seasonal basis. Proximity to a navigable river or the sea allowed access to the wider market.

Cyprus is generally well suited to the production and distribution of cereals. During the early 20th c., when bare fallow cultivation was still widely practiced and before chemical fertilizers were introduced, the wheat yield for the whole of Cyprus averaged 740 kg per ha. The annual variation of 12% was significantly less than the 20% or more recorded for Syria and Turkey.[20] Today some of the island's best farming soils occur in the broad alluvial basins of the S central and eastern regions. The Mesarka bottomlands in the lower Mesaoria have been described as the "nearest approach to Nilotic conditions Cyprus has to show", with perhaps 0.30 m of alluvium deposited each century. Annual rainfall in these areas can reach 400-500 mm, which compares favorably with much of the Near East mainland.[21] Agricultural conditions in parts of the Vasilikos valley may not have been quite as promising in antiquity. The mean annual rainfall is about 600 mm, which exceeds the minimum for dry farming of cereals (240 mm per annum with 40% variation), yet historically wheat production has been rather low, perhaps a third of that estimated for parts of Roman N Africa.[22] Assuming a minimum annual consumption of about 120,000 kg of wheat (at 237 kg per person), the inhabitants of Late Roman Kopetra would have needed to cultivate about 500 ha to cover basic human needs. The tradition of leaving fields fallow in alternate years doubles this area to 1000 ha, or 10 km^2.

All this establishes the central place of cereal crops in early Cypriot agriculture and the likelihood that they were raised in the Vasilikos valley for wider markets as well as local consumption. Grain surpluses are known to have been shipped from Cyprus to the Aegean in the 5th to 3rd c. B.C. and to Egypt under Ptolemy III Euergetes.[23] Pliny (*NH* 18.12.67-68) notes the export of Cypriot wheat to Rome, and Galen says that both wheat and barley were raised and consumed on the island.[24] The mid 7th-c. Life of Spyridon speaks of rural storerooms bulging with wheat.[25] Under the late empire much of the surplus probably followed the Egyptian grain-supply to provision Constantinople.[26] The island may have exported wheat to Galatia as late as the 7th c., for a donation of wheaten bread (*katharos artos*) from Cyprus is said to have reached Sykeon during a shortage.[27] The interruption of the Egyptian supply by the Persian and Arab invasions of the 7th c. certainly would have increased the island's importance as a supplier of the late empire. Admittedly the fragmentary historical sources provide little direct evidence for understanding the mechanics of the grain supply in the 7th c.,

---

19 Foxhall and Forbes 1982: 72; cf. Harvey 1989: 180-81 for more modest assumptions in the Middle Ages.

20 Christodoulou 1959: 125-28, fig. 64; A. J. Legge in Peltenburg 1982: 14-17; Hopkins 1983: 91 Table 1; Halstead 1987: 82; J. M. Wagstaff in Todd 1979a: 291-92; cf. for Greece Sarpaki 1992: 62-69.

21 Savile 1878: 38; Christodoulou 1959: 15, 19-33 and 41-45 (quoted here); Thirgood 1987: 22-24, fig. 1; Kaplan 1992: map 1.

22 J. M. Wagstaff in Todd 1987: 5, 8; cf. P. Ørsted in Ørsted *et al.* 2000: 146-47.

23 Thompson 1983: 74; Casson 1984: 70-72, who groups Cyprus with Egypt and Cyrene as one of three main sources of grain; Garnsey 1988: 153, 164.

24 *Nat. Fac.* 6.501, in Garnsey 1988: 51; Wallace and Orphanides 1990: 228; Michaelides 1996: 146.

25 van den Ven 1953: 12-13; Papacostas 2001: 112.

26 Teall 1959: 91-96; Pryor 1988: 15-20; Durliat 1990: 226-28; Sirks 1991; Bakirtzis 1995; Kingsley and Decker 2001b: 4-5.

27 Festugière 1970: 13, 26 and 83; cited in Harvey 1989: 166.

when needs must have been addressed on an increasingly *ad hoc* basis.[28] Following its recapture by Nikephoros Phocas in 965, Cyprus again supplied the capital with grain in the 11th c. Byzantine monastic documents and Arab geographers note the importance of cereal crops among island exports.[29] Occasional shortfalls in times of drought and infestation are noted in saints' lives and the Chronicle of Leontios Makhaeras.[30] Wheat and especially barley continued to be among the leading exports under the Lusignans, Venetians, and Ottomans.[31]

Other products

Other domestic crops supplemented the needs of local inhabitants (Ionas 1993-94: 440-41). Residential gardens are mentioned in the Life of Spyridon of Trimithos (van den Ven 1953: 109; Kaplan 1992: 63 and n.302). Cultivated and gathered crops would have included vegetables, wild greens, mushrooms, and bulbs.[32] Leontius of Neapolis identifies legumes as a favorite of the holy man Symeon (Krueger 1996: 96-99). Locally grown flax and perhaps cotton were spun and dyed for clothing.[33] Most agricultural by-products would have found ready use in house or stable (Foxhall 1998).

Such crops as wheat, legumes, and flax leave scant trace in the archaeological record. All were grown on an annual basis with minimal equipment that left little environmental impact. Threshing surfaces (*alonia*) are difficult to detect in the field; in more recent times, communally-owned or shared threshing surfaces were located around the village periphery.[34] Amphoras may have been used on occasion to measure, store, and transport grain, but non-ceramic containers were more suitable.[35] It is unlikely that many amphoras were re-used for this purpose. Some degree of recycling is possible in remote locations without access to good clays and large kilns, but few amphoras are known to have been used for secondary commercial transport.[36]

Copper was another important product of the Vasilikos area. The mines near *Petra* and *Spilios*, c.4 km above Kopetra and 8 km from the sea, were worked from at least the Late Bronze Age. Visible remains include some of the largest slag heaps (*skouries*) on the island, with an estimated mass of over 700 tons of slag. Radiocarbon-dated charcoal and pottery found near these slag heaps indicate that some level of extraction and refining was underway in Classical, Hellenistic, and Late Roman times.[37] The scale of Cypriot copper-production in late antiquity is unclear — certainly Spanish, Balkan, and Anatolian mines were better known to contemporary writers.[38] The contribution of the island to the late empire's copper supply nevertheless may be greater than is often recognized. Small-scale mining and smelting operations are known to have functioned at various sites in the west, especially around Soloi and Arsinoë (Polis) on Khrysokhou Bay.[39] Recent work by the Sydney Cyprus Survey Project (SCSP) has called attention to a number of Late Roman activity areas scattered among the N slopes

28 Teall 1959: 97-102, 135-37; Durliat 1990: 271-75; Kingsley and Decker 2001b: 5-9.

29 Ibn Hauqal in Kramers and Wiet 1964: 199; Malamut 1988: 396 and 411.

30 Dawkins 1932: 2-5, 622-25; Thirgood 1987: 59.

31 Savile 1878: 99-102; Richard 1977: 337-38 and 346; Aristidou 1995: 267; Arbel 1996: 185-86; Martin 1998; Given 2000: 213.

32 Foxhall and Forbes 1982; Richard 1977: 331-32; Sarpaki 1992: 70-73

33 Savile 1878: 102-4; Christodoulou 1959: 136-39 and 142-44; Jones 1964: 836 and 849; Rautman 2001b: 258 n.20.

34 White 1970: 173-89; Aurenche *et al.* 1993: 216; Whittaker 1999.

35 Rickman 1980: 120-22; cf. Hautumm 1981: 106-8; Bass 1982: 164-65; Rossiter and Freed 1991: 173; Reynolds 1995: 108.

36 Parker 1990: 343-45; id. 1992b: 93-95; van Alfen 1996: 202-3 and 209.

37 Bear 1963: 60-64; Pantazis 1967; Koucky and Steinberg 1982a; iid. 1982b: 128-29; Muhly 1996; Stos-Gale *et al.* 1998: 252, Tables 3 and 5.

38 Edmondson 1989; for insular production during the Roman period and later, Wallace and Orphanides 1990; Michaelides 1996; 144; Raptou 1996: 252-54; Kassianidou 2000.

39 Pliny, *NH* 34.2.20-22; Raber 1987: 305-6; Stos-Gale *et al.* 1998: Tables 1 and 4.

(Larnaca axis region) of the Troodos mountains, where a major portion of surface slag, with its distinctively high levels of manganese, appears to be of Roman or later date.[40] Numerous mines are known above Amathus in the vicinity of Armenochori, Yerasa, and Parekklishia, not far from *Petra* and *Spilios*.[41] The export potential of this region is clearly illustrated by the proximity of mines to coastal facilities for shipping; indeed, the close relationship is unmatched elsewhere on the island (compare maps in Leonard 1995b: fig. 11 and Stos-Gale *et al.* 1998: fig. 2). The wide distribution and small scale of many of these mining and smelting operations suggest the increasingly important rôle of local landowners and entrepreneurs in Late Roman copper-production (Matschke 2002: 117). Some quantity of bronze coinage in fact was struck briefly on Cyprus at Salamis-Constantia under Phocas (608-10) and Heraclius (615-18 and 626/27).[42] As was the case with cereals and other non-liquid foodstuffs, processed copper ore from these mines would usually have been transported in bags or baskets.[43]

Local outcrops of gypsum were quarried in late antiquity for local use and perhaps wider distribution. As a building material, gypsum was cheap and available across much of the island, and probably no less often employed than in recent village construction.[44] Fine-grained gypsum was burned and crushed before being used as structural cement or decorative plaster (above, p. 46). Coastal deposits of high quality gypsum like those in the Vasilikos valley would have offered attractive sources for large-scale exploitation. Bags containing gypsum in its relatively lightweight, powdered form could easily have been carted down the valley road to ships anchored offshore near *Petrini*. Ongoing production of gypsum near Kopetra today suggests that its export in antiquity may also have been economically viable (below, Appendix 6).

Kopetra and other contemporary villages no doubt supported small-scale manufacturing as well (cf. Ionas 1993-94: 433-36). Large storage jars and coarse-fabric Corinthian-style rooftiles were made from local clays. Heavy *pithos* sherds appear across the valley as well as in Late Roman levels at Kopetra. The variety of ornamental patterns on the collars and rims of these simple, handmade jars suggests they were shaped by many hands and open-fired at various locales over several generations (Devos *et al.* 1999: 87-91; Ionas 2002). Handmade cooking wares from 7th-c. contexts at Kopetra and elsewhere in the valley attest another dimension of local production, probably carried out at the neighborhood or even household level. The manufacture of handmade pottery was one of the few options available to rural families seeking to mitigate their exposure to agricultural risk occasioned by uncertainties of environment or market, and in this light the potter appears as "the most necessary craftsman of the countryside".[45] As in traditional Cypriot society, women in late antiquity probably played a prominent rôle in such domestic activities.[46] The production of a nearly infinite range of household crafts, ranging from farm tools and domestic implements to family clothing and children's toys — the realia of daily lives — can be assumed despite their scarcity in the material record.

The busy Cypriot countryside: a synthesis of recent work

Roman Cyprus was best known to classical authors as a passive landscape regarded for its mineral resources and agricultural bounty. Strabo (*Geog.* 14.6.5) characterizes the province as 'not inferior in fertility to any of the islands, for it produces both good wine and good oil, and also enough grain for its own use', as well as copper and silver from its well-known mines. Ammianus Marcellinus (14.8.14) speaks of Cyprus as so fertile and bountiful that it possessed

---

40 Koucky and Steinberg 1982a, 1982b: 129; Knapp *et al.* 1994; Knapp 1997: 43; Stos-Gale *et al.* 1998: 257, fig. 2.

41 Ovid, *Met.* 10.220-502; Petit *et al.* 1996: 178-79, plan 20; Stos-Gale *et al.* 1998: fig. 2, Table 3.

42 Grierson 1968: 209 and 327-30; Hendy 1985: 415-17.

43 For preserved Cypriot examples, Bruce 1937: 659 and 662, figs. 360 and 363-64.

44 Bear 1963: 146-47, fig. 6; Wright 1992: 392-96.

45 Gallant 1991: 12-13; Rautman 1998: 97; Vroom 2000: 255, quoting the 10th-c. *Geoponika* 85.20.

46 Johnston 1974: 138; Vincentelli 2000: 135-37.

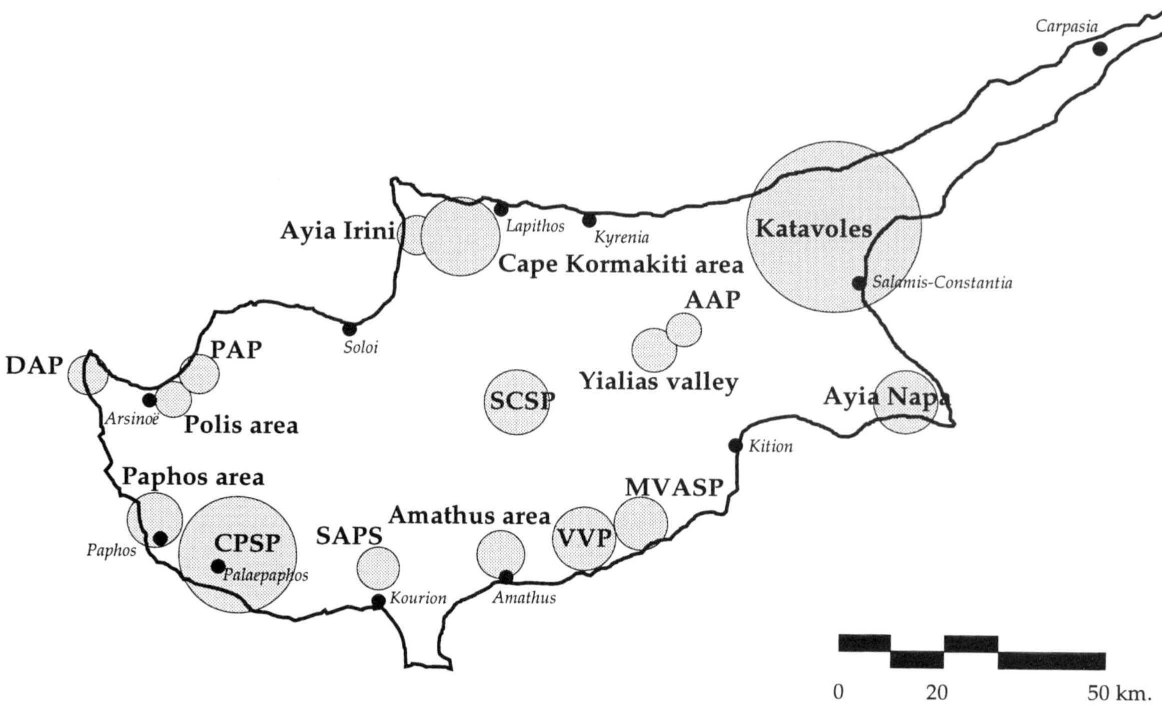

Fig. 7.6. Late Roman Cyprus with major cities and archaeological survey regions.

all the resources needed to build and equip transport ships. Timber from the mountains was readily available for fuel, architecture, and ship building as well as for shoring mineshafts.[47] From at least the 1st c., grain, oil, and wine were regarded as the island's most important agricultural products; they were distributed as far as Rome under the early empire and in later antiquity reached Constantinople (Pliny, *NH* 18.12.67-68; Hendy 1985: 562). Other products included almonds, figs, and various fruits, while many local plants and minerals were credited with healthful and medicinal properties.[48] Cyprus continued to play an important economic rôle in the late empire, with John Lydus (*de Mag.* 2.29) including the island among the most prosperous of 6th-c. provinces (Papacostas 2001).

Available evidence from the Vasilikos valley generally agrees with these perceptions of the Cypriot *chora*, but how representative is this of other parts of the island? The Kyrenia and Troodos mountains dominate the island's complex geography and shape a number of distinct valley systems (fig. 3.75). The jagged Kyrenia range extends along the N coast, separating it from the broad Mesaoria plain that crosses the island's interior. In the west, the forest-covered slopes of the Troodos define a radiating series of valleys, with steep foothills reaching to the shore and a broad plain stretching along the S coast. As a result, sharp physical and historical contrasts exist between inland and coast, mountains and plain, which are only accentuated by the insular setting.[49] Archaeological work carried out in different areas has identified points of both constancy and variability within the landscape, and provides a broad framework for understanding the early history of the Vasilikos region (fig. 7.6).

Much of the long N coast, that fertile strip lying in the shadow of the Kyrenia mountains, is known to have been extensively occupied in early Roman times and again during late antiquity. Reconnaissance in the 1950s by the Archaeological Survey office identified an "almost unbroken succession of settlement remains" of the period extending from Cape Kormakiti east to

---

47 Bruce 1937: 650-62; Christodoulou 1959: 50-51; Thirgood 1987: 70-72; Raptou 1996: 254-56; Burnet 1997.

48 For an overview Michaelides 1996: 144-46; additional sources in Wallace and Orphanides 1990; Roberts 2000.

49 Christodoulou 1959: 7-18; Malamut 1988: 26-31; Alcock 1993b: 168-69; Held 1993; Patton 1996: 1-34.

Cape Andreas (Megaw 1955: 41; id. 1957: 43; id. 1958: 25). The W part of this rugged coastland, including the Myrtou plain west of Lapithos, has been briefly reported.[50] The large number of small activity areas includes farmsteads (several with remains of olive-pressing equipment), hamlets, and villages stretching along the narrow coastal plain. Many of these sites were identified by the presence of building stones and rooftiles and were dated by surface pottery. Small churches were noted at some of the larger sites, although none of these was characterized as constituting more than a substantial village. Several caves in the Kyrenia foothills were found to be occupied at this time and salvage excavations at Dhiorios-*Mersineri* identified a sizeable pottery workshop. The manufacture of a limited series of cooking pots here and at nearby *Ianou* and *Mahainia* suggests the existence of a well-developed distribution network for local products. Trial excavation at Kormakiti-*Panayia* noted a small settlement that may have been occupied into the 8th c. (Megaw 1958: 30 and 34; Catling 1972: 79). The area's greatest prosperity, originally assigned to the 7th and 8th c., can now be placed in the years leading up to 650.[51] Not all of this part of Cyprus was occupied with uniform intensity, however. Settlement of the rocky coastland S of Cape Kormakiti apparently contracted with the abandonment of Melabron (Paleokastro) in the 2nd c. (Quilici Gigli 1971; Quilici 1985; id. 1989). Survey along the E part of the N coast, near Phlamoudhi, similarly located the peak of local settlement in the Hellenistic and Roman periods, with "times of difficulty" ensuing during the Late Roman and early Byzantine periods (Symeonoglou 1972: 196; Catling 1973).

Extensive fieldwalking of the eastern Kyrenia range and lower Mesaoria plain from Cape Andreas to Cape Greco has noted a similarly diffuse settlement-pattern. Reconnaissance in 1973-74 identified a total of 260 sites spread over an area of about 400 km^2 in the Famagusta district (Hadjisavvas 1991). Settlement apparently declined after the early Iron Age but expanded again from Hellenistic into Late Roman times. Many of the identified sites show a high degree of continuity through the 7th c. Two-thirds (41 of 62) of the Hellenistic sites continued to be occupied in the Roman period, and about half (32 of 63) of the Roman sites persisted into late antiquity, when nearby Salamis served as provincial capital. By contrast, the widespread displacement of population during the Dark Ages (7th to 9th c.) is apparent in the small number of Late Roman sites (6 of 60) reportedly occupied in Byzantine and mediaeval times. Many of the larger sites had small basilicas, some featuring mosaics and stone architectural elements. A similar distribution of sites extends into the Cape Greco region (Hadjisavvas 1983: 316-17; id. 1997).

The picture of rural settlement in W Cyprus appears broadly comparable, although the strikingly different topography introduces some important variations. Much of this area consists of narrow valleys shaped by the W- and S-facing slopes of the Troodos mountains. The dominant city from Hellenistic times was Paphos, which functioned as the island's capital and primary W port until devastated by earthquakes in the mid 4th c. Occupation of the city's immediate environs grew during the 1st and 2nd c. A.D., declined under the High Empire, and revived in the 5th and 6th c. (Rupp 1997). The Akamas peninsula west of Paphos saw similar growth around this time. A number of small sites, not closely dated but including tombs, farmsteads, and minor settlements, can be found scattered along the coastal plain north and west of the city.[52] Surveying an area of 15 km^2 on the western promontory, the Danish Akamas Project (DAP) observed that this rugged landscape's occupation contracted between the 2nd and 4th c. but rebounded during the 5th and early 6th c., reaching its peak about 550 (Fejfer 1995: 22-24 and 58-62, with reference to previous surveys). Farther north, reconnaissance around Arsinoë (Polis) on Khrysokhou Bay found that the number of activity areas, many of which showed signs of copper-working, may have reached its peak during the Hellenistic and early Roman

50 Catling and Dikigoropoulos 1970: 39-40, fig. 1; Catling 1972: 4-5 [quoted here], fig. 1; Stanley-Price 1979: 61-62, fig. 13; Şevketoğlu 2000.

51 Dikigoropoulos 1978: 6-9; cf. Hayes 1980b: 377; Megaw 1986: 505.

52 Hadjisavvas 1977: 225-27; Wallace 1984; Baird 1985: 346.

periods before dropping off sharply in the Middle Ages.[53] More recent work along the coastal plain to the north observed the steady presence of habitation in Roman times. Of the 40 settlement sites noted between 1992 and 1997 by the Polis-Pyrgos Archaeological Project (PAP), at least three were identified as Roman, 4 as Late Roman, and 5 as Byzantine or mediaeval in date.[54] Without exception, these were less than 1 ha in area. Many of the sites discovered in the region appear to be modest in size, measuring only 1-2 ha in area.[55] Recent excavations at Ayios Kononas provide a view of one small settlement located on a low plateau *c.*1.7 km from the shore. Identified buildings stretch 200 m along one side of a quarry, for a total inhabited area of *c.*1.5 ha. Several houses were occupied mostly during the later 5th and early 6th c., and a small basilica may have been built as late as 600. Preliminary assessment of coins and pottery suggests that the hamlet began to decline after 550 and was abandoned, along with other nearby settlements, during the 7th c.[56]

The Canadian Palaipaphos Survey Project (CPSP), which focused on a large coastal area east of Paphos, offers the most detailed available information for any Cypriot landscape (Rupp *et al.* 1984; Rupp 1986; Sørensen and Rupp 1993). A 635-km^2 area of the Ezousas, Xero Potamos, Dhiarizos, and Khapotami river-valleys was surveyed by random quadrant sampling in 1979-86. Surface pottery documents the tremendous growth of rural activity during the Hellenistic and early Roman periods, with almost 20% of all identified sites dating to this time (when Paphos rose to prominence), followed by an abrupt decline in the 2nd c. A.D. The area saw a significant revival in late antiquity (7-8% of all identified sites date to this period) but never attained the suburban density seen during the 1st c. A.D.[57] Most of these sites were identified as farmsteads smaller than 1.5 ha, with far fewer village-size settlements observed. The detailed publication of the CPSP pottery chronicles the occupation of this coastal landscape and offers a set of quantified data that can be compared with Kopetra. Figures 7.7 and 7.8 summarize the distribution of the main fine ware forms recovered by the two surveys (excavated finds are omitted in order to maintain sampling uniformity). In both cases Cypriot Red Slip is the most common fine ware, with form 9 making up over half of all classified sherds. The relatively later career of Kopetra is seen in the larger number of forms 8 and 11, compared with the greater popularity of forms 1 and 2 among the CPSP finds. Phocean Red Slip provides a complementary picture: the three variants of form 10 account for over half of the Kopetra examples, while the earlier forms 1, 2, and especially 3 are better represented in the CPSP area. The gradual decline that set in *c.*550 is seen most clearly in dwindling quantities of Phocean Red Slip, with the supply of Cypriot Red Slip trailing off in the later 7th c.[58] Considerable caution is needed in comparing data from a broad region with a single site, yet the general impression is that few places in the CPSP area were occupied as late as Kopetra.

Perhaps the most extensively scrutinized part of Cyprus is the S central coast, extending from Pissouri east to Cape Greco. Several projects have found that rural settlement expanded with the growth of Kourion, Amathus, and Kition during the Roman era. As noted for the Late Bronze Age, the importance and wealth of the area "was wholly disproportionate to its natural resources, and must have been largely due to its accessibility to the routes along which travelled the trade of the E Mediterranean and the Levant" (Catling 1962: 134). Survey of the immediate vicinity of Kourion observed a clear gap among the fine wares between the early Roman and late Roman centuries (Leonard 1987: 100-11). Recent sampling of the wider environs has placed the time of greatest rural activity in the Roman and especially Late Roman periods, with a small number of farmsteads (ranging from 0.03 to 0.064 ha in extent) emerging from

53 Adovasio *et al.* 1975: 349; Raber 1987: 305-6.

54 Maliszewski 1994, 1995, and 1999; although note that all the Late Roman sites were identified during inland survey in the most recent season.

55 E.g., Baird 1985: 346; Rupp 1986; id. 1997: 247-48, cf. 259 n.11.

56 Fejfer and Mathiesen 1992; Fejfer 1995: 73-86; Fejfer and Hayes 1995: 67-69.

57 Rupp 1986: 35-38, Table 1; Lund 1993: 135-43, figs. 54-55.

58 Cf. Rupp 1986: 38; Lund 1993: fig. 54.1-2.

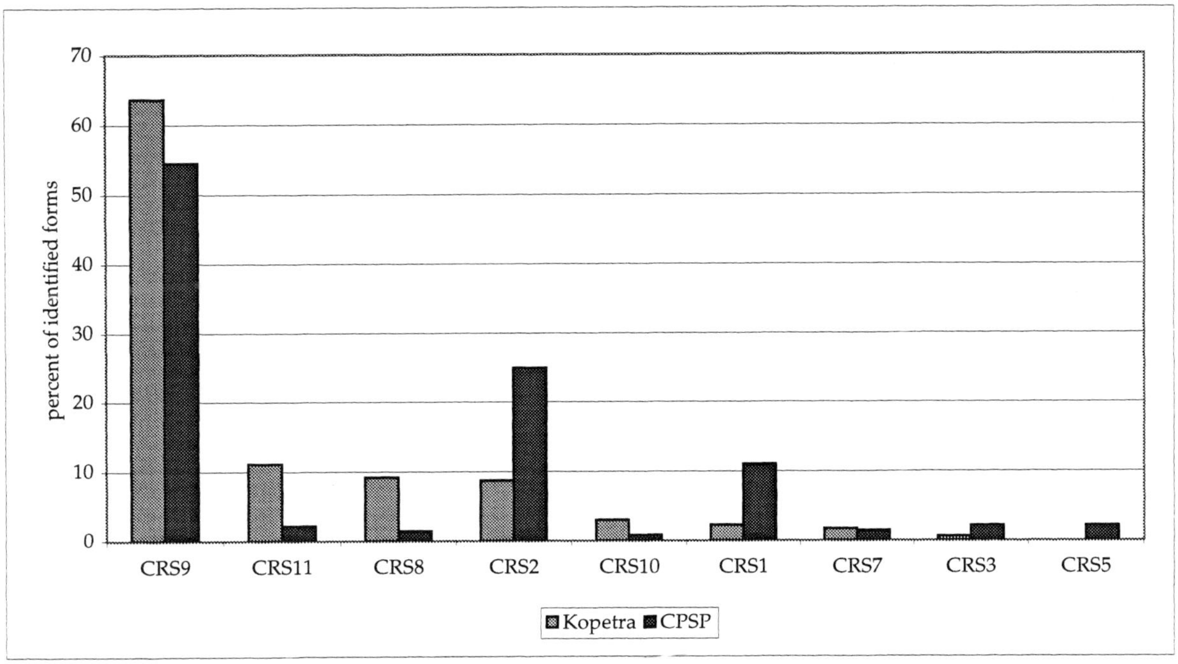

Fig. 7.7. Comparison of identified Cypriot Red Slip forms recovered by the Kopetra area survey (n=369) and the Canadian Palaipaphos Survey Project (n=145).

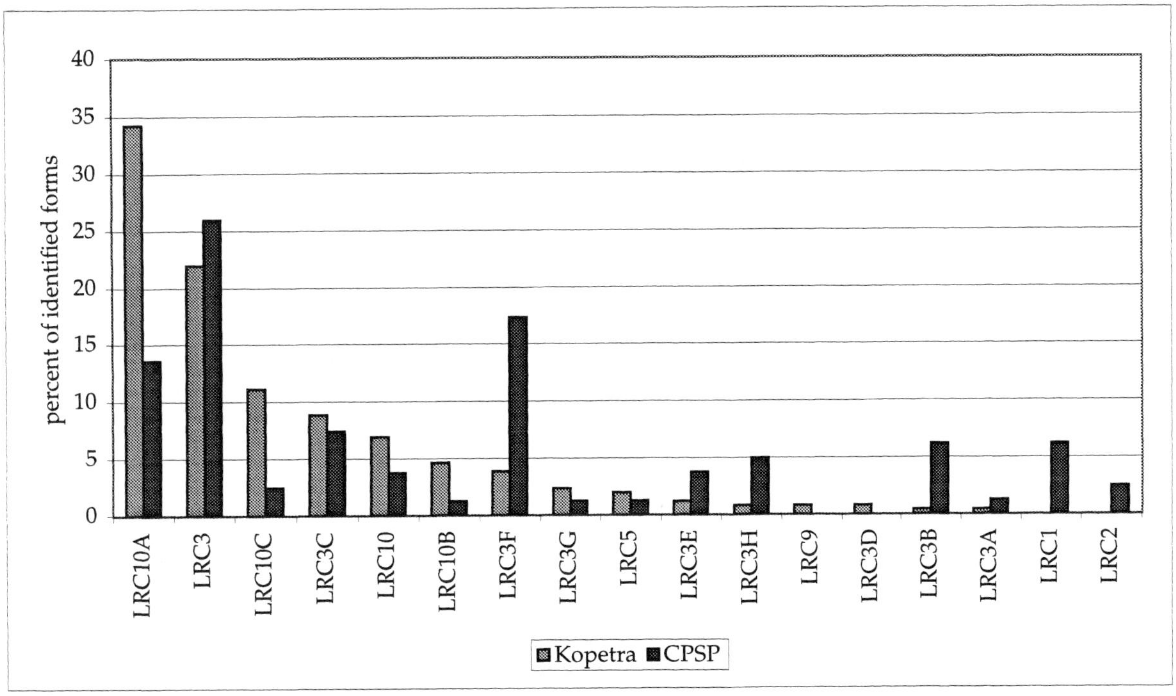

Fig. 7.8. Comparison of identified Phocean Red Slip forms recovered by the Kopetra area survey (n=260) and the Canadian Palaipaphos Survey Project (n=81).

a scattering of local Roman and post-Roman plain wares (Held 1988; Swiny and Mavromatis 2000). In the Amathus hinterland, immediately west of the Vasilikos valley, the École française d'Athènes has found that settlement fluctuated between dispersion and nucleation. Ten sites were dated to the early Iron Age, 5 or 6 Archaic and Classical sites are known, and at least 27 sites were occupied in Hellenistic times. The number of inhabited places fell sharply during the early empire with none assignable to the later 2nd and 3rd c.; but a general return to the countryside took place in the 5th to 7th c., when at least 28 sites were occupied (Petit *et al.* 1989; 1991; and 1996: 176-79, plan 20). Working just east of the Vasilikos valley, the Maroni

Valley Archaeological Survey Project (MVASP) has discovered a similar pattern of rural activity with a number of small sites scattered across the coastal plain. Excavation at one of these sites, Maroni-*Petrera,* located a small church complex with coins and pottery dating primarily to the late 6th and early 7th c. (Manning and Conwell 1992; Manning *et al.* 1994: 356-67; iid. 2002). A conjectural settlement around *Petrera,* which lies barely 2 km from the shore, would have offered a useful gathering-point for surrounding farmsteads and hamlets, perhaps similar to *Sokopra* in the Vasilikos valley. A sizeable contemporary site has been noted at Maroni-*Fouches,* which lies near the Ayios Minas river *c.*1 km to the south. A possible anchorage has been noted at nearby Maroni-*Vrysoudhia* (Manning *et al.* 2000: 253, fig. 1).

Inland Cyprus is a more variable environment that has received less attention. The Analiondas region of the Yalias valley, southeast of Nicosia, has seen a number of surveys as well as multiple excavations at the important Archaic city of Idalion.[59] This urban center dominated the valley during the early Iron Age. Little sign of Classical activity has been found locally, but rural population apparently expanded between the Hellenistic and late Roman periods. Twenty-two sites with 4 small basilicas have been dated to late antiquity. Few new settlements were set out in the Late Roman period and some may have been abandoned before the mid 7th c. The general impression of a modest level of activity contrasts markedly with the densely occupied N coast (Catling 1982: 233). Renewed occupation of several sites in the mediaeval period suggests that some might have been inhabited during the intervening Dark Ages as well.

Farther east, the Malloura valley near Athienou was no more extensively occupied in Roman times. Exploration by the Athienou Archaeological Project (AAP) has noted a small number of buildings, tombs, and minor activity areas in the area. The Archaic sanctuary at Athienou-*Malloura* continued to be used in the 1st c. A.D. but in late antiquity was superceded by a rural settlement. Excavation of several domestic buildings identified imported pottery and established that they were abandoned, perhaps following a fire, around the middle of the 7th c. (Toumazou *et al.* 1998: 175). The basilica at Athienou-*Yiorkous* dates to the same general period (Bakirtzis 1976). No evidence was found at *Malloura* for subsequent occupation until the mediaeval period.

The N-facing slopes of the Troodos mountains, southwest of Nicosia, have become the focus of renewed attention in recent years (Wallace 1982). The Sydney Cyprus Survey Project (SCSP) has sought to trace long-term activity patterns in the copper-rich region near Mitsero and Politiko. Systematic survey of a 65-km^2 area has identified a number of early historic sites across these slopes, which is characterized by the high presence of Late Roman pottery ("virtually omnipresent") from a variety of sites, including probable mining camps, agricultural hamlets, and villages.[60]

These multiple survey projects, conducted over the last 50 years and employing varied methods and goals, provide patchwork coverage of Cyprus and a cursory view of its settlement history. Inherent limitations of the available data should not be minimized.[61] Work has been carried out under a variety of circumstances, often necessitating rapid coverage of large areas by only a few people. Techniques have ranged from casual fieldwalking to quantified 'vacuum' samples along grids and transects. Tremendous methodological advances have been made since 1950 in geographic analysis, pottery study, and computer-based data processing. None of these projects can be said to be fully published and the records of the Cyprus Survey office in particular await systematic study. While all these circumstances urge caution in interpretation, the available evidence suggests that the island's rural settlement-pattern generally expanded in the late Hellenistic and early Roman periods and again during late antiquity. This

59 Megaw 1957: 43; Stanley-Price 1972; Walker and Bieber 1974; Catling 1982; Stager and Walker 1989.

60 Knapp *et al.* 1992 and 1994; Knapp 1997: 43; Stos-Gale *et al.* 1998: 237-42; Given *et al.* 1999 and 2002; Given and Knapp forthcoming.

61 Stanley-Price 1979: 54-58; Alcock 1993a: 49-53; Knapp 1997: 36-38; Bintliff 2000: 38-41; Şevketoğlu 2000: 23-24.

impression is not uniform: some parts of the island, especially isolated coastal areas in the far west and northeast as well as central inland regions, may not have seen significant growth in late Roman times. Limited natural resources, rugged topography, and difficult access are factors that would have hindered the development of urban as well as rural settlement in these areas, as they had during the Hellenistic period (Alcock 1993b: 168-69). Such exceptions underscore the sustained levels of increased activity apparent across much larger regions, however, from the long N and S shorelines to the wooded slopes of the Kyrenia and Troodos mountains.

Much of this rural expansion began in the later 5th c. Pottery from the CPSP in the southwest shows a steady increase during the 4th c., with the greatest activity occurring between 450 and 650 (Lund 1993: 139-40). Most finds from the Kopetra survey date to the same period (above, p. 28). In both cases this conclusion rests primarily on the fine wares, the ready identification of which extends this picture across the island. The foundation of churches offers another, more approximate guide to rural growth. Several basilicas were built during the 5th c., but many more are assignable to the later 5th and 6th c. (above, p. 147). The example of Kopetra suggests that many of these buildings attest not new but growing rural communities, the ongoing economic success of which made possible their construction. The widespread appearance of small churches reflects the rising importance of villages as centers of habitation and investment.

The prosperity of the Cypriot countryside resembles a broader picture of rural growth across the E Mediterranean. By the 6th c., a dense network of villages and market towns covered much of the countryside, stretching from the Near East to the Aegean and beyond (below, p. 256). In Cyprus, rural expansion apparently reflected a rising population, with cultivation pressing onto previously unworked lands and seemingly sustained by favorable climatic conditions. The arrival of relocated peoples may have contributed to this growth, with thousands of refugees fleeing the mainland in the late 6th and early 7th c. The emperor Maurice, for example, is said to have assigned dispersed Cypriot lands to a Monophysite community from Syria in 577. Other refugees were displaced to the island by the Persian advance across Syria and Egypt.[62] Significantly, this period of expansion in Cyprus coincided with environmental and demographic stress in other parts of the Roman world. Contemporary reports of climatic fluctuation and atmospheric epiphenomena have been speculatively linked with a variety of global-scale incidents, coinciding with (and possibly contributing to) repeated outbreaks of plague beginning in the 540s. First reported at Pelousion in Egypt in 542, the plague is well attested in Syria, Constantinople, and elsewhere during the following years, yet its extent and social consequences remain under discussion (for a recent summary, Morrisson and Sodini 2002: 193-95). It has yet to be demonstrated that any of these events seriously affected life in Cyprus before the 8th c. Unlike many parts of the late empire, much of the island's urban infrastructure was maintained through the 6th and early 7th c. The expansion of Kopetra and other rural settlements reinforces this picture of insular stability based on multiple factors, including the changing relationship of cities and countryside brought about by the late empire's increasing economic integration.

The variety of imported fine wares, amphoras, and rooftiles found in rural Cyprus attests a continuous network of commercial exchange, grounded primarily in farming, herding, and mining, that joined these small places with each other and the mainland. Quantitative pottery data from a number of different sites are needed to clarify the nature of this rural economy. Comparative study of the date, variety, and function of objects from second-tier habitation centers holds great potential for studying the inter-relationships of different regions. At this early stage it is uncertain whether contrasts among parts of the island are due to uneven data or reflect subtle but genuine variations of settlement and land-use. If available information cannot provide answers to such questions, it can at least show directions for future research.

---

62 Cameron 1992: 29-31; Krueger 1996: 11-12; Rautman 2001a: 314.

At present, the two most intensively examined parts of the Cypriot countryside are the SW and S central coastlands. The SW area encompasses the environs of Paphos stretching from the rocky Akamas peninsula to the hills above Palaipaphos. Ongoing publication of recent surveys by the CPSP and DAP provides a wealth of information about the early history of this area. The S central coastlands include the hinterlands of Amathus with the Vasilikos and Maroni valleys. Each of these neighboring valleys has been surveyed and discussed in detailed preliminary reports, which share broadly similar findings. In both cases the impression derived from surface survey is grounded in stratified excavations of local sites.

Survey information from the hinterland of Paphos demonstrates its primacy as a central place within its sub-regional setting. This commercial, political, and religious center clearly dominated W Cyprus in Roman times. Many small habitation sites have been identified outside the city but few of these are strongly differentiated hierarchically (Rupp 1997: 247-48). Most sites visited by the CPSP and DAP surveys appear to be farmsteads, hamlets, or agricultural villages with an area of 1-2 ha. The rural economy presumably aimed at self-sufficiency with any surplus directed to markets near Paphos. Activity apparently peaked around 550 and declined gradually during the later 6th and early 7th c.

The most important exception to this picture is the seaside town identified at Peyia-*Ayios Georgios* on Cape Drepanon, *c.*25 km west of Paphos. The settlement flourished primarily during the 500s and was at least partially inhabited until the mid 7th c. Several large buildings, including a bath complex and no fewer than three churches, were built around this time. One indication of the site's 6th-c. affluence is the extensive use of Proconnesian marble for building, decorating, and furnishing its churches, which constitute a unique group in Cypriot architecture (Megaw 1960; id. 1974: 71-72; Pallas 1977: 275-80). Survey of the surrounding countryside suggests that the settlement's sudden prosperity derived less from its agricultural hinterland than proximity to the sea. Ch. Bakirtzis (1995, 1997, and 2000) has proposed that the town's location at the SW point of Cyprus offered a key landmark for many of the ships plying the grain route from Egypt to the Aegean. In general, the Alexandrian sea-lane probably kept closer to the mainland and followed the coast of Cilicia and Lycia when heading west. Yet while the open-sea crossing from south to north may have been riskier at certain times of year, it also carried its own advantages, especially in the face of rising military instability along the coast. The return route from the Aegean past Rhodes and Cyprus on the way to Alexandria is better attested.[63] The particular importance of the Egyptian grain supply, and the need for its re-organization, is stressed by Justinian's legislation of the *annona civica* in the 530s. Specific arrangements remain unclear, but it seems likely that his measures introduced a greater degree of flexibility in managing regional traffic in order to adapt more readily to situational (economic, environmental, military, even religious) demands (Bowersock 2000: 18-19). The late and rapid growth of the Peyia settlement supports the idea that a greater part of this traffic now passed along the W and S coasts. The economic basis of Peyia's 6th-c. boom, as well as its demise in the 7th c., will ultimately be clarified by publication of its pottery.[64] Already it appears that some urban areas were abandoned before the site was destroyed *c.*650 (Christou 1997: 925-26; Hadjisavvas 1998: 697). To judge by the example of Ayios Kononas and other nearby places, Peyia's brief moment of prosperity had only limited effect on regional settlement.

The valleys of the S central coast, stretching east from Amathus toward Kition, differ in several important ways. The Pentakomo valley constitutes the immediate Amathusian hinterland, and the Vasilikos and Maroni valleys probably lay within that city's *territorium* as well (cf. Rupp 1997: fig. 3 for hypothetical settlement boundaries). A series of independent surveys has found that occupation of these neighboring valleys expanded rapidly between the

63 In general Teall 1959: 91-96; Rickman 1980: 128-32; Pryor 1988: 95-97; Hohlfelder 1995: 192; Murray 1995: 39; Sodini 2000: 195.

64 For examples of Cypriot Red Slip forms 10-12 from Peyia see Hayes 1972: 382-85.

5th and early 7th c. In the Vasilikos valley alone, over 40 Late Roman sites have been observed. The later phases of this rural prosperity appear most clearly at Kopetra, an otherwise unexceptional market village whose occupation peaked around 600 but remained strong until the mid 7th c.

More work is needed to verify the broad contrast between these different island regions, although it should be noted that this reconstruction emerges from no fewer than 6 separate surveys. Did a genuine difference exist between the economic régimes of the two areas? In many ways SW and S central Cyprus present very different environments. Rugged, sloping terrain characterizes much of the environs of Paphos. Cultivation of this rocky landscape probably was relatively specialized and marginally profitable, with any surplus directed to Paphos and Peyia. The two main regional settlements were ports whose economies may have depended largely on the traffic of goods between distant centers, such as Alexandria and Constantinople. This precarious arrangement appears especially vulnerable to instability along this primary sea-lane. By contrast, S central Cyprus depended less on a single path of external exchange. Communication was possible along the coastal highway and by the many small ships stopping at seaside anchorages as they sailed between Amathus, Kition, and Salamis, about a day's distance to the east.[65] All three ports would have provided markets for area products as well as access to wider exchange with the mainland. Local villages enjoyed a diversified production base founded on cereal farming and supplemented by olive cultivation and copper mining, yielding commodities that became increasingly scarce elsewhere during the early 7th c. The prosperity seen at Kopetra indicates the success with which one small community mediated this demand. In essence, the broad coastal plain and nearby hills — together with the cross-roads location — may have presented local residents with a more resilient resource base during times of economic transition.

Cyprus in the E Mediterranean

The web of cultural and economic relations that spanned Cyprus extended equally onto the mainland. The surrounding sea offered the island both security and hazard by simultaneously isolating it and providing access from its neighbors.[66] Its geographical centrality in the E Mediterranean had ensured the interest of competing regional powers since the Bronze Age, and much of Cypriot history reads as a palimpsest of external relations (Catling 1979). This insular reality is fundamental to understanding perceptions of Cyprus in late antiquity and the Middle Ages. Strabo's celebration of the new Roman province was reiterated by later authors like Eustathius of Thessaloniki, who calls Cypriots the most fortunate of islanders.[67] Other Byzantine writers took a harder look at this distant territory. Eutropius was banished briefly to the island by the emperor Arcadius.[68] Like many other islands, Cyprus could serve as a place of lonely exile. Theophanes (*Chron.* 445, in Mango and Scott 1997: 614) describes the removal of Thrakesian monks and nuns to the island in *c.* 770, and Constantine Manasses acutely felt his isolation here in the mid 12th c. (in Jenkins 1953: 1012; Pohlsander 1999: 128-29). Writing in the mid 11th c., Michael Psellus characterized Cyprus as neither populous nor fertile but oppressively hot.[69] More positive assessments come from Arab geographers and Lusignan and Venetian travelers.[70] The cumulative record offered by written sources and material remains

---

65 Cf. 15th- and 17th-c. sailing accounts in Cobham 1908: 52 and 77, and in general Martin 1998; for a map of likely anchorage sites see Leonard 1995b: fig. 11.

66 See variously Braudel 1972: 148-54; Kolodny 1973; Pryor 1988: 12-24; Held 1993; Broodbank 2000: 16-23; Horden and Purcell 2000: 224-30.

67 In Müller 1855: 245, 312-13; Malamut 1988: 36; Pohlsander 1999: 129-30.

68 Philostorgios, *Hist. eccl.* 11.8; Zosimos, *Hist. nova* 5.18.1-3; in Pohlsander 1999: 21, 44.

69 In Kurtz and Drexl 1941: 186; Malamut 1988: 30, 36-37 and 133; cf. Victorian attitudes in Demetriou 1997: 7-9; Martin 1998.

70 Al-Muqaddasi in Miquel 1963: 229; Ibn Hauqal in Kramers and Wiet 1964: 199; Richard 1977; Malamut 1988: 133-34; Gounaridis 1996; Gertwagen 1995; Roberts 2000.

illustrates Fernand Braudel's (1972: 149-51) observation that Mediterranean island societies lie open to the outer world while remaining closed upon themselves. The corollary of his "great insular contradiction" is that the network of Mediterranean commerce presents opportunities for both prosperity and disaster in those places where exchange is externally controlled and not designed for the benefit of the island.[71] This precarious insularity seems central to understanding the place of Cyprus in the late empire.

In many respects the occupation of rural Cyprus at this time resembles the mainland countryside, about which much more is known from written and archaeological evidence. Extensive surveys carried out across Cilicia, Syria, Palestine, and Egypt allow a detailed view of Roman-era habitation along the Mediterranean coast to the inland frontier.[72] A range of environmental factors and historical circumstances affects the decisions of people where to live and how to use the land, and the need to distinguish sub-regional developments precludes sweeping generalizations. While clearly distinct from Cyprus, this varied picture of the Near Eastern countryside provides essential background for understanding island villages like Kopetra.

One consistent feature is the expansion of rural settlement during the 5th and 6th c.[73] A vast network of farmsteads, villages, and towns grew up along the E Mediterranean shore and across the rugged inland plains. The remains of hundreds of such occupied sites survive in the N Syrian countryside around Antioch, Apamea, and Boroea, while farther south similar, less well-preserved settlements have been noted near Bostra in the Hauran and among the neighboring cities of the Decapolis. The majority were minor agricultural communities populated by farmers who apparently maintained themselves while provisioning nearby cities. A typical site might include 40-50 houses with about 100 rooms and as many as 5 agricultural presses.[74] The growing number, variety, and size of such places, even while many urban centers began to stagnate or decline, reflect the increasing autonomy of rural settlements across the late empire.

Various levels have been distinguished within the spectrum of mainland habitation, ranging from cities to isolated farmsteads and seasonal encampments. Settlement hierarchies, it should be noted, are relative yet abstract geographic constructs whose boundaries are both time-bound and dynamic. Late Roman documents do not consistently differentiate the physical features and social functions of kinds of settlements, which varied over time and by region. Cities (*poleis* or *civitae*) and towns (*vici*) occupy the upper levels of such hierarchies and usually can be identified by their specialized administrative and juridical functions and episcopal status, as well as their complex architectural form.[75] Farmsteads, either in isolation or gathered in small hamlets, are implied but neglected both in written sources and on the ground. Villages (*komai*, later *choria* with added fiscal connotations) occupy the intermediate range of settlement and perhaps were home to the largest number of rural inhabitants.[76] Late Roman authors mention upon occasion larger or extended villages (*komopoleis*, *metrokomiai*, or *komai megalai* in Libanius, *'ayarot* in the Rabbinic sources) on the basis of size and specialized economic functions. Such large villages could include 1000-3000 inhabitants covering an area up to 10-15 ha; baths and other public buildings might be built emulating the traditions of urban euergetism. The accumulation of multiple churches at Khirbat al-Samra (8), Umm el-Jimal (8),

---

71 Kolodny 1973: 19-25 and 127-37; Malamut 1988: 133-34; Horden and Purcell 2000: 229-30.

72 E.g., Tchalenko 1953-58; Villeneuve 1985; Tate 1992; Cameron 1993: 177-80; MacAdam 1994; Schick 1994; Tsafrir 1996; Walmsley 1996; Foss 1997; Dauphin 1998; Blanton 2000; Graf 2001.

73 In general, Lemerle 1979: 1-26; Kaplan 1992: 89-134; Lefort 1993: 104-5; Morrisson and Sodini 2002: 177-84.

74 Tate 1992: 206-20 and 264; Decker 2001: 81.

75 Whittaker 1990; Keay 1994; Christie and Loseby 1996; Haldon 1997: 99-102; id. 1999; Ward-Perkins 1996: 4-6; Brandes 1999.

76 In general Patlagean 1977: 236-45; Kaplan 1992: 89-104; Haldon 1997: 132-41; for the E Mediterranean mainland Dagron 1979; Villeneuve 1985: 75-89; Dauphin 1987; Gatier 1994: 26; Hirschfeld 1997; Graf 2001.

and Rihab (9) in Arabia, and Burdg Heidar (6) in Syria reflects the growth of these villages over time. Such settlements could on occasion even develop into towns, from which they can be hard to distinguish (e.g., Umm el-Jimal; de Vries 1998); indeed, the total area of some large villages approaches the extent of small cities. Run-of-the-mill villages (*komai* or *kfar*) were smaller settlements without specialized quarters or shops. Rabbinic sources sensibly recommend that villages be situated near a principle road and a water source with a wide view for defense. Excavated settlements in Galilee and the Golan feature close-built houses turned inward and forming a continuous exterior wall around the village. In most cases there were no specialized public buildings apart from one or more churches and a synagogue. Ovens and presses occupied residential courtyards, which often stabled animals as well. Certain activities (e.g., the tanning of hides) as well as burial were set well apart from the inhabited area (Dauphin 1987; Gatier 1994: 37-40).

Contemporary authors, never particularly generous when dealing with rural matters, were hard pressed to keep up with the proliferation of inhabited sites across the countryside. This expansion was apparent not only in the number of rural places but also in their social complexity and financial organization. The uncertainty of sources reflects the increasingly important rôle played by villages. Municipal *curiales* watched their control over urban affairs and fiscal matters dwindle at the same time that they were losing authority over their wider urban territories. Country markets operated as loci of rural exchange increasingly apart from the cities.[77] The growing independence of many villages, seen in the rise of councils that were responsible collectively for tax revenues, gradually became codified in law.[78] At the same time, the Church acquired greater authority in the *chora*. A bishop's domain transcended conventional civic boundaries to encompass all manner of habitation within the limits of an episcopal see. The presence in even the smaller villages of a church — much less two or more — implies an administrative and economic presence with clergy actively participating in local affairs.[79]

Much of the written evidence for understanding this transformation of rural society pertains to Asia Minor, with additional information coming from Syria, Palestine, and Egypt, yet the broader trends apply equally to Cyprus. Surveys and excavations demonstrate that the insular countryside became increasingly active between the 5th and 7th c. The distribution of villages and farmsteads within individual valleys suggests agricultural régimes that focused primarily on raising subsistence crops for local consumption.[80] Fortunate years produced surpluses, especially in cereals and olives, which were supplemented to some extent by the production of copper, pottery, and other manufactured goods. This productivity generated sufficient income to support a growing number of specialized market towns and an island-wide program of church building. Nowhere does the successful exploitation of this provincial landscape appear more clearly than at Kopetra.

Two inescapable factors conditioned rural settlement in Cyprus. The province stood physically apart from the mainland. Contact with the wider Roman world was necessarily by water, which varied with season and weather. The island's separation was more than geographic; it was underscored by its ecclesiastical independence from the late 5th c. and by its administrative status, re-assigned from Antioch to the *quaestura Justiniani exercitus* in 536 (Lokin 1986: 7; Chrysos 1993: 3-7). Its large area notwithstanding, Cyprus remained an island and its population developed a high level of self-sufficiency. In architecture this appears in the evolution of a distinctive approach to building and decoration based on locally available materials (i.e.,

77 Cf. Libanius, *Or.* 11.230; in MacMullen 1970: 335; Morrisson and Sodini 2002: 179-80.

78 Lemerle 1979: 27-67; Haldon 1997: 132-41.

79 Kaplan 1992: 202 and 230.

80 Cf. for Syria Villeneuve 1985: 121-25; Tate 1992: 243-47; for Cilicia Blanton 2000; for Crete Raab 2001: 31-44; and, for traditional rural economies in Cyprus, Aurenche *et al.* 1993: 215-25; Ionas 1993-94; Grivaud 1996.

little marble but plentiful gypsum). At least two independent rooftile traditions emerged at opposite ends of the island. The appearance of an indigenous fine pottery industry in W Cyprus met the growing demand for high-quality household goods among prospering rural residents and eventually took over the local market.

Located at the hub of the E Mediterranean, within a few hours of the shore stretching from Cilicia to Egypt, Cyprus also was uniquely linked with the mainland. Most city-dwellers lived along the coast, whose several good ports and many more serviceable anchorages provided ready contact with other parts of the island. The two-week walk along its length could be accomplished by boat in little over a day.[81] Since sea-travel was the most economical and safest mode of transport, Cyprus became closely integrated into the vast exchange-networks of the late empire. The circulation of pottery preserves the main paths of activity (above, fig. 5.22). The most important was along the Egyptian grain route, which brought fine pottery and amphoras from N Africa and the Aegean, while carrying Cypriot table wares and amphoras to Egypt and the west. Most traffic from Cilicia, Syria, and Palestine was agricultural in nature, involving primarily oil and wine, while Cypriot fine wares and amphoras followed the short return routes. The scale and organization of this activity remain unclear. While officially sponsored long-distance exchange may be the easiest to gauge, this would have rested on a broader foundation of intense economic activity among intermediate settlements and regions, which took the form of inter-valley cabotage.[82] Sub-regional dynamism encouraged specialization: wine, fine pottery, and perhaps copper were among the main products of W Cyprus, while cereals and olives probably dominated the Mesaoria and coastal valleys in the east. Distinctive kinds of rooftiles, amphoras, and cooking pottery were made at opposite ends of the island as well as at a few places in between. From this perspective the prosperity of the S coastal valleys, founded on a combination of cultivation, herding, and mining, reflects the resilience of a generous resource base and ready access to multiple markets.

Yet, on a pragmatic level, most Cypriots were members of an E Mediterranean *koine* whose daily routines differed little from their mainland counterparts. These were primarily farmers, free or tenant laborers who lived in small villages within 2-3 km of their scattered fields.[83] They cultivated gardens and fields to meet household needs while hoping for a modest surplus to pay taxes and acquire domestic goods. Families kept small flocks of sheep and goats to graze fallow and cropped fields in the lower plains, and spent summers in the cool upper valleys. Most goods were exchanged, probably through barter or similar means, in local markets and seasonal fairs. The sea, omnipresent yet remote, could be ignored by most villagers; few would have traveled by water as far as the nearest city, much less made the journey to the mainland. Still in the early 20th c. it was held that on Cyprus "most people died without having ever set eyes on the sea".[84] This degree of self-sufficiency adds another dimension to the view of Strabo, Ammianus, and others that the island offered enough resources to meet the needs of its inhabitants, who then re-created the social structures of the outside world. As on the mainland, most Cypriots in late antiquity pursued the possibilities and limitations of life within the valley of their birth.

The 'Dark Ages' on a sunny island

The 7th c. marks an important transition in the history of Cyprus. Many parts of the island experienced sustained demographic and economic growth through the early 600s, despite the

81 Although the length of the trek appears overstated by Arab geographers like al-Muqaddasi in Miquel 1963: 229, and Edrisi in Jaubert 1836-40: 128; cf. sailing accounts in Cobham 1908: 52 and 77.

82 Ahrweiler 1974; Horden and Purcell 2000: 150-52; Sodini 2000: 195-96; Ward-Perkins 2001: 169-74.

83 For rural commuting distances in prehistoric and Ottoman times see Wagstaff 1988: 66-67; Given 2000: 215.

84 Christodoulou 1959: 62 [quoted here]; Malamut 1988: 383-85; and similar anecdotes cited by P. P. Hayes and O. Thomsen in Fejfer 1995: 52; Karageorghis 1999: 12.

earlier environmental disruptions, outbreaks of plague, and social unrest reported elsewhere in the Mediterranean. Writing in the 640s, Leontius of Neapolis set his Life of Symeon the Fool against a background of urban well-being, with little sense of decline or nostalgia for a lost past (Krueger 1996: 9-10). Excavations in the coastal cities have documented the bustle of metropolitan life, with public building projects underway at Amathus and Salamis. Much of the countryside was widely and more or less intensively occupied, with a growing number of habitation sites like Kopetra providing detailed evidence of rural prosperity. Urban and rural, coastal and inland, almost all of these places were touched by events that took place during the 7th c., of which the most consequential were the Persian invasions and Arab conquest of Syria, Palestine, and Egypt, followed by attacks on Cyprus itself beginning in 649. Over the span of two or three generations, the island's political status shifted from a prosperous Late Roman province to an unstable frontier territory, balanced uneasily between Constantinople and Damascus.[85] Military campaigns, shifting economic patterns, and other circumstances seriously affected settlement-patterns and quality of life. By century's end, most coastal cities had been dramatically reduced in scale, their buildings damaged by earthquake, war, or neglect, and their populations scattered. Many villages and farmsteads across the island apparently were abandoned in favor of more ephemeral inland encampments (Catling 1962: 146; id. 1972: 4-5; Papageorghiou 1993). Despite the modern tendency to overdraw the contrast, there is little doubt that for many Cypriots life changed a great deal between the relative stability of late antiquity and the poorly documented centuries that followed.

Military conflict was the most obvious aspect of the period, with the Persian campaigns on the mainland followed by the wider conquests of the Arabs. These two conflicts had profoundly different implications for Cyprus. Persia opened its assault on Rome's eastern frontier in 603, arriving in Damascus in 613 and in Jerusalem the next year. In 619 the Persians captured Alexandria and by 620 controlled Egypt.[86] It has been suggested that the invaders may have reached Cyprus itself, although any such attack went unremarked by contemporary chroniclers and left little lasting effect. Even if the Persians did not actually land on the island, the perceived threat and wider consequences of their campaigns directly touched its inhabitants.[87]

It has been insufficiently remarked that this clash, "the last world war of antiquity," may have benefited the island in a tangible way. The key position Cyprus occupied in the E Mediterranean was obvious. Its apparent security, surrounded by water, attracted a considerable if uncertain number of refugees from the mainland in the late 6th and early 7th c.[88] Located only 100 km from the Syro-Palestinian shore, the island also offered Heraclius a strategic outpost for his campaign of reconquest on the mainland. The defenses of several port cities were renewed around this time. The Crusader castle at Kyrenia incorporates the remains of an earlier fortress perhaps built under Heraclius.[89] Traces of a defense wall about the harbor district of Paphos apparently date to the years just before the Arab campaigns.[90] At Amathus a late gate in the acropolis walls was reinforced and a lime kiln built nearby, probably in connection with other repairs in the area.[91] A long aqueduct was erected to supply Salamis in the 620s and a hastily built fortification with cistern surrounded a neighborhood near the church of Ayios Epiphanios.[92] Such projects of military necessity suggest that from a strategic standpoint Cyprus may never have been as vital to Constantinople as in the early 600s.

---

85 In general Dikigoropoulos 1940-48; Papageorghiou 1964; Browning 1977-79; Kyrris 1984 and 1994-98; Megaw 1986; Cameron 1992; Papadopoulos 1993.

86 Recent overviews in Whittow 1996: 69-82; Haldon 1997: 41-48; Kaegi 1998.

87 Foss 1975: 724; Chrysos 1984; id. 1993: 12-13; cf. Sodini 1998: 632; Bowersock 2000: 20.

88 Mango 1976: 4; Cameron 1992: 28-31; Krueger 1996: 11-12.

89 Megaw 1952: 116-17; id. 1985a: 214; id. 1986: 513, fig. 10.

90 Kyrris 1984: 157-58; Megaw 1986: 514-16 fig. 11; id. 1988: 143-45.

91 Megaw 1985a: 201-3; 1986: 509; P. Aupert and P. Leriche in Aupert 1996: 150.

92 Megaw 1985a: 201; id. 1986: 508 fig. 3; for the date, Callot 1985: 335-39; Sodini 1998: 622 and 633.

The island's importance at this time was cultural as well as military. The independence of the Church of Cyprus, recognized by the emperor Zeno in the late 5th c., effectively distanced the island from the growing Monophysite community in Cyprus.[93] This orthodox autonomy helped attract notable religious leaders to the island, especially following the capture of the patriarchal sees of Antioch, Jerusalem, and Alexandria. Sophronios (later patriarch of Jerusalem), John Moschus, Maximus the Confessor, and others are known to have visited in the early 7th c. Senior clerics like John the Almsgiver, Patriarch of Alexandria from 610 and author of a panegyric in honor of St. Tychon, returned to his native island following the Persian victories of 619. Monks, hermits, stylites, and other ascetics from Palestine and Egypt sought refuge here. Beginning amid these troubled times, the writings of John the Almsgiver and Leontius of Neapolis herald the golden age of Cypriot hagiography.[94]

The Persian campaigns also had important economic consequences. The path of conquest cut off the late empire from several of its key agricultural resources, especially N Syria, an important producer of olive oil, and the breadbasket of Egypt. Regional supplies of wine and cotton were interrupted as well. These circumstances would only have increased the Roman market for Cypriot products. Since 536 the island's surplus had been attached to the *quaestura Justiniani exercitus*, based perhaps for a time in Samos but ultimately stationed in Constantinople, in order to provision directly troops stationed along the N Balkan frontier.[95] Wheat and oil presumably were among the main westward exports at this time. Few texts specify how the army or capital was supplied, but the fluid circumstances must have necessitated varied *ad hoc* measures.[96] With the heightened military presence in the E Mediterranean, most Cypriot exports would have been redirected to troops stationed in Cilicia and in Cyprus itself as they prepared for their mainland campaigns. Rural products probably entered these paths of State distribution by a combination of official expropriation and market purchase. Both mechanisms provided incentive to extend cultivation onto suitable lands across much of the island, especially in the eastern and S central valleys.

Heraclius' efforts against the Persians won only short-lived success that fell before the Arab sweep across Syria, Palestine, and Egypt in the 630s. Conflicting Roman and Arab accounts permit no clear understanding of the mainland campaigns, and the situation in Cyprus is especially problematic.[97] In 649 Mu'awiya, the emir of Syria, launched the first attack on Cyprus and sacked Salamis-Constantia, Soloi, and other places across 'the whole island'.[98] Either the next year (*to epelthonti chrono*) or shortly afterwards, the Arabs returned under Abul 'l-Awar to besiege Paphos, Lapithos, Carpasia, and Salamis.[99] Tens of thousands of Cypriots are said to have been taken as prisoners to the mainland. A military garrison was established at or near Paphos. Subsequent generations, among the least well known in the island's history, were governed by a treaty of neutrality or dual allegiance to Constantinople and Damascus.

These events resulted in a fundamental reconfiguration of the E Mediterranean frontier and the place of Cyprus as a province of the late empire. Following the loss of Arados (Arwad) in 650, Constantinople effectively abandoned the region in order to concentrate its defenses in the

93 Hackett 1901: 23-26; Hill 1940: 276-78; Bowersock 2000: 17-18.

94 Hackett 1901; Catling and Dikigoroupolis 1970: 59-60; Krueger 1996: 11-18; Falkenhausen 1999: 22-31.

95 Hill 1940: 258-59; Chrysos 1993: 3-7; van Alfen 1996: 211; for the supply of LR1 and LR2 amphoras to the region see now Curta 2001: 208-10; Karagiorgou 2001: 154-55.

96 Lopez 1959; Teall 1959: 135-37; Hendy 1985: 619-26; Sirks 1991: 21-22.

97 In general Kaegi 1992; Cameron and Conrad 1992; Whittow 1996: 82-89; Howard-Johnston 1999; for Cyprus, Hill 1940: 326-29; Browning 1977-79; Kyrris 1984; Cameron 1992.

98 Theophanes, *Chron.* 344, in Mango and Scott 1997: 478; Pohlsander 1999: 75.

99 Hill 1940: 285-86; de Groot 1980: 302; Kyrris 1984: 154-57; des Gagniers and Tran Tam Tinh 1985: 115-25; Bowersock 2000: 21-23; cf. for the date Feissel 1987: 380-81, although not all agree that the second attack followed so soon; see Kyrris 1994-98: 185-89, 196-97 n.1.

Aegean (Cameron 1992: 41-42; Conrad 1992). Whether the Arab raids on Cyprus should be considered a symptom or cause of Roman weakness is less clear than the result: the island was reduced from a strategic military and economic outpost to the abbreviated terminus of an obsolete trade route. Its unique neutrality carried with it a dual tax burden, which would have cut by at least half the available exports for Constantinople (leaving more than 7,000 gold pieces owed both powers; Theophanes, *Chron.* 363, in Mango and Scott 1997: 506). The demise of grain route and military corridor would have left the island without easy access to ships sailing to and from the Aegean. Travel to the mainland still took place and Cyprus remained a stop for pilgrims bound for Palestine, but its economic integration into the late empire clearly was reduced.[100] Arab merchants who were active on the island may not have ventured much beyond the major ports.[101]

These conflicting written accounts are complemented by a meager archaeological record for the later 7th and 8th c. The concealing of bronze, silver, and gold coin hoards under Heraclius and Constans II attests the general insecurity of the times and is prelude to the sharp drop of monetary currency under Constantine IV (above, p. 159; Dikigoropoulos 1940-48 and 1956). The same period saw the end of large-scale fine pottery production, an industry that had relied on Mediterranean-wide networks of distribution. The most striking evidence comes from the coastal cities: all were significantly reduced and some substantially abandoned around this time. Widespread signs of destruction usually have been attributed to the Arab campaigns, yet it is also possible that earthquakes and broader social upheaval may have contributed to the damage. The documented deportation of large numbers of urban residents, either to Syria under Mu'awiya or to Cyzicus by Justinian II, must have had a major impact as well.

As revealing as the extensive physical damage sustained by Cypriot cities is the nature of the urban response. The few signs of recovery appear primarily among the churches, the most prominent and best studied of contemporary buildings. Following the raid of 649, the bishop of Soloi organized repairs to the large basilica B, which he commemorated in a long mosaic floor inscription. The renovated building may have survived into the 8th or 9th c.[102] Other churches were less ambitiously tended. Repairs to the southeast basilica at Amathus suggest that only part of the central aisle was occupied into the 8th c.[103] At Salamis, a chapel was installed in the sanctuary of the church of Ayios Epiphanios and a small basilica was built over the saint's tomb.[104] A few peripheral parts of the Campanopetra complex remained open.[105] At least one earlier townhouse was briefly used for habitation and agricultural processing, and in 723 the place generally struck the pilgrim Willibald as little more than a large village.[106] Not far inland the church of Ayios Barnabas was rebuilt with a multi-domed superstructure.[107] At Aphendrika, Lythrankomi, Morphou, and Polis, piers or solid walls were added to buttress the central aisles of early basilicas, which were then or somewhat later vaulted.[108] Basilicas at Paphos, Carpasia, and elsewhere may have seen limited repairs before being replaced. New vaulted churches were built in such coastal centers as Larnaca and Yeroskippos as well as a few inland settlements like Leukosia and Peristerona.[109]

The wider impact of these events appears in the dislocation of Late Roman lifeways across the island. The number of rural sites seems to have dropped everywhere during the later 7th

100 Malamut 1988: 434-36; Pryor 1988: 102-5; Papadopoulos 1993.
101 Jenkins 1953: 1007; Kyrris 1984 and 1994-98.
102 des Gagniers and Tran Tam Tinh 1985: 115-25; Megaw 1986: 512.
103 Christou 1996a: 1069; id. 1997: 904-5.
104 Jeffery 1928: 345-47; Megaw 1957: 49-50, fig. 3; id. 1974: 78; id. 1986: 508-9 and 516.
105 Hayes 1980b: 379; Roux 1998: 250-51.
106 Argoud *et al.* 1980; Megaw 1986: 508-9.
107 Megaw 1974: 78-79; id. 1986: 516-17.
108 Megaw 1946; id. 1958: 34; Megaw and Hawkins 1977: 32; Ćurčić 1999: 73-75.
109 Megaw 1974: 79-82; Papageorghiou 1985: 325-27; Wharton 1988: 61-66.

and 8th c., but the decline was especially pronounced in the hinterlands of the coastal cities. The fate of these suburban residents, like most city-dwellers, remains unclear. Many of them may have reassembled in new and smaller communities located in the upper valleys or farther inland; already by the 9th c. the author of the Life of Demetrianos describes a variety of villages, towns, and cities with churches and monasteries stretching across the island (Ryden 1993: 192-201). Regional surveys have confirmed that a number of Late Roman sites saw at least some activity in later mediaeval times, and perhaps during the interim as well. In the vicinity of Lapithos and the lower Mesaoria plain, for example, *c.*10% of rural sites were occupied both before and after the 8th-9th c.[110] Almost 20% of the Late Roman sites in the Vasilikos valley show some sign of mediaeval activity (Todd 1989: 50; id., forthcoming). Survey of the Palaipaphos region has identified greater resettlement, with perhaps 30% of the Late Roman sites on the coastal plain and lower valleys re-occupied in the Middle Ages (Gregory 1987: 200; id. 1993: fig. 60). A slightly higher level (nearly 40%) of resumed settlement in the Yalias valley suggests that this inland region may have seen even wider mediaeval activity (Catling 1982: 234). Our experience at Kopetra shows that such indirect data, unsupported by excavation, provide weak grounds for identifying sites of 8th- and 9th-c. habitation. On the sub-regional scale, however, these survey trends suggest that a range of rural activities — some stationary and constant, others varying with setting and season — continued in different parts of the island. Certainly the emergence of a new settlement hierarchy, including the growth of cities in the upper Mesaoria as well as along the S coast, points to changing patterns of rural land-use and communication. In the absence of large-scale mining and long-distance commerce, most of the island's tax-burden would have been raised by agricultural labor based in small, independent villages and gradually supplemented by inter-regional trade in specialty crops, animal products, and household crafts. Much of this historical reconstruction remains unclear, and its refinement depends on the study of minor habitation sites of the interior, together with different kinds of material culture. Yet the present, limited evidence indicates that the decline of the coastal cities did not prevent many Cypriots from living and even thriving elsewhere on the island.

Kopetra illustrates an intermediate stage in this evolving landscape. This small settlement, a place of no great antiquity or special consequence, prospered amid good times and bad until the events of the mid 7th c. brought instability and isolation. Its reduction and subsequent abandonment reflect not only one village's reaction to localized damage but its tentative effort at economic retrenchment. Inter-regional communication was profoundly affected by the uneasy neutrality that now prevailed on the island. Travel to the mainland continued but the scale of earlier exchange, and especially the sponsoring rôles of State and Church, were sharply curtailed. Within this re-oriented economy the topographic centrality and permanence of existing market towns lost much of their purpose. The full impact of these changes was broadly evident but would have been especially clear at places like Kopetra, with the most marginal and specialized communities facing the greatest exposure. The abandonment of such secondary centers reflects an adaptive response by village families to the challenges of a precarious island existence. Confronting social and economic uncertainties, rural inhabitants met their needs for food, shelter, craft, and faith through less materially conspicuous strategies — increasingly self-sufficient and transient in nature — that they formulated within the wider context of their valley. The people glimpsed here, neglected by classical authors and modern historians alike, provide a thread of cultural continuity that stretches from antiquity into the Middle Ages.

---

110 Catling 1972; Dikigoropoulos 1978: 9; Hadjisavvas 1991.

APPENDIX 1
Fieldwork participants

compiled by Murray C. McClellan

Project staff:

Co-directors: Murray C. McClellan (1987-91), Marcus Rautman (1987-91)

Architect: Virginia Delaney (1988), Marcus Rautman (1989-91)

Conservator: Claire Dean (1988, 1990), Sharon Taylor (1989), Howard Wellman (1991)

Database manager: William Andreas (1988-91)

Draftsperson: Janie Ravenhurst (1990-91)

Geomorphologist: Basil Gomez (1989, 1991)

Physical anthropologist: Sherry C. Fox (1989-91)

Registrar: Karen Walker (1988), Maria Holt (1989)

Survey coordinator: Susan Langdon (1987-89)

Topographic surveyors: Guy Sanders (1987), Lee Ann Turner (1987)

Trench supervisors: William Andreas (1988-91), Lisa Benson (1989-91), Larry Bruce (1988-89), Veronica Demko (1990), Jacqueline Eyl (1988-89), Mark Greco (1991), Sotiri Hadjicharalambous (1988-91), Sebastian Heath (1991), Susan Langdon (1988, 1991), John Leonard (1989), Rena Nestoros (1989, 1991), Victoria Nevius (1988), Danielle Parks (1989-91), Nancy Parish (1990), Matt Rigsby (1991), Lisa Rupp (1989), Paul Scotton (1990), James Terry (1990-91), Karen Walker (1988), Bennet Witt (1988), Louisa Zembyla (1988).

Earthwatch volunteers, field school members, and other participants:

1988: Katherine Baer, Yvette Baer, Betty J. Boetger, Paul Bugg, Pieter Burgess-Berbee, Tom Burgess, Linda Clougherty, Joseph Cullen, Mary Anne Garbarini, Ruth A. Gorham, Betsy Gray, Lloyd E. Hawkinson, Richard L. Huber, Roberta Huber, Emile Jorgenson, William Lawrence, Eileen J. Newhouse, John Niles, Michael E. Pasek, Raynor R. Pollack, Mary J. Proteau, Barbara Ross, Steve Stoffle.

1989: Bernice Cardy and Margaret Morden (Brock University Practicum leaders); Everett Allgood (Emory University field school assistant); Sylvia Baube, Robert Berzok, Douglas Burgess, Gabriella Cadeddu, Julie Coburn, Stevie Cody, Robert Colburn, John Critchley, Charlotte Dawson, Catherine Deans-Barrett, Murray Deason, Veronica Demko, Shawna Dye, Lisa Fechtel, Barbara Fegan, Kevin Fisher, Tracey Fudge, Rollie Graham, John Gray, Jackie Hollmann, Jo Isenberg, Edward Jenny, Carl Johnson, Reed Johnston, Monica Kezar, Lee Liggett, Nancy Mahony, Edna McMullan, Nancy Meshkoof, Tracy Nott, Nancy Parrish, Kristen Peterson, Christine Petruniak, Don Roberts, Ruth Roberts, Cary Ross, Joan Salmons, Diane Tineu, Klara Vogel, Robert A. Wilson.

1990: Nancy Mahoney (Emory University field school assistant), Achilleas Achilleos, Georgios Achilleos, Rudiieard Alcocer, Catherine Deans-Barrett, Lauren Ganck, Mark Greco, Tina Joines, Sue King, Angela Marshall, Tom Mathews, Erin Miller, Neil Petty, Mark Pharo, Antonis Pissiaras, Jennifer Strauss, Laurie Tedesco.

1991: Achilleas Achilleos, Georgios Achilleos, Robert Bolt, Stefan Claeson, Gwen Cohen, Stephanie Donchatz, Elizabeth Fakazis, Mary Jo Farren, Lucinda Ferguson, Jane Jalutkewicz, Elaine Greiner, Dana Leonard, John Morales, Elizabeth McMullen, Ghida el Osman, Antonis Pissiaras, Maressa Pollen, Amy Jo Riordan, Michael Scheidt, Belle Waring.

APPENDIX 2
Alluvial sedimentation and landscape stability

Basil Gomez

The Vasilikos is one of a series of rivers that drain the SE slopes of the Troodos Massif and flow southward into the Mediterranean. Its catchment has an area of 151 km^2. Igneous rocks of the Troodos Ophiolite complex underlie the upper reaches of the catchment, which lie between 200 and 1200 m asl; the lower reaches are underlain by Upper Cretaceous chalks and marls, and Pliocene sandstones (Bagnall 1960; Pantazis 1967). Coarse, thin calcareous soils mantle the chalk hills but rich, colluvial and alluvial soils, which today offer the most potential for agriculture, have developed on the valley floor and behind the extensive terrace systems which help retain sediment in tributary valleys (Wagstaff 1992). At the base of the hillslopes along the E boundary of the floodplain colluvial sediments interdigitate with the alluvial sediments on the valley floor. The colluvium forms a massive, homogeneous, autochthonous unit that is not readily subdivided. Trial excavations undertaken in the vicinity of Kalavasos-*Kopetra* in 1989 and 1991 indicated that the colluvium is between 1 and 2 m deep and contains sherds throughout, most of which date to the period of Late Roman occupation.

Gomez (1987) examined the alluvial fills in the lower Vasilikos valley. The bedrock valley floor is located at an average depth of 15 m beneath the flood plain. Borehole logs and excavations indicate that the igneous conglomerates beneath the floodplain are composed of two distinct units, which may be differentiated on the basis of the presence or absence of rounded igneous boulders. Remnants of the coarser (lower) component of the fill remain in evidence up to 10 m above the contemporary floodplain as the Kalavasos Terrace. It is composed of very poorly sorted igneous boulders, cobbles, gravels, and sands with scattered sub-angular chalk cobbles and gravels. The upper 7 m of the alluvial fill, which are nested within the coarser deposits, exhibit a composition that is similar to deposits in the contemporary channel in that igneous boulders rarely are present. The deposits in the contemporary channel consist of unstratified, clast-supported, poorly sorted, rounded igneous cobbles, gravels, and sands. Poorly sorted, horizontally bedded and cross-stratified igneous cobble, gravel, and sand conglomerates, which commonly fine upwards and are overlain by well-sorted sands, are associated with the development of meander lobes. The channel varies between 10 m and 20 m in width and the bed lies 1 m to 2 m below the level of the floodplain, which in the vicinity of Kopetra is *c.*250 m wide. Immediately adjacent to the channel the floodplain is mantled with up to 1 m of flat-bedded sands and silts overlain by a thin calcareous soil. Pits excavated in various locations along the W edge of the floodplain revealed a 0.5- to 6-m thick sequence of laminated silts overlying a poorly sorted igneous, cobble, gravel, and sand conglomerate. Estimates of the age of mature olive trees on the floodplain suggest that the surface has been stable for much of the period following the establishment of the Crusader Kingdom of Cyprus (*c.*1200).

Vita-Finzi (1969) developed a generalized model to describe the chronology of the alluvial fills that he observed to be forming valleys throughout the Mediterranean basin. An 'Older Fill', deposited between 50,000 and 10,000 years B.P., and a 'Younger Fill', deposited between 2,000 and 300 years B.P., characterized the deposits. The alluvial deposits in the lower Vasilikos valley in the vicinity of Kopetra broadly correspond with Vita-Finzi's sequence of 'Older' and 'Younger' fills. However, the 'Younger Fill' in the lower Vasilikos valley differs markedly from the deposits he described. First, it is composed of two (not one) distinct units: a coarse channel zone and a fine floodplain deposit. Secondly, C^{14} dating (Gomez 1987) suggests that overbank sedimentation already was underway at the time that the nearby Aceramic Neolithic site of Kalavasos-*Tenta* was occupied *c.*6330 ± 100 B.P. These observations support the results of other workers who have argued that the sequence of Holocene fills in Mediterranean valleys cannot be differentiated on the basis of a simple two-fold (coarse/fine) division, and that the date for the onset of deposition of the 'Younger Fill' almost certainly was not synchronous throughout the basin (van Andel and Zangger 1990).

Butzer (1980) presented arguments for anthropogenically-controlled Mediterranean valley alluviation resulting from accelerated soil erosion, beginning locally during the Bronze Age and becoming more widespread after the economic decline of the Roman Empire. He argued that climatic variations may have favored erosive activity (cf. Grove 2001), but the unprecedented extent and scope of the hill slope and valley changes that have occurred within the Holocene are inconceivable without a primarily cultural impetus (Butzer 1974: 138). However, as Wagstaff (1981) has pointed out, many investigations of the 'Younger Fill' (including those undertaken in the Vasilikos valley) lack enough stratigraphical detail to gain an appreciation either of the local depositional environment or of the subtle changes in rainfall characteristics that may have promoted increased erosional activity. Nevertheless, the stratigraphic investigations of the

'Younger Fill' that have been undertaken in the lower Vasilikos valley shed light on the local depositional environment and the probable controls on sedimentation of the late Holocene fill. Floodplains in semiarid regions are constructed by different processes, depending on whether the channel is fixed or migrates laterally. In discontinuous channels, where the long profile characteristically is punctuated by knick points and exhibits a step form, sediment production is limited and deposition is localized and episodic. Continuous channel networks extend directly back to the surrounding hill slopes. Sediment is derived from weathering and erosion of the hill slopes and generally is introduced directly into the channel system. High-gradient, low-order channels, with small drainage areas, typically are associated with the production and transport of sediment. Low-gradient high-order channels, with large drainage areas, represent storage sites where floodplain formation occurs in response to lateral and/or vertical accretion (Nanson and Croke 1992).

The rapidity with which a floodplain is constructed and its longevity appear primarily to be functions of a variety of factors including sediment availability and the magnitude and frequency of overbank flooding. In general, a succession of high magnitude floods appears to inspire channel instability and high sediment yields, while a series of low magnitude floods appears to reduce sediments fields and to favor floodplain alluviation and channel stability (Hereford 1984). Thus, Nanson and Croke (1992) argue for a continuum of floodplain environments. At the high-energy end of the spectrum, either floodplains appear to form and erode episodically in the absence of channel migration, or channels migrate rapidly across the floodplain. At the low-energy end of the range, channel migration is inhibited and valley fills form through the overbank deposition of the suspended load from quiescent flows over low-gradient floodplains.

Although the contemporary drainage network of the Vasilikos is discontinuous, agricultural terraces constructed across tributary valleys largely are responsible for disconnecting the tributaries from the main channel (Wagstaff 1992), and in the past the drainage network was more continuous than it appears at present. Floodplain alluviation occurs only along high-order, low-gradient reaches of the Vasilikos where the slope of the channel is of the order of 1%. The stratigraphy of the overbank deposits present in the lower Vasilikos valley gives the overall impression that they were deposited by vertical accretion in a low-energy environment. Beds appear to be laterally continuous in transverse sections. Contacts between individual beds generally are gradiational, most are not massively bedded, and there is a general absence of epsilon surfaces. Typically, single units are between 10 and 100-150 mm thick. The onset of the major phase of overbank alluviation in the lower Vasilikos valley occurred during the Aceramic Neolithic occupation *c.*6330 ± 100 B.P. (Gomez 1987). Excavations in the floodplain suggest that a maximum of 5.5 m of overbank sediments has accumulated since that time. This equates with an average overbank sedimentation rate of *c.*0.9 mm per year. This rate is similar to that observed in modern alluvial systems where the floodplain experiences slow, cumulative vertical aggradation, and the fine-grained overbank deposits are formed by episodic overbank flooding of a dominant master channel (Simm 1995). Note, however, that an average rate provides no indication of the significance of the contribution of individual flood events to overbank sedimentation, and also implies that sedimentation continued at the same rate throughout the period in question. There is no evidence at any of the sites that Gomez (1987) examined of any stripping of the overbank sediments, or of prolonged periods of floodplain inactivity. However, up to 1.5 m of the alluvium may have been deposited since the 15th c., suggesting that the average overbank sedimentation rate during the last 500 years was *c.*3 mm per year. The increase in overbank sedimentation rates occurred in conjunction with downcutting of the channel, and may reflect the intensification of agricultural activity in the historical period (Thirgood 1987).

Long-term aggradation (or degradation) trends across floodplains are the result of changes in the external factors governing the amount of sediment and water that is available within a drainage basin. The climatic and environmental conditions that have prevailed in the lower Vasilikos valley for most of the Holocene are largely indeterminate (A. Kingsnorth in Todd 1982; B. Gomez *et al.* in Todd 1987: 3-8). The natural vegetation probably consisted of a dense, mixed pine and oak forest on the igneous rocks in the upper reaches of the catchment, and maquis on calcareous rocks in the lower reaches of the Vasilikos valley. The vegetation cover was probably disrupted locally by the Aceramic and Ceramic Neolithic and Chalcolithic societies that originally inhabited the valley. Late Bronze Age mining and smelting activity in the valley must also have depleted the hardwood forests. The extensive agricultural terrace-systems in the lower Vasilikos valley have clearly acted to prevent some soil loss from the hillslopes and the tributary valley networks (Wagstaff 1992), but dates for the construction of the various structures remain to be determined.

In summary, the available evidence suggests progressive clearance of the vegetation cover and cultivation probably increased sediment yields and induced erosion and floodplain aggradation in the lower Vasilikos valley. The change from a meandering gravel-bed river system, where deposition occurred primarily within the channel zone, to a predominantly overbank depositional system appears to have been initiated at about the time the valley was first occupied in the Aceramic Neolithic. There is no apparent evidence of any significant phase(s) of valley alluviation. Instead, the floodplain appears to have been active throughout the entire period that the valley has been occupied. Enhanced sedimentation rates since the 15th c. are commensurate with observations of increased agricultural activity (and by implication, accelerated hillslope erosion) in the historical period. These observations raise additional questions about the rate of Holocene overbank sedimentation in the lower Vasilikos valley and origins of the 'Younger Fill'. Firstly, how do sedimentation rates in the lower Vasilikos valley compare with those in other Cypriot river valleys, and with sedimentation rates in other parts of the Mediterranean basin during the late Holocene? Secondly, is it correct to assume that sedimentation rates in the lower Vasilikos valley remained relatively stable during the entire *c.*6000-year period prior to the 15th c. (after which time they appear to increase), or was there a progressive increase in sedimentation rates through the period? Thirdly, if sedimentation rates were not stable during the period up to the 15th c., at what point did they start to increase appreciably; and what precipitated the increase? More detailed stratigraphical investigations are required to address these questions.

APPENDIX 3
Compositional study of ceramics from Kopetra
Marcus Rautman, Hector Neff, Michael D. Glascock

The prominence of pottery and rooftiles in Kopetra's material record encouraged us to begin a systematic program of compositional analysis during the final season of excavation (1991). Our primary objective was to examine the main fabric categories present in the Vasilikos valley in order to clarify the nature of local pottery manufacturing and determine source areas for non-local ceramics. In subsequent years we enlarged our sample of representative materials with pottery, rooftiles, and raw clays from across the island and, for comparative purposes, from several mainland sites. Most of our analysis was carried out using instrumental neutron activation analysis (INAA) at the MU Research Reactor Center (MURR) at the University of Missouri. Major funding for our work came from the Getty Grant Program and the National Science Foundation, with additional support by the University of Missouri-Columbia and Indiana State University.

Our investigations build on a well-developed foundation of analytical work with Cypriot pottery. Over the last 20 years techniques of compositional analysis have come to play an increasingly prominent rôle in studies of archaeological ceramics and in exploring the related issues of ancient trade. The geological diversity of the E Mediterranean has been shown to be well suited for such investigations, with Cyprus occupying a central place in regional production and exchange networks from prehistory through the Middle Ages (Bieber 1977, 1989; Jones 1986: 523-625; for a recent review Schneider 2000). The distinctive fine wares that traveled between the island and the mainland during the Bronze Age have received special attention (King 1987; Bieber 1989; Knapp and Cherry 1994; Bryan *et al.* 1997). At the time we began our study relatively little work had been devoted to Cypriot pottery of Roman and later times. Our analysis of representative Chalcolithic through post-Roman materials from the Vasilikos valley reveals elements of both continuity and transformation within regional patterns of ceramic exchange (Rautman *et al.* 1993; Gomez *et al.* 2002).

This report is based on the analysis by INAA of a total of 648 samples (Table 1). Of this number, 260 are finished ceramics from Kopetra and other Late Roman sites in the Vasilikos valley. We also assembled a selection of 97 Chalcolithic and Late Bronze Age sherds from the valley in order to establish a baseline of information about local production and exchange in prehistory. For comparative purposes we obtained a total of 134 ceramic specimens ranging from Chalcolithic to modern from across the island, most of which were kindly provided by the directors and staff of other archaeological projects (above, pp. 13-14). In 1994 B. Gomez undertook the systematic investigation of representative Cypriot clay sources, from which 147 samples were analyzed. Finally, 10 examples of Roman-era fine pottery and amphoras were obtained from mainland sites; these and comparable data from other projects allowed us to comment on the variability of these wares across the E Mediterranean. Subsequent petrographic and scanning electron microscopic study underscored the mineralogic basis for our major group divisions. Throughout the project we focused primarily on Cypriot pottery and for this reason largely excluded wares known to have originated off the island — for example, in N Africa, the Aegean region, Palestine or Egypt (e.g., Jones 1986; Taylor and Robinson 1996).

TABLE 1. PROVENANCE AND TYPE OF INAA SAMPLES (N=648)

Vasilikos valley			*Other Cyprus*			*Mainland*
Pre-Roman	*Roman*	*Soils*	*Pre-Roman*	*Roman*	*Soils*	*Roman*
97	260	8	31	103	139	10

Analytical procedures

With its standardized preparation techniques, sensitivity to minute elemental concentrations, and automated recording procedures, INAA continues to offer one of the most reliable means for the compositional investigation of archaeological ceramics. Methods of sample preparation and material analysis used at MURR have been reviewed at length elsewhere (Rautman *et al.* 1993 and 1999; Slane *et al.* 1994). Ceramic samples are powdered, dried, and weighed before being subjected to two irradiations. Three gamma-ray spectra are collected, one following a short, 5-second irradiation, and two after a long, 24-hour irradiation. The procedure used at MURR yields data for 33 elements in the majority of samples. In the present study, 9 elements were dropped from consideration either because too many specimens had missing values or because they had not been determined in the comparative data-sets to which we had access. The remaining 24 elements used for pattern-recognition and statistical analysis are lanthanum (La), lutetium (Lu), neodymium (Nd), sam-

TABLE 2. CRS/RED TILE GROUP MEMBERS

Source	*CS*	*CRS*	*Red Tiles*	*Plain B*	*sum*
Vasilikos valley		26	30	7	63
Maroni-*Petrera*	9	10	3		22
Amathus		1	2		3
Pyla		3			3
Athienou	1	1			2
Dhiorios	1				1
Paphos	5	5	2		12
Peyia		2	1		3
Ayios Kononas			2		2
Cape Arnauti		1		1	2
Polis-Marion		2	1		3
(Marina)	5				5
TOTAL	21	51	41	8	121

arium (Sm), ytterbium (Yb), cerium (Ce), cobalt (Co), chromium (Cr), cesium (Cs), europium (Eu), iron (Fe), hafnium (Hf), rubidium (Rb), scandium (Sc), tantalum (Ta), terbium (Tb), thorium (Th), zinc (Zn), calcium (Ca), dysprosium (Dy), potassium (K), manganese (Mn), sodium (Na), and titanium (Ti). The basic quantitative procedures used to recognize subgroups in the chemical data are described by Neff (2002).

Principal components analysis (PCA) was used together with inspection of bivariate plots in order to recognize potential subgroups in the data. These groups were evaluated by calculating Mahalanobis distances of all analyzed specimens to the group centroids. Specimens whose Mahalanobis distances placed them outside the 1% probability cut-off relative to all groups were left unassigned. Groups whose small size made it impossible to estimate multivariate group parameters (specimen-to-variate ratio less than one) or for which small size rendered parameter estimates unreliable (specimen-to-variate ratio only slightly greater than one) were evaluated by inspecting numerous bivariate projections of the data (PCA plots and bivariate elemental concentration plots). We also had access to comparative data from other regional sites analyzed at Lawrence Berkeley Laboratory (LBL) using procedures described by Perlman and Asaro (1969; also see Artzy *et al.* 1976; Gunneweg *et al.* 1983). The LBL data were calibrated for compatibility with MURR data.

Group definition and provenance determination

Three major reference groups emerged within the initial sample of 225 specimens and were confirmed by further analysis (figs. 1-2). The first (CRS/Red Tile) comprises exclusively specimens of Cypriot Red Slip ware and red-fabric Laconian-style rooftiles. The second (originally identified as YT but more accurately described as a collection of calcareous subgroups) consists primarily of yellow-fabric Corinthian-style rooftiles and LR1 amphoras. The third (Other Tile, = OT) encompasses mainly coarse-fabric Corinthian-style roofiles, thick-walled *pithos* sherds, and handmade cooking pots. Subsequent analysis allowed us to enlarge and refine these initial groupings. Similarities with other ceramics of demonstrated or presumed provenance and with unlevigated clays of known derivation led us to propose general source areas for a few of the individual wares. These suggestions received further support from consideration of the ceramic petrology in relation to the composition of raw materials in Cyprus and the E Mediterranean.

Only members of the OT group seem to have originated in the vicinity of Kopetra. Members of this group include *pithoi*, large Corinthian-style rooftiles, and handmade cooking pots, all of which have a fabric that varies considerably in the amount of coarse igneous sand and gravel particles (*RDAC* 1993: pl. LXI.1-2). The wide range of fabric colors suggests that open-firing methods may have been preferred for the manufacture of these wares. While the coarse-fabric tiles are relatively consistent in size, the cooking pots seem to be of non-standard size and shape, probably reflecting small-scale production at the neighborhood or household level (above, p. 212; Rautman 1998). Under such circumstances, the addition of coarse temper would have helped cope with the thermal stress of variable firing conditions as well as daily domestic use. The alluvial sand and gravel deposits of the lower Vasilikos river and its terraces include a variety of igneous temper that may have been used for this purpose. The dynamic nature of these formations (above, Appendix 2), coupled with the likelihood of multiple manufacturing venues, obviously complicates the search for surviving soils with this compositional profile. Yet suggestive indirect evidence of a local source comes from the upper Vasilikos valley, where a production site of Late Bronze Age White Slip II pottery was discovered accidentally at

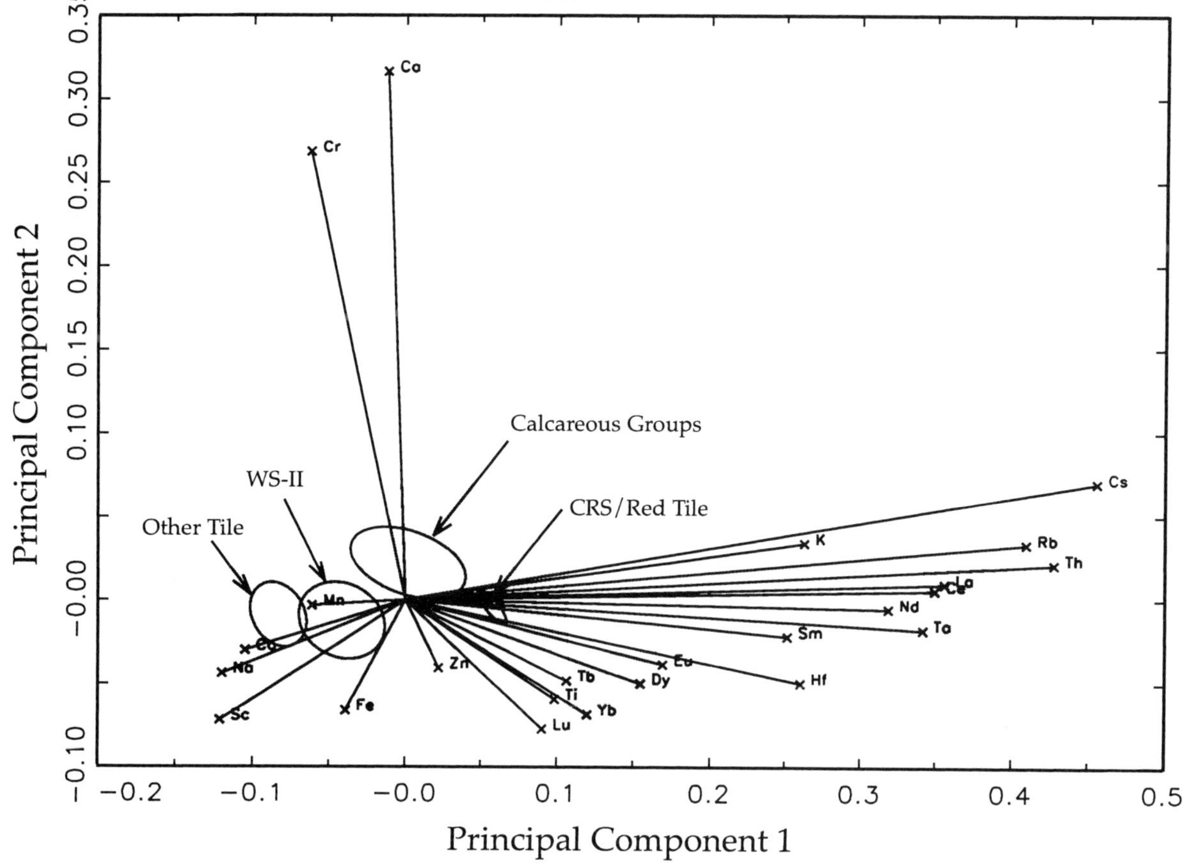

Fig. 1. Biplot of principal components correlation matrix of complete Cyprus data set with variables coordinates.

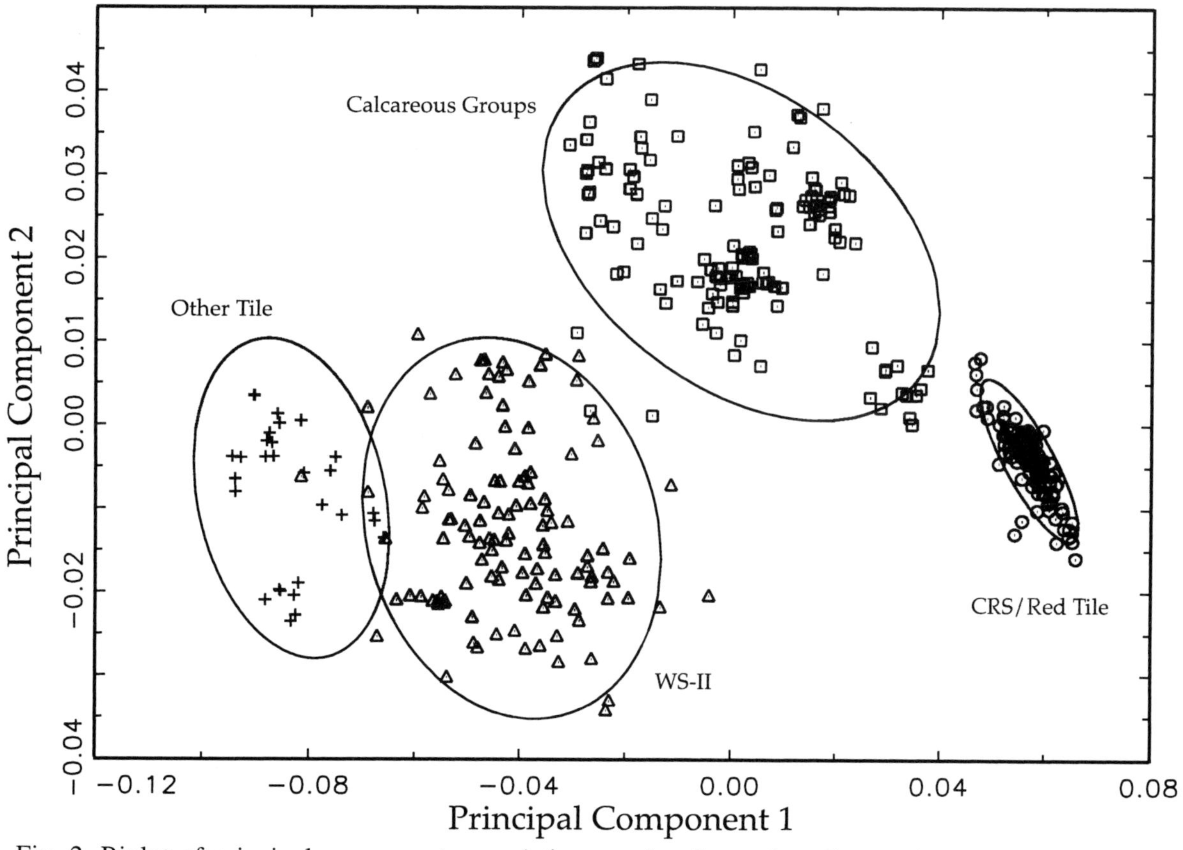

Fig. 2. Biplot of principal components correlation matrix of complete Cyprus data set with individual specimens.

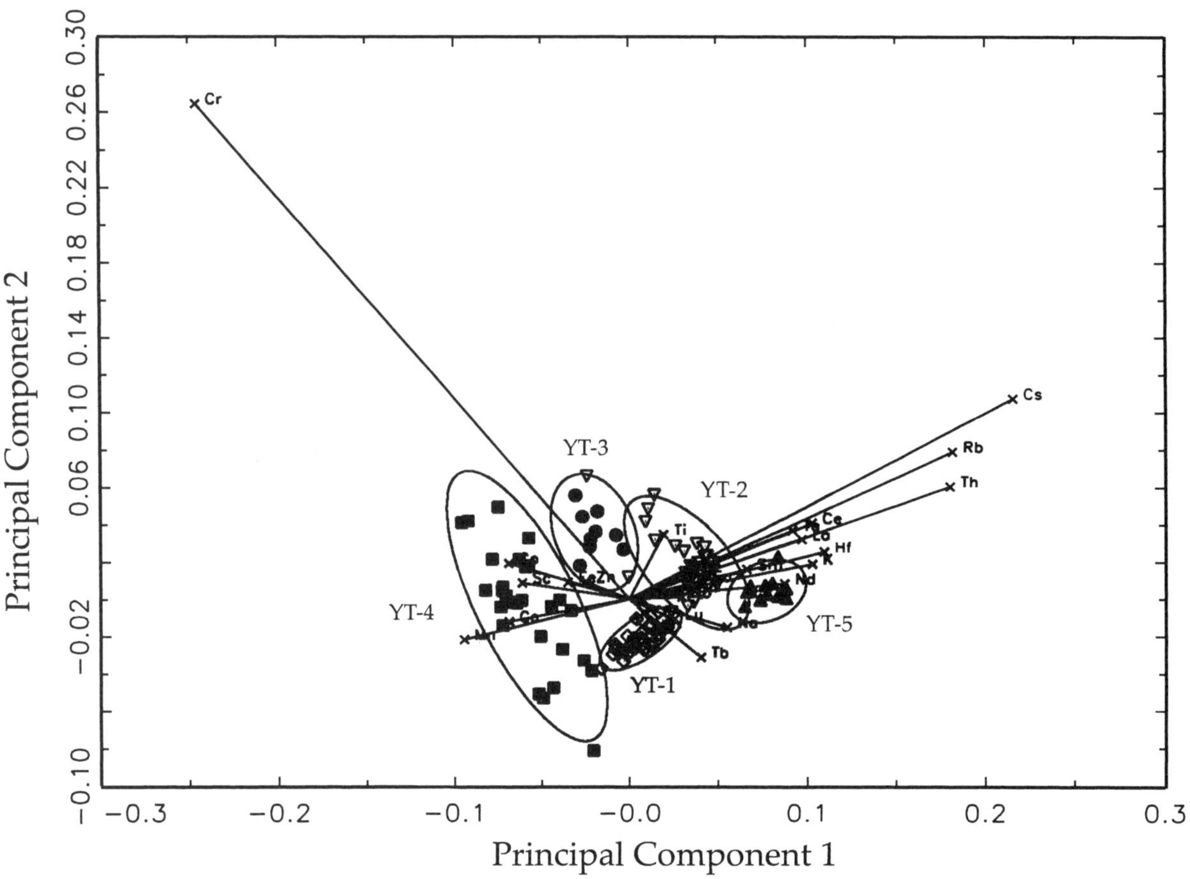

Fig. 3. Biplot of principal components correlation matrix of calcareous subgroups (YT-1 to YT-5).

Sanida-*Moutti tou Agiou Serkou* (Todd and Pilides 1993; Todd 2000). Soil samples from Sanida and other primary deposits developed on ultrabasic rocks of the Troodos massif revealed a close relationship with White Slip II sherds from throughout Cyprus and elsewhere, including the Ulu Burun shipwreck (Gomez *et al.* 1996 and 2002; Rautman *et al.* 1993: 259). Like members of the OT group, this distinctive Late Bronze Age ware exhibits a consistent composition that is relatively depleted in rare earth elements (fig. 1). We infer that ceramics of both the Other Tile and White Slip II groups were derived from ultrabasic parent materials, presumably the altered and weathered ultrabasic rocks that underlie the upper Vasilikos valley.

Further study of the CRS/RT group proceeded in two directions. Additional examples of both Cypriot Red Slip pottery and the distinctive red-fabric rooftiles were collected from other sites (Table 2). We noted that a number of specimens of unslipped table vessels closely resembled this group, which remains very homogeneous in its composition. A selection of early Roman Cypriot Sigillata sherds drawn from several locales on and off the island was found to fall within the range of variation of the CRS/RT reference group. This compositional uniformity corresponds with the consistent visual appearance of most specimens, and suggests that a single well-developed industry was responsible for their manufacture. While a Cypriot provenance for the fine wares has long been assumed, other mainland sources have been suggested for Cypriot Sigillata (Hayes 1967 and 1972; cf. Gunneweg *et al.* 1983). New evidence for a probable source area in the W part of the island was provided by representative soils recovered near Paphos, although clear matches with the CRS/RT group were not identified (Gomez *et al.* 1995). Quantifiable variations among the surviving soils, Cypriot Sigillata specimens, and examples of Cypriot Red Slip and red-fabric rooftiles may be interpreted as arising from both the erosion of clay sources and the evolution of manufacturing methods during the Roman and Late Roman periods (cf. Meyza 1995; Schneider 2000: 533-34).

Members of the calcareous (YT) subgroups exhibit a varied yet distinctive composition (fig. 3). The broad distinction between calcareous (i.e., high-calcium/low-aluminum) and non-calcareous (low-calcium/high-aluminum) ceramics has been observed in Bronze Age contexts as well and appears characteristic of Cypriot pottery making traditions (Barlow and Idziak 1989). Group members include examples of yellow-fabric roofiles, terracotta water pipes, LR1 amphoras, assorted *pithoi*, and Chalcolithic pottery from the lower Vasilikos valley (Table 3). The individual amphora fabrics (LR1[1], LR1[2], LR1[3], and LR1[5]) exhibited considerable variation, apparently reflecting their production at multiple sites along the coast of Cilicia and N Syria as well as Cyprus (Empereur and Picon 1988: 33; iid. 1989: 236-43; Rauh and Slane 2000; Demesticha

TABLE 3. CALCAREOUS FABRIC GROUP MEMBERS

Source	*LR1*	*LR13*	*KAmp1*	*KAmp2*	*Yellow Tiles*	*waterpipe*	*sum*
Kopetra	48		4	10	30	5	97
Zygi-*Petrini*	3						3
Maroni-*Petrera*					3		3
Amathus	2		1				3
Pyla	3			1	5		9
Paphos	5	5					10
(Sardis)	9						9
TOTAL	70	5	5	11	38	5	134

and Michaelides 2001). These analyses allowed us to distinguish 6 subgroups (YT-1 to YT-6). Source areas for these fabric subgroups can be proposed on comparison with surviving soils and the regional geomorphology (Rautman *et al.* 1999).

YT-1, which comprises almost all analyzed examples of yellow-fabric rooftiles, can be associated with the lower Mesaoria valley, not far from Salamis-Constantia. The association is based on compositional similarities with presumably local pottery from the Late Bronze Age site of Enkomi (Artzy *et al.* 1976; Gunneweg 1984) and, even more convincingly, by similarities with a clay recently used by potters from the village at Varoşa (Ionas 2000: 154-55). The infrequent occurrence and very weathered nature of the reworked igneous and bioclastic material contained in the clays are also consistent with the characteristics of the calcareous, fine-grained, clay-rich, shallow-marine Neogene and Pleistocene sediments that outcrop in the Mesaoria Plain. The YT-3 subgroup, which includes mostly specimens of KAmp1 and LR1(3) amphoras, resembles the YT-1 subgroup and, like the yellow tiles, probably originates among the Pliocene and recent sediments of the Mesaoria plain. Ceramics of the YT-4 subgroup, to which belong primarily LR1(1) and LR1(5) amphoras, can be assigned to S central Cyprus on the basis of two clay samples from the lower Vasilikos valley and igneous inclusions probably deriving from the gabbros and pyroxenites exposed on the S flanks of the Troodos Massif.

Amphoras and rooftiles of the YT-2 and YT-5 subgroups, by contrast, do not resemble any known Cypriot clay or ceramic ware and apparently did not originate on the island. The more homogeneous YT-5 subgroup includes all 11 examples of KAmp2 amphoras, whose angular, glassy inclusions are inconsistent with a Cypriot source; Empereur and Picon (1989: 232) have proposed a source for these amphoras near Seleucia-Pieria. The broadly defined YT-2 subgroup consists almost entirely of LR1(2) and LR1(3) amphoras, which have been assigned on the basis of quartz, crypto-crystalline limestone, serpentine, and pyroxene inclusions to a source area with outcrops of both ultra-basic and sedimentary rocks, as found in Cilicia and N Syria (Williams 1987). Chemical, optical petrographic, and SEM data for the YT-2 subgroup reinforce the connection with the diverse geology of the Anatolian and Syrian coastlands.

Conclusion

Compositional analysis offers a powerful means of approaching questions of pottery provenance and manufacture. Study of pottery from Cyprus and other parts of the E Mediterranean over the last 25 years has produced a large body of data with which to explore the production and exchange of ceramics in antiquity and the Middle Ages. Despite recent advances, uncertainties still remain concerning the compositional variability of individual wares — especially those of historic date — as well as their specific areas of production. The association of ceramic fabrics with raw materials is often complicated by differing methods of clay preparation, which removed many geographically distinctive impurities while also adding temper to native clays. The rapid advance of laboratory techniques with increasingly fine levels of precision can hinder the intercalibration of fresh analytical results with older data. An even more serious challenge is the continuing erosion of the archaeological record in Cyprus, as activity contexts and natural deposits of raw materials increasingly are overwhelmed by modern development. By documenting a variety of ceramic materials and surviving clay sources from across the island, our work adds to the expanding information-base and emphasizes the pressing need for further inquiry in the region.

APPENDIX 4
Marine and fresh-water shells
David S. Reese

This small shell collection includes 23 marine individuals and 20 fresh-water bivalve individuals from Areas I, II, and VI (Table 1). It includes:

- 9 *Donax trunculus* Linnaeus, 1758 individuals (1 early-mid 7th c.?, 3 mid 7th c., 1 third quarter of 7th c.?, 2 post-mediaeval, 1 topsoil, 1 undated). The (Abrupt) Wedge-shell is probably a minor food source, although 1 mid 7th-c. shell was picked up dead on the beach.
- 3 *Mytilus galloprovincialis* Lamarck, 1819 (early 7th c., early to mid 7th c., and topsoil); the Mussel is probably a minor food item.
- 2 *Cerastoderma (=Cardium) edule glaucum* (Bruguière, 1789) (mid 7th c. and post-medieval). The latter Cockle has a hole below the umbo and is probably an ornament.
- 2 fragmentary *Charonia nodifera* (Lamarck, 1822) (mid 7th c. and topsoil). There is no evidence that these Trumpet or Triton shells were modified to make a trumpet or vessel.
- 1 fresh *Euthria cornea* (Linnaeus, 1758), a whelk (early 7th c.).
- 1 *Dentalium dentalis* Linnaeus, 1767 (topsoil). This Tooth or Tusk shell is probably an ornament.
- 1 *Turritella communis* (Risso, 1826), a Turret or Tower shell (topsoil). It has a hole on its side and is probably an ornament.
- 1 broken fresh *Phulium (=Semicassis, =Cassis, =Tylocassis)* sp. fragment, a Helmet shell (topsoil).
- 1 water-worn *Thais (=Purpura) haemastoma* Linnaeus, 1748 (Oyster drill, Rock shell) with a holed body (topsoil). It is probably an ornament.
- 1 water-worn *Murex (=Truncularioposis, =Hexaplex, =Phyllonatus) trunculus* (Linnaeus, 1758) (post-mediaeval deposit). This Rock Murex could be strung as an ornament.
- 1 water-worn and naturally holed *Arcularia (=Nassarius, =Nassa) gibbosulus* (Linnaeus, 1759) (early to mid 7th c.?). This Nassa or Basket shell is probably an ornament.
- 14 *Unio* individuals, a small-to-medium sized fresh-water bivalve (1 late 6th c., 2 early 7th c., 1 early to mid 7th c., 3 mid 7th c., 3 mid 7th c.?, 1 third-quarter of 7th c.?, 2 undated, and 1 topsoil).
- 6 large fresh-water bivalve individuals (1 early 7th c., 2 7th c., 1 7th c., 1 7th c.?, and 1 undated). The fresh-water bivalves could have been consumed, their nacre (mother-of-pearl) utilized, or merely have come to the site with drinking water.
- 2 fossil shells, probably forms naturally occurring in the local building stone.

TABLE 1. MARINE AND FRESH-WATER SHELLS

Area I

Lot I-1: Topsoil.

Mytilus fragments, with umbo (8530/6015 1.1)

Mytilus — 2 fragments (8535/5995 1.1)

Dentalium — large, fresh, l. 45, d. 8 (8540/6010 1.1)

Unio fragments (8520/6010 3.1)

Unio fragment — right valve (8535/6010S 1.1)

Lot I-2: Basilica, upper collapse, 7th c.

large fresh-water bivalve — broken, right valve (8525/6000 3.3)

Lot I-5: Basilica, construction, late 6th c.

2 *Unio* fragments — small piece (8530/5995 3.1)

Lot I-7: Crypt, lower fall, early to mid 7th c.

Mytilus — umbonal end fragment (8525/5995 4.2)

Unio fragments (8525/5995 4.2)

fossil shell fragment in matrix (8525/5995 4.2)

Lot I-13: Space II, collapse, early 7th c.

Unio fragments (8525/6010 2.2)

Lot I-18: Space III, collapse, mid 7th c.?

Unio fragments (8520/6015E 3.1)

Lot I-19: Space III, destruction, date inconclusive.

large fresh-water bivalve fragment (8520/6015 4.1)

Lot I-20: Space III, construction, early 7th c.

Euthria — broken body, broken apex (8520/6015 5.2)

Unio fragment — with recent hole (8520/6015 5.1)

Unio fragments (8520/6015 5.1)

Unio fragments (8520/6015 5.2)

large fresh-water bivalve fragments (8520/6015 5.1)

large fresh-water bivalve fragment — distal end (8520/6015 5.1)

large fresh-water bivalve fragments (8520/6015 5.2)

large fresh-water bivalve fragments — right valve (8520/6015 5.2)

Lot I-21: Space IV, collapse, 7th c.?

large fresh-water bivalve fragment — right valve (8520/6020S 2.1)

Lot I-28: Courtyard, collapse, mid 7th c.

Cerastoderma fragment — fresh (8525/6010E 2.1)

Unio fragments (8525/6010E 2.1)

Unio fragments (8525/6015 3.2)

Unio fragment (8520/6010S 2.1)

large fresh-water bivalve — broken, right valve (8525/6010 2.1)

Area II

Lot II-1: Topsoil.

unidentifiable fragment of marine gastropod (8335/5940 1.1)

Turritella — fresh, no apex or distal end, l. 25+, hole on side 2 x 1.5 (8335/5935 1.1)

Phalium — 2 fragments, fresh (8335/5935 1.1)

Donax — fragment, right valve (8335/5940 1.1)

Charonia columella/mouth fragment (8335/5940 1.1)

Thais — large, water-worn, ancient hole in center of body, l. 101.5, w. 73.5, hole 33.5 x 18 (8355/5930 1.1)

fossil venerid bivalve — very large, umbonal fragment, left valve (8335/5940 1.1)

Lot II-2: Surface pit, post-medieval.

Donax — right, w. 27.5, slightly worn (8335/5940 2.1)

Donax — left valve, w. 24.5 (8335/5940 2.1)

Murex — water-worn, no apex, could be strung, l. 49.5+ (8335/5940 2.1)

Cerastoderma — left valve, h. 16.75, w. 18, hole below umbo 2.25 x 1.5 (8335/5940 2.1)

Lot II-6: South aisle, upper collapse, third quarter of 7th c.?

Donax — fragment, right valve (8345/5940 3.1)

Unio fragments (8335/5935 3.2)

Lot II-13: Bema, lower collapse, mid 7th c.

Donax — fragment, left valve (8345/5940 4.1)

Donax — fragment, right valve (8345/5940 4.1)

Donax — fragment, water-worn (8345/5940 4.1)

2 *Donax* — 2 left, 1 with a w. of 23, 1 broken (8345/5940 4.1)

Unio fragment (8345/5940 4.1)

Lot II-15: East room, upper collapse, mid 7th c.

Unio fragment — left valve (8350/5940 6.1)

Lot II-19: Center aisle, collapse, early to mid 7th c.?

Donax — broken, left valve (8335/5940 3.1)

Donax — right valve, w. 32 (8335/5940 3.1)

Arcularia — water-worn, natural holes on body and below apex, l. 13.75 (8335/5940 3.1)

Lot II-20: Center aisle, west end, burning level, mid 7th c.?

Donax — right valve, w. 25.5 (8335/5940 3.4)

Lot II-27: West room, lower collapse, mid 7th c.

Unio — right valve, broken (8335/5930 3.1)

Area VI

Lot VI-2: Upper collapse, disturbed, mid 7th c.?

Unio fragment — right valve (8280/6058 4.1)

Lot VI-3: Upper collapse, 7th c.?

Unio fragments (8280/6058 3.1)

Lot VI-5: Room 2, upper collapse, mid 7th c.

Charonia — fresh, broken apex, recent hole on body, l. 230+, w. 129 (8280/6055 4.1)

Lot VI-9: Room 1, lower collapse, early to mid 7th c.?

2 *Unio* fragments (8289/6050 4.1)

Lot VI-11: Room 3, lower collapse, mid 7th c.

Unio fragments (8280/6058 4.1)

large fresh-water bivalve — broken, left valve (8280/6058 4.1)

large fresh-water bivalve — broken, probably right valve, h. *c.* 56 (8280/6060 4.1)

Lot VI-15: Room 2, second phase surface, early 7th c.

Mytilus — umbonal end, broken (8280/6058 2.1)

N.B., All measurements are in millimeters.

APPENDIX 5
The human skeletal remains: a preliminary report

Sherry C. Fox

Human skeletal remains from a minimum of 21 individuals were recovered at various locations, including a limestone sarcophagus, 4 tombs, and a cistern. The sarcophagus, cistern, and Tombs 1 and 2 were excavated at the east church complex at *Sirmata* in 1988 and 1989. Tomb 3 at the south church was excavated in 1990, while Tomb 4 at the north church was examined in 1991. The human skeletal remains from Tomb 1 were recovered by excavation staff in 1988. The author excavated or assisted in the excavation of the human skeletal material from Tombs 2, 3, and 4. She also analyzed the human bones recovered from the *Sirmata* cistern in 1989 and from a sarcophagus that was accidentally unearthed prior to 1987. The following report is preliminary in nature. It provides information about the condition of the human remains; basic demographic data including determinations of the minimum number and sex of individuals; estimations of age-at-death and living statures; and analyses of dentition, anomalies, and paleopathological lesions. Integration of archaeological data is attempted when possible, and common Cypriot burial practices during this era are discussed. The human remains from Kopetra are presently housed at the Larnaca District Archaeological Museum.

Condition and completeness

The condition of the remains ranges from poor to good. Much more information was gained, especially from the poorly preserved remains, by the author's participation in excavation of Tombs 2-4 than would have been possible from her analysis of the bones alone. Soil pH measures were taken from *Sirmata* at locations where human bones were in contrasting states of preservation. Analysis by the Cyprus Department of Agriculture indicated that the soil pH varied little between locations and in general the pH was neutral. Both acidic and alkaline soils are known to be detrimental to human bone preservation, whereas a neutral pH is considered desirable. Thus, factors other than soil pH were responsible for the varying condition of the human remains. The alternating hot, dry summers and cool, damp winters of this part of Cyprus constitute a fluctuating environment that is not generally conducive to bone preservation (Angel 1945). Some of the taphonomic variables affecting bone preservation include the local burial environment (i.e., the type of tomb), water drainage, damage caused by roots and salts adhering to the bone (salts were present in Tombs 1 and 4 in particular), and physical damage caused by the weight of overlying features. The human remains from Tomb 4 were poorly preserved. The bottle-shaped cistern at *Sirmata* provided a micro-environment that was conducive to bone preservation. By contrast, the weight of overburden from the collapsed Tomb 4 at Area V probably hastened the deterioration of the human remains. The bones from Tomb 2 in the crypt at *Sirmata* were fairly well preserved, but this tomb was constructed of gypsum slabs and the skeletal material near its bottom was partially encased in gypsum plaster; as a result, the bones proved very difficult to excavate.

Most of the human skeletal remains were nearly complete. Both of the skeletons from the sarcophagus (Individuals 1 and 2) are missing portions of the leg bones, since part of the sarcophagus had been damaged by earthmoving equipment prior to its discovery; these two skeletons were never completely excavated and were not fully studied. The skeleton of the juvenile from Tomb 2 (Individual 7) is incomplete since this individual, the last interred in the tomb, suffered the greatest post-mortem damage when it collapsed. The left arm is missing post-mortem from the less completely recovered adult from Tomb 3 (Individual 11).

A number of the human bones from Kopetra were treated with a 10% solution of Paraloid in acetone, a bone preservative, to aid in the recovery and identification of the human remains.

Burial practice

The remains from Tomb 1 were somewhat commingled owing to repeated flooding and perhaps also reuse of the tomb. Reconstructing individuals from these remains is difficult; in fact, Tomb 1 was originally thought to be an ossuary. The tomb was subdivided into quadrants during excavation, which permits the reconstruction of some of the circumstances of burial. Only the upper body bones originated from the two northern quadrants of the tomb, and (apart from some hand bones) only lower body bones were found in the two southern quadrants. Photographs taken prior to excavation confirmed suspicions that the supposed ossuary was in fact a tomb containing primary burials that had been disturbed post-mortem. All of the individuals had been interred with their heads positioned to the north. Individual 9 was interred prior to

Individual 8, and Individual 8 was interred prior to Individual 7. It is not known whether these individuals were buried at one time, or if the tomb was re-used, perhaps as many as three times, following the initial burial.

Like the individuals from Tomb 1, the occupant of Tomb 4 was also buried in a supine and extended position with his head to the north. The individuals from Tombs 2 and 3 were buried in supine and extended positions with their heads to the W and elbows slightly flexed with their hands roughly folded across their abdomens. This body position and orientation reflect common practice in Cyprus today.

By far the most unusual deposition of human remains was within the *Sirmata* cistern, where something out of the ordinary clearly occurred. At least 9 individuals were recovered, ranging from late fetal to adult ages. The articulated condition of the skeletal remains indicates that these were primary interments. Gross examination identified no clear evidence that any of the individuals suffered from a traumatic bone injury at or around the time of death. For example, there are no observable cut-marks on the bones. It is possible that this mass burial reflects violent conflict since historical accounts speak of Arab raids on Cyprus around the mid 7th c. and Kopetra was largely abandoned around this time. An alternate explanation might be an epidemic such as the plague under Justinian, which is said to have lasted 52 years. According to Procopius, at the peak of the epidemic "more than 10,000 people died each day, and it became impossible to bury all the bodies", with half the inhabitants of the Byzantine empire dying by 565 (Patrick 1967: 246); but since viral epidemics rarely leave any detectable evidence on bones, interpretation of the physical evidence remains speculative.

Minimum number of individuals

At least 21 individuals were recovered from Kopetra. This is based upon duplication of skeletal elements and/or representation of individuals of different ages or sexes. Both the sarcophagus and Tomb 3 contained the remains of at least two individuals. Three individuals were recovered from Tomb 2 and 4 from Tomb 1, whereas just one individual was recovered from Tomb 4. The cistern contained the remains of at least 9 individuals.

Sex

Sex was determined by accepted morphological methods (Stewart 1979; Krogman and Iscan 1986; Bass 1995). Sex determination of subadults was not attempted. Two individuals could not be sexed either morphologically or metrically; femoral head diameters could be taken for both Individuals 12 and 20, but these dimensions fell within the 'indeterminate' range of both Pearson (1917-19) and (Thieme 1957; both cited in Bass 1995).

Age-at-death

The age-at-death of the subadults was estimated largely on the basis of the dental chart developed by Schour and Massler (1944), although measurements of long bone lengths were used to estimate the age of the fetal (Fazekas and Kosa 1978) and neonatal (Johnston 1962) remains. Adults were aged utilizing morphological assessments of the pubic symphysis (Katz and Suchey 1986), and sternal rib ends (Iscan *et al.* 1984). The late adolescent was aged according to the degree of epiphyseal fusion following Angel (1986: 186-87 Table 5.3). The age of Individual 12 from Tomb 4 could be aged generally by the degree of ossified thyroid cartilage (Cerny 1983: fig. 2; after Vlcek 1974, 1980; cited in Iscan 1989: 120-23).

Stature

Estimations were based upon the formulae developed from a modern Greek collection devised by Eliakis *et al.* (1966). Stature could be estimated for 8 (62%) of the 13 adults (possibly all male) from the site. It is possible that the stature reconstructions for Individuals 20 and 21 come from a single person, but the disparity in reconstructed stature was so great as to suggest assigning the statures to two individuals. The right humerus (max. length = 32.9 cm) was used to reconstruct stature for Individual 1 from the sarcophagus; the right radius (max. length = 23.8 cm) from Individual 5(?) from Tomb 1; the right tibia (maximum length = 33.1 cm) for Individual 8 from Tomb 2; the left femur (max. length = 44.6 cm) for Individual 9 from Tomb 2; max. lengths of the left femora for both individuals from Tomb 3 (Individual 10: 47.0 cm; Individual 11: 44.8 cm); the right humerus (max. length = 31.6 cm) for Individual 20 from the cistern and the left ulna (max. length = 27.4 cm) for Individual 21. Male formulae were used for individual 20 who is of unknown sex.

Anomalies

A few anomalies, including metopism, extrasutural bones, and exostoses, were detected among the individuals, but more dental anomalies undoubtedly exist (the teeth from the site are not yet fully studied). Three individuals (14%), all adults, demonstrate metopism: an individual from Tomb 1 as well as one each from Tomb 2 (Individual 9) and the cistern. Extrasutural bones, including the most common location along the lambdoidal suture, were observed but not quantified on a number of individuals. An exostosis of the humerus or supracondylar process has been observed on two individuals (with a prevalence of 10%).

Pathological lesions

Trauma, disease, and degenerative changes are seen on some of the human skeletal remains. The leading traumatic injury was fracture. The right scapula and clavicle both demonstrate healed fractures from the more superficial of the two males recovered from Tomb 3 (Individual 10). Two thoracic vertebrae from Individual 10 were ankylosed at the posterior vertebral arches. These pathological lesions probably resulted from a single traumatic incident, such as a fall. An adult from the cistern of unknown sex (Individual 21) had a fractured right clavicle that had formed a pseudarthrosis — not uncommon for this bone as the shoulder is such a mobile joint. Two cervical vertebrae (C-3/C-4) from Individual 21 also demonstrate traumatic arthritis evidently incurred at the same time as the clavicular fracture resulting from a fall.

An adult male (Individual 1) from the sarcophagus, *c.*37 years of age (±10 years), demonstrates evidence of a disruption in growth in the form of linear enamel defects in a few of his teeth (enamel hypoplasias). This disruption occurred very early in his life, during the time of enamel formation, producing a permanent record of this growth disruption. Enamel hypoplasias can be caused by fever, malnutrition, or a constitutional disorder.

The individual of unknown sex from Tomb 4 (Individual 12) demonstrates osteophytic lipping of some vertebral bodies. This individual was probably over 40 years. This osteophytic lipping can be the result of simple degenerative or age-related changes.

Results

All of the adults that could be sexed were thought to be male, with the possible exception of a female of late adolescent age recovered from the cistern (Table 1). A disproportionate number of males are present, but this is not unusual for those buried within churches at this period. Both individuals recovered from Tombs 13 and 14 (though possibly mediaeval in date) in the basilica at Alassa-*Ayia Mavri* were sexed as male. Females outnumbered males from burials outside the basilica at Alassa.

Estimated ages ranged from 9 lunar months to possibly 55 years for those with available criteria. The age-range is comparable to that at Alassa-*Ayia Mavri*. Eight (38%) of the 21 individuals from Kopetra were subadults. Only one subadult, the last to be interred in Tomb 2, was recovered from outside the cistern. The remaining 7 subadults, including two of late fetal age (viable if born alive), a neonate, three children, and an adolescent were all recovered from the cistern. The fetuses, however, may have been stillborn and the neonate, if born alive, succumbed shortly after birth. Infant mortality therefore could include these three individuals (14%). An additional 4 individuals (19%) succumbed during childhood (4-11 years). A single adolescent (5%) did not achieve adulthood. The average age at death of the adults (possibly all male) for whom ages could be estimated (6 individuals) is 37.6 years, older than the average of 29 years noted for the three ageable individuals at Alassa-*Ayia Mavri* (Fox 1996).

The average stature of the recovered individuals is 168.6 cm (*c.*5′6″). This is greater than that found at Alassa-*Ayia Mavri*, where stature could be estimated for only one at 155.6 cm, the same average figure as was estimated for the 4 females there.

Three different osseous anomalies are identified among the human remains from the site and a similar number of pathological lesions. The most notable traumatic injuries are fractures to the right clavicle, observed in two adult males. These were probably the results of falls and both men probably incurred other injuries simultaneously.

Summary

A total of 21 individuals were recovered from Kopetra. The condition of the human remains ranged from poor to good depending upon the micro-environment of each deposition. The skeletal remains of most indivi-

TABLE 1. SUMMARY OF RESULTS

Tomb type	*Individual*	*Sex*	*Age*	*Preservation*	*Stature*	*Pathology*
Sarcophagus	1	M	27-47 y	Fair	164.08±7.53cm	EH
	2	M	Adult	Fair		
Tomb 1	3	M?	Adult	Poor		
	4	M?	Adult	Poor		
	5	M	25-35 y	Poor	169.14±9.07cm?	
	6	M?	35-45 y	Poor		
Tomb 2	7	?	9-11 y	Poor		
	8	M	Adult	Fair	161.71±8.77cm	
	9	M	Adult	Fair	171.68±7.96cm	
Tomb 3	10	M	33-55 y	Good	178.69±7.96cm	Yes (1)
	11	M	Adult	Good	169.69±7.96cm	
Tomb 4	12	?	40+ y	Poor		osteophytosis
Cistern	13	?	~9 lm	Good		
	14	?	~9 lm	Good		
	15	?	Neonate	Good		
	16	?	4-6 y	Good		
	17	?	7-9 y	Good		
	18	?	8-10 y	Good		
	19	F?	16-19 y	Good		
	20	?	30-40 y	Good	160.84±7.53cm	Yes (2)
	21	M	Adult	Good	172.85±8.25cm?	

Key:
?=indeterminate,
y=years,
lm=lunar month,
EH=enamel hypoplasia

(1) Healed fractures of the right scapula and clavicle and fusion of two thoracic vertebral posterior arches.
(2) Pseudarthrosis from fractured right clavicle and traumatic arthritis of C-3/C-4 cervical vertebral pedicles. This individual also demonstrated a partial sacralization of the 5th lumbar vertebra.

duals are complete. The burials appear to have been primary, although some bones were slightly disturbed post-mortem. The skeletons from the tombs and sarcophagus were found in supine and extended positions, with pronated forearms and hands possibly clasped or folded. Interments were single (Tomb 4), double (Tomb 3), triple (Tomb 2) and quadruple (Tomb 1). The sarcophagus contained two individuals. The cistern, an unusual burial place, contained the remains of 9 individuals, at least some of which were deposited intact, as some remains were recovered articulated. They probably point to a catastrophic event All of the adults that could be sexed were classified as male. The only possible exception is the adolescent, a possible female. Ages ranged from 9 lunar months to possibly 55 years. Apart from one case of an episode of arrested growth (as evidenced by linear hypoplasias) and a possible degenerative condition (vertebral lipping), all of the other pathological lesions are traumatic in origin.

The dental remains need to be studied in greater detail. Chemical studies, including isotopic analyses for dietary reconstruction, should be attempted, as well as ancient DNA studies to determine, for example, relatedness among individuals. Further work would entail comparison with the community's still-to-be-located cemetery.

Acknowledgements

I am grateful for the invitation to participate in the excavations and analysis of the human skeletal remains from Kopetra, the approval by the Cyprus Department of Antiquities to undertake the work, and the support of the American Schools of Oriental Research through its Charles U. and Janet C. Harris Fellowship at CAARI (1992). Dr. Alexandros Kanakas generously radiographed some of the pathological bones.

APPENDIX 6
Present-day production of gypsum plaster in the Vasilikos valley

Murray C. McClellan

The production of slaked plaster from the Kalavasos-*Kafkalies* gypsum deposits in the Vasilikos valley has been renewed in recent times in order to serve the needs of nearby Portland cement plants at Vasiliko and Moni. Study of a local production-center for gypsum plaster has detailed a process that probably resembles that used in late antiquity. The operation is located *c.*500 m to the southwest of the village of Kalavasos and is run by Mr Kyriakos together with a crew that usually includes one of his sons, his son-in-law, and one or two paid laborers. They collect large gypsum blocks at the *Kafkalies* quarry, which is dynamited monthly by industrial quarrymen from the Moni factory, and transport the stone in a flatbed truck to their furnace. The gypsum is stacked in the upper chamber and heated by a wood fire built in the lower chamber. The furnace can hold 12 metric tons of gypsum blocks and requires two tons of wood for a single firing, which usually lasts around 12 hours and attains temperatures in the upper chamber of 120-180° C. After firing, the dehydrated gypsum is crushed by a machine, the resulting 10.8 tons of gypsum plaster is put into 20-kg bags, and the bags are sold to the Vasiliko cement factory and local consumers. In 1990 the prevailing price per bag was CY£0.75 (about US$1.60). This process creates a heavy demand for fuel, which is obtained by scavenging dead olive or carob trees and abandoned pieces of lumber. In 1992 Mr Kyriakos replaced his old wood-burning furnace with a new electric furnace.

Certain aspects of this production process obviously differ from ancient methods. By using dynamite at the quarry, trucks to transport stone from quarry to furnace and plaster from furnace to place of consumption, and a durable concrete furnace and crushing machinery, Mr Kyriakos's modest production center operates on a larger scale and more efficiently than could any Roman process. On the other hand, the production of gypsum plaster for Late Roman Kopetra could well have been undertaken by an extended family group that opportunistically scavenged stone from the *Kafkalies* quarry and wood from the surrounding region.

APPENDIX 7
Concordance of inventoried objects

Site inventory	*Lot*	*Catalogue*	*Fig.*
KK88-1	I-6		not illustrated
KK88-2	I-1	**C4**	4.2
KK88-3	I-1	**I-1-2**	3.21
KK88-7	II-1		3.44.13
KK88-8	surface		2.12.5
KK88-9	surface		2.12.6
KK88-12	SG71A		2.12.9
KK88-13	I-3		3.25.12
KK88-15	I-2		3.25.10
KK88-16	I-1		3.25.9
KK88-21A	I-1		3.25.6
KK88-23	I-1		3.25.11
KK88-26A-B	V-1		3.54.3
KK88-28	I-7		*RDAC* 1989: 165 no. 15, fig. 7:3
KK88-29	I-7	**290**	6.7
KK88-30	I-7	**255**	6.3
KK88-40	I-2		*RDAC* 1989: 165 no. 10, fig. 6
KK88-41	I-2		*RDAC* 1989: 165 no. 11, fig. 6
KK88-43	I-2		*RDAC* 1989: 165 no. 13, fig. 6
KK88-45	I-3		3.25.7
KK89-4	I-20		not illustrated
KK89-8	I-18	**I-18-1**	3.21
KK89-11	II-2	**C9**	4.2
KK89-12	II-1	**C11**	4.2
KK89-13	II-13	**C8**	4.2
KK89-15	II-6		3.45.28
KK89-17	I-3	**I-3-1**	3.21
KK89-21	I-1		not illustrated
KK89-24	I-6	**I-6-1**	3.21
KK89-25	I-1	**I-1-1**	3.21
KK89-28	I-32		3.24.8
KK89-30	II-2	**C13**	4.2
KK89-33	I-1		3.24.1
KK89-34	II-12		3.37
KK89-35	II-6		3.44.21
KK89-36	I-1		3.24.3
KK89-38A	II-6		3.44.14
KK89-39	I-11		*RDAC* 1989: 165 no. 9, fig. 6
KK89-42	I-11		*RDAC* 1989: 165 no. 12, fig. 6
KK90-1A	II-6		3.44.16
KK90-1B	II-6		3.44.17
KK90-4	SG73A		2.12.10
KK90-8	I-1		3.24.2
KK90-9	II-6		3.45.33
KK90-11	II-8		3.44.19
KK90-12	II-11		3.43.4
KK90-4	SG73A		2.12.10
KK90-8	I-1		3.24.2
KK90-9	II-6		3.45.33
KK90-11	II-8		3.44.19
KK90-12	II-11		3.43.4
KK90-13A	II-10		3.43.3
KK90-13C	II-10		3.43.2
KK90-15A-B	II-11		3.42.8
KK90-18	II-6		3.45.32
KK90-19	II-6		3.44.18
KK90-20	II-7		3.44.20
KK90-21A-C	II-8, 10, 14		3.42.7
KK90-22A-B	II-11, 12		3.42.3
KK90-25	II-12		3.44.15
KK90-26	II-1		3.43.8
KK90-29	II-6		3.43.5
KK90-33	II-26	**C10**	4.2
KK90-37	II-1	**C1**	4.2
KK90-39	II-3		3.42.2
KK90-40	II-2		3.42.1
KK90-41	II-1		3.45.24
KK90-43	II-14		3.42.5
KK90-44	II-9		3.42.6
KK90-45	II-6		3.44.22
KK90-46	II-8		3.45.31
KK90-48	II-5	**II-5-1**	3.41
KK90-49	II-5	**II-5-2**	3.41
KK90-50	II-5	**II-5-3**	3.41
KK90-51	II-5	**II-5-4**	3.41
KK91-3	VI-2	**C6**	not illustrated
KK91-4	VI-5	**C7**	4.2
KK91-7	II-3	**C12**	4.2
KK91-13	V-3	**C2**	4.2
KK91-14	VI-6	**C5**	4.2
KK91-15	II-3	**C3**	4.2
KK91-20	II-19	**II-19-1**	3.41
KK91-21	VI-11	**VI-11-3**	3.67
KK91-22	V-2	**V-2-1**	3.54
KK91-23	VI-13	**VI-13-2**	3.67
KK91-24	VI-5	**VI-5-5**	3.67
KK91-26	V-5		not illustrated
KK91-27	VI-5	**VI-5-6**	3.67
KK91-28	VI-5	**VI-5-7**	3.67
KK91-29	II-27	**II-27-1**	3.41
KK91-30	VI-15	**VI-15-1**	3.67
KK91-31	V-3		not illustrated
KK91-32	VI-5	**VI-5-8**	3.67
KK91-33	V-3		not illustrated
KK91-34	V-3	**V-3-2**	3.54

Site inventory	*Lot*	*Catalogue*	*Fig.*
KK91-35	II-21	**II-21-1**	3.41
KK91-37	VI-11	**VI-11-4**	3.67
KK91-38	VI-11	**VI-11-5**	3.67
KK91-40	V-3		3.54.7
KK91-41	II-1		3.45.23
KK91-42	II-6		3.45.25
KK91-43	II-6		3.45.26
KK91-44	II-6		3.45.27
KK91-45	II-6		3.45.29
KK91-46	II-32		3.45.30
KK91-47	II-1		3.43.7
KK91-49	V-2		3.54.5
KK91-51	II-19		3.43.1
KK91-53	V-1		3.54.8
KK91-54	V-2		3.54.2
KK91-55	VI-6	**103**	5.8
KK91-56	K-gen	**51**	5.4
KK91-58	SG58		2.12.3
KK91-59	V-1		3.54.4
KK93-1	K-gen	**3**	5.1
KK93-2	II-5	**17**	5.2
KK93-3	VI-5	**VI-5-1**	3.67
KK93-4	I-32	**I-32-3**	3.23
KK93-6	K-gen	**25**	5.2
KK93-7	I-28	**27**	5.3
KK93-8	K-gen	**23**	5.2
KK93-9	VI-11	**VI-11-2**	3.67
KK93-10	VI-7	**26**	5.2
KK93-11	VI-11	**198**	5.16
KK93-12	VI-6	**195**	5.16
KK93-13	VI-5	**144**	5.11
KK93-14	II-15	**143**	5.11
KK93-15	K-gen	**213**	5.17

Site inventory	*Lot*	*Catalogue*	*Fig.*
KK93-16	SG56A	**212**	5.17
KK93-18	SG75	**214**	5.17
KK93-19	SG31A	**206**	5.17
KK93-20	SG7A	**205**	5.17
KK94-1	K86-Tr. G	**32**	5.3
KK94-2	K-gen	**33**	5.3
KK94-3	II-3	**34**	5.3
KK94-4	I-20	**I-20-2**	3.22
KK94-5	K-gen	**4**	5.1
KK94-6	SG57	**29**	5.3
KK94-7	I-1	**30**	5.3
KK94-8	SG64	**31**	5.3
KK94-9	II-8	**II-8-1**	3.41
KK94-10	K-gen	**148**	5.11
KK94-12	K-gen	**151**	5.12
KK94-13	VI-11	**153**	5.12
KK94-14	K-gen	**191**	5.15
KK94-15	SG77	**192**	5.15
KK94-16	VI-6, 7	**193**	5.15
KK94-17	VI-7	**194**	5.15
KK94-18	II-27, 28	**197**	5.16
KK94-19	K-gen	**211**	5.17
KK94-25	II-1		3.43.6
KK94-28A-E	I-3		3.24.4
KK94-28F-G	I-1		3.24.5
KK94-28H	I-2		3.24.7
KK94-28I	I-3		3.24.6
KK94-33	SG33		not illustrated
KK94-38	IV-2		not illustrated
KK94-42	IV-13		not illustrated
KK94-44	VI-2		not illustrated

Bibliography

Abadie-Reynal, C. 1989. "Céramique et commerce dans le bassin égéen du IVè au VIIe siècle," in *Hommes et richesses dans l'empire byzantin* I, *IVe-VIIe siècle* (Paris) 143-59.

Abadie-Reynal, C. and J.-P. Sodini 1992. *La céramique paléochrétienne de Thasos* (Études thasiennes XIII).

Acconci, A. 1998. "Elements of the liturgical furniture," in M. Piccirillo and E. Alliata (edd.), *Mount Nebo. New archaeological excavations, 1967-1997* (Studium Biblicum Franciscanum coll. maior 27, Jerusalem) 468-542.

Adan-Bayewitz, D. 1986. "The pottery from the late Byzantine building (stratum 4) and its implications," in L. I. Levine and E. Netzer, *Excavations at Caesarea Maritima. 1975, 1976, 1979 — Final report* (Qedem 21) 90-129.

Adovasio, J. M., G. F. Fry, J. D. Gunn, and R. F. Maslowski 1975. "Prehistoric and historic settlement patterns in western Cyprus," *WorldArch* 6, 339-64; republished in *RDAC* 1978, 39-57.

Ahrweiler, H. 1974. "L'escale dans le monde byzantin," in *Recueils de la Société Jean Bodin* 32, 161-78; repr. in ead., *Byzance, les pays et les territoires* (London 1976).

Alcock, S. E. 1991. "Urban survey and the polis of Phlius," *Hesperia* 60, 421-63.

Alcock, S. E. 1993a. *Graecia capta. The landscapes of Roman Greece* (Cambridge).

Alcock, S. E. 1993b. "Surveying the peripheries of the Hellenistic world," in Bilde *et al.* 1993, 162-75.

Alcock, S. E., J. F. Cherry, and J. L. Davis 1994. "Intensive survey, agricultural practice and the classical landscape of Greece," in I. Morris (ed.), *Classical Greece: ancient histories and modern archaeologies* (Cambridge) 137-70.

Allen, P. S. 1989. "Dhali: a traditional community in transition," in Stager and Walker 1989, 425-46.

Ammerman, A. J. and M. W. Feldman 1978. "Replicated collection of site surfaces," *AmAnt* 43, 734-40.

Angel, J. L. 1945. "Skeletal material from Attica," *Hesperia* 14, 279-363.

Angel, J. L. 1986. "Age at death estimated from the skeleton and viscera," in M. R. Zimmerman and J. L. Angel (edd.), *Dating and age determination of biological materials* (London) 186-87.

Arbel, B. 1996. "The economy of Cyprus during the Venetian period (1473-1571)," in Karageorghis and Michaelides 1996, 185-92.

Argoud, G. 1980. "Fours à pain et fours à chaux byzantins de Salamine," in *Salamine de Chypre* 329-39.

Argoud, G., O. Callot, and B. Helly 1980. *Salamine de Chypre* XI. *Une résidence byzantine, "l'Huilerie"* (Paris).

Aristidou, E. 1995. "Trade and port development in Cyprus during the Latin period," in Karageorghis and Michaelides 1995, 263-70.

Arthur, P. and E. D. Oren 1998. "The North Sinai survey and the evidence of transport amphorae for Roman and Byzantine trading patterns," *JRA* 11, 193-212.

Artzy, M., I. Perlman, and F. Asaro 1976. "Alasiya of the Amarna letters," *JNES* 35, 171-82.

Åström, P. (ed.) 1992. *Acta Cypria. Acts of an int. congress on Cyriote archaeology held in Göteborg, 1991* (Jonsered).

Aupert, P. 1980. "Objets de la vie quotidienne à Argos en 585 ap. J.-C. V. Verrerie," in *Études argiennes* (*BCH* Suppl. 6) 443-49.

Aupert, P. (ed.) 1996. *Guide de l'Amathonte* (Sites et monuments XV, Paris).

Aurenche, O. *et al.* 1993. "Un village et son terroir: Episkopi (Paphos). Premiers résultats d'une enquête ethnoarchéologique à Chypre," in Yon 1993, 205-54.

Auth, S. H. 1975. "Roman glass," in C. W. Clairmont, *Excavations at Salona, Yugoslavia (1969-1972)* (Park Ridge, NJ) 145-80.

Bachmann, H.-G. 1982. *The identification of slags from archaeological sites* (London).

Bagatti, B. 1969. *Excavations in Nazareth* I. *From the beginning till the XII century*, transl. E. Hoade (Studium Biblicum Franciscanum pub. 17, Jerusalem).

Bagatti, B. and J. T. Milik 1958. *Gli scavi del "Dominus Flevit"*, I. *La necropoli del periodo romano* (Studium Biblicum Franciscanum pub. 13, Jerusalem).

Bagnall, P. S. 1960. *The geology and mineral resources of the Pano Lefkara-Larnaca area* (Nicosia).

Baird, D. 1985. "Survey in Peyia village territory, Paphos, 1983," *RDAC* 340-49.

Bakirtzis, Ch. 1976. "Παλαιοχριστιανική βασιλική στους Γιορκούς ΒΑ της Αθηαίνου," *RDAC* 260-66.

Bakirtzis, Ch. 1995. "The role of Cyprus in the grain supply of Constantinople in the Early Christian period," in Karageorghis and Michaelides 1995, 247-53.

Bakirtzis, Ch. 1996. "Description and metrology of some clay vessels from Agios Georgios, Pegeia," in Karageorghis and Michaelides 1996, 153-61.

Bakirtzis, Ch. 1997. "Η Θαλάσσια διαδρομή Κύπρου-Αιγαίου στα παλαιοχριστιανικά χρόνια," in *Proc. int. archaeological conference "Cyprus and the Aegean in antiquity from the prehistoric period to the 7th century A.D.," Nicosia, 1995* (Nicosia) 327-32.

Bakirtzis, Ch. 2000. "Αποτελέσματα ανασκαφών στον Άγιο Γεώργιο Πέγειας (Ακρωήτριον Δρέπανον) 1991-1995," in *Πρακτικά του τρίτου διεθνούς Κυπριολογικού συνεδρίου, Λευκοσία, 1996*, vol. II (Nicosia) 155-70.

Ballet, P. 1995. "Relations céramiques entre l'Égypte et Chypre à l'époque gréco-romaine et byzantine," in Meyza and Mlynarczyk 1995, 11-25.

Ballet, P. and M. Picon 1987. "Recherches préliminaires sur les origines de la céramique des Kellia (Égypte). Importations et productions égyptiennes," *Cahiers de la céramique égyptienne* 1, 17-48.

Ballet, P. *et al.* 1991. "Artisanat de la céramique dans l'Égypte romaine tardive et byzantine. Prospections d'ateliers de potiers de Minia à Assouan," *Cahiers de la céramique égyptienne* 2, 129-43.

Barag, D. 1967. "The glass," in M. W. Prausnitz, *Excavations at Shavei Zion* (Monografie de archeologia e d'arte II, Rome) 65-70.

Barag, D. 1970. "Glass pilgrim vessels from Jerusalem, part I," *JGS* 12, 35-63.

Barag, D. 1971. "Glass pilgrim vessels from Jerusalem, parts II and III," *JGS* 13, 45-63.

Barag, D. 1983. "Glass vessels," in V. Tzaferis, "The excavations of Kursi-Gergesa," *'Atiqot*, Eng. ser., 16, 37-38.

Barker, G. 1991. "Approaches to archaeological survey," in Barker and Lloyd 1991, 1-9.

Barker, G. and J. Lloyd (edd.) 1991. *Roman landscapes. Archaeological survey in the Mediterranean region* (British School at Rome monog. 2).

Barlow, J. A. and P. Idziak 1989. "Selective use of clays at a Middle Bronze Age site in Cyprus," *Archaeometry* 31, 66-76.

Bass, G. F. 1982. "The pottery," in id. and F. H. van Doorninck, Jr. (edd.), *Yassi Ada* I. *A seventh-century Byzantine shipwreck* (College Station, TX) 155-88.

Bass, W. M. 1995. *Human osteology. A laboratory and field manual* (Missouri Arch. Soc. spec. pub. 2, Columbia).

Baur, P. V. C. 1938. "Glassware. B. Other glass vessels," in Kraeling 1938, 513-46.

Bear, L. M. 1963. *The mineral resources and mining industry of Cyprus* (Bulletin no. 1, Nicosia).

Bekker-Nielsen, T. 1993. "Centres and road networks in Hellenistic Cyprus," in Bilde *et al.* 1993, 176-91.

Belke, K. *et al.* (edd.) 2000. *Byzans als Raum. Zu Methoden und Inhalten der historischen Geographie des östlichen Mittelmeerraumes* (VTIB 7, Vienna).

Bellinger, A. R. 1966. *Catalogue of the Byzantine coins in the Dumbarton Oaks collection and in the Whittemore collection.* I. *Anastasius I to Maurice, 491-602* (Washington, D.C.).

Ben Lazreg, N. and D. J. Mattingly (edd.) 1992. *Leptiminus (Lamta): a Roman port city in Tunisia, Report no. 1* (*JRA* Suppl. 4).

Benson, J. L. 1956. "Spirally fluted columns in Cyprus," *AJA* 64, 385-87.

Bieber, A. M., Jr. 1977. *Neutron activation analysis of archaeological ceramics from Cyprus* (Ph.D. diss., Univ. of Connecticut).

Bieber, A. M., Jr. 1989. "Neutron activation analysis of Cypriot pottery," in Stager and Walker 1989, 357-97.

Bilde, P. *et al.* (edd.) 1993. *Centre and periphery in the Hellenistic world* (Studies in Hellenistic civilization 4, Aarhus).

Bintliff, J. L. 1999. "Studying needles in haystacks. Surface survey and the rural landscape of central Greece in Roman times," *Pharos* 7, 51-91.

Bintliff, J. L. 2000. "Reconstructing the Byzantine countryside: new approaches from quantitative landscape archaeology," in Belke *et al.* 2000, 37-63.

Bintliff, J. and A. Snodgrass 1988a. "The end of the Roman countryside: a view from the east," in R. F. J. Jones *et al.* (edd.), *First millennium papers. Western Europe in the first millennium A.D.* (BAR S401, Oxford) 175-217.

Bintliff, J. and A. Snodgrass 1988b. "Mediterranean survey and the city," *Antiquity* 62, 57-71.

Biscop, J.-L. 1997. *Deir Déhès. Monastère d'Antiochène, étude architecturale* (BAHBeyrouth 148).

Blakeley, J. A. 1988. "Ceramics and commerce: amphorae from Caesarea Maritima," *BASOR* 271, 31-50.

Blakeley, J. A. 1996. "Toward the study of economics at Caesarea Maritima," in A. Raban and K. G. Holum (edd.), *Caesarea Maritima. A retrospective after two millennia* (Leiden) 327-45.

Blanton, R. E. 2000. *Hellenistic, Roman and Byzantine settlement patterns of the coast lands of western Rough Cilicia* (BAR S879, Oxford).

Boardman, J. 1989. "The pottery," in M. Balance *et al.*, *Excavations in Chios 1952-1955. Byzantine Emporio* (British School of Archaeology at Athens, suppl. 20) 88-121.

Boismier, W. A. 1997. *Modelling the effects of tillage processes on artefact distributions in the ploughzone* (BAR 259, Oxford).

Bowersock, G. W. 2000. *The international role of late antique Cyprus* (14th annual lecture on the history and archaeology of Cyprus, Nicosia).

Bradley, R. and M. Fulford 1980. "Sherd size in the analysis of occupation debris," *BullInstArchLon* 17, 85-94.

Brandes, W. 1999. "Byzantine cities in the seventh and eighth centuries — different sources, different histories?" in Brogiolo and Ward-Perkins 1999, 25-57.

Braudel, F. 1972. *The Mediterranean and the Mediterranean world in the age of Philip II* (transl. S. Reynolds, New York).

Brill, R. H. 1967. "A great glass slab from ancient Galilee," *Archaeology* 20, 88-95.

Brodribb, G. 1987. *Roman brick and tile* (Gloucester).

Brogiolo, G. P. and B. Ward-Perkins (edd.) 1999. *The idea and ideal of the town between late antiquity and the early Middle Ages* (Leiden).

Broodbank, C. 1999. *An island archaeology of the early Cyclades* (Cambridge).

Browning, R. 1977-79. "Byzantium and Islam in Cyprus in the early Middle Ages," *Επετηρίς του Κέντρου Επιστημονικών Ερευνών Κύπρου* 9, 101-16.

Bruce, J. L. 1937. "Appendix V. Antiquities in the mines of Cyprus," in E. Gjerstad *et al.*, *Swedish Cyprus Expedition. Finds and results of the excavations in Cyprus 1927-1931,* III (Stockholm) 639-71.

Bryan, N. D. *et al.* 1997. "Pottery sources in Bronze Age Cyprus: a provenance study by neutron activation," *RDAC* 31-64.

Bryer, A. A. M. and G. S. Georghallides (edd.) 1993. *"The sweet land of Cyprus." Papers given at the twenty-fifth jubilee spring symposium of Byzantine studies, Birmingham, 1991* (Nicosia).

Buchholz, H.-G. 1985. "Die deutschen Ausgrabungen in Tamassos von 1970 bis heute," in *Πρακτικά του δεύτερου διεθνούς Κυπριολογικού συνεδρίου, Λευκοσία, 1982,* vol. I (Nicosia) 229-71.

Buchwald, H. 1995. "Notes on the design of aisled basilicas in Asia Minor," in B. Borkopp, B. Schellewald, and L. Theis (edd.), *Studien zur byzantinischen Kunstgeschichte. Festschrift für Horst Hallensleben zum 65. Geburtstag* (Amsterdam) 19-30; repr. in H. Buchwald, *Form, style and meaning in Byzantine church architecture* (Aldershot 1999).

Buechner, T. S. 1960. "The glass from Tarrha," *Hesperia* 29, 109-17.

Burnet, J. E. 1997. "Sowing the four winds. Targeting the Cypriot forest resource in antiquity," in S. Swiny, R. L. Hohlfelder, and H. W. Swiny (edd.), *Res maritimae. Cyprus and the eastern Mediterranean from prehistory to late antiquity* (CAARI monog. 1) 59-69.

Burns, T. S. and J. W. Eadie (edd.) 2001. *Urban centers and rural contexts in late antiquity* (East Lansing, MI).

Butler, H. C. 1929. *Early churches in Syria, fourth to seventh centuries* (ed. E. B. Smith; Princeton).

Butzer, K. W. 1974. "Accelerated soil erosion: a problem of man-land relationships," in I. R. Manners and M. W. Mikesell (edd.), *Perspectives on environment* (Association of American Geographers publ. 13, Washington, D.C.) 57-78.

Butzer, K. W. 1980. "Holocene alluvial sequences: problems of dating and correlation," in R. A. Cullingford, D. A. Davidson, and J. Lewin (edd.), *Timescales in geomorphology* (Chichester) 131-42.

Cadogan, G. 1992. "Maroni VI," *RDAC* 51-58.

Callot, O. 1980. "Présentation des décors en stuc du bâtiment dit de "l'Huilerie" à Salamine," in *Salamine de Chypre* 341-73.

Callot, O. 1984. *Huileries antiques de Syrie du nord* (BAHBeyrouth 118).

Callot, O. 1985. "Salamine-Constantia. Note de numismatique et de topographie d'époque byzantine," *RDAC* 335-39.

Calvi, M. C. 1965. "La coppa vitrea di Aristeas nella collezione Strada," *JGS* 7, 9-16.

Cameron, A. 1992. "Cyprus at the time of the Arab conquests," *Επετηρίς της Κυπριακή Εταιρείας Ιστορικόν Σπούδων* 1, 27-49; repr. in ead., *Changing cultures in early Byzantium* (Aldershot 1996).

Cameron, A. 1993. *The Mediterranean world in late antiquity, A.D. 395-600* (London).

Campbell, S. 1988. *The mosaics of Antioch* (Subsidia mediaevalia 15, Toronto).

Campbell, S. 1991. *The mosaics of Aphrodisias in Caria* (Subsidia mediaevalia 18, Toronto).

Campbell, S. 1998. *The mosaics of Anemurium* (Subsidia mediaevalia 25, Toronto).

Casson, L. 1984. *Ancient trade and society* (Detroit, MI).

Catling, H. W. 1962. "Patterns of settlement in Bronze Age Cyprus," *OpAth* 4, 129-69.

Catling, H. W. 1972. "An early Byzantine pottery factory at Dhiorios in Cyprus," *Levant* 4, 1-82.

Catling H. W. 1973. "Observations on the archaeological survey in the area of Phlamoudhi, Cyprus," *RDAC* 107-15.

Catling, H. W. 1979. "Reflections upon the interpretation of the archaeological evidence for the history of Cyprus," in Karageorghis 1979, 194-205.

Catling, H. W. 1982. "The ancient topography of the Yalias valley," *RDAC* 227-36.

Catling, H. W. and A. I. Dikigoropoulos 1970. "The Kornos cave: an early Byzantine site in Cyprus," *Levant* 2, 37-62.

Chalkia, E. 1991. *Le mense paleocristiane. Tipologia e funzioni delle mense secondarie nel culto paleocristiano* (Studi di antichità cristiana 47, Vatican City).

Chavane, M.-J. 1975. *Salamine de Chypre* VI. *Les petits objets* (Paris).

Cherry, J. F., J. L. Davis, and E. Mantzourani 1991. *Landscape archaeology as long-term history. Northern Keos in the Cycladic islands from earliest settlement until modern times* (Monumenta archaeologica 16, Los Angeles).

Childs, W. A. P. 1988. "First preliminary report on the excavations at Polis Chrysochous by Princeton University," *RDAC* 2, 121-30.

Childs, W. A. P. 1999. "Princeton excavations at Polis Chrysochous, 1994-1997: interim report," *RDAC* 223-36.

Chollot, M. 1973. "Perspectives d'archéologie sous-marine au Liban," *CahArchSubaq* 2, 147-56.

Christie, N. and S. T. Loseby (edd.) 1996. *Towns in transition. Urban evolution in late antiquity and the early Middle Ages* (Aldershot).

Christodoulou, D. 1959. *The evolution of the rural land use pattern in Cyprus* (Bude, Cornwall).

Christou, D. 1994. "Chronique des fouilles et découvertes archéologiques à Chypre en 1993," *BCH* 118, 647-93.

Christou, D. 1995. "Chronique des fouilles et découvertes archéologiques à Chypre en 1994," *BCH* 119, 799-838.

Christou, D. 1996a. "Chronique des fouilles et découvertes archéologiques à Chypre en 1995," *BCH* 120, 1051-1100.

Christou, D. 1996b. *Kourion. Its monuments and local museum* (Nicosia).

Christou, D. 1997. "Chronique des fouilles et découvertes archéologiques à Chypre en 1996," *BCH* 121, 891-933.

Chrysos, E. 1984. "Ο Ηράκλειος στην Κύπρο (609/10)," in K. N. Konstantinides (ed.), *Πρακτικά συμποσίου Κυπριακές ιστορίας, Λευκωσία, 1983* (Ioannina) 53-62.

Chrysos, E. 1993. "Cyprus in early Byzantine times," in Bryer and Georghallides 1993, 3-14.

Clarke, J. and I. A. Todd 1993. "The field survey of Kalavasos-*Pamboules*," *RDAC* 11-27.

Clerc, G. 1991. "Aegyptiaca," in V. Karageorghis, O. Picard, and Ch. Tytgat (edd.), *La nécropole d'Amathonte. Tombes 110-385*, V (Études chypriotes XIII, Nicosia) 1-157.

Cobham, C. D. 1908. *Excerpta Cypria: materials for a history of Cyprus* (Cambridge; repr. New York 1969).

Conrad, L. I. 1992. "The conquest of Arwad: a source-critical study in the historiography of the early medieval Near East," in A. Cameron and L. I. Conrad (edd.), *The Byzantine and early Islamic Near East,* I. *Problems in the literary source material* (Princeton) 317-401.

Conrad, L. I. 1994. "Epidemic disease in central Syria in the late sixth century. Some new insights from the verse of Hassan ibn Thabit," *BMGS* 18, 12-58.

Constable-Maxwell 1979. *Catalogue of the Constable-Maxwell collection of ancient glass.* Sotheby Parke Bernet sale auction, 4-5 June, 1979 (London).

Constantinou, G. 1980. *Annual report of the Geological Survey Department for the year 1979* (Nicosia).

Coureas, N. and J. Riley-Smith (edd.) 1995. *Cyprus and the Crusades. Papers given at the int. conference "Cyprus and the Crusades," Nicosia, 1994* (Nicosia).

Cox, D. H. 1959. *Coins from the excavations at Curium, 1932-1953* (American Numismatic Notes and Monog. 145).

Crowfoot, G. M. 1957. "Glass," in J. W. Crowfoot, G. M. Crowfoot, and K. M. Kenyon, *The objects from Samaria* (London) 403-22.

Crowfoot, G. M. and D. B. Harden 1931. "Early Byzantine and later glass lamps," *JEA* 17, 196-208.

Ćurčić, S. 1999. "Byzantine architecture on Cyprus: an introduction to the problem of the genesis of a regional style," in Ševčenko and Moss 1999, 71-91.

Curta, F. 2001. "Peasants as 'makeshift soldiers for the occasion': sixth-century settlement patterns in the Balkans," in Burns and Eadie 2001, 199-217.

Dagron, G. 1979. "Entre village et cité: la bourgade rurale des IVe-VIIe siècles en Orient," *Koinonia* 3, 29-52; repr. in id., *La romanité chrétienne en Orient: héritages et mutations* (London 1984).

Daszewski, W. A. 1970. "Polish excavations at Kato (Nea) Paphos. Second preliminary report: seasons 1968 and 1969," *RDAC* 112-41.

Dauphin, C. 1987. "Les 'komai' de Palestine," *Proche Orient chrétien* 37, 251-67.

Dauphin, C. 1998. *La Palestine byzantine. Peuplement et populations* (BAR S726, Oxford).

Davidson, G. R. 1952. *Corinth* XII. *The minor objects* (Princeton).

Dawkins, R. M. 1932. *Leontios Makhairas. Recital concerning the sweet land of Cyprus entitled "Chronicle"* (Oxford).

Decker, M. 2001. "Food for an empire: wine and oil production in North Syria," in Kingsley and Decker 2001a, 69-86.

de Groot, A. H. 1980. "Kubrus," in *Encyclopaedia of Islam* 5 (Leiden) 301-9.

de Ligt, L. 1993. *Fairs and markets in the Roman empire* (Amsterdam).

Delougaz, P. and R. C. Haines 1960. *A Byzantine church at Khirbat al-Karak* (Oriental Institute publ. 85).

Delvoye, Ch. 1972. "La place de Chypre dans l'architecture paléochrétienne de la Méditerranée," in *Πρακτικά του τρίτου διεθνούς Κυπριολογικού συνεδρίου, Λευκωσία, 1969,* vol. II (Nicosia) 17-21.

Delvoye, Ch. 1976. "L'art paléochrétien de Chypre," in *XVe Congrès int. d'études byzantines, Athènes, 1976, Rapports et co-rapports* (Athens).

Demesticha, S. 2000. "The Paphos kiln. Manufacturing techniques of LR1 amphoras," *RCRF Acta* 36, 549-54.

Demesticha, S. and D. Michaelides 2001. "The excavation of a Late Roman 1 amphora kiln in Paphos," in Villeneuve and Watson 2001, 289-96.

Demetriou, K. 1997. "Victorian Cyprus: society and institutions in the aftermath of the Anglo-Turkish convention, 1878-1891," *BMGS* 21, 1-29.

des Gagniers, J. and Tran Tam Tinh 1985. *Soloi. Dix campagnes de fouilles, 1964-1974,* I (Ste. Foy, Québec).

Devos, G., P. De Paepe, and F. Vermeulen 1999. "The *pithoi* from the ancient Anatolian city of Pessinus. An integrated archaeological and petrographical study," *BABesch* 74, 79-110.

de Vries, B. 1998. *Umm el-Jimal. A frontier town and its landscape in Northern Jordan,* I. *Fieldwork 1972-1981* (*JRA* Suppl. 26).

di Cesnola, L. P. 1877. *Cyprus. Its ancient cities, tombs, and temples* (London).

di Cesnola, L. P. 1894. *A descriptive atlas of the Cesnola collection of Cypriote antiquities in the Metropolitan Museum of Art,* II (New York).

Diederichs, C. 1980a. "Plats estampés d'époque byzantine," in *Salamine de Chypre* 389-93.

Diederichs, C. 1980b. *Salamine de Chypre* IX. *Céramiques hellénistiques, romaines et byzantines* (Paris).

Dikaios, P. 1936. "The excavations at Erimi, 1933-35: a final report," *RDAC* 1, 1-81.

Dikigoropoulos, A. I. 1940-48. "The political status of Cyprus A.D. 648-965," *RDAC* 94-114.

Dikigoropoulos, A. I. 1956. "A Byzantine hoard from Kharcha, Cyprus," *NC* 6.16, 255-65.

Dikigoropoulos, A. I. 1978. "Agrarian conditions and the demography of Cyprus during the period of the Arab wars A.D. 648-965," *Γεογραφικά χρονικά* 8, 3-14.

Donceel-Voûte, P. 1988. *Les pavements des églises byzantines de Syrie et du Liban. Décor, archéologie et liturgie* (Louvain-la-Neuve).

Donceel-Voûte, P. 1995. "Syro-Phoenician mosaics of the 6th century," in R. Ling (ed.), *Fifth int. colloquium on ancient mosaics held at Bath, England, 1987* (*JRA* Suppl. 9.2) 88-100.

Dore, J. N. 1992. "First report on the pottery," in Ben Lazreg and Mattingly 1992, 115-56.

Downey, S. B. 1977. *The stone and plaster sculpture. Excavations at Dura-Europos. Final report* III, 1.2 (Monumenta archaeologica 5, Los Angeles).

du Bouetiez, E. *et al.* 1991. "Rapport sur les travaux de l'École française à Amathonte de Chypre en 1990. La basilique de l'acropole," *BCH* 115, 751-59.

Dunnell, R. C. and J. F. Simek 1995. "Artifact size and plowzone processes," *JFA* 22, 305-19.

Durliat, J. 1990. *De la ville antique à la ville byzantine. Le problème des subsistances* (CollÉFR 136).

Duval, N. 1994. "L'architecture chrétienne et les pratiques liturgiques en Jordanie en rapport avec la Palestine: recherches nouvelles," in Painter 1994, 149-212.

Edmondson, J. C. 1989. "Mining in the later Roman empire and beyond: continuity or disruption?" *JRS* 79, 84-102.

Egloff, M. 1977. *Kellia. La poterie copte. Quatre siècles d'artisanat et d'échanges en Basse-Egypte* (Geneva).

Eliakis C., E. Eliakis, and P. Iordanidis 1966. "Détermination de la taille d'après la mensuration des os longs," *Annales de médecine légale* 46, 403-21.

Elliott, C., C. Xenophontos, and J. G. Malpas 1986. "Petrographic and mineral analyses used in tracing the provenance of Late Bronze Age and Roman basalt artefacts from Cyprus," *RDAC* 80-96.

Empereur, J.-Y. 1985. "Rapport sur les travaux de l'École française à Amathonte de Chypre en 1984. Le port," *BCH* 109, 984-89.

Empereur, J.-Y. and Y. Garlan (edd.) 1986. *Recherches sur les amphores grecques. Actes du colloque int. Athènes, 1984* (*BCH* Suppl. XIII).

Empereur, J.-Y. and M. Picon 1988. "The production of Aegean amphorae: field and laboratory studies," in R. E. Jones and H. W. Catling (edd.), *New aspects of archaeological science in Greece* (Fitch Laboratory occ. pap. 3, Athens) 33-38.

Empereur, J.-Y. and M. Picon 1989. "Les régions de production d'amphores impériales en méditerranée orientale," in *Amphores romaines et histoire économique* (CollÉFR 114) 223-48.

Empereur, J.-Y. and M. Picon 1998. "Les ateliers d'amphores du lac Mariout," in J.-Y. Empereur (ed.), *Commerce et artisanat dans l'Alexandrie hellénistique et romaine* (*BCH* Suppl. 33) 75-91.

Empereur, J.-Y. and C. Verlinden 1987. "The underwater excavation at the ancient port of Amathus in Cyprus," *IJNA* 16, 7-18.

Engvig, O. T. and P. Åström 1975. *Hala Sultan Tekke* II. *The Cape Kiti Survey. An underwater archaeological survey* (SIMA 45.2).

Engvig, O. T. and M. Beichmann 1984. "Underwater activities and the situation at Cape Kiti, Cyprus," *OpAth* 15, 181-86.

Falkenhausen, V. von 1999. "Bishops and monks in the hagiography of Byzantine Cyprus," in Ševčenko and Moss 1999, 21-33.

Fazekas, I. G. and F. Kósa 1978. *Forensic fetal osteology* (Budapest).

Feissel, D. 1987. "Bulletin épigraphique. Inscriptions chrétiennes et byzantines," *REG* 100, 347-87.

Fejfer, J. (ed.) 1995. *Ancient Akamas* I. *Settlement and environment* (Aarhus).

Fejfer, J. and P. P. Hayes 1995. "Ancient Akamas and the abandonment of sites in 7th century A.D. Cyprus," in P. W. Wallace (ed.), *Visitors, immigrants, and invaders in Cyprus* (Albany, NY) 62-69.

Fejfer, J. and H. Mathiesen 1991. "The Danish Akamas Project. The first two seasons of work (1989-1990)," *RDAC* 211-23.

Fejfer, J. and H. E. Mathiesen 1992. "Ayios Kononas. A Late Roman/early Byzantine site in the Akamas," in Åström 1992, vol. 2, 67-83.

Felten, F. 1975. "Die christliche Siedlung," in H. Walter (ed.), *Alt-Ägina* I, part 2 (Mainz) 55-80.

Festugière, A.-J. (ed.) 1970. *Vie de Théodore de Sykéôn* (Subsidia hagiographica 48).

Fitzgerald, G. M. 1931. *Beth Shan excavations 1921-1923. The Arab and Byzantine levels* (Philadelphia).

Fitzwilliam Museum 1978. *Glass at the Fitzwilliam Museum* (Cambridge).

Flourentzos, P. 1988. "Tombs at Kalavassos: new cippi types and rare pottery forms," *Levant* 20, 235-38.

Flourentzos, P. 1996. *Excavations in the Kouris valley, II. The basilica of Alassa* (Nicosia).

Forsyth, G. H. and K. Weitzmann 1973. *The monastery of Saint Catherine at Mount Sinai. The church and fortress of Justinian* (Ann Arbor).

Foss, C. 1975. "The Persians in Asia Minor and the end of antiquity," *EHR* 90, 721-47.

Foss, C. 1997. "Syria in transition, A.D. 550-750: an archaeological approach," *DOP* 51, 189-269.

Fossey, J. M. 1986. "Répartition de la céramique en surface du site," in J. M. Fossey and J. Morin (edd.), *Khóstia 1983. Rapport préliminaire sur la seconde campagne de fouilles canadiennes à Khóstia en Béotie, Grèce centrale* (Amsterdam) 43-63.

Fox, S. C. 1996. "The human skeletal remains from Alassa-*Ayia Mavri*," in Flourentzos 1996, 39-64.

Fox, W. A. and D. A. Perlman 1987. "Threshing sledge production in the Paphos district, Cyprus," in Rupp 1987, 227-34.

Foxhall, L. 1998. "Snapping up the unconsidered trifles. The use of agricultural residues in ancient Greek and Roman farming," *Environmental archaeology* 1, 35-40.

Foxhall, L. and H. A. Forbes 1982. "Σιτομετρεία: the role of grain as a staple food in classical antiquity," *Chiron* 12, 41-90.

Frankel, R. 1997. "Presses for oil and wine in the southern Levant in the Byzantine period," *DOP* 51, 73-84.

Frankovich, R., H. Patterson, and G. Barker (edd.) 2000. *The archaeology of Mediterranean landscapes, 5. Extracting meaning from ploughsoil assemblages* (Oxford).

Frantz, A. 1988. *The Athenian Agora* XXIV. *Late antiquity: A.D. 267-700* (Princeton).

Fraser, P. M. and E. Matthews 1987. *A lexikon of Greek personal names,* I. *The Aegean islands, Cyprus, Cyrenaica* (Oxford).

Freshfield, E. 1873. "On Byzantine churches, and the modifications made in their arrangements owing to the necessities of the Greek ritual," *Archaeologia* 44, 383-92.

Fulford, M. G. 1987. "Economic interdependence among urban communities of the Roman Mediterranean," *WorldArch* 19, 58-75.

Fulford, M. G. 1989. "To east and west: the Mediterranean trade of Cyrenaica and Tripolitania in antiquity," *LibSt* 20, 169-91.

Fulford, M. G. and D. P. S. Peacock 1984. *Excavations at Carthage: the British Mission* I, 2. *The Avenue du Président Habib Bourguiba, Salammbo: the pottery and other ceramic objects from the site* (Sheffield).

Gaffney, C. F. and V. L. Gaffney 1986. "From Boeotia to Berkshire: an integrated approach to geophysics and rural field survey," *Prospezione archeologiche* 10, 65-70.

Gallant, T. W. 1991. *Risk and survival in ancient Greece: reconstructing the rural domestic economy* (Stanford).

Garnsey, P. 1988. *Famine and food supply in the Graeco-Roman world* (Cambridge).

Gatier, P.-L. 1994. "Villages du Proche-Orient protobyzantin (4ème-7ème s.). Étude régionale," in King and Cameron 1994, 17-48.

Gertwagen, R. 1995. "Maritime activity concerning the ports and harbours of Cyprus from the late 12th to the 16th centuries (1191-1571)," in Coureas and Riley-Smith 1995, 511-38.

Giangrande, C. *et al.* 1987. "Cyprus underwater survey, 1983-1984. A preliminary report," *RDAC* 185-97.

Giudice, F. *et al.* 1993. "Paphos, Garrison's camp. Campagna 1989," *RDAC* 279-327.

Giudice, F. *et al.* 1994. "Paphos, Garrison's camp. Campagna 1990," *RDAC* 215-68.

Giudice, F. *et al.* 1998. "Paphos, Garrison's camp. Va campagna (1992)," *RDAC* 187-202.

Giudice, F. *et al.* 1999. "Pafos, Garrison's camp. VIa campagna," *RDAC* 279-314.

Giudice, F. *et al.* 2000. "Paphos, Garrison's camp. VIIa campagna," *RDAC* 259-98.

Given, M. 2000. "Agriculture, settlement and landscape in Ottoman Cyprus," *Levant* 32, 209-30.

Given, M. and A. B. Knapp forthcoming. *The Sydney Cyprus Survey Project. Social approaches to regional archaeological survey.*

Given, M. *et al.* 1999. "The Sydney Cyprus Survey Project: an interdisciplinary investigation of long-term change in the north central Troodos, Cyprus," *JFA* 26, 19-39.

Given, M. *et al.* 2002. "Troodos Archaeological and Environmental Survey Project, Cyprus: report on the 2001 season," *Levant* 34, 25-38.

Gjerstad, E. *et al.* 1934. *Swedish Cyprus Expedition. Finds and results of the excavations in Cyprus 1927-1931,* I (Stockholm).

Gomez, B. 1987. "The alluvial terraces and fills of the lower Vasilikos valley, in the vicinity of Kalavasos, Cyprus," *Transactions, Institute of British Geographers* 12, 345-59.

Gomez, B. *et al.* 1995. "Clays related to the production of White Slip ware," *RDAC* 113-18.

Gomez, B. *et al.* 1996. "Clays used in the manufacture of Cypriot Red Slip pottery and related ceramics," *RDAC* 69-82.

Gomez, B. *et al.* 2002. "Source provenance of Bronze Age and Roman pottery from Cyprus," *Archaeometry* 44, 23-36.

Goodwin, J. C. 1984. *An historical toponymy of Cyprus* (4th edn., Pano Lakatamia).

Gough, M. (ed.) 1985. *Alahan. An Early Christian monastery in southern Turkey* (Toronto).

Gounaridis, P. 1996. "The economy of Byzantine Cyprus: Cyprus, an ordinary Byzantine province," in Karageorghis and Michaelides 1996, 175-84.

Graf, D. F. 2001. "Town and countryside in Roman Arabia during late antiquity," in Burns and Eadie 2001, 219-40.

Green, J. N. 1973. "An underwater archaeological survey of Cape Andreas, Cyprus, 1969-70. A preliminary report," in D. J. Blackman (ed.), *Marine archaeology* (London) 141-78.

Gregory, T. E. 1985. "An early Byzantine complex at Akra Sophia near Corinth," *Hesperia* 54, 411-28.

Gregory, T. E. 1986. "Intensive archaeological survey and its place in Byzantine studies," *Byzantine studies/Études byzan-*

tines 13, 155-75.

Gregory, T. E. 1987. "Circulation of Byzantine and medieval pottery in southwestern Cyprus," in Rupp 1987, 199-213.

Gregory, T. E. 1993. "Byzantine and medieval pottery," in Sørensen and Rupp 1993, 157-75.

Gregory, T. E. and P. N. Kardulias 1990. "Geophysical and surface surveys in the Byzantine fortress at Isthmia, 1985-1986," *Hesperia* 59, 467-511.

Grierson, P. 1968. *Catalogue of the Byzantine coins in the Dumbarton Oaks collection and in the Whittemore collection, II. Phocas to Theodosius III, 602-717* (Washington, D.C.).

Grierson, P. 1982. *Byzantine coins* (Berkeley).

Grierson, P. and M. Mayes 1992. *Catalogue of Late Roman coins in the Dumbarton Oaks collections and in the Whittemore collection* (Washington, D.C.).

Grivaud, G. 1996. "Population et peuplement rural à Chypre (fin XIIe siècle–milieu du XVIe)," in J. Fridrich *et al.* (edd.), *Ruralia* I. *Conference ruralia I — Prague, 1995* (Prague) 217-26.

Grossmann, P. 1973. *S. Michele in Africisco zu Ravenna. Baugeschichtliche Untersuchungen* (Mainz).

Grove, A. T. 2001. "The Little Ice Age and its geomorphological consequences in Mediterranean Europe," *Climatic Change* 48, 121-36.

Guillou, A. 1998. "La géographie historique de l'île de Chypre pendant la période byzantine," in *Matériaux pour une histoire de Chypre (IVe-XXe s.)* (Études balkaniques 5, Paris) 11-32.

Gunneweg, J. 1984. "The origin of Eastern Terra Sigillata-A and Hayes' 'Cypriot Sigillata' (on the basis of Neutron Activation Analysis)," *RCRFActa* 23-24, 111-15.

Gunneweg, J., I. Perlman, and J. Yellin 1983. *The provenience, typology, and chronology of Eastern Terra Sigillata* (Qedem 17).

Habas, L. 1999. "The marble furniture," in Hirschfeld 1999, 119-32.

Hackett, J. 1901. *A history of the Orthodox Church of Cyprus* (London).

Hadjichristophi, F. 1989. "Rapport sur les travaux de l'École française à Amathonte de Chypre en 1988. Les tuiles de la basilique," *BCH* 113, 875-78.

Hadjichristophi, F. 1997. "Το δάπεδο του Αγίου Προκοπίου στη Σύγκραση," *RDAC* 277-83.

Hadjichristophi, F. 1998. "L'île aux cent basiliques," *Le monde de la Bible* 112, juillet-août 1998.

Hadjichristophi, F. 2000. "Les pavements du VIe siècle à Chypre," in *Πρακτικά του τρίτου διεθνούς Κυπριολογικού συνεδρίου, Λευκοσία, 1996*, vol. I (Nicosia) 531-44.

Hadjisavvas, S. 1977. "The archaeological survey of Paphos. A preliminary report," *RDAC* 222-31.

Hadjisavvas, S. 1983. "New light on the history of the Ayia Napa region," *RDAC* 315-18.

Hadjisavvas, S. 1988. "Olive oil production in ancient Cyprus," *RDAC* 2, 111-20.

Hadjisavvas, S. 1991. *Καταβολές I. Η αρχαιολογική επισκόπηση 20 κατεχομένων σήμερα χωριών της επαρχίας Αμμοχώστου* (Nicosia).

Hadjisavvas, S. 1992. *Olive oil processing in Cyprus from the Bronze Age to the Byzantine period* (SIMA 99).

Hadjisavvas, S. 1996. "The economy of the olive," in Karageorghis and Michaelides 1996, 127-37.

Hadjisavvas, S. 1997. *Ayia Napa. Excavations at Makronisos and the archaeology of the region* (Nicosia).

Hadjisavvas, S. 1998. "Chronique des fouilles et découvertes archéologiques à Chypre en 1997," *BCH* 122, 663-703.

Hadjisavvas, S. 1999. "Chronique des fouilles et découvertes archéologiques à Chypre en 1998," *BCH* 123, 599-633.

Hadjisavvas, S. 2000. "Chronique des fouilles et découvertes archéologiques à Chypre en 1999," *BCH* 124, 665-99.

Haldon, J. F. 1997. *Byzantium in the seventh century. The transformation of a culture* (rev. edn. Cambridge).

Haldon, J. F. 1999. "The idea of the town in the Byzantine empire," in Brogiolo and Ward-Perkins 1999, 1-23.

Halstead, P. 1987. "Traditional and ancient rural economy in Mediterranean Europe: plus ça change? *JHS* 107, 77-87.

Harden, D. B. 1935. "Romano-Syrian glasses with mould-blown inscriptions," *JRS* 25, 163-86.

Harden, D. B. 1936. *Roman glass from Karanis found by the University of Michigan Archaeological Expedition in Egypt, 1924-29* (Ann Arbor).

Harden, D. B. 1944-45. "Two tomb-groups of the first century A.D. from Yahmour, Syria, and a supplement to the list of Romano-Syrian glass with mould-blown inscriptions," *Syria* 24, 81-95.

Harden, D. B. 1961. "Domestic window glass: Roman, Saxon and Medieval," in E. M. Jope (ed.), *Studies in building. Essays in recognition of the work of B. H. St. J. O'Neil* (London) 39-63.

Harden, D. B. 1962. "Glass," in H. D. Colt (ed.), *Excavations at Nessana* I (Princeton) 76-91.

Harrison, R. M. 1986. *Excavations at Saraçhane in Istanbul* 1. *The excavations* (Princeton).

Harrison, R. M. and M. V. Gill 1986. "The mosaics," in Harrison 1986, 182-96.

Harvey, A. 1989. *Economic expansion in the Byzantine empire, 900-1200* (Cambridge).

Hassan, F. A. 1981. *Demographic archaeology* (New York).

Hautumm, W. 1981. *Studien zu Amphoren der spätrömischen und frühbyzantinischen Zeit* (Fulda).

Hayes, J. W. 1967. "'Cypriot sigillata,'" *RDAC* 65-77.

Hayes, J. W. 1972. *Late Roman pottery* (London).

Hayes, J. W. 1975. *Roman and pre-Roman glass in the Royal Ontario Museum* (Toronto).

Hayes, J. W. 1980a. *A supplement to* Late Roman Pottery (London).

Hayes, J. W. 1980b. "Problèmes de la céramique des VIIème-IXème siècles à Salamine et à Chypre," in *Salamine de Chypre* 375-87.

Hayes, J. W. 1985. "Hellenistic to Byzantine fine wares and derivatives in the Jerusalem corpus," in Tushingham 1985, 179-94.

Hayes, J. W. 1991. *Paphos* III. *The Hellenistic and Roman pottery* (Nicosia).

Hayes, J. W. 1992. *Excavations at Saraçhane in Istanbul* 2. *The pottery* (Princeton).

Hayes, J. W. 1998a. "Pottery of the 6th and 7th centuries," in N. Cambi and E. Marin (edd.), *Acta XIII Congressus int. archaeologiae christianae, Split-Poreč 1994*, vol. II (Vatican City) 541-50.

Hayes, J. W. 1998b. "The study of Roman pottery in the Mediterranean: 23 years after *Late Roman Pottery*," in Saguì 1998, vol. 1, 9-21.

Hayes, J. W. 2001a. "Early Christian pottery from Knossos: the 1978-1981 finds from the Knossos medical faculty site," *BSA* 96, 431-54.

Hayes, J. W. 2001b. "Late Roman fine wares and their successors: a Mediterranean Byzantine perspective (with reference to the Syro-Jordanian situation)," in Villeneuve and Watson 2001, 275-82.

Hayes, J. W. forthcoming. "The pottery and clay lamps," in Megaw forthcoming.

Held, S. O. 1988. "Sotira-*Kaminoudia* survey: preliminary report of the 1983 and 1984 seasons," *RDAC* 53-62.

Held, S. O. 1993. "Insularity as a modifier of culture change. The case of prehistoric Cyprus," *BASOR* 292, 25-33.

Hellenkemper, H. 1989. "Ein byzantinisches Baumaß," *IstMitt* 39, 181-90.

Hellenkemper, H. 1994. "Early church architecture in southern Asia Minor," in Painter 1994, 213-38.

Hellström, P. 1965. *Labraunda* II, 1. *Pottery of classical and later date* (Lund).

Helly, B. 1973. "Monnaies d'or et d'argent byzantines et médiévales," in *Salamine de Chypre* IV. *Anthologie Salaminienne* (Paris) 197-200.

Hendy, M. F. 1985. *Studies in the Byzantine monetary economy, c.300-1450* (Cambridge).

Hereford, R. 1984. "Climate and ephemeral-stream processes: twentieth-century geomorphology and alluvial stratigraphy of the Little Colorado river, Arizona," *Geological Society of America Bulletin* 95, 654-68.

Hermary, A. 1987. "Statuettes, sarcophages et stèles décorées," in V. Karageorghis, O. Picard, and Ch. Tygat (edd.), *La nécropole d'Amathonte. Tombes 113-367*, vol. III (Études chypriotes IX) 55-75.

Hill, G. 1940. *A history of Cyprus* I. *To the conquest by Richard Lion Heart* (Cambridge).

Hill, S. 1996. *The early Byzantine churches of Cilicia and Isauria* (Birmingham Byzantine and Ottoman monog. 1).

Hirschfeld, Y. 1992. *The Judean desert monasteries in the Byzantine period* (New Haven).

Hirschfeld, Y. 1995. *The Palestinian dwelling in the Roman-Byzantine period* (Jerusalem).

Hirschfeld, Y. 1997. "Farms and villages in Byzantine Palestine," *DOP* 51, 33-71.

Hirschfeld, Y. 1999. *The early Byzantine monastery at Khirbet ed-Deir in the Judean Desert. The excavations in 1981-1987* (Qedem 38).

Hogarth, D. G. 1889. *Devia Cypria. Notes of an archaeological journey in Cyprus in 1888* (London).

Hohlfelder, R. L. 1992. "The Paphos ancient harbour explorations, 1991," *RDAC* 255-56.

Hohlfelder, R. L. 1995. "Ancient Paphos beneath the sea. A survey of the submerged structures," in Karageorghis and Michaelides 1995, 191-210.

Hopkins, K. 1983. "Models, ships and staples," in P. Garnsey and C. R. Whittaker (edd.), *Trade and famine in classical antiquity* (Cambridge) 84-109.

Horden, P. and N. Purcell 2000. *The corrupting sea. A study of Mediterranean history* (Oxford).

Howard-Johnston, J. 1999. "Heraclius' Persian campaigns and the revival of the east Roman empire," *War in History* 6, 1-44.

Huffstot, J. 1987. "Rooftiles," in Soren 1987, 263-99.

Ionas, I. 1988. *La maison rurale de Chypre (XVIIIe-XXe siècle). Aspects et techniques de construction* (Nicosia).

Ionas, I. 1993-94. "Subsistence economy in Cyprus," *Επετηρίς του Κέντρου Επιστημονικών Ερευνών Κύπρου* 21, 1-13.

Ionas, I. 1998. *Pottery in the Cyprus tradition* (Nicosia).

Ionas, I. 2000. *Traditional pottery and potters in Cyprus* (Aldershot).

Iscan, M. Y. 1989. *Age markers in the human skeleton* (Springfield, IL).

Iscan, M. Y., S. R. Loth, and R. K. Wright 1984. "Age estimation from the rib by phase analysis: white males," *Journal of Forensic Sciences* 29, 1094-1104.

Isings, C. 1957. *Roman glass from dated finds* (Groningen).

Jasny, N. 1944. *The wheats of classical antiquity* (Baltimore).

Jaubert, P.-A. (ed.) 1836-40. *La géographie d'Édrisi* (Paris).

Jeffery, G. E. 1928. "The basilica of Constantia, Cyprus," *AntJ* 8, 344-49.

Jeffery, J. G. 1918. *A description of the historic monuments of Cyprus* (Nicosia).

Jenkins, R. J. H. 1953. "Cyprus between Byzantium and Islam, A.D. 688-965," in G. E. Mylonas (ed.), *Studies presented to David Moore Robinson* II (St. Louis) 1006-14; repr. in R. J. H. Jenkins, *Studies in Byzantine history of the 9th and 10th centuries* (London 1970).

Johnson, B. L. 1986. "Syro-Palestinian bag-shaped amphoras in the Athenian Agora and Corinth collections," in Empereur and Garlan 1986, 589-97.

Johnson, B. L. 1988. "The pottery," in Weinberg 1988, 137-226.

Johnston, F. E. 1962. "Growth of the long bones of infants and young children at Indian Knoll," *American Journal of Physical Anthropology* 20, 249-54.

Johnston, R. H. 1974. "The Cypriot potter," in Stager, Walker, and Wright 1974, 131-39.

Jones, A. H. M. 1964. *The later Roman empire, 284-602* (Oxford).

Jones, F. F. 1950. "The pottery," in H. Goldman (ed.), *Excavations at Gözlü Kule, Tarsus*, I (Princeton) 149-296.

Jones, J. D. forthcoming. "Glass from el-Lejjun: final report," in S. T. Parker (ed.), *The Roman frontier in Central Jordan. Final report on the Limes Arabicus Project, 1980-1989.*

Jones, R. E. 1986. *Greek and Cypriot pottery. A review of scientific studies* (Fitch Laboratory occ. pap. 1, Athens).

Kaegi, W. E. 1992. *Byzantium and the early Islamic conquests* (Cambridge).

Kaegi, W. E. 1998. "Egypt on the eve of the Muslim conquest," in C. F. Petry (ed.), *The Cambridge history of Egypt* I. *Islamic Egypt, 640-1517* (Cambridge) 34-61.

Kaplan, M. 1992. *Les hommes et la terre à Byzance du VIe au XIe siècle. Propriété et exploitation du sol* (Byzantina Sorbonensia 10).

Karageorghis, V. 1960. "Chronique des fouilles et découvertes archéologiques à Chypre en 1959," *BCH* 84, 242-99.

Karageorghis, V. 1962. "Chronique des fouilles et découvertes archéologiques à Chypre en 1961," *BCH* 86, 327-414.

Karageorghis, V. 1963. "Chronique des fouilles et découvertes archéologiques à Chypre en 1962," *BCH* 87, 325-87.

Karageorghis, V. 1964. "Chronique des fouilles et découvertes archéologiques à Chypre en 1963," *BCH* 88, 289-379.

Karageorghis, V. 1969. "Chronique des fouilles et découvertes archéologiques à Chypre en 1968," *BCH* 93, 431-569

Karageorghis, V. 1976. "Chronique des fouilles et découvertes archéologiques à Chypre en 1975," *BCH* 100, 839-906.

Karageorghis, V. (ed.) 1979. *Studies presented in memory of Porphyrios Dikaios* (Nicosia).

Karageorghis, V. (ed.) 1985a. *Archaeology in Cyprus 1960-1985* (Nicosia).

Karageorghis, V. 1985b. "The Cyprus Department of Antiquities, 1935-1985," in Karageorghis 1985a, 1-10.

Karageorghis, V. (ed.) 1986. *Acts of the int. archaeological symposium "Cyprus between the Orient and the Occident," Nicosia, 1985* (Nicosia).

Karageorghis, V. 1999. *Excavating at Salamis in Cyprus, 1952-1974* (Athens).

Karageorghis, V. and D. Michaelides (edd.) 1995. *Proc. int. symposium "Cyprus and the sea," Nicosia, 1993* (Nicosia).

Karageorghis, V. and D. Michaelides (edd.) 1996. *The development of the Cypriot economy from the prehistoric period to the present day* (Nicosia).

Karagiorgou, O. 2001. "LR2: a container for the military *annona* on the Danubian border?" in Kingsley and Decker 2001a, 129-66.

Kardulias, P. N., T. E. Gregory, and J. Sawmiller 1995. "Bronze Age and late antique exploitation of an islet in the Saronic Gulf, Greece," *JFA* 22, 3-21.

Karouzis, G. 1977. *Landownership in Cyprus, past and present* (Nicosia).

Kassianidou, V. 2000. "Hellenistic and Roman mining in Cyprus," in *Πρακτικά του τρίτου διεθνούς Κυπριολογικού συνεδρίου, Λευκοσία, 1996*, vol. I (Nicosia) 745-56.

Katz, D. and J. M. Suchey 1986. "Age determination of the male *Os pubis*," *American Journal of Physical Anthropology* 69, 427-35.

Keay, S. J. 1984. *Late Roman amphorae in the western Mediterranean. A typology and economic study: the Catalan evidence* (BAR S196, Oxford).

Keay, S. J. 1994. "Towns in the Roman world: economic centers or cultural symbols?" in *La ciutat en el món Romà. Actes, XIVè Congrès Int. d'Arqueologia Classica, Tarragona, 1993*, I (Tarragona) 253-59.

Keay, S., J. Creighton, and D. Jordan 1991. "Sampling ancient towns," *OJA* 10, 371-83.

Keller, D. R. and D. W. Rupp (edd.) 1983. *Archaeological survey in the Mediterranean area* (BAR S155, Oxford).

Keswani, P. S. 1989. "The pithoi and other plain ware vessels," in South, Russell, and Keswani 1989, 12-21.

King, G. R. D. and A. Cameron (edd.) 1994. *The Byzantine and early Islamic Near East II. Land use and settlement patterns* (Princeton).

King, R. H. 1987. "An investigation of the geographical origins of pottery from southwestern Cyprus and the source of materials used in their manufacture," in Rupp 1987, 215-26.

Kingsley, S. A. 1999. "The Sumaqa pottery assemblage: classification and quantification," in S. Dar, *Sumaqa. A Roman and Byzantine Jewish village on Mount Carmel, Israel* (BAR S815, Oxford) 263-329.

Kingsley, S. A. 2001. "The economic impact of the Palestinian wine trade in late antiquity," in Kingsley and Decker (edd.) 2001a, 44-68.

Kingsley, S. A. and M. Decker (edd.) 2001a. *Economy and exchange in the east Mediterranean during late antiquity* (Oxford).

Kingsley, S. A. and M. Decker 2001b. "New Rome, new theories on inter-regional exchange. An introduction to the east Mediterranean economy in late antiquity," in Kingsley and Decker 2001a, 1-27.

Kingsley, S. A. and K. Raveh 1996. *The ancient harbour and anchorage at Dor, Israel. Results of the underwater surveys 1976-1991* (BAR S626, Oxford).

Knapp, A. B. 1997. *The archaeology of Late Bronze Age Cypriot society: the study of settlement, survey and landscape* (Glasgow).

Knapp, A. B. and J. F. Cherry 1994. *Provenience studies and Bronze Age Cyprus* (Madison).

Knapp, A. B. *et al.* 1992. "The Sydney-Cyprus Survey Project. First preliminary report (1992)," *RDAC* 319-36.

Knapp, A. B. *et al.* 1994. "The Sydney-Cyprus Survey Project (SCSP). Second preliminary report (1993)," *RDAC* 329-43.

Kolodny, E. Y. 1973. *La population des îles de la Grèce. Essai de géographie insulaire en Méditerranée orientale* (Aix-en-Provence).

Koucky, F. L. and A. Steinberg 1982a. "Ancient mining and mineral dressing on Cyprus," in T. A. Wertime and S. F. Wertime (edd.), *Early pyrotechnology: the evolution of the first fire-using industries* (Washington, D.C.) 149-80.

Koucky, F. L. and A. Steinberg 1982b. "The ancient slags of Cyprus," in J. D. Muhly, R. Maddin, and V. Karageorghis (edd.), *Acta of the int. archaeological symposium "Early metallurgy in Cyprus, 4000-500 B.C."* (Nicosia) 117-37.

Koucky, F. L. and A. Steinberg 1989. "Ancient mining and mineral dressing on Cyprus," in Stager and Walker 1989, 275-327.

Kraeling, C. H. 1938. *Gerasa. City of the Decapolis* (New Haven).

Kramers, J. H. and G. Wiet (edd.) 1964. *Ibn Hauqal, Configuration de la terre (Kitab Surat al-Ard)* (Paris).

Krogman, W. M. and M. Y. Iscan 1986. *The human skeleton in forensic medicine* (Springfield, IL).

Krueger, D. 1996. *Symeon the holy fool. Leontius's "Life" and the late antique city* (Berkeley).

Kurtz, E. and F. Drexl (edd.) 1941. *Michaelis Pselli scripta minora*, vol. 2 (Milan).

Kyrris, C. P. 1983. "Cyprus as a trade station between east and west in the Middle Ages," *Επετηρίς του Κέντρου Επιστημονικών Ερευνών Κύπρου* 12, 1-3.

Kyrris, C. P. 1984. "The nature of the Arab-Byzantine relations in Cyprus from the middle of the 7th to the middle of the 10th century A.D.," *Graeco-Arabica* 3, 149-75.

Kyrris, C. P. 1994-98. "Byzantium, Cyprus and the Arabs from the mid-7th to the early 8th century," *EpetByz* 49, 185-236.

Lafontaine-Dosogne, J. 1993. "Aspects de l'architecture monastique à Byzance du VIIIe au Xe siècle. Topographie et disposition liturgique," *Revue Bénédictine* 103, 186-208.

Laiou, A. E. (ed.) 2002. *The economic history of Byzantium from the seventh through the fifteenth century* (Washington, D.C.).

Landgraf, J. 1980. "Keisan's Byzantine pottery," in J. Briend and J.-B. Humbert (edd.), *Tell Keisan (1971-1976). Une cité phénicienne en Galilée* (Fribourg) 51-99.

Lassus, J. 1947. *Sanctuaires chrétiens de Syrie* (BAHBeyrouth 42).

Last, J. S. 1975. "Kourion: the ancient water supply," *ProcAm PhilSoc* 119, 39-72.

Lefort, J. 1993. "Rural economy and social relations in the countryside," *DOP* 47, 101-13.

Lemerle, P. 1979. *The agrarian history of Byzantium from the origins to the twelfth century* (Galway).

Leonard, A., Jr. 1987. "A brief survey," in Soren 1987, 80-116.

Leonard, J. R. 1995a. "The anchorage at Kioni," in Fejfer 1995, 133-70.

Leonard, J. R. 1995b. "Evidence for Roman ports, harbours and anchorages in Cyprus," in Karageorghis and Michaelides 1995, 228-46.

Levi, D. 1947. *Antioch mosaic pavements* (Princeton).

Lewarch, D. E. and M. J. O'Brien 1981. "The expanding role of surface assemblages in archaeological research," in M. B. Schiffer (ed.), *Advances in archaeological method and theory*, 4 (New York) 297-342.

Lightfoot, C. S. 1989. *A catalogue of glass vessels in Afyon Museum* (British Institute of Archaeology at Ankara monog. 10; BAR S530, Oxford).

Lokin, J. H. A. 1986. "Administration and jurisdiction in Cyprus in the sixth century A.D.," in *Πρακτικά του δεύτερου διεθνούς Κυπριολογικού συνεδρίου, Λευκωσία, 1982*, vol. II (Nicosia) 1-9.

London, G. 1991. "Ethnoarchaeological evidence of variation in Cypriot ceramics and its implications for the taxonomy of ancient pottery," in J. A. Barlow, D. L. Bolger, and B. Kling (edd.), *Cypriot ceramics: reading the prehistoric record* (Philadelphia) 221-35.

London, G., F. Egoumenidou, and V. Karageorghis 1990. *Töpferei auf Zypern damals-heute/Traditional pottery in Cyprus* (Mainz).

Lopez, R. S. 1959. "The role of trade in the economic readjustment of Byzantium in the seventh century," *DOP* 13, 67-85.

Loverance, R. 1990. "Early Byzantine marble church furnishings: some examples from the episcopal basilica of Kourion in Cyprus," in R. Morris (ed.), *Church and people in Byzantium. Twentieth spring symposium of Byzantine studies, Manchester, 1986* (Birmingham) 225-43.

Lund, J. 1992. "Centuries of darkness? A ceramic sidelight on Cyprus and the eastern Mediterranean between A.D. 200 and A.D. 350," in Åström 1992, vol. 2, 193-213.

Lund, J. 1993. "Pottery of the Classical, Hellenistic and Roman periods," in Sørensen and Rupp 1993, 79-155.

Lund, J. 1995. "Hellenistic, Roman and Late Roman fine wares from the Segermes valley — forms and chronology," in S. Dietz, L. L. Sebaï, and H. Ben Hassen (edd.), *Africa Proconsularis. Regional studies in the Segermes valley of northern Tunesia* II (Copenhagen) 447-629.

Lund, J. 1996. "From archaeology to history? Reflections on the chronological distribution of ceramic fine wares in southwestern and southern Asia Minor from the 1st to the 7th c. A.D.," in M. Herfort-Koch, U. Mandel, and U. Schädler (edd.), *Hellenistische und kaiserzeitliche Keramik des östlichen Mittelmeergebietes. Kolloquium Frankfurt, 1995* (Frankfurt) 105-25.

MacAdam, H. I. 1994. "Settlements and settlement patterns in northern and central Transjordania, ca. 550-750," in King and Cameron 1994, 49-93.

Mackensen, M. 1984. *Resafa* I. *Eine befestigte spätantike Anlage vor den Stadtmauern von Resafa* (Mainz).

Mackensen, M. 1991. "Zur Datierung mediterraner Sigillata aus der spätantiken Befestigung Iatrus an der unteren Donau. Die Chronologie der Late Roman C – Formen Hayes 3A-E," *Germania* 69.1, 79-96.

Mackensen, M. 1993. *Die spätantiken Sigillata- und Lampentöpfereien von el Mahrine (Nordtunesien)* (Munich).

Mackensen, M. 1998. "Centres of African red slip ware production in Tunisia from the late 5th to the 7th century," in Saguì 1998, vol. 1, 23-39.

MacMullen, R. 1970. "Market-days in the Roman empire," *Phoenix* 24, 333-41.

Magness, J. 1993. *Jerusalem ceramic chronology circa 200-800 C.E.* (JSOT 9, Sheffield).

Maier, H. G. 1985. *Alt-Paphos auf Cypern. Ausgrabungen zur Geschichte von Stadt und Heiligtum 1966-1984* (Mainz).

Majcherek, G. 1992. "The Late Roman ceramics from sector 'G' (Alexandrie 1980-1987)," *ÉtTrav* 16, 81-117.

Majcherek, G. 1993. "Roman amphorae from Marina el-Alamein," *MittKairo* 49, 215-20.

Majcherek, G. 1995. "Gazan amphorae: typology reconsidered," in Meyza and Mlynarczyk 1995, 163-78.

Malamut, E. 1988. *Les îles de l'empire byzantin, VIIIe-XIIe siècles* (Byzantina Sorbonensia 8).

Malinowski, R. 1998. "Chemical composition of ancient mortars found in Cyprus," in P. Åström, *Hala Sultan Tekke* 10. *The wells* (SIMA 45.10) 135.

Maliszewski, D. 1994. "Polis-Pyrgos Archaeological Project. A preliminary report," *RDAC* 167-74.

Maliszewski, D. 1995. "Polis-Pyrgos Archaeological Project. Second preliminary report," *RDAC* 311-16.

Maliszewski, D. 1999. "Polis-Pyrgos Archaeological Project. Fourth preliminary report," *RDAC* 339-49.

Mango, C. 1972. *Art of the Byzantine empire, 312-1453. Sources and documents* (Englewood Cliffs, NJ).

Mango, C. 1976. "Chypre, carrefour du monde byzantin," in *XVe Congrès int. d'études byzantines, Athens, 1976, Rapports et co-rapports*, V.5 (Athens) 3-13; repr. in id., *Byzantium and its image* (London 1984).

Mango, C. and R. Scott (edd.) 1997. *The chronicle of Theophanes Confessor. Byzantine and Near Eastern history A.D. 284-813* (Oxford).

Manning, S. W. and D. H. Conwell 1992. "Maroni Valley Archaeological Survey Project: preliminary report on the 1990-1991 field seasons," *RDAC* 271-83.

Manning, S. W. *et al.* 1994. "Maroni Valley Archaeological Survey Project: preliminary report on the 1992-1993 seasons," *RDAC* 345-67.

Manning, S. W. *et al.* 2000. "Late Roman type 1a amphora production at the Late Roman site of Zygi-*Petrini*, Cyprus," *RDAC* 233-57.

Manning, S. W. *et al.* 2002. *The Late Roman church at Maroni-Petrera. Survey and salvage excavations 1990-1997, and other traces of Roman remains in the lower Maroni Valley, Cyprus* (Nicosia).

Martin, D. W. (ed.) 1998. *Sources for the history of Cyprus* V. *English texts: Frankish and Turkish periods* (Altamont, NY).

Martin, D. W. (ed.) 1999. *Sources for the history of Cyprus* VI. *English texts: British period to 1900* (Altamont, NY).

Martini, W. and C. Steckner 1993. *Samos XVII. Das Gymnasium von Samos. Das frühbyzantinische Klostergut* (Bonn).

Matheson, S. B. 1980. *Ancient glass in the Yale University Art Gallery* (New Haven).

Mathews, T. F. 1971. *The early churches of Constantinople* (University Park, PA).

Matschke, K.-P. 2002. "Mining," in Laiou 2002, 115-20.

Mattingly, D. J. 1992. "The field survey: strategy, methodology, and preliminary results," in Ben Lazreg and Mattingly 1992, 89-114.

Mattingly, D. J. 1996. "First fruit? The olive in the Roman world," in G. Shipley and J. Salmon (edd.), *Human landscapes in classical antiquity* (London) 213-53.

Mayerson, P. 1985. "The wine and vineyards of Gaza in the Byzantine period," *BASOR* 257, 75-80.

Mayet, F. and M. Picon 1986. "Une sigillée phocéenne tardive ('Late Roman C ware') et sa diffusion en Occident," *Figlina* 7, 129-42.

McCaslin, D. 1978. "The 1977 underwater report," in G. Hult and D. McCaslin, *Hala Sultan Tekke* 4 (SIMA 45.4) 97-157.

McClellan, M. C. 1984. *Core-formed glass from dated finds* (Ph.D. diss., Univ. of Pennsylvania).

McClellan, M. C. 1993. "Glass fragments," in Sørensen and Rupp 1993, 215-17.

McClellan, M. C. and M. L. Rautman 1989. "The 1987 and 1988 field seasons of the Kalavasos-*Kopetra* Project," *RDAC* 157-66.

McClellan, M. C. and M. L. Rautman 1991. "The 1990 field season at Kalavasos-*Kopetra*," *RDAC* 225-36.

McClellan, M. C. and M. L. Rautman 1994. "The 1991-1993 field seasons at Kalavasos-*Kopetra*," *RDAC* 289-307.

McClellan, M. C., P. J. Russell, and I. A. Todd 1988. "Kalavasos-*Mangia*. Rescue excavations at a Late Bronze Age cemetery," *RDAC* 1, 201-22.

McNicoll, A., R. H. Smith, and B. Hennessy 1982. *Pella in Jordan* 1 (Canberra).

McWhirr, A. (ed.) 1979. *Roman brick and tile* (BAR S69, Oxford).

Mee, C. and H. Forbes (edd.) 1997. *A rough and rocky place: the landscape and settlement history of the Methana peninsula, Greece* (Liverpool).

Megaw, A. H. S. 1946. "Three vaulted basilicas in Cyprus," *JHS* 66, 48-56.

Megaw, A. H. S. 1951. "Archaeology in Cyprus, 1949-1950," *JHS* 71, 258-60.

Megaw, A. H. S. 1952. "Archaeology in Cyprus, 1951," *JHS* 72, 113-17.

Megaw, A. H. S. 1953. "Archaeology in Cyprus, 1952," *JHS* 73, 133-37.

Megaw, A. H. S. 1955. "Archaeology in Cyprus, 1955," *AR 1955*, 41-46.

Megaw, A. H. S. 1956. "Archaeology in Cyprus, 1956," *AR 1956*, 24-31.

Megaw, A. H. S. 1957. "Archaeology in Cyprus, 1957," *AR 1957*, 43-50.

Megaw, A. H. S. 1958. "Archaeology in Cyprus, 1958," *AR 1958*, 25-34.

Megaw, A. H. S. 1960. "Early Byzantine monuments in Cyprus in light of recent discoveries," in F. Dölger and H.-G. Beck (edd.), *Akten des XI. int. Byzantinistenkongresses, München, 1958* (Munich) 345-51.

Megaw, A. H. S. 1971. "Excavations at 'Saranda Kolones', Paphos. Preliminary report on the 1966-67 and 1970-71 seasons," *RDAC* 117-46.

Megaw, A. H. S. 1972. "Supplementary excavations on a castle site at Paphos, Cyprus, 1970-1971," *DOP* 26, 322-43.

Megaw, A. H. S. 1974. "Byzantine architecture and decoration in Cyprus: metropolitan or provincial?" *DOP* 28, 57-88.

Megaw, A. H. S. 1976a. "Excavations at the episcopal basilica of Kourion in Cyprus in 1974 and 1975: a preliminary report," *DOP* 30, 345-71.

Megaw, A. H. S. 1976b. "Interior decoration in Early Christian Cyprus," *XVe Congrès int. d'études byzantines, Athens, 1976, Rapports et co-rapports* V.4 (Athens) 1-29.

Megaw, A. H. S. 1985a. "Le fortificazioni bizantine a Cipro," *CCARB* 32, 199-231.

Megaw, A. H. S. 1985b. "Mosaici parietali paleobizantini di Cipro," *CCARB* 32, 173-98.

Megaw, A. H. S. 1986. "'Betwixt Greeks and Saracens,'" in Karageorghis 1986, 505-19.

Megaw, A. H. S. 1988. "Reflections on Byzantine Paphos," in J. Chrysostomides (ed.), *Καθηγήτρια. Essays presented to Joan Hussey for her 80th birthday* (Athens) 135-50.

Megaw, A. H. S. 1993. "The episcopal precinct at Kourion and the evidence for re-location," in Bryer and Georghallides 1993, 53-67.

Megaw, A. H. S. 1997. "The Aegean connections of Cypriot church-builders in late antiquity," in *Proc. int. archaeological conference "Cyprus and the Aegean in antiquity from the prehistoric period to the 7th century A.D.," Nicosia, 1995* (Nicosia) 343-52.

Megaw, A. H. S. 2000. "The Soloi basilicas reconsidered," in *Πρακτικά του τρίτου διεθνούς Κυπριολογικού συνεδρίου, Λευκωσία, 1996*, vol. II, 171-80 (Nicosia).

Megaw, A. H. S. (ed.) forthcoming. *The episcopal basilica at Kourion* (Washington, D.C.).

Megaw, A. H. S. and E. J. W. Hawkins 1977. *The church of the Panagia Kanakariá at Lythrankomi in Cyprus: its mosaics and frescoes* (Washington, D.C.).

Megaw, A. H. S. and R. E. Jones 1983. "Byzantine and allied pottery: a contribution by chemical analysis to problems of origin and distribution," *BSA* 78, 235-63.

Metcalf, D. M. 1995. *Coinage of the Crusaders and the Latin East in the Ashmolean Museum Oxford* (2nd edn., Royal Numismatic Society spec. pub. 28).

Meyer, C. 1988. "Glass from the north theater Byzantine church, and soundings at Jerash, Jordan, 1982-1983," *BASOR* Suppl. 25, 175-222.

Meyers, E. M., A. T. Kraabel, and J. F. Strange 1976. *Ancient synagogue excavations at Khirbet Shema', Upper Galilee, Israel, 1970-1972* (AASOR 42).

Meyza, H. 1995. "Cypriot Sigillata and Cypriot Red Slip ware: problems of origin and continuity," in Meyza and Mlynarczyk 1995, 179-202.

Meyza, H. 2000. "Cypriot Red Slip. Development of the ware (an attempt at refinement)," in *Πρακτικά του τρίτου διεθνούς Κυπριολογικού συνεδρίου, Λευκωσία, 1996*, vol. I (Nicosia) 507-29.

Meyza, H. and J. Mlynarczyk (edd.) 1995. *Hellenistic and Roman pottery in the eastern Mediterranean — Advances in scientific studies (Acts of the II Nieborów pottery workshop, 1993)* (Warsaw).

Michaelides, D. 1987. *Cypriot mosaics* (Nicosia).

Michaelides, D. 1988. "Mosaic pavements from Early Christian cult buildings in Cyprus," in W. A. Daszewski and D. Michaelides, *Mosaic floors in Cyprus* (Bologna) 81-153.

Michaelides, D. 1989. "Cypriot mosaics: local traditions and external influences," in E. Peltenburg (ed.), *Early society in Cyprus* (Edinburgh) 272-92.

Michaelides, D. 1993. "*Opus sectile* in Cyprus," in Bryer and Georghallides 1993, 69-113.

Michaelides, D. 1996. "The economy of Cyprus during the Hellenistic and Roman periods," in Karageorghis and Michaelides 1996, 139-52.

Michaelides, D. 1998. "Archeologia paleocristiana a Cipro," *CCARB* 44, 179-239.

Millett, M. 2000. "The comparison of surface and stratified artefact assemblages," in M. Pasquinucci and F. Trémont (edd.), *The archaeology of Mediterranean landscapes, 4. Non-destructive techniques applied to landscape archaeology* (Oxford) 216-22.

Miquel, A. (ed., transl.) 1963. *Al-Muqaddasi, La meilleure répartition pour la connaissance des provinces* (Damascus).

Mitford, T. B. 1980. "Roman Cyprus," in *ANRW* II.7.2, 1285-1384.

Morris, C. E. and A. A. D. Peatfield 1987. "Pottery from the Cyprus underwater survey, 1983," *RDAC* 199-212.

Morrisson, C. 1986. "Byzance au VIIe siècle. Le témoignage de la numismatique," in N. A. Stratos (ed.), *Byzantium. Tribute to Andreas N. Stratos* I (Athens) 149-63.

Morrisson, C. and J.-P. Sodini 2002. "The sixth-century economy," in Laiou 2002, 171-220.

Muhly, J. D. 1996. "The significance of metals in the Late Bronze Age economy of Cyprus," in Karageorghis and Michaelides 1996, 45-60.

Müller, K. (ed.) 1855. *Geographi Graeci minores* (Paris).

Murray, W. M. 1995. "Ancient sailing winds in the eastern Mediterranean: the case for Cyprus," in Karageorghis and Michaelides 1995, 33-44.

Myres, J. L. 1914. *Handbook of the Cesnola collection of antiquities from Cyprus* (New York).

Nanson, G. C. and J. C. Croke 1992. "A genetic classification of floodplains," *Geomorphology* 4, 459-86.

Neff, H. 2002. "Quantitative techniques for analyzing ceramic compositional data," in D. M. Glowacki and H. Neff (edd.), *Ceramic production and circulation in the greater Southwest* (Los Angeles) 15-36.

Negev, A. 1978. "The Greek inscriptions from 'Avdat (Oboda)," *LibAnn* 28, 87-126.

Nicolaou, I. 1989. "Inscriptiones Cypriae alphabeticae XXIII, 1988," *RDAC* 141-50.

Nicolaou, I. 1990. *Paphos* II. *The coins from the House of Dionysos* (Nicosia).

Nicolaou, I. 1991. "Inscriptions from the necropolis of Amathus," in Karageorghis, Picard, and Tytgat 1991, 195-208.

Nicolaou, K. 1976. *The historical topography of Kition* (SIMA 43).

Oleson, J. P. *et al.* 1994. *The harbours of Caesarea Maritima. Results of the Caesarea Ancient Harbour Excavation Project 1980-85*, vol. II. *The finds and the ship* (BAR S594, Oxford).

Orlandos, A. K. 1952-54. *Η ξυλόστεγος παλαιοχριστιανική βασιλική της μεσογειακής λεκάνης* (Athens).

Ørsted, P. *et al.* (edd.) 2000. *Africa Proconsularis. Regional studies in the Segermes valley of northern Tunisia* III (Aarhus).

Orton, C., P. Tyers, and A. Vince 1993. *Pottery in archaeology* (Cambridge).

Ovadiah, A. 1970. *Corpus of the Byzantine churches in the Holy Land* (Bonn).

Ovadiah, R. and A. Ovadiah 1987. *Hellenistic, Roman and early Byzantine mosaic pavements in Israel* (Rome).

Owsley, D. W. and B. Bradtmiller 1983. "Mortality of pregnant females in Arikara villages: osteological evidence," *American Journal of Physical Anthropology* 61, 331-36.

Oziol, T. 1977. *Salamine de Chypre* VII. *Les lampes du Musée de Chypre* (Paris).

Oziol, T.-J. and J. Pouilloux 1969. *Salamine de Chypre* I. *Les lampes* (Paris).

Painter, K. (ed.) 1994. *"Churches built in ancient times." Recent studies in Early Christian archaeology* (Soc. Ant. Occ. Pap. 16.1).

Pallas, D. 1977. *Les monuments paléochrétiens de Grèce découverts de 1958-1973* (Rome).

Pallas, D. 1979-80. "Monuments et textes. Remarques sur la liturgie dans quelques basiliques paléochrétiennes de l'Illyricum oriental," *EpetByz* 44, 37-116.

Panella, C. 1986. "Oriente et occidente. Considerazioni su alcune anfore 'egee' di età imperiale a Ostia," in Empereur and Garlan 1986, 609-36.

Pantazis, T. M. 1967. *The geology and mineral resources of the Pharmakas-Kalavasos area* (Memoir no. 8, Nicosia).

Papacostas, T. 2001. "The economy of late antique Cyprus," in Kingsley and Decker 2001a, 107-28.

Papadopoulos, Th. 1993. "Frontier status and frontier processes in Cyprus," in Bryer and Georghallides 1993, 15-24.

Papageorghiou, A. 1963. "Η βασιλική Μαραθοβούνου," *RDAC* 84-101.

Papageorghiou, A. 1964. "Les premières incursions arabes à Chypre et leurs conséquences," in *Αφιέρωμα εις τον Κωνσταντίνον Σπυριδάκιν* (Nicosia) 152-58.

Papageorghiou, A. 1985. "L'architecture paléochrétienne de Chypre," *CCARB* 32, 299-324.

Papageorghiou, A. 1986. "Foreign influences on the Early Christian architecture of Cyprus," in Karageorghis 1986, 490-504.

Papageorghiou, A. 1993. "Cities and countryside at the end of antiquity and the beginning of the Middle Ages in Cyprus," in Bryer and Georghallides 1993, 27-51.

Parker, A. J. 1990. "Classical antiquity: the maritime dimension," *Antiquity* 64, 335-46.

Parker, A. J. 1992a. *Ancient shipwrecks of the Mediterranean & the Roman provinces* (BAR S580, Oxford).

Parker, A. J. 1992b. "Cargoes, containers and stowage: the ancient Mediterranean," *IJNA* 21, 89-100.

Patlagean, E. 1977. *Pauvreté économique et pauvreté social à Byzance 4e-7e siècles* (Paris).

Patrich 1988a. "Architectural sculpture and stone objects," in Tsafrir *et al.* 1988, 97-133.

Patrich 1988b. "The glass vessels," in Tsafrir *et al.* 1988, 134-41.

Patrick, A. 1967. "Disease in antiquity: ancient Greece and Rome," in D. Brothwell and A. T. Sandison (edd.), *Disease in antiquity* (Springfield, IL).

Patterson, H. 2000. "The current state of early medieval and medieval ceramic studies in Mediterranean survey," in Frankovich, Patterson, and Barker 2000, 110-20.

Patton, M. 1996. *Islands in time. Island sociogeography and Mediterranean prehistory* (New York).

Peacock, D. P. S. 1979. "An ethnoarchaeological approach to the study of Roman bricks and tiles," in McWhirr 1979, 5-10.

Peacock, D. P. S., F. Bejaoui, and N. Ben Lazreg 1990. "Roman pottery production in central Tunisia," *JRA* 3, 59-84.

Peacock, D. P. S. and D. F. Williams 1986. *Amphorae and the Roman economy. An introductory guide* (London).

Pearson, K. 1917-19. "A study of the long bones of the English skeleton, I. The femur," in *University of London, University College, Department of Applied Statistics, Company research, Memoirs, Biometric series* X, chapts. 1-4.

Peleg, M. 1989. "Domestic pottery," in V. Tzaferis, *Excavations at Capernaum* I. *1978-1982* (Winona Lake, IN) 31-113.

Peleg, M. and R. Reich 1992. "Excavations of a segment of the Byzantine city wall of Caesarea Maritima," *'Atiqot*, Eng. ser. 21, 137-222.

Peltenburg, E. J. 1979. "The prehistory of west Cyprus: Ktima lowlands investigations 1976-1978," *RDAC* 69-99.

Peltenburg, E. J. 1982. *Vrysi. A subterranean settlement in Cyprus. Excavations at prehistoric Ayios Epiktitos Vrysi, 1969-73* (Warminster).

Peltenburg, E. J. *et al.* 1983. "The prehistory of west Cyprus: Ktima lowlands investigations 1979-82," *RDAC* 9-55.

Perlman, I. and F. Asaro 1969. "Pottery analysis by Neutron Activation," *Archaeometry* 11, 21-52.

Petit, C., P.-Y. Péchoux, and P. Aupert 1991. "Rapport sur les travaux de l'École française à Amathonte de Chypre en 1990. La campagne de prospection," *BCH* 115, 775-87.

Petit, C., P.-Y. Péchoux, and Ch. Dieulafait 1996. "Amathonte et son territoire à travers les âges," in Aupert (ed.) 1996, 173-82.

Petit, C. *et al.* 1989. "Rapport sur les travaux de l'École française à Amathonte de Chypre en 1988. Première campagne d'exploration du royaume (du Amathonte)," *BCH* 113, 889-99.

Photos, E. 1982. "Conservation and preliminary scientific examination of the Kalavasos-*Tenta* human burials," in Todd 1982, 74-76.

Picard, O. 1993. "Chypre et l'École française d'Athènes," in Yon 1993, 39-54.

Pinder-Wilson, R. H. and G. T. Scanlon 1973. "Glass finds from Fustat: 1964-71," *JGS* 15, 12-30.

Ploug, G. 1985. *Hama. Fouilles et recherches 1931-1938,* III, part 1. *The Graeco-Roman town* (Copenhagen).

Pohlsander, H. A. (ed.) 1999. *Sources for the history of Cyprus* VII. *Greek texts of the fourth to thirteenth centuries* (Altamont, NY).

Pralong, A. 1991. "Rapport sur les travaux de l'École française à Amathonte de Chypre en 1990. Dépose de l'*opus sectile* et des placages muraux," *BCH* 115, 759-66.

Pralong, A. 1993. "Rapport sur les travaux de l'École française à Amathonte de Chypre en 1992. La basilique," *BCH* 117, 694-96.

Pralong, A. 1994a. "La basilique de l'acropole d'Amathonte (Chypre)," *RACrist* 70, 411-55.

Pralong, A. 1994b. "Rapport sur les travaux de l'École française à Amathonte de Chypre en 1993. Basilique paléochrétienne de l'acropole," *BCH* 118, 485-90.

Pralong, A. and J.-M. Saulnier 1986. "Rapport sur les travaux de l'École française à Amathonte de Chypre en 1985. La basilique," *BCH* 110, 884-99.

Pralong, A. and J.-M. Saulnier 1987. "Rapport sur les travaux de l'École française à Amathonte de Chypre en 1986. La basilique," *BCH* 111, 741-54.

Pralong, A. and J.-M. Saulnier 1989. "Rapport sur les travaux de l'École française à Amathonte de Chypre en 1988. Les structures paléochrétiennes," *BCH* 113, 860-71.

Pralong, A. and J.-M. Saulnier 1999. "Rapport sur les travaux de l'École française à Amathonte de Chypre en 1998. La basilique de l'acropole," *BCH* 123, 502-14.

Price, J. 1991. "Decorated mould-blown glass tablewares in the first century A.D.," in M. Newby and K. Painter (edd.), *Roman glass: two centuries of art and invention* (Soc. Ant. Occ. Pap. 13) 56-75.

Prokopiou, E. 1995. "Αμαθούντα. Ανατολική νεκρόπολη. Τάφος-οστεοφυλάκιο του 7ου μ.Χ. αιώνα," *RDAC* 249-79.

Prokopiou, E. 1996. "Δύο τάφοι-οστεοφυλάκια του 7ου μ.Χ. αιώνα στην ανατολική νεκρόπολη της Αμαθούντας," *RDAC* 273-84.

Prokopiou, E. 1997a. "Βυζαντινές πόρπες από την Αμαθούντα και την παλαιά συλλογή του Κυπριακού Μουσείου," in *Proc. int. archaeological conference "Cyprus and the Aegean in antiquity from the prehistoric period to the 7th century A.D.," Nicosia, 1995* (Nicosia) 333-42.

Prokopiou, E. 1997b. "Λεμεσός. Οδός Ζικ-Ζακ. Έκθεση αποτελεσμάτων σωστικής ανασκαφικής έρευνας 1993," *RDAC* 285-322.

Pryor, J. H. 1988. *Geography, technology, and war. Studies in the maritime history of the Mediterranean, 649-1571* (Cambridge).

Quilici, L. 1985. "La mission italienne à Ayia Irini (Kyrenia)," in Karageorghis 1985a, 182-92.

Quilici, L. 1989. "Poleografia e popolamento della penisola di Kormakiti a Cipro," *FelRav* 137-38, 7-23.

Quilici Gigli, S. 1971. "Prima perlustrazione topografica," in *Studi ciprioti e rapporti di scavo* I (Rome) 13-34.

Raab, H. A. 2001. *Rural settlement in Hellenistic and Roman Crete. The Akrotiri peninsula* (BAR S984, Oxford).

Raber, P. 1987. "Early copper production in the Polis region, Western Cyprus," *JFA* 14, 297-312.

Rackham, O. and J. A. Moody 1992. "Terraces," in Wells 1992, 123-30.

Rahmani, L. Y. 1960. "The ancient synagogue of Ma'on (Nirim). B. The small finds and coins," in *Louis M. Rabinowitz Fund for the Exploration of Ancient Synagogues, Bulletin* 3, 14-18.

Raptou, E. 1996. "Contribution to the study of the economy of ancient Cyprus: copper–timber," in Karageorghis and Michaelides 1996, 249-60.

Rasson, A.-M. and J. Seigne 1989. "Une cisterne byzantino-omeyyade sur le sanctuaire de Zeus," *Syria* 66, 117-51.

Rauh, N. K. and K. W. Slane 2000. "Possible amphora kiln sites in W Rough Cilicia," *JRA* 13, 319-30.

Rautman, M. L. 1995a. "Neutron activation analysis of Cypriot and related ceramics at the University of Missouri," in

Meyza and Mlynarczyk 1995, 331-49.

Rautman, M. L. 1995b. "Two Late Roman wells at Sardis," *AASOR* 53, 37-84.

Rautman, M. L. 1998. "Handmade pottery and social change: the view from Late Roman Cyprus," *JMA* 11, 81-104.

Rautman, M. L. 2000. "The busy countryside of Late Roman Cyprus," *RDAC* 317-31.

Rautman, M. L. 2001a. "The context of rural innovation: an early monastery at Kalavasos-*Sirmata*," *RDAC* 307-18.

Rautman, M. L. 2001b. "Rural society and economy in Late Roman Cyprus," in Burns and Eadie 2001, 241-62.

Rautman, M. L. and M. C. McClellan 1987. "Cyprus at the end of antiquity: investigations at Kalavasos-*Kopetra*," *Muse* 21, 45-54.

Rautman, M. L. and M. C. McClellan 1988. "Kalavasos-*Kopetra*, 1988," *Muse* 22, 51-63.

Rautman, M. L. and M. C. McClellan 1989-90. "Kalavasos-*Kopetra*, 1989-1990," *Muse* 23-24, 14-29.

Rautman, M. L. and M. C. McClellan 1990. "The 1989 field season at Kalavasos-*Kopetra*," *RDAC* 231-38.

Rautman, M. L. and M. C. McClellan 1991. "Kalavasos-*Kopetra*, 1991," *Muse* 25, 10-20.

Rautman, M. L. and M. C. McClellan 1992. "Excavations at Late Roman *Kopetra*, Cyprus," *JRA* 5, 265-71.

Rautman, M. L. *et al.* 1993. "Neutron activation analysis of Late Roman ceramics from Kalavasos-*Kopetra* and the environs of the Vasilikos valley," *RDAC* 233-64.

Rautman, M. L. *et al.* 1999. "Amphoras and rooftiles from Late Roman Cyprus: a compositional study of calcareous fabric ceramics from Kalavasos-*Kopetra*," *JRA* 12, 377-91.

Redman, C. L. 1987. "Surface collection, sampling, and research design. A retrospective," *AmAnt* 52, 249-65.

Restle, M. 1979. *Studien zur frühbyzantinischen Architektur Kappadokiens* (VTIB 3, Vienna).

Reynolds, P. 1995. *Trade in the western Mediterranean, A.D. 400-700: the ceramic evidence* (BAR S604, Oxford).

Richard, J. 1977. "Une économie coloniale? Chypre et ses ressources agricoles au Moyen-Âge," *ByzForsch* 5, 331-52.

Rickman, G. 1980. *The corn supply of ancient Rome* (Oxford).

Riley, J. A. 1975. "The pottery from the first session of excavation in the Caesarea hippodrome," *BASOR* 218, 25-63.

Riley, J. A. 1979. "The coarse pottery from Berenice," in J. A. Lloyd (ed.), *Excavations at Sidi Khrebish, Benghazi (Berenice)*, II (*LibAnt* Suppl. II) 91-467.

Rizopoulou-Egoumenidou, E. and K. Seretis 2000. "Folk art stone carvings in traditional houses in the village of Mitsero," *RDAC* 407-31.

Roberts, L. (ed.) 2000. *Sources for the history of Cyprus* VIII. *Latin texts from the first century B.C. to the seventeenth century A.D.* (Altamont, NY).

Robinson, H. S. 1959. *The Athenian Agora* V. *Pottery of the Roman period* (Princeton).

Rodziewicz, M. 1976. *Alexandrie* I. *La céramique romaine tardive d'Alexandrie* (Warsaw).

Rodziewicz, M. 1984. *Alexandrie* III. *Les habitations romaines tardives d'Alexandrie* (Warsaw).

Rosenthal-Heginbottom, R. 1982. *Die Kirchen von Sobota und die Dreiapsidenkirchen des Nahen Ostens* (Göttinger Orientforschungen II.7).

Rosser, J. 1985. "Excavations at Saranda Kolones, Paphos, Cyprus, 1981-1983," *DOP* 39, 81-97.

Rossiter, J. J. and J. Freed 1991. "Canadian-Turkish excavations at Domuztepe, Cilicia (1989)," *ÉchCl* 35, 145-74.

Roux, G. 1973. "Tables chrétiennes en marbre découvertes à Salamine," in *Salamine de Chypre* IV. *Anthologie Salaminienne* (Paris) 133-96.

Roux, G. 1998. *Salamine de Chypre* XV. *La basilique de la Campanopétra* (Paris).

Rowe, A. H. 1998. "A current Late Roman site in Nea Paphos, Cyprus," *NEA* 61, 179.

Rowe, A. H. 1999. "A Late Roman streetscape in Nea Pafos," *RDAC* 269-78.

Ruggieri, V. 1991. *Byzantine religious architecture (582-867): its history and structural elements* (Orientalia Christiana Analecta 237, Rome).

Rupp, D. W. 1986. "The Canadian Palaipaphos (Cyprus) Survey Project. Third preliminary report, 1983-1985," *ActaArch* 57, 27-45.

Rupp, D. W. (ed.) 1987. *Western Cyprus: connections. An archaeological symposium held at Brock University, 1986* (SIMA 77).

Rupp, D. W. 1997. "'Metro' Nea Paphos: suburban sprawl in southwestern Cyprus in the Hellenistic and earlier Roman periods," in W. E. Aufrecht, N. A. Mirau, and S. W. Gauley (edd.), *Urbanism in antiquity from Mesopotamia to Crete* (JSOT Suppl. 244, Sheffield) 236-62.

Rupp, D. W. *et al.* 1984. "Canadian Palaipaphos (Cyprus) Survey Project: second preliminary report, 1980-1982," *JFA* 11, 133-54.

Rupp, D. W. *et al.* 1992. "Canadian Palaipaphos Survey Project: 1991 field season," *RDAC* 285-317.

Russell, J. 1982. "Byzantine *instrumenta domestica* from Anemurium: the significance of context," in R. L. Hohlfelder (ed.), *City, town and countryside in the early Byzantine era* (Boulder, CO) 133-63.

Russell, J. C. 1958. *Late antique and medieval populations* (TransAmPhilSoc 48.3).

Ryden, L. 1993. "Cyprus at the time of the condominium as reflected in the Lives of Sts Demetrianos and Constantine the Jew," in Bryer and Georghallides 1993, 189-202.

Saguì, L. (ed.) 1998. *Ceramica in Italia: VI-VII secolo. Atti del convegno in onore di John W. Hayes, Roma, 1995* (Florence).

Salamine de Chypre. Histoire et archéologie 1980 (Colloques int. du CNRS 578, Paris).

Saller, S. J. 1941. *The memorial of Moses on Mount Nebo* (Studium Biblicum Franciscanum pub. 1, Jerusalem).

Salles, J.-F. 1983. *Kition-Bamboula* II. *Les égouts de la ville classique* (Paris).

Salles, J.-F. 1993. *Kition-Bamboula* IV. *Les niveaux hellénistiques* (Paris).

Sarpaki, A. 1992. "The palaeoethnobotanical approach. The Mediterranean triad or is it a quartet?" in Wells 1992, 61-75.

Savile, A. R. 1878. *Cyprus. Compiled in the intelligence branch, Quarter-master-general's department, horse guards* (London).

Savvides, A. 1995. "The consolidation of Byzantine power on Cyprus on the eve of the First Crusade and the first decade of the empire's relations with the Crusaders," in Coureas and Riley-Smith 1995, 3-18.

Schick, R. 1994. "The settlement pattern of southern Jordan: the nature of the evidence," in King and Cameron 1994, 133-54.

Schilbach, E. 1970. *Byzantinische Metrologie* (Byzantinisches Handbuch 4, Munich).

Schlumberger, G. 1878. *Numismatique de l'Orient latin* (Paris).

Schneider, G. 2000. "Chemical and mineralogical studies of late Hellenistic to Byzantine pottery production in the eastern Mediterranean," *RCRFActa* 36, 525-36.

Schour, I. and M. Massler 1944. *Development of the human dentition* (chart, American Dental Association).

Schuring, J. M. 1984. "Studies on Roman amphorae II. Amphorae from the San Sisto Vecchio in Rome," *BABesch* 59, 147-95.

Seefried, M. 1986. "Glass in Cyprus from the Late Bronze Age to Roman times," *RDAC* 146-49.

Segal, A. 1983. *The Byzantine city of Shivta* (BAR S179, Oxford).

Ševčenko, N. P. and C. Moss (edd.) 1999. *Medieval Cyprus. Studies in art, architecture, and history in memory of Doula Mouriki* (Princeton).

Şevketoğlu, M. 2000. *Archaeological field survey of the Neolithic and Chalcolithic settlement sites in Kyrenia district, north Cyprus* (BAR S834, Oxford).

Shennan, S. 1985. *Experiments in the collection and analysis of archaeological survey data: the East Hampshire survey* (Sheffield).

Simm, D. J. 1995. "The rates and patterns of overbank deposition on a lowland floodplain," in I. D. L. Foster, A. M. Gurnell, and B. W. Webb (edd.), *Sediment and water quality in river catchments* (Chichester) 247-64.

Sinos, S. 1984. "The folk architecture and art of Cyprus," *RDAC* 354-74.

Sinos, S. 1986. "Types of rural dwellings in Cyprus," in Karageorghis 1986, 520-33.

Sirks, B. 1991. *Food for Rome* (Amsterdam).

Slane, K. W. 2002. "Corinth's Roman pottery. Quantification and meaning," in C. K. Williams, II and N. Bookidis (edd.), *Corinth* XX. *The centenary, 1896-1996* (Princeton) 307-22.

Slane, K. W. *et al.* 1994. "Compositional analysis of Eastern Sigillata A and related wares from Tel Anafa (Israel)," *JArchSci* 21, 51-64.

Smith, R. H. and L. P. Day 1989. *Pella of the Decapolis* 2. *Area IX, the civic complex, 1979-1985* (Wooster, OH).

Sodini, J.-P. 1986. "Les 'tombes privilégiés' dans l'Orient chrétien (à l'exception du diocèse d'Egypt)," in Y. Duval and J.-Ch. Picard (edd.), *L'inhumation privilégiée du IVe au VIIIe siècle en Occident* (Paris) 233-43.

Sodini, J.-P. 1989a. "Le commerce des marbres à l'époque protobyzantine," in *Hommes et richesses dans l'empire byzantin*, I. *IVe-VIIe siècle* (Paris) 163-89.

Sodini, J.-P. 1989b. "Les églises de Syrie du nord," in J.-M. Dentzer and W. Orthmann (edd.), *Archéologie et histoire de la Syrie* II. *La Syrie de l'époque achéménide à l'avènement de l'Islam* (Saarbrücken) 347-72.

Sodini, J.-P. 1998. "Les inscriptions de l'aqueduc de Kythrea à Salamine de Chypre," in *ΕΥΨΥΧΙΑ. Mélanges offerts à Hélène Ahrweiler* I (Byzantina Sorbonensia 16) 619-34.

Sodini, J.-P. 2000. "Productions et échanges dans le monde protobyzantin (IVe-VIIe s.): le cas de la céramique," in Belke *et al.* 2000, 181-208.

Sodini, J.-P. and K. Kolokotsas 1984. *Aliki* II. *La basilique double* (Études thasiennes X).

Sodini, J.-P. and E. Villeveuve 1992. "Le passage de la céramique byzantine à la céramique omeyyade en Syrie du nord, en Palestine et en Transjordanie," in P. Canivet and J.-P. Rey-Coquais (edd.), *La Syrie de Byzance à l'Islam, VIIe-VIIIe siècle* (Damascus) 195-218.

Sodini, J.-P. *et al.* 1980. "Déhès (Syrie du nord). Campagnes I-III (1976-1978). Recherches sur l'habitat rural," *Syria* 57, 1-304.

Soren, D. (ed.). 1987. *The sanctuary of Apollo Hylates at Kourion, Cyprus* (Tucson).

Sørensen, L. W. *et al.* 1998. "Third preliminary report of the Danish archaeological excavations at Panayia Ematousa, Aradippou, Cyprus," *Proc. Danish Institute Athens* 2, 319-81.

Sørensen, L. W. and D. W. Rupp (edd.) 1993. *The land of the Paphian Aphrodite* 2. *The Canadian Palaipaphos Survey Project. Artifact and ecofactual studies* (SIMA 104.2).

South, A. K. 1984. "Kalavasos-*Ayios Dhimitrios* 1983," *RDAC* 14-41.

South, A. K., P. Russell, and P. S. Keswani 1989. *Kalavasos-Ayios Dhimitrios* II. *Ceramics, objects, tombs, specialist studies* (VVP 3, SIMA 71.3).

Stager, L. E. and A. M. Walker (edd.) 1989. *American Expedition to Idalion, Cyprus. 1973-1980* (Oriental Institute communications 24).

Stager, L. E., A. Walker, and G. E. Wright (edd.) 1974. *American Expedition to Idalion, Cyprus. First preliminary report: seasons of 1971 and 1972* (*BASOR* Suppl. 18).

Stanley-Price, N. P. 1972. "A prehistoric survey of the Analiondas region," *RDAC* 15-21.

Stanley-Price, N. P. 1979. *Early prehistoric settlement in Cyprus. A review and gazetteer of sites, c.6500-3000 B.C.* (BAR S65, Oxford).

Stern, E. M. 1985. "Ancient and medieval glass from the necropolis church at Anemurium," in *Annales du 9e congrès int. d'étude historique du verre, Nancy, 1983* (Liège) 35-64.

Stewart, T. D. 1979. *Essentials of forensic anthropology* (Springfield, IL).

Stillwell, R. (ed.) 1941. *Antioch-on-the-Orontes* III. *The excavations, 1937-1939* (Princeton).

Stos-Gale, S., G. Maliotis, and N. Gale 1998. "A preliminary survey of the Cypriot slag heaps and their contribution to the reconstruction of copper production on Cyprus," in T. Rehren, A. Hauptmann, and J. D. Muhly (edd.), *Metallurgica antiqua in honour of Hans-Gert Bachmann and Robert Maddin* (Bochum) 235-62.

Sullivan, A. P. 1992. "Investigating the archaeological consequences of short-duration occupations," *AmerAnt* 57, 99-115.

Sumner, W. M. 1989. "Population and settlement area: an example from Iran," *American Anthropologist* 91, 631-41.

Sussman, V. 1976. "A burial cave at Kefa 'Ara," *'Atiqot*, Eng. ser. 11, 92-101.

Swiny, H. W. (ed.) 1982. *An archaeological guide to the ancient Kourion area and the Akrotiri peninsula* (Nicosia).

Swiny, S. and Ch. Mavromatis 2000. "Land behind Kourion. Results of the 1997 Sotira Archaeological Project survey," *RDAC* 433-52.

Symeonoglou, S. 1972. "Archaeological survey in the area of Phlamoudhi, Cyprus," *RDAC* 187-98.

Tate, G. 1992. *Les campagnes de la Syrie du nord du IIe au VIIe siècle*, I (BAHBeyrouth 133).

Tatton-Brown, V. A. 1984. "The glass," in H. R. Hurst and S. P. Roskams (edd.), *Excavations at Carthage: the British Mission* I, 1. *The Avenue du Président Habib Bourguiba, Salammbo: the site and finds other than pottery* (Sheffield) 194-212.

Tatton-Brown, V. A. 1985. "Archaeology in Cyprus 1960-1985: Classical to Roman periods," in Karageorghis 1985a, 60-72.

Tatton-Brown, V. A. 1994. "The glass," in H. R. Hurst (ed.), *Excavations at Carthage: the British Mission* II, 1. *The circular harbour, north side: the site and finds other than pottery* (Oxford) 282-90.

Taylor, J. 2000. "Cultural depositional processes and post-depositional problems," in Francovich, Patterson, and Barker 2000, 16-26.

Taylor, J. du Plat 1933. "A water cistern with Byzantine paintings, Salamis, Cyprus," *AntJ* 13, 97-108.

Taylor, J. du Plat 1934. "Paphos — Roman cistern," *RDAC* 15-16.

Taylor, J. du Plat and A. H. S. Megaw 1981. "Excavations at Ayios Philon, the ancient Carpasia. Part II. The Early Christian buildings," *RDAC* 209-50.

Taylor, R. J. and V. J. Robinson 1996. "Neutron Activation Analysis of Roman African Red Slip ware kilns," *Archaeometry* 38, 231-43.

Tchalenko, G. 1953-58. *Villages antiques de la Syrie du nord. Le massif du Bélus à l'époque romaine* (BAHBeyrouth 50).

Teall, J . L. 1959. "The grain supply of the Byzantine empire, 330-1025," *DOP* 13, 87-139.

Thieme, F. P. 1957. "Sex in negro skeletons," *Journal of Forensic Medicine* 4, 72-81.

Thirgood, J. V. 1987. *Cyprus. A chronicle of its forests, land, and people* (Vancouver).

Thompson, D. J. 1983. "Nile grain transport under the Ptolemies," in P. Garnsey, K. Hopkins, and C. R. Whittaker (edd.), *Trade in the ancient economy* (Cambridge).

Todd, I. A. 1979a. "Vasilikos Valley Project: third preliminary report, 1978," *JFA* 6, 265-300.

Todd, I. A. 1979b. "Vasilikos Valley Project, 1977-1978: an interim report," *RDAC* 13-68.

Todd, I. A. 1982. "Vasilikos Valley Project: fourth preliminary report, 1979-1980," *JFA* 9, 35-77.

Todd, I. A. 1985. "Excavations in the Vasilikos valley," in Karageorghis 1985a, 81-91.

Todd, I. A. 1987. *Excavations at Kalavasos-Tenta* I (VVP 6, SIMA 71.6).

Todd, I. A. 1989. "The 1988 field survey in the Vasilikos valley," *RDAC* 41-50.

Todd, I. A. 2000. "Excavations at Sanidha, a Late Bronze Age ceramic manufacturing centre," *Πρακτικά του τρίτου διεθνούς Κυπριολογικού συνεδρίου, Λευκοσία, 1996*, vol. I (Nicosia), 301-25.

Todd, I. A. forthcoming. *The field survey of the Vasilikos valley* (VVP 9, SIMA 71.9).

Todd, I. A. and P. Croft forthcoming. *Excavations at Kalavasos-Ayious* (VVP 8, SIMA 71.8).

Todd, I. A. and D. Pilides 1993. "Excavations at Sanida 1992," *RDAC* 97-146.

Tomber, R. 1987. "Evidence for long-distance commerce: imported bricks and tiles at Carthage," *RCRFActa* 25/26, 161-74.

Tomber, R. 1993. "Quantitative approaches to the investigation of long-distance trade," *JRA* 6, 142-66.

Touma, M. 1989. "La céramique protobyzantine d'Amathonte: remarques sur le matériel trouvé en 1988," *BCH* 113, 871-75.

Touma, M. 2001. "Quelques témoignages de la céramique sur les échanges syro-chypriotes à la période byzantine," in Villeneuve and Watson 2001, 49-58.

Toumazou, M. K., R. W. Yerkes, and P. N. Kardulias 1998. "Athienou Archaeological Project: investigations in the Malloura valley, Cyprus, 1990-1995," *JFA* 25, 163-82.

Tsafrir, Y. 1988. "The northern church," in Tsafrir *et al.* 1988, 22-77.

Tsafrir, Y. 1990. "On the pre-planning of ancient churches and synagogues. A test case: the northern church at Rehovot in the Negev," in G. C. Bottini, L. Di Segni, and E. Alliata (edd.), *Christian archaeology in the Holy Land. New discoveries* (Studium Biblicum Franciscanum coll. maior 36, Jerusalem) 535-44.

Tsafrir, Y. 1996. "Some notes on the settlement and demography of Palestine in the Byzantine period: the archaeological evidence," in J. D. Seger (ed.), *Retrieving the past* (Winona Lake, IN) 269-83.

Tsafrir, Y. *et al.* 1988. *Excavations at Rehovot-in-the-Negev* I. *The northern church* (Qedem 25).

Tubb, J. N. 1986. "The pottery from a Byzantine well near Tell Fara," *PEQ* 118, 51-65.

Tushingham, A. D. 1985. *Excavations in Jerusalem, 1961-1967*, I (Toronto).

Tzaferis, V. 1982. "The ancient synagogue at Ma'oz Hayyim," *IEJ* 32, 215-44.

Tzori, N. 1973. "The house of Kyrios Leontis at Beth-Shean," *Eretz-Israel* 11, 229-47 [Hebrew].

Ulbert, Th. 1986. *Resafa* II. *Die Basilika des Heiligen Kreuzes in Resafa-Sergiupolis* (Mainz).

Underwood, P. A. 1948. "Some principles of measure in the architecture of the period of Justinian," *CahArch* 3, 64-74.

Vaag, L. E. 2001. "The stamped decoration on Phocaean Red Slip ware," in J. Fleischer, J. Lund, and M. Nielsen (edd.), *Late antiquity. Art in context* (Acta Hyperborea 8) 215-33.

van Alfen, P. G. 1996. "New light on the 7th-c. Yassi Ada shipwreck: capacities and standard sizes of LR1 amphoras," *JRA* 9, 189-213.

van Andel, T. H. and E. Zangger 1990. "Landscape stability and destabilisation in the prehistory of Greece," in S. Bottema, G. Entjes-Nieborg, and W. van Zeist (edd.), *Man's role in the shaping of the eastern Mediterranean landscape* (Rotterdam) 159-82.

van den Ven, P. (ed.) 1953. *La légende de S. Spyridon, évêque de Trimithonte* (Bibliothèque du Muséon 33, Louvain).

Vann, R. L. 1989. "Pre-cast gypsum as a building material," in R. I. Curtis (ed.), *Studia Pompeiana & classica in honor of Wilhelmina F. Jashemski* II. *Classica* (New Rochelle, NY) 241-53.

Vessberg, O. 1953. "Hellenistic and Roman lamps in Cyprus," *OpAth* 1, 115-29.

Vessberg, O. 1956. "Glass," in Vessberg and Westholm 1956, 128-75 and 193-219.

Vessberg, O. and A. Westholm 1956. *Swedish Cyprus Expedition* IV, 3. *The Hellenistic and Roman periods in Cyprus* (Lund).

Villeneuve, E. and P. M. Watson (edd.) 2001. *La céramique byzantine et proto-islamique en Syrie-Jordanie (IVe-VIIIe siècles apr.*

J.-C.). Actes du colloque tenu à Amman, 1994 (BAHBeyrouth 159).

Villeneuve, F. 1985. "L'économie rurale et la vie des campagnes dans le Hauran antique (Ier siècle av. J.-C. – VIIe siècle ap. J.-C.). Une approche," in J.-M. Dentzer (ed.), *Hauran I. Recherches archéologiques sur la Syrie du sud a l'époque hellénistique et romaine* (Paris) 63-136.

Vincentelli, M. 2000. *Women and ceramics: gendered vessels* (Manchester).

Vita-Finzi, C., 1969. *The Mediterranean valleys. Geological changes in historic times* (Cambridge).

von Saldern, A. 1980. *Ancient and Byzantine glass from Sardis* (Sardis M6, Cambridge, MA).

Vroom, J. 2000. "Piecing together the past. Survey pottery and deserted settlements in medieval Boeotia (Greece)," in Belke *et al.* 2000, 245-59.

Waagé, F. O. 1948. "Hellenistic and Roman tableware of north Syria," in id. (ed.), *Antioch-on-the-Orontes* IV, part 1. *Ceramics and Islamic coins* (Princeton) 1-60.

Wagstaff, J. M. 1981. "Buried assumptions: some problems in the interpretation of the 'Younger Fill' raised by recent data from Greece," *JAS* 8, 247-64.

Wagstaff, J. M. 1988. "The Tenta catchment: resource exploitation in Neolithic Cyprus," in J. L. Bintliff, D. A. Davidson, and E. G. Grant (edd.), *Conceptual issues in environmental archaeology* (Edinburgh) 64-71.

Wagstaff, M. 1992. "Agricultural terraces: the Vasilikos valley, Cyprus," in M. Bell and J. Boardman (edd.), *Past and present soil erosion* (Oxford) 155-61.

Walker, A. M. and A. M. Bieber, Jr. 1974. "Surface survey of the lower city," in Stager, Walker, and Wright 1974, 27-41.

Wallace, P. W. 1982. "Survey of the Akhera area," *RDAC* 237-43.

Wallace, P. W. 1984. "The Akamas promontory of Cyprus," *RDAC* 341-47.

Wallace, P. W. and A. G. Orphanides (edd.) 1990. *Sources for the history of Cyprus, I. Greek and Latin texts to the third century* (Albany, NY).

Walmsley, A. 1996. "Byzantine Palestine and Arabia: urban prosperity in late antiquity," in Christie and Loseby 1996, 126-58.

Ward-Perkins, B. 1996. "Urban continuity?" in Christie and Loseby 1996, 4-17.

Ward-Perkins, B. 2001. "Specialisation, trade, and prosperity: an overview of the economy of the late antique eastern Mediterranean," in Kingsley and Decker 2001a, 167-78.

Watkins, T. F. 1979. "Kataliondas-*Kourvellos*. The analysis of surface-collected data," in Karageorghis 1979, 12-20.

Webb, J. M. 1986. *Corpus of Cypriote antiquities* 12. *Cypriote antiquities in the Abbey Museum, Queensland, Australia* (SIMA 20.12).

Weinberg, G. D. (ed.). 1988. *Excavations at Jalame. Site of a glass factory in Late Roman Palestine* (Columbia).

Wells, B. (ed.) 1992. *Agriculture in ancient Greece. Proc. 7th int. symposium at the Swedish Institute at Athens, 1990* (Stockholm).

Wharton, A. 1988. *Art of empire. Painting and architecture on the Byzantine periphery* (University Park, PA).

White, K. D. 1970. *Roman farming* (Ithaca, NY).

Whitehouse, D. *et al.* 1985. "The Scola Praeconum II," *PBSR* 53, 163-210.

Whittaker, C. R. 1990. "The consumer city revisited: the *vicus* and the city," *JRA* 3, 110-18.

Whittaker, J. C. 1999. "*Alonia*. The ethnoarchaeology of Cypriot threshing floors," *JMA* 12, 7-25.

Whittow, M. 1996. *The making of Byzantium, 600-1025* (Berkeley).

Wickham, C. 1988. "Marx, Sherlock Holmes, and Late Roman commerce," *JRS* 78, 183-93.

Williams, C. 1977. "A Byzantine well-deposit from Anemurium (Rough Cilicia)," *AnatSt* 27, 175-90.

Williams, C. 1989. *Anemurium. The Roman and early Byzantine pottery* (Subsidia mediaevalia 16, Toronto).

Williams, D. F. 1987. "Roman amphorae from Kourion, Cyprus," *RDAC* 235-38.

Woods, A. J. 1986. "Form, fabric and function: some observations on the cooking pot in antiquity," in W. D. Kingery (ed.), *Ceramics and civilization*, II. *Technology and style* (Columbus, OH) 157-72.

Woolf, G. 1992. "Imperialism, empire and the integration of the Roman economy," *WorldArch* 23, 283-93.

Wright, G. R. W. 1985. *Ancient building in south Syria and Palestine* (Handbuch der Orientalistik, Leiden).

Wright, G. R. W. 1992. *Ancient building in Cyprus* (Handbuch der Orientalistik, Leiden).

Wright, J. C. *et al.* 1990. "The Nemea Valley Archaeological Project: a preliminary report," *Hesperia* 59, 579-659.

Yannopoulos, P. A. 1983. "Chypre au milieu du VIIe siècle à la lumière des sources numismatiques," *Επετερίς του Κέντρου Επιστημονικών Ερευνών Κύπρου* 12, 69-77.

Yon, M. (ed.) 1993. *Kinyras. L'archéologie française à Chypre. Table-ronde tenue à Lyon, 1991* (Lyon).

Young, S. H. 1993. "A preview of seventh-century glass from the Kourion basilica, Cyprus," *JGS* 35, 39-47.

Young, S. H. forthcoming. "The glass," in Megaw forthcoming.

Zemer, A. 1977. *Storage jars in ancient sea trade* (Haifa).

Zori, N. 1967. "The ancient synagogue at Beth-Shean," *Eretz-Israel* 8, 149-67 [Hebrew].

Zorn, J. R. 1994. "Estimating the population size of ancient settlements: methods, problems, solutions, and a case study," *BASOR* 295, 31-48.